UNITED STATES
Territorial Expansion

Lake of the Woods

MINNESOTA (1858)

St. Paul

Lake Superior

Mississippi R.

WISCONSIN (1848)

Madison

Lake Michigan

Lake Huron

MICHIGAN (1837)

Lansing

IOWA (1846)

Des Moines

ORIGINAL UNITED STATES
(By treaty with Britain, 1783)

OHIO (1803)

Columbus

ILLINOIS (1818)

Springfield

INDIANA (1816)

Indianapolis

1900

1950

Topeka

MISSOURI (1821)

Missouri R.

Jefferson City

2000

Ohio R.

1850

Charleston

WEST VIRGINIA (1863)

Frankfort

KENTUCKY (1792)

Nashville

Lake Erie

Lake Ontario

St. Lawrence R.

MAINE (1820)

Augusta

VT. (1791)

Montpelier

N.H. (1788)

Concord

Boston

NEW YORK (1788)

Albany

MASS. (1788)

Providence

Hartford

R.I. (1790)

CONN. (1788)

PENN. (1787)

Harrisburg

Trenton

N.J. (1787)

1800

1790

MD. (1788)

Annapolis

Dover

DEL. (1787)

Washington, D.C.

VIRGINIA (1788)

Richmond

Chesapeake Bay

ORIGINAL THIRTEEN COLONIES

Raleigh

NORTH CAROLINA (1789)

ATLANTIC OCEAN

SOUTH CAROLINA (1788)

Columbia

● Geographical center of population per Census year

TENNESSEE (1796)

Tennessee R.

ARKANSAS (1836)

Arkansas R.

Little Rock

Mississippi R.

Atlanta

GEORGIA (1788)

ALABAMA (1819)

MISSISSIPPI (1817)

Montgomery

Jackson

Red R.

Baton Rouge

LOUISIANA (1812)

(Seized from Spain, 1810, 1813)

Tallahassee

FLORIDA
(By treaty with Spain, 1819)

FLORIDA (1845)

Lake Okeechobee

PUERTO RICO
(From Spain, 1898)

ATLANTIC OCEAN

San Juan

★ Charlotte Amalie

VIRGIN ISLANDS
(From Denmark, 1917)

| 0 | 50 | 100 Miles |
| 0 | 50 | 100 Kilometers |

Gulf of Mexico

BAHAMAS

CUBA

| 0 | 150 | 300 Miles |
| 0 | 150 | 300 Kilometers |

CONCISE SIXTH EDITION

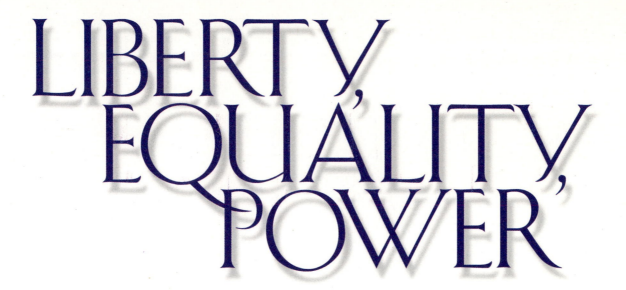

LIBERTY, EQUALITY, POWER

A HISTORY OF THE AMERICAN PEOPLE

Volume 1: To 1877

JOHN M. MURRIN
PRINCETON UNIVERSITY, EMERITUS

PAUL E. JOHNSON
UNIVERSITY OF SOUTH CAROLINA, EMERITUS

JAMES M. MCPHERSON
PRINCETON UNIVERSITY, EMERITUS

ALICE FAHS
UNIVERSITY OF CALIFORNIA, IRVINE

GARY GERSTLE
VANDERBILT UNIVERSITY

EMILY S. ROSENBERG
UNIVERSITY OF CALIFORNIA, IRVINE

NORMAN L. ROSENBERG
MACALESTER COLLEGE

WADSWORTH
CENGAGE Learning·

Australia · Brazil · Japan · Korea · Mexico · Singapore · Spain · United Kingdom · United States

WADSWORTH
CENGAGE Learning·

Liberty, Equality, Power: A History of the American People, Concise Sixth Edition, Volume 1: To 1877
Murrin/Johnson/McPherson/Fahs/Gerstle/Rosenberg/Rosenberg

Editor-in-Chief: Lyn Uhl
Senior Publisher: Suzanne Jeans
Senior Sponsoring Editor: Ann West
Senior Development Editor:
   Margaret McAndrew Beasley
Assistant Editor: Megan Chrisman
Editorial Assistant: Kati Coleman
Media Editor: Kate MacLean
Brand Manager: Melissa Larmon
Marketing Development Manager: Kyle Zimmerman
Marketing Coordinator: Lorreen R. Towle
Senior Content Project Manager: Carol Newman
Senior Art Director: Cate Rickard Barr
Print Buyer: Sandee Milewski
Senior Rights Acquisition Specialist:
   Jennifer Meyer Dare
Cover Designer: Cabbage Design
Cover Image:
   The Schuyler Family, 1824 (w/c on paper) by Ambrose
   Andrews (1805-1859) ©Collection of the New-York
   Historical Society, USA /The Bridgeman Art Library
Production Service and Compositor:
   Integra Software Services, Inc.

For product information and technology assistance, contact us at
Cengage Learning Customer & Sales Support, 1-800-354-9706

For permission to use material from this text or product,
submit all requests online at **www.cengage.com/permissions**.
Further permissions questions can be emailed to
permissionrequest@cengage.com.

Library of Congress Control Number: 2012935928

Student Edition:
ISBN-13: 978-1-133-94773-8
ISBN-10: 1-133-94773-5

Wadsworth
20 Channel Center Street
Boston, MA 02210
USA

Cengage Learning is a leading provider of customized learning solutions with office locations around the globe, including Singapore, the United Kingdom, Australia, Mexico, Brazil and Japan. Locate your local office at **international.cengage.com/region**

Cengage Learning products are represented in Canada by Nelson Education, Ltd.

For your course and learning solutions, visit **www.cengage.com**.

Purchase any of our product at your local college store
or at our preferred online store **www.cengagebrain.com**.

Instructors: Please visit **login.cengage.com** and log in to access instructor-specific resources.

Printed in the United States of America
1 2 3 4 5 6 7 16 15 14 13 12

John M. Murrin

Princeton University, Emeritus

John M. Murrin studies American colonial and revolutionary history and the early republic. He has edited one multivolume series and five books, including two essay collections, *Colonial America: Essays in Politics and Social Development*, Sixth Edition (2010), and *Saints and Revolutionaries: Essays in Early American History* (1984). His own essays range from ethnic tensions, the early history of trial by jury, the emergence of the legal profession, and the political culture of the colonies and the new nation, to the rise of professional baseball and college football in the 19th century. He served as president of the Society for Historians of the Early American Republic in 1998–1999.

Paul E. Johnson

University of South Carolina,
Distinguished Professor Emeritus

A specialist in early national social and cultural history, Paul E. Johnson is also the author of *The Early American Republic, 1789–1829* (2006); *Sam Patch, the Famous Jumper* (2003); and *A Shopkeeper's Millennium: Society and Revivals in Rochester, New York, 1815–1837*, 25th Anniversary Edition (2004). He is coauthor (with Sean Wilentz) of *The Kingdom of Matthias: Sex and Salvation in 19th-Century America* (1994), and editor of *African-American Christianity: Essays in History* (1994). He has been awarded the Merle Curti Prize of the Organization of American Historians (1980), the Richard P. McCormack Prize of the New Jersey Historical Association (1989), and fellowships from the National Endowment for the Humanities (1985–1986), the John Simon Guggenheim Foundation (1995), the Gilder Lehrman Institute (2001), and the National Endowment for the Humanities We the People Fellowship (2006–2007).

James M. McPherson

Princeton University, Emeritus

James M. McPherson is a distinguished Civil War historian and was president of the American Historical Association in 2003. He won the 1989 Pulitzer Prize for his book *Battle Cry of Freedom: The Civil War Era*. His other publications include *Marching Toward Freedom: Blacks in the Civil War*, Second Edition (1991); *Ordeal by Fire: The Civil War and Reconstruction*, Third Edition (2001); *Abraham Lincoln and the Second American Revolution* (1991); *For Cause and Comrades: Why Men Fought in the Civil War* (1997), which won the Lincoln Prize in 1998; *Crossroads of Freedom: Antietam* (2002); and *Tried by War: Abraham Lincoln as Commander in Chief* (2008), which won the Lincoln Prize for 2009.

Alice Fahs

University of California, Irvine

Alice Fahs is a specialist in American cultural history of the 19th and 20th centuries. Her 2001 *The Imagined Civil War: Popular Literature of the North and South, 1861–1865* was a finalist in 2002 for the Lincoln Prize. Together with Joan Waugh, she published the edited collection *The Memory of the Civil War in American Culture* in 2004; she has also edited Louisa May Alcott's *Hospital Sketches* (2004), an account of Alcott's nursing experiences during the Civil War first published in 1863. Fahs has been published on the cultural history of the Civil War and gender in such journals as the *Journal of American History and Civil War History*. Her honors include an American Council of Learned Societies Fellowship and a Gilder Lehrman Fellowship, as well as fellowships from the American Antiquarian Society, the Newberry Library, and the Huntington Library. She is currently at work on a study of popular literary culture in the late 19th and early 20th centuries, focused on the emergence of mass-market newspapers during an age of imperialism.

Gary Gerstle

Vanderbilt University

Gary Gerstle is the James G. Stahlman Professor of American History at Vanderbilt. A historian of the 20th-century United States, he is the author, coauthor, and coeditor of six books and the author of more than 30 articles. His books include *Working-Class Americanism: The Politics of Labor in a Textile City, 1914–1960* (1989); *American Crucible: Race and Nation in the Twentieth Century* (2001), winner of the Saloutos Prize for the best work in immigration and ethnic history; *The Rise and Fall of the New Deal Order, 1930–1980* (1989); and *Ruling America: Wealth and Power in a Democracy* (2005). He has served on the board of editors of both the *Journal of American*

History and *The American Historical Review*. His honors include a National Endowment for the Humanities Fellowship, a John Simon Guggenheim Memorial Fellowship, the Harmsworth Professorship of American History at the University of Oxford, and membership in the Society of American Historians.

context of international finance, American culture, and gender ideology. She has served on the board of the Organization of American Historians, on the board of editors of the *Journal of American History*, and as president of the Society for Historians of American Foreign Relations.

EMILY S. ROSENBERG

University of California, Irvine

Emily S. Rosenberg specializes in U.S. foreign relations in the 20th century and is the author of *Spreading the American Dream: American Economic and Cultural Expansion, 1890–1945* (1982); *Financial Missionaries to the World: The Politics and Culture of Dollar Diplomacy* (1999), which won the Ferrell Book Award; and *A Date Which Will Live: Pearl Harbor in American Memory* (2004). Her other publications include (with Norman L. Rosenberg) *In Our Times: America Since 1945*, Seventh Edition (2003), and numerous articles dealing with foreign relations in the

NORMAN L. ROSENBERG

Macalester College

Norman L. Rosenberg specializes in legal history with a particular interest in legal culture and First Amendment issues. His books include *Protecting the "Best Men": An Interpretive History of the Law of Libel* (1990) and (with Emily S. Rosenberg) *In Our Times: America Since 1945*, Seventh Edition (2003). He has published articles in the *Rutgers Law Review, UCLA Law Review, Constitutional Commentary, Law & History Review*, and many other journals and law-related anthologies.

BRIEF CONTENTS

CONTENTS

3   ENGLAND DISCOVERS ITS COLONIES: EMPIRE, LIBERTY, AND EXPANSION   58

15 SECESSION AND CIVIL WAR, 1860–1862   335

16 A NEW BIRTH OF FREEDOM, 1862–1865   360

LIST OF MAPS

HISTORY THROUGH FILM

MUSICAL LINKS TO THE PAST

LINKS TO THE PAST

VISUAL LINKS TO THE PAST

WHY STUDY HISTORY?

Why take a course in American history? This is a question that many college and university student ask. In many respects, students today are like the generations of Americans who have gone before them: optimistic and forward looking, far more eager to imagine where we as a nation might be going than to reflect on where we have been. If anything, this tendency has become more pronounced in recent years, as the Internet revolution has accelerated the pace and excitement of change and made even the recent past seem at best quaint, at worst uninteresting and irrelevant.

But it is precisely in these moments of change that a sense of the past can be indispensable in guiding our actions in the present and future. We can find in other periods of American history moments, like our own, of dizzying technological change and economic growth, rapid alterations in the concentration of wealth and power, and basic changes in patterns of work, residence, and play. How did Americans at those times create, embrace, and resist these changes? In earlier periods of American history, the United States was home, as it is today, to a broad array of ethnic and racial groups. How did earlier generations of Americans respond to the cultural conflicts and misunderstandings that often arise from conditions of diversity? How did immigrants of the early 1900s perceive their new land? How and when did they integrate themselves into American society? To study how ordinary Americans of the past struggled with these issues is to gain perspective on the opportunities and problems that we face today.

History also provides an important guide to affairs of state. What role should America assume in world affairs? Should we participate in international bodies such as the United Nations, or insist on our ability to act autonomously and without the consent of other nations? What is the proper role of government in economic and social life? Should the government regulate the economy? To what extent should the government enforce morality regarding religion, sexual practices, drinking and drugs, movies, TV, and other forms of mass culture? And what are our responsibilities as citizens to each other and to the nation? Americans of past generations have debated these issues with verve and conviction. Exploring these debates, and how they were resolved, will enrich our understanding of the policy possibilities for today and tomorrow.

History, finally, is about stories—stories that we all tell about ourselves; our families; our communities; our ethnicity, race, region, and religion; and our nation. They are stories of triumph and tragedy, of engagement and flight, and of high ideals and high comedy. When telling these stories, "American history" is often the furthest thing from our minds. But, often, an implicit sense of the past informs what we say about grandparents who immigrated many years ago; the suburb in which we live; the church, synagogue, or mosque at which we worship; or the ethnic or racial group to which we belong. How well, we might ask, do we really understand these individuals, institutions, and groups? Do our stories about them capture their history and complexity? Or do our stories wittingly or unwittingly simplify or alter what these individuals and groups experienced? A study of American history helps us first to ask these questions and then to answer them. In the process, we can embark on a journey of intellectual and personal discovery and situate ourselves more firmly than we had thought possible in relation to those who came before us. We can gain a firmer self-knowledge and a greater appreciation for the richness of our nation and, indeed, of all humanity.

Astronomers investigate the universe through telescopes. Biologists study the natural world by collecting plants and animals in the field and then examining them with microscopes. Sociologists and psychologists study human behavior through observation and controlled laboratory experiments.

Historians study the past by examining historical "evidence" or "source" materials—government documents; the records of private institutions ranging from religious and charitable organizations to labor unions, corporations, and lobbying groups; letters, advertisements, paintings, music, literature, movies, and cartoons; buildings, clothing, farm implements, industrial machinery, and landscapes—anything and everything written or created by our ancestors that gives clues about their lives and the times in which they lived.

Historians refer to written material as "documents." Excerpts of dozens of documents appear throughout the textbook—within the chapters and in the "Discovery" sections. Each chapter also includes many visual representations of the American past in the form of photographs of buildings, paintings, murals, individuals, cartoons, sculptures, and other historical evidence. As you read each chapter, the more you examine this "evidence," the more you will understand the main ideas of this book and of the course you are taking. The better you become at reading evidence, the better historian you will become.

"Discovery" sections at the end of each chapter assist you in practicing these skills by taking a closer look at specific images, quotes, or maps that will help you to connect the various threads of American history and to excel in your course.

DISCOVERY

What kind of culture emerged out of the market revolution that was discussed in Chapter 9? What was the impact on American families of the popular culture discussed in Chapter 10?

In thinking about this question, begin by breaking it down into the components shown below. A discussion of the significance of each component should appear in your answer.

The Impact of the Market on Family Life

Look at the illustration of domestic life on page 230. What does it suggest about how middle-class Americans saw their lives and their daily activities? What did the family want to reveal about their life at home? How does the illustration reflect the artist's definitions of *domesticity* and *sentimentality*? What would a photograph of your family suggest to future generations about the way you lived?

The Impact of the "New Popular Culture" on Family Life

Examine the image of an evening at the theater in the early 19th century. Does this activity seem to attract more men or women? How do you account for this gender difference? Is this gender difference important?

AN EARLY PRINT OF "JIM CROW" RICE AT NEW YORK'S BOWERY THEATER

Liberty, Equality, Power is a textbook admired for its successful integration of political, cultural, and social history; its thematic unity; its narrative clarity and eloquence; its extraordinary coverage of pre-Columbian America; its attention to war and conquest; its extended treatment of the Civil War; its history of economic growth and change; and its robust map and illustration programs. We have preserved and enhanced all these strengths in this Concise Sixth Edition. The concise version is intended to make the textbook more accessible to a broad range of students and give instructors maximum flexibility in their teaching. A brief edition, for example, makes it easier for instructors both to reach out to students who might be discouraged by a longer narrative and to supplement the textbook with readings, Web-based exercises, movies, and related materials of their own choosing.

THE *LIBERTY, EQUALITY, POWER* APPROACH

In this book we tell many small stories, and one large one: how America transformed itself, in a relatively brief era of world history, from a land inhabited by hunter-gatherer and agricultural Native American societies into the most powerful industrial nation on earth. This story has been told many times before, and those who have told it in the past have usually emphasized the political experiment in liberty and equality that took root here in the 18th century. We, too, stress the extraordinary and transformative impact that the ideals of liberty and equality exerted on American politics, society, and economics during the American Revolution and after. We show how the creation of a free economic environment, one that nourished entrepreneurship and technological innovation, underpinned American industrial might. We emphasize, too, the successful struggles for freedom that, over the course of the last 230 years, have brought—first to all white men, then to men of color, and finally to women—rights and opportunities that they had not previously known. But we have also identified a third factor in this pantheon of American ideals: power. We examine power in many forms—the accumulation of economic fortunes that dominated the economy and politics; the dispossession of Native Americans from land that they regarded as theirs; the enslavement of millions of Africans and their African American descendants for a period of almost 250 years; the relegation of women and of racial, ethnic, and religious minorities to subordinate places in American society; and the extension of American control over foreign peoples, such as Latin Americans and Filipinos, who would have preferred to be free and self-governing. We do not mean to suggest that American power has always been turned to negative purposes. To the contrary: Subordinate groups have themselves marshaled power to combat oppression, as in the abolitionist and civil rights crusades, the campaign for woman's suffrage, and the labor movement. In the 20th century, the federal government used its power to moderate poverty and to manage the economy in the interests of general prosperity. While one form of power sustained slavery over many generations, another, greater power abolished the institution in four years. Later, the federal government mobilized the nation's military might to defeat Nazi Germany, World War II Japan, the Cold War Soviet Union, and other enemies of freedom. The invocation of power as a variable in American history forces us to widen the lens through which we look at the past and to complicate the stories we tell. Ours has been a history of freedom and domination, of progress toward democracy and of delays and reverses, of abundance and poverty, of wars to free peoples from tyranny and battles to put foreign markets under American control.

In complicating our master narrative in this way, we think we have rendered American history more exciting and intriguing. Progress has not been automatic, but has been instead the product of ongoing struggles.

In this book we have also tried to capture the diversity of the American past, both in terms of outcomes and in terms of the variety of groups who have participated in America's making. We have not presented Native Americans simply as the victims of European aggression, but as a people diverse in their own ranks, with a variety of systems of social organization and cultural expression. We give equal treatment to the industrial titans of American history—the likes of Andrew Carnegie and John D. Rockefeller—and to those, such as small farmers and skilled workers, who resisted the corporate reorganization of economic life. We dwell on the achievements of 1863, when African Americans were freed from slavery, and of 1868, when they were made full citizens of the United States. But we also note how a majority of African Americans had to wait another 100 years, until the civil rights movement of the 1960s, to gain full access to American freedoms. We tell similarly complex stories about women, Latinos, and groups of ethnic Americans.

Political issues, of course, are only part of America's story. Americans have always pursued individuality and happiness and, in the process, have created the world's most vibrant popular culture. They have embraced technological innovations, especially those promising to make their lives easier and more fun. In light of this history, we have devoted considerable space to a discussion of popular culture, from the founding of the first newspapers in the 18th century to the rise of movies, jazz, and comics in the 20th century, to the cable television and Internet revolutions of recent years. We have pondered, too, how American industry has periodically altered home and personal life by making new products— such as clothing, cars, refrigerators, and computers— available to consumers. In such ways we hope to give our readers a rich portrait of how Americans spent their time, money, and leisure at various points in our history.

NEW TO THIS EDITION

In preparing for this revision, we solicited feedback from professors and scholars throughout the country, many of whom have used the comprehensive or concise editions of *Liberty, Equality, Power* in their classrooms. Many of their suggestions have been incorporated into the Concise Sixth Edition. Thus, for example, at the prompting of reviewers, we have expanded our primary source program to include new "Visual Links to the Past," described below. We have also undertaken for this edition a major reorganization and overhaul of Chapters 19 and 20. The new Chapter 19 now brings together and reworks material on late 19th-century economics, technology, and labor that in earlier editions had appeared in multiple chapters. The new Chapter 20, in turn, focuses on cities, peoples, and cultures during that same period of time. Much of the material in Chapter 20 is new and deepens our textbook's engagement with cultural and intellectual history. Chapters 29, 30, and 32 have also been significantly revised and reorganized to provide new perspectives on the most recent past.

Finally, we have scrutinized each page of the textbook, making sure our prose is clear, the historical issues are well presented, and the scholarship is up to date. This review, guided by the scholarly feedback we received, caused us to make numerous revisions and additions. A list of notable content changes follows.

SPECIFIC REVISIONS TO CONTENT AND COVERAGE

Chapter 1 New Link to the Past feature, Miguel León-Portilla, *The Broken Spears*. Deleted "Brazil" section.

Chapter 2 Condensed "Dutch and Swedish Settlements" section by shifting focus to the Dutch. New Link to the Past feature, "A City upon a Hill."

Chapter 3 New Visual Link to the Past feature, *A Pictish Man Holding a Human Head*, by John White; new map of Pueblo Revolt, 1680. Streamlined "Demographic Differences" section.

Chapter 4 New Visual Link to the Past feature, Benjamin West's *Benjamin Franklin Drawing Electricity from the Sky* (circa 1817). Rearranged and streamlined "Political Culture in the Colonies" section.

Chapter 5 Deleted sections on "The Feudal Revival and Rural Discontent" and "Regulator Movements in the Carolinas."

Chapter 6 Streamlined material on loyalists.

Chapter 7 New Link to the Past feature, "Washington's Republican Court."

Chapter 8 Deleted references to "safety-first" agriculture; condensed "The Decline of Patriarchy" section and moved to Chapter 12.

Chapter 9 New Visual Link to the Past feature, "A Southern View of Slavery"; increased coverage of crops and regions other than cotton; revised treatment of Denmark Vesey takes into account work of Michael Johnson; condensed treatment of government role in settlement; discussion of invention of the cotton gin revised to give less exclusive credit to Eli Whitney; added Link to the Past feature, "A Slave Mother and the Slave Trade"; revised Map 9.2 Distribution of Slave Population, 1790, 1820, and 1860.

Chapter 10 New Musical Link to the Past feature, "Oh Susannah"; moved discussions of *Uncle Tom's Cabin* and American Colonization Society to Chapter 12; deleted section entitled "Southern Entertainments" in response to reviewer feedback.

Chapter 11 Reworked Conclusion; added Focus Questions.

Chapter 12 New Visual Link to the Past feature, "An Abolitionist View of Slave Society"; reworked Introduction and Conclusion; deleted section on "Appetites"; expanded and revised treatments of antislavery movement and women's rights with increased emphasis on influence of blacks and women; condensed treatment of economic development.

Chapters 13 and 14 Added material in sections on Manifest Destiny, the Gold Rush, the Oregon Trail, and Harriet Beecher Stowe; Chapter 13 includes a new Visual Link to the Past feature, "Manifest Destiny."

Chapter 15 Condensed material on foreign relations, eliminating the section on the Trent affair.

Chapter 16 New Link to the Past feature, "'We Cannot Escape History': Abraham Lincoln."

Chapter 17 Condensed material on the Treaty of Washington. New Link to the Past feature, "Frederick Douglass on the Supreme Court and Civil Rights."

Chapter 18 New material on mining; condensed material on ranching and cowboys; new Visual Link to the Past feature, "Indian Children at the Hampton Institute."

Chapter 19 (MAJOR REVISION) Completely revised and reorganized. Now titled "The Rise of Corporate America, 1865–1914," it incorporates material from Fifth Edition Chapters 19 and 20 so that the story of the growth of American corporations is told in one place. New Visual Link to the Past feature, "The New Woman."

Chapter 20 (MAJOR REVISION) New title, Introduction, and Conclusion; added two substantial sections, "The Rise of the City" and "Reimagining American Nationality"; substantially revised section, "Working-Class and Commercial Culture" (formerly, "The Joys of the City"); new Musical Link to the Past feature, "Ragtime"; new History through Film feature, *Coney Island* (1917); added Focus Questions and glossary terms.

Chapter 21 Added sections on the IWW and Frederick W. Taylor and scientific management; added Focus Questions;

reduced number of major headings. New Link to the Past feature, "Humor and the Woman Suffrage Movement."

Chapter 23 New Link to the Past feature, "A Storm of Our People toward the North."

Chapter 24 Moved History through Film feature on *The Jazz Singer* here from Chapter 20.

Chapter 25 Condensed material on the Federal Reserve Board and the tariff; added Focus Questions.

Chapter 26 Streamlined and revised prose to provide stronger narrative; condensed sections on European and Pacific theaters into one; increased attention to role of West in "Business and Finance" section; expanded coverage of Japanese internment and added mention of Italian and German internees; revised Focus Questions; added History through Film feature, *Saving Private Ryan* (1998); new Link to the Past feature, "Civil Liberties in Wartime: *Korematsu v. United States.*"

Chapter 27 Revised Korean War section, giving greater emphasis to war's impact; substantially revised discussion of containment; updated material on McCarthy; added material on farm issues; revised Fair Deal section; added discussion of integration of armed forces; revised end of chapter in light of recent scholarship on significance of election of 1952; new Visual Link to the Past feature, "It's Okay—We're Hunting Communists"; revised Focus Questions.

Chapter 28 Combined coverage of civil rights movement into one section; revised coverage of conservatism in sections "Debating the Role of Government" and "The Case for a More Active Government"; refocused final section of chapter; reorganized and streamlined the section "The Third World"; added material on rural America and farm policy; new Link to the Past feature, "A Warning about the Future: President Dwight Eisenhower's Farewell Address, 1961."

Chapter 29 (MAJOR REVISION) Streamlined and reorganized to clarify and focus narrative; reframed section, "A Crisis of Governance, 1972–1974"; reworked civil rights material; added discussion of environmentalism; revised accounts of 1964 election and Gulf of Tonkin; revised Focus Questions; new Visual Link to the Past feature, "Shocking Images."

Chapter 30 (MAJOR REVISION) Completely reorganized chapter along thematic lines; new section, "The Reagan Revolution, 1981–1992," includes a more focused discussion of the central themes of the administration of Ronald Reagan; added Link to the Past feature, "Cultural Disagreements: Equality for Women?"

Chapter 31 Revised section on the financial sector.

Chapter 32 (MAJOR REVISION) Revised and updated entire chapter; reworked economic discussion; new Visual Link to the Past feature, "The Future of Print Media?"; new History through Film feature, *The Big Lebowski* (1998); revised Focus Questions.

FEATURES

The success of our **Musical Link to the Past** feature has inspired us to expand our primary source program in new directions for this edition: We have added an entirely new feature, **Visual Link to the Past.** Each of the new Visual Links focuses on a single piece of art, material culture, or photography that reveals something important about the historical era in which it was produced. In an extended caption we explore the historical significance of the object in question, and then pose a question for students to answer. Examples include "Benjamin West's *Benjamin Franklin Drawing Electricity from the Sky* (circa 1817)" (Chapter 4); "Indian Children at the Hampton Institute" (Chapter 18); "The New Woman," featuring a John Singer Sargent portrait (Chapter 19); and a political cartoon "It's Okay—We're Hunting Communists" (Chapter 27).

The Concise Sixth Edition also incorporates some of the **Link to the Past** features that have appeared in the comprehensive version for several editions. These features explore important written documents from the American past and include an assignable question for individual response or classroom discussion. Featured documents include an 1852 letter from an enslaved woman to her husband expressing distress at the recent sale of their son (Chapter 9), a poem which takes a lighthearted look at woman suffrage (Chapter 21), and an excerpt from President Eisenhower's Farewell Address, warning about escalating the Cold War arms race (Chapter 28).

We've retained the Musical Link to the Past features, which cover a great range of songs and artists: from revolutionary era odes to liberty to 20th-century country music laments about women's domestic burdens; from John Philip Sousa to Duke Ellington and Grandmaster Flash. The Concise Sixth Edition includes two new entries: Stephen Foster, "Oh Susannah" (Chapter 10); and Scott Joplin, "Maple Leaf Rag" (Chapter 20). Dr. Harvey Cohen, a specialist in American cultural history who teaches at King's College London, drafted the texts of these musical features, and we wish to recognize his important contributions to this textbook. To make the Musical Links come alive in classrooms, we have assembled a **Musical Links to the Past CD** containing many of the musical selections that we discuss. All instructors who adopt our textbook are encouraged to request a free copy of this CD to play in their classrooms. In combination, the three Links features—musical, visual, and textual—endow our Concise Sixth Edition with one of the most comprehensive, diverse, and intriguing programs of primary sources available in a U.S. history textbook.

The popular **History through Film** essays summarize a film, note interesting historical questions that it raises, and offer commentary on the accuracy or inaccuracy of historical figures and events as seen through the lens of a camera. The Concise Sixth Edition includes 15 History through Film features, including *A Midwife's Tale* (Chapter 8), *Amistad* (Chapter 11), a new feature on *Coney Island* (Chapter 20), and *Saving Private Ryan* (Chapter 26).

Visually engaging **Timelines** help students understand the relationships among the events and movements of a particular era. Many chapter sections open with **Focus Questions** to aid students in grasping overarching themes and to organize the knowledge that they are acquiring. These reappear at the end of each chapter in the **Chapter Review**, which is supplemented by **Critical Thinking Questions** that encourage students to range widely and imaginatively in their thinking about what they have just learned. **Identification** lists at the end of the chapter highlight the key terms for study and review.

Quick Reviews and **Glossary Terms** further contribute to the emphasis we have placed on pedagogy. Quick Reviews appear periodically in the margins to summarize major events, ideas, and movements discussed in the text. Glossary Terms—individuals, ideas, events, legislation, and movements that we have deemed particularly important to an understanding of the historical period in question—appear boldface in the text and then are briefly defined in the margins.

SUPPLEMENTS

FOR THE INSTRUCTOR

The Instructor's Companion Web Site provides instructors access to all of the features of the Student Companion Web Site, along with the eInstructor's Resource Manual. This manual has many features, including instructional objectives, chapter outlines and summaries, lecture suggestions, suggested debate and research topics, cooperative learning activities, and suggested readings and resources.

The PowerLecture with ExamView and JoinIn, [ISBN: 9781285059334] a dual-platform, all-in-one multimedia resource, includes the Instructor's Resource Manual; Test Bank, revised by D. Antonio Cantù of Bradley University (includes key term identification, multiple-choice, short answer, essay, and map questions); Microsoft® PowerPoint® slides of both lecture outlines and images and maps from the text that can be used as offered, or customized by importing personal lecture slides or other material; and JoinIn® Power-Point® slides with clicker content. Also included is ExamView, an easy-to-use assessment and tutorial system that allows instructors to create, deliver, and customize tests in minutes. Instructors can build tests with as many as 250 questions using up to 12 question types, and using ExamView's complete word-processing capabilities, they can enter an unlimited number of new questions or edit existing ones.

Cengage Learning's History **CourseMate** brings course concepts to life with interactive learning, study, and exam preparation tools that support the printed textbook. Watch student comprehension soar as your class works with the printed textbook and the textbook-specific Web site. History CourseMate includes an integrated eBook, interactive teaching and learning tools including quizzes, revised by Thomas Born of Blinn College, flashcards, videos, and more, and EngagementTracker, a first-of-its-kind tool that monitors student engagement in the course. Learn more at www.cengagebrain.com.

Aplia™ is an online interactive learning solution that improves comprehension and outcomes by increasing student effort and engagement. Founded by a professor to enhance his own courses, Aplia provides automatically graded assignments with detailed, immediate explanations on every question and innovative teaching materials. Our easy-to-use system has been used by more than one million students at over 1,800 institutions. Features include "flip-book" navigation that allows students to easily scan the contents; chapter assignments, developed specifically for your textbook and customizable for your course, that are automatically graded and provide detailed responses to students; a course management system so you can post announcements, upload course materials, host student discussions, e-mail students, and manage your gradebook; and personalized support from a knowledgeable and friendly team. Our support team also offers assistance in customizing our assignments to your course schedule. To learn more, visit www.aplia.com.

FOR THE STUDENT

The Student Companion Web Site allows students to access a wide assortment of resources to help them master the subject matter. The Web site includes a glossary, flashcards, tutorial quizzes, essay questions, critical thinking exercises, Web links, and suggested readings. Throughout the text, icons direct students to relevant exercises and self-testing material located on the student companion Web site.

The History Handbook, Second Edition [ISBN: 9780495906766], by Carol Berkin of Baruch College, City University of New York, and Betty Anderson of Boston University, teaches students both basic and history-specific study skills such as how to read primary sources, research historical topics, and correctly cite sources. Substantially less expensive than comparable skill-building texts, *The History Handbook* also offers tips for Internet research and evaluating online sources.

Doing History: Research and Writing in the Digital Age, Second Edition [ISBN: 9781133587880], by Michael J. Galgano, J. Chris Arndt, and Raymond M. Hyser of James Madison University, is a perfect guide whether you are starting down the path of a history major or simply looking for a straightforward, systematic guide to writing a successful paper. This text is an indispensable handbook to historical research. Its "soup-to-nuts" approach to researching and writing about history addresses every step of the process, from locating your sources and gathering information, to writing clearly and making proper use of various citation styles to avoid plagiarism. You'll also learn how to make the most of every tool available to you—especially the technology that helps you conduct the process efficiently and effectively. The Second Edition includes a special appendix linked to CourseReader (see below), where you can examine and interpret primary sources online.

The Modern Researcher, Sixth Edition [ISBN: 9780495318705], by Jacques Barzun and Henry F. Graff of Columbia University, a classic introduction to the techniques of research and the art of expression, is used widely in history courses but is also appropriate for writing and research method courses in other departments. Barzun and Graff thoroughly cover every aspect of research, from the selection of a topic through the gathering, analysis, writing, revision, and publication of findings, presenting the process not as a set of rules but through actual cases that put the subtleties of research in a useful context. Part One covers the principles and methods of research; Part Two covers writing, speaking, and getting one's work published.

Rand McNally Atlas of American History, Second Edition [ISBN: 9780618842018], is a comprehensive atlas that features more than 80 maps, with new content covering global perspectives, including events in the Middle East from 1945 to 2005, as well as population trends in the United States and around the world. Additional maps document voyages of discovery; the settling of the colonies; major U.S. military engagements, including the American Revolution and World Wars I and II; and sources of immigrations, ethnic populations, and patterns of economic change.

Our new **CourseReader** lets you create a customized electronic reader in minutes. With our easy-to-use interface and assessment tool, you can choose exactly what your students will be assigned—simply search or browse Cengage Learning's extensive document database to preview and select your customized collection of readings.

Once you've made your choice, students will always receive the pedagogical support they need to succeed with the materials you've chosen: Each source document includes a descriptive headnote that puts the reading into context, and every selection is further supported by both critical thinking and multiple-choice questions designed to reinforce key points.

ACKNOWLEDGMENTS

We recognize the contributions of these reviewers, who have provided feedback on *Liberty, Equality, Power*, Concise Edition:

David Arnold, Columbia Basin College
Mary Ann Bodayla, Southwest Tennessee Community College
Betty Brandon, University of Southern Alabama
Janet Brantley, Texarkana College
April L. Brown, NorthWest Arkansas Community College
B. R. Burg, Arizona State University
Gary Damron, Seward County Community College
Randy Finley, Georgia Perimeter College
Michael P. Gabriel, Kutztown University
Steven C. Garvey, Muskegon Community College
Wendy Gordon, SUNY Plattsburgh
Sally Hadden, Florida State University
Kevin E. Hall, University of South Florida
Ian Harrison, University of Nevada, Las Vegas
Mary Ann Heiss, Kent State University
Terry Isaacs, South Plains College
Volker Janssen, California State University, Fullerton
Catherine Kaplan, Arizona State University
Timothy K. Kinsella, Ursuline College
Greg Kiser, NorthWest Arkansas Community College

C. Douglas Kroll, College of the Desert
David F. Krugler, University of Wisconsin, Platteville
Joseph Lapsley, Columbia College of Art
Marianne F. McKnight, Salt Lake Community College
Joel McMahon, Baker College
Salvatore R. Mercogliano, Central Carolina Community College
Caryn E. Neumann, Miami University of Ohio
Margaret E. Newell, Ohio State University
Thomas Ott, University of North Alabama
George S. Pabis, Georgia Perimeter College
Birte Pfleger, California State University, Los Angeles
Geoffrey Plank, University of Cincinnati
G. David Price, Santa Fe Community College (FL)
John Putman, San Diego State University
Akim D. Reinhardt, Towson University
Jason Ripper, Everett Community College
Jerry Rodnitzky, University of Texas, Arlington
John Paul Rossi, Penn State Erie
Steven T. Sheehan, University of Wisconsin, Fox Valley
Megan Taylor Shockley, Clemson University
Adam M. Sowards, University of Idaho
Evelyn Sterne, University of Rhode Island
Kristen L. Streater, Collin County Community College, Preston Ridge Campus
Sean Taylor, Minnesota State University, Moorhead
Jerry Tiarsmith, Georgia Perimeter College
Leslie V. Tischauser, Prairie State College
Paul S. Vickery, Oral Roberts University
Stephen Webre, Louisiana Tech University
Bryan Wuthrich, Santa Fe Community College (FL)

We also wish to thank Carol Newman, senior content project manager, and other members of the Wadsworth staff who capably guided the revision and production of this edition. Special thanks to Ann West, senior sponsoring editor, for her wisdom, support, and mastery of textbook publishing, and to Rob Heinrich, freelance editor, for the quality of his editing. Our greatest debt once again is to our longtime developmental editor, Margaret McAndrew Beasley. Margaret's editing skills, organizational expertise, good sense, and belief in this book and its authors keep us going.

John M. Murrin
Paul E. Johnson
James M. McPherson
Alice Fahs
Gary Gerstle
Emily S. Rosenberg
Norman L. Rosenberg

LIBERTY, EQUALITY, POWER

C H A P T E R

1

WHEN OLD WORLDS COLLIDE: CONTACT, CONQUEST, CATASTROPHE

When Christopher Columbus crossed the Atlantic, he did not know where he was going, and he died without realizing where he had been. Yet he changed history forever. In the 40 years after 1492, Europeans conquered the Americas, not just with sails, gunpowder, and steel, but also with their plants, livestock, and, most of all, their diseases. By 1600, they had created the first global economy in history and had inflicted upon the native peoples of the Americas, for the most part unintentionally, the greatest known catastrophe that human societies have ever experienced.

In the 15th century the Americas were in some ways a more ancient world than Western Europe. At a time when Paris and London were insignificant, huge cities were thriving in the Andes and **Mesoamerica** (the area embracing Central America and southern and central Mexico). Which world was old and which was new is a matter of perspective. Each already had its own distinctive past.

1

TIMELINE

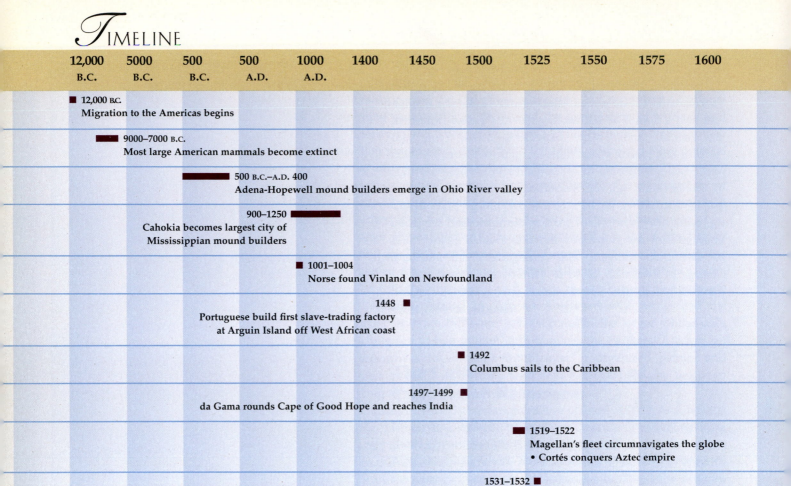

12,000 B.C.	5000 B.C.	500 B.C.	500 A.D.	1000 A.D.	1400	1450	1500	1525	1550	1575	1600

■ 12,000 B.C.
Migration to the Americas begins

9000–7000 B.C.
Most large American mammals become extinct

500 B.C.–A.D. 400
Adena-Hopewell mound builders emerge in Ohio River valley

900–1250
Cahokia becomes largest city of Mississippian mound builders

■ 1001–1004
Norse found Vinland on Newfoundland

1448 ■
Portuguese build first slave-trading factory at Arguin Island off West African coast

■ 1492
Columbus sails to the Caribbean

1497–1499 ■
da Gama rounds Cape of Good Hope and reaches India

■ 1519–1522
Magellan's fleet circumnavigates the globe
• Cortés conquers Aztec empire

1531–1532 ■
Pizarro conquers Inca empire

1580 ■
Philip II unites Spanish and Portuguese empires

PEOPLES IN MOTION

By the time **Christopher Columbus** sailed west from Spain in 1492, four waves of immigrants had already swept over the Americas. Three came from Asia. The last, from northern Europe, did not survive.

From Beringia to the Americas

Mesoamerica *Area encompassing Central America and southern and central Mexico.*

Christopher Columbus *Genoese mariner who persuaded Queen Isabella of Spain to support his voyage of discovery across the Atlantic to East Asia in 1492. Instead, he discovered America.*

Before the most recent ice age ended 12,000 years ago, glaciers covered huge portions of the Americas, Europe, and Asia. The ice captured so much of the world's water that sea levels fell drastically when they melted and created a land bridge 600 miles wide across the Bering Strait between Siberia and Alaska. For more than 10,000 years after 23,000 BCE, this exposed area—now called **Beringia**—was dry land on which plants, animals, and humans lived. These first immigrants to the Americas hunted for meat and furs and probably built small fishing vessels. They made snug homes to keep themselves warm through the fierce winters. As the glaciers further receded, people drifted from Asia in small bands and spread throughout the Americas. By 8000 BCE, they had reached **Tierra del Fuego** at the southern tip of South America.

These Asians probably came in three waves. Those in the first wave, beginning around 12,000 BCE, spread over most of the two continents and spoke **Amerind,** the forerunner of the Algonquian, Iroquoian, Muskogean, Siouan, Nahuatl (Aztec), Mayan, and all South American tongues. Those in the middle wave, which came a few thousand years later, spoke a language that eventually gave rise to the various Athapaskan languages of the Canadian Northwest as well as the Apache, Navajo, and related tongues in the American Southwest. The last to arrive, the ancestors of the Inuits (called Eskimos by other Indians), crossed after 7000 BCE, when Beringia was again underwater. About 4,000 years ago, these people began to migrate across the northern rim of North America and then across the North Atlantic to Greenland, where they encountered the first Europeans migrating westward—the Norsemen.

The Great Extinction and the Rise of Agriculture

As the climate warmed, the people who had wandered south and east found an environment teeming with game. Imperial mammoths, huge mastodons, woolly rhinoceroses, a species of enormous bison, and giant ground sloths roamed the plains and forests. These animals had no instinctive fear of the two-legged intruders, who became ever more skillful at hunting them. A superior spear point, the Clovis tip, appeared in the area around present-day New Mexico and Texas some time before 9000 BCE. As its use spread throughout the Americas over the next thousand years, the big game died off. Overhunting was a major factor, along with climatic change.

The hemisphere was left with a severely depleted number of animal species. The largest beasts were bears, buffalo, and moose; the biggest cat was the jaguar. The extinction of giant species probably led to a sharp decline in the human population as people scrambled for new food sources. Some Indians raised guinea pigs, turkeys, or ducks, but apart from dogs, they domesticated no large animals except for llamas (useful for hauling light loads in mountainous terrain) and alpacas (valued for their wool), both in South America. The peoples of the Pacific Northwest sustained themselves through fishing, hunting, and the gathering of nuts, berries, and other edible plants. Men fished and hunted; women gathered. Hunter-gatherers also lived in Brazil, Florida, and New England.

Most Indians could not depend solely on hunting and gathering food, however. Some of them, almost certainly women, began to plant and harvest crops. In Asia and Africa, this practice was closely linked to the domestication of animals and

Beringia *Land bridge during the last ice age across the Bering Strait between Siberia and Alaska, where plants, animals, and humans lived.*

Tierra del Fuego *Region at the southern tip of South America.*

Amerind *Forerunner of the vast majority of Indian languages in the Americas.*

Clovis tip *A superior spear point developed before 9000 BCE. Its use produced an improvement in hunting ability that contributed to the extinction of most large mammals.*

© Werner Forman/Art Resource, NY

INUIT FACE MASK. *Despite their forbidding arctic climate, Inuits developed their own art forms. The face on this mask represents the spirit of the moon, the wood surrounding it is air, and the feathers are stars.*

happened quickly enough to be called the **Neolithic** (new or late Stone Age) revolution. But in the Americas the rise of farming had little to do with animals, occurred gradually, and might better be termed the Neolithic *evolution*. Somewhere between 4000 and 1500 BCE, permanent farm villages began to dominate parts of Peru, Mexico, and the southwestern United States. The first American farmers grew amaranth (a cereal), manioc (tapioca), chili peppers, pumpkins, sweet potatoes, several varieties of beans, and, above all, maize, or Indian corn.

By 900 CE, the temperature in North America and northern Europe had risen two or three degrees. Agriculture became the primary means of support in most of North America. In the northeastern woodlands, peoples settled into semisedentary communities, where they raised and stored their crops, erected dwellings, and then dispersed for part of the year to hunt or fish. Population increased. Climate began to cool again in the 14th century, a trend that became more severe in the 16th and 17th centuries and provoked frequent droughts in Europe and North America.

The Norsemen

Europeans also began trekking long distances. Pushed by fierce invaders from central Asia, Germanic tribes overran the western provinces of the Roman Empire. The Norse, a Germanic people, occupied Scandinavia. For centuries their Viking warriors raided the coasts of the British Isles and France. Their sleek longboats, propelled by both sails and oars, enabled them to challenge the contrary currents of the north Atlantic.

Beginning in 874 CE, Vikings occupied Iceland. In 982 and 983, Erik the Red, accused of manslaughter in Norway and then outlawed for committing more mayhem in Iceland, led his Norse followers farther west to Greenland. There they established permanent settlements.

Leif, Erik's son, sailed west from Greenland in 1001 and explored the coast of North America. He made three more voyages, the last in 1014, and started a colony that he called "Vinland" on the northern coast of Newfoundland. After driving off the local Indians, the Norse quarreled among themselves and destroyed the colony. They abandoned Vinland but continued to visit North America for another century, probably to get wood.

Several centuries later, not long before Columbus sailed in 1492, the last Norse settler in Greenland died a lonely death. The colony had suffered a population decline, gradually lost contact with the homeland, and slowly withered away. Despite their spectacular exploits, the Norse had no impact on the later course of American history.

EUROPE AND THE WORLD IN THE 15TH CENTURY

Nobody in the year 1400 could have foreseen the course of European expansion that was about to begin. At that time Europe stood at the edge, not the center, of world commerce.

China: The Rejection of Overseas Expansion

By just about every standard, China under the Ming Dynasty was the world's most complex culture. The government of China, staffed by well-educated bureaucrats, ruled 100 million people. The Chinese had invented the compass, gunpowder, and early

---

Neolithic *Period known also as the late Stone Age when agriculture developed, and stone, rather than metal, tools were used.*

QUICK REVIEW

SETTLEMENT OF THE AMERICAS DURING AND AFTER THE LAST ICE AGE

- Migration and settlement across Beringia

- Spread of settlement and the great extinction as climate warmed

- Rise of agriculture

- Exploration and brief settlement of America by the Norsemen

FOCUS QUESTION

What enabled relatively backward European societies to establish dominance over the oceans of the world?

forms of printing and paper money. Foreigners coveted China's silks, teas, and other fine products, but they had little to offer in exchange. Most of what Europe knew about China came from *The Travels* of Marco Polo, a merchant from the Italian city-state of Venice who reached the Chinese court in 1271 and served the emperor, Kublai Khan, for the next 20 years. Marco insisted that the Khan's capital city (today's Beijing) was the world's largest and grandest and that China outshone Europe and all other cultures.

The Chinese agreed. Between 1405 and 1434 a royal eunuch, Cheng Ho, led six large fleets from China to the East Indies and the coast of East Africa, trading and exploring along the way. His ships were large enough to sail around the southern tip of Africa and "discover" Europe. Had China thrown its resources into overseas expansion, the subsequent history of the world would have been vastly different. But most of what the Chinese learned about the outside world confirmed their belief that other cultures had little to offer. No one followed Cheng Ho's lead after he died. The emperor banned the construction of oceangoing ships and later forbade anyone to own a vessel with more than two masts. China turned inward. It did not need the rest of the world.

Christian Europe Challenges Islam

Compared with China or the Islamic world, Western Europe suffered severe disadvantages in 1400. Its location on the Atlantic rim of the Eurasian continent had always made access to Asian trade difficult and costly. Islamic societies controlled overland trade with Asia and the only known seaborne route through the Persian Gulf. In 1400, Arab mariners were the world's best. Europeans coveted East Indian spices, but because they produced little that Asians wished to buy, they had to pay for these imports with scarce silver or gold.

While Europe's sphere of influence was shrinking, and while China seemed content with what it already had, Islamic states embarked on another great phase of expansion. The Ottoman Turks took Constantinople in 1453, overran the Balkans by the 1520s, and threatened Vienna. The Safavid Empire in Iran (Persia) rose to new splendor at the same time. Other Moslems carried the Koran to Indonesia and northern India.

By 1300 more than 100 million people were living in Europe, but Europe's farms could not sustain further growth. Lean years and famines ensued, leaving people undernourished. Then, in the late 1340s, the Black Death (bubonic plague) reduced the population by more than a third. Recurring bouts of plague kept the population low until about 1500.

During this long decline of the 15th century, however, overworked soil regained its fertility, and per capita income rose among people who now had stronger immunities to disease. By then European metallurgy and architecture were quite advanced. The Renaissance, which revived interest in the art and literature of ancient Greece and Rome, also gave a new impetus to European culture, especially after Johannes Gutenberg invented the printing press and movable type in the 1430s. This revolution in communications permitted improvements in ship design and navigational techniques to become a self-reinforcing process. The Arabs, by contrast, had borrowed printing from China in the 10th century but gave it up by 1400.

Unlike China, none of Europe's kingdoms was a self-contained economy. All had to trade with one another and with the non-Christian world. No single state had a monopoly on the manufacture of firearms or on the flow of capital, a situation that proved advantageous in the long run. During the 15th century European societies began to compete with one another to gain access to these resources and to master new **maritime** and military techniques. As a result, European armies were far more formidable by 1520 than a century before, and European fleets could outsail and outfight all rivals.

maritime *Of, or relating to, the sea.*

The Legacy of the Crusades

Quite apart from the Norse explorers, Europe had a heritage of expansion that derived from the efforts of crusaders to wrest the Holy Land from Islam. Crusaders had established their own Kingdom of Jerusalem, which was finally retaken in 1244. This overseas venture taught Europeans important lessons. To make Palestine profitable, the crusaders had taken over sugar plantations and worked them with a combination of free and slave labor. After they were driven from the Holy Land, they retreated to the Mediterranean islands of Cyprus, Malta, Crete, and Rhodes, where they used slaves to grow sugar cane and grapes.

Long before Columbus, then, these planters had created the economic components of overseas expansion. They assumed that colonies should produce a staple crop, at least partly through slave labor, for sale in Europe. The first slaves were Moslem captives. In the 14th and 15th centuries, planters turned to pagan Slavs (hence the word *slave*) from the Black Sea area and the Adriatic. Some black Africans were also acquired from Arab merchants who controlled the caravan trade across the Sahara Desert.

The Unlikely Pioneer: Portugal

In 1400 Portugal, a small kingdom of fewer than a million people, had been united for less than a century. Its maritime traditions lagged behind those of the Italian states, France, and England, and it had little capital.

Yet Portugal enjoyed internal peace and an efficient government at a time when its neighbors endured war and internal upheaval. Moreover, it was located at the intersection of the Mediterranean and Atlantic worlds. At first, Portuguese mariners were interested in short-term gains rather than in some all-water route to Asia. They knew that Arab caravans crossed the Sahara to bring gold and slaves from black Africa to Europe. The Portuguese believed that an Atlantic voyage to coastal points south of the Sahara would undercut Arab traders. The greatest problem they faced in this quest was Cape Bojador, with its treacherous shallows, awesome waves, and strong northerly winds.

In 1420 a member of the Portuguese royal family, Prince Henry, sponsored 15 voyages along the African coast. In 1434, one of his captains finally sailed past Cape Bojador, explored the coastline, and then headed west into the Atlantic until he met favorable winds that carried him back to Europe. Other captains pushed farther south along the African coast.

During the 15th century Portuguese navigators mapped the prevailing winds and currents over most of the globe. They collected geographic information. They studied the superior designs of Arab vessels, copied them, and then improved on them. They borrowed the lateen (triangular) sail from the Arabs and combined it with square rigging in the right proportion to produce a superb oceangoing vessel, the caravel. Portuguese captains used the compass and adopted the Arabs' astrolabe, a device that permits accurate calculation of latitude, or distances north and south. They also learned how to mount heavy cannon on the decks of their ships. In an age when others fought naval battles by grappling and boarding enemy vessels, Portuguese ships could stand farther off and literally blow their opponents out of the water.

After 1450 Portuguese mariners explored ever farther along the African coast. South of the Sahara they found the wealth they had been seeking: gold, ivory, and slaves.

staple crop *Crops, such as tobacco and sugar, grown for commercial sale, usually produced in a colonial area and sold in Europe.*

caravel *New type of oceangoing vessel that could sail closer to a headwind than any other sailing ship and make speeds of 3 to 12 knots.*

astrolabe *Device that permitted accurate calculation of latitude, or distances north and south.*

Africa, Colonies, and the Slave Trade

West Africans had been supplying Europe with most of its gold for hundreds of years through indirect trade across the Sahara. West Africa's political history had seen the rise and decline of a series of large inland states. The most recent was the empire of Mali. As the Portuguese advanced past the Sahara, their commerce began to pull trade away from the desert caravans, weakening Mali and other interior states. By 1550, the empire had fallen apart.

The Portuguese also founded offshore colonies along the way, settling in the Madeira Islands, the Azores, the Cape Verde Islands, and São Tomé. Like exploration, colonization turned a profit. Beginning in the 1440s Portuguese island planters produced sugar or wine, increasingly with slave labor imported from nearby Africa.

The Portuguese initially acquired their slaves by landing on the African coast, attacking villages, and carrying off everyone they could catch, but these raids enraged coastal peoples and made other forms of trade more difficult. In the decades after 1450, the slave trade assumed its classic form. The Portuguese established small posts, or **factories**, along the coast or on small offshore islands. Operating out of these bases, traders would buy slaves from the local rulers, who usually acquired them by waging war. Throughout the history of the **Atlantic slave trade**, nearly every African shipped overseas had first been enslaved by other Africans.

Slavery had long existed in Africa, but in a form less brutal than what the Europeans would impose. In Africa, slaves were not forced to toil endlessly to produce staple crops, and their descendants often became fully assimilated into the captors' society. Slaves were not isolated as a separate caste. By the time African middlemen learned about the cruel conditions of slavery under European rule, the trade had become too lucrative to stop. When the rulers of the Kongo embraced Catholicism in the 16th century, they protested against the Atlantic slave trade, only to see their own people become vulnerable to enslavement by others. The non-Christian kingdom of Benin learned the same lesson.

The Portuguese made the slave trade profitable by exploiting rivalries among the more than 200 small states of West and Central Africa. Despite many cultural similarities among these groups, West Africans had never thought of themselves as a single people. Nor did they share a universal religion, such as Islam, that might have restrained them from selling their fellow believers into slavery. The Christian Western European traders believed that enslaving fellow Christians was immoral. Enslaving pagan or Moslem Africans was another matter. Some Europeans even persuaded themselves that they were doing the enslaved a favor by making their souls eligible for salvation.

Portugal's Asian Empire

In the 1480s the Portuguese government supported the quest for an all-water route to Asia. In 1487 Bartolomeu Dias reached the Cape of Good Hope at the southern tip of Africa and headed east toward the Indian Ocean, but his crew rebelled in those stormy waters, and he turned back. Ten years later Vasco da Gama led a small fleet around the Cape of Good Hope and sailed on to the southwestern coast of India. In a voyage that lasted more than two years, he bargained and fought for spices that yielded a 20-to-1 profit.

To secure their Asian trade, the Portuguese established a chain of naval bases from East Africa to the Persian Gulf, to the west coast of India, and from there to the Moluccas, or East Indies. Portuguese missionaries even penetrated Japan. The Moluccas, with their profitable spices, became the Asian center of the Portuguese

factories *Small posts established for the early slave trade along the coast of Africa or on small offshore islands.*

Atlantic slave trade *A European commerce that led to the enslavement of millions of people, who were shipped from their African homelands to European colonies in the Americas.*

Map 1.1 Africa and the Mediterranean in the 15th Century. *The Mediterranean islands held by Europeans in the late Middle Ages, the Atlantic islands colonized by Portugal and Spain in the 15th century, the part of West Africa from Cape Blanco to Angola that provided the main suppliers of the Atlantic slave trade, and the Portuguese all-water route to India after 1497.*

seaborne empire. Beyond assuring its continued access to spices, however, Portugal made little effort to govern its colonies. In all their Asian holdings, the Portuguese remained heavily outnumbered by native peoples. Only in the Western Hemisphere—in Brazil, discovered accidentally by Pedro Álvares Cabral in 1500 when he was blown off course while trying to round the Cape of Good Hope—had settlement become a major goal by the late 16th century.

Early Lessons

As the Norse failure showed, the ability to navigate the high seas gave no guarantee of lasting success. Sustained expansion overseas required the support of a home government and ready access to what other states had learned. The desire for precious metals provided the initial economic stimulus behind colonization, but staple crops and slavery kept that impetus alive. Before the 19th century, more than two-thirds of the people who crossed the Atlantic were enslaved Africans, not free European settlers.

Spain, Columbus, and the Americas

In January 1492 Isabella and Ferdinand completed the reconquest of Spain by taking Granada, the last outpost of Islam on the Iberian Peninsula. Just over half of Spain's 80,000 Jews were evicted, and, a decade later, Ferdinand and Isabella also expelled all unconverted Moors, or Spanish Moslems. Spain entered the 16th century as Europe's most fiercely Catholic society, an attitude that accompanied its soldiers and settlers to America.

Columbus

A talented navigator from Genoa named Christopher Columbus had been pleading for years with the courts of Portugal, England, France, and Spain to give him the ships and men to attempt an unprecedented feat: He planned to reach eastern Asia by sailing west across the Atlantic.

Columbus's proposed voyage was controversial, but not because he assumed the earth is round. Learned men already agreed on that point, but they disagreed about its size. Columbus put its circumference at only 16,000 miles, whereas the Portuguese calculated it, correctly, at about 26,000 miles.

The fall of Granada gave Columbus another chance to plead his case. Isabella now had men and resources to spare. She put him in charge of a fleet of two caravels, the *Niña* and the *Pinta*, together with a larger, square-rigged vessel, the *Santa María*, which became his flagship.

Columbus's motives were both religious and practical. As the "Christ-bearer" (the literal meaning of his first name), Columbus was convinced that he had a role to play in bringing on the **Millennium**, the period at the end of history when Jesus would return and rule with his saints for 1,000 years. But Columbus was not averse to acquiring wealth and glory along the way.

Embarking in August 1492, Columbus headed south to the Canaries, picked up provisions, and started west across the Atlantic. Despite his assurances that they had not sailed very far, the crews grew restless in early October. Columbus pushed on. Land was finally spotted on October 12. The Spaniards splashed ashore on San Salvador, now Watling's Island in the Bahamas. Convinced that he was somewhere in the East Indies, Columbus called the local inhabitants "Indians." When the peaceful Tainos (or Arawaks) claimed that the Carib Indians on nearby islands were cannibals, Columbus interpreted their

FOCUS QUESTION

How could Columbus, who never understood what he had found, transform world history despite the carnage that he provoked?

Millennium *Period at the end of history when Christ is expected to return and rule with his saints for a thousand years.*

word for "Carib" to mean the great "Khan" or emperor of China, known to him through Marco Polo's *Travels*. Columbus set out to find the Caribs. For several months he poked about the Caribbean. Then, on Christmas, the *Santa María* ran onto rocks and had to be abandoned. A few weeks later Columbus sailed for Spain on the *Niña*, leaving some of the crew as a garrison on the island of Hispaniola. Soon the Tainos had seen enough of the European invaders. Before Columbus returned on his second voyage in late 1493, they had killed every man he had left behind.

The voyage had immediate consequences. In 1493, Pope Alexander VI (a Spaniard) issued a decree that divided all non-Christian lands between Spain and Portugal. A year later, the two kingdoms adjusted the dividing line, with Spain eventually claiming most of the Western Hemisphere, plus the Philippines, and Portugal most of the Eastern Hemisphere, including the African coast, plus Brazil. As a result, Spain never acquired direct access to the African slave trade.

Columbus made three more voyages in quest of China and also served as governor of the Spanish Indies. The colonists often defied him, and in 1500, after his third voyage, they shipped him back to Spain in chains. Although later restored to royal favor, he died in 1506, a bitter, disappointed man.

THEODORE DE BRY'S ENGRAVING OF FIRST CONTACT BETWEEN SPANIARDS AND TAINOS (1596). *This illustration, made about a century after the event itself, depicts the Indians as far more eager to welcome the Spaniards than they actually were.*

Spain and the Caribbean

By then, overseas settlement had acquired a momentum of its own as thousands of ex-soldiers, minor nobles, and assorted adventurers drifted across the Atlantic. They carried with them seeds for Europe's cereal crops and livestock, including horses, cows, sheep, goats, and pigs. On islands without fences, the animals roamed freely, eating everything in sight, and soon threatened the Tainos' food supply. Unconcerned, the Spaniards forced the increasingly malnourished Indians to work for them, mostly panning for gold. Under these pressures, even before the onset of major infectious diseases, the Indian population declined catastrophically throughout the Caribbean. A whole way of life all but vanished from the earth, to be replaced by sugar, slaves, and livestock. African slaves, acquired from the Portuguese, soon arrived to replace the dead Indians as a labor force.

The Spaniards continued their explorations. Juan Ponce de León tramped through Florida in quest of a legendary fountain of youth. Vasco Núñez de Balboa became the first European to reach the Pacific Ocean, after crossing the Isthmus of Panama in 1513. But Spain gained little wealth from these new possessions. One geographer concluded that Spain had found a whole new continent, which he named "America" in honor of his informant, the explorer Amerigo Vespucci. For those who doubted, Ferdinand Magellan, a Portuguese mariner serving the king of Spain, settled the issue when his fleet sailed around the world between 1519 and 1522. (Magellan himself never completed the voyage; he was killed in the Philippines.)

During the same three years, **Hernán Cortés** sailed from Cuba, invaded Mexico, and found the treasure that Spaniards had been seeking. In 1519, he landed at a place he named Veracruz (The True Cross) and over the next several months tracked down the fabulous empire of the **Aztecs**, high in the Valley of Mexico. Moctezuma, the Aztec "speaker" or ruler, sent rich presents to persuade the Spaniards to leave, but the gesture had the opposite effect. When the small army of 400 men first laid eyes on the Aztec capital of **Tenochtitlán** (a metropolis of 200,000, much larger than any urban center in Western Europe), they wondered if they were dreaming.

Hernán Cortés *Spanish conquistador who vanquished the Aztecs.*

Aztec *Last pre-Columbian high culture in the Valley of Mexico. It was conquered by the Spaniards in 1519–1521.*

Tenochtitlán *Huge Aztec capital city destroyed by Cortés.*

QUICK REVIEW

SPAIN CREATED AN ATLANTIC EMPIRE

- Columbus tried to reach Asia by sailing west across the Atlantic
- Early Spanish exploration of the Caribbean threatened peoples and ecosystems
- Cortés discovered the wealth of the Aztec empire

THE EMERGENCE OF COMPLEX SOCIETIES IN THE AMERICAS

The high cultures of the Americas had been developing for thousands of years before Cortés found one of them. Their wealth fired the imagination of Europe and aroused the envy of Spain's enemies. The fabulous Aztec and **Inca** empires became the magnets that turned European exploration into empires of permanent settlement.

The Rise of Sedentary Cultures

After 4000 BCE, agriculture slowly transformed the lives of most Indians. As farming became the principal source of food in the Americas, settled villages grew into large cities. Indians became completely **sedentary** (nonmigratory) only in the most advanced cultures. Most of those living north of Mexico were migratory for part of each year. After a tribe chose a site, the men chopped down some trees, girdled others, burned away the underbrush, and often planted tobacco, a mood-altering sacred crop grown exclusively by men.

FOCUS QUESTION

How could the advanced societies of pre-Columbian America, which lacked wheeled vehicles, pulleys, and large domesticated animals, build larger cities that were in some respects more elegant than any in Western Europe?

Inca *Last and most extensive pre-Columbian empire that arose in the Andes and along the Pacific coast of South America.*

INDIAN WOMEN AS FARMERS. *In this illustration, a French artist depicted 16th-century Indian women in southeastern North America.*

Courtesy of the John Carter Brown Library at Brown University

Burning the underbrush fertilized the soil with ash and gave the community years of high productivity. Indian women usually erected the dwellings and planted and harvested food crops. In the fall, either the men alone or entire family groups went off hunting or fishing.

Because this **slash-and-burn** system of agriculture slowly depleted the soil, the whole tribe had to move to new fields after 10 or 20 years. In this semisedentary way of life, few Indians cared to acquire more personal property than the women could carry. This limited interest in consumption would profoundly condition their response to capitalism after contact with Europeans.

Even sedentary Indians did not own land as individuals. Clans or families guarded their "use rights" to land that had been allocated to them by their chiefs. In sedentary societies both men and women worked in the fields, and families accumulated surpluses for trade. Although not all sedentary peoples developed monumental architecture and elaborate state forms, such examples of cultural complexity emerged primarily among sedentary populations.

The spread of farming produced another population surge among both sedentary and semisedentary peoples. Estimates vary greatly, but at least 50 million people were living in the Western Hemisphere by 1492—and perhaps as many as 70 million, or one-seventh of the world's population. Despite their large populations, even the most complex societies in the Americas remained Stone Age cultures. The Indians made some use of metals, but they had not learned how to make bronze (a compound of copper and tin), nor found any use for iron. Nearly all of their tools were made of stone or bone, and their sharpest weapons were made from obsidian, a hard, glassy, volcanic rock. Nor did they use the wheel or devices based on the wheel, such as pulleys or gears.

sedentary *Societies that are rooted locally or are nonmigratory. Semisedentary societies are migratory for part of the year.*

slash and burn *System of agriculture in which trees were cut down, girdled, or in some way destroyed. The underbrush then was burned, and a crop was planted. The system depleted the fertility of the soil, and the tribe would move to a new area after 10 or 20 years.*

The Andes: Cycles of Complex Cultures

Despite these technological limitations, Indians accomplished a great deal. During the second millennium BCE, elaborate urban societies began to take shape in the Andes and along Mexico's Gulf Coast. Ancient Andean societies devised productive agricultural systems at 12,000 feet above sea level, far above the altitude at which anyone else has ever been able to raise crops. Lands using the Andean canal system never had to lie fallow. This type of irrigation took hold around Lake Titicaca about 1000 BCE and spread throughout the region.

Between 3000 and 2100 BCE, monumental architecture and urbanization took hold along the Peruvian coast and in the interior. Some of the earliest temples were immense pyramids. The one at Sechin Alto near Lima, more than 10 stories high, was built between 1800 and 1500 BCE. This "Pre-Classic" Chavin culture was well established by 1000 BCE, only to collapse suddenly around 300 BCE.

Chavin culture had two offshoots that together constitute the "Classic" phase of pre-Columbian history in South America. The Mochica culture, which emerged around 300 CE on the northwest coast of Peru, produced finely detailed pottery, much of it erotic, and built pyramids as centers of worship. At about the same time, another Classic culture arose in the mountains around the city of Tiwanaku, 12,000 feet above sea level. Terraces at various altitudes enabled the community to raise crops from different climatic zones. At the lowest levels, Tiwanakans planted cotton in the hot, humid air. Farther up the mountain, they raised maize (corn) and other crops suitable to a temperate zone. At still higher elevations, they grew potatoes and grazed their alpacas and llamas.

The Classic Andean cultures collapsed between the 6th and 11th centuries CE, possibly after a conquest of the Mochica region by the Tiwanakans. The disruption that followed this decline was not permanent, for complex Post-Classic cultures soon thrived both north and west of Tiwanaku.

Inca Civilization

Around 1400 the Inca (the word applies both to the ruler and to the empire's dominant nation) emerged as the new imperial power in the Andes. From their capital at Cuzco, high in the mountains, the Inca controlled an empire that eventually extended more than 2,000 miles from south to north, and they bound it together with an efficient network of roads and suspension bridges.

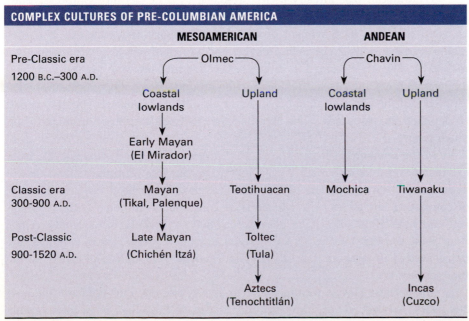

COMPLEX CULTURES OF PRE-COLUMBIAN AMERICA

	MESOAMERICAN		ANDEAN	
Pre-Classic era 1200 B.C.–300 A.D.	— Olmec —		— Chavin —	
	Coastal lowlands	Upland	Coastal lowlands	Upland
	Early Mayan (El Mirador)			
Classic era 300–900 A.D.	Mayan (Tikal, Palenque)	Teotihuacan	Mochica	Tiwanaku
Post-Classic 900–1520 A.D.	Late Mayan (Chichén Itzá)	Toltec (Tula)		
		Aztecs (Tenochtitlán)		Incas (Cuzco)

© Cengage Learning

Map 1.2 Inca Empire and Principal Earlier Cultures.
The Pacific coast of South America, showing the location of the Mochica, Chavin, Tiwanaku, and Nazca cultures and finally the Inca empire, which covered a much larger area than its predecessors.

They had no written language; high-altitude runners, who memorized the Inca's oral commands, raced along the roads to deliver their ruler's decrees over vast distances. The Inca also invented a decimal system and used it to keep accounts on a device they called a *quipu*. By 1500, the Inca empire ruled 8 to 12 million people. No other nonliterate culture has ever matched that feat.

Mesoamerica: Cycles of Complex Cultures

Mesoamerica experienced a similar cycle of change.

The **Olmecs**, who appeared along the Gulf Coast around 1200 BCE, were the oldest pre-Columbian high culture to appear in what is now Mexico. They built the first pyramids and the first ballparks in Mesoamerica. They also learned how to write and developed a dual calendar system. It took 52 years for the two calendars to complete a full cycle, after which the first day of the "short" calendar would again coincide with the first day of the "long" one. Olmecs faced the closing days of each cycle with dread, lest the gods allow the sun to be destroyed—something that the Olmecs believed had already happened several times. They believed that the sacrifice of a god had been necessary to set the sun in motion in each new creation cycle and that only human sacrifice could placate the gods and keep the sun moving. The arrival of Cortés created a religious as well as a political crisis, because 1519 marked the end of a 52-year cycle.

The Olmecs were succeeded by two Classic cultures. The city and empire of Teotihuacan emerged in the mountains not far from modern Mexico City. **Mayan** culture took shape mostly in the southern lowlands of Yucatán.

Teotihuacan was already a city of 40,000 by 1 CE. Its most impressive art form was its brightly painted murals, of which only a few survive. Teotihuacan invested resources in apartment dwellings for ordinary residents, not in monuments or inscriptions to rulers. It probably had a form of senate government, not a monarchy. The city extended its influence throughout Mesoamerica and remained a powerful force until its sudden destruction around 750 CE, when its shrines were toppled and the city was abandoned. In all likelihood, Teotihuacan's growth had so depleted the resources of the area that the city could not have sustained itself much longer.

In the lowlands, Classic Mayan culture went through a similar cycle from expansion to ecological crisis. It was also urban but less centralized than that of Teotihuacan. For more than 1,000 years, Mayan culture rested upon a network of competing city-states. The city of Tikal controlled commerce with Teotihuacan and housed 100,000 at its peak before 800 CE. Twenty other smaller cities flourished throughout the region. Mayan engineers built canals to water the crops needed to support this urban system, which was well established by the first century BCE.

The earliest Mayan writings date to 50 BCE, but few survive from the next 300 years. Around 300 CE, Mayans began to record their history in considerable

Olmec *Oldest pre-Columbian high culture to appear in what is now Mexico.*

Maya *Literate, highly urbanized Mesoamerican civilization that flourished for more than a thousand years before its sudden collapse in the 9th century CE.*

detail. Since 1960 scholars have been able to decipher most Mayan inscriptions. Mayan art and writings reveal their religious beliefs, including the place of human sacrifice in their cosmos and the role of ritual self-mutilation in their worship. Scholars have learned, for example, about the long reign of Pacal the Great, king (or "Great Sun") of the elegant city of Palenque, who was born on March 26, 603, and died on August 31, 683. Other monuments tell of the Great Suns of other cities whom Pacal vanquished and sacrificed to the gods.

Classic Mayan culture began to collapse about 50 years after the fall of Teotihuacan, which disrupted Mayan trade with the Valley of Mexico. The last date recorded at Tikal was 869; the last in the southern lowlands came 40 years later. The Mayan aristocracy had grown faster than the ability of commoners to support it, until population outstripped local resources. Frequent wars hastened the decline.

After 900, the Post-Classic era saw a kind of Mayan renaissance in the northern lowlands of the Yucatán, where many refugees from the south had fled. Chichén Itzá, a city that had existed for centuries, preserved many distinctive Mayan traits but merged them with new influences from the Valley of Mexico, where the Toltecs had become dominant in the high country and

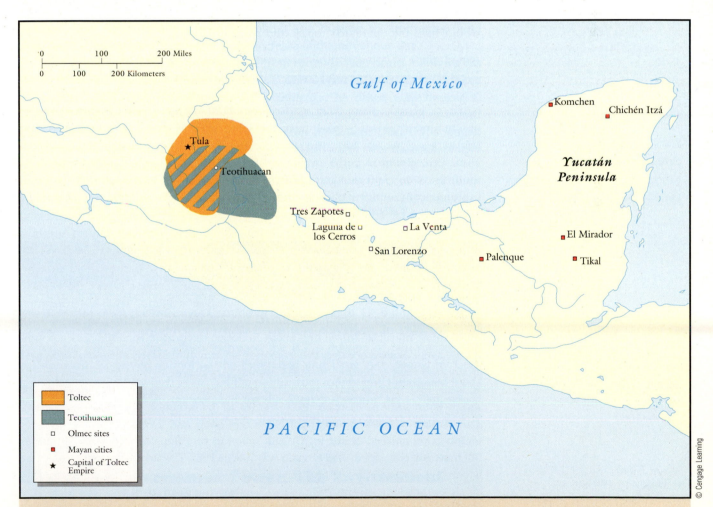

Map 1.3 Ancient Mesoamerica. *The location of the three principal Olmec cities, Teotihuacan, several major Mayan cities, and the Toltec capital of Tula.*

may even have conquered Chichén Itzá. The fierce Toltecs controlled the Valley of Mexico for almost three centuries, until about 1200, when they too declined.

The Aztecs and Tenochtitlán

By 1400, power in the Valley of Mexico was passing to the Aztecs, a warrior people who had migrated from the north about two centuries earlier and had settled on the shore of Lake Texcoco. They built a great city, Tenochtitlán, out on the lake. Its only connection with the mainland was by several broad causeways. The Aztecs raised their agricultural productivity by creating **chinampas**, or floating gardens, right on the water. Yet their mounting population strained the food supply, and in the 1450s the threat of famine was severe.

As newcomers to the region, the Aztecs felt a need to prove themselves worthy heirs to the ancient culture of the Valley of Mexico. They adopted the old religion but practiced it with a terrifying intensity. Human sacrifice was an ancient ritual in Mesoamerica, familiar to everyone, but the Aztecs practiced it on an unprecedented scale. They waged perpetual war to gain captives for their ceremonies. At the dedication of the Great Pyramid of the Sun in 1487 they sacrificed about 14,000 people. The need for thousands of victims each year created potential enemies everywhere. After 1519, many Mesoamerican peoples would help the Spaniards topple the Aztecs.

North American Mound Builders

North of Mexico, from 3000 BCE to about 1700 CE, the earliest distinct cultures of "mound builders" arose near the Ohio and Mississippi rivers and their tributaries. One of the most notable mound-building cultures, the Adena-Hopewell, emerged between 500 BCE and 400 CE in the Ohio River valley. Its mounds were elaborate burial sites, indicating belief in an afterlife. Mound-building communities participated in a commerce that spanned most of the

chinampas Highly productive gardens built on Lake Texcoco by the Aztecs.

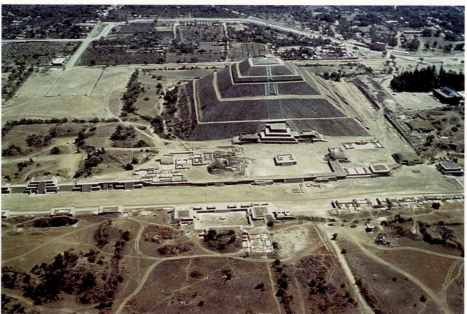

THE TEMPLE OF THE SUN AT TEOTIHUACAN. *The giant, stepped pyramid shown here is one of pre-Columbian America's most elegant pyramids.*

continent between the Appalachians and the Rockies, the Great Lakes and the Gulf of Mexico. Obsidian from the Yellowstone Valley in the Far West, copper from the Great Lakes basin, and shells from the Gulf of Mexico have all been found buried in the Adena-Hopewell mounds. Both the mound building and the long-distance trade largely ceased after 400 CE, for reasons that remain unclear.

Mound building revived in a final Mississippian phase between 1000 and 1700. This culture dominated the Mississippi River valley from modern St. Louis to Natchez, with the largest center at **Cahokia,** in Illinois near modern St. Louis. Cahokia flourished from 900 to 1250 and may have had 30,000 residents at its peak, making it the largest city north of Mexico. Cahokia's enormous central mound, 100 feet high, is the world's largest earthenwork.

Urban Cultures of the Southwest

Other complex societies emerged in North America's semiarid southwest—among them the Hohokam, the **Anasazi**, and the Pueblo. The Hohokam Indians settled in what is now central Arizona somewhere between 300 BCE and 300 CE. Their irrigation system, consisting of several hundred miles of canals, produced two harvests a year. They wove cotton cloth, made pottery with a distinctive red color, and traded with places as distant as California and Mesoamerica. Perhaps because unceasing irrigation had increased the salinity of the soil, this culture declined by 1450.

Even more tantalizing and mysterious is the brief flowering of the Anasazi, a cliff-dwelling people who have left behind some remarkable artifacts at such sites as Chaco Canyon in New Mexico and Mesa Verde in Colorado. In their caves and cliffs they constructed apartment houses five stories high, with as many as 500 dwellings and with elegant and spacious *kivas*, or meeting rooms for religious functions. They built an elaborate network of roads that ran in several directions. The Anasazi were also superb astronomers whose calendar tracked the 19-year cycles of the moon. They flourished for about two centuries and then, in the last quarter of the 13th century, apparently overwhelmed by a prolonged drought and by hostile invaders, they abandoned their principal sites. The Pueblo Indians claim descent from them.

CONTACT AND CULTURAL MISUNDERSTANDING

After the voyage of Columbus, the peoples of Europe and America, both with ancient pasts, confronted each other. Nothing in the histories of Europeans or Indians had prepared either of them for the encounter.

Religious Dilemmas

Christians had trouble understanding how Indians could exist at all, as the Bible never mentioned them. Some theologians tried to resolve this dilemma by arguing that Indians were animals without souls, not human beings. The pope and the royal courts of Portugal and Spain listened instead to a Dominican missionary, Fray

Cahokia *Largest city created by Mississippian mound builders. Located in Illinois near modern St. Louis, it thrived from 900 to 1250 CE.*

Anasazi *Advanced pre-Columbian cliff-dwelling culture that flourished for two centuries in what are now the states of Arizona, New Mexico, Utah, and Colorado before these sites were abandoned in the late 13th century CE.*

QUICK REVIEW

PRE-COLUMBIAN AMERICA
- Cycles of Pre-Classic, Classic, and Post-Classic cultures emerged in the Andes and Mesoamerica
- Cycles of mound-building cultures developed in the North American heartland
- Complex cultures emerged in what is now the southwestern United States
- Contact with Europeans led to cultural misunderstandings about religion, war, and gender

FOCUS QUESTION

Why were the native peoples of the Americas extremely vulnerable to European diseases, instead of the other way around?

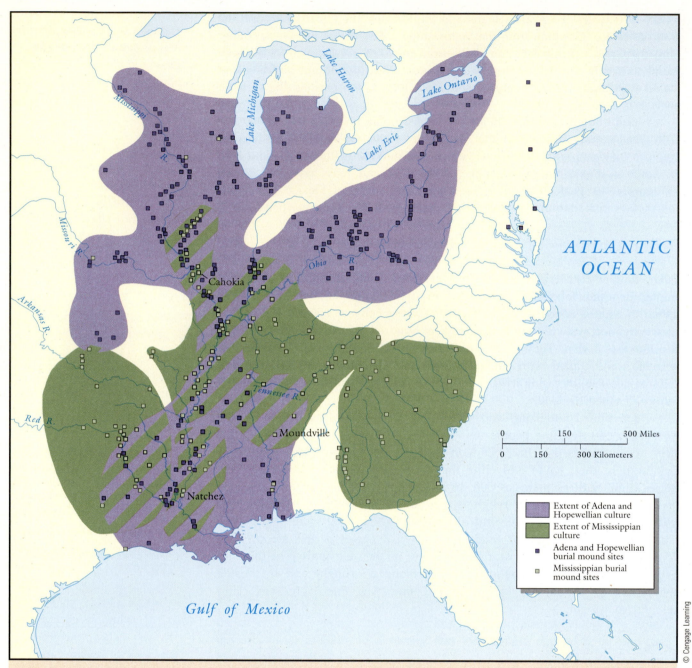

Map 1.4 **Mound-Building Cultures of North America.** *Early Adena and Hopewell burial sites and later Mississippian sites and the areas that these cultures influenced.*

Bartolomé de Las Casas, who insisted on the Indians' humanity. But, asked Europeans, if Indians did possess immortal souls, would a compassionate God have failed to make the Gospel known to them? Some early Catholic missionaries concluded that one of the apostles must have visited America (and India), and that the natives must have rejected his message.

To Europeans, the sacrificial temples, skull racks, and snake motifs of Mesoamerica led to only one conclusion: The Aztecs worshiped Satan. Human sacrifice and ritual cannibalism were widespread throughout the Americas. The Incas, whose creation myth resembled that of Mesoamerica, offered an occasional victim to the sun or to some other god. The Indians of eastern North America frequently

AZTEC SKULL RACK ALTAR. *This rack held the skulls of hundreds of sacrificial victims and shocked the invading Spaniards.*

Moctezuma's Mexico, by David Carrasco and Eduardo Mato Moctezuma. ©1992 University Press of Colorado. Photographs by Salvador Guilliem Arroyo.

tortured to death their adult male captives. Christians were shocked by human sacrifice and found cannibalism revolting, but Indians regarded certain European practices with equal horror. Between 1500 and 1700, Europeans burned or hanged up to 100,000 people, usually old women, for conversing with the wrong spirits— that is, for witchcraft. The Spanish Inquisition burned thousands of heretics and blasphemers. To the Indians, these incinerations looked like human sacrifices to a vengeful god.

Even the Christians' moral message was ambiguous. Missionaries brought news of how Christ had died to save mankind from sin. Catholic worship, then as now, centered on the Mass and the Eucharist, in which a priest transforms bread and wine into the literal body and blood of Christ. Most Protestants also accepted this sacrament but interpreted it symbolically, not literally. To the Indians, Christians seemed to be a people who ate their own god but grew outraged at the lesser matter of sacrificing a human being to please an Indian god.

When Europeans tried to convert Indians to Christianity, the Indians concluded that the converts would spend the afterlife with the souls of Europeans, separated forever from their own ancestors, whose memory they revered. Neither side fully recognized these obstacles to mutual understanding. Although early Catholic missionaries converted thousands of Indians, the results were mixed at best. Most converts adopted some Christian rites but continued many of their old rituals, often in secret.

War as Cultural Misunderstanding

Such misunderstandings multiplied as Indians and Europeans came into closer contact. Both waged war, but with different objectives. Europeans tried to settle matters on the battlefield and expected to kill many enemies. Indians fought mostly to obtain captives, whether for sacrifice (as with the Aztecs) or to replace tribal losses through adoption (as with the Iroquois). To Indians, massive deaths on the battlefield were an atrocity that could in no way appease the gods. Europeans and Indians also differed profoundly on what acts were outrageous. The torture and ritual sacrifice of captives horrified Europeans; the slaughter of women and children, which Europeans brought to America, appalled Indians.

Gender and Cultural Misunderstanding

Indian social organization also differed fundamentally from that of Europeans. European men owned almost all property, set the rules of inheritance, farmed the land, and performed nearly all public functions. Among many Indian peoples, descent was **matrilineal** (traced through the maternal line), and women owned nearly all movable property. European men felt incomplete unless they acquired authority over other people, especially the other members of their households. Indian men had none of these patriarchal ambitions. Women did the farming in semisedentary Indian cultures, and they often could demand a war or try to prevent one, although the final decision rested with men. When Europeans tried to change warriors into farmers, Indian males protested that they were being turned into women. Only over fully sedentary peoples could Europeans impose direct rule by building on the existing social hierarchy, division of labor, and system of tribute.

matrilineal *Society that determines inheritance and roles in life based on the female or maternal line.*

CONQUEST AND CATASTROPHE

Spanish *conquistadores*, or conquerors, led small armies that rarely exceeded 1,000 men. Yet they subdued two empires much larger than Spain itself and then looked around for more worlds to overrun. There, beyond the great empires, Indians had more success in resisting them.

The Conquest of Mexico and Peru

When Cortés entered Tenochtitlán in 1519, he seized Moctezuma as prisoner and hostage. Although overwhelmingly outnumbered, Cortés and his men destroyed Aztec religious objects, replacing them with images of the Virgin Mary or other Catholic saints. In response, while Cortés was away, the Aztecs rose against the intruders, Moctezuma was killed, and the Spaniards were driven out with heavy losses. But then the smallpox the Spaniards left behind began killing Aztecs by the thousands. Cortés found refuge with the nearby Tlaxcalans, an independent people who had never submitted to Aztec rule. With thousands of their warriors, he returned the next year and destroyed Tenochtitlán. With royal support from Spain, the *conquistadores* established themselves as new imperial rulers in Mesoamerica, looted all the silver and gold they could find, and built Mexico City on the ruins of Tenochtitlán.

Rumors abounded about an even richer empire far to the south, and in 1531 and 1532 Francisco Pizarro finally located the Inca empire high in the Andes. Pizarro captured the reigning Inca, Atahualpa, and managed to win a few allies from among the Inca's recent enemies. Atahualpa paid a huge ransom, but Pizarro had him strangled anyway. Tens of thousands of angry Indians besieged the outnumbered Spaniards for months in Cuzco, the Inca capital, but Pizarro managed to hold out and finally prevailed. The Spanish established a new capital at Lima on the coast.

Despite these dramatic conquests, only in the 1540s did the Spanish finally locate the bonanza they had been seeking. The silver mines at Potosí in present-day Bolivia, and other lodes in Mexico, sustained Spain's military might in Europe for the next 100 years.

conquistadores Spanish word for conquerors.

LINK TO THE PAST

Miguel Leon-Portilla, *The Broken Spears: The Aztec Account of the Conquest of Mexico*

An Aztec lamentation after the Spanish destroyed Tenochtitlán:

Broken spears lie in the roads;
We have torn our hair in our grief.
The houses are roofless now, and their walls
are red with blood.
Worms are swarming in the streets and plazas,
and the walls are splattered with gore.
The Water has turned red, as if it were dyed,
and when we drink it,
it has the taste of brine.
We have pounded our hands in despair
against the adobe walls,
for our inheritance, our city, is lost and dead.

The shields of our warriors were its defense,
but they could not save it.
We have chewed dry twigs and salt grasses;
we have filled our mouths with dust and bits of
adobe;
we have eaten lizards, rats and worms.

Q The Aztecs were the most brutal and violent society in pre-Columbian America. How do you account for the sensitivity in this poetic lamentation?

Source: From *The Broken Spears* by Miguel Leon-Portilla. Copyright © 1962, 1990 by Miguel Leon-Portilla. Expanded and Updated Edition © 1992 by Miguel Leon-Portilla. Reprinted by permission of Beacon Press, Boston.

North American *Conquistadores* and Missionaries

The exploits of the *conquistadores* seemed so wondrous that anything became believable, including rumors that cities of gold existed in the interior of North America. Alvar Núñez Cabeza de Vaca, a survivor of a disastrous Spanish expedition to Florida, made his way back to Mexico City in 1536 after an overland journey of eight years that took him through Texas and northern Mexico. In an account of his adventures, he mentioned Indian tales of great cities to the north, and this reference soon became stories of "golden cities." Hernando de Soto landed in Florida in 1539 and roamed through much of what is now the southeastern United States in quest of these treasures. Farther west, Francisco Vasquez de Coronado marched into New Mexico and Arizona, where he encountered several Pueblo towns but no golden cities. The expedition reached the Grand Canyon, then headed east into Texas and as far north as Kansas before returning to Mexico, leaving behind diseases that severely afflicted Indians of the interior.

After the *conquistadores* departed, Spanish priests did their best to convert thousands of North American Indians to the Catholic faith. In 1570, the Jesuits even established a mission in what is now Virginia, but local Indians soon wiped it out. The Jesuits withdrew, and Franciscans took their place.

In 1573, Philip II issued the Royal Orders for New Discoveries that made it illegal to enslave Indians or even attack them. He expected unarmed priests to bring them together into missions and convert them into loyal Catholic subjects of the Spanish Crown. Franciscans had no success among the nomadic residents of central and southern Florida. They had to build their missions within the permanent villages of northern Florida or the Pueblo communities of New Mexico. Even then they needed some soldiers nearby to protect them. By 1630, about 86,000 Pueblo, Apache, and Navajo Indians of New Mexico had accepted baptism. By midcentury, 30 missions in Florida contained about 26,000 baptized Indians.

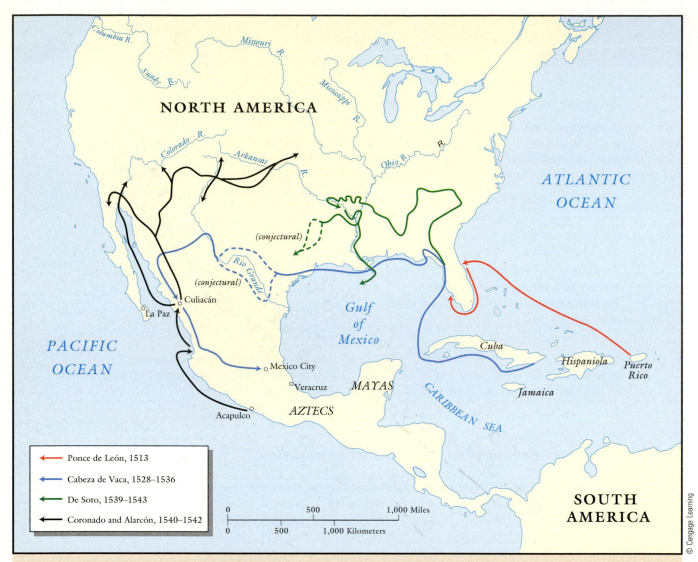

Map 1.5 **Principal Spanish Explorations of North America.** *Four Spanish expeditions marched through much of the interior of North America between 1513 and 1543.*

The Spanish Empire and Demographic Catastrophe

By the late 16th century the Spanish Empire had emerged as a system of direct colonial rule in Mexico and Peru, protected by a strong defensive perimeter in the Caribbean and surrounded by frontier missions extending into Florida and New Mexico. The Spaniards also brought new systems of labor and new religious institutions to their overseas colonies.

The first Spanish rulers in Mexico and Peru relied on a form of labor tribute called *encomienda*. This system permitted the holder, or *encomendero*, to claim labor from an Indian district for a stated period of time. *Encomienda* worked because it resembled the way the Aztecs and the Incas had levied labor for their own massive public buildings and irrigation projects. In time, the king intervened to correct abuses and to limit labor tribute to Crown projects, such as mining or building churches. Spanish settlers shifted from demanding labor to claiming land. In the countryside the *hacienda*, a large estate with its own crops and herds, became a familiar institution.

encomienda *System of labor introduced into the Western Hemisphere by the Spanish that permitted the holder, or encomendero, to claim labor from Indians in a district for a stated period of time.*

haciendas *Large, landed estates established by the Spanish.*

TRIBUTE LABOR (*MITA*) IN THE SILVER MINES. *The silver mines of Potosí, in the Andes, are about two miles above sea level. The work, as depicted in this 1603 engraving by Theodore de Bry, was extremely onerous and often dangerous.*

As missionaries acquired land and labor, they began to exhibit less zeal for Indian souls. The Franciscans—in Europe, the gentlest of Catholic religious orders—systematically tortured their Mayan converts whenever they caught them worshiping their old gods. To the Franciscans, the slightest lapse could signal a reversion to Satan worship, with human sacrifice a likely consequence.

Most important of all, the Spaniards brought deadly microbes with them. Smallpox, which could be fatal but which most Europeans survived in childhood, devastated the Indians, who had almost no immunity to it. When Cortés arrived in 1519 the Indian population of Mexico probably exceeded 15 million. In the 1620s, after waves of killing epidemics, it bottomed out at 700,000. Peru's population plummeted from perhaps 10 million to 600,000. For the hemisphere as a whole, any given region probably lost 90 or 95 percent of its population within a century of sustained contact with Europeans.

Global Colossus, Global Economy

American silver made the king of Spain the most powerful monarch in Christendom. Philip II (1556–1598) commanded the largest army in Europe. In 1580, after the king of Portugal died with no direct heir, Philip claimed his throne, thus uniting

FOCUS QUESTION

How important was the establishment of an oceanic system of commerce that linked East and South Asia with Europe and the Americas?

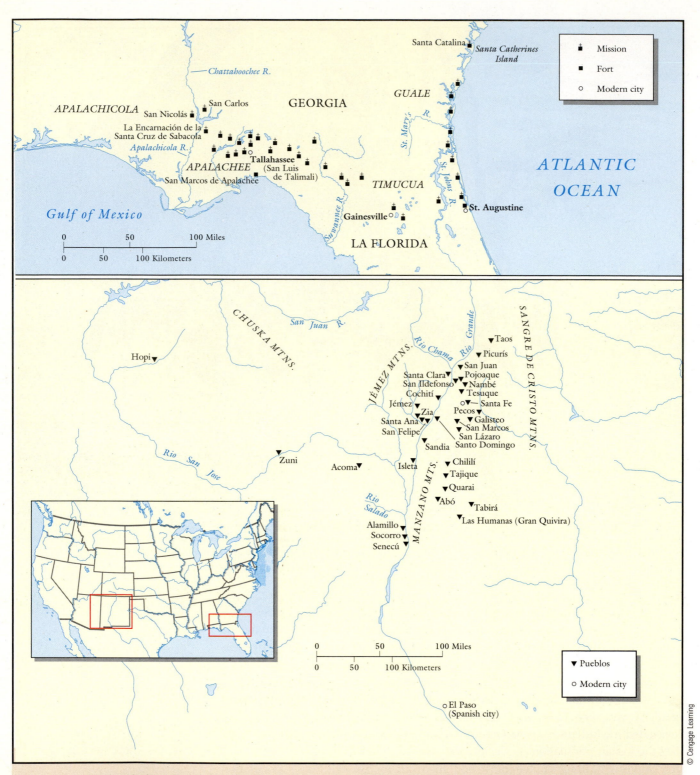

Map 1.6 **Spanish Missions in Florida and New Mexico, circa 1675.** *Franciscan friars established missions in Florida from the Atlantic to the Gulf of Mexico and in New Mexico along the Rio Grande Valley and, in a few cases, farther inland.*

Serfdom *Early medieval Europe's predominant labor system that tied peasants to their lords and the land. They were not slaves because they could not be sold from the land.*

under his own rule Portugal's Asian empire, Brazil, Spain's American possessions, and the Philippines. This colossus was the greatest empire the world had ever seen. It also sustained the first truly global economy, because the Portuguese used Spain's American silver to pay for the spices and silks they imported from Asia.

The Spanish colossus became part of an even broader economic pattern. **Serfdom**, which tied peasants to their lords and to the land, had been declining

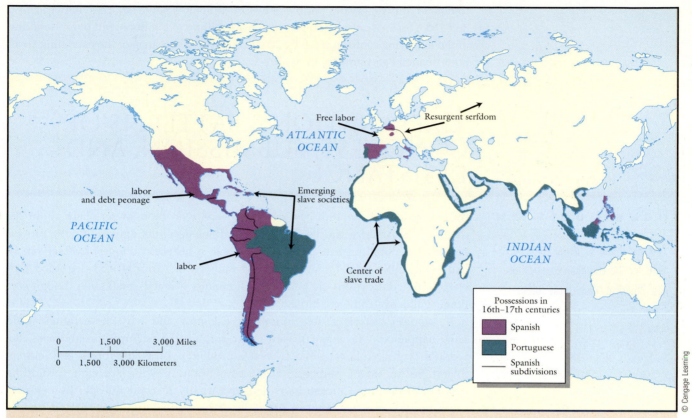

Map 1.7 Spanish Empire and Global Labor Systems. *While Western European states were becoming free-labor societies, they created or encouraged the establishment of societies that required various unfree labor systems to prosper in the Americas, the Caribbean, Africa, and Eastern Europe.*

in Europe since the 12th century and was nearly gone by 1500. A system of free labor arose in its place, and overseas expansion strengthened that trend within Western Europe. Conversely, unfree labor systems took root all around Europe's periphery. In general, free labor reigned where populations were dense and still growing. Large pools of labor kept wages low. But where land was cheap and labor expensive, coercive systems became the only efficient way for Europeans to extract from those areas the products they desired.

The forms of unfree labor varied greatly. In New Spain, the practice of *encomienda* slowly yielded to debt peonage. Unpayable debts kept Indians tied to the *haciendas* of the countryside. The mining of precious metals, on the other hand, was so dangerous and unpleasant that it almost always required a coercive system of labor tribute, called *mita* in the Andes. Similarly, any colonial region that devoted itself to the production of staple crops for sale in Europe also turned to unfree labor and eventually to overt slavery.

Sugar production first reduced Indians to bondage in the Caribbean and Brazil and then, as they died off, led to the importation of African slaves by the millions. Tobacco, rice, cotton, and coffee followed similar patterns. At first these crops were considered luxuries and commanded high prices, but as they became widely available on the world market, their prices fell steeply, profit margins contracted, and planters turned overwhelmingly to coerced labor. Even in Eastern Europe, which began to produce cereal crops for sale in the West, serfdom revived.

Spain's rise had been spectacular, but its empire was vulnerable. The costs of continuous conflict, the inflation generated by a steady influx of silver, and the need

QUICK REVIEW

THE SPANISH CONQUESTS

- Hugely outnumbered, Cortés and Pizarro conquered the Aztecs and the Inca

- *Conquistadores* de Soto and Coronado led the fruitless search for cities of gold

- Spanish missionaries in North America attempted to convert Indians

- Demographic catastrophe through disease, overwork, and war

- Emergence of a global economy sustained by unfree labor systems

to defend a much greater perimeter absorbed Spain's new resources. Between 1492 and 1580, Spain's population grew from 4.9 million to 8 million, but over the course of the following century, it fell by 20 percent, mostly because of the escalating costs, both financial and human, of Spain's wars.

EXPLANATIONS: PATTERNS OF CONQUEST, SUBMISSION, AND RESISTANCE

FOCUS QUESTION

Can you think of better explanations for the European conquest of the Americas than those offered here?

By the middle of the 18th century, Europeans who thought seriously about the discovery of America and its global implications generally agreed that the process had been a moral outrage, possibly the worst in history. Conquest and settlement had killed millions of Indians, enslaved millions of Africans, and degraded Europeans. By comparison, the benefits to humanity seemed small even though economic gains by 1750 were large.

Modern historians, less moralistic, ask how and why these things could have happened. One major reason is geographical. The Eurasian landmass, the world's largest, follows an east-west axis that permits life-forms and human inventions to travel immense distances without passing through forbidding changes of climate. Chinese inventions eventually reached Europe. By contrast, the Americas and sub-Saharan Africa lie along north-south axes that do impose such barriers. Another compelling explanation for European success focuses on the prolonged isolation of the Americas from the rest of the world. If two communities of equal ability are kept apart, the one with the larger and more varied population will invent more things and learn more rapidly over time. More than any other technological edge, far more than firearms or even horses, steel made military conquest possible. European armor stopped Indian spears and arrows, and European swords killed enemies swiftly without any need to reload.

The biological consequences of isolation were even more momentous than the technological. The Indians' genetic makeup was more uniform than that of Europeans, Africans, or Asians. Indians were descended from a small sample of the total gene pool of Eurasia. The Indians first encountered by Europeans were bigger, stronger, and—at first contact—healthier than the newcomers, but with almost no resistance to new diseases, they died in enormous numbers.

European plants, such as Kentucky bluegrass, also thrived at the expense of native vegetation. And European animals prevailed over potential American rivals. Horses multiplied at an astonishing rate in America, and wild herds moved north from Mexico faster than the Spaniards, transforming the way of life of the Apaches and the Sioux. But some life-forms also moved from the Americas to Europe, Asia, and Africa. Indians probably gave syphilis to the first Europeans they met. Other American exports, such as corn, potatoes, and tomatoes, were far more benign and have enriched the diet of the rest of the world.

Conclusion

For thousands of years the Americas had been cut off from the rest of the world. The major cultures of Eurasia and Africa had existed in relative isolation, engaging in direct contact only with their immediate neighbors. Islamic states, which shared borders with India, the East Indies, black Africa, and Europe, had been the principal mediators among these cultures. Then suddenly, in just 40 years, daring European navigators joined the world together and challenged the Moslems' mediating role. Between 1492 and 1532, Europe, Africa, Asia, the Spice Islands, the Philippines, the Caribbean, Aztec Mexico, Inca Peru, and other parts of the Americas came into intense and often violent contact with one another. Spain acquired a military advantage within Europe that would last for a century. Nearly everybody else suffered, especially in the Americas and Africa.

Spain spent the rest of the 16th century trying to create an imperial system that could impose order on this turbulent reality. But Spain had many enemies. They too would find the lure of wealth and land overseas irresistible.

CHAPTER REVIEW

Review Questions

1. What enabled relatively backward European societies to establish dominance over the oceans of the world?
2. How could Columbus, who never understood what he had found, transform world history despite the carnage that he provoked?
3. How could the advanced societies of pre-Columbian America, which lacked wheeled vehicles, pulleys, and large domesticated animals, build larger cities that were in some respects more elegant than any in Western Europe?
4. Why were the native peoples of the Americas extremely vulnerable to European diseases, instead of the other way around?
5. Why did the free-labor societies of Western Europe generate unfree labor systems all around their periphery?
6. How important was the establishment of an oceanic system of commerce that linked East and South Asia with Europe and the Americas?
7. Can you think of better explanations for the European conquest of the Americas than those offered here?

Critical Thinking Questions

1. European expansion inflicted enormous destruction upon the peoples of sub-Saharan Africa and the Americas. Is there any way that this vast projection of European power overseas also contributed to an eventual expansion of liberty?
2. Had Europeans been willing to treat Indian peoples as potential equals, would Christian missionaries have been in a stronger position to win converts?

Identifications

Review your understanding of the following key terms, people, and events for this chapter.

Mesoamerica, p. 1
Christopher Columbus, p. 2
Beringia, p. 2
Tierra del Fuego, p. 2
Amerind, p. 3
Clovis tip, p. 3
Neolithic, p. 4

maritime, p. 5
staple crop, p. 6
caravel, p. 6
astrolabe, p. 6
factories, p. 7
Atlantic slave trade, p. 7
Millennium, p. 9
Hernán Cortés, p. 11

Aztec, p. 11
Tenochtitlán, p. 11
Inca, p. 11
sedentary, p. 11
slash and burn, p. 12
Olmec, p. 14
Maya, p. 14
chinampas, p. 16

Cahokia, p. 17
Anasazi, p. 17
matrilineal, p. 20
conquistadores, p. 20
encomienda, p. 22
haciendas, p. 22
Serfdom, p. 24

DISCOVERY

How did the differences between the societies in the Americas and the ones in Europe lead to conflict and ultimately devastation for the cultures of the Americas?

In thinking about this question, begin by breaking it down into the components shown below. A discussion of the significance of each component should appear in your answer.

Geography

Look at the map, "Mound-Building Cultures of North America." Note the expanse of territory covered by these communities—from the Appalachians to the Rockies and the Great Lakes to the Gulf of Mexico. Based on the geographic evidence, would you characterize these Native American societies as unified or separate? How did their patterns of settlement contribute to the eventual and quick conquest of these Native American societies by Europeans?

Religion and Philosophy

Imagine what you might think if you traveled to a distant place and discovered a sacrificial site such as the "Aztec Skull Rack Altar" (see page 19). Considering your own thoughts as well as the section on "Religious Dilemmas," explain how religious differences led to cultural misunderstandings and even to war. Give specific examples.

Government and Law

Look at the map, "Spanish Empire and Global Labor Systems," and the section titled "Global Colossus, Global Economy" (pages 23–26). Why did the European nations that were becoming free-labor societies generate unfree labor systems all around their periphery? How did the European view of Native American civilization affect their treatment of those people? Was this seen in European treatment of other civilizations around the world?

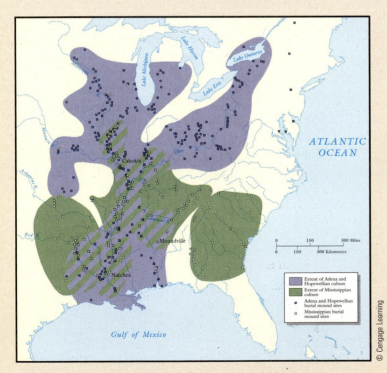

Map 1.4 Mound-Building Cultures of North America

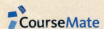

Visit the CourseMate website at www.cengagebrain.com for additional study tools and review materials for this chapter.

2

THE CHALLENGE TO SPAIN AND THE SETTLEMENT OF NORTH AMERICA

France, the Dutch Republic, and England challenged Spanish power in Europe and overseas. None of them planted a permanent settlement in North America before 1600. In the quarter-century after 1600, they all did. Spain's rivals created colonies of different kinds. Virginia and Barbados grew staple crops with indentured servants and African slaves. New France and New Netherland pursued trade with the Indians without trying to rule them. In New England, labor was provided by families of settlers. English Quakers created another free-labor society in the Delaware valley.

1610	1620	1630	1640	1650	1660	1670	1680	1690	1700	1710

...ther begins Protestant Reformation

■ 1607
English settlement at Jamestown begins

■ 1608
Champlain founds Quebec

■ 1613–1614
Rolfe grows tobacco, marries Pocahontas

■ 1619
First Africans arrive in Virginia • House of Burgesses and headright system created

■ 1620
Pilgrims adopt Mayflower Compact, settle at Plymouth

■ 1626
Minuit founds New Amsterdam

■ 1630
Puritan "great migration" to New England begins

■ 1664
English conquer New Netherland

1670 ■
First permanent English settlements in South Carolina

■ 1681
Penn receives charter for Pennsylvania

1683 ■
Pennsylvania and New York adopt Charters of Liberty

1705 ■
Virginia adopts comprehensive slave code

© Cengage Learning

THE PROTESTANT REFORMATION AND THE CHALLENGE TO SPAIN

FOCUS QUESTION

Why did the number of Indians who chose to become Catholics far exceed the number who accepted Protestantism?

Protestant Reformation

Religious movement begun by Martin Luther in 1517 that led to the repudiation of the Roman Catholic Church in large parts of northern and central Europe.

By the time its enemies challenged Spain overseas, the **Protestant Reformation** had shattered the religious unity of Europe. In November 1517, not long before Cortés landed at Vera Cruz, Martin Luther nailed his 95 Theses to the door of the Castle Church at Wittenberg and touched off the Reformation. Luther insisted that salvation comes through God's grace alone, and that God grants redemption and forgiveness to those who hear his Word and have faith.

John Calvin, a French Protestant who took control of the Swiss city of Geneva, also embraced justification by faith alone. He rejected the pope and all Catholic rituals and sacraments (except baptism and the Eucharist). Instead, he gave central importance to **predestination**. According to that doctrine, God has already decreed who will be saved and who will be damned. Because salvation was beyond human power to alter, Calvinists felt a compelling need to recognize in themselves a conversion experience, the process by which God's elect discovered that they had received divine grace.

The Reformation ensured that powerful Protestant movements would influence France, the Netherlands, and England as they challenged Catholic Spain's power in Europe and abroad.

Theodore de Bry

Spaniards Torturing Indians, as Depicted by Theodore de Bry, Late 16th Century. *Among Protestants in northern Europe, images such as this one merged into a "black legend" of Spanish cruelty, which in turn helped justify their own challenge to Spanish power overseas. But in practice, the behavior of Protestant settlers toward Indians was often as harsh as anything the Spaniards had done.*

NEW FRANCE

In 1500 France had three times the population of Spain. The French made a few stabs at overseas expansion before 1600, but with little success.

Early French Explorers

The earliest French explorers focused on Canada. In 1524, King Francis I sent Giovanni da Verrazano, an Italian, on a fruitless search for a northwest passage to Asia. Between 1534 and 1543, Jacques Cartier made three voyages to North America. He explored the St. Lawrence Valley without finding any fabulous wealth. Harsh Canadian winters made him give up.

These failures convinced the French to ignore Canada after 1550 and instead turn to warmer climates. **Huguenots** sacked Havana, prompting Spain to fortify it as a naval base, commanded by Admiral Pedro Menéndez de Avilés. After Huguenots settled on the Atlantic coast of Florida, Menéndez attacked them in 1565, and then executed every adult male who refused to accept the Catholic faith.

France's Wars of Religion blocked further expansion efforts for the rest of the century. King Henry IV (1589–1610), a Protestant, converted to Catholicism and restored peace, while granting limited toleration to Huguenots through the Edict of Nantes in 1598. A *politique*, Henry insisted that the survival of the state take precedence over religious differences and that survival required toleration.

Missions and Furs

Catholic soldier and explorer Samuel de Champlain also believed that Catholics and Huguenots could work together, Europeanize the Indians, convert them, and even marry them. Before his death in 1635, he made 11 voyages to Canada. During his second trip (1604–1606), he planted a predominantly Huguenot settlement in Acadia (Nova Scotia). In 1608, he sailed up the St. Lawrence River, established friendly relations with the Indians, and founded Quebec. Many Frenchmen

predestination *Theory that God had decreed, even before he created the world, who would be saved and who would be damned.*

Huguenots *French Protestants who followed the beliefs of John Calvin.*

politique *One who believed that the survival of the state took precedence over religious differences.*

cohabited with Indian women, but only 15 formal marriages took place between them in the 17th century. Champlain's friendliness toward these Indians also drew him into their wars with the Iroquois Five Nations. At times, Iroquois hostility almost destroyed New France.

Champlain failed to unite Catholics and Protestants. Huguenots were eager to trade with Canada, but few settled there. Their ministers showed no interest in converting Indians, whereas Catholic priests became zealous missionaries. In 1625, the French Crown declared that only Catholicism could be practiced in New France, and Acadia soon went Catholic as well. Early New France is a tale of missionaries and furs, of attempts to convert the Indians, and, equally important, of efforts to trade with them. The carousing *coureurs de bois* (roamers of the woods) did much for the fur trade but made life difficult for missionaries.

After 1630, Jesuit missionaries made heroic efforts to bring Christ to the Indians. Uncompromising in their opposition to Protestants, Jesuits were more flexible in dealing with non-Christian peoples. Other missionaries insisted that Indians must be Europeanized before they could be converted, but the Jesuits saw nothing contradictory about converts who retained some native customs.

The Jesuits converted 10,000 Indians in 40 years, most of them members of the five confederated Huron nations. They mastered Indian languages, lived in Indian villages, and accepted most Indian customs. But their successes antagonized some Indians who were still attached to their own rituals. For example, when smallpox devastated the Hurons in the 1640s, Jesuits baptized hundreds of dying victims to ensure their salvation. Indian survivors suspected witchcraft and resisted even more fiercely. Eventually the Jesuits' efforts lost ground to the fur trade, especially after the Crown assumed control of New France in 1663.

coureur de bois French phrase interpreted as "a roamer of the woods," referring to French colonists who participated in the fur trade with the Indians and lived part of the year with them.

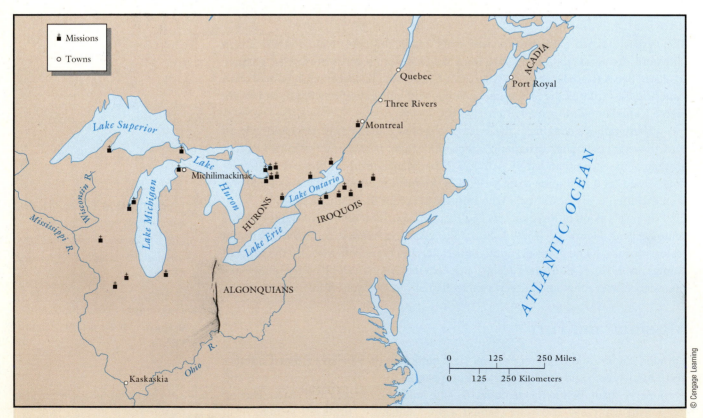

Map 2.1 New France and the Jesuit Missions. *The Jesuits established Indian missions near Montreal and far into the interior of North America, most of them well beyond the range of French military aid in any emergency.*

New France under Louis XIV

After 1663, Louis XIV and his minister, Jean-Baptiste Colbert, took charge of the colony. Colbert immediately attempted to increase the population. He sent 774 young women to the St. Lawrence to provide brides for settlers and soldiers. He offered bonuses to large families and fined those who failed to marry. Between 1663 and 1700, the population of New France rose from 3,000 to about 14,000. Roughly one-fourth of the population concentrated in three cities: Three Rivers, Quebec, and Montreal.

Colbert tried to confine the fur trade to annual fairs at Montreal and Quebec, thus bringing the Indians to the settlers, not the settlers to the Indians. This effort to eliminate the *coureurs de bois* failed, leading instead to a quiet rebellion in the West. Several hundred Frenchmen settled in the Mississippi valley between the missions of Cahokia and Kaskaskia in what became the Illinois country. These settlers rejected Colbert's policies of feudal dues, compulsory militia service, and church **tithes**, even though the tithe was set at half its rate in Europe. They did, however, import African slaves from Louisiana. Many prospered as wheat farmers, and many married Christian Indian women from the missions.

But Canada did not long remain the center of French overseas activity. Most of the French who crossed the Atlantic preferred the Caribbean. At first the French in the West Indies joined with other enemies of Spain to prey as buccaneers upon Spanish colonies and ships. Then they transformed the island colonies of Saint-Domingue (modern Haiti), Guadeloupe, and Martinique into centers of sugar and coffee production, where a small planter class prospered from the labor of thousands of slaves. The sugar islands generated more wealth than Canada or any other colony in the world.

tithe *Portion of one's income, usually one-tenth, that is owed to the church.*

THE DUTCH SETTLEMENTS

For most of the 17th century, the Dutch were more active overseas than the French. The Dutch Republic, whose two million people inhabited the most densely populated part of Europe, moved ahead of all rivals in finance, shipping, and trade. With Protestant dissenters from many countries, a sizable Jewish community, and a large Catholic minority, the Dutch Republic was actually a polyglot confederation. Amsterdam's merchant republicanism—which stressed religious toleration and free trade—competed with the orthodox Calvinist Dutch Reformed Church for the allegiance of the people. This tension carried over into New Netherland.

The East and West India Companies

Profit was the dominant motive in Dutch expansion. In 1602, the **States General** chartered the Dutch East India Company, which pressured Spain where it was weakest, in the Portuguese East Indies. Elbowing the Portuguese out of the Spice Islands, the Dutch set up their own capital at Batavia (now Jakarta) on the island of Java. The Atlantic and North America also attracted the Dutch. In 1609, Henry Hudson, an Englishman in Dutch service, sailed up what the Dutch called the North River (the English later renamed it the Hudson) and claimed the area for the Netherlands. In 1614, Lutheran refugees from Amsterdam built a fort near modern Albany to trade with Indians for furs, but they did not settle permanently.

In 1621 the States General chartered the Dutch West India Company and gave it jurisdiction over the African slave trade, Brazil, the Caribbean, and North

States General *Legislative assembly of the Netherlands.*

America. The company captured Portugal's slave-trading posts in West Africa, and it occupied Portuguese Angola and the richest sugar-producing region of Brazil until the 1640s.

In North America the Dutch claimed the Delaware, Hudson, and Connecticut river valleys. The company put most of its effort into the Hudson valley. The first permanent settlers arrived in 1624. Two years later, Deacon Pierre Minuit, leading 30 Walloon (French-speaking) Protestant refugee families, bought Manhattan Island from the Indians and founded the port of New Amsterdam. The Dutch established Fort Orange (modern Albany) 150 miles upriver for trade with the Iroquois. Much like New France, New Netherland depended on the goodwill of nearby Indians. But unlike in New France, few Dutchmen ventured into the deep woods. There were no *coureurs de bois* and no missionaries. The Indians brought their furs to Fort Orange and exchanged them for firearms and other goods that the Dutch sold cheaply.

New Netherland as a Pluralistic Society

New Netherland became North America's first experiment in ethnic and religious pluralism. The Dutch were a people with a Flemish (Dutch-speaking) majority and a Walloon minority. Both came to the colony. So did Danes, Norwegians, Swedes, Finns, Germans, and Scots.

The colony's government tried to utilize this diversity. On the one hand, it appealed to religious refugees by emphasizing the West India Company's Protestant identity. On the other hand, the company sometimes recognized that acceptance of religious diversity might stimulate trade. At first, Minuit and Governor Pieter Stuyvesant embraced the religious formula for unity and resisted toleration even for the benefit of commerce.

After Minuit returned to Europe in 1631, the emphasis shifted from piety to trade. The Dutch sold muskets to the Iroquois to expand their own access to the fur trade and exported grain to the Caribbean. In 1643, however, Willem Kieft, a stubborn and quarrelsome governor, slaughtered a tribe of Indian refugees to whom he had granted asylum from other Indians. This Pavonia Massacre, which took place across the Hudson from Manhattan, set off a war with nearby Algonquian nations that nearly destroyed New Netherland. By the time Stuyvesant replaced Kieft in 1647, the colony's population had fallen to about 700. Stuyvesant made peace and then strengthened town governments and the Dutch Reformed Church. During his administration, the population rose to more than 6,000. Most newcomers arrived as families who reproduced rapidly, enabling the population to double every 25 years.

English Encroachments

But New Netherland would soon face problems from the outside. The English, already entrenched in Virginia and New England, threatened to overwhelm the Dutch as they moved onto Long Island and into what is now Westchester County, New York. Kieft welcomed them in the 1640s and gave them local privileges greater than those enjoyed by the Dutch. Stuyvesant regarded these **Yankees** (a Dutch word that probably meant "land pirates") as good Calvinists. They agitated for a more active role in government, but their loyalty was questionable. If England attacked the colony, would these Puritans side with their Dutch Calvinist neighbors or the Anglican invaders? Stuyvesant would learn the unpleasant answer when England attacked in 1664.

Yankees *Dutch word for New Englanders that originally meant something like "land pirate."*

THE CHALLENGE FROM ELIZABETHAN ENGLAND

England's interest in America emerged slowly. In 1497, Henry VII (1485–1509) sent Giovanni Cabato (John Cabot), an Italian mariner who had moved to Bristol, to search for a northwest passage to Asia. Cabot probably reached Newfoundland, which he took to be part of Asia. He sailed again in 1498 with five ships but was lost at sea. Only one vessel returned, but Cabot's voyages gave England a vague claim to portions of the North American coast.

The English Reformation

When interest in America revived during the reign of Elizabeth I (1558–1603), England was rapidly becoming a Protestant kingdom. Elizabeth's father, Henry VIII (1509–1547), desperate for a male heir, had broken with the pope to divorce his queen. He remarried, proclaimed himself the "Only Supreme Head" of the Church of England, confiscated monastic lands, and inadvertently opened the way for committed Protestant reformers. Under Elizabeth's younger brother Edward VI (1547–1553), the government embraced Protestantism. When Edward died, Elizabeth's older sister Mary I (1553–1558) reimposed Catholicism. She burned hundreds of Protestants at the stake and drove thousands into exile, where many became Calvinists. Elizabeth, however, accepted Protestantism, and the exiles returned. The Church of England became Calvinist in doctrine but remained largely Catholic in structure, liturgy, and ritual.

Some Protestants demanded the eradication of Catholic vestiges and the replacement of the **Anglican** Book of Common Prayer with sermons and psalms as the dominant mode of worship. These **Puritans** played a major role in England's overseas expansion. More extreme Protestants, called **Separatists**, denied that the Church of England was a true church and began to set up independent congregations of their own. Some of them would found the small colony of **Plymouth**.

Hawkins and Drake

In 1560 England was a rather backward country of three million people. Its chief export was woolen cloth. During the 16th century the numbers of both people and sheep grew rapidly, competing for the same land. After 1600, internal migration fueled overseas settlement. But before then, interest in America centered not in the rapidly growing London but in the southwestern ports already involved in the Newfoundland fishery.

Taking advantage of friendly relations that still prevailed between England and Spain, John Hawkins of Plymouth made three voyages to New Spain between 1562 and 1569. On his first trip he bought slaves from the Portuguese in West Africa and sold them to the Spaniards in Hispaniola, where he tried to set up as a legitimate trader. Spanish authorities disapproved, and on his second voyage he had to trade at gunpoint. On his third trip, the Spanish viceroy sank four of his six ships. Hawkins and his kinsman Francis Drake escaped, both vowing vengeance.

Drake even began to talk of freeing slaves from Spanish tyranny. His most dramatic exploit came between 1577 and 1580 when he rounded Cape Horn and plundered Spanish possessions along the Pacific coast of Peru. Knowing that the Spaniards would be waiting for him if he returned by the same route, he sailed

Anglican *Member of the legally established Church of England, or that church itself.*

Puritans *English religious group that followed the teachings of John Calvin and wanted to purify the Church of England of its surviving Catholic ceremonies and vestments.*

Separatists *One of the most extreme English Protestant groups that followed the teachings of John Calvin. They began to separate from the Church of England and form their own congregations.*

Plymouth *England's first permanent colony in New England, founded by Separatists in 1620.*

north, explored San Francisco Bay, and continued west around the world to England. Elizabeth rewarded him with a knighthood.

Gilbert, Ireland, and America

By the 1560s the idea of permanent colonization intrigued several Englishmen. England had a model in Ireland, which the English Crown had claimed for centuries. After 1560, the English tried to impose their agriculture, language, local government, legal system, aristocracy, and Protestant religion upon the Irish. The Irish responded by becoming more intensely Catholic.

Sir Humphrey Gilbert was one of the most brutal of Elizabeth's captains in the Irish wars of the 1560s. In subduing Munster in 1569, Gilbert killed nearly everyone in his path and destroyed all the crops, a strategy that the English later employed against Indians. Gilbert next began to think about colonizing America. He proposed that England grab control of Newfoundland fisheries and urged settlements that could become bases for plundering New Spain. After a failed first attempt in 1578, Gilbert's fleet arrived to claim Newfoundland in 1583. The crews of 22 Spanish and Portuguese fishing vessels and 18 French and English ships listened in astonishment as Gilbert read his royal patent to them. He then sailed away to explore more of the American coast. His own ship went under during a storm.

Ralegh, Roanoke, and War with Spain

Sir Walter Ralegh *Elizabethan courtier who, in the 1580s, tried but failed to establish an English colony on Roanoke Island in what is now North Carolina.*

Jamestown *First permanent English settlement in North America (1607) and the capital of Virginia for most of the 17th century.*

Gilbert's half-brother, **Sir Walter Ralegh** (or Raleigh), obtained his own patent from the queen and tried twice to plant a colony in North America. In 1585, he sent a large expedition to Roanoke Island in what is now North Carolina, but the settlers planted no crops and exasperated the Indians with demands for food during a drought. In June 1586, the English killed the local chief, Wingina, who had threatened to resettle his people on the mainland and leave the colonists to starve—or work. Days later, when the expected supply vessels failed to arrive on schedule, the colonists sailed back to England on the ships of Sir Francis Drake, who had just burned the Spanish city of St. Augustine with the support of Florida Indians, whom he freed. The supply ships reached Roanoke a little later, only to find the site abandoned. They left a small garrison there and sailed off in quest of Spanish plunder. The garrison was never heard from again.

Ralegh sent a second expedition to Roanoke in 1587, one that included some women, a sign that he envisioned a permanent colony. When the governor went back to England for more supplies, his return to Roanoke was delayed by the assault of the Spanish Armada on England in 1588. By the time he returned to Roanoke in 1590, the settlers had vanished, leaving a cryptic message— "CROATOAN"—carved on a tree. The colonists may have settled among the Chesapeake nation of Indians near the entrance to Chesapeake Bay. Sketchy evidence suggests that the powerful Powhatans wiped out the Chesapeakes, along with any English living with them, in the spring of 1607, just as the first **Jamestown** settlers were sailing into the bay.

The Spanish armada touched off a war that lasted until 1604 and strained the resources of England. Although the plundering exploits of Hawkins, Drake, Gilbert, and Ralegh continued to pay, the English could not afford to sustain a colony like Roanoke until it could return a profit. But beginning in the 1590s, London became intensely involved in American affairs by launching privateering fleets against Spain. This marriage of London capital and explorer ambition would make permanent colonization possible.

TABLE 2.1

THE PATTERN OF SETTLEMENT IN THE ENGLISH COLONIES UP TO 1700				
	Immigrants (or settlers) (in thousands)		U.S. Population in 1700 (in thousands)	
Region	Europeans	Africans	European Americans	African Americans
West Indies	220 (29.6%)	316 (42.5%)	33 (8.3%)	115 (28.8%)
South	135 (18.1%)	30 (4.0%)	82 (20.5%)	22 (5.5%)
Mid-Atlantic	20 (2.7%)	2 (0.3%)	51 (12.8%)	3 (0.8%)
New England	20 (2.7%)	1 (0.1%)	91 (22.8%)	2 (0.5%)
Total	395 (53.1%)	349 (46.9%)	257 (64.4%)	142 (35.6%)

© Cengage Learning

The Swarming of the English

In the 17th century more than 700,000 people crossed the Atlantic to the English colonies in North America and the Caribbean. Most European migrants were single young men who arrived as servants. And, at first, some Africans were regarded as servants, not slaves.

The Europeans who settled in New England or the Hudson and Delaware valleys were the most fortunate. Because Puritans and Quakers migrated as families into healthy regions, their populations flourished. The descendants of this small, idealistic minority soon became a substantial part of the total population and played a role in American history far out of proportion to their original numbers.

As Table 2.1 shows, the New England and Middle Atlantic colonies together attracted only 5.4 percent of the immigrants, but by 1700 they contained 36 percent of all the people in the English colonies and 55 percent of the Europeans.

THE CHESAPEAKE AND WEST INDIAN COLONIES

In 1606 King James I of England (1603–1625) chartered the Virginia Company with authority to colonize North America between the 34th and 45th parallels. The company had two headquarters. One, in the English city of Plymouth, received jurisdiction over the northern portion of the grant. Known as the Plymouth Company, it planted a colony at Sagadahoc on the coast of Maine in 1607. But after the Abenaki Indians refused to trade with the settlers, they abandoned the site in September 1608.

The other branch, based in London, chose to colonize the Chesapeake Bay area. In 1607, the London Company sent out three ships carrying 104 settlers. They landed at a peninsula on what they called the James River, built a fort and other crude buildings, and named the settlement Jamestown. Investors hoped to find gold or silver, a northwest passage to Asia, a cure for syphilis, or other valuable products for sale in Europe. The settlers expected to compel local Indians to work for them. If the Indians proved hostile, the settlers were told to form alliances with more distant Indians and subdue those who resisted. Company officials did not realize that a war chief named Powhatan ruled virtually all of the Indians whom the English believed they could enlist as allies.

FOCUS QUESTION

Why did the English, crossing the Atlantic at nearly the same time, create such radically different societies in the Chesapeake, the West Indies, and New England?

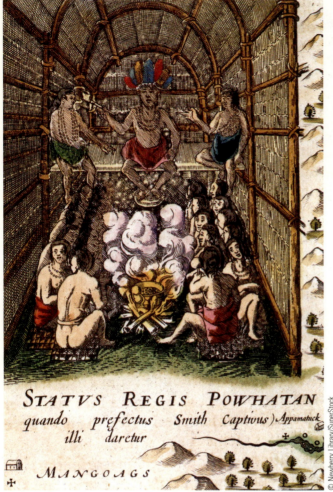

STATVS REGIS POWHATAN
quando   prefectus   Smith   Captivus) Appamatuck
illi   daretur

MANGOAGS

© Newberry Library/SuperStock

REGAL STATE. *Illustration of Emperor Powhatan with tobacco pipe enthroned in his lodge, from vignette embellishing Smith's map of Virginia, first published in 1612.*

Captain John Smith *Member of the Virginia Council whose strong leadership from 1607 to 1609 probably saved the colony from collapse.*

joint-stock company *Form of business organization that resembled a modern corporation in that individuals invested in the company through the purchase of shares, although each stockholder had one vote regardless of how many shares he owned.*

The Jamestown Disaster

The colony was a deathtrap. Every summer the river around Jamestown became contaminated and sent out killing waves of dysentery and typhoid fever. Before long, malaria also set in. Only 38 of the original 104 settlers survived the first year. Of the 325 who came before 1609, fewer than 100 remained alive in the spring of that year.

The survivors owed their good fortune to the resourcefulness of **Captain John Smith**, a soldier and adventurer who took charge. After his explorations uncovered neither riches nor any quick route to Asia, he concentrated instead on sheer survival. He tried to awe Powhatan, maintain friendly relations with him, and buy corn. Through the help of Pocahontas, Powhatan's 12-year-old daughter, he avoided war. Though Smith gave conflicting versions of the story later on, he clearly believed that Pocahontas saved his life in December 1607. But food remained scarce. The colony had too many members who considered farming beneath their dignity. Over their protests, Smith set them to work raising grain for four hours a day.

In 1609 the London Company sent out 600 more settlers under Lieutenant Governor Thomas Gates, but his ship ran aground on Bermuda, and the crew spent a year building another vessel. About 400 new settlers reached Virginia before Gates arrived. Smith, after suffering a severe injury in an explosion, sailed back to England, and the colony lacked firm leadership for the next year. When Gates finally reached Jamestown in June 1610, he found only 60 settlers alive.

He also found himself in the middle of the colony's first Indian war. Wearying Powhatan with their endless demands for corn during a drought, the settlers had provoked the violence that Smith had avoided. From 1609 to 1614, Powhatan's warriors picked off any settlers who strayed far from Jamestown. The English retaliated by slaughtering whole villages in hopes of intimidating others. The war finally ended after the English captured Pocahontas and used her as a hostage to negotiate peace. She converted to Christianity and married John Rolfe, a widower.

Despite the Indian war, the colony's prospects improved. Through Rolfe's efforts Jamestown began to produce a cash crop. In 1613, he imported a mild strain of tobacco from the West Indies. It brought such a good price in England that the king, who had insisted no one could build a colony "upon smoke," was proved wrong. Soon everyone was growing tobacco.

Reorganization, Reform, and Crisis

In 1609 a new royal charter extended Virginia's boundaries to the Pacific. A third charter in 1612 made the London Company a **joint-stock company**. It resembled a modern corporation except that each stockholder had only one vote.

The company adopted an ambitious reform program for Virginia. It encouraged economic diversification, such as planting grapevines and raising silkworms. English common law replaced martial law. The settlers were allowed to elect their own assembly, the **House of Burgesses**, to meet with the governor and his council and make local laws. Finally, settlers were permitted to own land. Under this **headright** system, a colonist received 50 acres for each person whose passage to Virginia he financed. By 1623, the company had shipped 4,000 settlers to Virginia, but the economic diversification program failed. Only tobacco found a market.

The flood of newcomers strained the food supply and soured relations with the Indians, especially after Powhatan died and was succeeded by his militant brother,

> **House of Burgesses** *Assembly of early Virginia elected by settlers that met with the governor and his council and enacted local laws. It first met in 1619.*

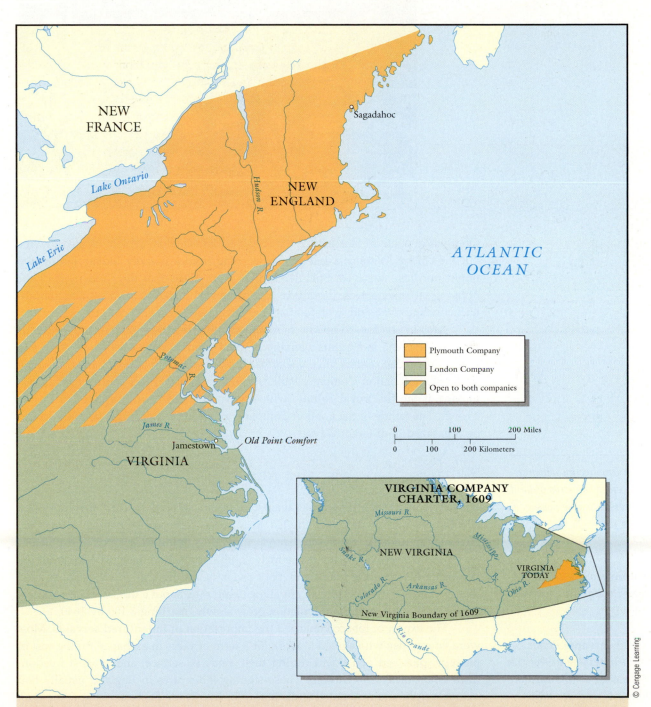

Map 2.2 Virginia Company Charter, 1606. *This charter gave the Plymouth Company jurisdiction over what would become New England and New York, and the London Company jurisdiction over most of what became Virginia and North Carolina. They shared jurisdiction over the intervening area. The insert map shows Virginia's revised sea-to-sea boundaries laid out in the 1609 charter.*

© Cengage Learning

THE OPECHANCANOUGH MASSACRE OF 1622. *This famous event, as portrayed in an engraving from the workshop of Theodore de Bry, depicts the warriors as treacherous, bloodthirsty savages and the settlers as innocent victims.*

Opechancanough. In March 1622, the new chief launched an attack intended to wipe out the colony. Without a last-minute warning from a friendly Indian, Jamestown might not have survived. Still, 347 settlers were killed that day, and most of the outlying settlements were destroyed. Newcomers who arrived in subsequent months had nowhere to go and, with food again scarce, hundreds died over the winter.

Back in London, company shareholders withdrew their capital, and asked the king to intervene in Virginia's affairs. A royal commission visited the colony and found only 1,200 settlers alive out of 6,000 sent over since 1607. In 1624, the king declared the London Company bankrupt and assumed direct control of Virginia, making it the first **royal colony**, with a governor and council appointed by the Crown. The failure of the London Company guaranteed that future colonies would be organized in different ways.

Tobacco, Servants, and Survival

headright *Practice by which a colonist received 50 acres of land for every person whose passage to America he financed.*

royal colony *Colony controlled directly by the English monarch.*

indentured servants *People who had their passage to America paid by a master or ship captain. They agreed to work for their master for a term of years in exchange for cost of passage, bed and board, and small freedom dues when their terms were up.*

For ten years the settlers warred against Opechancanough. In 1623, they poisoned 200 Indians whom they had invited to a peace conference. In most years they attacked the Indians just before harvest time, destroying their crops and villages. By the time both sides made peace in 1632, all Indians had been expelled from the peninsula between the James and York rivers below Jamestown. Virginia proved that it could survive. Despite an appalling death rate, about a thousand new settlers arrived each year, and the population grew slowly, reaching 8,100 by 1640.

The export of tobacco financed the importation of **indentured servants**. Most were young men who agreed to work for a term of years in exchange for the cost of passage, plus bed and board during their years of service, and modest freedom dues when their term expired. Those signing indentures in England usually had valuable skills and negotiated terms of four or five years. Those arriving without an indenture, most of whom were younger and less skilled, were sold by the ship captain to a planter. Those over age 19 served five years. Those under 19 served until age 24. The system turned servants into freemen who hoped to prosper on their own.

Until 1660, many former servants managed to acquire land, and some even served on the county courts and in the House of Burgesses. As tobacco prices fell after 1660, however, upward mobility became more difficult. Political offices usually went to the richest settlers. Government became a self-perpetuating **oligarchy**, and resentment grew among those who were shut off from power and unable to prosper.

Maryland

A second colony on the Chesapeake Bay, Maryland, arose from the social and religious vision of Sir George Calvert and his son, Cecilius, who saw America as a refuge for persecuted English and Irish Catholics. Sir George, a prominent office-holder, had invested in the London Company. When he resigned his royal office after becoming a Catholic, the king made him Baron Baltimore in the Irish peerage.

The Maryland charter of 1632 made Baltimore "lord proprietor" of the colony, the most sweeping delegation of power that the Crown could make. After 1630, most new colonial projects were **proprietary colonies**. Many of them embodied the distinctive social ideals of their founders.

George Calvert died as the Maryland patent was being issued, and Cecilius inherited Maryland and the peerage. Like Champlain, he believed that Catholics and Protestants could live in peace in the same colony. But he expected the servants, most of whom were Protestants, to continue to serve the Catholic gentlemen of the colony (he made them manor lords) after their indentures expired.

Those plans were never fulfilled. The condition of English Catholics improved under Charles I (1625–1649) and his queen, Henrietta Maria, a French Catholic for whom the colony was named. Because few Catholics emigrated, most settlers were Protestants. The civil war that erupted in England in 1642 soon spread to Maryland. Protestants overthrew Lord Baltimore's regime several times between 1642 and 1660, but the English state always sided with him.

The manorial system did not survive these upheavals. Protestant servants, after their indentures expired, acquired their own land rather than become tenants under Catholic manor lords, most of whom died or returned to England. When Maryland's unrest ended around 1660, the colony was raising tobacco, corn, and livestock and was governed by county courts similar to those in Virginia.

Chesapeake Family Life

At first, European men outnumbered women in Virginia by 5 to 1. Among new immigrant servants as late as the 1690s, the ratio was still 5 to 2. Population became self-sustaining about 1680, when live births finally began to outnumber deaths. Until 1700, most prominent people were immigrants.

Life expectancy slowly improved, but it still remained much lower than in England. The Chesapeake immigrants had survived childhood diseases in Europe, but men at age 20 could expect to live only to about 45, with 70 percent dead by age 50. Women died even younger, especially during pregnancy. About 70 percent of the men never married or, if they did, produced no children. Women could not marry until they had finished their indentures. About one-fifth had illegitimate children, despite legal penalties, and one-third were pregnant on their wedding day. In a typical Chesapeake marriage, the groom was in his 30s and the bride eight or ten years younger. This age gap meant that the husband usually died before his wife, who then quickly remarried. Orphans were a major community problem. Stepparents were common. Few lived long enough to become grandparents.

oligarchy *Society dominated by a few persons or families.*

proprietary colony *Colony owned by an individual(s) who had vast discretionary powers.*

Under these circumstances, family loyalties tended to focus on uncles, aunts, cousins, and older stepbrothers or stepsisters. Patriarchy remained weak. Because fathers died young, even the elite that took shape after 1650 had difficulty passing its status to its sons. Only toward the end of the century were the men who held office likely to be descended from fathers of comparable distinction.

The West Indies and the Transition to Slavery

Before 1700 far more Englishmen went to the West Indies than to the Chesapeake. Between 1624 and 1640 they settled the tiny Leeward Islands (St. Christopher, Nevis, Montserrat, and Antigua) and Barbados. At first, English planters grew tobacco there using the labor of indentured servants. Then, beginning around 1645 in Barbados, sugar replaced tobacco. Sugar required a heavy investment in slaves and mills, and large planters with many slaves soon dominated the islands. Ex-servants found little employment, and most of them moved to the mainland or joined the buccaneers. In 1660, Europeans outnumbered slaves in the islands by 33,000 to 22,000. By 1700, the number of slaves had increased sixfold. Planters often worked slaves to death: Of the 316,000 Africans imported before 1700, only 115,000 remained alive in that year. Observers were depressed by the moral climate on the islands, yet they generated

SLAVES ON A SUGAR PLANTATION IN ANTIGUA. *Sugar was an even more demanding crop than tobacco, partly because workers could easily cut themselves on the sharp edges of the cane stalks and also because planters tried to compel workers to toil almost around the clock at harvest time so that the cane could be crushed in a mill and the juice boiled before it could spoil. A weary slave could easily lose fingers or an arm while trying to feed the mill.*

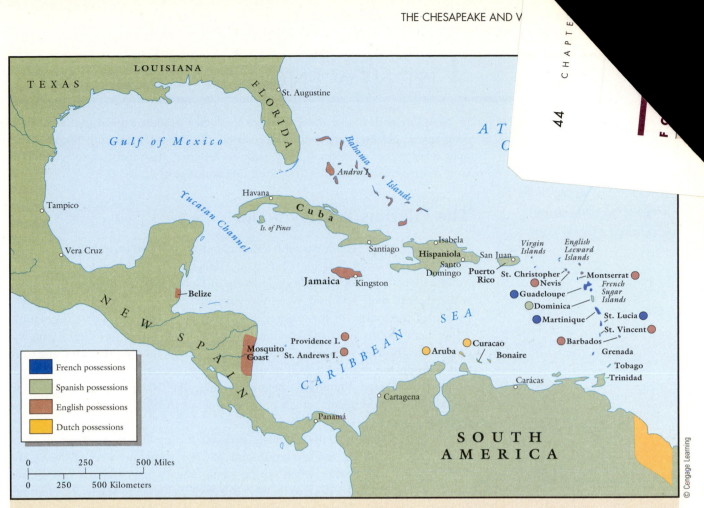

Map 2.3 **Principal West Indian Colonies in the 17th Century.** *Spain retained control of the large islands of Cuba, Hispaniola, and Puerto Rico, while its English, French, and Dutch rivals settled the smaller but fertile islands east of Puerto Rico or south of Cuba.*

enormous wealth for the English empire, far more than the mainland colonies well into the 18th century.

The Rise of Slavery in North America

Africans reached Virginia in 1619 when, John Rolfe reported, a Dutch ship "sold us twenty Negars." In the Chesapeake some Africans were treated as servants and won their freedom after several years, including perhaps 30 percent of those on Virginia's eastern shore as late as the 1660s. But most Africans were already serving for life, and that pattern soon prevailed.

In the generation after 1680, the caste structure of the Chesapeake colonies became firmly set. Fewer indentured servants reached the Chesapeake from England, as the Delaware valley and the expanding English army and navy competed for the same young men. Slaves took their place. They cost more to buy, but they served for life. In 1705, the Virginia legislature forbade the whipping of a white servant without a court's permission, a restriction that did not apply to the punishment of slaves. To attract more whites, Virginia also promised every ex-servant 50 acres of land. The message was obvious: Every white was now superior to any black. Racial caste became the organizing principle of Chesapeake society.

QUICK REVIEW

THE ENGLISH IN VIRGINIA, MARYLAND, AND THE CARIBBEAN

- Problems of survival due to disease, disorganization, and warfare in Virginia

- Tobacco production financed the importation of servants

- Maryland founded by Calvert family, English and Irish Catholics

- Sugar revolution in the West Indies required heavy investment in slaves and mills

- Shift to African slavery in the Chesapeake as numbers of indentured servants decreased

THE NEW ENGLAND COLONIES

In the Chesapeake colonies, why did Africans eventually become hereditary slaves serving for life instead of indentured servants bound only for several years?

In New England, unlike the Chesapeake colonies, settlers reproduced the mixed economy of old England, with minor variations. Their quarrel with England was over religion, not economics. They came to America, they insisted, to worship as God commanded, not as the Church of England required.

The Pilgrims and Plymouth

The **Pilgrims** were Separatists who left England for the Netherlands between 1607 and 1609, convinced that the Church of England was no true daughter of the Reformation. They hoped to worship freely in Holland. After 10 years there, they realized that their children were growing up Dutch, not English. That fear prompted a minority of the congregation to move to America. After negotiating rather harsh terms with the London Company, they sailed for Virginia on the *Mayflower*. The ship was blown off course late in 1620, landing first on Cape Cod, and then on the mainland well north of the charter boundaries of Virginia, at a site they named Plymouth. Before landing, the 100 passengers agreed to the Mayflower Compact, which bound them all to obey the decisions of the majority.

Short on supplies, the colonists suffered during the first winter. Half of them died, including the governor and all but three married women. The settlers fared much better when spring came. The Patuxet Indians of the area had been wiped out by disease in 1617, but their fields were ready for planting. Squanto, the only Patuxet to survive, had been kidnapped and carried to England by coastal traders in 1614. He had just made his way home and showed up at Plymouth in March 1621. He taught the settlers Indian methods of fishing and growing corn. He also introduced them to Massasoit, the powerful Wampanoag *sachem* whose people celebrated the first thanksgiving feast with the settlers after the 1621 harvest. By 1630, the settlers numbered about 300. They had paid off their London creditors, thus gaining political autonomy and private ownership of their flourishing farms.

Covenant Theology

Pilgrims *Pious, sentimental term used by later generations to describe the Separatist settlers who sailed on the* Mayflower *in 1620 and founded Plymouth Colony.*

sachem *Algonquian word that meant "chief."*

covenant theology *Belief that God made two personal covenants with humans: the covenant of works and the covenant of grace.*

A much larger Puritan exodus settled Massachusetts Bay between 1630 and 1641. To Puritans the stakes were immense by the late 1620s. God's wrath would visit England, they warned. During that early phase of Europe's Thirty Years' War (1618–1648), Catholic armies seemed about to crush the German Reformation. Charles I blundered into a brief war against both Spain and France, raised money for the war by dubious means, and dissolved Parliament when it protested.

Puritans embraced what they called **covenant theology**. According to this system, God had made two biblical covenants with humans: the covenant of works and the covenant of grace. In the covenant of works, God had promised Adam that if he kept God's law he would never die—but Adam disobeyed. All of his descendants remain under the same covenant, but because of his fall can never be capable of keeping the law; they deserve damnation. But God was merciful and answered sin with the covenant of grace. God will save his chosen people; everyone else will be damned. Even though the covenant of works can no longer bring eternal life, it remains in force and establishes the strict moral standards that every Christian must strive to follow. A Christian's inability to keep the law usually triggered the conversion experience by demonstrating that only faith, not works, could save.

At this level, covenant theology merely restated Calvinist orthodoxy, but the Puritans gave it a novel social dimension by pairing each personal covenant with a communal counterpart. The social equivalent of the covenant of grace was the church covenant. Each congregation organized itself into a church, a community of **the elect**. The founders of each church, after satisfying one another of their own conversions, agreed that within their church discipline would be strictly maintained. God, in turn, promised to bestow saving grace within that church—not to everyone, but presumably to most of the children of the elect. The communal counterpart of the covenant of works was the "national" covenant. It determined not who was saved or damned but the rise and fall of nations or peoples. As a people, New Englanders agreed to obey the law, and God promised them prosperity. If their **magistrates** enforced God's law and the people supported these efforts, God would not punish the whole community. But if sinners escaped public account, God's anger would be terrible. In England, the government had refused to assume a godly role. Puritans fleeing to America hoped to escape the divine wrath that they believed threatened England.

Massachusetts Bay

In 1629 English Puritans obtained a royal charter for the **Massachusetts Bay Company**. Led by Governor John Winthrop, they carried the charter to America, beyond the gaze of Charles I. They used it not to organize a business corporation but as the constitution for the colony. In the 1630s, the General Court created by the charter became the Massachusetts legislature.

New England settlers came from the broad middle range of English society. Most had owned property in England. When they sold it to go to America, they probably raised far more capital than the London Company had invested in Virginia.

An advance party that sailed in 1629 took over a fishing village on the coast and renamed it Salem. The Winthrop fleet brought 1,000 settlers in 1630. In small groups they scattered around the bay, founding Dorchester, Roxbury, Boston, Charlestown, and Cambridge. Each town formed around a minister and a magistrate. The local congregation was the first institution to take shape. From it evolved the town meeting. Soon the colonists were raising European livestock and growing English wheat and other grains, along with corn. Perhaps 30 percent of them perished during the first winter. A few hundred others grew discouraged and returned to England. Then conditions rapidly improved, as they had at Plymouth a decade earlier. About 13,000 persons settled in New England by 1641, most as families—a unique event in Atlantic empires to that time.

Puritan Family Life

After the first winter, deaths in rural areas were rare. The bracing climate proved healthy, and families grew rapidly as 6 or even 10 children reached maturity. For the founders and their children, life expectancy far exceeded the European norm.

the elect *Those selected by God for salvation.*

magistrate *Official who enforced the law. In colonial America, this person was usually a justice of the peace or a judge in a higher court.*

Massachusetts Bay Company *Joint-stock company chartered by Charles I in 1629. It was controlled by Non-Separatists who took the charter with them to New England and converted it into a written constitution for the colony.*

A City upon a Hill

Governor John Winthrop preached a lay sermon entitled "A Model of Christian Charity" to his fellow passengers aboard the *Arbella* as they sailed to New England in 1630. The following passage has become the most famous part of any sermon by a New Englander in the 17th century:

> For we must consider that we shall be as a City upon a Hill, the eyes of all people are upon us; so that if we shall deal falsely with our God in this work we have undertaken, and so cause Him to withdraw His present help from us, we shall be made a story and a by-word through the world. We shall open the mouths of enemies to speak evil of the ways of God and all professors [i.e., professing Christians] for God's sake; we shall shame the faces of many of God's worthy servants, and cause their prayers to be turned into Curses upon us till we be consumed out of the good land where we are going. . . . Beloved, there is now set before us life and good, death and evil, in that we are commanded this day to love the Lord our God, and to love one another, to walk in His ways and to keep His Commandments and His Ordinances and His Laws, and the Articles of our Covenant with Him that we may live and be multiplied, and that the Lord our God may bless us in the land where we go. . . .

Q American popular culture regards this sermon as a celebration of the Puritan sense of mission, but why did Winthrop issue such a stark warning about the consequences of failure?

Source: *Life and Letters of John Winthrop*, ed. by John C. Winthrop, Vol. 2, Boston (Ticknor and Fields, 1867).

More than one-fifth of the men who founded Andover lived past age 80. Infant mortality fell, and few mothers died in childbirth. Because people lived so long, New England families became intensely patriarchal. Many fathers refused to grant land titles to their sons before their own deaths. In the early years settlers often moved, looking for the richest soil, the best neighbors, and the most inspiring minister. By about 1645, migration into or out of country towns became much lower than in England, and the New England town settled into a tight community that slowly became an intricate web of cousins. Once the settlers had formed a typical farming town, they grew reluctant to admit "strangers" to their midst. They largely avoided slavery, mostly to keep outsiders from contaminating their religion.

Conversion, Dissent, and Expansion

The vital force behind Puritanism was the quest for conversion. But after the mid-1630s, stirred by the sermons of Boston's John Cotton, converts turned from analyzing the legitimacy of their own conversions to assessing the validity of someone else's. Churches began to test for regeneracy, or conversion, and the standards of acceptance escalated rapidly.

The conversion experience was deeply ambiguous to a Puritan. Anyone who found no inner trace of saving grace was damned. Anyone absolutely certain of salvation was also damned. Conversion took months, even years, to achieve. It began with the discovery that one could not keep God's law and that one deserved damnation, not for an occasional misdeed but for what one was at one's best—a wretched sinner. It progressed through despair to hope, which had to rest on passages of scripture that spoke to that person's condition. A "saint" at last found reason to believe that God had saved him or her. The whole process involved a painful balance between assurance and doubt. A saint was sure of salvation, but never too sure.

This quest for conversion generated dissent and new colonies. In the mid-1630s, Reverend Thomas Hooker, alarmed by Cotton's preaching, led his people west to the Connecticut River, where they founded Hartford and other towns south of the charter boundary of Massachusetts. John Winthrop Jr. built Saybrook Fort at the mouth of the river, and it soon merged with Hooker's towns into the colony of Connecticut.

The residents of most New England towns agreed on the kind of worship they preferred, but some settlers made greater demands. Roger Williams was a Separatist who refused to worship with anyone who did not explicitly repudiate the Church of England. Nearly all Massachusetts Puritans were **Non-Separatists** who claimed only to be reforming the Anglican Church. In 1636, after Williams challenged the king's right as a Christian to grant Indian lands to anyone at all, the colony banished him. He fled to Narragansett Bay with a few disciples and founded Providence. He developed eloquent arguments for religious liberty and the complete separation of church and state.

Anne Hutchinson, an admirer of John Cotton, claimed that virtually all other ministers were preaching only the covenant of works, not the covenant of grace, and were leading people to hell. She won a large following in Boston. At her trial there, she claimed to have received direct messages from God (the Antinomian heresy). Banished in 1638, she and her followers also fled to Narragansett Bay, where they founded Newport and Portsmouth. These towns united with Providence to form the colony of Rhode Island. They too accepted the religious liberty and separation of church and state that Williams advocated.

This territorial expansion reflected not just religious idealism, but also a quest for land that threatened neighboring Indians. Connecticut and Massachusetts waged a war of annihilation against the Pequot Indians, who controlled the fertile Thames River valley in eastern Connecticut. In May 1637, New England soldiers debated with their chaplain which of two Pequot forts to attack, the one held by warriors or the one containing mostly women, children, and the elderly. The Puritan army chose the second fort, set fire to all the wigwams, and shot everyone who tried to flee. The godly had their own uses for terror.

Congregations, Towns, and Colony Governments

These struggles shaped New England's basic institutions. Congregations abolished Anglican forms of worship. The sermon became the dominant rite, and each congregation chose and ordained its own minister. No singing was permitted, except of psalms. Congregations sometimes sent ministers and laymen to a synod, but its decisions were advisory, not binding.

The New England town had become something distinct from the congregation. Town meetings decided who got how much land. It was distributed broadly but never equally. In some villages, town meetings made most of the decisions, and left only the details to a board of elected "selectmen." In others the selectmen did most of the governing. All adult males usually participated in local decisions, but Massachusetts and New Haven restricted the vote for offices to men who were full church members, a decision that greatly narrowed the electorate by the 1660s.

Non-Separatists *English Puritans who insisted that they were faithful members of the Church of England while demanding that it purge itself of its surviving Catholic rituals and vestments.*

Anne Hutchinson *Religious radical who attracted a large following in Massachusetts. She warned that nearly all of the ministers were preaching a covenant of works instead of covenant of grace. Convicted of the Antinomian heresy, she and her most loyal followers were banished to Rhode Island in 1638.*

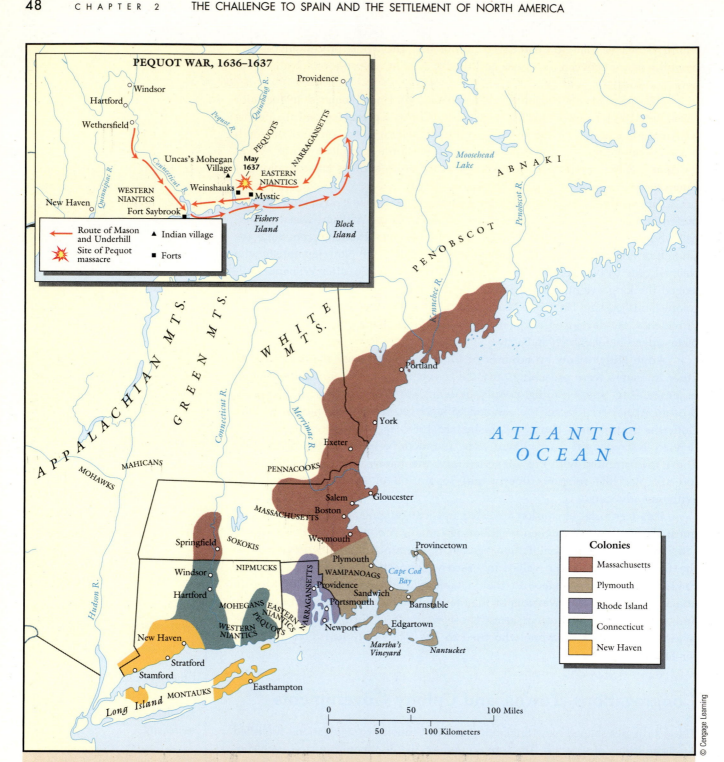

Map 2.4 New England in the 1640s. *The five Puritan colonies spread over the Atlantic coast and nearby islands, the shores and islands of Narragansett Bay, both sides of Long Island Sound, and much of the Connecticut valley. Although New Hampshire and Maine (not named as such on this map) were not founded by Puritans, Massachusetts extended its government over their settlers during the English civil wars. The insert map shows the principal military campaign of the Pequot War.*

bicameral legislature

Legislature with two houses or chambers.

Massachusetts had a **bicameral legislature** by the 1640s. It defined its legal system in the "Body of Liberties" of 1641 (which may actually be history's first bill of rights) and in a comprehensive law code of 1648 that was widely imitated in other colonies. Unlike England, Massachusetts seldom executed anyone for a crime against property. Other distinctive features of the system included the swift punishment of crime and an explicit recognition of the liberties of women, children, servants, foreigners, and even "the Bruite Creature," or animals.

New England also transformed the traditional English jury system. New Haven abolished juries altogether because the Bible does not mention them, but the other colonies vastly expanded the role of civil (noncriminal) juries. Except in capital trials, however, the criminal jury—a fixture of English justice—almost disappeared in New England. The punishment of sin involved fidelity to the covenant and was too important to leave to 12 ordinary men. This system worked well because even most sinners shared its values. Most offenders appeared in court and accepted their punishments. Acquittals were rare, yet hardly anyone ran away to avoid trial or punishment.

Infant Baptism and New Dissent

Although most founders of the New England colonies became church members during the fervor of the 1630s, their children had trouble achieving conversion. They had never lived as part of a beleaguered minority in England, nor had they experienced the joy of joining with other holy refugees in founding their own church. They had to find God on their own and then persuade their elders that their conversions were authentic. Most failed. They grew up, married, and requested baptism for their children. A 1648 synod declared that only "saints" (the converted) and their children could be baptized. But what about the grandchildren of the saints if their own parents had not yet experienced conversion? By 1660 this problem was becoming acute.

Dissenters offered two answers. In the 1640s, some settlers became Baptists. They argued that only converted adults should receive baptism. Their position challenged the logic of a covenanted community by implying that the community was a mass of sinners from whom God would randomly choose the saints. Prominent Baptists were arrested and expelled. Even more alarming to the Puritan establishment were the Quakers (see later section in this chapter), who invaded the region from England in the 1650s. Quakers found salvation within themselves—through the Inner Light present in all people. To Puritans the Quaker answer to the conversion dilemma seemed blasphemous and Antinomian. Massachusetts hanged four Quakers who refused to stop preaching, including Mary Dyer, once a disciple of Anne Hutchinson.

The clergy's answer to the lack of conversions, worked out at a synod in 1662, became known as the **Half-Way Covenant**. Parents who had been baptized but had not yet experienced conversion could bring their children before the church, "own the covenant" (that is, subject themselves and their offspring to the doctrine and discipline of the church), and have their children baptized. In practice, women often experienced conversion before age 30, men closer to 40, but many never did. In most churches women also began to outnumber men as full members. Despite the urging of the clergy, aging church members resisted the Half-Way Covenant, but as the founders died off in the 1670s and 1680s, it took hold and soon led to something like universal baptism. Almost every child had an ancestor who had been a full church member.

Half-Way Covenant *The Puritan practice whereby parents who had been baptized but had not yet experienced conversion could bring their children before the church and have them baptized.*

FROM CIVIL WAR TO THE FIRST RESTORATION COLONIES

England fell apart in the 1640s. After governing without Parliament from 1629 to 1640, Charles I tried to impose the Anglican Book of Common Prayer upon Presbyterian Scotland. The Scots revolted and invaded England. Charles had to summon Parliament, but in 1642 they took up arms against each other. Parliament won the military struggle. In 1649 it executed the king, abolished the House of Lords, and proclaimed England a Commonwealth (or republic). In 1653 the army named its most successful general, Oliver Cromwell, Lord Protector of England, but he died in 1658. As the Protectorate collapsed, part of the army invited Charles II to return from exile and accept the throne. By then the Church of England had nearly disintegrated. For two decades, no new bishoprics had been created.

The new Restoration government did its best to restore the old order. It brought back the House of Lords and reestablished the Church of England under its episcopal form of government. The English state, denying any right of dissent, persecuted both Catholics and Protestant dissenters: Presbyterians, Congregationalists, Baptists, and Quakers.

England had founded 6 of the original 13 colonies before 1640. Six others were founded or came under English rule during the **Restoration era** (1660–1688). The last, Georgia, was settled in the 1730s (see Chapter 4). All were proprietary in form. Except for **William Penn**, the new proprietors were **Cavaliers** who had supported Charles II and his brother James, duke of York, during their long exile. Charles owed them something, and a colonial charter cost nothing to grant. Except for Pennsylvania, the Restoration colonies were all founded by men with big ideas and small purses. The proprietors tried to attract settlers from the older colonies because importing them from Europe was expensive. They made it easy for settlers to acquire land, and they competed by offering guarantees of civil and political liberties. They all promised either toleration or full religious liberty, at least for Christians. Whereas Virginia and New England (except Rhode Island) were still homogeneous societies, the Restoration colonies all attracted a mix of religious and ethnic groups. No colony found it easy to create political stability out of this diversity.

Carolina, Harrington, and the Aristocratic Ideal

In 1663 eight courtiers obtained a charter by which they became the board of proprietors for a colony called "Carolina" in honor of the king. Most settlers came from two sources. Former servants from Virginia and Maryland, many in debt, claimed land around Albemarle Sound in what eventually became North Carolina. Other former servants came from Barbados. They settled the area that became South Carolina, 300 miles south of Albemarle.

To the proprietors in England, these scattered settlements made up a single colony. They drafted the Fundamental Constitutions of Carolina in 1669, an incredibly complex plan for organizing the new colony. (A young secretary, philosopher John Locke, helped write the document.) The Fundamental Constitutions drew on the work of Commonwealth England's most prominent republican thinker, James Harrington, author of *Oceana* (1656). Harrington argued that how land was distributed ought to determine whether power should be lodged in one man (monarchy), a few men (aristocracy), or many (a republic). Where ownership of land was

Restoration era *Period that began in 1660 when the Stuart dynasty under Charles II was restored to the throne of England and ended with the overthrow of James II in 1688–1689.*

William Penn *A convert to the Society of Friends in the 1660s, Penn acquired a charter for Pennsylvania in 1681, and then launched a major migration of Friends to the Delaware valley.*

Cavaliers *Supporters of the Stuart family of Charles I during the civil wars.*

widespread, he insisted, absolute government could not prevail. He proposed several other republican devices, such as frequent rotation of officeholders (called "term limits" today), the secret ballot, and a bicameral legislature.

Using Harrington's principles, the proprietors hoped to create an ideal aristocratic society in Carolina. But the Fundamental Constitutions proposed a government far more complex than any colony could sustain. England had three supreme courts; Carolina would have eight. A legislature of nobles and commoners would make laws. The nobles would control 40 percent of the land. The document guaranteed religious toleration to all who believed in God, but everyone had to join a church or lose his citizenship. The document also envisioned a class of lowly whites, "leetmen," who would live on small tracts and serve the great landlords—and it accepted slavery.

Conditions were bleak on Barbados for ex-servants, but not bleak enough to make the Fundamental Constitutions attractive to the Barbadians who settled in Carolina. In the 1680s, tired of resistance from the predominantly Anglican Barbadians, the proprietors shipped 1,000 dissenters from England and Scotland to South Carolina. These newcomers made religious diversity a social fact, but they never grew strong enough to win approval for the Fundamental Constitutions.

Carolina presented its organizers with other unanticipated obstacles to these aristocratic goals. The proprietors assumed that land ownership would be the key to everything else, including wealth and status, but many settlers prospered in other ways. Settlers in Albemarle exploited the virgin forests all around them to produce masts, turpentine, tar, and pitch for sale to English shipbuilders. Other settlers raised cattle and hogs by letting them run free on open land. Some of South Carolina's enslaved Africans were probably America's first cowboys. The settlers also traded with the Indians. As in New France and New Netherland, the Indian trade sustained a genuine city, Charleston, the first in the American South, founded in 1680. Carolina traders allied themselves with Indians to kidnap Indian women and children to Charleston for sale as slaves. Until 1715, the Indian slave trade was the colony's biggest business.

In the early 18th century South Carolina and North Carolina became separate colonies, and South Carolina's economy moved in a new direction. Charleston merchants increasingly invested their capital, acquired in the Indian trade, in rice plantations. In the 1690s, planters learned how to grow rice from slaves who had cultivated it in West Africa. It quickly became the staple export of South Carolina and triggered a sharp growth of slavery. In 1700, nearly half of the colony's population of 5,700 were African or Indian slaves. By 1730, two-thirds of its 30,000 people were African slaves, most toiling on rice plantations.

New York: An Experiment in Absolutism

In 1664 James, duke of York, obtained a charter from his royal brother for a colony between the Delaware and Connecticut rivers. Charles II claimed that the territory of New Netherland was rightfully England's because it was included in the Virginia charter of 1606. James sent a fleet to Manhattan, and the English settlers on Long Island rose to support his claim. Stuyvesant surrendered without resistance. The English renamed the province New York. New Amsterdam became New York City, and Fort Orange became Albany. New York also inherited New Netherland's role as mediator between the settlers and the Iroquois Five Nations.

The transition from a Dutch to an English colony did not go smoothly. The duke boldly tried to do in New York what he and the king did not dare attempt in England—to govern without an elective assembly. This policy made it difficult to attract English colonists to New York, especially after New Jersey granted settlers the right to elect an assembly, which made that colony far more attractive to English settlers. The creation of New Jersey also slowed the flow of Dutch settlers across the Hudson and thus helped to keep New York Dutch. Although English soldiers abused many Dutch civilians, official policy toward the Dutch was conciliatory. Those who chose to leave could take their property with them. Those who stayed retained their property and were assured of religious toleration. Most stayed.

James expected his English invaders to assimilate the conquered Dutch, but the reverse was more common. Most Englishmen who settled in New York after the conquest married Dutch women (few unmarried English women were available) and sent their children to the Dutch Reformed Church. In effect, the Dutch were assimilating the English. Nor did the Dutch give up their loyalty to the Netherlands. In 1673, when a Dutch fleet threatened the colony, the Dutch refused to assist the English garrison of Fort James at the southern tip of Manhattan. Much like Stuyvesant nine years earlier, the garrison gave up without resistance. New York City now became New Orange.

New Orange survived for 15 months, until the Dutch Republic again concluded that the colony was not worth its cost and returned it to England in 1674, at the end of the Third Anglo-Dutch War. The new governor, Major Edmund Andros, arrested seven prominent Dutch merchants and tried them as aliens after they refused to swear an oath of loyalty to England that might oblige them to fight other Dutchmen. Faced with the confiscation of their property, they gave in. Andros also helped secure bilingual ministers for Dutch Reformed pulpits. Ordinary Dutch settlers looked with suspicion on the new ministers and on wealthier Dutch families who socialized with the governor or sent their sons to New England to learn English.

The English (but not Dutch) towns on Long Island joined in the demand for an elective assembly, an urgent matter now that William Penn's much freer colony on the Delaware threatened to drain away the small English population of New York. The duke finally relented and conceded an assembly. When it met in 1683 it adopted a Charter of Liberties that proclaimed government by consent. Although the flight of English settlers to Pennsylvania declined, few immigrants came to New York at a time when thousands were landing in Philadelphia. Philadelphia's thriving trade cut into New York City's profits. New York remained a Dutch society with a Yankee enclave, governed by English intruders.

BROTHERLY LOVE: THE QUAKERS AND AMERICA

The most fascinating social experiment of the Restoration era took place in the Delaware valley, where Quakers led another family-based, religiously motivated migration of more than 10,000 people between 1675 and 1690. The Society of Friends expanded dramatically in the 1650s as it went through a heroic phase of missionaries and martyrs, including the four executed in Massachusetts. After the Restoration, persecution in England finally prompted Quakers to seek refuge in America.

Quaker Beliefs

pacifist *Person opposed to war or violence. The religious group most committed to pacifism was the Quakers.*

Quakers infuriated other Christians. They insisted that God, in the form of the Inner Light, is present in all people, who can become good—even perfect—if only they will let that light shine forth. They became **pacifists**, enraging Catholics and most other Protestants, all of whom had found ways to justify war. Quakers also denounced oaths as sinful. Again, other Christians reacted with horror because their judicial systems rested on oaths.

Although orderly and peaceful, Quakers struck others as dangerous radicals whose beliefs would bring anarchy. For instance, slavery made them uncomfortable, though they did not embrace abolitionism until a century later. Further, in what they called "the Lamb's war" against human pride, Quakers refused to doff their hats to social superiors. Hats symbolized the social hierarchy of Europe. Every man knew his place so long as he understood whom to doff to, and who should doff to him. And Quakers refused to accept or to confer titles. They called everyone "thee" or "thou," familiar terms used by superiors when addressing inferiors.

The implications of Quaker religious beliefs appalled other Christians. The Inner Light seemed to obliterate predestination, original sin, maybe even the Trinity. Quakers had no sacraments, not even an organized clergy. They denounced Protestant ministers as "hireling priests." Quakers also held distinctive views about revelation. If God speaks directly to Friends, that Word must be every bit as inspired as anything in the Bible. Quakers compiled books of their "sufferings," which they thought were the equal of the Acts of the Apostles in the New Testament, a claim that seemed blasphemous to others.

Contemporaries expected the Society of Friends to fall apart as each member followed his or her own Light in some unique direction. In the 1660s, however, Quakers found ways to deal with discord. The heart of Quaker worship was the "weekly meeting" of the local congregation. There was no sermon or liturgy; people spoke whenever the Light inspired them. But because a few men and women spoke often and with great effect, they became recognized as **public friends**, the closest the Quakers came to having a clergy. The weekly meetings within a region sent representatives to a "monthly meeting," which resolved questions of policy and discipline. The monthly meetings sent delegates to the "yearly meeting" in London. At every level, decisions had to be unanimous because God would convey the same message to all. This insistence on unanimity provided safeguards against schism.

Quaker Families

Quakers transformed the traditional family as well. Women enjoyed almost full equality, and some of them, such as Mary Dyer, became exceptional preachers, even martyrs. Women held their own formal meetings and made important decisions about discipline and betrothals. Quaker reforms also affected children, whom most Protestants saw as tiny sinners whose wills must be broken by discipline. But once Quakers stopped worrying about original sin, their children became innocents in whom the Light would shine if only they could be protected from worldly corruption. In America, Quakers created affectionate families and worked hard to acquire land for all their children. Earlier than other Christians, they began to limit family size to give more love to the children they did have. Quakers seldom socialized with non-Quakers, and the needs of their own children were paramount. To marry an outsider meant expulsion from the Society.

Persecution in England helped to drive Quakers across the ocean, but the need to provide for their children was another powerful motive for emigration. By 1700, about half of the Quakers in England and Wales had moved to America.

public friends *Men and women who spoke most frequently and effectively for the Society of Friends. They were as close as the Quakers came to having a clergy.*

West New Jersey

In 1674, the New Jersey proprietors split their holding into two colonies. Sir George Carteret claimed what he now called East New Jersey, a province near New York City. Lord Berkeley claimed the western portion and promptly sold it to Quakers, who then founded two colonies in America: West New Jersey and Pennsylvania.

West Jersey Quakers believed that godly people could live together in love—without war, lawyers, or internal conflict. They kept government close to the people, made land easy to acquire, and promised freedom of worship to everyone. But as social and religious diversity grew, the system broke down. Non-Quakers increasingly refused to cooperate. In the 1690s, the courts became impotent, and Quaker rule collapsed some years before the Crown took over the colony in 1702.

Pennsylvania

By 1681 Quaker attention was shifting to the west bank of the Delaware River, where William Penn launched a much larger, if rather more cautious, "holy experiment." The son of a Commonwealth admiral, Penn grew up surrounded by privilege. He knew well both Charles II and the duke of York, attended Oxford and the **Inns of Court** (England's law schools), and began to manage his father's Irish estates. Then something happened that embarrassed his family. "Mr. William Pen," reported a neighbor in December 1667, "is a Quaker again, or some very melancholy thing." Penn often traveled to the continent on behalf of the Society of Friends, winning converts and recruiting settlers in the Netherlands and Germany.

Penn was no ordinary colonizer. Using his contacts at court, he converted an old debt (owed to his father by the king) into a charter for a proprietary colony that Charles named "Pennsylvania" in honor of the deceased admiral. The emerging imperial bureaucracy disliked the project and, after failing to block it, inserted legal and trade restrictions into the charter. Contemporaries said little about the most striking innovation attempted by the Quaker colonists: They entered America unarmed. Pennsylvanians did not even organize a militia until the 1740s. Friendly relations with Indians were essential to the project's success, and Penn was careful to deal fairly with the Lenni Lenape, or Delaware Indians.

More thought went into the planning of Pennsylvania than into the creation of any other colony. Twenty drafts survive of Penn's First Frame of Government, his 1682 constitution for the province. Under this plan, the settlers would elect a council of 72 men to staggered three-year terms. The council would draft all legislation and submit copies to the voters. In the early years the voters would meet to approve or reject these bills in person, but as the province expanded, such meetings would become impractical. Voters would then elect an assembly of 200, which would increase gradually to 500. Penn gave up the power to veto bills but retained control of the distribution of land. Capital punishment for crimes other than murder was abolished. Religious liberty, trial by jury, and habeas corpus all received strong guarantees. When the colonists persuaded Penn that the First Frame was too cumbersome for a small colony, he initiated the Second Frame, or the Pennsylvania Charter of Liberties of 1683, which reduced the council to 18 men and the assembly to 36.

Inns of Court *England's law schools.*

PENN'S TREATY WITH THE INDIANS, BY BENJAMIN WEST. *This 1771 painting celebrates William Penn's efforts, nearly a century earlier, to establish peaceful relations with the Delaware Indians.*

In 1691 the Society of Friends suffered a brief schism in the Delaware valley. A Quaker schoolteacher, George Keith, urged all Quakers to systematize their beliefs and even wrote his own catechism, only to encounter the opposition of the public friends, who included the colony's major officeholders. When he attacked them directly, he was convicted and fined for abusing civil officers. In contrast to Massachusetts in the 1630s, no one was banished, and Pennsylvania remained a haven for all religions.

Pennsylvania's politics remained turbulent and unstable into the 1720s. Yet Quaker families prospered, and the colony's policy of religious freedom attracted thousands of outsiders. Some were German pacifists who shared the major goals of the Society of Friends. Others were Anglicans and Presbyterians who warned London that Quakers were unfit to rule—anywhere.

Conclusion

In the 16th century, France, the Netherlands, and England all challenged Spanish power in Europe and across the ocean. After 1600, all three founded their own colonies in North America and the Caribbean. New France became a land of missionaries and traders. New Netherland also was founded to participate in the fur trade. Both colonies slowly acquired an agricultural base.

The English, by contrast, desired the land itself. The southern mainland and Caribbean colonies produced staple crops for sale in Europe, first with the labor of indentured servants and then with enslaved Africans. The Puritan and Quaker colonies became smaller versions of England's mixed economy, with an emphasis on family farms. After conquering New Netherland, England controlled the Atlantic seaboard from Maine to South Carolina, and by 1700 the population of England's mainland colonies was doubling every 25 years. England was beginning to emerge as the biggest winner in the competition for empire.

CHAPTER REVIEW

Review Questions

1. Why did the number of Indians who chose to become Catholics far exceed the number who accepted Protestantism?
2. Why did Englishmen, crossing the Atlantic at roughly the same time, create such radically different societies in the Chesapeake, the West Indies, and New England?
3. In what ways did the Restoration colonies differ from those founded earlier in the Chesapeake and New England?

Critical Thinking Questions

1. Does the splintering of New England into multiple colonies, each with a somewhat different vision of the Puritan mission, indicate that religious uniformity could be maintained only under the strong government of a single state?
2. In the 17th century, Quakers came closer than any other group to affirming equality as a positive value. Does their experience in England and America suggest how difficult it might be to persuade an entire society to embrace that value?

Identifications

Review your understanding of the following key terms, people, and events for this chapter.

Protestant Reformation, p. 30
predestination, p. 30
Huguenots, p. 31
politique, p. 31
coureur de bois, p. 32
tithe, p. 33
States General, p. 33
Yankees, p. 34
Anglican, p. 35
Puritans, p. 35

Separatists, p. 35
Plymouth, p. 35
Sir Walter Ralegh, p. 36
Jamestown, p. 36
Captain John Smith, p. 38
joint-stock company, p. 38
House of Burgesses, p. 39
headright, p. 39
royal colony, p. 40
indentured servants, p. 40

oligarchy, p. 41
proprietary colony, p. 41
Pilgrims, p. 44
sachem, p. 44
covenant theology, p. 44
the elect, p. 45
magistrate, p. 45
Massachusetts Bay Company, p. 45
Non-Separatists, p. 47

Anne Hutchinson, p. 47
bicameral legislature, p. 48
Half-Way Covenant, p. 49
Restoration era, p. 50
William Penn, p. 50
Cavaliers, p. 50
pacifist, p. 52
public friends, p. 53
Inns of Court, p. 54

DISCOVERY

What were the differences and similarities between various colonizing countries' approaches to colonial development? In particular, how did the colonies of France and England differ in their dealings with indigenous Indian populations?

In thinking about this question, begin by breaking it down into the components shown below. A discussion of the significance of each component should appear in your answer.

Geography

Look at the maps "New France and the Jesuit Missions" (page 32) and "New England in the 1640s" (page 48). Where in particular did the French and English choose to colonize? Which settlements made it easier to retain close ties with their home country? What does Map 2.1 (and the map legend) suggest about France's motivation for overseas expansion? What does Map 2.4 (and the map insert) suggest about England's motivation?

Social and Cultural Aspects

Look at the illustration, "The Opechancanough Massacre of 1622." What does this image say about the English colonists' view of the Native Americans? Based on your reading of the chapter, how accurate do you think this portrayal is in this instance? What would have been the motive in creating such a picture? Who, if anyone, might have paid to have this image engraved?

Courtesy of the John Carter Brown Library at Brown University

THE OPECHANCANOUGH MASSACRE OF 1622

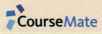

Visit the CourseMate website at www.cengagebrain.com for additional study tools and review materials for this chapter.

CHAPTER 3

ENGLAND DISCOVERS ITS COLONIES: EMPIRE, LIBERTY, AND EXPANSION

I n 1603, England was still a weak power on the fringes of Europe. By 1700, England was a global giant. It possessed 20 colonies in North America and the Caribbean and controlled much of the African slave trade. This transformation occurred during a century of domestic upheaval. King and Parliament fought a long struggle entailing civil war, the execution of one king, and the overthrow of another, but resulting in a unique constitution that established parliamentary supremacy and responsible government under the Crown. The English colonies formed not a single type, but a spectrum of settlement with contrasting economies, social relationships, and institutions. Nevertheless, by 1700 England had created a system of regulation that respected colonial liberties while asserting imperial power.

TIMELINE

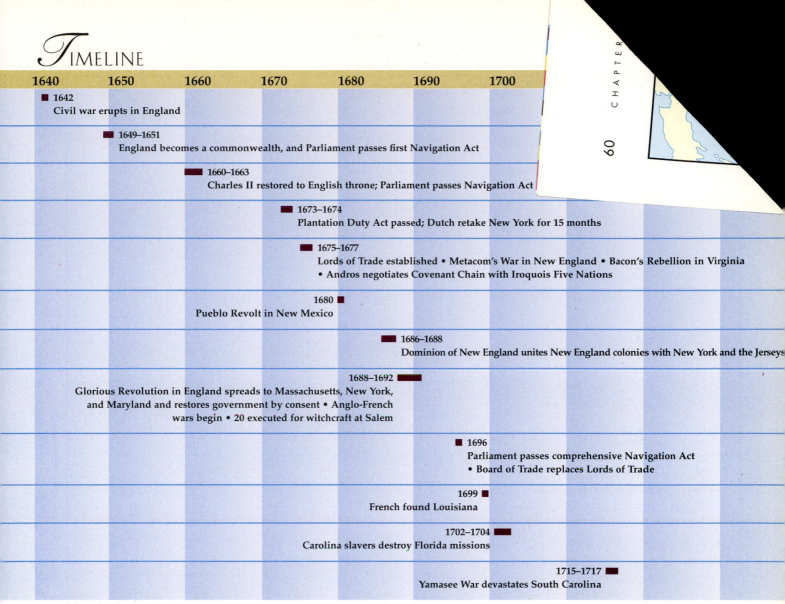

1640	1650	1660	1670	1680	1690	1700

■ **1642**
Civil war erupts in England

■ **1649–1651**
England becomes a commonwealth, and Parliament passes first Navigation Act

■ **1660–1663**
Charles II restored to English throne; Parliament passes Navigation Act

■ **1673–1674**
Plantation Duty Act passed; Dutch retake New York for 15 months

■ **1675–1677**
Lords of Trade established • Metacom's War in New England • Bacon's Rebellion in Virginia
• Andros negotiates Covenant Chain with Iroquois Five Nations

1680 ■
Pueblo Revolt in New Mexico

■ **1686–1688**
Dominion of New England unites New England colonies with New York and the Jerseys

1688–1692 ■
Glorious Revolution in England spreads to Massachusetts, New York,
and Maryland and restores government by consent • Anglo-French
wars begin • 20 executed for witchcraft at Salem

■ **1696**
Parliament passes comprehensive Navigation Act
• Board of Trade replaces Lords of Trade

1699 ■
French found Louisiana

1702–1704 ■
Carolina slavers destroy Florida missions

1715–1717 ■
Yamasee War devastates South Carolina

© Cengage Learning

THE ATLANTIC PRISM AND THE SPECTRUM OF SETTLEMENT

Over thousands of years, the Indians of the Americas had become diversified into hundreds of distinct cultures and languages. The colonists of 17th-century North America and the Caribbean were following much the same course. America divided them. The Atlantic and their connection to England gave them what unity they could sustain.

If we imagine England as a source of white light, and the Atlantic as a prism refracting that light, 17th-century America becomes a spectrum of settlement, with each color merging imperceptibly into the shade next to it. Each settlement had much in common with its neighbors but shared few traits with more distant colonies.

Demographic Differences

The most pronounced differences involved life expectancy, the ratio of men to women, and family structure. In the sugar islands, European men often died by age 40, and slaves even sooner. Female settlers were scarce, and families hardly existed. In Virginia

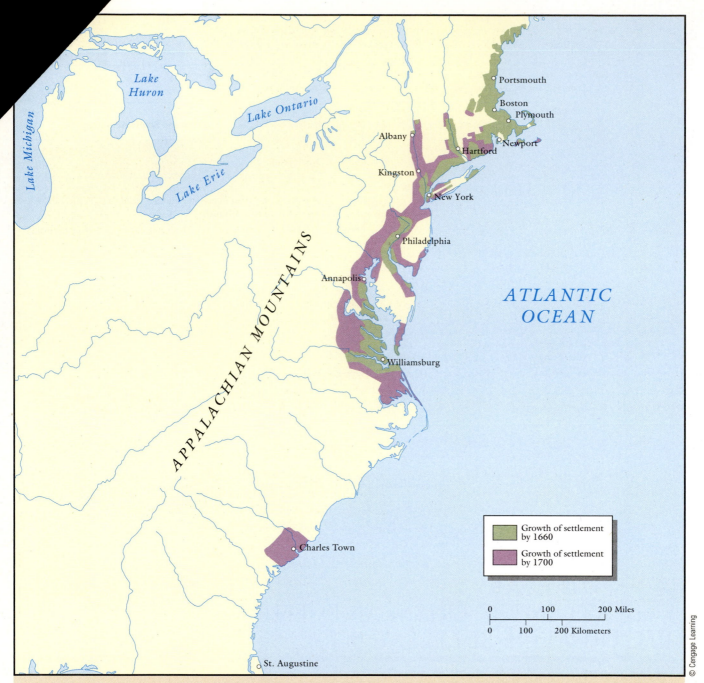

Map 3.1 **Area of English Settlement by 1700.** *This map differentiates the areas settled before 1660 from those settled between 1660 and 1700, or roughly the Restoration era.*

and Maryland, men who survived childhood diseases lived to an average age of about 45 years during the last half of the 17th century. Then, as natural increase replaced immigration as the main source of population growth after 1680, women became more numerous, married earlier, and raised larger families.

The northern colonies were much healthier. In the Delaware valley, a man who reached adulthood could expect to live past 60. New England was one of the healthiest places in the world. Because the sex ratio rapidly approached equality and because the economy permitted couples to marry earlier than in England, population exploded. Canada followed a similar pattern. By 1700, the birthrate in New France caught up with New England's, and population grew at a comparable pace.

TABLE 3.1

THE SPECTRUM OF SETTLEMENT: DEMOGRAPHY, ETHNICITY, ECONOMY, 1650–1700						
Category	West Indies	Lower South	Chesapeake	Mid-Atlantic	New England	New France
Life expectancy for men, at age 20	40	42	45	60+	Late 60s	60s
Family size	Below replacement rate	About two children	Rising after 1680	Very large	Very large	Very large
Race and ethnicity	Black majority by circa 1670s	Black majority by circa 1710	Growing black minority	Ethnic mix, N.W. Europe, English a minority	Almost all English	Almost all French
Economy	Sugar	Indian slave trade, then rice	Tobacco	Furs, farms	Farms, fishing, shipbuilding	Furs, farms

© Cengage Learning

These demographic differences had major consequences. For example, the Caribbean and southern colonies were youthful societies in which men with good connections could expect to achieve high office while in their 30s. By contrast, a New England man was not likely to become even a selectman before his 40s. Despite the appalling death rate in the sugar and tobacco colonies, young men remained optimistic about their futures. In New England, people were more despondent, even though they lived much longer.

Race, Ethnicity, and Economy

The degree of racial and ethnic mixture also varied from region to region. The West Indies already had a large slave majority by 1700. African slaves became a majority in South Carolina around 1710, and they would comprise 40 percent of Virginia's population by the 1730s. Africans were less numerous in the Delaware and Hudson valleys, although slavery became deeply entrenched in New York City and parts of New Jersey. In the Middle Atlantic region, settlers from Europe created an ethnic mosaic. English colonists were probably always a minority, outnumbered at first by the Dutch and later by Germans, Scots, and Irish. New England was in every sense the most English of the colonies. New France was as French as New England was English. The farther south one went, the more diverse the population; the farther north, the more uniform.

Slavery and staple crops went together. Slave societies raised sugar, rice, or tobacco. General farming and family labor also went together. By 1700, the Middle Atlantic was the wheat belt of North America. New Englanders farmed and exported fish, livestock, and lumber to the West Indies.

Religion and Education

Religious observance across the spectrum of settlement ranged from irreverence and indifference in the West Indies to intense piety in Pennsylvania, New England, and New France. By 1710, the established church of the mother country was the legally established church in the West Indies and in the southern mainland colonies. Toleration prevailed in New York and full religious liberty in Pennsylvania. In New England, Old World dissent became the New World establishment. Public support for the clergy, and hence the proportion of ministers, was much greater in the north than in the south.

Along the spectrum, literacy and education, like piety, usually grew stronger from south to north. Colonists everywhere tried to prevent slaves from learning to read, and low literacy prevailed wherever slavery predominated. Chesapeake settlers provided almost no formal schooling for their children prior to the 1690s. By contrast, the Dutch maintained several good schools in New Netherland. Massachusetts required every town to have a writing school. In New France, a seminary (now Laval University) was established in the 1660s, but lay literacy remained low.

Local and Provincial Governments

Forms of government also varied. At the local level, settlers drew on their English experience and chose to organize as parishes, boroughs (towns), and counties. At the provincial level, the West Indian colonies all had royal governments by the 1660s. Proprietary forms dominated the mainland south of New England, except for royal Virginia. Until the 1680s, New England relied on corporate forms of government in which all officials, even governors, were elected. This system survived in Connecticut and Rhode Island beyond independence.

Unifying Trends: Language, War, Law, and Inheritance

Despite this diversity, unifying trends developed in the 17th century. Language became more uniform in America than in England. Londoners went to all the colonies, and London English softened the contrasts among the emerging regional dialects. Another area of uniformity involved war. Colonists waged it with short-term volunteers who often utilized terror against Indian women and children. Europe was moving toward limited wars; colonists demanded quick and total victories.

Law became a simpler version of England's complex legal system—in fact, an organized legal profession did not emerge until the 18th century. Also, no mainland American colony rigidly followed English patterns of inheritance. Instead, some women got the chance to acquire property, usually by inheritance from a deceased husband. Single women who crossed the Atlantic as servants and stayed alive could marry landowners and reach the respectability never available to them in England. In every colony, younger sons also found their situation improved. They thus showed little inclination to preserve institutions that had offered them no landed inheritance in England.

THE BEGINNINGS OF EMPIRE

FOCUS QUESTION

How important was England's mercantilistic system in gaining effective control over the colonies and in projecting English power against its European rivals?

In the chaotic 1640s the English realized that their colonies overseas were bringing them few benefits. England had no coherent colonial policy.

Upheaval in America: The Critical 1640s

England's civil wars rocked its emerging empire, politically and economically. As royal power collapsed in the 1640s, the West Indian colonies demanded and received elective assemblies. The Dutch financed much of the sugar revolution in Barbados and seized control of trade in and out of England's West Indian and Chesapeake colonies. By 1650, most sugar and tobacco exports were going through Amsterdam, not London.

During the civil wars, nobody in England exercised effective control over the colonies. The king had declared that their trade was to remain in English hands, but no agency existed to enforce that policy. The new elective assemblies of Barbados and the Leeward Islands preferred to trade with the Dutch, even after the English

A Pictish Man Holding a Human Head, by John White, Late 16th Century

In the ancient world, the Picts on the island of Great Britain had been known for their ferocity. Also, they were among the ancestors of the English and the Scots. John White, who painted many Indian scenes on Roanoke Island in the 1580s, believed that these progenitors of the English people had been "savages" not all that long ago and that American Indians, like the English some centuries earlier, could progress to "civility." His American experience made him think of "progress."

Q Why did White's expectations fail to take hold?

Q Why did Indians become, to European colonists, symbols of unconquerable backwardness and barbarity rather than potential vessels of progress?

Q Also, this particular warrior was carrying the severed head of an enemy he presumably had killed. Europeans often beheaded men who were convicted of and executed for treason. Why then would they have regarded this Pict's victory trophy, and his painted body, as symbols of his savagery?

© The Trustees of The British Museum/Art Resource, NY

Crown took over those colonies in 1660. The mainland colonies already governed themselves; only Virginia had a royal governor.

Indians viewed the chaos in England as an opportunity to resist the settlers. Between 1643 and 1647, Indian wars almost destroyed New France, New Netherland, and Maryland. In Virginia in 1644, the aging warrior Opechancanough staged another massacre, killing 500 settlers without warning. But the settlers recovered, took Opechancanough prisoner, and murdered him. They broke up his chiefdom and imposed treaties of dependency on its member tribes. Only New England avoided war with the Indians, and even there tensions between the settlers and the Narragansett Indians remained high.

Mercantilism as a Moral Revolution

What happened in the colonies seemed of little interest to the English people in the turbulent 1640s. But as the civil wars ended and the extent of Dutch commercial domination became obvious, the English turned their eyes westward.

During the 17th century most of the European powers followed a set of policies often called "mercantilism." Mercantilists argued that power derived ultimately from the wealth of a country, that the increase of wealth required vigorous trade, and that colonies had become essential to economic growth. Clearly, a state had to control the commerce of its colonies, but mercantilists disagreed over the best ways to promote growth. The Dutch favored virtual free trade within Europe, whereas England preferred state regulation of the domestic and imperial economy. Early mercantilists assumed that the world contained a fixed supply of wealth. A state, to augment its own power, would have to expropriate the wealth of a rival. Trade wars would replace religious wars.

Mercantilism gradually became associated with the emerging idea of unending progress. To Europeans, the opening of the Americas had already reinforced two visions of progress, one associated with Renaissance humanism, the other explicitly Christian. Humanists knew that the distant ancestors of Europeans had all been "barbarians" who had advanced over the centuries toward "civility." Encounters with the peoples of Africa, Ireland, and America underscored this view by revealing new "savages" who seemed inferior to the "civilized" colonists. Committed Christians shared these convictions, but they also believed that human society was progressing toward a future Millennium. The discovery of millions of **heathens** in the Americas stimulated this thinking: God had chosen this moment to open a new hemisphere to Christians because the Millennium was near.

According to both the humanist and the Christian notions of progress, however, humanity would advance to a certain level, and progress would cease. Mercantilism, by contrast, marked a revolution of the human imagination precisely because it could arouse visions of endless progress. To that end, mercantilists developed a concept of law as a way to change society.

The First Navigation Act

During a depression in the 1620s, English merchants concluded that a nation's wealth depended on its **balance of trade**, that a healthy nation ought to export more than it imports, and that the difference—or balance—could be converted into military strength. They also believed that a state needed colonies to produce essential commodities unavailable at home. And they argued that a society ought to export luxuries, not import them.

London merchants clamored for measures to stifle Dutch competition. In 1650, Parliament responded by banning foreign ships from English colonies. A year later, it passed its first Navigation Act. Under this law, Asian and African goods could be imported into the British Isles or the colonies only in English-owned ships, and the master and at least half of each crew had to be Englishmen. European goods could be imported into Britain or the colonies in either English ships or the ships of the producing country, but foreigners could not trade between one English port and another.

These restrictions angered English colonists who prospered by selling their crops to the Dutch, who offered the lowest freight rates. Barbados greeted the Navigation Act by proclaiming virtual independence. Virginia continued to welcome Dutch and Yankee traders. To stifle this dissent, England dispatched a naval force to America in 1651. It compelled Barbados to submit to Parliament and forced Virginia and Maryland to capitulate in 1652. But with no resident officials to enforce English policy, trade with the Dutch continued.

By 1652 England and the Netherlands were at war, the first of three Anglo-Dutch conflicts between 1652 and 1674. For two years the English navy dealt heavy blows to the Dutch. Finally, in 1654, Oliver Cromwell sent Parliament home and made peace. A militant Protestant, he preferred to fight Catholic Spain rather than the Netherlands. He sent a fleet that failed to take Hispaniola but did seize Jamaica in 1655.

heathens *Term used by Christians to refer to people who did not worship the God of the Bible.*

balance of trade *Relationship between imports and exports. A favorable balance of trade meant that exports exceeded imports.*

Restoration Navigation Acts

By the Restoration era, mercantilist thinking was widespread. Although the new royalist Parliament invalidated all legislation passed during the Commonwealth period, these "Cavaliers" reenacted and extended the original Navigation Act. The Navigation Act of 1660 required that all colonial trade be carried on English ships, but the master and *three-fourths* of the crew had to be English. The act also created a category of **enumerated commodities,** of which sugar and tobacco were the most important, permitting these products to be shipped from the colony of origin *only* to England or to another English colony.

In a second measure, the Staple Act of 1663 declared that, with few exceptions, products from Europe or Asia could not be delivered to the settlements unless they had first been landed in England. A third measure, the Plantation Duty Act of 1673, required captains of colonial ships to post bond in the colonies that they would deliver all enumerated commodities to England, or else pay on the spot the duties that would be owed in England (the "plantation duty"). This measure, England hoped, would eliminate all incentives to smuggle. To make it effective, England for the first time sent customs officers to the colonies to collect the duty and prosecute violators. They won little compliance at first.

Within half a century, however, the Navigation Acts dislodged the Dutch and establish English hegemony over Atlantic trade. In 1600, about 90 percent of England's exports consisted of woolen cloth. By 1700, colonial and Asian commerce accounted for 30 to 40 percent of England's overseas trade, and London had become the largest city in western Europe. By 1700, Britain had the most powerful navy in the world. By 1710 or so, virtually all British colonial trade was carried on British (including colonial) ships. Sugar, tobacco, and other staple crops all passed through Britain on their way to their ultimate destinations. Nearly all imported manufactured goods consumed in the colonies were made in Britain.

Few government policies have ever been as successful as England's Navigation Acts, but England achieved these results without pursuing a steady course toward increased imperial control. For example, in granting charters to Rhode Island and Connecticut in 1662–1663, Charles II approved elective governors and legislatures in both colonies. These elective officials could not be dismissed for failure to enforce the Navigation Acts. Moreover, the Crown also chartered several new Restoration colonies (see Chapter 2), whose organizers had few incentives to obey the new laws.

QUICK REVIEW

TOWARD EMPIRE

- Upheaval in England and the colonies, Indian challenges, and Dutch competition revealed incoherent colonial policy

- Parliament passed first Navigation Act, went to war with the Netherlands

- England's Restoration government extended the Navigation Act system

enumerated commodities
Colonial staple crops, such as sugar and tobacco, that had to be shipped from the colony of origin to England or another English colony.

INDIANS, SETTLERS, UPHEAVAL

As of 1670 no sharp boundaries separated Indian lands from colonial settlements. Boston, the largest city north of Mexico, was only 15 miles from an Indian village. The outposts on the Delaware River were islands in a sea of Indians. Nearly every European settlement was vulnerable to attack.

Indian Strategies of Survival

By the 1670s, depopulation magnified the tribes' need for captives, thus intensifying warfare among Indian peoples. The Iroquois, hard hit by smallpox and other maladies, acquired muskets from the Dutch and used them, first to attack other Iroquoian peoples and then **Algonquians**. These **mourning wars** were often initiated by female relatives of a deceased loved one. Male kin would launch raids

FOCUS QUESTION

Contrast the failure of New England and Virginia to preserve peaceful relations with neighboring Indians in 1675–1676 with New York's success in the same decade and later.

and bring back captives. Although adult male prisoners were usually tortured to death, most women and children were adopted and assimilated. Adoption worked because the captives shared the cultural values of their captors. They became Iroquois. As early as the 1660s, a majority of the Indians in the Five Nations were adoptees. The confederacy remained strong; its rivals declined.

In some ways, America became as much a new world for the Indians as it did for the colonists. European cloth, muskets, hatchets, knives, and pots spread far into the interior. Indians who used them gradually abandoned traditional skills and became dependent on European goods. Drunkenness, a by-product of this trade, became a social problem.

Settlers whose prosperity depended on the fur trade tried to stay on good terms with the Indians. Pieter Stuyvesant put New Netherland on such a course, and the English governors of New York followed his lead. Edmund Andros, governor from 1674 to 1680, cultivated the friendship of the **Iroquois League**, in which the five member nations had promised not to wage war against one another. In 1677, Andros and the Five Nations agreed to make New York the easternmost link in what the English called the **Covenant Chain of Peace**. This huge defensive advantage helped lightly populated New York avoid the conflicts that nearly destroyed New England and Virginia beginning in 1675.

Puritan Indian Missions

Puritan efforts to convert Indians to Protestantism began in the 1640s on the island of Martha's Vineyard under Thomas Mayhew and his son, Thomas, Jr., and in Massachusetts under John Eliot, pastor of the Roxbury church. The Mayhews worked with local sachems and even won over some of the tribal **powwows** (prophets or medicine men). They encouraged Indian men to teach settlers how to hunt whales, an activity that made them productive members of the settlers' economy without threatening their identity as men.

Eliot, by contrast, attacked the authority of both sachems and powwows and insisted on turning Indian men into farmers, a female role in Indian society. Yet he did translate the Bible and a few other religious works into the Massachusett language. By the early 1670s, more than 1,000 Indians, nearly all of them survivors of coastal tribes that had been decimated by disease, lived in a string of seven "praying towns," and Eliot got busy organizing five more. By 1675, about 2,300 Indians, perhaps one-quarter of all those living in southeastern New England, were in various stages of conversion to Christianity, but only 160 of them had achieved the kind of conversion experience that Puritans required for full church member-ship. Few Indians shared the Puritan sense of sin. The more powerful nations felt threatened by this pressure to convert, and resistance to Christianity became one cause of the war that broke out in 1675. Other causes were the settlers' lust for Indian lands, the encroachment of livestock onto Indian cornfields, and the fear of young warriors that their way of life was threatened.

Metacom's (or King Philip's) War

Metacom (whom the English called King Philip) shared these fears. He was *sachem* of the Wampanoags and the son of Massasoit, who had celebrated the first thanks-giving feast with the Pilgrims. What came to be known as **Metacom's War** began in the frontier town of Swansea in June 1675, after settlers killed an Indian they found looting an abandoned house. When the Indians demanded satisfaction, the settlers laughed in their faces. The Indians took revenge, and the violence escalated into war.

Algonquians *Indian peoples who spoke some dialect of the Algonquian language family.*

mourning war *Indian war often initiated by a widow or bereaved relative who insisted that her male relatives provide captives to compensate for her loss.*

Iroquois League *Confederation of five Indian nations centered around the Mohawk valley and active in the fur trade.*

Covenant Chain of Peace *Agreement negotiated by Governor Edmund Andros in 1677 that linked the colony of New York to the Iroquois Five Nations and was later expanded to include other colonies and Indian peoples.*

powwow *Originally, a word used to identify tribal prophets or medicine men. Later it was also used to describe their ceremonies.*

Metacom's War (King Philip's War) *War that devastated much of southern New England in 1675–1676. It began as a conflict between Metacom's Wampanoags and Plymouth Colony but soon engulfed all of the New England colonies and most of the region's Indian nations.*

The settlers were confident of victory, but since the 1630s the Indians had acquired firearms. They had become skilled marksmen and built forges to make musket balls and repair their weapons. The settlers, armed with older guns, were terrible shots. In the tradition of European armies, they discharged volleys without aiming. To the surprise of the colonists, Metacom won several engagements against the Plymouth militia, usually by ambushing the noisy intruders. He then escaped from Plymouth Colony and fled to the upper Connecticut valley, where the local Indians, after being ordered by magistrates to disarm, joined him instead. Together they burned five towns in three months.

Massachusetts and Connecticut joined the fray. As winter approached, rather than attack Metacom's Wampanoags, they went after the Narragansetts, who had welcomed some Wampanoag refugees while trying to remain neutral. In the Great Swamp Fight of December 1675, a Puritan army attacked an unfinished Narragansett fort during a blizzard and massacred hundreds of Indians, most of them women and children, but not before the Indians had picked off a high percentage of the officers. The surviving warriors joined Metacom. Altogether about 800 settlers were killed during the war, and two dozen towns were destroyed or badly damaged.

The settlers finally pulled together and won the war in 1676. Governor Andros of New York persuaded the Mohawks to attack Metacom's winter camp and disperse his people, who by then were short of gunpowder. The New Englanders, working closely with Mohegan and Christian Indian allies, adopted Indian tactics to attack Metacom's war parties, kill hundreds of Indians, including Metacom, and sell hundreds more into West Indian slavery. The struggle had turned into a civil war among the Indian peoples of southern New England, with all of the colonies supporting Metacom's enemies.

Virginia's Indian War

In 1675 the Doegs, a dependent Indian nation in the Potomac valley, demanded payment of an old debt from a Virginia planter. When he refused, they ran off some of his livestock. After his overseer killed one of the Indians, the others fled but later returned to ambush and kill the man. The county militia mustered and followed the Doegs across the Potomac into Maryland. At a fork in the trail, the militia split into two parties. Each found a group of Indians in a shack a few hundred yards up the path. Both parties fired at point-blank range, killing 11 at one cabin and 14 at the other. One of the bands was Doeg, but the other was comprised of Susquehannocks, a strong Iroquoian-speaking people with firearms who had moved to Maryland to escape Iroquois attacks.

Hoping to avoid war, Virginia governor Sir William Berkeley sent John Washington with some Virginia militia to investigate the killings and, if possible, to set things right. But Washington preferred vengeance. His Virginia militia joined with a Maryland force, and together they besieged a formidable fort on the north bank of the Potomac. When the Indians sent out five or six sachems to negotiate, the militia murdered them and then laid siege to the fort for six weeks. The Indians, short of

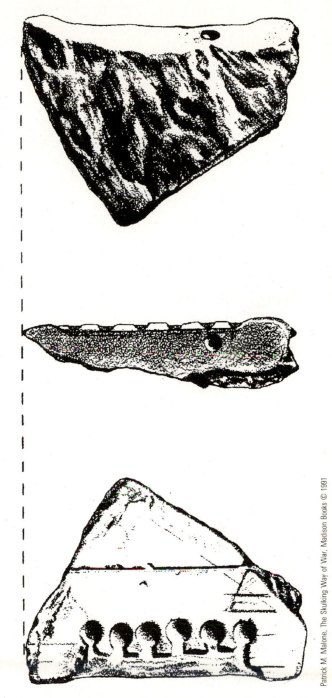

Patrick M. Malone, The Skulking Way of War, Madison Books © 1991

BULLET MOLD IN USE AMONG NEW ENGLAND INDIANS, CIRCA 1675. *Indians could make bullets and repair muskets, but they remained dependent on Europeans for their supply of gunpowder. In early 1676, the Indian leader Metacom ran low on gunpowder after failing to acquire more from New France. Over the next several months, he lost the war.*

provisions, finally broke out one night with all their people, killing several militiamen. After hurling taunts of defiance and promises of vengeance, they disappeared into the forest. In January 1676, they killed more than 30 Virginians. The colonists began to panic.

Berkeley favored a defensive strategy against the Indians. In March 1676, he summoned a special session of the Virginia legislature to approve the creation of a string of forts. Berkeley also hoped to maintain a distinction between the clearly hostile Susquehannocks and other Indians who might still be neutral or friendly. Finally, to avoid further provocation, Berkeley restricted the fur trade to a few of his close associates. To the men excluded from that circle, his actions looked like favoritism. To new settlers in frontier counties, whose access to land was blocked by Indians and who now had to pay higher taxes, Berkeley's strategy seemed intolerable.

Bacon's Rebellion

The colonists demanded an offensive campaign waged by unpaid volunteers, who would take their rewards by plundering and enslaving any Indians they could seize. In April, they found a reckless leader in newcomer Nathaniel Bacon. Using his political connections (he was the governor's cousin by marriage), he got himself appointed to the council soon after his arrival in the colony in 1674, but he was now excluded from the Indian trade under Berkeley's new rules.

Ignoring Berkeley's orders, Bacon marched his frontiersmen south in search of the elusive Susquehannocks. After several days his weary men reached a village of friendly Occaneechees, who offered them shelter and volunteered to attack a nearby Susquehannock camp. They surprised and defeated the Susquehannocks and returned with their captives to celebrate the victory with Bacon. But after they fell asleep, Bacon's men massacred them and seized their furs and prisoners.

By then, Berkeley had outlawed Bacon, dissolved the legislature, and called the first general election since 1661. Voters from Bacon's home county of Henrico elected the rebel leader to the House of Burgesses. Berkeley had Bacon arrested when he reached Jamestown and made him apologize on his knees for his disobedience. The governor then forgave him and restored him to his seat in the council. While the burgesses were passing laws to reform the county courts, the vestries, and the tax system, Bacon slipped home, summoned his followers again, and marched on Jamestown. At gunpoint, he forced Berkeley to commission him as general of volunteers and compelled the legislature to authorize another expedition against the Indians.

Berkeley retreated downriver to Gloucester County and mustered its militia, but they refused to follow him against Bacon. They would fight only Indians. Mortified, Berkeley fled to the eastern shore, the only part of the colony still loyal to him. He raised his own force there by promising the men an exemption from taxes for 21 years and the right to plunder the rebels. Unlike the situation in New England, few Indians killed other Indians during **Bacon's Rebellion**. This civil war pitted settlers against each other.

While Bacon was slaughtering and enslaving the unresisting Pamunkeys along the frontier, Berkeley assembled a small fleet and retook Jamestown in August 1676. Bacon and his men rushed east and laid siege to Jamestown. After suffering only a few casualties, the governor's men grew discouraged, and in early September they returned to the eastern shore. Bacon then burned Jamestown to the ground.

But Bacon's Rebellion faltered when its leader died of dysentery in October. Berkeley regained control of Virginia using the ships of the London tobacco fleet. Ignoring royal orders to show clemency, the governor executed 23 rebels. A new assembly repudiated the reforms of 1676, and in many counties the governor's men

QUICK REVIEW

UPHEAVALS OF THE 1670S

- Iroquois strategy for survival included adoption, assimilation, merger

- Puritan missionary efforts among the Indians and encroachments onto Indian land created tensions in New England

- Metacom's (King Philip's) War devastated both settlers and Indians

- Virginia's war with the Susquehannocks led to Bacon's Rebellion

- Bacon's Rebellion revealed fissures within Virginia's governing elite and between social classes

- New York negotiated a "Covenant Chain of Peace" with the Iroquois Five Nations to avoid frontier war

Bacon's Rebellion *The most serious challenge to royal authority in the English mainland colonies prior to 1775. It erupted in Virginia in 1676 after the governor and Nathaniel Bacon, the principal rebel, could not agree on how best to wage war against frontier Indians.*

used their control of the courts to plunder the Baconians for years through confiscations and fines. Berkeley, summoned to England to defend himself, died there in 1677 before he could present his case.

CRISIS IN ENGLAND AND THE REDEFINITION OF EMPIRE

Bacon's Rebellion helped trigger a political crisis in England. Because Virginia produced little tobacco during the uprising, English customs revenues fell sharply, and the king asked Parliament for more money. Parliament's response was tempered by the much deeper problem of the royal succession. Charles II had fathered many bastards, but his royal marriage was childless. After the queen reached menopause in the mid-1670s, his brother James, duke of York, became his heir. By then James had become a Catholic. When Charles dissolved the Parliament that had sat from 1661 until 1678, he knew he would have to deal with a new House of Commons terrified by the prospect of a Catholic king.

FOCUS QUESTION

Did the crisis in England do more to undermine or to encourage liberty and equality in the English mainland colonies?

The Popish Plot, the Exclusion Crisis, and the Rise of Party

In this atmosphere of distrust, a cynical adventurer, Titus Oates, fabricated the sensational story that he had uncovered a sinister "Popish Plot" to kill Charles and bring James to the throne. In the wake of these accusations, the king's ministry fell, and the parliamentary opposition won majorities in three successive elections between 1678 and 1681. Organized by Lord Shaftesbury (the Carolina proprietor), the opposition demanded that James, a Catholic, be excluded from the throne in favor of his Protestant daughters, Mary and Anne. It also called for a guarantee of frequent elections and for an independent electorate not under the influence of wealthy patrons. The king's men castigated Shaftesbury's followers as **Whigs,** an obscure sect of Scottish religious extremists urging the assassination of both Charles and James. Whigs denounced Charles's courtiers as **Tories,** a term for Irish Catholic bandits who murdered Protestant landlords. Both labels stuck.

Charles ended three years of turmoil in 1681. After getting secret financial support from King Louis XIV of France, he dissolved Parliament and ruled without one for the last four years of his reign.

The Lords of Trade and Imperial Reform

English politics of the 1670s and 1680s had a profound impact on the colonies. The duke of York emerged from the Third Anglo-Dutch War (1672–1674) as the most powerful shaper of imperial policy. At his urging, the government created a new agency in 1675, the Lords Committee of Trade and Plantations, or more simply, the Lords of Trade. The Lords enforced the Navigation Acts and administered the colonies.

The instruments of royal government first took shape in the West Indies. In the 1660s, the king appointed the governor and upper house of Barbados, Jamaica, and the Leeward Islands; the settlers elected an assembly. The Privy Council in England issued a formal commission and a lengthy set of instructions to each royal governor. From the Crown's point of view, the governor's commission *created* the constitutional structure of each colony, a claim that few settlers accepted. Most colonists believed they had an inherent right to constitutional rule. And Crown lawyers eventually agreed that these

Whigs *Obscure sect of Scottish religious extremists who favored the assassination of Charles and James of England. The term was used to denote one of the two leading political parties of late 17th-century England.*

Tories *Term for Irish Catholic peasants who murdered Protestant landlords. It was used to describe the followers of Charles II and became the name of the other major political party in England.*

instructions were binding only on the governor, not on the colony as a whole. In short, royal instructions never acquired the force of law.

London also insisted that each colony pay for its own government. This requirement, ironically, strengthened colonial claims to self-rule. In 1681, the Crown imposed a compromise in Jamaica that had broad significance for all the colonies. The Lords of Trade threatened to make the Jamaica assembly as weak as the Irish Parliament, which could debate and approve only those bills that had first been adopted by the English Privy Council. Under the compromise, the Jamaica assembly retained its power to initiate and amend legislation, in return for agreeing to a long-term revenue act that later became permanent, a measure that freed the governor from financial dependence on the assembly.

Metacom's War and Bacon's Rebellion lent urgency to these reforms and speeded up their use in the mainland colonies. The Lords of Trade ordered soldiers to Virginia along with a royal commission to investigate grievances there. In 1676, they also sent an aggressive customs officer, Edward Randolph, to Massachusetts. He recommended that the colony's charter be revoked. Possessing no effective instruments for punishing violators of the Navigation Acts in North America, the Lords had reason for concern. The king could demand and reprimand, but not command.

Although the Jamaica model was becoming the norm for the Lords of Trade, James's real preference emerged after the English Court of Chancery revoked the Massachusetts charter in 1684. Charles II died, and his brother became King James II in early 1685. The possibility of an autocracy in America suddenly reappeared.

The Dominion of New England

Absolutist New York now became the king's model for reorganizing New England. James disallowed New York's Charter of Liberties of 1683 (see Chapter 2) and abolished the colony's assembly, but kept the permanent revenue act in force. In 1686, he sent now former New York governor Sir Edmund Andros to Massachusetts to take over a new government called the Dominion of New England. James added New Hampshire, Plymouth, Rhode Island, Connecticut, New York, and both Jerseys to the Dominion. Andros governed this vast domain through an appointive council and a superior court that rode a circuit, dispensing justice. There was no elective assembly. Andros also imposed religious toleration on the Puritans.

At first, Andros won support from merchants who had been denied the suffrage by the Puritan requirement that they be full church members, but his enforcement of the Navigation Acts soon alienated them. When he tried to compel New England farmers to take out new land titles that included annual **quitrents,** he enraged the whole countryside.

THE GLORIOUS REVOLUTION

Events in England and France undermined the Dominion of New England. James II proclaimed toleration for both Protestant dissenters and Catholics and, in violation of recent laws, began to name Catholics to high office. In 1685, Louis XIV revoked the 1598 Edict of Nantes that had granted toleration to Protestants and launched a vicious persecution of the Huguenots. About 160,000 fled the kingdom. James II tried to suppress the news of Louis's persecution, which made his own professions of toleration seem hypocritical, even though his commitment was probably genuine. Then in 1688 James II's queen gave birth to a son who would clearly be raised

QUICK REVIEW

IMPERIAL REFORMS IN AN ERA OF POLITICAL CRISIS

- Whigs and Tories emerged while Parliament debated the royal succession

- Lords of Trade enforced Navigation Acts and developed Jamaica model of royal government, which reduced power of local assemblies

- Edward Randolph recommended revocation of Massachusetts charter

- James II united the northern colonies in the autocratic Dominion of New England

quitrent *Small annual fee attached to a piece of land. It differed from other rents in that nonpayment did not lead to ejection from the land but to a suit for debt.*

FOCUS QUESTION

On what common principles did English political culture begin to converge in both the mother country and the colonies after the Glorious Revolution?

Catholic, thus imposing a Catholic *dynasty* on England. Several Whig and Tory leaders swallowed their mutual hatred and invited William of Orange, the *stadholder* (captain general) of the Netherlands, to England. The husband of the king's older Protestant daughter Mary by James's first marriage, William had become the most prominent Protestant soldier in Europe during a long war against Louis XIV.

William landed in England in November 1688. Most of the English army sided with him, and James fled to France. Parliament declared that James had abdicated the throne and named William III (1689–1702) and Mary II (1689–1694) as joint sovereigns. It also passed a Toleration Act that gave Protestant dissenters (but not Catholics) the right to worship publicly and a Declaration of Rights that guaranteed a Protestant succession to the throne and condemned as illegal many of the acts of James II. This **Glorious Revolution** also brought England and the Netherlands into war against Louis XIV, who supported James.

The Glorious Revolution in America

Andros's attempt to suppress the news that William had landed in England convinced the Puritans that he was part of a global Popish Plot to undermine Protestant societies everywhere. The Boston militia overthrew him in April 1689.

In May and June, the New York City militia took over Fort James at the southern tip of Manhattan and renamed it Fort William. Most of the active rebels in New York City were Dutch Calvinists, who had little experience with traditional English liberties. Their leader, Jacob Leisler, dreaded conquest by Catholics from New France and began to act like a Dutch *stadholder* in a nominally English colony.

Defense became Leisler's highest priority, but his demands for supplies soon alienated even his Yankee supporters on Long Island. Although he summoned an elective assembly, he made no effort to revive the Charter of Liberties of 1683 while continuing to collect duties under the revenue act. He showed little respect for the legal rights of his opponents. Complaints against his administration reached the Crown in London.

In Maryland, Protestants overthrew Lord Baltimore's Catholic government in 1689. The governor of Maryland refused to proclaim William and Mary king and queen, even after all the other colonies had done so. To Lord Baltimore's dismay, the messenger he had sent from England to Maryland with orders to accept the new monarchs died en route. Had he arrived, the government might have survived the crisis.

The English Response

England responded in different ways to each of these upheavals. The Maryland rebels won the royal government they requested from England and soon established the Anglican Church in the colony. Catholics could no longer worship in public, hold office, or run their schools, but they did receive unofficial toleration.

In New York, Leisler and his Dutch followers watched helplessly as their enemies manipulated the Dutch king of England into undermining his loyal Dutch supporters in New York. The new governor arrested Leisler and his son-in-law in 1691, tried both for treason, and had them hanged, drawn (disemboweled), and quartered. The assembly elected that year was controlled by Anti-Leislerians, most of whom were English. It passed a modified version of the Charter of Liberties of 1683, this time denying toleration to Catholics. Like its predecessor, it was later disallowed.

Another complex struggle involved Massachusetts. In 1689, the Reverend Increase Mather, the colony's agent in London, failed to persuade Parliament to restore the charter of 1629. Over the next two years he negotiated a new charter, which gave

Glorious Revolution *Bloodless overthrow in 1688 of King James II by Whigs and Tories, who invited William of Orange to England. He and his wife Mary became king and queen.*

the power to veto laws, to hear judicial appeals, and to appoint governors, d militia officers. The 1691 charter also granted toleration to all Protestants voting rights on property qualifications, not church membership. Liberty ty had triumphed over godliness.

lem Witch Trials

er sailed into Boston Harbor with the new charter in May 1692, he found e besieged by witches. The accusations arose in Salem Village (modern nong a group of girls that included a young daughter and a niece of the r, Samuel Parris. They then spread to older girls, some of whom had been uring the Indian wars. The girls howled, barked, and stretched themselves contortions. With adult encouragement, they accused many neighbors of witchcraft, mostly people who did not approve of Parris. The number of accused escalated in April after 14-year-old Abigail Hobbs confessed that she had made a compact with the devil in Maine in 1688 just before the outbreak of the Indian war that devastated northern New England. Altogether about 150 people were accused in Essex County and beyond. Satan, supported by Indian warriors on the frontier and witches within the colony, seemed determined to destroy Massachusetts.

The trials began in June. The court hanged 19 people, pressed one man to death because he refused to stand trial, and allowed several others to die in jail. Everyone executed claimed to be innocent. Of 50 who confessed, none was hanged. The governor finally halted the trials after someone accused his wife of witchcraft. By then, public support for the trials was collapsing. The **Salem witch trials** provided a bitter finale to the era of political uncertainty that had afflicted Massachusetts since the loss of the colony's charter in 1684. Along with the new charter, the trials brought the Puritan era to a close.

The Completion of Empire

The Glorious Revolution guaranteed that royal colonies would have representative governments. Any colony settled by the English would elect an assembly to vote taxes and pass laws. Governors would be appointed by the Crown or a lord proprietor. (Governors remained elective in Connecticut and Rhode Island.) Even the New Jersey and Carolina proprietors surrendered their powers of government to the Crown. By the 1720s, Maryland and Pennsylvania (along with Delaware, which became a separate colony under the Penn proprietorship in 1704) were the only surviving proprietary provinces on the mainland.

This transition to royal government seems smoother in retrospect than it did at the time. London almost lost control of the empire in the 1690s. Overwhelmed by the pressures of the French war, the Lords of Trade could not keep pace with events in the colonies. When French privateers disrupted the tobacco trade, Scottish smugglers stepped in and began to divert it to Glasgow in defiance of the Navigation Acts.

William took action in 1696. Parliament passed a new, comprehensive Navigation Act that plugged loopholes in earlier laws and extended to America the English system of vice-admiralty courts, which dispensed quick justice without juries. When the new courts settled routine maritime disputes or condemned enemy merchant ships captured by privateers, the settlers appreciated these services. But when the courts tried to assume jurisdiction over the Navigation Acts, they aroused controversy.

Also in 1696, William replaced the Lords of Trade with a new agency, the Board of Trade. Its powers were almost purely advisory. It corresponded with governors and other officials in the colonies, listened to lobbyists in England, and

Salem witch trials *The 1692 outbreak of witchcraft accusations in a Puritan village marked by an atmosphere of fear, hysteria, and stress that led to 20 executions.*

made policy recommendations to governmental bodies. It marked an early attempt at government by experts.

Another difficult problem was resolved in 1707 when England and Scotland agreed to merge their separate parliaments and become the single kingdom of Great Britain. This union placed Scotland inside the Navigation Act system and legalized Scottish participation in the tobacco trade. By the middle of the 18th century, Scotland owed its growing prosperity to its colonial trade.

Imperial Federalism

The transformations that took place between 1689 and 1707 defined the structure of the British Empire until the American Revolution. Although Parliament claimed full power over the colonies, in practice it seldom regulated anything colonial except Atlantic commerce. Compliance was minimal to nonexistent when Parliament tried to regulate inland affairs. To get things done within the colonies, the Crown had to win the settlers' agreement through their lawful assemblies and unsalaried local officials. The empire had stumbled into a system of de facto federalism. Parliament exercised only limited powers, and the colonies controlled the rest. What seemed an arrangement of convenience in London soon acquired overtones of right in America: the right to consent to all taxes and local laws.

The Mixed and Balanced Constitution

After the Glorious Revolution, Britain quickly became a far more powerful state than the Stuart kings had been able to sustain with their pretensions to absolute monarchy. The British constitution, which made ministers legally responsible for their public actions, proved remarkably stable. In the ancient world, free societies had degenerated into tyrannies. England, it seemed, had defied history, retaining its liberty and growing stronger in the process.

The explanation, everyone agreed, lay in England's "mixed and balanced" constitution. Government by king, lords, and commons mirrored society itself—the monarchy, aristocracy, and commonality. As long as each freely consented to government measures, English liberty would be secure. But if one of the three acquired the power to dominate the other two, English liberty would be in peril. The danger to liberty lay in corruption—in the ability of Crown ministers to use their patronage to undermine the independence of the House of Commons.

After 1689 England raised larger fleets and armies than ever before. To support them, Parliament created for the first time a **funded national debt,** in which the state agreed to pay the interest due to its creditors ahead of all other obligations. This device gave Britain enormous borrowing power. In 1694, the government created the Bank of England to facilitate its own finances; the London Stock Exchange also emerged in the 1690s. To meet wartime expenses, Parliament levied a heavy land tax on the gentry and excises on ordinary people. These actions amounted to a financial revolution that enabled England to outspend France, despite having only one-fourth of France's population. And by giving public offices to members of Parliament, Crown ministers were almost assured of majority support for their measures.

Ever since the Popish Plot, public debates had pitted Court against Country. The Court favored policies that strengthened its war-making capabilities. The Country stood for liberty. Although the Tories had begun as Charles II's Court party, by 1720 most of them were part of a Country opposition. Whigs had defended Country positions in 1680, but by 1720 most of them advocated for the Court policies of George I

funded national debt
Agreement by the state to pay the interest due to its creditors before all other obligations.

GEORGE III (1760–1820) GOING INTO HIS PALACE BY A SIDE ENTRANCE. *In Court culture, even everyday events, such as the king entering or leaving his palace by a side gate, had to display the honor, splendor, and hierarchy surrounding the monarch.*

(1714–1727). Court spokesmen defended the military buildup, the financial revolution, and the new patronage as essential to victory over France and to sustain British strength in world politics. Their Country opponents denounced standing armies, attacked the financial revolution as an engine of corruption, favored an early peace with France, demanded more frequent elections, and tried to ban placemen (officeholders who sat in Parliament) from the House of Commons.

Court Whigs emerged victorious during the long ministry of Sir Robert Walpole (1721–1742), but their opponents were more eloquent and controlled more presses. The central theme of the opposition was corruption—the insidious means by which ministers threatened the independence of Parliament and English liberty. This debate over liberty soon reached America.

CONTRASTING EMPIRES: SPAIN AND FRANCE IN NORTH AMERICA

FOCUS QUESTION

What enabled sparsely settled New France to resist British expansion with great success for more than half a century, whereas Spanish Florida seemed almost helpless against a similar threat?

After 1689 Britain's enemies were France and Spain. These two nations shared a Catholic zeal for converting Indians that exceeded anything displayed by English Protestants, but their American empires had little else in common.

The Pueblo Revolt

In the late 17th century the Spanish missions of North America entered a period of crisis. Fewer priests took the trouble to master Indian languages, insisting instead that the Indians learn Spanish. For all of their pious intentions, the missionaries often whipped or shackled Indians for minor infractions. Disease also took its toll.

Indian population loss led to pressing labor demands by missionaries, and despite strong prohibitions, some Spaniards enslaved Indians.

The greatest challenge to Spain arose in New Mexico, where the Pueblo population had fallen from 80,000 to 17,000 since 1598. A prolonged drought, together with Apache and Navajo attacks, prompted many Pueblos to abandon Christianity and resume their old forms of worship. Missionaries responded with whippings and, in 1675, three executions. Popé, a San Juan Pueblo medicine man who had been whipped for his beliefs, moved north to Taos Pueblo, where he organized the most successful Indian revolt in American history. In 1680, in a carefully timed uprising, the Pueblos killed 400 of the 2,300 Spaniards in New Mexico and destroyed or plundered every Spanish building, including churches, in the province (see Map 1.6 on p. 24). They killed 21 of New Mexico's 40 priests. Spanish survivors of the **Pueblo Revolt** fled from Santa Fe down the Rio Grande to El Paso.

Popé lost his influence after traditional Pueblo rites failed to end the drought or stop Apache attacks. When the Spanish returned in the 1690s, the Pueblos were badly divided. When Santa Fe finally fell in December 1693, the Spanish executed 70 men and gave 400 women and children to the returning settlers as their slaves. Spain's attempt to create a demilitarized Christian frontier was proving a tragic failure.

New France and the Middle Ground

A different story unfolded along the western frontier of New France. There the Iroquois menace made possible an unusual accommodation between the colony and the Indians of the Great Lakes region. The survival of the Iroquois Five Nations depended on their ability to assimilate the thousands of captives they seized from western Indians. The Iroquois wars depopulated nearly all of what is now the state of Ohio and much of the Ontario peninsula. The Indians around Lakes Erie and Huron either fled west or were absorbed by the Iroquois. The refugees, mostly Algonquian-speaking peoples, founded new multiethnic communities farther west. But when the refugees disagreed with one another or came into conflict with the Sioux to their west, the absence of traditional tribal structures made it difficult to resolve their differences. Over time, French officials, soldiers, and missionaries began to mediate.

Pueblo Revolt *In the most successful Indian uprising in American history, the Pueblo people rose against the Spanish in 1680, killing most Spanish missionaries, devastating Spanish buildings, and forcing the surviving Spaniards to retreat down the Rio Grande.*

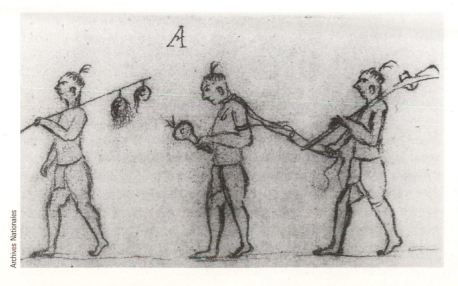

Archives Nationales

IROQUOIS WARRIORS LEADING AN INDIAN PRISONER INTO CAPTIVITY, 1660s. *Because Indian populations had been depleted by war and disease, a tribe's survival became dependent on its ability to assimilate captives. This is a French copy of an Iroquois pictograph.*

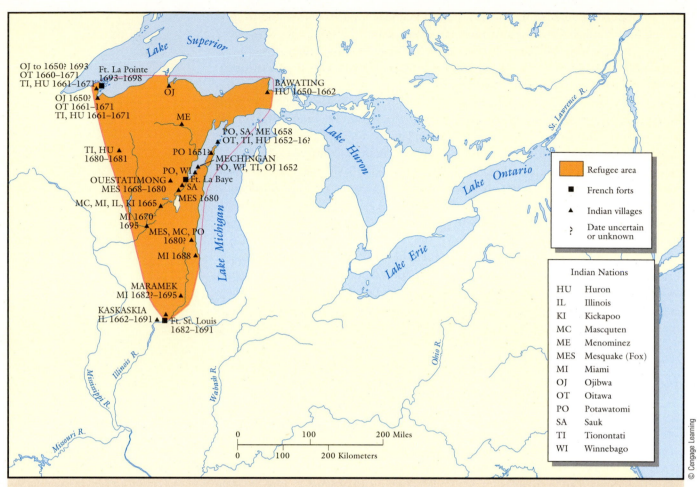

OJ to 1650? 1693
OT 1660-1671
TI, HU 1661-1671

Ft. La Pointe
1693-1698

OJ 1650?
OT 1661-1671
TI, HU 1661-1671

OJ

BAWATING
HU 1650-1662

ME

PO, SA, ME 1658
OT, TI, HU 1652-16?

TI, HU
1680-1681

PO 1651

MECHINGAN
PO, WI, TI, OJ 1652

PO, WI

OUESTATIMONG
MES 1668-1680

Ft. La Baye
SA
MES 1680

MC, MI, IL, KI 1665

MI 1670
1695

MES, MC, PO
1680?

MI 1688

MARAMEK
MI 1682?-1695

KASKASKIA
IL 1662-1691

Ft. St. Louis
1682-1691

	Refugee area
	French forts
	Indian villages
?	Date uncertain or unknown

Indian Nations	
HU	Huron
IL	Illinois
KI	Kickapoo
MC	Mascquten
ME	Menominez
MES	Mesquake (Fox)
MI	Miami
OJ	Ojibwa
OT	Oitawa
PO	Potawatomi
SA	Sauk
TI	Tionontati
WI	Winnebago

0   100   200 Miles
0   100   200 Kilometers

Map 3.2 **French Middle Ground in North America circa 1700.** *French power in North America rested mostly on the arrangements French governors worked out with refugee Algonquian Indians trying to resist Iroquois raids in the Great Lakes region.*

Middle Ground *Area of French and Indian cooperation west of Niagara and south of the Great Lakes, over which no one exercised sovereign power.*

Onontio *Algonquian word meaning "Great Mountain"; used by Indians of the Middle Ground to designate the governor of New France.*

The leaders of thinly populated New France were eager to erect an Algonquian shield against the Iroquois. The French supplied the Algonquians with brandy and other European goods, including the firearms the Algonquians needed to strike back against their enemies. By 1701, Iroquois losses had become so heavy that the Five Nations negotiated a peace treaty with the French and the western Indians. The Iroquois agreed to remain neutral in any war between France and England. France's Indian allies, supported by a new French fort erected at Detroit in 1701, began returning to the lands around Lakes Erie and Huron. That region became a **Middle Ground** over which no one could wield sovereign power, although New France exercised great influence within it.

France's success in the interior rested on negotiation, not force. Hugely outnumbered, the French knew that they could not impose their will on the Indians. They instead conducted diplomacy according to Indian, not European, rules. Algonquians called the governor of New France **Onontio** ("Great Mountain"), a supreme alliance chief whose persuasive power was backed by gifts. The respect accorded to peacetime chiefs was roughly proportionate to how much they gave away, not how much they accumulated. The English, by contrast, tried to "buy" land from the Indians and regarded the sale of the land as contractual. The French understood that agreements had to be renewed regularly, always with an exchange of gifts.

Middle Ground diplomacy came at a price: It involved New France in the Indian slave trade. Because Indians fought wars mostly to acquire captives, Onontio's western allies often presented captives to French traders, who realized that to refuse the gift would be an insult. By the 1720s, up to 5 percent of the colony's population consisted of enslaved Indians.

French Louisiana and Spanish Texas

In 1682 René-Robert Cavelier, *sieur* de La Salle traveled down the Mississippi to its mouth, claiming possession of the entire area for France and calling it Louisiana (for Louis XIV). Seven years later, the French returned to the Gulf of Mexico. Pierre le Moyne d'Iberville, a Canadian, landed with 80 men at Biloxi, built a fort, and began trading with the Indians. In 1702, he moved his headquarters to Mobile, closer to the more populous nations of the interior, especially the Choctaws. The Choctaws could still field 5,000 warriors but had suffered heavy losses from slaving raids organized by South Carolinians and carried out mostly by that colony's Chickasaw and Creek allies. Using the Choctaws to anchor their trading system, the greatly outnumbered French created a weaker, southern version of the Great Lakes Middle Ground, acting as mediators while trading brandy, firearms, and other European products for furs and food.

Spain, alarmed at any challenge to its monopoly on the Gulf of Mexico, founded Pensacola in 1698 and sent missionaries into eastern Texas in 1690, but they brought smallpox with them. They said the epidemic was God's "holy will"; the Tejas Indians told them to get out or be killed. They fled in 1693, leaving Texas to the Indians for another 20 years.

AN EMPIRE OF SETTLEMENT: THE BRITISH COLONIES

By 1700, when 250,000 settlers and slaves were already living in England's mainland colonies, the population was doubling every 25 years. New France matched that pace, but with only 14,000 people in 1700 it could not close the gap. The population of the Spanish missions continued to decline. In the struggle for empire, a growing population became Britain's greatest advantage.

The Engine of British Expansion: The Colonial Household

In England younger sons rarely owned land and clearly ranked below the oldest son. Daughters ranked behind both. By contrast, most colonial householders tried to pass on their status to all their sons and to provide dowries that would enable all their daughters to marry men of equal status. Nevertheless, colonial households were patriarchal. A mature male was expected to be the master of his family and perhaps of others. Above all, a patriarch strove to preserve his own economic independence. Although every household owed small debts or favors to its neighbors, these obligations seldom compromised a family's standing in the community.

Farmers tried to grow an agricultural surplus, if only as a hedge against drought or other unpredictable events. They often sold this surplus for cash to merchants. Farmers used the proceeds to pay taxes or their ministers' salaries

FOCUS QUESTION

Was England's advantage over Spain and France by 1713 in North America a result of London's conscious policies? Or did it illustrate instead the importance of the unintended consequences of many, perhaps most, historical endeavors?

and to buy British imports. These arrangements sometimes placed families in short-term debt to merchants, but most managed to avoid long-term debt. Settlers accepted temporary dependency among freemen—of sons on their parents, indentured servants on their masters, or apprentices on master craftsmen. A man who became permanently dependent on others lost the respect of his community.

The Voluntaristic Ethic and Public Life

The spirit of independence entered public life and shaped an ethic of voluntarism. Few freemen could be coerced into doing something of which they disapproved. Local officials serving without pay ignored orders that did not serve their interests or the interests of their community. For example, young men accepted military service only if it fitted their future plans. They would serve only under officers they knew, and then for only a single campaign. After serving, they used their bonus and their pay, and often the promise of a land grant, to speed their way to becoming householders themselves. Military service, for those who survived, could lead to the ownership of land and an earlier marriage.

Three Warring Empires, 1689–1716

When the three empires went to war after 1689, the Spanish and French fought to survive, while the British fought to expand their holdings. In King William's War (1689–1697), Sir William Phips of Massachusetts forced Acadia to surrender in 1690 (although the French soon regained it) and then sailed up the St. Lawrence to Quebec, where he was forced to retreat with heavy losses. Meanwhile, Indians devastated coastal New England.

In 1704, during Queen Anne's War (1702–1713), the French and their Indian allies destroyed Deerfield, Massachusetts, in a winter attack and marched most of its people off to captivity in Canada. Hundreds of New Englanders spent months, even years, as captives. As the war dragged on, New Englanders twice failed to take Port Royal in Acadia, but a combined British and colonial force finally succeeded in 1710, renaming the colony Nova Scotia. An effort to subdue Quebec the following year met with disaster when many of the British ships ran aground in a treacherous stretch of the St. Lawrence River.

Farther south, the imperial struggle was grimmer and even more tragic. Although the Franciscan missions of Florida were already in decline, mission Indians still attracted Carolina slavers, who invaded Florida between 1702 and

QUICK REVIEW

EMPIRES IN CONFLICT AFTER THE GLORIOUS REVOLUTION

- Pueblo Revolt challenged Spanish rule in New Mexico

- France succeeded in establishing Middle Ground diplomacy

- English colonies marked by continual expansion and their voluntaristic ethic

- Series of imperial wars between British and French empires

- South Carolina's slave traders destroyed Spanish missions in Florida but were devastated by Indians in the Yamasee War

TABLE 3.2

BRITISH WARS AGAINST FRANCE (AND USUALLY SPAIN), 1689–1763			
European Name	**American Name**	**Years**	**Peace**
War of the League of Augsburg	King William's War	1689–1697	Ryswick
War of the Spanish Succession	Queen Anne's War	1702–1713	Utrecht
War of Jenkins' Ear, merging with		1739–1748	
War of the Austrian Succession	King George's War	1744–1748	Aix-la-Chapelle
Seven Years' War	French and Indian War	1754–1763*	Paris

* The French and Indian War began in America in 1754 and then merged with the Seven Years' War in Europe, which began in 1756.

1704 with a large force of Indian allies, dragged off 4,000 women and children as slaves, and drove 9,000 Indians from their homes. The invaders failed to take the Spanish fortress of St. Augustine, but slaving raids spread devastation as far west as Choctaw country and far south along the Florida peninsula.

By 1715 South Carolina's greed for Indian slaves finally alienated the colony's strongest Indian allies, the Yamasees, who resented the mistreatment of Indian women by the traders. Fearing that they would be the next to be enslaved, the warriors killed all the colonial traders among them and aligned with other southeastern Indians to attack the colony. They almost destroyed it before being thrust back and nearly exterminated. Some of the Yamasees and a number of escaped African slaves fled as refugees to Spanish Florida.

The wars of 1689–1716 halted the movement of British settlers onto new lands in New England and the Carolinas. But in Pennsylvania, Maryland, and Virginia—colonies that had not been deeply involved in the wars—the expansive thrust continued.

SOUTH CAROLINA COLONISTS ENSLAVING AN INDIAN. *The colony enslaved thousands of Indians from 1680 through 1715, a practice that was finally abandoned after the Yamasee War nearly destroyed the colony.*

Conclusion

The diversity of the colonies posed a huge challenge to the English government. After 1650, it found ways to regulate trade, mostly for the mutual benefit of both England and the colonies. Beset by hostile Indians and internal discord, the colonies began to recognize that they needed protection that only England could provide. Once the Crown gave up its claims to absolute power, the two sides discovered much on which they could agree.

Political values in England and the colonies converged after the Glorious Revolution. Englishmen everywhere insisted that the right to property was sacred, that without it liberty could never be secure. They celebrated liberty under law, government by consent, and the toleration of all Protestants. In an empire dedicated to "liberty, property, and no popery," Catholics became big losers.

So did Indians and Africans. Racism directed against Indians mostly welled up from below, taking root among ordinary settlers who competed with Indians for land and other resources. Colonial elites tried, often ineffectually, to contain the popular rage that nearly tore New England and Virginia apart in 1675–1676. By contrast, racism directed against enslaved Africans was typically imposed from above and increasingly enforced by law. Ordinary settlers and Africans knew one another by name, made love, sometimes even married, stole hogs together, ran away together, and even fought together under Nathaniel Bacon's leadership. The men who were becoming great planters used their power to criminalize most of these activities. Bacon terrified them with the upheaval that ex-servants could create, and they hoped for greater stability from a labor force serving for life. They rewarded small planters and servants with white supremacy.

Still, by the 18th century, the British colonists had come to believe they were the freest people on earth. They attributed this fortune to their widespread ownership of land and to the English constitutional principles that they had incorporated into their own governments. In their minds, the British Empire had become the world's last bastion of liberty. Especially since the Glorious Revolution, it had asserted this liberty while greatly magnifying its power.

CHAPTER REVIEW

Review Questions

1. How important was England's mercantilistic system in gaining effective control over the colonies and in projecting English power against its European rivals?

2. Contrast the failure of New England and Virginia to preserve peaceful relations with neighboring Indians in 1675–1676 with New York's success in the same decade and later.

3. Did the crisis in England do more to undermine or to encourage liberty and equality in the English mainland colonies?

4. On what common principles did English political culture begin to converge in both the mother country and the colonies after the Glorious Revolution?

5. What enabled sparsely settled New France to resist British expansion with great success for more than half a century, whereas Spanish Florida seemed almost helpless against a similar threat?

6. Was England's advantage over Spain and France by 1713 in North America a result of London's conscious policies? Or did it illustrate instead the importance of the unintended consequences of many, perhaps most, historical endeavors?

Critical Thinking Questions

1. From the Restoration era to the American Revolution, most Englishmen and colonists understood politics as a perpetual struggle between power and liberty, one in which victory had almost always gone to power. How then was the British Empire able to increase both its power and its commitment to liberty over that period?

2. Discuss the changing forms of racism and the role they played in the English colonies between their founding and the Yamasee War.

Identifications

Review your understanding of the following key terms, people, and events for this chapter.

heathens, p. 64
balance of trade, p. 64
enumerated commodities, p. 65
Algonquians, p. 65
mourning war, p. 65

Iroquois League, p. 66
Covenant Chain of Peace, p. 66
powwow, p. 66
Metacom's War (King Philip's War), p. 66

Bacon's Rebellion, p. 68
Whigs, p. 69
Tories, p. 69
quitrent, p. 70
Glorious Revolution, p. 71
Salem witch trials, p. 72

funded national debt, p. 73
Pueblo Revolt, p. 75
Middle Ground, p. 76
Onontio, p. 76

DISCOVERY

What difficulties did England encounter while governing its overseas empire? How did it respond to these problems? What role did cultural perspectives play in England's "problems" with the Indians?

In thinking about this question, begin by breaking it down into the components shown below. A discussion of the significance of each component should appear in your answer.

Demography, Economy, and Government:

Look at Table 3.1, "The Spectrum of Settlement" (page 61). Why was life expectancy in many of the English colonies so low? How would this have created political and economic problems? How did race, ethnicity, and religion influence life expectancies? Compare and contrast New France and the English colonies. Based on this comparison, in which location would you most like to have lived in this period?

Culture and Society:

Examine the painting *A Pictish Man Holding a Human Head*. Did the portrayal of Native Americans by the colonists contribute to the latter's sense of cultural superiority? If so, how? How did European attitudes influence colonial policies toward Native Americans? What does an artist's depiction reveal about the artist and his or her beliefs?

A PICTISH MAN HOLDING A HUMAN HEAD

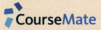

Visit the CourseMate website at www.cengagebrain.com for additional study tools and review materials for this chapter.

CHAPTER

PROVINCIAL AMERICA AND THE STRUGGLE FOR A CONTINENT

The British colonists, who thought they were the freest people on earth, faced a dilemma. To maintain the opportunity that settlers had come to expect, the colonies had to expand onto new lands. But provincial society also emulated the cultural values of Great Britain—its architecture, polite learning, religion, and politics. Relentless expansion made this emulation difficult because new settlements were not genteel. An anglicized province would become far more hierarchical than the colonies had been and might not even try to provide a rough equality of opportunity. The settlers' aspirations also brought them into renewed conflict with the Spanish and the French after 1739. In contrast to white colonists, slaves saw Spain as a beacon of liberty. In the eastern woodlands, most Indians identified France as the only ally committed to their survival and independence.

TIMELINE

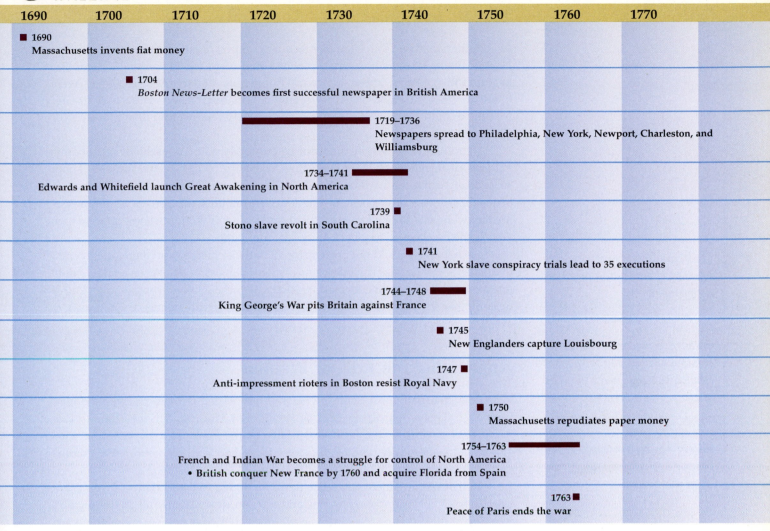

| 1690 | 1700 | 1710 | 1720 | 1730 | 1740 | 1750 | 1760 | 1770 |

■ **1690**
Massachusetts invents fiat money

■ **1704**
Boston News-Letter becomes first successful newspaper in British America

1719–1736
Newspapers spread to Philadelphia, New York, Newport, Charleston, and Williamsburg

1734–1741
Edwards and Whitefield launch Great Awakening in North America

1739 ■
Stono slave revolt in South Carolina

■ **1741**
New York slave conspiracy trials lead to 35 executions

1744–1748
King George's War pits Britain against France

■ **1745**
New Englanders capture Louisbourg

1747 ■
Anti-impressment rioters in Boston resist Royal Navy

■ **1750**
Massachusetts repudiates paper money

1754–1763
French and Indian War becomes a struggle for control of North America
• British conquer New France by 1760 and acquire Florida from Spain

1763 ■
Peace of Paris ends the war

© Cengage Learning

EXPANSION VERSUS ANGLICIZATION

In the 18th century many of the things the British colonists had left behind began to reappear. After 1740, for example, imports of British goods grew spectacularly. The gentry and the merchants dressed in the latest London fashions and embraced that city's standards of taste and elegance. Southern planters erected "big houses," such as Mount Vernon. Newspapers and learned professions based on English models proliferated.

But the population of British North America doubled every 25 years. Each generation required twice as many colleges, ministers, lawyers, physicians, craftsmen, printers, sailors, and unskilled laborers as the preceding generation. Without them, standards of "civility" would decline. As the 18th century progressed, the colonies experienced a contest between the pace of expansion and these anglicizing tendencies.

FOCUS QUESTION

Why was it difficult to sustain both continual expansion and the anglicization of the colonies at the same time?

Threats to Householder Autonomy

As population rose, some families acquired more prestige than others. Before 1700 ordinary farmers and small planters had often sat in colonial assemblies. In the 18th century, those active in public life above the local level were likely to be **gentlemen** who performed no manual labor. They had greater wealth, a more impressive lineage, and a better education than farmers or craftsmen.

By midcentury, despite the value colonists placed on householder autonomy, patterns of dependency were beginning to emerge. In tidewater Virginia, about 80 percent of the land was **entailed**—the owner could not divide it but had to bequeath it intact to his heir. In one Maryland county, 27 percent of the householders were tenants who worked small tracts of land without slaves or were men who owned a slave or two but had no claim to land.

Such families could not provide for all of their children and therefore reverted to English social norms. The inheritance rate for daughters fell. When a father could not support all his sons, he favored the eldest over the younger sons, who took up a trade or headed for the frontier. The goal of family independence continued to exercise great power, but it was under siege.

Anglicizing the Role of Women

When they married, most English women in propertied families received a **dowry** from their father, usually in cash or goods, not land. Under the common-law doctrine of **coverture,** the legal personality of the husband "covered" the wife, and he made all legally binding decisions. If he died first, his widow was entitled to **dower rights,** usually one-third of the estate.

In the colonies, there was some flexibility in the role and rights of women, at least at first. For example, New England women did virtually all of the region's weaving, a male occupation in Britain and the other colonies. Yet colonial women were also becoming more English in other ways. Until 1700 many Chesapeake widows inherited all of their husbands' property and administered their own estates. After 1700 such arrangements were rare. In New England, too, women suffered losses. Before 1700 courts had routinely punished men for sexual offenses, and many men had pleaded guilty and accepted their sentence. After 1700 almost no man would plead guilty except to making love to his wife before their wedding day. To avoid a small fine, some husbands humiliated their wives by denying that charge, even if their wives had already pleaded guilty after giving birth to a child that had obviously been conceived before the wedding. Europe's double standard of sexual behavior, which punished women for their indiscretions while tolerating male infractions, revived.

EXPANSION, IMMIGRATION, AND REGIONAL DIFFERENTIATION

gentleman *Term used to describe a person of means who performed no manual labor.*

entail *A legal device that required a landowner to keep his estate intact and pass it on to his heir.*

dowry *The cash or goods a woman received from her father when she married.*

coverture *A common-law doctrine under which the legal personality of the husband covered the wife, and he made all legally binding decisions.*

dower rights *The right of a widow to a portion of her deceased husband's estate (usually one-third of the value of the estate).*

FOCUS QUESTION

Why did production, not consumption, define regional differences?

After 1715, the settled portions of North America enjoyed an era of peace. Wars had emptied the borderlands of most inhabitants, and people poured into these areas, usually without provoking the Indians of the interior. As the colonies expanded, they evolved into distinct regions.

The Emergence of the Old South

In 1730 about 630,000 settlers and slaves lived in the mainland colonies. By 1775, another 248,000 Africans and 284,000 Europeans had landed, including 50,000 British convicts. Most of the voluntary immigrants settled in the middle or southern colonies. Almost 90 percent of the slaves went to the southern colonies. About 80 percent arrived from Africa on overcrowded, stinking, British-owned vessels. Most of the rest came from the West Indies on New England ships. This massive influx of slaves created the Old South, a society consisting of wealthy slaveholding planters, a much larger class of small planters, and thousands of slaves.

Slaves transformed the social structure of the southern colonies. In 1700, most members of Virginia's House of Burgesses were small planters who raised tobacco with a few indentured servants and a slave or two. After 1730 the typical burgess was a great planter who owned at least 20 slaves. By 1750, the rice planters of South Carolina were richer than any other group in British North America.

The lives of slaves in the upper South (Maryland, Virginia, and the Albemarle region of North Carolina) differed from those of slaves in the lower South (from Cape Fear in North Carolina through South Carolina and eventually Georgia). Chesapeake tobacco planters organized their slaves into closely supervised gangs and kept them in the fields all day. The planters, who saw themselves as benevolent paternalists, encouraged family life among their workers, who by the 1720s were achieving a rate of reproduction almost equal to that of the settlers.

Paternalism soon extended to religion. In the 1720s, for the first time on any significant scale, planters began to urge their slaves to convert to Christianity, mostly, it seems, because planters hoped that Christian slaves would be more dutiful. These efforts expanded despite a massive slave uprising. In 1730, a rumor spread that the British government had promised to emancipate any slave who converted and that the colony was suppressing the news. In September, about 300 slaves tried to escape through the Great Dismal Swamp. The planters hired Indians to track them, crushed the rebels, and hanged 29 of them.

South Carolina planters also began with paternalistic goals, but the rice swamps and mosquitoes defeated them. Whites supervising slave gangs in the rice fields caught malaria, which left them vulnerable to other diseases that often killed them. Africans fared much better than whites in the marshy fields. (Modern medicine has shown that many Africans possess a **sickle cell** in their blood that protects against malaria but can expose their children to a deadly form of inherited anemia.) Carolina planters seldom ventured into the rice fields, and, with few exceptions, they made no effort to Christianize their slaves.

This situation altered work patterns. To produce a crop of rice, planters devised the **task system.** Slaves had to finish certain tasks each day, after which their time was their own. Slaves used this time to create an invisible economy, raising crops, hunting, or fishing. Therefore, although the huge profits from rice

© Snark/Art Resource, NY

BRITAIN'S AFRICAN SLAVE TRADE. *The captives were packed aboard the slave ship, often so tightly that they could scarcely move and had to suffer the humiliation of inhaling the stench of their own human waste. The most famous illustration of such a ship, the Brooks of Liverpool, was published by antislavery advocates in London in 1789 and gave a tremendous boost to what became Britain's abolitionist movement.*

sickle cell *A crescent or sickle-shaped red blood cell sometimes found in African Americans. It helped protect them from malaria but exposed some children to the dangerous and painful condition of sickle cell anemia.*

task system *A system of slave labor, used primarily on rice plantations, under which slaves had to complete specific assignments each day. After these assignments were finished, their time was their own.*

gang labor *A system used on tobacco plantations where planters organized their field slaves into gangs, supervised them closely, and kept them working in the fields all day.*

Gullah *A language spoken by newly imported African slaves. Originally a simple second language for everyone who spoke it, it evolved into modern black English.*

indigo *A blue dye, obtained from plants, that was used by the textile industry. The British government subsidized the commercial production of it in South Carolina.*

Ulster *The northern province of Ireland that provided 70 percent of the Irish immigrants in the colonial period. Nearly all of them were Presbyterians whose forebears had moved to Ireland from Scotland in the previous century. They sometimes are called Scots-Irish today.*

redemptioners *Servants with a contract of indenture that allowed them to find masters after they arrived in the colonies. Many German immigrant families were redemptioners and thus were able to stay together while they served their terms.*

backcountry *Term used in the 18th and early 19th centuries to refer to the western settlements and the supposed misfits who lived in them.*

condemned nearly all Carolina slaves to monotonous, unpleasant labor in the marshes, they preferred the task system to **gang labor**. Rice culture also gave slaves a lower rate of reproduction; their population did not grow by natural increase until the 1770s, half a century later than in the Chesapeake.

The task system slowed assimilation into the British world. African words and customs survived longer in South Carolina than in the Chesapeake colonies. Newly imported slaves spoke **Gullah,** a pidgin language (that is, a simple second language for everyone who spoke it). Gullah began with a few phrases common to many West African languages, gradually added English words, and became the natural language of subsequent generations, eventually evolving into modern black English.

The slavery system required brute force to maintain it. Slaves convicted of arson were often burned at the stake, an unthinkable punishment for a white person. Whippings were frequent. One South Carolina overseer killed five slaves in two or three years before 1712. If such extreme cruelty was rare, random acts of violence were common and, from a slave's perspective, unpredictable. William Byrd II was one of Virginia's most refined settlers and owned its largest library. His diary reveals that when he and his wife Lucy disagreed, the slaves could suffer. "My wife caused Prue to be whipped notwithstanding I desired it not," Byrd reported, "which provoked me to have Anaka whipped likewise who had deserved it much more, on which my wife flew into such a passion she hoped she would be revenged of me."

The southern colonies prospered in the 18th century by exchanging their staple crops for British imports. By 1775, over 90 percent of Chesapeake tobacco was reexported to Europe from Britain. South Carolina continued to export provisions to the sugar islands and deerskins to Britain. **Indigo**, used as a dye by the British textile industry, emerged at midcentury as a second staple crop, pioneered by a woman planter, Eliza Lucas Pinckney. Many Chesapeake planters turned to wheat as a second cash crop. Wheat required mills to grind it into flour, barrels in which to pack it, and ships to carry it away. The result was the growth of cities: Norfolk and Baltimore had nearly 10,000 people by 1775.

The Mid-Atlantic Colonies: The "Best Poor Man's Country"

The Mid-Atlantic colonies had been pluralistic societies from the start, and immigration added to this ethnic and religious diversity. After 1720 Ireland and Germany replaced England as the source of most free immigrants. About 70 percent of Ireland's emigrants came from **Ulster**. They were Presbyterians whose forebears had come to Ireland from Scotland in the 17th century. (Historians now call them the Scots-Irish, a term seldom used at the time.) Most left Ireland to avoid an increase in rents and to enjoy greater trading privileges than Parliament had allowed them. Roughly 80,000 Irish reached the Delaware valley before 1776.

Perhaps 70,000 of the free immigrants were Germans. Most arrived as **redemptioners,** a new form of indentured service attractive to married couples because it allowed them to find and bind themselves to the same master. After completing their service, most redemptioners streamed into the interior of Pennsylvania. Others moved on to the southern **backcountry** with the Irish.

These colonies grew excellent wheat and built their own ships to carry it abroad. When Europe's population surged around 1740, the middle colonies began to ship flour across the Atlantic. By 1760, both Philadelphia and New York City had overtaken Boston's stagnant population of 15,000. Philadelphia, with 32,000 people, was the largest city in British North America by 1775. By then Pennsylvania was the second most populous colony, trailing only Virginia.

The Backcountry

Many Scots-Irish and Germans pushed west into the mountains and up the river valleys into the interior parts of Virginia and the Carolinas. They brought their folkways with them and soon gave the region its own distinctive culture. Most farmed, but many became hunters or raised cattle. Unlike the coastal settlements, the backcountry had no newspapers, few clergymen or other professionals, and, in South Carolina's interior, almost no government. A visiting Anglican clergyman bemoaned "the abandon'd Morals and profligate Principles" of the settlers. Clannish and violent, backcountry settlers drank heavily and hated Indians. Once war with the Indians broke out, most backcountry men demanded their extermination.

New England: A Faltering Economy and Paper Money

New England's relative isolation in the 17th century began to have negative consequences after 1700. Life expectancy declined as diseases from Europe invaded the region. The first settlers had left these diseases behind, but lack of exposure in childhood made later generations vulnerable. When smallpox threatened to devastate Boston in 1721, Zabdiel Boylston, a self-taught doctor, began inoculating people with it on the theory that healthy people would survive the injection and become immune. The experiment worked. But a diphtheria epidemic in the 1730s and high military losses after 1740 took their toll. New England's rate of population growth fell behind that of other regions.

New England had prospered by exporting cod, grain, livestock, and barrel staves to the West Indies. An imbalance of trade, however, hurt the region's economy. A blight called the **wheat blast** appeared in the 1660s and slowly spread until wheat cultivation nearly ceased. After grain exports declined, the West Indian trade barely broke even. And after 1700, Yankees had trouble feeding themselves, much less others. They had to buy flour from New York and Pennsylvania and, eventually, wheat from Chesapeake Bay. Poverty grew, especially in Boston, where by the 1740s about one-third of all adult women were widows, many impoverished.

New England's experience with paper money further illustrates its economic difficulties. In response to a military emergency in 1690, Massachusetts invented **fiat money**—paper money backed only by the government's promise to accept it in payment of taxes. It worked well for 20 years, but then depreciation set in. Creditors attacked paper money as fraudulent. Only gold and silver, they claimed, had real value. Defenders retorted that, in most other colonies, paper was holding its value. The problem lay with the New England economy, which could not generate enough exports to pay for the region's imports. War disrupted shipping in the 1740s, and military expenditures sent New England currency to a new low. Then, in 1748, Parliament agreed to reimburse Massachusetts for these expenses at the 1745 exchange rate, and the legislature used the grant to retire all paper and convert to silver money. That decision was a drastic example of anglicization. Although fiat money was the colony's own invention, Massachusetts repudiated it in favor of British methods.

wheat blast *A plant disease that affected wheat and first appeared in New England in the 1660s. It spread until wheat production in New England nearly ceased.*

fiat money *Paper money backed only by the promise of the government to accept it in payment of taxes. It originated in Massachusetts after a military emergency in 1690.*

ANGLICIZING PROVINCIAL AMERICA

FOCUS QUESTION

How were the colonists able to embrace both the Enlightenment and evangelical religion at the same time?

Forms of production had made these regions diverse. They became more alike through what they imported from Britain. Although each region exported its own distinctive products, patterns of consumption became quite similar throughout the colonies. Their ability to consume ever-larger quantities of British goods was making the mainland colonies more valuable than the sugar islands to the empire. The mainland also welcomed English revivalists and absorbed much of Britain's intellectual and political culture.

The World of Print

Few 17th-century American settlers owned books. Only Massachusetts had printing presses before the 1680s. By 1740, Boston had eight printers; New York and Philadelphia each had two. A few others had one.

Boston thus led the way in newspaper publishing. John Campbell, the city's postmaster, established the *Boston News-Letter* in 1704. By the early 1720s, two more weekly papers had opened in Boston. Philadelphia and New York City had each acquired one. The *South Carolina Gazette* was founded in Charleston in 1732 and the *Virginia Gazette* at Williamsburg in 1736. These papers devoted nearly all of their space to European news, usually reprinted from the *London Gazette*. But beginning in the 1720s the *New England Courant* also began to reprint political essays, including the angry and immensely popular writings, mostly aimed at religious bigotry and political and financial corruption, of "Cato," a pen name used jointly by John Trenchard and Thomas Gordon.

Benjamin Franklin personified the **Enlightenment** values that the newspapers were spreading. As a boy, he skipped church in Puritan Boston to read newspapers and to perfect his prose style. As a young printer with his brother's *New England Courant* in the 1720s, he helped to publish the writings of John Checkley, an Anglican whom the courts twice prosecuted in a vain attempt to silence him. After 1729, he made his *Pennsylvania Gazette* the best-edited and most widely read paper in America.

Franklin always sought ways to improve society. In 1727, he and some friends founded a debating club that later evolved into the American Philosophical Society. Franklin was a founder of North America's first Masonic lodge in 1730, the Library Company of Philadelphia a year later, the Union Fire Company in 1736, the Philadelphia Hospital in 1751, and an academy that became the College of Philadelphia (now the University of Pennsylvania) in the 1750s. But his greatest fame came from his electrical experiments during the 1740s and 1750s. He invented the Franklin stove and the lightning rod. By 1760, he had become the most celebrated North American in the world.

The Enlightenment in America

Enlightenment *The new learning in science and philosophy that took hold, at least in England, between 1660 and the American Revolution. Nearly all of its spokesmen were religious moderates who were more interested in science than religious doctrine and who favored broad religious toleration.*

The English Enlightenment exalted man's capacity for knowledge and social improvement. Enlightened writers celebrated Sir Isaac Newton's laws of motion as one of the greatest intellectual achievements of all time, joined the philosopher John Locke in calling for social improvements, and began to suspect that

MUSICAL LINK TO THE PAST

He Could Make a Lass Weep

Composers: Francis Hopkinson (music), Thomas Parnell (lyrics)
Title: "My Days Have Been So Wondrous Free" (1759)

Until almost the American Revolution, American music was European music, especially English music, and most of it was church music. Francis Hopkinson was America's earliest secular songwriter, and "My Days Have Been So Wondrous Free" was probably the first American secular song. Although the title and the song's rhythm suggest a jaunty mood, the song is not as upbeat as a superficial listen might indicate. Hopkinson's music complemented and added depth to lyrics written decades earlier by Thomas Parnell. A romantic and bittersweet yearning permeates the song, although whether such yearning is directed toward communing with nature or with a romantic companion is uncertain.

Hopkinson wrote American secular songs in an environment in which no tradition, publisher, or demand existed. He was a multitalented Renaissance man in the style of his contemporaries and friends Thomas Jefferson and Benjamin Franklin, with expertise in music, painting, inventing, writing, the law, and politics: a delegate to the Continental Congress, he signed the Declaration of Independence.

"My Days" represents an early example of two important traditions in American songwriting. First, Hopkinson purposely crafted compositions that untrained amateurs could perform and enjoy. "The best of [my songs] is that they are so easy that any Person who can play at all may perform them without much Trouble, & I have endeavour'd to make the melodies pleasing to the untutored Ear," he explained. Second, his songs meant to arouse emotion and emanated from "the Imagination of an Author who composes from his Heart, rather than his Head."

Although Hopkinson's songs did not attain large popularity, they did fulfill his elevated purposes in at least one family. After Hopkinson sent Jefferson some of his songs, Jefferson replied: "Accept my thanks … and my daughter's … I will not tell you how much they have pleased us, nor how well the last of them merits praise for its pathos, but relate a fact only, which is that while my elder daughter was playing it on the harpsichord, I happened to look toward the fire, & saw the younger one in tears. I asked her if she was sick? She said 'no; but the tune was so mournful.'"

Q Why do you think the colonists took more than a hundred years to develop their own popular songs, relying instead on material imported from England and the rest of Europe?

 Listen to an audio recording of this music on the *Musical Links to the Past* CD.

---

moderns had surpassed the ancients in learning and wisdom. John Tillotson, archbishop of Canterbury before his death in 1694, preached morality rather than dogma. He had a way of defending the doctrine of eternal damnation that left his listeners wondering how a merciful God could have ordained such a cruel punishment.

Enlightened ideas won an elite constituency in the colonies. Tillotson's sermons appeared in numerous southern libraries and made a deep impression on the tutors at Harvard College, including John Leverett, Jr., who became Harvard's president in 1707. Tillotson's ideas became entrenched in the curriculum. Harvard-trained ministers stressed the similarities between Anglicans and Congregationalists and favored religious toleration. After 1800, most Harvard-educated ministers became Unitarians who no longer believed in hell or the divinity of Jesus.

The legal and medical professions also spread Enlightenment ideas in America. Most Massachusetts lawyers before 1760 were either Anglicans or young men who

VISUAL LINK TO THE PAST

Benjamin West's *Benjamin Franklin Drawing Electricity from the Sky* (circa 1817)

To educated Europeans, Franklin's scientific experiments made him the most famous man in North America until rivaled by George Washington. Franklin showed lightning was a form of electricity, a phenomenon that, at the time, was just being studied by Europeans. He invented the lightning rod, which quickly brought spectacular benefits to the Atlantic world by protecting buildings from fires started by lightning. His fellow Americans also admired him, but more as a self-made man of numerous talents than as a scientific pioneer. West's painting, completed about a generation after Franklin's death, brought Europe's understanding of Franklin into closer alignment with America's appreciation of him.

Q Franklin lacked a formal education and may have taken up science, at least in part, because it did not require classical language or a college degree. Do modern innovators, such as Bill Gates, have similar backgrounds? Gates has a college degree, but has it had much to do with his creation of Microsoft?

© Philadelphia Museum of Art/CORBIS

---

had rejected the ministry as a career. By the 1790s, lawyers saw themselves as the cultural vanguard of the new republic. Poet William Cullen Bryant and writer Washington Irving even gave up law to write full time. In medicine, Benjamin Rush brought the latest Scottish techniques to the Philadelphia Hospital. He became an enlightened reformer, and many other colonial physicians embraced radical politics.

Georgia: The Failure of an Enlightenment Utopia

In the 1730s Anglican humanitarianism and the Enlightenment belief in social improvement converged and led to the founding of Georgia. The sponsors of this project hoped to create a society that could make productive use of England's "worthy" poor. They also intended to shield South Carolina's slave society from Spanish Florida by populating Georgia with disciplined, armed freemen. They planned to produce silk and wine, items that no other British colony had yet succeeded in making. They prohibited hard liquor as well as slavery.

A group of trustees set themselves up as a nonprofit corporation and announced that they would give land away. Led by James Oglethorpe, they obtained a 20-year charter from Parliament in 1732. The trustees recruited foreign

Protestants, a small number of Moravian Brethren (a German pacifist sect), and French Huguenots. In England, they interviewed many prospective settlers to distinguish the worthy poor from the unworthy.

As refined men, the trustees believed they knew what the colony needed and refused to consult the settlers on what might be good for them or for Georgia. They governed through "regulations" instead of laws. An elective assembly, the trustees promised, would come later, after Georgia's character had been firmly established.

The land system never worked as planned. The trustees gave 50 acres to every male settler whose passage was paid for out of charitable funds, but ordinary farmers could not support a family on 50 acres of the sandy soil around Savannah. Because the trustees envisioned every landowner as a soldier, women could not inherit land, nor could landowners sell their plots. The settlers failed to grow grapes or produce silk. They smuggled rum into the colony and insisted that Georgia would never thrive until it had slaves.

By the mid-1740s, enough people had died or left to reduce the population by more than half. Between 1750 and 1752, the trustees dropped their ban on alcohol, allowed the importation of slaves, summoned an elective assembly (but only to consult, not legislate), and finally surrendered their charter to Parliament. With the establishment of royal government in 1752, Georgia became what it was never meant to be—a smaller version of South Carolina, producing rice and indigo with slave labor. By then, ironically, the colony had done more to spread revivalism than to vindicate Enlightenment ideals.

THE GREAT AWAKENING

Between the mid-1730s and the early 1740s, an immense religious revival, the **Great Awakening,** swept across the Protestant world. It shattered denominational loyalties in the colonies and enabled the Methodists and the Baptists to surge ahead of all Protestant rivals after 1780.

Origins of the Revivals

Some of the earliest **revivals** originated in the colonies. In New England, **evangelical** minister Solomon Stoddard of Northampton presided over six revivals between the 1670s and his death in 1729. Jonathan Edwards, his grandson and successor, touched off a revival in 1734 and 1735 that rocked dozens of Connecticut valley towns. Edwards's *A Faithful Narrative of the Surprising Work of God* (1737) explained what a revival was—an emotional response to God's Word that brought sudden conversions to scores of people.

In England, John Wesley set the pace. At Oxford University, Wesley and his brother Charles founded the Holy Club, a High Church society whose members sometimes fasted until they could barely walk. These methodical practices prompted scoffers to call them "Methodists." Wesley went to Georgia as a missionary in 1735, but the settlers rejected his ascetic piety. In 1737, on his return voyage to England, some Moravians convinced him that he had never grasped the central Protestant message of justification by faith alone. He was also deeply moved by Edwards's *Faithful Narrative*. Soon, Wesley found his life's mission—the conversion of sinners—and it launched him on an extraordinary 50-year preaching career.

FOCUS QUESTION

What sort of dissatisfaction with existing Protestant denominations can explain the religious upheaval of the Great Awakening?

Great Awakening *An immense religious revival that swept across the Protestant world in the 1730s and 1740s.*

revival *A series of emotional religious meetings that led to numerous public conversions.*

evangelical *A style of Christian ministry that includes much zeal and enthusiasm. Evangelical ministers emphasized personal conversion and faith rather than religious ritual.*

Whitefield Launches the Transatlantic Revival

George Whitefield, a talented amateur actor in his youth, joined the Holy Club at Oxford and became an Anglican minister. He followed Wesley to Georgia, founded an orphanage, then returned to England and preached all over the kingdom to raise money for it. He too began to preach the "new birth"—the necessity of a conversion experience. When pastors banned him from their pulpits, he preached in open fields. Newspapers reported these controversies, and Whitefield's admirers began to notify the press of his whereabouts on any given day. Colonial newspapers also followed his activities.

In 1739 Whitefield made his second trip to America, and thousands flocked to hear him preach. After landing in Delaware, he preached his way northward through Philadelphia, New Jersey, and New York City, then headed south through the Chesapeake colonies and into South Carolina. In September 1740, he sailed to Newport and for two months toured New England. Using his acting skills, he imitated Christ on the cross, shedding "pious tears" for poor sinners. When he wept, so did his audience. When he condemned them, they fell to the ground in agony.

Long-Term Consequences of the Revivals and the Denominational Realignment

Amid the enthusiasm of Whitefield's tour, the number of women church members soared, and in some congregations they acquired an informal veto over the choice of the minister. Although more men than usual had joined a church, after another year or two, men became hard to convert. Partly in reaction to the revivals, thousands of men became Freemasons, often instead of joining a church. They nearly turned these societies into a religion of manliness, complete with secret and mysterious rituals that extolled sobriety, industry, brotherhood, benevolence, and citizenship. This movement peaked during and after the Revolution.

The revivals destroyed the unity of New England's Congregational Church. Evangelicals seceded from dozens of congregations to form their own "Separate" churches, many of which went Baptist by the 1760s. In the middle colonies, where most people did not belong to a church in the 1730s, the revivals prompted many to become **New Side** (evangelical) Presbyterians, **Old Side** (antirevival) Presbyterians, or unevangelical Anglicans. The southern colonies were less affected, although evangelical Presbyterians made modest gains in Virginia after 1740. Finally, in the 1760s, the Baptists began to win thousands of converts, to be followed and overtaken by the Methodists during and after the Revolution.

As Anglicans split into Methodists and Latitudinarians, Congregationalists into **New Lights** (pro-revival) and **Old Lights** (antirevival), and Presbyterians into comparable New Side and Old Side synods, evangelicals discovered that they had more in common with revivalists in other denominations than with antirevivalists in their own.

The revivals therefore transformed American religious life. In 1700, the three strongest denominations had been the Congregationalists in New England, the Quakers in the Delaware valley, and the Anglicans in the South. By 1800, all three had lost ground to newcomers: the Methodists, the Baptists, and the Presbyterians. Methodists and Baptists did not expect their preachers to attend college, and they recruited ministers from a much broader segment of the population than their rivals could tap. They demanded only personal conversion, integrity, knowledge of the Bible, and a talent for preaching.

New Side *Term used to describe evangelical Presbyterians.*

Old Side *Antirevival Presbyterians.*

New Lights *Term used to describe pro-revival Congregationalists.*

Old Lights *Antirevival Congregationalists.*

POLITICAL CULTURE IN THE COLONIES

In politics, as in other activities, the colonies became more like Britain during the 18th century. Colonists agreed that they were free because they were British, because they too had mixed constitutions that united monarchy, aristocracy, and democracy in almost perfect balance.

By the 1720s every colony except Connecticut and Rhode Island had an appointive governor, a council, and an elective assembly. The governor stood for monarchy and the council for aristocracy. In Massachusetts, Rhode Island, and Connecticut the council or upper house was elected (indirectly in Massachusetts). In all other colonies except Pennsylvania, an appointive but not hereditary council played an active legislative role. Yet especially in Virginia, some councilors served for life and might be succeeded by their sons.

FOCUS QUESTION

Why did Britain's "Country" values prevail in most southern colonies while "Court" politics took hold in most northern provinces?

The Rise of the Assembly and the Governor

In all 13 colonies the settlers elected the assembly. The right to vote was more widely shared than in England, where two-thirds of adult males were disfranchised. In the colonies, about three-fourths of free males could vote at some point in their adult lives. The frequency of elections varied, from every year in a few colonies to every seven years in others. As the century advanced, legislatures sat longer and passed more laws, and the lower house, the assembly, usually initiated major bills. The rise of the assembly was a major political trend of the era.

Every royal colony except New York and Georgia already had an assembly with a strong sense of its own privileges when the first royal governor arrived, but the governors also grew more powerful. Because the governor's instructions usually challenged some existing practices, clashed occurred. The first royal governors never got all of their demands, but they did win concessions over the years. The most successful governors learned to depend less on their royal prerogatives than on their ability to win over the assembly through persuasion or **patronage**.

Early in the century, conflicts between governor and assembly were legalistic. Each side cited technical precedents to justify the governor's prerogatives or the assembly's privileges. Later on, when conflict spilled over into pamphlets and newspapers, it often pitted an aggrieved minority against the governor and assembly. These conflicts were ideological. The opposition accused the governor of corrupting the assembly, and he denounced them as a "faction." Everyone condemned factions, or political parties, as selfish and destructive.

"Country" Constitutions: The Southern Colonies

In most southern colonies, the "Country" principles of the British opposition (see Chapter 3) became the common assumptions of public life, acceptable to both governor and assembly, typically after a failed attempt to impose the "Court" alternative. When a governor such as Virginia's Alexander Spotswood (1710–1722) used his patronage to fill the assembly with his own "placemen," the voters turned them out at the next election. Just as Spotswood learned that he could not manipulate the house through patronage, the assembly discovered that it could not coerce a governor who had a permanent salary. Accordingly, Virginia and South Carolina cultivated the **politics of harmony**, a system of ritualized mutual flattery. Governors

patronage *The act of appointing people to government jobs or awarding them government contracts, often based on political favoritism rather than on abilities.*

politics of harmony *A system in which the governor and the colonial assembly worked together through persuasion rather than through patronage or bullying.*

found that they could accomplish more through persuasion than through patronage, and the assemblies responded by showing their appreciation. Factions disappeared, allowing the governor and the assembly to pursue the "common good" in an atmosphere free of rancor or corruption. Georgia adopted similar practices in the 1750s.

In Virginia, public controversy all but ceased. South Carolina's politics became almost as placid into the 1760s, even as serious social problems began to emerge in the unrepresented backcountry. By contrast, the politics of harmony never took hold in Maryland, where the lord proprietor always tried to seduce assemblymen with his lavish patronage; nor in North Carolina, where tobacco and rice planters fought each other and the backcountry distrusted both.

"Court" Constitutions: The Northern Colonies

QUICK REVIEW

THE IMPACT OF BRITAIN'S COURT AND COUNTRY VALUES ON COLONIAL POLITICS

• Colonial versions of Britain's mixed and balanced constitution

• Both royal governors and elected assemblies became more powerful

• "Country" constitutions: the politics of harmony in Virginia, South Carolina, and Georgia, but not in Maryland or North Carolina

• "Court" constitutions: patronage systems took hold in Massachusetts, New Hampshire, and New York for a time, but not in Pennsylvania

With many economic interests and ethnic groups to satisfy, the northern colonies often gave rise to political factions. Governors used patronage to reward some groups and discipline others. Although Pennsylvania kept its provincial governor weak, patronage systems took hold in Massachusetts, New Hampshire, and New York. William Shirley, governor of Massachusetts from 1741 to 1756, used judicial and militia appointments and war contracts to build a majority in the assembly. Ineffective opposition accused the governor of corrupting the assembly, but Shirley claimed that his actions were essential to the colony's needs.

The opposition, though seldom able to implement its demands at the provincial level, was important nonetheless. It kept settlers alert to any infringements on their liberties. In Boston, artisans engaged in ritualized mob activities that had a sharp political edge. On Guy Fawkes Day (November 5) every year, a North End mob and a South End mob burned effigies of the pope, the devil, and the Stuart pretender to the British throne. These men were celebrating liberty, property, and no popery—the British constitution as they understood it. The violence made many wealthy merchants nervous, and by 1765 some of them would become its targets.

Colonists both north and south absorbed the ideology of the British opposition, which warned that those in power were usually trying to destroy liberty and that corruption was their most effective weapon. By 1776, that view would justify independence and the repudiation of a "corrupt" king and Parliament. Before 1760, however, it served different purposes. In the south, this ideology celebrated Anglo-American harmony. In the north, it became the language of frustrated minorities unable to defeat the governor or control the assembly.

THE RENEWAL OF IMPERIAL CONFLICT

FOCUS QUESTION

Why did Britain, despite its naval superiority and its huge population advantage in North America, fail to dominate the Spanish and the French in King George's War?

A new era of imperial war began in 1739 and continued, with only a brief interruption, until 1763. The colonies, New Spain, New France, and the Indians of the eastern woodlands all became involved.

Challenges to French Power

In the decades of peace after 1713 the French tried to strengthen their position in North America. They erected the continent's most formidable fortress, Louisbourg,

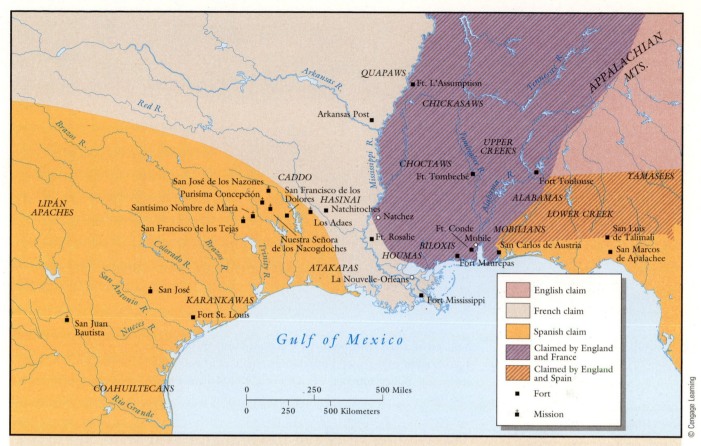

Map 4.1 French Louisiana and Spanish Texas, circa 1730. *In this part of North America, French and Spanish settlers and missionaries were spread quite thinly over a vast area and surrounded by much larger numbers of Indian peoples.*

on Cape Breton Island. A naval force stationed there could guard the approaches to the St. Lawrence River. The French also built Fort St. Frédéric (the British called it Crown Point) on Lake Champlain and maintained their Great Lakes posts at Forts Frontenac, Michilimackinac, and Detroit. In 1718 the French founded New Orleans, which became the capital of Louisiana in 1722.

Despite these efforts, the French hold on the interior began to weaken. Indians returned to the Ohio valley, mostly to trade with pacifist Pennsylvania or with Fort Oswego, a new British post on Lake Ontario. Many Indians founded what the French disparagingly called **republics,** villages outside the French alliance system that were eager for British trade. They accepted people from all tribes—Delawares from the east, Shawnees from the south and east, Mingoes (Iroquois who had left their homeland) from the north, and other Algonquians of the Great Lakes region to the west.

Sometimes the French system of mediation broke down. In the southwest an arrogant French officer decided to take over the lands of the Natchez Indians and ordered them to move. While pretending to comply, the Natchez planned a counterstroke and, on November 28, 1729, killed every French male in the vicinity. French and Choctaw retaliation destroyed the Natchez—the last of the mound builders—as a distinct people.

In 1730, the French barely averted a massive slave uprising in New Orleans. To stir up hatred between Indians and Africans, the French turned over some of the African leaders to the Choctaws to be burned alive. Unable to afford enough gifts to

republics *Independent Indian villages that were willing to trade with the British and remained outside the French system of Indian alliances.*

hold an alliance with both the Choctaws and the Chickasaws, the French encouraged hostilities between both nations. Instead of weakening the pro-British Chickasaws, this policy touched off a Choctaw civil war. France lost both influence and prestige.

The Danger of Slave Revolts and War with Spain

The Spanish presence in Florida proved troublesome to South Carolina. On several occasions after 1680, Spanish Florida had promised freedom to slaves who escaped from Carolina and were willing to accept Catholicism. In 1738 the governor established, just north of St. Augustine, a new town, Gracia Real de Santa Teresa de Mose (or Mose for short, pronounced *Moe*-shah) and made it the first community of free blacks in what is now the United States.

In 1739 the governor of Spanish Florida offered liberty to slaves in the British colonies who could make their way to Florida. This manifesto, and rumors about Mose, touched off the Stono Rebellion in South Carolina, the most violent slave revolt in the history of the 13 colonies. A force of 20 slaves attacked a store at Stono (south of Charleston), killed the owner, seized weapons, and moved on to assault homes and attract recruits. Heading toward Florida, they killed another 25 settlers. The militia caught them at the Edisto River and killed about two-thirds of the growing force. In the weeks that followed, white settlers killed another 60. No rebels reached Florida, but, as the founders of Georgia had foreseen, South Carolina was indeed vulnerable in any dispute with Spain.

Georgia was supposed to protect South Carolina. General Oglethorpe, its governor, retaliated against the Spanish by invading Florida in 1740. He dispersed the black residents of Mose and occupied the site, but the Spaniards mauled his garrison in a surprise counterattack. Oglethorpe retreated without taking St. Augustine and brought back some disturbing reports. Spain, he said, was sending blacks into the British colonies to start slave uprisings, and Spanish priests in disguise were joining the black conspirators. This news set off panics in the rice and tobacco colonies, but it had its biggest impact in New York City.

By 1741, New York City's 2,000 slaves were the largest concentration of blacks in British North America outside of Charleston. When several suspicious fires broke out, the settlers grew nervous. Some of the fires probably provided cover for an interracial larceny ring that operated out of the tavern of John Hughson, a white man. When the New York Supreme Court offered freedom to Mary Burton, a 16-year-old Irish servant girl at the tavern, in exchange for her testimony, she swore that the tavern was the center of a "Popish Plot" to murder the city's adult white males, free the slaves, and make Hughson king of the Africans. Some free black Spanish sailors, after capture and enslavement by **privateers,** were also accused, partly for insisting they were free men. The New York conspiracy trials continued from May into August 1741. Four whites and 18 slaves were hanged, 13 slaves were burned alive, and 70 were banished to the West Indies.

In 1742 King Philip V of Spain sent 36 ships and 2,000 soldiers from Cuba with orders to devastate Georgia and South Carolina and free the slaves. The invaders outnumbered the entire population of Georgia, but Oglethorpe raised 900 men and met the Spaniards on St. Simons Island. After he ambushed two patrols, Spanish morale collapsed. The Spanish force departed, leaving the British colonies once again as a safe haven for liberty, property, no popery— and slavery.

France versus Britain: King George's War

In 1744, when France joined Spain in the war against Britain, the action shifted to the north. After the French laid siege to Annapolis Royal, the capital of Nova Scotia, Governor Shirley of Massachusetts intervened to save the small garrison, and the French withdrew. Shirley then planned an attack on Fortress Louisbourg. With only a few lightly armed Yankee vessels at his disposal, he asked the commander of the British West Indian squadron, Sir Peter Warren, for assistance. But Shirley's expedition, which included about one-sixth of the adult males of Massachusetts, set out before Warren could respond. Warren reached Cape Breton in the nick of time; had he not, nearly every family in New England could have lost a close relative. The British navy drove off the French fleet, and on June 16, 1745, untrained Yankees subdued the mightiest fortress in America.

After that, nothing went right. Plans to attack Quebec by sea in 1746 and 1747 came to nothing because no British fleet arrived. French and Indian raiders assaulted the weakly defended frontier. Bristol County farmers rioted against high taxes. When the Royal Navy finally arrived in Boston in late 1747, its commander sent gangs of sailors ashore to compel anyone they could seize into serving with the fleet. An angry crowd descended on the sailors, took some officers hostage, and controlled the streets of Boston for three days before the commander released all the Massachusetts men he had impressed. Finally, Britain returned Louisbourg to France under the Treaty of Aix-la-Chapelle, which ended the war in 1748.

The Impending Storm

The war had driven back the frontiers of British settlement in North America, but the colonies had promised land grants to many volunteers. Thus peace touched off a frenzy of expansion. In 1749, the British established the town of Halifax, which became the new capital of Nova Scotia. Yankees swarmed north

privateers *A privately owned ship that was authorized by a government to attack enemy ships during times of war. The owner and crew of the ship claimed a portion of whatever was captured.*

King George's War *Popular term in North America for the third of the four Anglo-French wars before the American Revolution (1744–1748).*

PORTRAIT OF CHIEF HENDRIK OF THE MOHAWKS. *Hendrik's ultimatum to New York in 1753 precipitated the summoning of the Albany Congress a year later.*

into Maine and New Hampshire and west into the middle colonies. In 1754, Connecticut's delegation to the Albany Congress (discussed in the next section) used bribes to acquire an Indian title to all of northern Pennsylvania, which Connecticut claimed on the basis of its sea-to-sea charter of 1663. The blatant encroachments of New York speculators and settlers on Mohawk lands so infuriated the Mohawks' Chief Hendrik that he bluntly told the governor of New York that "the Covenant Chain is broken between you and us [the Iroquois League]." New York, Pennsylvania, and Virginia competed for trade with the new Indian "republics" between Lake Erie and the Ohio River. Virginians, whom the Indians called **long knives,** were particularly aggressive. They organized the Ohio Company of Virginia in 1747 to settle the Ohio valley and established their first outpost at the site where the Monongahela and Allegheny Rivers converge to form the Ohio River (the site of modern Pittsburgh).

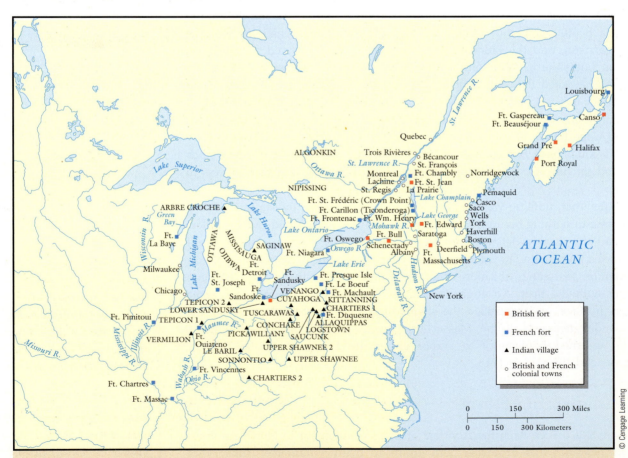

Map 4.2 **France versus Britain in North America by 1755.** *North of the Ohio River, much of North America was becoming a series of fortresses along the frontiers, separating New France from the British colonies.*

The French began to panic. They rebuilt Louisbourg and erected Fort Beauséjour on the neck that connects mainland Canada to Nova Scotia and Fort Carillon (Ticonderoga to the British) on Lake Champlain to protect Crown Point.

In a more controversial move, the French launched two expeditions into the area between the Great Lakes and the Ohio. In 1749 Pierre-Joseph Céloron de Blainville led several hundred men down the Allegheny to the Ohio, then up the Miami and back to Canada. Along the way Blainville buried plaques, claiming the area for France. The Indians removed them. Marquis Duquesne sent 2,000 Canadians, with almost no Indian support, to erect a line of posts from Fort Presque Isle (now Erie, Pennsylvania) to Fort Duquesne (now Pittsburgh).

The French intended to prevent British settlement west of the Alleghenies. To Duquesne, this policy was so obviously beneficial to the Indians that it needed no explanation. Yet the Mingoes warned him not to build a fort in their territory, and a delegation of Delawares and Shawnees asked the Virginians if they would be willing to expel the French from the Ohio country and then go back home. Instead Virginia sent George Washington to the Ohio country in 1753 to warn Duquesne to withdraw, and a small Virginia force began building its own fort at the forks of the Ohio. Duquesne ignored Washington, advanced toward the Ohio, expelled the Virginians, took over their fort, and finished building it. Virginia sent Washington back to the Ohio in 1754. On May 28, after discovering a French patrol nearby, Washington launched an attack. That command started a world war.

THE WAR FOR NORTH AMERICA

In 1755, France and Britain intervened in North America on an unprecedented scale. Colonists called this struggle the **French and Indian War.**

The Albany Congress and the Onset of War

In the spring of 1754 Britain ordered New York to host an intercolonial congress at Albany to meet with the Iroquois and redress their grievances. At this **Albany Congress,** Benjamin Franklin presented a plan for union. He called for a "President General" to be appointed by the Crown as commander in chief and to administer the laws of the union, and for a "Grand Council" to be elected for three-year terms by the lower houses of each colony. The union would have power to raise soldiers, build forts, levy taxes, regulate the Indian trade, purchase land from the Indians, and supervise western settlements until the Crown organized them as new colonies. To take effect, the plan would require approval by the Crown, by each colonial legislature, and finally by Parliament. The Albany Congress adopted an amended version of Franklin's proposal.

Newspapers ignored the Albany Plan, and every colony rejected it. As Franklin later explained, the colonies feared that the President General might become too powerful. But they also distrusted one another. Despite the French threat, they did not yet see themselves as "Americans" ready to put aside their differences and unite.

The Board of Trade responded by drafting its own plan, which resembled Franklin's, except that the Grand Council could only requisition—instead of tax—and colonial union would not require Parliament's approval. After news

FOCUS QUESTION

What made the war for North America (1754–1763) so much more decisive than the three earlier Anglo-French wars?

long knives *Term Indians used to describe Virginians.*

French and Indian War *Popular name for the struggle between Britain and France for the control of North America from 1754 to 1763, in which the British conquered New France. It merged into Europe's Seven Years' War (1756–1763) that pitted Britain and Prussia against France, Austria, and Russia.*

BENJAMIN FRANKLIN'S SNAKE CARTOON. *One of the first newspaper cartoons in colonial America, this device appeared in* the Pennsylvania Gazette *in May 1754. The cartoon called for colonial union on the eve of the Albany Congress and drew on the folk legend that a snake, cut into pieces, could revive and live if it somehow joined its severed parts together before sundown.*

arrived that Washington had surrendered his small force to the French at Great Meadows in July 1754, Britain decided that the colonies were incapable of uniting in their own defense. Even if they could, the precedent would be dangerous. Instead, London sent redcoats to Virginia—two regiments commanded by General Edward Braddock. For Britain, colonial union and direct military aid were policy *alternatives*. Although military aid was more expensive to the British government than the proposed union, it seemed the safer choice.

Britain's Years of Defeat

In 1755 London hoped that a quick British victory at the forks of the Ohio would keep the war from spreading. But Governor Shirley persuaded Braddock to accept New England's much broader war objectives. Instead of a single expedition aimed at one fort, the campaign of 1755 became four distinct offensives designed to crush the outer defenses of New France and leave it open to British invasion.

The redcoats were disciplined professional soldiers trained to fight other professional armies. **Irregular war** in American forests made them nervous. Provincial soldiers, by contrast, were young volunteers who enlisted only for a single campaign. They knew little about military drill, expected to serve under the officers who had recruited them, and sometimes refused to obey orders. Provincials admired the courage of the redcoats but were shocked by the brutal discipline imposed on them. Nevertheless, several thousand colonists also enlisted in the British army.

Under the enlarged plan of 1755, Nova Scotia's redcoats together with New England provincials would assault Fort Beauséjour. New England and New York provincials would attack Crown Point, while Shirley, who had been commissioned as a British colonel, would lead two regiments of New England redcoats to Niagara and cut off New France from the western Indians. Braddock would take Fort Duquesne.

Fort Duquesne's commander could muster only 72 French, 146 Canadians, and 637 Indians against the 1,400 British regulars and 450 Virginia provincials, including Washington. They clashed on July 9, 1755, along a narrow path with thick forest and brush on either side. The French and Indians took cover on the British flanks. Braddock's rear elements rushed toward the sound of the guns. There, massed together, they formed a gigantic red bull's eye. The Indians and the French poured round after round into them while the British fired wild volleys at the trees. The British lost 977 killed or wounded, along with their artillery. Braddock was killed. Only 39 French and Indians were killed or wounded. The redcoats finally broke and ran.

In Nova Scotia, Fort Beauséjour fell on June 17, 1755. When the Acadians refused to take an oath that might have obliged them to bear arms against other Frenchmen, the British and Yankees rounded up between 6,000 and 7,000 of them, forced them aboard ships, and expelled them from the province, to be scattered among the 13 colonies, none of which was prepared for the influx. A second roundup in 1759 caught most of the families that had evaded the first one.

Albany Congress *An intercolonial congress that met in Albany, New York, in June 1754. The delegates urged the Crown to assume direct control of Indian relations beyond the settled boundaries of the colonies, and they drafted a plan of confederation for the continental colonies. Every colony rejected it.*

Irregular war *A type of war using men who were not part of a permanent or professional regular military force. It also can apply to guerilla-type warfare, usually against the civilian population.*

The government of Nova Scotia confiscated the Acadians' land and redistributed it to Protestant settlers. About 3,000 Acadian refugees, after spending miserable years as unwanted Catholic exiles in a Protestant world, made it to French Louisiana, where their descendants became known as Cajuns.

Meanwhile William Johnson led his provincials against Crown Point. On September 8, the French commander, Jean-Armand, Baron Dieskau, drove the provincials back to the improvised Fort William Henry near Lake George. Although the provincials held the field and wounded and captured Dieskau, Johnson failed to take Crown Point. Shirley's Niagara campaign got no farther than Oswego on Lake Ontario and then stopped for the winter. Oswego was soon cut off by heavy snows. Malnutrition and disease ravaged the garrison.

A World War

With the death of Braddock and the capture of Dieskau, military amateurs took over both armies: Shirley in the British colonies and Governor-General Pierre de Rigaud de Vaudreuil in New France. Vaudreuil was a Canadian who understood his colony's weakness without Indian support. The white population of the 13 colonies outnumbered that of New France by 13 to 1. Vaudreuil knew that if the British Empire could concentrate its resources in a few strategic places, it had a good chance of overwhelming New France. A frontier war waged by New France against ordinary settlers remained the most effective way to force the British colonies to disperse their resources.

As long as Vaudreuil was in charge, New France kept winning. Even so, the French government decided that New France needed a professional general and sent Louis-Joseph, marquis de Montcalm, in 1756. Shocked and repelled by the brutality of frontier warfare, Montcalm tried to turn the conflict into a traditional European struggle of sieges and battles. This shift in tactics gave the advantage (as Vaudreuil well understood) to the British. When Fort William Henry fell the next year, Montcalm promised to let the British garrison march unmolested to Fort Edward, but his Indian allies, mostly in pursuit of plunder, killed or carried off 308 of the 2,300 prisoners, an event that colonial newspapers called the Fort William Henry Massacre. The British blamed Montcalm for the outrage; the western Indians resented his interference and never again provided him with significant support. Meanwhile, Braddock's defeat convinced the British government that the struggle with France could not be limited to a few outposts. Britain declared war on France in 1756, and the French and Indian War in the colonies merged with a general European struggle, the Seven Years' War (1756–1763).

Reluctant to antagonize Britain, Spain remained neutral for most of the war. Spain's neutrality prevented the opening of another theater of conflict and permitted Britain to concentrate an overwhelming force against New France.

Imperial Tensions: From Loudoun to Pitt

When London suddenly realized in 1755 that Shirley, an amateur, had taken command of the British army in North America, it dispatched General John Campbell, earl of Loudoun, to replace him and began pouring in reinforcements. Loudoun had a special talent for alienating provincials. Colonial units believed they had a contractual relationship with *their* officers; they had never agreed to serve under Loudoun's professionals. Many British officers, in turn, despised the provincials. "The Americans are in general the dirtiest most contemptible cowardly dogs that you can conceive," snarled General James Wolfe.

Loudon tried to impose authoritarian solutions on the other problems he faced: the quartering (or housing) of British soldiers, the relative rank of British and provincial officers, military discipline, revenue, and smuggling. When he sent redcoats into a city, he demanded that the assembly pay to quarter them or else he would take over public buildings by force. He tried to make any British major superior in rank to every provincial officer, and he ordered New England troops to serve directly under British officers. If a colonial assembly refused to vote adequate supplies, Loudoun urged Parliament to tax the colonies directly. He sometimes imposed embargoes on colonial shipping, partly to stamp out smuggling with French colonies. Loudoun built up his forces but otherwise accomplished little.

In 1757 William Pitt came to power as Britain's war minister. He understood that consent worked better than coercion in the colonies. Colonial assemblies, when asked, built barracks to house British soldiers. Pitt declared that every provincial officer would rank immediately behind the equivalent British rank but above all lesser officers, British or provincial. Provincial units under the command of their own officers cooperated with the British army, and the officers began to impose something close to British discipline on them.

Rather than levy a parliamentary tax, Pitt set aside £200,000 beginning in 1758 and told the colonies that they could claim a share of it in proportion to their contribution to the war effort. He persuaded the colonies to compete voluntarily in support of his stupendous mobilization. The subsidies covered less than half of the cost of fielding 20,000 provincials each year from 1758 to 1760 and smaller numbers in 1761 and 1762 as operations shifted to the Caribbean. Finally, British conquests soon reduced the smuggling problem. By 1762, Canada, Martinique, and Guadeloupe, as well as Spanish Havana, were all in British hands.

Pitt had no patience with military failure. He replaced Loudoun with James Abercrombie, and he put Jeffrey Amherst in charge of a new Louisbourg expedition. By 1758, the British Empire had finally put together a military force capable of overwhelming New France and knew how to use it.

The Years of British Victory

By 1758 the Royal Navy had cut off Canada from reinforcements and supplies. Britain had sent more than 30 regiments to North America. Combined with 20,000 provincials, thousands of **bateau** men rowing supplies into the interior, and swarms of privateers preying on French commerce, Britain had mustered 60,000 men for the final assault. Most of them now closed in on the 75,000 people of New France.

Spurred on by Quaker mediators, the British and colonial governments made peace with the western Indians in 1758 by promising not to seize their lands. But neither settlers nor officials had noticed a new trend: Few Indians in the northeastern woodlands were willing to kill one another. In 1755, for example, some Senecas fought with New France and some Mohawks with the British, but they avoided confronting each other. A sense of pan-Indian identity began to emerge.

Peace with the western Indians in 1758 permitted the British to revive the grand military plan of 1755, except that this time the overall goal was clear—the conquest of New France. Amherst and James Wolfe besieged Louisbourg, and it fell in September, enabling Nova Scotia to annex Cape Breton Island. Colonel John Bradstreet's 3,000 provincials took Fort Frontenac on Lake Ontario, cutting off the French in the Ohio valley from their supplies. A powerful force of regulars under John Forbes and provincials under Washington marched west through

bateau *A light, flat-bottomed boat with narrow ends that was used in Canada and the northeastern part of the colonies.*

Map 4.3 Conquest of Canada, 1758–1760. *In three campaigns, the British, with strong colonial support, first subdued the outer defenses of New France, then took Quebec in 1759 and Montreal in 1760.*

Pennsylvania to attack Fort Duquesne, but the French blew up the fort and retreated north just before they arrived. The British erected Fort Pitt on the ruins.

In June 1759, Wolfe with 8,000 redcoats and colonial rangers laid siege to Quebec, defended by Montcalm with 16,000 regulars, Canadian militia, and Indians. Wolfe mounted howitzers across the river from Quebec and began reducing most of the city to rubble. Frustrated by the French refusal to fight, he turned loose his American rangers, who ravaged and burned more than 1,400 farms. Still the French held out.

By September both Wolfe and Montcalm realized that the British fleet would soon have to depart or risk being frozen in during the long winter. Wolfe made a last desperate effort. His men silently sailed up the St. Lawrence, climbed a formidable cliff above the city in darkness, and on the morning of September 13, 1759, deployed on the Plains of Abraham behind Quebec. Montcalm panicked. Instead of using his artillery to defend the walls from inside, he marched out of Quebec onto the plains. Both generals now had what they craved most, a set-piece European battle. Wolfe and Montcalm were both mortally wounded, but the British took Quebec. Montreal fell in 1760, and Canada surrendered.

The Cherokee War and Spanish Intervention

In December 1759 the Cherokees, who had been allies and trading partners of South Carolina, reacted to a long string of violent incidents by attacking backcountry settlers and driving the frontier back 100 miles. British regular soldiers arrived in South Carolina and laid waste the Cherokee Lower Towns in the Appalachian foothills. When that expedition failed to bring peace, another one devastated the Middle Towns farther west. The Cherokees made peace in December 1761, but the backcountry settlers, left brutalized and lawless, became a political problem for South Carolina.

Only then, in January 1762, after the French and the Cherokees had been defeated, did Spain finally enter the war. British forces quickly took Havana and even Manila in the distant Philippines. France and Spain sued for peace.

The Peace of Paris

In 1763 the **Peace of Paris** ended the war. Britain returned Martinique and Guadeloupe to France. France surrendered to Great Britain several minor West Indian islands and all of North America east of the Mississippi, except New Orleans. In exchange for Havana, Spain ceded Florida to the British and also paid a large ransom for the return of Manila. To compensate its Spanish ally, France gave all of Louisiana west of the Mississippi, including New Orleans, to Spain.

British colonists were jubilant. Britain and the colonies could now develop their vast resources in an imperial partnership that would bring unprecedented prosperity. But the western Indians angrily rejected the peace settlement. No one had conquered them, and they denied the power of France to surrender their lands to Great Britain. They began to plan their own war of liberation.

Conclusion

Cherokee War *Between December 1759 and December 1761, the Cherokee Indians devastated the South Carolina backcountry. The British army intervened and in turn inflicted immense damage on the Cherokee.*

Between 1713 and 1754 expansion and renewed immigration pushed North American settlement ever farther into the interior. With a population that doubled every 25 years, many householders no longer had the opportunity to give all of their sons and daughters the level of economic success that they themselves enjoyed. As in England, many families had to favor sons over daughters and the eldest son over his younger brothers. The colonies anglicized in other ways as well. Newspapers and the learned professions spread the English Enlightenment to the colonies. English revivalists had a tremendous impact in North America, and British political values reshaped both northern and southern colonies, though in different ways.

Peace of Paris *The 1763 treaty ended the war between Britain on the one side, and France and Spain on the other. France surrendered New France to Britain. Spain ceded Florida to Britain, and France compensated its ally by ceding Louisiana to Spain.*

In 1739 the imperial wars resumed. The threat of internal upheaval kept King George's War indecisive in the 1740s, but when Spain remained neutral as Britain and France went to war after 1754, the British mobilized their full resources and conquered New France.

The war left powerful memories behind. Provincials admired the courage of the redcoats and the victories they won but hated their arrogant officers. The concord and prosperity that were supposed to follow Britain's great imperial victory yielded instead to bitter strife.

CHAPTER REVIEW

Review Questions

1. Why was it difficult to sustain both continual expansion and the anglicization of the colonies at the same time?
2. Why did production, not consumption, define regional differences?
3. How were the colonists able to embrace both the Enlightenment and evangelical religion at the same time?
4. What sort of dissatisfaction with existing Protestant denominations can explain the religious upheaval of the Great Awakening?
5. Why did Britain's "Country" values prevail in most southern colonies while "Court" politics took hold in most northern provinces?
6. Why did Britain, despite its naval superiority and its huge population advantage in North America, fail to dominate the Spanish and the French in King George's War?
7. What made the War for North America (1754–1763) so much more decisive than the three earlier Anglo-French conflicts?

Critical Thinking Questions

1. "How is it that we hear the loudest yelps for liberty among the drivers of Negroes?" asked Dr. Samuel Johnson, a towering literary figure in 18th-century England, on the eve of the Revolutionary War. Thomas Jefferson, George Washington, Patrick Henry, James Madison, and many other prominent spokesmen for the American cause owned dozens, even hundreds, of slaves. Is there any way that being a large slaveholder might have increased a planter's commitment to liberty as it had come to be understood in England by that time? Did Johnson have a point?
2. The duc de Choiseul, who negotiated the Treaty of Paris that ended the Seven Years' War in 1763, and the comte de Vergennes, who negotiated the Franco-American Alliance of 1778, both claimed that France's decision to cede Canada to Great Britain in 1763 was a masterstroke of French policy because, with no enemy to fear on their borders, the colonies would no longer need British protection and would soon move toward complete independence. By contrast, the leaders of colonial resistance after 1763 always insisted that Britain's postwar policies provoked both the resistance and independence. Who was right?

Identifications

Review your understanding of the following key terms, people, and events for this chapter.

gentleman, p. 84	indigo, p. 86	evangelical, p. 91	King George's War, p. 97
entail, p. 84	Ulster, p. 86	New Side, p. 92	long knives, p. 98
dowry, p. 84	redemptioners, p. 86	Old Side, p. 92	French and Indian War, p. 99
coverture, p. 84	backcountry, p. 86	New Lights, p. 92	Albany Congress, p. 99
dower rights, p. 84	wheat blast, p. 87	Old Lights, p. 92	irregular war, p. 100
sickle cell, p. 85	fiat money, p. 87	patronage, p. 93	bateau, p. 102
task system, p. 85	Enlightenment, p. 88	politics of harmony, p. 93	Cherokee War, p. 104
gang labor, p. 86	Great Awakening, p. 91	republics, p. 95	Peace of Paris, p. 104
Gullah, p. 86	revival, p. 91	privateers, p. 97	

DISCOVERY

What social and political changes occurred in the first half of the 1700s that would help spur the later revolutionary movement?

In thinking about this question, begin by breaking it down into the components shown below. A discussion of the significance of each component should appear in your answer.

Warfare

Look at Map 4.3 on page 103, "Conquest of Canada, 1758–1760." What advantages can you see that the British possessed based solely on geographic position of their settlements? Consider also what you have read in the section "The Years of British Victory" (page 102). What role did the colonists and Indians play in the French and Indian War?

Government and Law

What do the letters G, SC, NC, and so on mean in Benjamin Franklin's snake cartoon? Based on your reading in this chapter and the cartoon, what do you think might have motivated Franklin to create and print this cartoon in his newspaper instead of explaining his opinion in an essay? What kinds of people do you think agreed with him about the advantage of colonial unity? Who might have opposed this kind of union? Why?

The Historical Society of Pennsylvania

BENJAMIN FRANKLIN'S SNAKE CARTOON

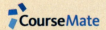

Visit the CourseMate website at www.cengagebrain.com for additional study tools and review materials for this chapter.

5

REFORM, RESISTANCE, REVOLUTION

Britain left an army in North America after 1763 and taxed the colonies to pay part of its cost. The colonists agreed that they should contribute to their own defense but insisted that taxation without representation violated their rights as Englishmen. Three successive crises, provoked by parliamentary taxation, shattered Britain's North American empire. Neither the colonies nor the Crown dared back down, and repeated confrontations eventually led to armed violence. War broke out in April 1775. Fifteen months later the colonies declared their independence.

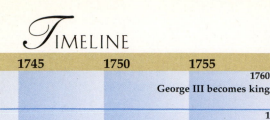

| 1745 | 1750 | 1755 | 1760 | 1765 | 1770 | 1775 | 1780 |

1760
George III becomes king

1763–1765
Grenville ministry enacts reform program for America

1765–1766
Colonists resist Stamp Act and force its repeal

1767–1771
Townshend Revenue Act provokes another round of colonial resistance
• Boston Massacre and repeal of all Townshend duties except that on tea (1770)

1772–1773
12 colonies establish committees of correspondence

1773–1774
Tea Act passes • Boston Tea Party • American Quakers prohibit slaveholding • Parliament passes Coercive (Intolerable) Acts and Quebec Act • First Continental Congress meets in Philadelphia

1775
Revolutionary War begins at Lexington and Concord • Second Continental Congress creates Continental Army • Olive Branch Petition fails and George III issues Proclamation of Rebellion

1776
Paine publishes *Common Sense* • British forced to evacuate Boston • Congress proclaims American independence

© Cengage Learning

IMPERIAL REFORM

In 1760, George III (1760–1820) inherited the British throne at the age of 22. His pronouncements on behalf of religion and virtue at first won him admirers in North America, but the political coalition leading Britain to victory over France fell apart. The king's new ministers set out to reform the empire.

Grenville's Policies

Britain's national debt had nearly doubled during the war with France. The sheer scale of Britain's victory required more revenue just to police the new conquests. In April 1763, **George Grenville** (William Pitt's brother-in-law) became first lord of the treasury, although the king distrusted him and found him barely acceptable. Continuing the policy of his predecessor, John Stuart, earl of Bute, Grenville left 20 battalions (about 7,000 men) in America. Because the colonists would receive the benefit of this protection, Grenville argued, they ought to pay a reasonable portion of the cost, and eventually all of it. He never asked the colonies to contribute anything to Britain's national debt or to urgent domestic needs.

Instead of building on the voluntaristic measures that Pitt had used to win the war, Grenville reverted to the demands for coercive reforms that had characterized Britain's years of defeat from 1755 to 1757. To Grenville, the willing cooperation of the colonies after 1758 exposed the empire's weakness, not its strength. He thought that London had to establish its authority before the colonies slipped completely out of control. He thus set in motion a self-fulfilling prophecy

FOCUS QUESTION

Why was the British Empire more successful in defeating powerful France in a global war than in imposing rather modest reform upon the North American colonies after the victory?

George Grenville *As head of the British government from 1763 to 1765, Grenville passed the Sugar Act, Quartering Act, Currency Act, and the Stamp Act, provoking the imperial crisis of 1765–1766.*

whereby the British government brought about precisely what it was determined to prevent.

Indian Policy and Pontiac's War

The king's **Proclamation of 1763** set up governments in Canada, Florida, and other conquered colonies. It created the so-called Proclamation Line along the Appalachian watershed to regulate the pace of western expansion. No settlements could be planted west of that line unless Britain first purchased the land from the Indians. Settlers would be encouraged to move instead to Nova Scotia, northern New England, Georgia, or Florida. But General Jeffrey Amherst had stopped distributing gifts to the Indians, and his contempt for Indian customs deprived Britain of most of its leverage with them just when their ability to unite had become stronger than ever.

In 1761 Neolin, a western Delaware, reported a vision in which God commanded Indians to return to ancestral ways. Neolin called for an end to Indian dependence on the Anglo-Americans. With unprecedented unity, the Indians struck in 1763. **Pontiac**'s War, named for an Ottawa chief, combined Seneca, Mingo, Delaware, Shawnee, Wyandot, Miami, Ottawa, and other warriors. They attacked 13 British posts in the West, defeated most of them, and besieged Detroit and Fort Pitt. They hoped to drive British settlers back to the eastern seaboard.

Enraged, Amherst ordered the commander at Fort Pitt to distribute smallpox-infested blankets among the western nations, contributing to a lethal epidemic. In 1764, British and provincial forces ended resistance and restored peace. The British then reluctantly accepted the role that the French had played in the Great Lakes region by distributing gifts and mediating differences.

But 10 years of conflict had brutalized the frontiersmen. Perhaps sensing the Indians' growing revulsion against warring with one another, many settlers began to assume that all Indians must be the enemies of all whites. In December 1763, the Scots-Irish of Paxton Township, Pennsylvania, murdered six unarmed Christian Indians—two old men, three women, and a child—at nearby Conestoga. Two weeks later, the "Paxton Boys" slaughtered 14 more Christian Indians at Lancaster. After Governor John Penn removed 140 Moravian mission Indians to Philadelphia for safety, the Paxton Boys marched on the capital, determined to kill them all.

Denouncing the Paxton Boys as "Christian white Savages," Benjamin Franklin led a delegation from the assembly and persuaded them to go home. The Moravian Indians had been spared, but efforts to bring the murderers to justice failed, and Pennsylvania and Virginia frontiersmen virtually declared an open season on Indians that continued for years.

The Sugar Act

In a step that settlers found ominous, Grenville's Sugar Act of 1764 placed duties on Madeira wine, coffee, and other products. Grenville expected the greatest revenue to come from the molasses duty of threepence per gallon. The Molasses Act of 1733 had been designed to keep French molasses out of North America by imposing a prohibitive duty of sixpence per gallon. Instead, merchants had paid a bribe to get French molasses certified as British. By 1760, more than 90 percent of all molasses imported into New England came from the French islands, and nobody seemed to have any interest in stopping the trade.

Proclamation of 1763 *English attempt to prevent the colonists from encroaching upon Indian lands by prohibiting settlement west of the Appalachian watershed unless the government first purchased those lands by treaty.*

Pontiac *An Ottawa chief whose name has been attached to the great Indian uprising against the British in 1763–1764.*

Map 5.1 **Pontiac's War and the Proclamation Line of 1763.** *Britain claimed possession of North America east of the Mississippi, only to face an extraordinary challenge from the Indians of the interior, who wiped out eight garrisons but could not take Detroit, Niagara, or Fort Pitt.*

New England merchants said they were willing to pay a duty of one penny (what bribes were costing them), but Grenville insisted on three. The Sugar Act also targeted smugglers by increasing the paperwork required of ship captains and permitting seizures of ships for what owners considered to be mere technicalities. Finally, it encouraged customs officers to prosecute violators in **vice-admiralty courts**, which did not use juries.

The Currency Act and the Quartering Act

Grenville passed several other imperial measures. The Currency Act of 1764 responded to wartime protests of London merchants against Virginia's paper money, which had lost 15 percent of its value between 1759 and 1764. The act forbade the colonies to issue paper money as legal tender. The money question was urgent because the Sugar Act (and, later, the Stamp Act) required that all duties be paid in **specie** (silver or gold). Supporters of those taxes argued that the new duties would keep the specie in America to pay the army, but the colonists replied that the drain of specie from some colonies would hurt others. While Grenville saw "America" as a single region in which specie would circulate to the benefit of all, the colonists knew better. As of 1765, "America" existed only in British minds, not yet in colonial hearts.

The Quartering Act of 1765, requested by Sir Thomas Gage, Amherst's successor as army commander, asked for authority to quarter soldiers in private homes. Parliament ordered colonial assemblies to vote specific supplies, such as beer and candles, for the troops, which the assemblies were already doing. But it also required the army to quarter its soldiers only in public buildings, such as taverns, which existed in large numbers only in cities. The Quartering Act solved no problems; it created several new ones.

The Stamp Act

In early 1764, when Parliament passed the Sugar Act, Grenville announced that a stamp tax on legal documents and publications might also be needed. Because Parliament had never levied a direct tax on the colonies, however, he knew that he must persuade the settlers that a stamp tax would not be a constitutional innovation. The measure, his supporters insisted, did not violate the principle of no taxation without representation. Each member of Parliament, they argued, represented the entire empire, not just his constituency. The colonists were no different than the large nonvoting majority of subjects within Great Britain. All were **virtually represented** in Parliament. Grenville also denied that any legal difference existed between **external taxes** (port duties, such as that on molasses) and **internal** (or inland) **taxes**, such as the proposed stamp tax.

Grenville indicated that, if the colonies could devise a better revenue plan, he would listen. All 13 colonial assemblies drafted petitions objecting to the **Stamp Act** as a form of taxation without representation. With few exceptions, they also rejected the distinction between internal and external taxes. While agreeing that they ought to contribute to their own defense, they urged the government to return to the traditional method of requisitions, in which the Crown asked a colony for a specific sum, and the assembly decided how (or whether) to raise it.

Parliament refused to receive these petitions. Grenville argued that requisitions had often been tried but had not worked efficiently and never would. He rejected the petitions with a clear conscience. But to the colonists, he had acted in bad faith by asking their advice and then refusing even to consider it.

The Stamp Act passed in February 1765, to go into effect on November 1. All contracts, licenses, commissions, and most other legal documents would be void unless they were executed on officially stamped paper. A stamp duty was put on all newspapers and pamphlets. Playing cards and dice were also taxed.

vice-admiralty courts *These royal courts handled the disposition of enemy ships captured in time of war, adjudicated routine maritime disputes, and occasionally tried to decide cases involving parliamentary regulation of colonial commerce. This last category was the most controversial. These courts did not use juries.*

specie *Also called "hard money" as against paper money. In colonial times, it usually meant silver, but it could also include gold coins.*

virtual representation *The English concept that members of Parliament represented the entire empire, not just a local constituency and its voters. According to this theory, settlers were represented in Parliament in the same way that nonvoting subjects in Britain were represented.*

THE STAMP ACT CRISIS

FOCUS QUESTION

Colonists opposed all taxes by a central legislature that, they claimed, did not represent them. They violently nullified the Stamp Act. Why, in 1766, did they stop resisting and rejoice in its repeal even though the Revenue Act of 1766 continued to tax molasses?

external taxes *Taxes based on oceanic trade, such as port duties. Some colonists thought of them more as a means of regulating trade than as taxes for revenue.*

internal taxes *Taxes that were imposed on land, on people, on retail items, or on legal documents and newspapers (such as the Stamp Act). Most colonists thought that only their elective assemblies had the constitutional power to impose internal taxes.*

Stamp Act *Passed by the administration of George Grenville in 1765, the Stamp Act imposed duties on most legal documents in the colonies and on newspapers and other publications. Massive colonial resistance to the act created a major imperial crisis.*

Liberty Tree *A term for the gallows on which enemies of the people deserved to be hanged. The best known was in Boston.*

nonimportation agreements *Agreements not to import goods from Great Britain. They were designed to put pressure on the British economy and force the repeal of unpopular parliamentary acts.*

Colonial resistance to the Stamp Act began in the spring of 1765. Patrick Henry, a newcomer to the Virginia House of Burgesses, introduced five resolutions on May 30 and 31. His resolves passed by narrow margins; one was rescinded the next day. Henry had two more in his pocket that he decided not to introduce. But over the summer the *Newport Mercury* printed six of Henry's seven resolutions, and the *Maryland Gazette* printed all of them. Neither paper reported that some had not passed. To other colonies, then, Virginia's position seemed far more radical than it really was. The last resolve printed in the *Maryland Gazette* claimed that anyone defending Parliament's right to tax Virginia "shall be Deemed, an Enemy to this his Majesty's Colony."

Eight colonial legislatures passed resolutions condemning the Stamp Act. Nine colonies sent delegates to the Stamp Act Congress, which met in New York in October. It passed resolutions affirming colonial loyalty to the king and "all due subordination" to Parliament but condemned the Stamp and Sugar Acts. By now, nearly all colonial spokesmen agreed that the Stamp Act was unconstitutional and should be repealed. They accepted the idea of virtual representation *within* the colonies—their assemblies, they said, represented both voters and nonvoters in each colony—but they ridiculed the argument when it was applied across the Atlantic. A disfranchised Englishman who acquired sufficient property could become a voter, but no colonist could ever vote for a member of Parliament. Members of Parliament paid the taxes that they levied on people within Britain, but they would never pay any tax they imposed on the colonies.

Nullification

Resolutions and pamphlets alone could not defeat the Stamp Act. Street violence might, however, and in Boston men calling themselves the "Sons of Liberty" showed the way. On August 14 the town awoke to find an effigy of Andrew Oliver, the stamp distributor, hanging on what became the town's **Liberty Tree** (a gallows for hanging effigies of enemies of the people). After dark a crowd of men roamed the streets, shouted defiance at the governor and council, demolished a new building Oliver was erecting, beheaded and burned Oliver's effigy, and invaded his home. He had already fled.

On August 26, an even angrier crowd all but demolished the mansion of Lt. Governor Thomas Hutchinson, whom they believed had helped to draft the Stamp Act in letters to British friends. In fact, he had opposed it. The militia finally appeared to police the streets, but when Governor Francis Bernard tried to arrest those responsible for the first riot, he got nowhere. Bostonians deplored the events of August 26 but approved those of August 14. No one was punished for either riot.

Everywhere except Georgia, the stamp master was forced to resign before the law took effect on November 1. With no one to distribute the stamps, the act could not be implemented. Merchants adopted **nonimportation agreements** to pressure the British into repeal. In other cities the Sons of Liberty followed Boston's lead and took control of the streets. Violent resistance worked. The Stamp Act was nullified—even in Georgia, eventually.

Repeal

The next move was up to Britain. Charles Watson-Wentworth, marquess of Rockingham, had succeeded Grenville as first lord of the treasury in October 1765. Rockingham came to believe that the only alternative to repeal was a ruinous civil war in America, but he could hardly tell Parliament that the world's greatest empire must yield to unruly mobs. Needing a better reason, he began to mobilize British merchants and manufacturers who traded with America. They petitioned Parliament for repeal of the Stamp Act, which had been an economic disaster for them. Their arguments gave Rockingham the leverage he needed. When William Pitt eloquently demanded repeal in the House of Commons on January 14, 1766, Rockingham gained a powerful, though temporary, ally. Rockingham brought the king around by threatening to resign, which would have forced the king to bring back Grenville, whom he hated.

Three pieces of legislation ended the crisis. The first, the Declaratory Act, affirmed that Parliament had "full power and authority to make laws and statutes of sufficient force and validity to bind the colonies...in all cases whatsoever." Rockingham resisted pressure to insert the word "taxes" along with "laws and statutes." That omission permitted the colonists, who drew a sharp distinction between legislation (which, they conceded, Parliament had a right to pass) and taxation (which it could not), to interpret the act as an affirmation of their position, while nearly everyone in Britain read precisely the opposite meaning into the phrase "laws and statutes." The colonists saw the Declaratory Act as a face-saving gesture that made repeal possible.

The second measure repealed the Stamp Act as "greatly detrimental to the commercial interests" of the empire. The third, the Revenue Act of 1766, reduced the duty on molasses from threepence per gallon to one penny, but imposed it on all

"THE REPEAL OR THE FUNERAL OF MISS AMERICA-STAMP." *This London cartoon of 1766 shows George Grenville carrying the coffin of the Stamp Act with Lord Bute behind him. Contemporaries would easily have identified the other personalities.*

Courtesy of the John Carter Brown Library at Brown University

molasses, British or foreign. Although the act was more favorable to the molasses trade than any other law yet passed by Parliament, it was clearly a revenue measure, and it generated more income for the empire than any other colonial tax. Few colonists attacked it for violating the principle of no taxation without representation. In Britain it seemed that the colonists objected only to internal taxes but would accept external duties.

The colonists greeted repeal with wild celebrations. Yet neither side fully appreciated the significance of the misunderstandings that had made repeal possible. Both sides had rejected the distinction between internal and external taxes. They could find no legal or philosophical basis for condemning the one while approving the other. Parliament had tried to extend its authority over the internal affairs of the colonies and had failed, but it continued to collect port duties in the colonies, some to regulate trade, others for revenue. No one could justify this division of authority, but the external-internal cleavage marked the boundary between what Parliament could do on its own and what the Crown could do only with the consent of the colonists.

Another misunderstanding was equally grave. Only the riots had created a crisis severe enough to push Parliament into repeal. Both sides, however, preferred to believe that economic pressure had been decisive. For the colonies, this conviction set the pattern of resistance for the next two imperial crises.

THE TOWNSHEND CRISIS

FOCUS QUESTION

If the colonists condemned all parliamentary taxes for revenue, why did effective resistance to the Townshend Revenue Act take so long to organize, and why did it cease before achieving total repeal?

The goodwill created by repeal did not last. In 1766, the king dismissed Rockingham and persuaded William Pitt to form a government. Pitt's ministry faced serious opposition within Parliament. Pitt compounded that problem by accepting a peerage as earl of Chatham, a decision that removed his compelling oratory from the House of Commons and left Charles Townshend as his spokesman in that chamber. A witty, extemporaneous speaker, Townshend had betrayed every leader he ever served. The only consistent policy in his political career had been his hard-line attitude toward the colonies.

The Townshend Program

A central aspect of Townshend's annual budget was the **Townshend Revenue Act** of 1767, which imposed new duties on imports that the colonies could legally buy only from Britain: tea, paper, glass, red and white lead, and painter's colors. But Townshend also removed more duties on tea within Britain than he could offset with the new revenue collected in the colonies. His real goal, clearly, was to use the new revenues to pay the salaries of governors and judges in the colonies, thereby freeing them from dependence on the assemblies. This devious strategy convinced many colonists that men in the British government were plotting to deprive them of their liberties.

The British army also began to withdraw from nearly all frontier posts and concentrate near the coast. Although the primary motive was to save money, the implications were striking: An army far distant from the frontier presumably existed only to police the colonists themselves. Why should they pay costs to enforce policies that would undermine their liberties?

Townshend ridiculed the distinction between internal and external taxes but declared that he would honor it anyway. Then, having won approval for his

Townshend Revenue Act
Passed by Parliament in 1767, this act imposed import duties on tea, paper, glass, red and white lead, and painter's colors. It provoked the imperial crisis of 1767–1770. In 1770 Parliament repealed all of the duties except the one on tea.

program, he died suddenly in September 1767 and passed on to others the dilemmas he had created. Frederick, Lord North, replaced him as chancellor of the exchequer. Chatham resigned, and the duke of Grafton became prime minister.

Resistance: The Politics of Escalation

Defeating the Townshend Revenue Act would prove tougher than nullifying the Stamp Act. Parliament had never been able to impose its will on the internal affairs of the colonies, as the Stamp Act fiasco demonstrated, but it did control the seas. Goods subject to duties might be aboard any of hundreds of ships arriving from Britain each year, but screening the cargo of every vessel threatened to impose enormous burdens on the Sons of Liberty. General nonimportation would be easier to implement, but British trade played a bigger role in the colonial economy than North American trade did in Britain's.

To hurt Britain a little, the colonies would have to harm themselves a lot. In October 1767, the Boston town meeting encouraged greater use of home manufactures and authorized the voluntary nonconsumption of British goods. But no organized resistance developed, and the Townshend duties became operative in November with little opposition. A month later, John Dickinson, a Philadelphia lawyer, tried to rouse his fellow colonists to action through 12 urgent letters printed in nearly every colonial newspaper. These anonymous *Letters from a Farmer in Pennsylvania* denied the distinction between internal and external taxes and insisted that all parliamentary taxes for revenue violated the colonists' rights.

Massachusetts again set the pace of resistance. In February 1768, its assembly petitioned the king, but not Parliament, against the new measures. Without waiting for a reply, it also sent a Circular Letter to the other assemblies, urging them to pursue "constitutional measures" of resistance against the Quartering Act, the new taxes, and their use in paying the salaries of governors and judges.

Wills Hill, earl of Hillsborough and secretary of state for the American colonies (an office created in 1768), responded so sharply that he turned tepid opposition into serious resistance. He directed the Massachusetts assembly to rescind the Circular Letter and ordered all governors to dissolve any assembly that accepted it. In June 1768, the Massachusetts House voted 92 to 17 not to rescind. Even assemblies that had shown little interest in the Townshend program, particularly in the southern colonies where governors already had fixed salaries, bristled when told what they could or could not debate. They took up the Circular Letter or began to draft their own. One by one, the assemblies were dissolved until government by consent seemed in serious peril.

In response, colonists pursued both economic sanctions and street protests. Nonimportation agreements at last began to take hold, first in Boston and New York in March 1768, and then in Philadelphia on January 1, 1769. Spurred on by the popular but mistaken belief that the nonimportation agreement of 1765 had forced Parliament to repeal the Stamp Act, the colonists hoped that economic activism could subvert the Townshend duties.

On the streets, the next escalation again came from Boston. On March 18, 1768, the town's celebration of the anniversary of the Stamp Act's repeal grew so raucous that the governor and customs officials asked Hillsborough for troops. He ordered General Gage, based in New York, to send two regiments to Boston from Nova Scotia. On June 10, before Gage could respond, Bostonians rioted after customs collectors seized John Hancock's sloop *Liberty* for smuggling Madeira wine (taxed under the Sugar Act) on its *previous* voyage. By waiting until the ship had a new cargo, informers and customs officials could split larger shares when the sloop

PAUL REVERE'S ENGRAVING OF THE BRITISH ARMY LANDING IN BOSTON, 1768. *The navy approached the city in battle array, a sight familiar to veterans of the French wars. To emphasize the peaceful, Christian character of Boston, Revere exaggerated the height of the church steeples.*

was condemned. Terrified by the fury of the popular response, the commissioners fled to Castle William in Boston Harbor and again petitioned Hillsborough for troops. He sent two more regiments from Ireland.

The public response stunned Governor Bernard. The Boston town meeting asked him to summon the legislature, which he had dissolved in June after it stood by its Circular Letter. When Bernard refused, the Sons of Liberty asked the other towns to elect delegates to a "convention" in Boston. The convention had no legal standing in the colony's government. When it met, it accepted Boston's definition of colonial grievances but refused to sanction violence.

An Experiment in Military Coercion

In early October, the British fleet entered Boston Harbor in battle array and landed 1,000 soldiers. Massachusetts had built barracks—in Castle William, miles away on an island in Boston Harbor, where soldiers could hardly function as a police force. Since the Quartering Act prohibited attempts to quarter soldiers on private property, the soldiers pitched their tents on Boston Common and eventually took over a building that had been the Boston poorhouse. The regiments from Ireland joined them later.

Colonial newspapers reported almost every clash between soldiers and civilians in Boston. When news of the Massachusetts convention reached Britain, the House of Lords passed a set of resolutions calling for the deportation of colonial political offenders to England for trial. Instead of quashing dissent, this threat to colonial political autonomy infuriated the southern colonies. Virginia, Maryland, and South Carolina now adopted nonimportation agreements. Up and down the continent, the feeble resistance of mid-1768 became more formidable in 1769.

The Boston Massacre

In late 1769 the Boston Sons of Liberty turned to direct confrontation with the army, and the city again faced a crisis. Under English **common law**, soldiers could not fire on civilians without an order from a civil magistrate, except in self-defense when their lives were in danger. By the fall of 1769, no magistrate dared to issue such a command.

By 1770 the soldiers often felt under siege, and, in March, tensions between soldiers and citizens reached a fatal climax. Off-duty soldiers often supplemented their meager wages with part-time employment, a practice that angered local **artisans** who resented the competition. On Friday, March 2, 1770, three soldiers visited John Hancock's wharf. "Soldier, will you work?" asked Samuel Gray, a ropemaker. "Yes," replied one. "Then go and clean my shit house," sneered Gray. After an ugly brawl, Gray's employer persuaded their colonel to confine his men to barracks. Peace prevailed through the Puritan Sabbath, but everyone expected trouble on Monday, March 5.

After dark on Monday, civilians and soldiers clashed at several places. A crowd hurling snowballs and rocks closed in on the lone sentinel guarding the hated customs house. The guard called for help. Eight soldiers rushed to his aid and loaded their weapons. Captain Thomas Preston took command and ordered the soldiers to drive the attackers slowly back with fixed bayonets. The crowd taunted the soldiers, daring them to fire. One soldier apparently slipped, discharging his musket into the air as he fell. The others then fired into the crowd, killing five and wounding six. One of the victims was Samuel Gray; another was Crispus Attucks, a man of African and Indian ancestry.

Preston and six of his men stood trial for murder and were defended, brilliantly, by two radical patriot lawyers, John Adams and Josiah Quincy Jr., who believed that every accused person ought to have a proper defense. Preston and four of the soldiers were acquitted. The other two were convicted only of manslaughter, branded on the thumb, and released. The **Boston Massacre**, as the Sons of Liberty called this encounter, represented the failure of Britain's first attempt at military coercion.

Partial Repeal

The day of the massacre marked a turning point in Britain as well, for on March 5 Lord North, now the prime minister, asked Parliament to repeal the Townshend duties, except the one on tea. He claimed to be retaining only a vestige of the Townshend Revenue Act while repealing the substance. In fact, he did the opposite. Tea provided nearly three-fourths of the revenue under the act. By repealing all other duties but retaining that on tea, North kept the substance but gave up the shadow.

This news reached the colonies just after nonimportation had achieved its greatest success in 1769 (see Table 5.1). The colonies reduced imports by about one-third from what they had been in 1768, but the impact on Britain was slight. North had hoped that partial repeal, although it would not placate all the colonists, would at least divide them. It did. Most merchants favored renewed importation of everything but tea, while the Sons of Liberty, most of whom were artisans, still supported broad nonimportation to sustain demand for their own manufactures. North's repeal was followed by an orgy of importation of British goods, setting record highs everywhere.

common law *The heart of the English legal system was based on precedents and judicial decisions. Common-law courts offered due process through such devices as trial by jury, which usually consisted of local men.*

artisan *A skilled laborer who works with his or her hands. In early America, artisans often owned their own shops and produced goods for general sale or for special order.*

Boston Massacre *The colonial term for the confrontation between colonial protestors and British soldiers in front of the customs house on March 5, 1770. Five colonists were killed and six wounded.*

TABLE 5.1

EXPORTS IN £000 STERLING FROM ENGLAND AND SCOTLAND TO THE AMERICAN COLONIES, 1766–1775										
Colony	1766	1767	1768	1769	1770	1771	1772	1773	1774	1775
New England	419	416	431	224	417	1,436*	844	543	577	85.0
New York	333	424	491	76	480	655*	349	296	460	1.5
Pennsylvania	334	383	442	205	140	747*	526	436	646	1.4
Chesapeake†	520	653	670	715	997*	1,224*	1,016	589	690	1.9
Lower South‡	376	292	357	385*	228	515*	575*	448	471	130.5
Totals	1,982	2,168	2,391	1,605	2,262	4,577*	3,310	2,312	2,844	220.3

Average total exports, 1766–1768 = £2,180

1769 = 73.6% of that average, or 67.1% of 1768 exports

1770 = 103.8% of that average, or 94.6% of 1768 exports

*These totals surpassed all previous highs.

†Chesapeake = Maryland and Virginia.

‡Lower South = Carolinas and Georgia.

Source: U.S. Bureau of the Census, *Historical Statistics of the United States, Colonial Times to 1970* (Washington, DC, 1975), II, 1176–78, as corrected by the original compiler, Jacob Price.

© Cengage Learning

Disaffection

The Quartering Act expired quietly in 1770; some of the more objectionable features of the vice-admiralty courts were softened; and the Currency Act of 1764 was repealed in stages between 1770 and 1773. Yet North had not restored confidence in the justice and decency of the British government. To a degree now difficult to appreciate, the empire ran on trust, or voluntarism, what people at the time called "affection." Its opposite, *dis*affection, had a more literal and dangerous meaning to them than it does today.

Many colonists blamed one another for failing to win complete repeal. Bostonians, for example, lamented the "immortal shame and infamy" of New Yorkers for abandoning resistance. These recriminations, gratifying as they seemed to British officials, masked a vast erosion of trust in the imperial government. The colonists were angry with one another for failing to appreciate how menacing British policy still was. The tea duty remained a sliver in a wound that would not heal.

That fear sometimes broke through the surface calm between 1770 and 1773. In 1772, a predatory customs vessel, the *Gaspée*, ran aground in Rhode Island while pursuing peaceful coastal ships. After dark, men with blackened faces boarded the *Gaspée*, wounded its captain, and burned the ship. British efforts to find the perpetrators failed because no one would talk.

Twelve colonial assemblies considered the threat so ominous that they created permanent **committees of correspondence** to keep in touch with one another and *anticipate* new threats to their liberties. When Governor Hutchinson announced in 1773 that Massachusetts Superior Court justices would receive their salaries from the imperial treasury, Boston created its own committee of correspondence and urged other towns to do the same. Most towns of any size followed Boston's lead. Even moderates now believed that the British government was conspiring to destroy liberty in America.

committees of correspondence
Bodies formed on both the local and colonial levels that played an important role in exchanging ideas and information. They spread primarily anti-British material and were an important step in the first tentative unity of people in different colonies.

The Boston Massacre trials and the *Gaspée* affair convinced London that it was pointless to prosecute individuals for politically motivated crimes. At the same time, the use of force against entire communities could lead to outright war. The spread of committees of correspondence throughout the colonies suggested that settlers who had been unable to unite against New France at Albany in 1754 now deemed unity against Britain essential to their liberties. By 1773, several New England newspapers were calling on the colonies to create a formal union.

In effect, the Townshend crisis never ended. With the tea duty standing as a symbol of Parliament's right to tax the colonies without their consent, genuine imperial harmony was becoming impossible. This crisis was a far more accurate predictor of future behavior than response to the Stamp Act had been. Nearly everyone had denounced the Stamp Act. By contrast, most merchants and lawyers who resisted nonimportation in 1768 became loyalists by 1775. Artisans, merchants, and lawyers who supported the boycotts, especially those who favored continuing them past 1770, became patriots.

The Contagion of Liberty: Slaves and Women

All the talk of liberty led some colonists to question the persistence of slavery in their midst. Around the middle of the 18th century, an antislavery movement on both sides of the Atlantic attracted both future patriots and loyalists. In the 1740s and 1750s, Quaker abolitionists urged their brethren to free their slaves. In the 1750s, the Quaker Yearly Meeting placed the slave trade off limits and finally, in 1774, forbade slaveholding altogether. Any Friend who did not comply by 1779 would be disowned. Britain's Methodist leader John Wesley also attacked slavery, as did several colonial disciples of Jonathan Edwards. Many evangelicals began to agree that slavery was a sin.

By the 1760s, supporters of slavery found that they now had to defend the institution. Hardly anyone had bothered to do so earlier, but as equal rights became a popular topic, some colonists suggested that *all* people could claim these rights. Slavery, declared Patrick Henry, "is as repugnant to humanity as it is inconsistent with the Bible and destructive of liberty." In England, Granville Sharp, an early abolitionist, brought the Somerset case before the Court of King's Bench in 1771 and compelled a famous judgment, that slavery was incompatible with the "free air" of England. That decision enabled many of England's 10,000 or 15,000 blacks to claim their freedom.

New Englanders began to head in similar directions. Two women played leading roles in the movement. Sarah Osborn, a widow in Newport, Rhode Island, opened a school in 1744 to support her family. She also taught women and blacks and began holding evening religious meetings, which turned into a large revival. At one point in the 1760s about one-sixth of Newport's Africans were attending her school. That made them the most literate African population in the colonies, although they were living in the colonial city most deeply involved in the African slave trade. Osborn's students supported abolition of the slave trade and, later, of slavery itself.

In 1761, an eight-year-old girl who would become known as **Phillis Wheatley** arrived in Boston from Africa and was purchased by wealthy John Wheatley as a servant for his wife, Susannah, who treated her more like a daughter than a slave and taught her to read and write. In 1767, Phillis published her first poem in Boston, and she visited London as a celebrity in 1773 after a volume of her poetry was published there. Her poems deplored slavery but rejoiced in the Christianization of Africans. The Wheatleys emancipated her after her return to Boston.

Phillis Wheatley *Wheatley, a slave, published her first poem in Boston in 1767. In 1773, she visited London to celebrate the publication there of a volume of her poetry, an event that made her a transatlantic sensation.*

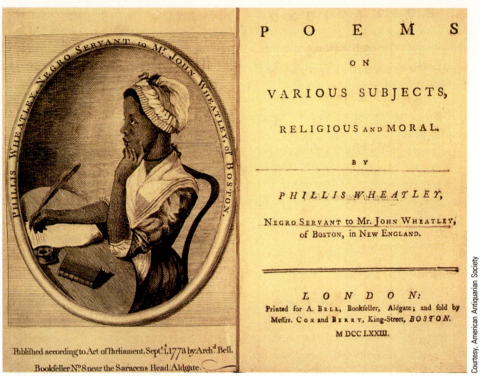

PHILLIS WHEATLEY. *Engraving of Phillis Wheatley opposite the title page of her collected poems, published in 1773.*

Soon many of Boston's blacks sensed an opportunity for emancipation. On several occasions in 1773 and 1774 they petitioned the legislature or the governor for freedom, pointing out that, although they had never forfeited their natural rights, they were being "held in slavery in the bowels of a free and Christian Country." When the legislature passed a bill on their behalf, Governor Hutchinson vetoed it. Boston slaves made it clear to General Gage, Hutchinson's successor, that they would serve him as a loyal militia in exchange for their freedom. Many patriots began to rally to their cause.

The patriots could look to another group of allies as well. Many women became indispensable to the broader resistance movement. They could not vote or hold office, but without their willing support, nonimportation would have been a fiasco. In thousands of households, women joined the discussions about liberty and agreed to make homespun clothing to take the place of imported British textiles. Freedom's ferment made a heady wine. After 1773, any direct challenge to British power would trigger enormous social changes within the colonies.

THE LAST IMPERIAL CRISIS

FOCUS QUESTION

Why did the colonists start a revolution after the Tea Act of 1773 lowered the price of tea?

The surface calm between 1770 and 1773 ended when Lord North moved to save the East India Company from bankruptcy. Without solving the company's problems, North created a crisis too big for Britain to handle.

The Tea Crisis

The East India Company was being undersold in England and the colonies by smuggled Dutch tea. North's Tea Act of 1773 repealed import duties on tea in England but retained the Townshend duty in the colonies. In both places, North estimated, legal tea would be cheaper than anyone else's. The company would be saved, and the settlers, to get cheap legal tea, would accept Parliament's right to tax them.

Another aspect of the Tea Act antagonized most colonial merchants. It gave the company a monopoly on the shipping and distribution of tea in the colonies. Only a few consignees in each port would have the exclusive right to sell it. The combined dangers of taxation and monopoly again forged the coalition of artisans and merchants that had helped to defeat the Stamp Act by 1766 and resist the Townshend Act by 1769. Patriots saw the Tea Act as a Trojan horse that would destroy liberty by seducing the settlers into accepting parliamentary sovereignty.

North also unintentionally gave an advantage to those determined to resist the Tea Act. He had devised an oceanic, or external, measure that the colonists could actually nullify despite British control of the seas. No one would have to police the entire waterfront looking for tea importers. The patriots had only to wait for the specially chartered tea ships and prevent their cargoes from landing.

Direct threats usually did the job. Most tea ships quickly departed—except in Boston. There, Governor Hutchinson decided to face down the radicals. He refused to grant clearance papers to three tea ships that, under the law, had to pay the Townshend duty within 21 days of arrival or face seizure. Hutchinson meant to force them to land the tea and pay the duty. This deadline led to urgent mass meetings for several weeks and, finally, a major crisis. Convinced that they had no other way to block the landing of the tea, the radicals organized the **Boston Tea Party**. Disguised as Indians, they threw 342 chests of tea, worth about £11,000 sterling (more than $700,000 in today's dollars), into Boston Harbor on the night of December 16, 1773.

Britain's Response: The Coercive Acts

This willful destruction of private property shocked both Britain and America. Convinced that severe punishment was essential to British credibility, Parliament passed four Coercive Acts during the spring of 1774. The Boston Port Act closed the port of Boston until the town paid for the tea. A new Quartering Act allowed the army to quarter soldiers among civilians if necessary. The Administration of Justice Act permitted a British soldier or official charged with a crime while carrying out his duties to be tried in another colony or in England. Most controversial of all, the Massachusetts Government Act overturned the Massachusetts Charter of 1691, made the council appointive, and restricted town meetings. In effect, it made Massachusetts like other royal colonies.

Parliament passed a fifth law, unrelated to the Coercive Acts but significant nonetheless. The Quebec Act established French civil law and the Roman Catholic Church in the Province of Quebec, provided for trial by jury in criminal but not in civil cases, gave legislative but not taxing power to an appointive governor and council, and extended Quebec's administrative boundaries to the area between the Great Lakes and the Ohio River. The colonists saw the Quebec Act as a deliberate revival of the power of New France and the Catholic Church on their northern border, now bolstered by Britain's naval and military might. The Quebec Act intensified the fear that evil ministers in London were conspiring to destroy British and colonial liberties. The settlers lumped the Quebec Act with the **Coercive Acts** and coined their own name for all of them—the **Intolerable Acts**.

The Radical Explosion

General Gage, already the commander of the British army in North America, took over as governor of Massachusetts in May 1774, before passage of the Massachusetts Government Act. In June, he closed the ports of Boston and Charlestown, just

Boston Tea Party *In December 1773, Boston's Sons of Liberty threw 342 chests of East India Company tea into Boston Harbor rather than allow them to be landed and the hated tea duty to be paid.*

Coercive (Intolerable) Acts *Four statutes passed by Parliament in response to the Boston Tea Party, including one that closed the port of Boston until the tea was paid for, and another that overturned the Massachusetts Charter of 1691. The colonists called them the Intolerable Acts and included the Quebec Act under that label.*

north of Boston. Colonists responded with calls for a colonial union and for immediate nonimportation and nonconsumption of British goods. In New York City, however, a mass meeting rejected immediate nonimportation in favor of an intercolonial congress. Philadelphia followed New York's lead. In both cities, cautious merchants hoped that a congress might postpone or prevent radical measures of resistance.

North assumed that the Coercive Acts would isolate Boston from the rest of the province, Massachusetts from the rest of New England, and New England from the other colonies. Instead, contributions began pouring in from all the colonies to help Boston survive. When royal governors outside Massachusetts dismissed their assemblies to prevent them from joining the resistance movement, the colonists elected **provincial congresses**, or conventions, to organize resistance. As the congresses took hold, royal government began to collapse almost everywhere. Numerous calls for a continental congress made the movement irresistible. By June, it was obvious that an intercolonial congress would adopt nonimportation.

News of the Massachusetts Government Act arrived on August 6. Gage's authority disintegrated when he tried to enforce the act. The councilors whom Gage appointed to the new upper house under the act either resigned or fled to Boston to seek the army's protection. The Superior Court could not hold its sessions because jurors refused to take an oath under the new act. At the county level (the real center of royal power in the colony), popular conventions closed the courts and took charge in August and September. In October, Massachusetts towns sent 200 delegates to Concord, where they organized the Massachusetts Provincial Congress. That body became the de facto government of the colony and implemented radical demands such as the creation of a special force of armed "minutemen" and the payment of taxes to the congress in Concord, not to Gage in Boston. The Provincial Congress also collected military stores at Concord.

By then, Gage's power was limited to the Boston area, which the army held. Thoroughly frustrated, he wrote North on October 30 that "a small Force rather encourages Resistance than terrifys." He stunned London by asking for 20,000 redcoats, nearly as many as had been needed to conquer Canada.

The First Continental Congress

Twelve colonies (all but Georgia) sent delegates to Philadelphia in September 1774 for the **First Continental Congress**. The delegates scarcely even debated nonimportation, which they agreed should finally be extended to molasses, and they were almost unanimous in adopting nonexportation if Britain did not redress colonial grievances by September 1775. Nonexportation was much more radical than nonimportation because it raised the threat of repudiating debts to British merchants, which colonial exports normally paid for.

The Congress spent three weeks trying to define colonial rights. Everyone insisted that the Intolerable Acts and all surviving revenue acts had to be repealed and that infringements on trial by jury had to be rejected. They affirmed the new principle of no *legislation* without consent—but added a saving clause that affirmed colonial assent to acts of Parliament that *only* regulated their trade.

Congress petitioned the king, not Parliament, because patriots no longer recognized Parliament as a legitimate legislature for the colonies. It agreed to meet again in May 1775 if the British response was inadequate. And it created the **Association**—with citizen committees in every community—to enforce its trade sanctions against Britain. In approving the Association, Congress began to act as a central government for the united colonies.

provincial congress *A type of convention elected by the colonists to organize resistance. They tended to be larger than the legal assemblies they displaced, and they played a major role in politicizing the countryside.*

First Continental Congress *This intercolonial body met in Philadelphia in September and October 1774 to organize resistance against the Intolerable Acts by defining American rights, petitioning the king, and appealing to the British and American people. It created the Association, local committees in each community to enforce nonimportation.*

Association *Groups created by the First Continental Congress as local committees to enforce its trade sanctions against Britain. Their creation signaled that Congress was beginning to act as a central government.*

Toward War

Lord North still hoped for a peaceful solution, but in January 1775, he made war inevitable. He ordered Gage to send troops to Concord, destroy the arms stored there, and arrest leading patriots John Hancock and Samuel Adams. Only after sending this dispatch did he introduce his Conciliatory Proposition. Parliament pledged that it would tax no colony that paid its share for imperial defense and gave proper salaries to its royal officials, but Britain would use force against delinquent colonies. To reassure hard-liners that he was not turning soft, North introduced the New England Restraining Act, which barred New Englanders from the Atlantic fisheries and banned all commerce between New England and any place except Britain and the British West Indies— precisely the trade routes that Congress was blocking through nonimportation.

North's orders to Gage arrived before the Conciliatory Proposition reached America, and Gage obeyed. He hoped to surprise Concord with a predawn march, but Boston radicals knew about the expedition almost as soon as the orders were written. They had already made careful preparations to alert the whole countryside. Their informant, in all likelihood, was Gage's wife, Margaret Kemble Gage, a New Jerseyan by birth. At 2 a.m. on April 19, about 700 elite troops began their march toward Concord. Paul Revere, a Boston silversmith, galloped west with the news that "The redcoats are coming!" When Revere was captured past Lexington by a British patrol, Dr. Samuel Prescott managed to get

ENGAGEMENT AT THE NORTH BRIDGE IN CONCORD, APRIL 19, 1775. *This 1775 painting by Ralph Earl is quite accurate in its details. It shows the first American military victory in the war when the militia drove the British back from Concord Bridge and eventually through Lexington and all the way to Boston.*

Battle of Lexington *The first military engagement of the Revolutionary War. It occurred on April 19, 1775, when British soldiers fired into a much smaller body of minutemen on Lexington Green.*

the message through to Concord. As the British approached Lexington Green at dawn, they found 60 to 70 militiamen drawn up to face them. The outnumbered militia began to withdraw. Then somebody—probably a colonial bystander but possibly a British solider—fired the first shot in what became the **Battle of Lexington**. The British line fired, killing eight and wounding nine. With fifes playing and drums beating (secrecy had become pointless), the British resumed their march to Concord. From every direction, like angry hornets, the whole countryside swarmed toward them.

THE IMPROVISED WAR

FOCUS QUESTION

How and why did a resistance movement dedicated to protecting the colonists' rights as Englishmen end by proclaiming American independence instead?

In April 1775, neither side had a plan for winning a major war. Gage sent soldiers to enforce acts of Parliament. The militia fought for a political regime that Parliament was trying to change. They drove the British from Concord Bridge and pursued them all the way to Boston. Had a relief force not met the battered British survivors near Lexington, all of them might have been lost.

Lacking an adequate command or supply structure, the colonists besieged Boston. After two months, Gage finally declared that all settlers bearing arms, and those who aided them, were rebels and traitors. He offered to pardon anyone (except John Hancock and Samuel Adams) who returned to his allegiance. Instead of complying, the besiegers escalated the struggle. They fortified the high ground on Breed's Hill (next to Bunker Hill), overlooking Boston. The British sent 2,400 men, one-fifth of the garrison, to take the hills on June 17. Secure behind their defenses, the settlers shot more than 1,000 redcoats before running out of ammunition and withdrawing. The defenders suffered about 370 casualties, nearly all during the retreat.

Well into 1776 both sides fought an improvised war. In May 1775, Vermont and Massachusetts militia took Fort Ticonderoga on Lake Champlain and seized the artillery and gunpowder that would be used months later to end the siege of Boston. Crown Point also fell. With nearly all of their forces in Boston, the British were too weak to defend other positions. The collapse of royal government meant that the rebels now controlled the militia and most of the royal powder houses.

The militia became the key to political allegiance. Compulsory service with the militia politicized many waverers, who decided that they really were patriots when redcoats shot at them or when they drove a loyalist into exile. The militia kept the countryside committed to the Revolution wherever the British army was too weak to overwhelm them.

QUICK REVIEW

THE THIRD IMPERIAL CRISIS

- Tea Act provoked Boston Tea Party

- Parliament responded with Boston Port Act, Massachusetts Government Act, and two other Coercive Acts

- Colonial reaction: Continental Congress imposed trade sanctions; Massachusetts nullified Massachusetts Government Act and collected military supplies at Concord

- War began after Governor Gage sent the army to confiscate those arms

- Second Continental Congress's failure of conciliation and the movement toward independence

The Second Continental Congress

The **Second Continental Congress** met in May 1775. For months it pursued conflicting strategies of resistance and conciliation. It voted to turn the undisciplined men besieging Boston into a Continental Army. On June 15, at the urging of John Adams of Massachusetts, Congress made George Washington of Virginia the army's commanding general. Washington was appalled at the soldiers' poor discipline and their casual familiarity with their officers. He insisted that officers behave with dignity and instill obedience. As the months passed, most of them won his respect. At year's end, however, nearly all of the men went home, and Washington had to train a new army for 1776. But enthusiasm for the cause remained strong and new volunteers soon filled his camp.

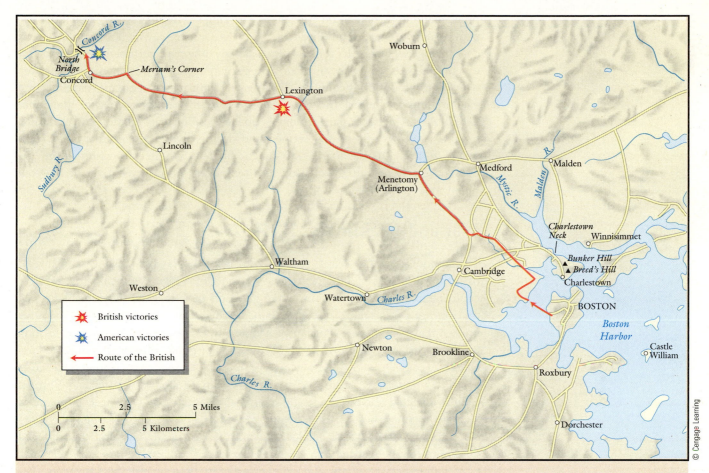

Map 5.2 **Lexington, Concord, and Boston, 1775–1776.** *The British march to Lexington and Concord on April 19, 1775, touched off the Revolutionary War. The colonists drove the redcoats back to Boston and then besieged the city for 11 months until the British withdrew.*

In June 1775, Congress authorized an invasion of Canada to win over the French before they could side with the British and attack New York or New England. Two forces moved northward. One, under General Richard Montgomery, took Montreal in November. The other, commanded by Colonel Benedict Arnold, laid siege to Quebec, where Montgomery joined Arnold in December. With enlistments about to expire, they decided to assault the city. Their attack in a blizzard on December 31 was a disaster. Nearly half of the 900 men still with them were killed, wounded, or captured. Montgomery was killed and Arnold wounded. Both were hailed as American heroes.

The colonial objective in this fighting was still to restore government by consent under the Crown. After rejecting Lord North's Conciliatory Proposition, Congress approved an Olive Branch Petition to George III on July 5, 1775, in the hope of ending the bloodshed. Moderates, led by John Dickinson, strongly favored the measure. The petition affirmed the colonists' loyalty to the Crown, did not even mention "rights," and implored the king to take the initiative in devising "a happy and permanent reconciliation." Another document, written mostly by Virginia's Thomas Jefferson, "The Declaration of the Causes and Necessities of Taking Up Arms," set forth the colonies' grievances and justified their armed resistance. Like the Olive Branch Petition, the declaration assured the British "that we mean not to dissolve that Union which has so long and so happily subsisted between us." It reached London along with news of Bunker Hill. George III replied with a formal

Second Continental Congress
The intercolonial body that met in Philadelphia in May 1775. It organized the Continental Army, appointed George Washington commander in chief, and simultaneously pursued policies of military resistance and conciliation. When conciliation failed, it chose independence in July 1776.

proclamation of rebellion on August 23. The king's refusal to receive this moderate petition strengthened the radicals.

Congress began to function increasingly like a government, but with few exceptions, it assumed royal rather than parliamentary powers, which were taken over by the individual colonies. Congress did not tax or regulate trade, beyond encouraging nonimportation. It passed no laws. It took command of the Continental Army, printed paper money, opened diplomatic relations with Indian nations, took over the postal service, and decided which government was legitimate in individual colonies—all functions that had been performed by the Crown. Congress thought of itself as a temporary plural executive for the continent, not as a legislature.

War and Legitimacy, 1775–1776

Throughout 1775, the British reacted with fitful displays of violence and threats of turning slaves and Indians against the settlers. When the weak British forces could neither restore order nor make good on their threats, they conciliated no one, enraged thousands, and undermined British claims to legitimacy. The navy burned Falmouth (now Portland), Maine, in October. On November 7, John Murray, earl of Dunmore and governor of Virginia, offered freedom to any slaves of rebel planters who would join his 200 redcoats. About 800 slaves mustered under his banner only to fall victim to smallpox after the Virginia militia defeated them in a single action. On January 1, Dunmore bombarded Norfolk in retaliation, setting several buildings ablaze. The patriots, who considered Norfolk a loyalist bastion, burned the rest of the city and then blamed Dunmore for its destruction.

Other British efforts met with disaster in Boston and the Carolinas. The greatest colonial victory came at Boston. On March 17, 1776, after Washington fortified Dorchester Heights south of the city and brought heavy artillery (from Ticonderoga) to bear on it, the British pulled out and sailed for Nova Scotia. A loyalist uprising by Highland Scots in North Carolina was crushed at Moore's Creek Bridge on February 27, and a British naval expedition sent to take Charleston was repulsed with heavy losses in June. Cherokee attacks against colonists in Virginia failed in 1776 because they occurred after Dunmore had left and did not fit into any larger general strategy. Before spring turned to summer, patriot forces had won control of the territory of all 13 colonies.

Independence

George III's dismissal of the Olive Branch Petition left moderates no option but to yield or fight. In late 1775, Congress created a committee to correspond with foreign powers. By early 1776, delegates from New England, Virginia, and Georgia already favored independence, but they knew that unless they won over all 13 colonies, the British would be able to divide them. The British attack on Charleston in June nudged the Carolinas toward independence.

Resistance to independence came mostly from the mid-Atlantic colonies, from New York through Maryland. None of the five legal assemblies in the mid-Atlantic region ever repudiated the Crown. All of them had to be overthrown along with royal (or proprietary) government itself.

In the struggle for middle colony loyalties, Thomas Paine's pamphlet, *Common Sense*, became a huge success. Published in Philadelphia in January 1776, it sold more than 100,000 copies within a few months. Paine, a recent immigrant from England, castigated George III as "the Royal Brute of Great Britain." He attacked monarchy and

HISTORY THROUGH FILM

1776 (1972)

Directed by Peter H. Hunt; starring William Daniels (John Adams), Virginia Vestoff (Abigail), Ken Howard (Thomas Jefferson), Howard da Silva (Benjamin Franklin), and Blythe Danner (Martha)

The musical *1776* does not pretend to be a historical recreation of actual events. It is, rather, an intelligent, offbeat, winning fantasy conceived by northeasterners at the expense, mostly, of Virginians.

The film version of *1776* is a screen adaptation of a musical comedy produced on the New York stage by Stuart Ostrow. Some scenes were filmed on location at Independence Hall in Philadelphia. Sherman Edwards's lively music and lyrics carry the drama from May 1776 to the signing of the Declaration of Independence on July 4.

Director Peter Hunt made his movie debut with *1776*. He also directed *Give 'em Hell, Harry* in 1975 and the 1997 Broadway version of *The Scarlet Pimpernel*, along with various films made for television.

The movie opens with John Adams (William Daniels) trying to force the Second Continental Congress into a serious debate on independence. The delegates respond in full chorus, shouting: "Sit down, John! Sit down, John! For God's sake, John, sit down!" while some of them complain about the flies and the oppressive heat. Adams stalks out and unburdens himself to his wife, Abigail (Virginia Vestoff), still at home in Massachusetts. Abigail, in her reply, urges him to "Tell the Congress to declare / independency. / Then sign your name, get out of there / And hurry home to me."

With Benjamin Franklin's help, Adams finally achieves his goal. The film's bite derives from its determination to move Adams to the center of the story, rather than Thomas Jefferson (Ken Howard), whom Adams and Franklin (Howard da Silva) finally maneuver into writing the first draft of the Declaration, much against his will. Adams declines to write the actual Declaration because, as he explains to Franklin and Jefferson, "If I'm the one to do it / They'll run their quill pens through it. / I'm obnoxious and disliked."

Jefferson also declines at first because he pines for Martha (Blythe Danner), his young bride, still in Virginia. "Mr. Adams, damn you Mr. Adams! / . . . once again you stand between me and my lovely bride. / Oh, Mr. Adams you are driving me to homicide!"

This outburst prompts the other members of the drafting committee to chorus: "Homicide! Homicide! We may see murder yet!" But instead, Jefferson accepts the burden. When he is unable to write, Adams and Franklin bring Martha to Philadelphia so that, after making love to her, he can concentrate his energies on the Declaration.

Some of the delegates appear as mere caricatures, especially Richard Henry Lee of Virginia and James Wilson of Pennsylvania, two articulate delegates who, in real life, played important roles in creating the new republic. The film addresses the slavery question by showing South Carolina's fierce opposition to inclusion of an antislavery clause, a point on which Adams, Jefferson, and Franklin reluctantly yield. The film, like the play on which it is based, works well to deliver an articulate, entertaining taste of history.

Columbia/THE KOBAL COLLECTION

1776. A lively musical, 1776 depicts events from May 1776 to the signing of the Declaration of Independence on July 4.

aristocracy as decadent institutions and urged Americans to unite under a simple republican regime of their own. "There is something very absurd," he insisted, "in supposing a Continent to be perpetually governed by an island."

The British continued to alienate the colonists. They hired 17,000 mercenaries from Hesse and other north German states. (The colonists called them all **Hessians**.) Disturbing (but false) rumors suggested that Britain and France were about to sign a "partition treaty" dividing the eastern half of North America between them. Many congressmen concluded that only independence could counter these dangers by engaging Britain's European enemies on America's side. As long as conciliation was the goal, France would not participate, because American success would restore the British Empire to its former glory. But Louis XVI (1774–1793) might help the colonies win their independence if that meant crippling Britain.

From April to June, about 90 communities issued calls for independence. Most of them did not look further back than 1775 to justify their demand. The king had waged war against the colonists and had hired foreigners to kill them. Self-defense demanded a permanent separation.

On May 15, 1776, Congress voted to suppress "every kind of authority" under the British Crown, thus giving radicals an opportunity to seize power in Pennsylvania and New Jersey. Moderates still controlled New York, Delaware, and Maryland, but they reluctantly accepted independence as inevitable. In early June, Congress named a committee of five, including Jefferson, John Adams, and Benjamin Franklin, to prepare a declaration that would vindicate America's decision to the whole world. Jefferson's draft justified independence on the lofty ground of "self-evident truths," including a natural right to "Life, Liberty, and the pursuit of Happiness." The longest section indicted George III as a tyrant.

With the necessary votes in place, Congress on July 2 passed Richard Henry Lee's resolution "that these United colonies are, and of right, ought to be, Free and Independent States; . . . and that all political connexion between them, and the state of Great Britain, is, and ought to be, totally dissolved." On the same day, the first ships of the largest armada yet sent across the Atlantic by any European state began landing British soldiers on Staten Island. Two days later, on July 4, 12 colonies, with New York abstaining to await instructions, unanimously approved Jefferson's **Declaration of Independence**, as amended by Congress.

Hessians *A term used by Americans to describe the 17,000 mercenary troops hired by Britain from various German states, especially Hesse.*

Declaration of Independence *Drafted primarily by Thomas Jefferson of Virginia, this document justified American independence to the world by affirming "that all men are created equal" and have a natural right to "Life, Liberty, and the pursuit of Happiness." The longest section of the Declaration condemned George III as a tyrant.*

Conclusion

Between 1763 and 1776 Britain and the colonies became trapped in a series of self-fulfilling prophecies. The British feared that without major reforms to guarantee Parliament's control of the empire, the colonies would drift toward independence. Colonial resistance to the new policies convinced the British that a movement for independence was already underway. The colonists denied that they desired independence, but they began to fear that the British government would deprive them of their rights as Englishmen. Britain's policy drove them toward a closer union with one another and finally provoked armed resistance. With the onset of war, both sides felt vindicated.

Both sides were wrong. The British had no systematic plan to destroy liberty in North America, and until winter 1775–1776, hardly any colonists favored independence. But the three imperial crises undermined mutual confidence and brought about an independent American nation. Unable to govern North America, Britain now faced the grim task of conquering it instead.

CHAPTER REVIEW

Review Questions

1. Why was the British Empire more successful in defeating powerful France in a global war than in imposing rather modest reform upon the North American colonies after the victory?

2. Colonists opposed all taxes by a central legislature that, they claimed, did not represent them. They violently nullified the Stamp Act. Why in 1766 did they stop resisting and rejoice in its repeal even though the Revenue Act of 1766 continued to tax molasses?

3. If the colonists condemned all parliamentary taxes for revenue, why did effective resistance to the Townshend Revenue Act take so long to organize, and why did it cease before achieving total repeal?

4. Why did the colonists start a revolution after the Tea Act of 1773 lowered the price of tea?

5. How and why did a resistance movement dedicated to protecting the colonists' rights as Englishmen end by proclaiming American independence instead?

Critical Thinking Questions

1. The colonists insisted that the right to property was essential to the preservation of liberty. Taxation without representation was unconstitutional precisely because it deprived them of their property without their consent. How then could they find it appropriate and legitimate to resist British policies by destroying the property of stamp distributors, Thomas Hutchinson, and the East India Company?

2. In 1775 Lord North promised that Parliament would not tax any colony that paid its share of the costs of imperial defense and gave adequate salaries to its civil officers, but the Second Continental Congress rejected the proposal out of hand. Had George Grenville offered something of the kind between 1763 and 1765, might Britain have averted the Revolution? Specifically, imagine if Grenville had praised Massachusetts men and Virginians for their vigorous cooperation with the empire during the French and Indian War while censuring Maryland and North Carolina for lack of cooperation. Would Boston have rioted and Patrick Henry have urged resistance if Parliament had decided to punish Maryland and North Carolina for failing to meet the standards set by Massachusetts and Virginia?

Identifications

Review your understanding of the following key terms, people, and events for this chapter.

George Grenville, p. 108
Proclamation of 1763, p. 109
Pontiac, p. 109
vice-admiralty courts, p. 110
specie, p. 111
virtual representation, p. 111
external taxes, p. 111

internal taxes, p. 111
Stamp Act, p. 111
Liberty Tree, p. 112
nonimportation agreements, p. 112
Townshend Revenue Act, p. 114
common law, p. 117
artisan, p. 117
Boston Massacre, p. 117

committees of correspondence, p. 118
Phillis Wheatley, p. 119
Boston Tea Party, p. 121
Coercive (Intolerable) Acts, p. 121
provincial congress, p. 122
First Continental Congress, p. 122

Association, p. 122
Battle of Lexington, p. 124
Second Continental Congress, p. 124
Hessians, p. 128
Declaration of Independence, p. 128

DISCOVERY

What principles were at stake during the period of the American Revolution?

In thinking about this question, begin by breaking it down into the components shown below. A discussion of the significance of each component should appear in your answer.

Government and Law

The section on "Independence" (page 126) lists some of the "self-evident" affirmations of the Declaration of Independence, such as that "all men are created equal" and have a natural right to "life, liberty, and the pursuit of happiness." Did the colonists fully embrace all of the principles set forth in the Declaration of Independence? If not, which principles were not fully embraced? Why were they not?

Culture and Society

Look at the title page of Phillis Wheatley's collected poems and note the inscription encircling the engraving of Wheatley. Why was it necessary to include such an inscription? How was her status affected by her gender or the fact that she was enslaved? Which groups were not included in the newfound ideas of independence and freedom? Why were they excluded? How did they attempt to have their voices heard?

PHILLIS WHEATLEY

Courtesy, American Antiquarian Society

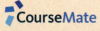

Visit the CourseMate website at www.cengagebrain.com for additional study tools and review materials for this chapter.

THE REVOLUTIONARY REPUBLIC

The Revolutionary War was a civil war. Neighbors were more likely to fight neighbors during the Revolution than they were between 1861 and 1865, when the geographical line separating the two sides would be much sharper. Twice, in 1776 and 1780, the British might have won, but in both campaigns the Americans rallied. The Americans won only by bringing in France as an ally. France brought in Spain.

During the war, Americans began to think, more than before, in crude racial categories. But they drafted state constitutions and bills of rights that reached far beyond the racism many of them felt. At the national level, the war demonstrated how weak Congress was, even after ratification of the Articles of Confederation in 1781. During the summer of 1787 the Philadelphia Convention drafted a new Constitution for the United States. It went into effect in April 1789.

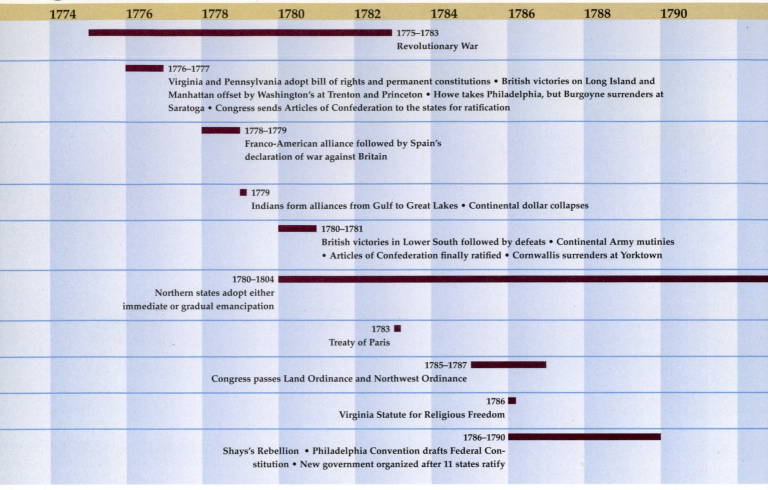

| 1774 | 1776 | 1778 | 1780 | 1782 | 1784 | 1786 | 1788 | 1790 |

1775–1783
Revolutionary War

1776–1777
Virginia and Pennsylvania adopt bill of rights and permanent constitutions • British victories on Long Island and Manhattan offset by Washington's at Trenton and Princeton • Howe takes Philadelphia, but Burgoyne surrenders at Saratoga • Congress sends Articles of Confederation to the states for ratification

1778–1779
Franco-American alliance followed by Spain's declaration of war against Britain

1779
Indians form alliances from Gulf to Great Lakes • Continental dollar collapses

1780–1781
British victories in Lower South followed by defeats • Continental Army mutinies • Articles of Confederation finally ratified • Cornwallis surrenders at Yorktown

1780–1804
Northern states adopt either immediate or gradual emancipation

1783
Treaty of Paris

1785–1787
Congress passes Land Ordinance and Northwest Ordinance

1786
Virginia Statute for Religious Freedom

1786–1790
Shays's Rebellion • Philadelphia Convention drafts Federal Constitution • New government organized after 11 states ratify

© Cengage Learning

HEARTS AND MINDS: THE NORTHERN WAR, 1776–1777

FOCUS QUESTION

What enabled American volunteers, fiercely committed to individual liberty, to believe that they could defeat Britain's disciplined professional army?

To keep the colonies, the men who ruled Britain raised more soldiers and larger fleets than ever before and more than doubled its national debt. Americans, too confident after their early successes, staggered under the onslaught.

The British Offensive

The first setback came in Canada. In May 1776, when a fresh British force sailed up the St. Lawrence River, the Americans, weakened by smallpox, had to retreat. By July, Sir Guy Carleton drove them back into northern New York, to Ticonderoga on Lake Champlain. Largely through Benedict Arnold's efforts, the Americans held, and Carleton returned to Canada for the winter.

Farther south, Richard, viscount Howe, admiral of the British fleet, and his brother General William Howe prepared an awesome striking force on Staten Island. They also acted as peace commissioners, with power to pardon rebels and restore colonies to the king's peace. They hoped to avoid using their huge army, but when they wrote George Washington to open negotiations, he refused to accept the letter because it did not address him as "General." To do so would have recognized the legitimacy of his appointment. Unable to negotiate, the Howes had to fight.

In New York City, Washington divided his inferior force of 19,000 and sent half of it from Manhattan to Long Island. The men dug in on Brooklyn Heights and waited for a frontal attack. The British invaded Long Island on August 27, 1776. While Hessians feinted a frontal assault, the flanking force crushed the American left and rear.

The Howes did nothing to prevent the evacuation of the rest of the American army to Manhattan, which occurred under the cover of a fierce nor'easter storm. Instead, on September 11 the British opened informal talks with several members of Congress on Staten Island. The talks collapsed when the Americans insisted that the British recognize their independence. Washington evacuated lower Manhattan. The British took New York City, much of which was destroyed by fire on September 21. The Howes offered a pardon to people willing to lay down their arms and return to British allegiance within 60 days. In southern New York State, several thousand complied.

From October through December the Howes pushed the American forces out of New York and across New Jersey. Demoralized, many American soldiers went home. In September, 27,000 Americans stood fit for duty in the northern theater; by December, only 6,000 remained. Many observers thought the war was all but over as sad remnants of the Continental army crossed the Delaware River into Pennsylvania. Even Jefferson began to think about terms on which a restoration of the monarchy might be acceptable.

The Trenton-Princeton Campaign

Washington knew he had to do something dramatic to restore morale and encourage his soldiers to reenlist. On Christmas night, 1776, he crossed the ice-choked Delaware and marched south, surprising the Trenton, New Jersey, garrison at dawn during another nor'easter. Nearly 1,000 Hessians surrendered. The British sent General Charles, earl Cornwallis, south with 8,000 men. They caught up with Washington at Trenton near sunset on January 2 but decided to wait until dawn before attacking. British patrols watched the Delaware to prevent another escape across the river, but Washington left his campfires burning, muffled the wheels of his wagons and guns, and stole around the British left flank, heading north. At dawn, he met a British regiment beginning its march from Princeton to Trenton. In the Battle of Princeton the Americans, with a 5-to-1 edge, mauled yet another garrison.

Washington's two victories had an enormous impact on the war. The Howes blundered in not hounding Washington's remnant of an army to its destruction after Princeton, if that was still possible. Instead, they called in their scattered garrisons and concentrated the army along the Raritan River from New Brunswick to the sea. As the British departed, the militia returned, asking who had sworn oaths to the king. Loyalists who had taken the oath now groveled, or fled to British lines. For the rest of the winter, the militia attacked and usually defeated British patrols foraging for supplies. By spring, the Howes' forces were reduced to less than half the strength they had been in August. Many invaders had aroused fierce hatred by looting and raping their way across New Jersey. The British and Hessians had lost the hearts and minds of the people.

General William Howe *Howe commanded the British army in North America from 1776 to 1778. He won major victories in New York and northern New Jersey in 1776, but Washington regained control of New Jersey after his Trenton-Princeton campaign. Howe took Philadelphia in September 1777 but was recalled in disgrace after Britain's northern army surrendered at Saratoga.*

George Washington *A veteran of the French and Indian War, Washington was named commander in chief of the Continental army by the Second Continental Congress in 1775 and won notable victories at Boston, Trenton, Princeton, and Yorktown, where Lord Cornwallis's army surrendered to him in 1781.*

Loyalists *People in the 13 colonies who remained loyal to Britain during the Revolution.*

QUICK REVIEW

UNABLE TO NEGOTIATE A RECONCILIATION, THE HOWE BROTHERS LAUNCH THEIR OFFENSIVE

- The British took New York City, swept across northern New Jersey

- Washington won victories at Trenton and Princeton

- After the British withdrew most of their outposts, the militia regained control

- Their foraging war cut the effective strength of the British army to less than half what it had been in August

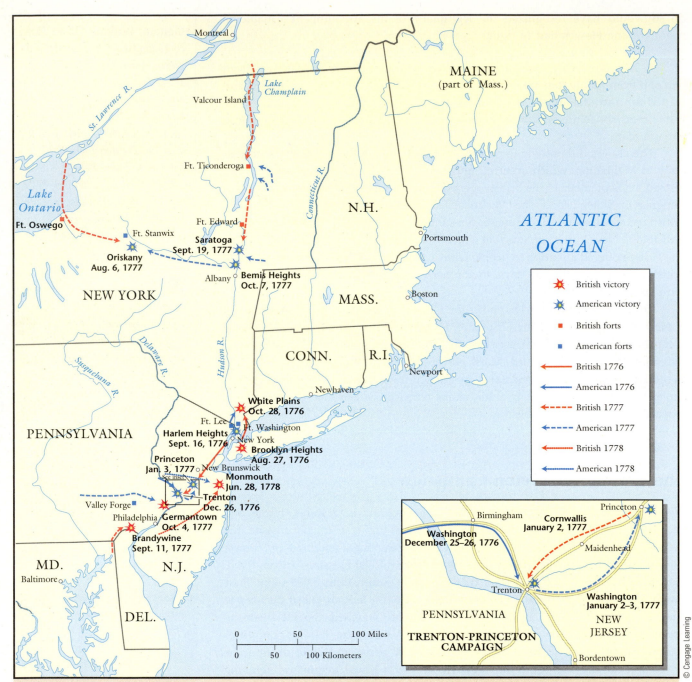

Map 6.1 Revolutionary War in the Northern States. *This map shows the campaigns in New York and New Jersey in 1776–1777, in northern New York and around Philadelphia in 1777, and at Monmouth, New Jersey, in 1778. The inset shows Washington's Trenton and Princeton campaigns after Christmas 1776.*

THE CAMPAIGNS OF 1777 AND FOREIGN INTERVENTION

FOCUS QUESTION

Why did France intervene after Britain took Philadelphia, the American capital, and forced Congress to flee?

In 1777, Lord George Germain, Britain's war minister, ordered General Howe to take Philadelphia. He also sent General John Burgoyne to Canada with orders to march his army south and link up with the garrison of New York City, commanded by Sir Henry Clinton. When few reinforcements reached the Howes, they rejected an overland march to Philadelphia as too risky and decided to invade by sea, a decision that allowed Washington to shift men north to oppose Burgoyne.

The Loss of Philadelphia

After Trenton and Princeton, Washington demanded longer terms of enlistment. Congress promised a cash bonus to anyone enlisting for three years and a land bounty to anyone serving for the duration. Congress never came close to raising the 75,000 men it hoped for, but these new policies did create the foundation for a more experienced army. As the 1777 recruits came in, the two northern armies, swelled by militia, grew to about 28,000 men fit for duty—17,000 in northern New York and 11,000 under Washington.

The Howes sailed south from New York with 13,000 men and landed the troops in Maryland on August 24. The British marched toward Philadelphia. After his experience in New York, Washington was wary of being trapped in a city. Instead of trying to hold Philadelphia, he took up positions at Brandywine Creek along the British route of march. On September 11, Howe again outmaneuvered him, drove in his right flank, and forced him to retreat. Congress fled to Lancaster, and the British occupied Philadelphia on September 26.

Washington headed west to Valley Forge, where the army endured a miserable winter.

"CONGRESS FLEEING PHILADELPHIA BY BALLOON," 1777. *This British cartoon mocked Congress as it fled from the British army in the 1777 campaign. Hot air balloon flights, still experimental, were becoming a popular rage in France and Britain. The first flight across the English Channel would occur in 1783.*

Saratoga

In northern New York, Ticonderoga fell to Burgoyne on June 2, 1777, but little went right for the British after that. Benedict Arnold forced a combined British and Indian force to retreat after they had defeated militia at Oriskany. Burgoyne's army of 7,800, advancing from Ticonderoga toward Albany, was overwhelmed in the upper Hudson valley. When he detached 700 Hessians to forage in the Green Mountains, they ran into 2,600 militia raised by John Stark of New Hampshire. Stark killed or captured nearly all of them. By the time Burgoyne's surviving soldiers reached the Hudson and started toward Albany, the Americans under Horatio Gates outnumbered them 3 to 1. After two costly battles, Burgoyne retreated to **Saratoga**, where he surrendered his entire army on October 17.

French Intervention and Spanish Assistance

In May 1776, Louis XVI authorized secret aid to the American rebels. Without these smuggled French supplies, the Americans could not have continued the war. In December 1776, Benjamin Franklin arrived in France as an agent of Congress. The 70-year-old Franklin took Parisian society by storm. He wore simple clothes, replaced his wig with a fur cap, and played to perfection the role of innocent man of nature that French *philosophes* associated with Pennsylvania. He kept the supplies flowing.

Saratoga *A major turning point in the Revolutionary War. American forces prevented John Burgoyne's army from reaching Albany, cut off its retreat, and forced it to surrender in October 1777. This victory helped bring France into the war.*

1777: YEAR OF DECISION

- Professionalism of the Continental army grew

- British took Philadelphia after defeating Washington at Brandywine

- Burgoyne, after he took Ticonderoga, was swamped by American forces and surrendered his army at Saratoga

- Franklin negotiated an alliance with France in 1778, and a year later France brought Spain into the war

Burgoyne's defeat convinced Louis that the Americans could win. Franklin and Foreign Minister Charles Gravier, comte de Vergennes, signed two treaties in February 1778. One, a commercial agreement, granted Americans generous trading terms with France. In the other, France made a perpetual alliance with the United States, recognized American independence, agreed to fight until Britain conceded independence, and disavowed all territorial ambitions on the North American continent.

Franklin's treaties stunned London. Lord North proposed a plan of conciliation that conceded virtually everything but independence. In 1775, such terms would have resolved the imperial crisis, but now Congress rejected them out of hand. In response, George III declared war on France, recalled the Howe brothers, and ordered General Clinton, the new commander, to abandon Philadelphia. Fearing a French invasion of the British Isles while most of the Royal Navy was in American waters, the British redeployed their forces on a global scale in 1778–1779.

The Americans also received indirect help from Spain, another nation eager to avenge old defeats against Britain. Although the Spanish king, Charles III (1759–1788), never made an alliance with the United States, in 1779 he joined France in its war against Britain, hoping to retake Gibraltar and to stabilize Spain's North American borders. Britain held Gibraltar, but Spain took West Florida. In 1783, Britain ceded East Florida as well, giving Spain control of the entire coastline of the Gulf of Mexico for the first time in a century.

THE RECONSTITUTION OF AUTHORITY

FOCUS QUESTION

How did American constitutionalism after 1776 differ from the British constitutional principles that the colonists had accepted and revered before 1776?

In 1776, the prospect of independence touched off an intense debate among Americans on constitutionalism. They agreed that every state needed a written constitution to limit the powers of government in terms more explicit than the precedents and customs that made up Britain's unwritten constitution. Over the next four years, they moved toward fuller expressions of **popular sovereignty**—the theory that all power must be derived from the people.

John Adams and the Separation of Powers

No one learned more from these debates than John Adams, who wrote *Thoughts on Government* in 1776. Adams was already moving away from the British notion of a "mixed and balanced" constitution, in which government by kings, lords, and commons embodied the social orders of British society. He was turning instead toward the **separation of powers**. Government, he affirmed, should be divided into three branches—an executive armed with veto power, a legislature, and a judiciary independent of both. The legislature must be bicameral, so that each house could expose the failings of the other. A free government need not embody distinct social orders to be stable. It could uphold republican values by being properly balanced within itself.

Governments exist to promote the happiness of the people, Adams declared. Happiness depends on "virtue," both public and private. **Public virtue** meant "patriotism," the willingness of citizens to value the common good above their personal interests. The form of government that rests entirely on virtue, Adams argued, is a republic. Americans must elect legislatures that would mirror society. Britain had put the nobility in one house and the commoners in another, but in

popular sovereignty *The theory that all power must derive from the people.*

separation of powers *The theory that a free government, especially in a republic, should have three independent branches capable of checking or balancing one another: the executive, the legislative (usually bicameral), and the judicial.*

America, everyone was a commoner. In what sense, then, could any government reflect American society?

In 1776 Adams knew only that the legislature should mirror society. **Unicameral legislatures,** such as Pennsylvania's, horrified him: "A single assembly, possessed of all the powers of government," he warned, "would make arbitrary laws for their own interest, execute all laws arbitrarily for their own interest, and adjudge all controversies in their own favor." Adams had not yet found a way to distinguish between everyday legislation and the power to create a constitution. While struggling to define what a republic ought to be, he and his admirers could not escape two assumptions of European politics—that government itself must be sovereign, and that it alone could define the rights of the people. A few ordinary settlers had already spotted the dangers of those assumptions. The citizens of Concord, Massachusetts, warned in October 1776, "A Constitution alterable by the Supreme Legislative [Power] is no Security at all to the Subject against any Encroachment of the Governing part on . . . their Rights and Privileges."

This concern would eventually prompt Americans to invent the embodiment of popular sovereignty in its purest form, the constitutional convention. But in 1776, most Americans still assumed that governments must be sovereign. In the early state constitutions, every state lodged **sovereign power** in its legislature and let it define the rights of citizens. The American reply to Britain's sovereign Parliament was 13 sovereign state legislatures—14, with Vermont.

The Virginia Constitution

In June 1776, Virginia became the first state to adopt a permanent, republican constitution. The legislature chose the governor, the governor's council, and all judges above the level of justice of the peace. The governor had no veto and little patronage. The lower house faced annual elections, but members of the upper house served four-year terms.

George Mason drafted a declaration of rights that the Virginia delegates passed before approving the constitution, on the theory that the people should define their rights before empowering the government. Mason's text affirmed the right to life, liberty, property, and the pursuit of happiness. The convention's amended text affirmed human equality, but not for enslaved people. The bill of rights also condemned hereditary privilege, called for rotation in office, provided guarantees for trial by jury and due process, and extolled religious liberty. Other states adopted variations of the Virginia model.

The Pennsylvania Constitution

In June 1776, Pennsylvania radicals overthrew Crown, proprietor, and assembly and elected artisans to office in Philadelphia and ordinary farmers in rural areas. Until 1776 most officeholders had either been Quakers or Anglicans. Now, Scots-Irish Presbyterians and German Lutherans or Calvinists replaced them. They summoned a special convention whose only task was to write a constitution. That document established a unicameral assembly and a plural executive of 12 men, one of whom would preside and thus be called "president." All freemen who paid taxes, and their adult sons living at home, could vote. Elections were annual, voting was by secret ballot, legislative sessions were open to the public, and no representative could serve for more than four years out of any seven. All bills were to be offered to the public for discussion before passage. Only at the next session of the legislature could they be passed into law, except in emergencies.

public virtue *Meant, to the revolutionary generation, patriotism and the willingness of a free and independent people to subordinate their interests to the common good and even to die for their country.*

unicameral legislature *A legislature with only one chamber or house.*

sovereign power *A term used to describe supreme or final power.*

The Pennsylvania constitution generated intense conflict in late 1776 as the British army drew near. In this emergency, the convention that drafted the constitution began to pass laws, destroying any distinction between itself and the legislature it was creating. The convention and the legislatures that succeeded it rarely delayed the enactment of a bill until voters could discuss it. Even more alarming, many residents, including the men driven from power in 1776, condemned the new constitution as illegitimate. The radicals, calling themselves Constitutionalists, required all citizens to uphold the constitution and disfranchised those who refused to support it, such as Quakers.

Some men (mostly leaders of the old Proprietary Party) took the oaths only to form an opposition party. Called Anticonstitutionalists at first (that is, opponents of the 1776 constitution), they soon took the name Republicans. In the 1780s, after the war emergency had passed, they won a majority in the assembly, secured ratification of the federal Constitution, and, in 1790, replaced the state's radical constitution with one that made the legislature bicameral and added an elected governor.

Massachusetts Redefines Constitutionalism

A bitter struggle occurred in Massachusetts. After four years of intense debate, Massachusetts found a way to lodge sovereignty with the people and not with government—that is, a way to distinguish a constitution from simple laws.

In response to the Massachusetts Government Act passed by Parliament in 1774, the colonists had prevented the royal courts from sitting (see Chapter 5). The courts remained closed until the British withdrew from Boston in March 1776 when the provincial congress moved into the city and reestablished itself as the General Court. The legislature then reapportioned itself. The new system let towns choose representatives in proportion to population. It rewarded the older, populous eastern towns at the expense of lightly settled western towns.

When the General Court also revived royal practice by appointing its own members as county judges and justices of the peace, the western counties exploded. They attacked the reapportionment act and refused to reopen the courts in Hampshire and Berkshire counties. Berkshire's radicals insisted on contracts or compacts as the basis of authority in both church and state and kept using county conventions in place of the courts. To Berkshire Constitutionalists, a **convention** was the purest expression of the will of the people, superior to any legislature.

In fall 1776, the General Court asked the towns to authorize it to draft a constitution. By a 2 to 1 margin, the voters agreed, a result that reflected growing *distrust* of the legislature. Six months earlier few would have questioned such a procedure. The legislature drafted a constitution over the next year and then, in an unusual precaution, asked the towns to ratify it. The voters rejected it by the stunning margin of 5 to 1. Chastened, the General Court urged the towns to postpone the question until after the war. Hampshire County reopened its courts in April 1778, but Berkshire farmers threatened to secede from the state unless it called a constitutional convention.

The General Court gave in, and a convention met in Boston in December 1779. John Adams drafted a constitution that the convention used as its starting point. A constitution now had to be drafted by a special constitutional convention and then ratified by the people.

convention *In England, a meeting, usually of the houses of Parliament, to address an emergency, such as the flight of James II to France in 1688. In the United States by the 1780s conventions had become the purest expression of the popular will, superior to the legislature, as in the convention that drafted the Massachusetts constitution of 1780.*

Like its Virginia counterpart, the Massachusetts constitution began with a bill of rights. Both houses would be elected annually. Members of the House of Representatives would be chosen by the towns. Senators would be elected by counties and apportioned according to property values, not population. The people would elect the governor, who would have a veto that two-thirds of both houses could override. Property qualifications rose as a man's civic duties increased. For purposes of ratification only, all free adult males were eligible to vote. Everyone (that is, all free men) would have a chance to consent to the basic social compact.

The new constitution went into effect during spring 1780 and, although often amended, is still in force today, making it the world's oldest written constitution. Beginning with New Hampshire, other states adopted the Massachusetts model.

Confederation

Congress began discussing the American union in summer 1776. It had been voting by state since the First Continental Congress in 1774. Delegates from large states favored representation according to population, but the small states insisted on being treated as equals. So long as Britain was ready to embrace any state that defected, small states had great leverage. In one early draft of the Articles of Confederation, John Dickinson rejected proportional representation in favor of state equality. He enumerated the powers of Congress, which did not include levying taxes or regulating trade. To raise money, Congress would have to print it or requisition specific amounts from the states. Congress then split over how to apportion these requisitions. Northern states wanted to count slaves in computing the ratios. Southern states wanted apportionment based on each state's free population. Western lands were another divisive issue. States with fixed borders pressured states with boundary claims stretching into the Ohio or Mississippi valleys to surrender their claims to Congress. Congress could not resolve these issues in 1776.

Debate resumed after Washington's victories at Trenton and Princeton. Thomas Burke of North Carolina introduced a resolution that eventually became part of the Articles of Confederation: "Each state retains its sovereignty, freedom and independence, and every power, jurisdiction, and right, which is not by this confederation expressly delegated to the United States in Congress assembled." Acceptance of Burke's resolution, with only Virginia dissenting, ensured that the Articles would contain a firm commitment to state sovereignty. In the final version, Congress was given no power over western land claims, and requisitions would be based on each state's free population. In 1781, Congress urged that each slave be counted as three-fifths of a person for the purpose of apportioning requisitions, but this amendment was never ratified.

In November 1777 Congress asked the states to ratify the Articles by March 10, 1778, but only Virginia met the deadline. By midsummer 10 had ratified. The three dissenters—Delaware, New Jersey, and Maryland—were small states without western land claims who feared the large states. Maryland held out for more than three years, until Virginia agreed to cede its land claims north of the Ohio River to Congress. The Articles finally went into force on March 1, 1781. By then, Congress had lost most of its power. As the states adopted their own constitutions, their legitimacy became more obvious than that of Congress.

THE CRISIS OF THE REVOLUTION, 1779–1783

FOCUS QUESTION

Why, despite the French alliance, did the United States nearly lose the war between 1779 and 1781?

Americans expected a quick victory under the French alliance. Instead, the struggle turned into a grim war of **attrition**. The British began to look to the Deep South as the likeliest recruiting ground for armed loyalists.

The Loyalists, White and Black

Loyalists embraced English ideas of liberty. They thought that creating a new American union was far riskier than remaining part of the British Empire. About one-sixth of the white population chose the British side in the war. Unlike most patriots, loyalists served long terms because they could not go home unless they won. By 1780, the number of loyalists under arms probably exceeded the number of Continentals by 2 to 1. State governments retaliated by banishing prominent loyalists under pain of death and confiscating their property.

In New England, where slaves sensed that they could gain freedom by joining the rebels, many volunteered for military service. Elsewhere, although some fought for the Revolution, they realized that their best chance of emancipation lay with the British army. During the war, more than 50,000 slaves (about 10 percent) fled their owners. This decision carried risks. In South Carolina during Clinton's 1776 invasion, hundreds reached the Sea Islands to join the British, only to face their owners' wrath when the British failed to rescue them. Others approached British units only to be treated as contraband (property) and face possible resale. But most slaves who reached British lines won their freedom. When the British left after the war, 20,000 blacks went with them, to Jamaica, Nova Scotia, London, or Sierra Leone.

The war created an enormous stream of refugees. In addition to former slaves, some 60,000 to 70,000 colonists left for other parts of the British Empire. A generous land policy, which required an oath of allegiance to George III, attracted thousands of new immigrants to Canada from the United States in the 1780s and 1790s. By the War of 1812, four-fifths of Upper Canada's 100,000 people were American-born.

The Indian Struggle for Unity and Survival

Indians of the eastern woodlands saw that an American victory would threaten their survival as a people on their ancestral lands. They supported Britain in the hope that a British victory might stem the flood of western expansion, and they achieved a level of unity without precedent in their history.

At first, most Indians tried to remain neutral. Only the Cherokees took up arms in 1776. Short on British supplies, they took heavy losses before making peace and accepting neutrality. A splinter group, the Chickamaugas, continued to resist. In the Deep South, only the Catawbas fought on the American side.

Burgoyne's invasion brought the Iroquois into the war. Mohawks in the east and Senecas in the west sided with Britain under the leadership of Joseph Brant, an educated Mohawk and a Freemason. His sister, Mary Brant, emerged as a skillful diplomat in the alliance between the Iroquois and the loyalists. A minority of Oneidas and Tuscaroras fought with the Americans. Despite severe strains during the revolution, the Iroquois League did not dissolve until after the war, when those who had fought for Britain migrated to Canada.

attrition *A type of warfare where an effort is made to exhaust the manpower, supplies, and morale of the other side.*

HISTORY THROUGH FILM

Mary Silliman's War (1993)

*Directed by Stephen Surjik; starring Nancy Palk (Mary Silliman),
Richard Donat (Selleck Silliman), Paul Boretski (David Holly), Joanne Miller (Amelia),
Elias Williams (Peter), and Allan Royal (Thomas Jones)*

Strong movies about the Revolutionary War are hard to find. *Mary Silliman's War* rests on the outstanding research of Joy Day Buel and Richard Buel, Jr., on the life of Mary Fish Noyes Silliman Dickinson, a Connecticut woman who was widowed three times in the course of a long life (1736–1818). The numerous letters and journals she left behind have made it possible to reconstruct and dramatize her life. Steven Schechter, who coproduced the film, also wrote most of the screenplay. It picks up Mary's story in 1779 when she is living in Fairfield, Connecticut, with her second husband, Gold Selleck Silliman, and their children. Selleck commands the militia that responds to emergencies, and he also serves as prosecuting attorney in his civilian capacity. In the northern states, the Revolutionary War has become mostly a series of destructive raids, with the British and loyalists based on Long Island and the patriots on the mainland. For good reason, both sides worry about traitors and spies in their midst.

As the film opens, Selleck is successfully prosecuting two loyalist townsmen. When they are sentenced to death, Mary objects that the war is turning neighbor against neighbor, but Selleck will not relent. In retaliation, the loyalists stage a night raid on the Silliman home, capture Selleck, and take him to New York City, the headquarters of the British army. The message seems clear. If the Fairfield loyalists are to be executed, Selleck will also die. Thomas Jones, a magistrate and perhaps the most prominent loyalist living on Long Island, has known Selleck since their undergraduate days at Yale College. He acts as an intermediary. When George Washington refuses to exchange a captured British officer for Selleck because Selleck is not an officer in the Continental army, Mary faces an unpleasant dilemma. An American privateer, Captain David Holly, offers to raid Long Island, capture Judge Jones, and force the British to negotiate an exchange. Mary dislikes privateers and does not approve of Holly, but after the British raid Fairfield and burn most of the town, she consents. The rest of the story explores the consequences of this decision. Mary's deep religious convictions are emphasized throughout the film.

The screenplay telescopes the chronology of these events somewhat, invents a romance between Amelia (a servant in the Silliman household) and Captain Holly, and uses the slave Peter to illustrate the dilemmas that African Americans faced during the war. But the central plot line follows a drama that is well documented in the historical record and exposes a side of the Revolutionary War of which few Americans are even vaguely aware. The struggle was a long, brutal conflict that brought liberty to many and equality to smaller numbers, but it also turned neighbor against neighbor.

Mary Fish Silliman at age 58, four years after the death of her second husband, Gold Selleck Silliman.

Courtesy of the Fairfield Historical Society

JOSEPH BRANT, PORTRAIT BY GILBERT STUART. *Brant, a Mohawk and a Freemason, was one of Britain's ablest commanders of loyalist and Indian forces. After the war, he led most of the Six Nations to Canada for resettlement.*

A minority of Shawnees, led by Cornplanter, and of Delawares, led by White Eyes and Killbuck, also pursued friendly relations with the Americans, but they refused to fight other Indians. Christian Moravian Indians in the Ohio country took a similar stance.

Frontier racism made Indian neutrality impossible. Backcountry settlers refused to accept the neutrals on their own terms. Indian warriors, especially young men influenced by nativist prophets, insisted that the Great Spirit had created whites, Indians, and blacks as separate peoples who ought to remain apart. Their militancy further enraged the settlers.

Hatred of Indians threatened to undercut the American war effort. In 1777, a Continental officer had Cornplanter murdered. In 1778, American militia killed White Eyes. Four years later, Americans used mallets to crush the skulls of 100 unarmed Moravian mission Indians, nearly all of them praying women and children, at Gnadenhutten, Ohio. Until then, most Indians had refrained from the ritual torture of prisoners, but after Gnadenhutten they resumed the custom by burning alive the captured leaders of the massacre.

Indians united to protect their lands. They won the frontier war north of the Ohio River. The Iroquois ravaged the Wyoming valley of Pennsylvania in 1778. When an American army devastated Iroquoia in 1779, the Indians fell back on the British post at Niagara and continued the struggle. In 1779 nearly all Indians from the Gulf Coast to the Great Lakes exchanged emissaries and planned to attack all along the frontier. They finally drove Virginia's "long knives" out of the Ohio country in 1782.

Attrition

After 1778, George III's determination to continue the war bitterly divided his kingdom. Political dissent rose and included widespread demand for the reduction of royal patronage and for electoral reforms. Desperate for men, the British army had been quietly recruiting Irish Catholics, and North supported a modest degree of toleration for English and Scottish Catholics. This leniency produced a surge of Protestant violence that discredited the reformers and gave North one last chance to win the war.

Attrition also weakened the United States. Raids by Indians and loyalists destroyed property and wore down the defenders. Military levies kept thousands of men away from productive work. Average household income plunged by more than 40 percent. Even some triumphs came at a high price. For example, Burgoyne's surrender left Americans with the burden of feeding his army for the rest of the war. These heavy demands led to the collapse of the Continental dollar in 1779–1780. Congress agreed to stop printing money and rely instead on requisitions from the states and on foreign and domestic loans, but without paper money it could not even pay the army.

Continental soldiers—unpaid, ill clothed, and often poorly fed—grew mutinous. The winter of 1779–1780, the worst of the century, marked a low point in morale. In

May 1780, two Connecticut regiments, without food for three days, threatened to go home, raising the danger that the whole army might dissolve. Their officers barely managed to restore control.

THE BRITISH OFFENSIVE IN THE SOUTH

By early 1780, the British had held Savannah for over a year and were ready to launch a major offensive. Clinton had finally devised a strategy for winning the war. He would send his New York army to Charleston and take it. Clinton would return to New York and land on the Jersey coast with a force three times larger than Washington's. By dividing this army into two columns, Clinton could break through both passes of the Watchung Mountains leading to Morristown, where he would destroy Washington and the Continental army. Clinton was also negotiating secretly with an angry and disgruntled Benedict Arnold (he had received little recognition for his heroics in the Saratoga campaign) for the surrender of West Point, which would open the Hudson River to British ships. Finally, if the French landed in Newport, Clinton would move against them with nearly his entire New York fleet and garrison. His remaining task would then be pacification, which he could leave to loyalists. But he told no one about his New Jersey plan.

Clinton's invasion of South Carolina began with great successes. While the British navy sealed off Charleston from the sea, an army of 10,000 closed off the land approaches to the city, forcing its 5,000 defenders to surrender on May 12. Loyalists led by Banastre Tarleton caught 350 remaining Continentals near the North Carolina border on May 29 and killed them all, including many prisoners. This calculated brutality was designed to terrorize civilians into submission. But Thomas Sumter began to fight back after loyalists burned his plantation. At Hanging Rock on August 6, Sumter's 800 men scattered 500 loyalists, killing or wounding nearly half of them.

Leaving Cornwallis in command of 8,300 men in South Carolina, Clinton sailed north with one-third of his Carolina army, only to learn that loyalists had already persuaded the temporary British commander in New York to land in New Jersey with 6,000 men on the night of June 6–7. Loyalists hoped that the militia was so weary from the harsh winter and numerous raids that it would not turn out to assist Washington. But the militia appeared in force on June 7. Only after an inconclusive engagement did the British learn that Clinton was on his way. They pulled back to the coast and waited, but they had lost the element of surprise.

Clinton attacked at Springfield on June 23, but a stout defense persuaded him to withdraw to New York. Arnold's attempt to betray West Point was thwarted. Clinton's emissary was captured and hanged, but Arnold fled to British lines and became a general in the British army.

Cornwallis's conquest of the Carolinas proceeded rapidly. He crushed American forces led by Horatio Gates at Camden on August 16. Two days later, Tarleton surprised Sumter's camp at Fishing Creek, killing 150 men and wounding 300. In four months, the British had destroyed the Continental forces in the Deep South and mauled Sumter's partisans. Cornwallis turned the pacification of South Carolina over to his loyalists and marched confidently on to "liberate" North Carolina.

FOCUS QUESTION

In the Carolinas, the war went radical in 1780 with an emphasis on guerilla tactics, but in Philadelphia, Congress grew more conservative, creating executive departments and moving toward European models of government finance. Were these trends contradictory?

The Partisan War

But resistance continued. In the west, frontier riflemen led by Daniel Morgan crossed the Blue Ridge and overwhelmed the loyalists at King's Mountain near the North Carolina border on October 7, 1780. In retaliation for Tarleton's atrocities, they shot many prisoners and hanged a dozen. Stunned, Cornwallis halted his drive into North Carolina.

In October 1780, Congress sent **Nathanael Greene** to the Carolinas with a small Continental force. After Sumter withdrew to nurse a wound, Francis Marion, a much abler leader, took his place. In the face of a superior enemy, Greene ignored a maxim of war and split up his force of 1,800 Continentals. He sent 300 men east to bolster Marion and ordered Morgan and 300 riflemen west to threaten the British outpost of Ninety-Six. Cornwallis divided his own army and sent Tarleton with a mixed force of British and loyalists after Morgan, who decided to stand with his back to a river at a place called Cowpens.

Tarleton attacked on January 17, 1781, but Morgan's men annihilated his legion. On March 15, Greene's now 4,400 men faced Cornwallis's 1,900 men at Guilford Court House. Even though the British retained possession of the battlefield, they lost one-quarter of their force. Cornwallis retreated to the coast to refit. He then marched into Virginia. Instead of following him, Greene returned to South Carolina, where he and Marion took the surviving British outposts. After the British evacuated Ninety-Six on July 1, 1781, they held only Savannah and Charleston in the Deep South.

Government Reform

While armed partisans were making the war more radical, politics became more conservative, moving toward the creation of European state forms, such as executive departments and a bank. Congress stopped printing money, abandoned its cumbersome committee system, and created separate executive departments of foreign affairs, finance, war, and marine. Robert Morris, a Philadelphia merchant, became secretary of finance, helped to organize the Bank of North America (America's first), and made certain that the Continental army was clothed and well fed. Congress began to requisition revenue from the states, which imposed heavy taxes but not enough to meet both their own and national needs. Congress tried to amend the Articles of Confederation in 1781 and asked the states for a 5 percent duty on all imports. Most states quickly ratified the "impost," but amendments to the Articles needed unanimous approval. In 1783 Rhode Island's opposition killed the impost. A new impost proposal was defeated by New York in 1786.

The reforms of 1781 barely kept a smaller army in the field for the rest of the war, but the new executive departments had an unforeseen effect. Congress had been a plural executive, America's answer to the imperial Crown. But once Congress created its own departments, it looked more like a feeble legislature. It began to pass not just "orders" and "resolves" but also "ordinances," which were meant to be permanent and binding. It still could not punish anyone for noncompliance, which may be why it never called any of its measures "laws."

From the Ravaging of Virginia to Yorktown and Peace

Nathanael Greene *A general from Rhode Island whose superb strategy of irregular war reclaimed the Lower South for the American cause in 1780–1781.*

Both Cornwallis and Washington believed that events in Virginia would decide the war. In January 1781, Clinton sent Arnold from New York with 1,600 men. They sailed up the James and gutted the new capital of Richmond. When Governor Thomas Jefferson called out the militia, few responded. Most Virginia freemen had already

Map 6.2 War in the Lower South, 1780–1781. *British victories in 1780 nearly restored Georgia and South Carolina to the Crown, but after Guilford Court House in March 1781, the Americans regained the advantage throughout the region.*

done service, if only as short-term militia, many as recently as 1780. They thought it was now someone else's turn. For months, there was no one else. Cornwallis took command in April, and Arnold departed for New York. But the raids continued into summer, sweeping as far west as Charlottesville, where Tarleton almost captured Jefferson. Many of Jefferson's slaves greeted the British as liberators. Washington sent the French marquis de Lafayette with 1,200 New England and New Jersey Continentals to contain the damage. Cornwallis withdrew to Yorktown.

Map 6.3 **Virginia and the Yorktown Campaign.** *After the British ravaged much of Virginia, Washington and a French fleet and army were able to trap Lord Cornwallis at Yorktown, force his surrender, and guarantee American independence.*

Yorktown *The last major engagement of the Revolutionary War. Washington's army, two French armies, and a French fleet trapped Lord Cornwallis at Yorktown and forced his army to surrender in October 1781.*

At last, Washington saw an opportunity. He learned that a powerful French fleet under François, comte de Grasse, with 3,000 soldiers would sail from St. Domingue for Chesapeake Bay on August 13. Cooperating closely with the French army commander, Jean Baptiste Donatien, comte de Rochambeau, Washington sprang his trap. Rochambeau led his 5,000 soldiers from Newport to the outskirts of New York, where they joined Washington's 5,000 Continentals. After feinting an attack to freeze Clinton in place, Washington led the combined armies south to tidewater Virginia, where they linked up with Lafayette's Americans and de Grasse's French army. After de Grasse beat back a British relief force at the Battle of the Capes on September 5, Washington besieged **Yorktown**. On October 19, 1781, Cornwallis surrendered his army of 8,000 men. Yorktown brought down the British government in March 1782. Lord North resigned. The British evacuated Savannah and Charleston and concentrated their remaining forces in New York City.

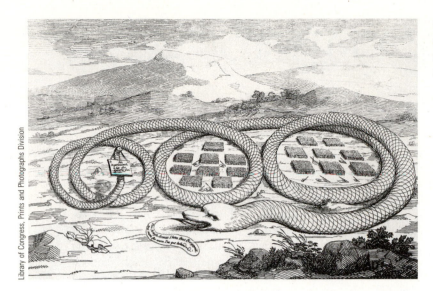

Library of Congress, Prints and Photographs Division

"The American Rattle Snake." *This 1782 cartoon celebrated the victory of Yorktown, the second time in the war that an entire British army had surrendered to the United States.*

Contrary to the French Treaty of 1778, John Jay and John Adams opened secret peace talks in Paris with the British. They won British recognition of the Mississippi, but without New Orleans, as the western boundary of the new republic. New Englanders retained the right to fish off Newfoundland. The treaty recognized the validity of prewar transatlantic debts, and Congress promised to urge the states to restore confiscated loyalist property. After the negotiations were far advanced, the Americans told Vergennes what they were doing. He feigned indignation, but the threat of a separate peace gave him the leverage he needed with Spain. Spain stopped demanding that France fight until Gibraltar surrendered. The Treaty of Paris ended the war in 1783. Western Indians were appalled to learn that the treaty gave their lands to the United States. They knew that they had not been conquered, whatever European diplomats might say. Their war for survival continued with few breaks into 1795.

Congress still faced ominous problems. In March 1783 many Continental officers threatened a coup d'état unless Congress granted them generous pensions. Washington, confronting them at their encampment at Newburgh, New York, fumbled for his glasses and remarked, "I have grown old in the service of my country, and now find that I am growing blind." Tears filled the eyes of his comrades in arms, and the threat of a coup vanished. Still, the Union's stability, even its survival, remained uncertain.

A REVOLUTIONARY SOCIETY

Independence transformed America. The biggest winners were free householders, who gained from the democratization of politics and the chance to colonize the West. Besides loyalists, the biggest losers were Indians, determined to resist settler expansion. Many slaves won freedom, and women struggled for greater dignity. Both succeeded only when their goals proved compatible with the ambitions of white householders.

Religious Transformations

Independence left the Anglican Church vulnerable, if only because George III was its "supreme head." Although most Anglican clergymen supported the Revolution

MUSICAL LINK TO THE PAST

No King but God!

Composer: William Billings
Title: "Independence" (1778)

William Billings, America's most important musical figure during its first two decades of independence, was the first native-born composer to spend all of his time on music—a luxury both then and now. Billings was also the first and perhaps the only person to compose songs inspired by the Revolution. While John Dickinson and Thomas Jefferson established political justifications for the American break with Great Britain, Billings in "Independence" offers a religious justification: "To the King they shall sing hallelujah / And all the continent shall sing: down with this earthly King / No King but God." Billings insists that Americans were not impetuous in declaring independence because they exhibited a great respect for God and proper social institutions. In this view, Britain and King George III placed themselves in a position above God by depriving Anglo-Americans of their rights as British subjects. For a new country that already had a long history of passionate commitment to religion, this argument for American independence was probably quite convincing.

Although the idea that Americans could create art equal to or of more worth than Europeans would not become commonplace until the 20th century, Billings viewed himself as a serious American artist. He was also the first major American composer to lobby for a copyright law. The lack of such a law cost Billings a fortune when his defiant song "Chester" became the most popular song of the American Revolution, and numerous publishers bootlegged it without permission. Under

pressure from Billings and a similarly plagiarized Noah Webster (the author of America's first dictionary), Congress passed its first copyright law in 1790. Because it failed to provide any U.S. protection for foreign artists and composers, however, American publishers released and promoted floods of European works on which they did not pay royalties. Because Congress was unable to protect what is now known as intellectual property, William Billings, the author of "Independence," did not make a living commensurate to the musical contribution he made to his country.

Q Early American artists such as William Billings had to shape the role of the artist in a democracy. Some American observers at the time and in the 19th century believed that creating art represented a frivolous and decadent occupation in the United States. Should artists in a democracy seek to create works that promote the goals and aspirations of the populace as a whole, or should they cultivate a more personal expression?

Q Do you think that today's practice of downloading music through the Internet presents a similar ethical problem to the unauthorized publishing of Billings's works that occurred during the early national period?

 Listen to an audio recording of this music on the Musical Links to the Past CD.

or remained neutral, an aggressive loyalist minority stirred the wrath of patriots. Religious dissenters disestablished the Anglican Church in every southern state. In 1786, Virginia passed Jefferson's Statute for Religious Freedom, which declared that efforts to use coercion in matters of religion "tend only to beget habits of hypocrisy and meanness." In Virginia, church attendance and the support of ministers became voluntary activities. Other states moved more slowly. Congregational churches supported the Revolution and were less vulnerable to attack. Disestablishment did not become complete until 1818 in Connecticut and 1833 in Massachusetts.

Although most states still restricted officeholding to Christians or Protestants, many people were coming to regard the coercion of anyone's conscience as morally wrong. Jews and Catholics both gained from the new atmosphere of tolerance.

The First Emancipation

The Revolution freed tens of thousands of slaves, but it also gave new vitality to slavery in the region that people were beginning to call "the South." Within a generation, slavery was abolished in the emerging "North." Race became a defining factor in both regions. In the South, most blacks remained slaves. In the North, they became free but not equal.

The British army enabled more than half the slaves of Georgia and perhaps one-quarter of those in South Carolina to free themselves. A similar process was under way in Virginia in 1781, only to be cut short at Yorktown. Hundreds of New England slaves won freedom through military service. After the Massachusetts bill of rights proclaimed that all people were "born free and equal," Elizabeth (Bett) Freeman sued her master in 1781 and won her liberty. Thereafter, most of the slaves in Massachusetts and New Hampshire simply walked away from their masters.

Elsewhere, legislative action was necessary. Pennsylvania led the way in 1780 with the modern world's first gradual **emancipation** statute. It declared that all children born to slaves would become free at age 28. The slaves, not masters or taxpayers, thus bore the costs of their own emancipation. This requirement left them unable to compete on equal terms with free whites, who usually entered adult life with inherited property. Some masters shipped their slaves south before emancipation, and some whites kidnapped freedmen and carried them south. The Pennsylvania Abolition Society existed largely to fight these abuses.

The Pennsylvania pattern took hold, with variations, in most other northern states. Where slaves constituted more than 10 percent of the population, as in southern New York and northeastern New Jersey, slaveholders' resistance delayed legislation for years. New York yielded in 1799, New Jersey in 1804.

In the upper South, Maryland and Virginia authorized the **manumission** of individual slaves. By 1810 more than one-fifth of Maryland's slaves had been freed, as had 10,000 of Virginia's 300,000 slaves, including 123 freed in Washington's will. Southern planters supported humane reforms such as the Christianization of their slaves, but they resisted emancipation, especially with the rise of cotton as a new cash crop after the war. General emancipation would have amounted to a social and economic revolution.

Maryland and Virginia banned the Atlantic slave trade, as did all states outside the Deep South. But Georgia and South Carolina reopened it to offset wartime losses and to raise cotton. South Carolina imported almost 60,000 more Africans before Congress prohibited that traffic in 1808.

The Challenge to Patriarchy

Nothing as dramatic as emancipation altered relations between the sexes. With the men away fighting, many women were left in charge of the household and had to work harder to keep it functioning. The war cut them off from most European consumer goods. Household manufactures, largely the task of women, filled the gap. Soaring food prices made women more assertive. In numerous food riots, women tried to force merchants to lower prices or stop hoarding grain.

Attitudes toward marriage were also changing. The common-law rule of coverture (see Chapter 4) still denied wives any legal personality, but a few persuaded state governments not to impoverish them by confiscating the property of their loyalist husbands. Many writers insisted that good marriages rested on mutual affection, not on property settlements. Parents were urged to respect the personalities of their children and to avoid severe discipline. Although few women

emancipation *Refers to release from slavery or bondage.*

manumission of slaves *The act of freeing a slave, done at the will of the owner.*

yet demanded equal political rights, the New Jersey Constitution of 1776 let them vote if they headed a household (usually as a widow) and paid taxes. This right was revoked in 1807.

Philosophers, clergymen, and even popular writers began treating women as morally superior to men. In the Northeast, the first female academies opened in the 1790s, and more women learned to read and write. By 1830 nearly all native-born women in the Northeast had become literate. The ideal of the "republican wife" and the "republican mother" took hold, giving wives and mothers an expanding educational role within the family. They encouraged diligence in their husbands and patriotism in their sons. The novel became a major cultural form in the United States. Its main audience was female, as were many of the authors.

Western Expansion, Discontent, and Conflict with Indians

Westward expansion continued during the Revolutionary War. With 30 axmen, **Daniel Boone** hacked out the Wilderness Road from Cumberland Gap to the Kentucky bluegrass country in early 1775. Because of the constant danger of conflict with Indians, only a few thousand settlers stuck it out until the war ended, when they were joined by swarms of newcomers. Speculators and absentees were already trying to claim the best lands. The Federal Census of 1790 listed 74,000 settlers and slaves in Kentucky and about half that many in Tennessee, where the Cherokees had ceded a large tract after their defeat in 1776. Those settlers thrived both because few Indians lived there and because British and Spanish raiders found it hard to reach them.

Americans had recruited soldiers with promises of land after the war. Now they needed Indian lands to fulfill these pledges. The Indian nations that supported the United States suffered the most. In the 1780s, after Joseph Brant led most of the Iroquois north to Canada, New York confiscated much of the land of the friendly Iroquois who stayed. South Carolina dispossessed the Catawbas of most of their lands. The states had a harder time seizing the land of hostile Indians who had Spanish or British aid.

Secessionist movements arose in the 1780s when neither Congress nor eastern state governments seemed able to solve western problems. Some Tennessee settlers seceded from North Carolina to maintain, briefly, the separate state of Franklin. Settlers in western Pennsylvania thought of setting up on their own after Spain closed the Mississippi to American traffic in 1784. When Congress refused to recognize Vermont's independence from New York, even the radical Green Mountain Boys sounded out Canadian officials about readmission to the British Empire as a separate province.

The Northwest Ordinance

After Virginia ceded its land claims north of the Ohio River to Congress, other states followed suit. In the Land Ordinance of 1785, Congress authorized the survey of the Northwest Territory and its division into townships six miles square, each composed of 36 "sections" of 640 acres. Surveyed land would be sold at auction starting at a dollar per acre. Alternate townships would be sold in sections or as a whole, to satisfy settlers and speculators, respectively.

In July 1787, Congress passed the **Northwest Ordinance**. It authorized the creation of from 3 to 5 states, to be admitted to the Union as equals of the original 13. Congress would appoint a governor and a council to rule until

Daniel Boone *A pioneer settler of Kentucky, Boone became the most famous American frontiersman of his generation.*

Northwest Ordinance *This ordinance established the Northwest Territory between the Ohio River and the Great Lakes. Adopted by the Confederation Congress in 1787, it abolished slavery in the territory and provided that it be divided into 3 to 5 states that would eventually be admitted to the Union as full equals of the original 13.*

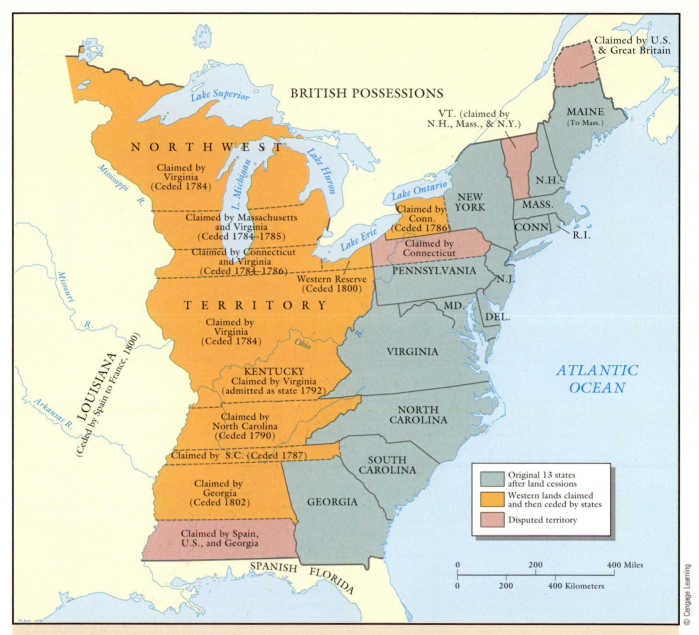

Map 6.4 Western Land Claims during the Revolution. *One of the most difficult questions that Congress faced was the competing western land claims of several states. After Virginia ceded its claims north of the Ohio to Congress, other states followed suit, creating the national domain and what soon became the Northwest Territory.*

population reached 5,000. At that point, the settlers could elect an assembly empowered to pass laws, but the governor had an absolute veto. When population reached 60,000, the settlers could draft their own constitution and petition Congress for statehood. The ordinance protected civil liberties, provided for public education, and prohibited slavery in the territory.

Southern delegates all voted for the Northwest Ordinance despite its antislavery clause. The clause may have been part of a larger Compromise of 1787, involving both the ordinance and the clauses on slavery in the federal Constitution. The Constitutional Convention in Philadelphia permitted states to count three-fifths of their slaves for purposes of representation and taxation. The antislavery concession to northerners in the ordinance was made at the same time that southern states

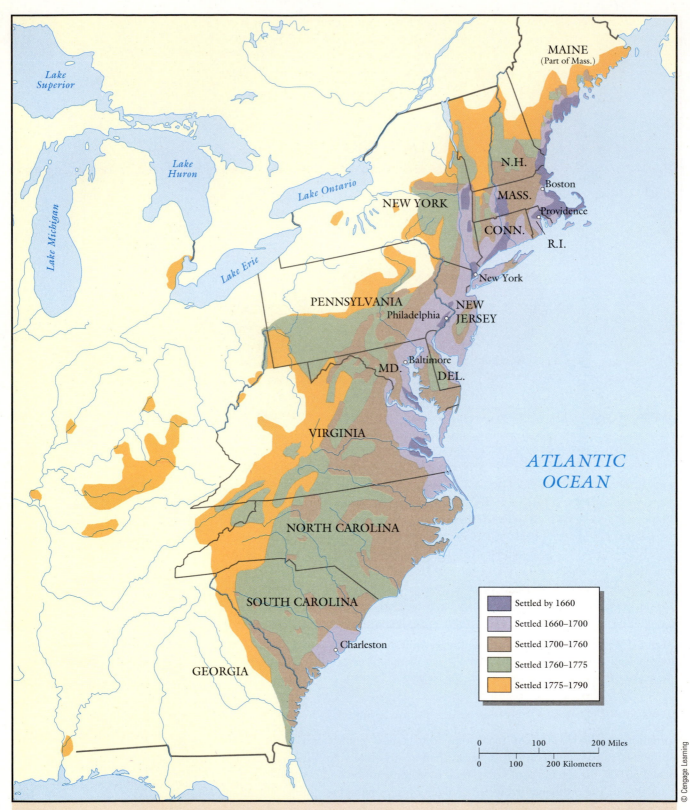

Map 6.5 Advance of Settlement to 1790. *Between 1760 and 1790 America's population grew from nearly 1.6 million to almost 4 million. The area of settlement was spreading west of Pittsburgh and into much of Kentucky and parts of Tennessee.*

won this concession in Philadelphia. Several congressmen were also delegates to the Constitutional Convention and traveled back and forth while these decisions were being made. They may have struck a deal.

When the first townships in Ohio were offered for sale in late 1787, there were few buyers. Yet by 1789, the Ohio Company had established the town of Marietta, and Kentuckians had founded Cincinnati. But without massive help from the new federal government, the settlers had little chance of overcoming stout Indian resistance.

A MORE PERFECT UNION

The 1780s were difficult times. The economy failed to rebound, debtors fought creditors, and state politics became bitter and contentious. Out of this ferment arose the demand to amend or even replace the Articles of Confederation.

Commerce, Debt, and Shays's Rebellion

In 1784, British merchants flooded American markets with exports worth £3.7 million, the greatest volume since 1771. But Americans could not pay for them. Exports to Britain that year were £750,000—less than 40 percent of the £1.9 million of 1774. Britain invoked the Navigation Acts to close the British West Indies to American ships. Because the French could not offer the long-term credit that the British had provided, trade with France remained disappointing. The American economy entered a deep depression. Private debts became a huge social problem, and farmers, faced with the loss of their farms, looked to their state governments for relief.

About half the states issued paper money, and many passed **stay laws** to postpone the date on which a debt would come due. Massachusetts rejected both options and raised taxes to new heights. In 1786, many farmers in Hampshire County took matters into their own hands. Crowds gathered to prevent the courts from conducting business, much as patriots had done against the British in 1774. In early 1787, the protestors, loosely organized under a Continental Army veteran, Captain Daniel Shays, threatened the federal arsenal at Springfield. Although they were scattered by militia, Shaysites won enough seats in the May elections to pass a stay law. **Shays's Rebellion** converted into nationalists many gentlemen and artisans who until then had opposed strengthening the central government.

Cosmopolitans versus Localists

The tensions racking Massachusetts surfaced elsewhere. Debtors in other states closed law courts or even besieged the legislature. State politics reflected a persistent rift between "cosmopolitan" and "localist" coalitions. Merchants, professional men, urban artisans, commercial farmers, southern planters, and former Continental Army officers made up the cosmopolitan bloc. They favored aggressive trade policies, hard money, payment of public debts, good salaries for executive officials and judges, and leniency to returning loyalists. Localists were farmers, rural artisans, and militia veterans who distrusted those policies. They demanded paper money, debtor relief, and generous salaries for representatives so that ordinary men could afford to serve.

In most states, localists usually defeated their opponents. Cosmopolitans lost so often that many of them despaired of state politics and became

stay laws *Laws that delay or postpone a proceeding. During the 1780s many states passed stay laws to delay the due date on debts because of the serious economic problems of the times.*

Shays's Rebellion *An uprising of farmers in western Massachusetts in the winter of 1786–1787. They objected to high taxes and foreclosures for unpaid debts. Militia from eastern Massachusetts suppressed the rebels.*

nationalists eager to strengthen the Union. In 1785 some of them tried to see what could be done outside Congress, which was faltering under its massive postwar debt. Prompted by James Madison, the Virginia legislature urged all the states to participate in a convention at Annapolis to explore ways to improve American trade. Four states ignored the call, and the New Englanders had not yet arrived when, in September 1786, the delegates from the four middle states and Virginia accepted a report drafted by Alexander Hamilton of New York. It asked all the states to send delegates to a convention at Philadelphia the next May "to devise such further provisions as shall appear to them necessary to render the constitution of the Federal Government adequate to the exigencies of the Union." Seven states responded positively before Congress endorsed the convention on February 21, 1787, and five accepted later. Rhode Island refused to participate.

The Philadelphia Convention

The convention opened in May 1787. The delegates, in four months of secret sessions, repeated the constitutional learning process that had taken four years to unfold at the state level after 1776.

With Washington presiding, Governor Edmund Randolph proposed the Virginia, or "large state," Plan. Drafted by Madison, it proposed a bicameral legislature, with representation in both houses apportioned according to population. The legislature would choose the executive and the judiciary. It would possess all powers currently lodged in Congress and the power "to legislate in all cases to which the separate States are incompetent." It could "negative all laws passed by the several States, contravening in [its] opinion . . . the articles of Union." The plan did not include explicit powers to tax or regulate trade.

In mid-June, delegates from the small states struck back. William Paterson proposed the New Jersey Plan, which gave the existing Congress the power to levy import duties and a stamp tax (as in Grenville's imperial reforms of 1764 and 1765), to regulate trade, and to use force to collect delinquent requisitions from the states (as in North's Conciliatory Proposition of 1775). As under the Articles, each state would have one vote.

The debate grew as hot as the summer weather. The small states warned that their voters would never accept a constitution that let the large states swallow them. The large states insisted on proportional representation in both houses. Then the Connecticut delegates announced that they would be happy with proportional representation in one house and state equality in the other.

In July, the delegates accepted this Connecticut Compromise and then completed the document by September. They finally realized that they were creating a government of laws, to be enforced on individuals through federal courts, and were not propping up a system of congressional resolutions to be carried out (or ignored) by the states. Terms for representatives were set at two years, and terms for senators at six, with each state legislature choosing two senators. The president would serve four years, could be reelected, and would be chosen by an **Electoral College**. Each state received as many electors as it had congressmen and senators combined, and the states were free to decide how to choose their electors.

In other provisions, free and slave states agreed to count only three-fifths of the slaves in apportioning both representation and direct taxes. The enumeration of congressional powers became lengthy and explicit and included taxation, the regulation of foreign and interstate commerce, and the catchall "necessary and proper"

Electoral College *The group that elects the president. Each state received as many electors as it had congressmen and senators combined. Each state could decide how to choose its electors.*

"THE HERO WHO DEFENDED THE MOTHERS WILL PROTECT THE DAUGHTERS."
Washington is hailed by young women near the bridge at Trenton on the way to his inauguration as first president of the United States, 1789.

© North Wind Picture Archives

clause. Madison's negative on state laws was replaced by the gentler "supreme law of the land" clause. Over George Mason's last-minute objection, the delegates refused to include a bill of rights.

With little debate, the convention approved a revolutionary proposal for ratifying the Constitution. This clause called for special conventions in each state and declared that the Constitution would go into force as soon as any nine states had accepted it, even though the Articles of Confederation required unanimous approval for all amendments. The delegates were proposing an illegal but peaceful overthrow of the existing legal order—that is, a revolution. If all the states approved, it would, they hoped, become both peaceful and legal. The Constitution would then rest on popular sovereignty in a way that the Articles never had. The **Federalists**, as supporters of the Constitution now called themselves, were willing to risk destroying the Union in order to save it.

Ratification

Back home, Federalist delegates made a powerful case for the Constitution in newspapers. Most Anti-Federalists, or opponents of the Constitution, were localists with little access to the press. Federalists gave them little time to organize. The first ratifying conventions met in December. Delaware ratified unanimously on December 7. Pennsylvania, New Jersey, Georgia, and Connecticut soon followed.

In Pennsylvania, Anti-Federalists eloquently demanded a federal bill of rights and major changes in the structure of the new government. The other victories came in small states, which, once they had equality in the Senate, saw many advantages in a strong central government. Under the new Constitution, import duties would go to the federal government, not to neighboring states—a clear gain for every small state but Rhode Island, which stood to lose import duties at both Providence and Newport.

The first hotly contested state was Massachusetts. Federalists won there by a slim margin (187 to 168) in February 1788 by promising to support a bill of rights through constitutional amendment *after* ratification. The Rhode Island legislature voted overwhelmingly against summoning a ratifying convention. Maryland and South Carolina ratified easily in April and May, bringing the total to eight of the

Federalists *Supporters of the Constitution during the ratification process. Anti-Federalists resisted ratification.*

nine states required. Then conventions met almost simultaneously in New Hampshire, Virginia, New York, and North Carolina. In each, a majority at first opposed ratification.

As resistance stiffened, the ratification controversy turned into the first great debate on what kind of a national government the United States ought to have. The Anti-Federalists argued that the new government would be too remote from the people to be trusted with such broad powers. They warned that in a House of Representatives divided into districts of 30,000 people (twice the size of Boston), only prominent men would be elected. The absence of a bill of rights also troubled them.

During the struggle over ratification, Hamilton, Madison, and Jay wrote a series of 85 essays, published first in New York newspapers, then widely reprinted elsewhere. They defended the Constitution almost clause by clause. Signing themselves "Publius," they later published the collected essays as *The Federalist Papers.* In *Federalist, no. 10,* Madison challenged 2,000 years of received wisdom when he argued that a large republic would be more stable than a small one. In small republics, he argued, majority factions could easily gain power, trample the rights of minorities, and ignore the common good. But in a huge republic as diverse as the United States, factions would seldom be able to forge a majority. "Publius" hoped that the new government would attract the talents of the wisest and best-educated citizens. To those who accused him of trying to erect an American aristocracy, he noted that the Constitution forbade titles and hereditary rule.

Federalists won a narrow majority (57 to 46) in New Hampshire on June 21, and Madison guided Virginia to ratification (89 to 79) five days later. New York approved, by 30 votes to 27, one month later, bringing 11 states into the Union, enough to launch the new government. North Carolina rejected the Constitution in July 1788 but finally ratified in November 1789 after the first Congress had drafted the Bill of Rights and sent it to the states. Rhode Island, after voting seven times not to call a ratifying convention, finally summoned one that ratified by a vote of 34 to 32 in May 1790.

Conclusion

Americans survived the most devastating war they had yet fought and won independence, but only with massive aid from France. Most blacks and Indians sided with Britain. During the struggle white Americans affirmed liberty and equality for themselves in their new state constitutions and bills of rights, but they rarely applied these values to Indians and blacks, even though every northern state adopted either immediate or gradual emancipation. The discontent of the postwar years created the Federalist coalition, which drafted and ratified a new national Constitution to replace the Articles of Confederation. Nothing resembling the American federal system had ever been tried before. It removed sovereignty from government and bestowed it on the people, who then empowered separate levels of government through their state and federal constitutions. As the Great Seal of the United States proclaimed, it was a *novus ordo seclorum*—a new order for the ages.

CHAPTER REVIEW

Review Questions

1. What enabled American volunteers, fiercely committed to individual liberty, to believe that they could defeat Britain's disciplined professional army?
2. Why did France intervene after Britain took Philadelphia, the American capital, and forced Congress to flee?
3. How did American constitutionalism after 1776 differ from the British constitutional principles that the colonists had accepted and revered before 1776?
4. Why, despite the French alliance, did the United States nearly lose the war between 1779 and 1781?
5. In the Carolinas, the war went radical in 1780 with an emphasis on guerilla tactics, but in Philadelphia, Congress grew more conservative, creating executive departments and moving toward European models of government finance. Were these trends contradictory?
6. In what ways did the values shared by independent householders limit the reforms that the Revolution could offer to other Americans?

Critical Thinking Questions

1. The Articles of Confederation favored small states, especially in giving each state one vote in Congress. Why then did large states ratify quickly while three small states held up final ratification for years? The Constitution shifted power to large states. Why then did most small states ratify quickly while every large state except Pennsylvania came close to rejecting the new government?
2. The federal Constitution dramatically increased the power of the central government of the United States. What about liberty and equality? Did the Constitution make them more secure, or did it sacrifice part of one or both in order to empower the new government?

Identifications

Review your understanding of the following key terms, people, and events for this chapter.

General William Howe, p. 132
George Washington, p. 132
loyalists, p. 133
Saratoga, p. 135
popular sovereignty, p. 136

separation of powers, p. 136
public virtue, p. 136
unicameral legislature, p. 137
sovereign power, p. 137
convention, p. 138
attrition, p. 140

Nathanael Greene, p. 144
Yorktown, p. 146
emancipation, p. 149
manumission of slaves, p. 149
Daniel Boone, p. 150
Northwest Ordinance, p. 150

stay laws, p. 153
Shays's Rebellion, p. 153
Electoral College, p. 154
Federalists, p. 155

DISCOVERY

Winning the War for Independence and solidifying the changes unleashed by the American Revolution were two different projects. In what ways did America change following the Revolution? What impact did this have on America's future?

In thinking about this question, begin by breaking it down into the components shown below. A discussion of the significance of each component should appear in your answer.

Geography

Look at the map concerning western land claims. What problems are apparent in the new territories? How did claims to those lands impede the work of an American government? On what basis were those claims made? What areas might cause the most problems for the new government? Look at the map concerning settlement patterns. In what western territories was settlement occurring most rapidly? Where do you think those settlers were coming from? In what ways do you think patterns of settlement might have affected the balance of territory and population between North and South in the first 50 years of the 19th century?

Map 6.4 Western Land Claims during the Revolution

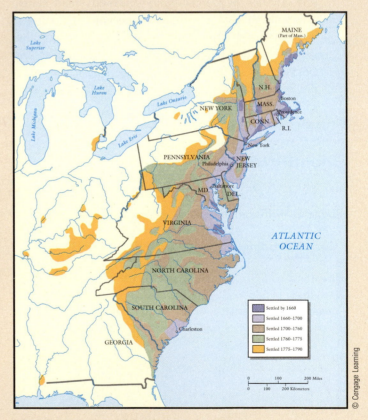

Map 6.5 Advance of Settlement to 1790

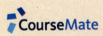

Visit the CourseMate website at www.cengagebrain.com for additional study tools and review materials for this chapter.

COMPLETING THE REVOLUTION, 1789–1815

Almost by acclamation, George Washington became the first president under the Constitution. Washington and his closest advisers (they would soon call themselves Federalists) believed that the balance between power and liberty had tipped toward anarchy after the Revolution. Federalists wanted the Constitution to counter democratic excesses, and they sought to make the national government powerful enough to command respect abroad and impose order at home. For the most part, they succeeded, but in the process they aroused a determined opposition. These self-styled Democratic Republicans (led almost from the beginning by Thomas Jefferson) were as firmly tied to revolutionary ideals of limited government and a citizenry of independent farmers as the Federalists were tied to visions of an orderly commercial republic with a powerful national state. The fight between Federalists and Democratic Republicans was conducted against a backdrop of international intrigue and war between France and Britain.

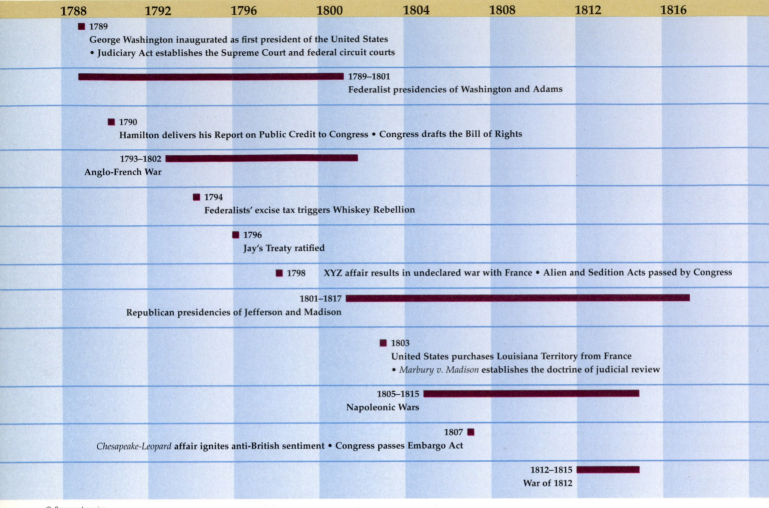

1788	1792	1796	1800	1804	1808	1812	1816

■ 1789
George Washington inaugurated as first president of the United States
• Judiciary Act establishes the Supreme Court and federal circuit courts

1789–1801
Federalist presidencies of Washington and Adams

■ 1790
Hamilton delivers his Report on Public Credit to Congress • Congress drafts the Bill of Rights

1793–1802
Anglo-French War

■ 1794
Federalists' excise tax triggers Whiskey Rebellion

■ 1796
Jay's Treaty ratified

■ 1798 XYZ affair results in undeclared war with France • Alien and Sedition Acts passed by Congress

1801–1817
Republican presidencies of Jefferson and Madison

■ 1803
United States purchases Louisiana Territory from France
• *Marbury v. Madison* establishes the doctrine of judicial review

1805–1815
Napoleonic Wars

1807 ■
Chesapeake-Leopard affair ignites anti-British sentiment • Congress passes Embargo Act

1812–1815
War of 1812

© Cengage Learning

ESTABLISHING THE NATIONAL GOVERNMENT

FOCUS QUESTION

What was the Federalist plan for organizing the national government and its finances? What were the Jeffersonian Republicans' principal objections to those plans?

George Washington left Mount Vernon for the temporary capital in New York City in April 1789. Militia companies and local dignitaries escorted him from town to town, crowds cheered, church bells marked his progress, and lines of girls in white dresses waved demurely as he passed. At Newark Bay, he boarded a flower-bedecked barge and crossed to New York City, where he was inaugurated on April 30.

Mr. President

Reporting for work, President Washington found the new government embroiled in its first controversy—an argument over the dignity that would attach to his office. Vice President John Adams had asked the Senate to create a title of honor for the president. Adams and others wanted a resounding title that would reflect the power of the new executive. They considered "His Highness," "His Elective Highness," "His Most Benign Highness," "His Majesty," and "His Highness, the President of the United States, and Protector of Their Liberties." The Senate debated the question for a month, until it became clear that the more democratic House of Representatives disliked titles. They settled on the austere dignity of "Mr. President."

Much was at stake in the argument over titles. What citizens called their president was part of the constellation of laws, customs, and forms of etiquette that would give the new government either a republican or a courtly tone. Many Federalists wanted to bolster presidential power against the localism and democracy that, they believed, had nearly killed the republic in the 1780s. Washington's inaugural tour, the endless round of formal balls and presidential dinners, the appearance of Washington's profile on some of the nation's coins—all dramatized the power and grandeur of the new government. The battle over titles was a revealing episode in the argument over how Americans would finally answer the questions of power and liberty they had debated since the 1760s.

GEORGE WASHINGTON IN 1796, NEAR THE END OF HIS PRESIDENCY. *The artist here captured the formal dignity of the first president and surrounded him with gold, red velvet, a presidential throne, and other emblems of kingly office.*

The First Congress

Under James Madison's leadership, the First Congress strengthened the new national government at every turn. First it passed a **tariff** on imports, which would be the government's chief source of income. Next, it turned to amendments to the Constitution demanded by the state ratifying conventions.

Madison proposed 19 constitutional amendments. The 10 that survived congressional scrutiny and ratification by the states became the **Bill of Rights**. The First Amendment guaranteed the freedoms of speech, press, and religion against federal interference. The Second and Third Amendments guaranteed the continuation of a militia of armed citizens and stated the specific conditions under which soldiers could be quartered in citizens' households. The Fourth through Eighth Amendments defined a citizen's rights in court and when under arrest. The Ninth Amendment stated that the enumeration of specific rights in the first eight amendments did not imply a denial of other rights. Finally, the Tenth Amendment stated that powers not assigned to the national government by the Constitution remained with the states and the citizenry.

Doubters at the ratifying conventions had called for amendments that would weaken the national government. By channeling their fears into the area of civil liberties, Madison soothed popular concerns while preserving governmental power. The Bill of Rights was an important guarantee of individual liberties. In the context in which it was written and ratified, however, it was an even more important guarantee of the power of the national government.

Congress then created the executive departments of war, state, and treasury. The heads of those departments and their assistants would be appointed by the president. With the Judiciary Act of 1789, Congress established a Supreme Court with six members, along with 13 district courts and three **circuit courts** of appeal. The act allowed for certain cases to be appealed from state courts to federal circuit courts presided over by traveling Supreme Court justices.

Hamiltonian Economics

Washington chose Henry Knox, an old comrade from the Revolution, to be secretary of war. The State Department went to his fellow Virginian, Thomas Jefferson. He chose **Alexander Hamilton** of New York to head the Department

tariff *A tax on imports.*

Bill of Rights *The first 10 amendments to the Constitution, which protect the rights of individuals from abuses by the federal government.*

circuit court *Court that meets at different places within a district.*

Alexander Hamilton *Secretary of the Treasury under Washington. He organized the finances of the new government and led the partisan fight against the Democratic Republicans.*

LINK TO THE PAST

Washington's "Republican Court"

George Washington did what he could to surround the office of the presidency with dignity and an aura of awe—something that more democratic members of the new government considered reminiscent of European court society. Here is a description of Washington at a formal reception:

> The president was dressed in black velvet; his hair in full dress, powdered and gathered behind in a large silk bag; yellow gloves on his hands; holding a cocked hat with cockade in it, and the edges adorned with a black feather about an inch deep. He wore knee and shoe buckles; and a long sword, with a finely wrought and polished steel hilt, which appeared at the left hip; the coat worn over the sword, so that the hilt, and the part below the folds of the coat behind, were in view. The scabbard was white polished leather.
>
> He stood always in front of the fireplace, with his face towards the door of entrance. . . . He received his visitor with a dignified bow, while his hands were so disposed of as to indicate, that the salutation was not to be accompanied with shaking hands. This ceremony never occurred in these visits.
> —William Sullivan

In 1804, Sir John Augustus Foster took over his duties as Secretary of the British Legation in Washington.

Here is his description of Jefferson at a formal government function:

> Having mentioned Mr. Jefferson, it may be interesting to the reader to have the following description of his person as he appeared to me on my arrival in the United States in the year 1804. He was a tall man with a very red freckled face and grey neglected hair, his manners goodnatured, frank and rather friendly though he had somewhat of a cynical expression of countenance. He wore a blue coat, a thick grey coloured hairy waistcoat with a red underwaistcoat lapped over it, green velveteen breeches with pearl buttons, yarn stockings and slippers down at the heel, his appearance being very much like that of a tall large-boned farmer. He said he washed his feet as often as he did his hands in order to keep off cold, and appeared to think himself unique in so doing.

Q How did the presidential personae of Washington and Jefferson differ? How did those personae relate to what the two men wanted to accomplish as president of the United States?

Q Why do you think Washington avoided shaking hands with his guests? Why do you think Jefferson felt free to talk about washing his feet?

of the Treasury. A brilliant economic thinker, an admirer of the British system of centralized government and finance, and a supremely arrogant and ambitious man, Hamilton more than any other cabinet member directed the making of a national government.

In 1789, Congress asked Secretary Hamilton to report on the public debt. The debt fell into three categories, Hamilton reported. The first was the $11 million owed to foreigners—primarily debts to France incurred during the Revolution. The second and third—roughly $24 million each—were debts owed by the national and state governments to American citizens who had supplied food, arms, and other resources to the revolutionary cause. Congress agreed that both justice and the credibility of the new government dictated that the foreign debts be paid in full, but the domestic debts raised troublesome questions. Those debts consisted of notes issued during the Revolution to soldiers, merchants, farmers, and others who had helped the war effort. Over the years, businessmen and speculators had purchased many of these notes at 10 to 30 percent of their original value. Full payment would bring them enormous windfall profits.

The Revolutionary War debts of the individual states had also been bought up by speculators. Many states, including all of the southern states except South Carolina, had paid off most of their notes in the 1780s; the other states still had significant outstanding debts. If the federal government assumed the state debts and paid them off at face value, as the nationalists wanted, money would flow out of the southern, middle, and western states into the Northeast.

That is precisely what Hamilton proposed in his Report on Public Credit, issued in January 1790. He urged Congress to assume the state debts and to combine them with the federal government's foreign and domestic debts into a consolidated national debt. He agreed that the foreign debt should be paid promptly, but he insisted that the domestic debt be a permanent, tax-supported fixture of government. Under his plan, the government would issue securities to its creditors and would pay an annual rate of interest of 4 percent. A permanent debt would encourage wealthy financiers to invest in government securities, allying them with the national state. Servicing the debt would also require an enlargement of the federal civil service, national financial institutions, and federal taxes. The national debt, in short, was at the center of Alexander Hamilton's plan for a powerful national state.

As part of that plan, Hamilton asked Congress to charter a Bank of the United States. The government would store its funds in the bank and would supervise its operations, but the bank would be controlled by directors representing private stockholders. The Bank of the United States would print and back the national currency and would regulate other banks. To fund the national debt, Hamilton called for a federal **excise tax** on wines, coffee, tea, and spirits. The tax on spirits would fall most heavily on the whiskey produced on the frontier. Its purpose was not only to produce revenue but also to establish the government's power to create an internal tax and to collect it in the most remote regions in the republic.

The Rise of Opposition

In 1789, nearly every federal officeholder wanted to make the new government work. In particular, Alexander Hamilton at Treasury and James Madison in the House of Representatives expected to continue their political partnership. Yet in the debate over the national debt, Madison led congressional opposition to Hamilton. Hamilton presented his national debt proposal as a solution to specific problems of government finance. Madison and other southerners opposed it because they did not want northern speculators to reap fortunes from notes bought at rock-bottom prices from soldiers, widows, and orphans.

The congressional opposition compromised. In exchange for accepting Hamilton's debt, they won his promise to locate the permanent capital of the United States at a site on the Potomac River. The compromise went to the heart of American revolutionary republicanism. Hamilton intended to tie northeastern commercial interests to the federal government. If New York or Philadelphia became the permanent capital, political and economic power might be concentrated there as it was in Paris and London—court cities in league against the countryside. The compromise would distance the commercial power of the cities from the federal government and would put an end to the "republican court" that had formed around Washington.

Jefferson versus Hamilton

When Hamilton proposed the Bank of the United States, Republicans in Congress immediately noted its similarity to the Bank of England and voiced deep suspicion. Thomas Jefferson joined the opposition, arguing that Congress had no

excise tax *Internal tax on goods or services.*

right to charter a bank. Hamilton responded with the first argument for expanded federal power under the clause in the Constitution empowering Congress "to make all laws which shall be necessary and proper" to the performance of its duties. President Washington and a majority in Congress sided with Hamilton.

Jefferson contended that the federal bank was unconstitutional, that a federal excise tax would arouse public opposition, and that funding the debt rewarded speculators and penalized ordinary citizens. More important, Jefferson charged, Hamilton used government securities and stock in the Bank of the United States to buy the loyalty not only of merchants and speculators but also of members of Congress. "The ultimate object of all this," said Jefferson, "is to prepare the way for a change, from the present republican form of government, to that of a monarchy, of which the English constitution is to be the model."

For their part, Hamilton and his supporters (who by now were calling themselves Federalists) insisted that the centralization of power and a strong executive were necessary to the survival of the republic. The alternative was a return to the localism and public disorder of the 1780s. Until late 1792, this argument over Hamilton's centralizing schemes was limited to government officials. Then, as both sides began to mobilize popular support, events in Europe came to dominate the politics of the American republican experiment.

THE REPUBLIC IN A WORLD AT WAR, 1793–1800

FOCUS QUESTION

What were the principal foreign and internal threats to the federal government in the years 1793–1797? How did Federalist administrations respond to those threats?

Late in 1792, French revolutionaries rejected monarchy and proclaimed the French Republic. They beheaded Louis XVI in January 1793. Eleven days later, the French declared war on Britain, thus launching a war between French republicanism and the British-led reaction that, with periodic outbreaks of peace, would embroil the Atlantic world until the defeat of France in 1815. In the United States, national politics was now subsumed within the struggle over international republicanism.

Americans and the French Revolution

As Britain and France went to war in 1793, President Washington declared American neutrality, thereby **abrogating** the 1778 treaties with the French. Washington and his advisers wanted to stay on good terms with Great Britain; both commerce and the financial health of the government depended on that relationship. Moreover, Federalists genuinely sympathized with the British in the war with France. They viewed Britain as the defender of hierarchical society and ordered liberty against the homicidal anarchy of the French.

Although they agreed that the United States should stay out of the war, Jefferson and his friends saw things differently. They applauded the French for carrying on the republican revolution Americans had begun in 1776, and they had no affection for the monarchical politics of the Federalists or for Americans' continued neocolonial dependence upon British trade. The faction led by Jefferson and Madison wanted to abandon the English mercantile system and trade

abrogating a treaty *Process of abolishing a treaty so that it is no longer in effect.*

freely with all nations. They did not care if that course of action hurt commercial interests (most of which supported the Federalists) or impaired the government's ability to centralize power in itself.

Citizen Genêt

In the end, both Great Britain and France intervened freely in American affairs and made neutrality impossible. In April 1793, the French sent Citizen Edmond Genêt to the United States to enlist American aid with or without the Washington administration's consent. After the president's proclamation of neutrality, Genêt openly commissioned American privateers to harass British shipping and enlisted Americans in intrigues against the Spanish outpost of New Orleans. Genêt then opened France's Caribbean colonies to American shipping, providing American shippers a choice between French free trade and British mercantilism.

The British responded with a promise to seize any ship trading with French colonies in the Caribbean. The Royal Navy also searched American ships for English sailors who had deserted. During these searches, some American sailors were kidnapped into the British navy—an assault on American sovereignty. Meanwhile, the British began promising military aid to the Indians north of the Ohio River.

Western Troubles

The summer and fall of 1794 saw an intensified threat from British and Indian forces in the west, as well as from settlers in that region. The Shawnee and allied tribes plotted with the British and talked of driving all settlers out of their territory. At the same time, frontier whites resented a national government that could neither pacify the Indians nor guarantee their free use of the Mississippi River. President Washington heard that 2,000 Kentuckians were armed and ready to attack New Orleans—a move that would have started a war with Spain. Settlers in Georgia were making unauthorized forays against the Creeks.

Worst of all, frontier settlers refused to pay the excise tax on whiskey—a direct challenge to federal authority. In July 1794, near Pittsburgh, 500 militiamen marched on the house of federal excise collector General John Neville. Neville, his family, and a few federal soldiers fought the militiamen, killing two and wounding six before they abandoned the house to be looted and burned. Two weeks later, 6,000 "Whiskey Rebels" met at Braddock's Field near Pittsburgh, threatening to attack the town.

Washington determined to defeat the Indians and the Whiskey Rebels by force. He sent General "Mad" Anthony Wayne against the northwestern tribes. Wayne's decisive victory at Fallen Timbers in August 1794 ended the Indian-British challenge in the Northwest for many years. The Treaty of Greenville forced the Native Americans to cede two-thirds of what now makes up Ohio and southeastern Indiana. In September, Washington ordered 12,000 militiamen to quell the **Whiskey Rebellion**. He promised amnesty to rebels who pledged to support the government and prison terms to those who did not. As the army marched west, they met no armed resistance. They arrested 20 suspected rebels in Pittsburgh and marched them back to Philadelphia for trial. In the end only two "rebels," both of them feeble-minded, were convicted. President Washington pardoned them, and the Whiskey Rebellion was over.

Whiskey Rebellion *Revolt in western Pennsylvania against the federal excise tax on whiskey.*

QUICK REVIEW

JAY'S TREATY

• British abandoned their northwestern forts

• Did not settle maritime disputes

• Established trade with Great Britain on a favored-nation basis

The Jay Treaty

While he sent armies against Indians and frontiersmen, President Washington capitulated to the British on the high seas. In 1794, he sent John Jay, chief justice of the Supreme Court, to negotiate the conflicts between the United States and Britain. Armed with news of Wayne's victory, Jay extracted a promise from the British to remove their troops from American territory in the Northwest. But on every other point of dispute he agreed to British terms. Jay's Treaty reestablished trade with Great Britain on a most-favored-nation basis (something that was certain to cause domestic opposition), and it made no mention of **impressment** or other violations of American maritime rights. Given Great Britain's power, it was the best that Americans could expect. The Senate ratified Jay's Treaty in June 1795 by a bare two-thirds majority. The House ratified it the following year, but only after an intense battle that featured pitched resistance from southern representatives who believed the Federalists wanted to subvert republicanism in both France and the United States.

Washington's Farewell and the Election of 1796

George Washington refused to run for reelection in 1796. He could be proud of his accomplishments. He had presided over the creation of a national government and made it evident that the government could and would control its most distant regions. He had also avoided war with Great Britain, although not without overlooking assaults on American sovereignty. His farewell address warned against long-term "entangling alliances" with other countries. America, he said, should act independently in international affairs. Washington also warned against internal political divisions. Of course, he did not regard his own Federalists as a "party." They were simply friends of the government. Washington's call for unity and an end to partisanship was in fact a parting shot at Jefferson's Democratic Republicans, who he viewed as a self-interested faction.

In 1796, Americans experienced their first contested presidential election. The Federalists chose as their candidate John Adams of Massachusetts, who had served as vice president. The Democratic Republicans nominated Thomas Jefferson. Since Adams would certainly carry Federalist New England, and Jefferson would carry the South, the election would be decided in Pennsylvania and New York. There, as in most states, state legislatures selected the presidential electors. Jefferson won in Pennsylvania, but Adams took New York, which had more electoral votes. Prior to the ratification of the Twelfth Amendment in 1804, the candidate with a majority of the electoral votes became president, and the second-place candidate became vice president. As a result, Adams was elected president and Jefferson became vice president.

Troubles with France, 1796–1800

As Adams entered office, an international crisis was already in full swing. France, regarding Jay's Treaty as an Anglo-American alliance, had broken off relations with the United States. During the presidential elections, the French had seized American ships trading with Britain, giving the Americans a taste of what would happen if they did not elect a government friendlier to France. When the election went to John Adams, the French gave up on the United States and set about

impressment *Removal of sailors from American ships by British naval officers.*

denying Britain its new de facto ally. In 1797, the French ordered that American ships carrying "so much as a handkerchief" made in England be confiscated and announced that American seamen serving in the British navy would be hanged if captured.

President Adams knew that the United States might not survive a war with France. He also knew that French grievances (including Jay's Treaty and the abrogation of the French-American treaties of 1778) were legitimate. He sent a high-level mission to France, which was at first ignored. Finally, three French officials (the correspondence identified them only as "X, Y, and Z," and the incident later became known as the **XYZ Affair**) hinted that France would receive the delegates if they paid a bribe of $250,000, arranged for the United States to loan $12 million to the French government, and apologized for unpleasant remarks that John Adams had made about France. The delegates refused and returned home.

After the outrage of the XYZ Affair, President Adams asked Congress to prepare for war. The French responded by seizing more American ships. Thus began, in April 1798, an undeclared naval war between France and the United States in the Caribbean. After nearly a year of fighting, with the British providing powder and shot for American guns, the U.S. Navy chased the French privateers out.

The Crisis at Home, 1798–1800

Disclosure of the XYZ correspondence, together with the quasi-war in the Caribbean, produced a surge of public hostility toward the French and their Republican friends in the United States. Many Federalists, led by Alexander Hamilton, wanted to use the crisis to destroy their political opponents. Without consulting President Adams, the Federalist-dominated Congress passed several wartime measures. The first was a federal property tax. Congress then passed four laws known as the Alien and Sedition Acts. The first three were directed at immigrants: They extended the **naturalization** period from 5 to 14 years and empowered the president to detain enemy **aliens** during wartime and to deport those he deemed dangerous to the United States. The fourth law—the Sedition Act—set jail terms and fines for persons who advocated disobedience to federal law or who wrote, printed, or spoke "false, scandalous, and malicious" statements against the government or the president.

President Adams never used the powers granted under the Alien Acts, but the Sedition Act resulted in the prosecution of 14 Republicans, most of them journalists. Republicans charged that the Alien and Sedition Acts violated the First Amendment, and they turned to the states for help. Jefferson provided the Kentucky legislature with draft resolutions, and Madison did the same for the Virginia legislature. Jefferson's Kentucky Resolves reminded Congress that the Alien and Sedition Acts gave the national government powers not mentioned in the Constitution and that the Tenth Amendment reserved such powers to the states. He also argued that the Constitution was a "compact" between sovereign states and that state legislatures could "nullify" federal laws they deemed unconstitutional.

Opposition to the Sedition Act ranged from popular attempts to obstruct the law to fistfights in Congress. But no other states followed the lead of Virginia and Kentucky, and talk of armed opposition to Federalist policies was limited to a few areas in the South.

XYZ Affair *Incident that precipitated an undeclared war with France when three French officials (identified as X, Y, and Z) demanded that American emissaries pay a bribe before negotiating disputes between the two countries.*

naturalization *Process by which people born in a foreign country are granted full citizenship with all of its rights.*

alien *Person from another country who is living in the United States.*

High Federalists *A term used to describe Alexander Hamilton and some of his less moderate supporters. They wanted the naval war with France to continue and also wanted to severely limit the rights of an opposition party.*

Aaron Burr *Vice president under Thomas Jefferson.*

lame-duck administration *Period of time between an incumbent party's or officeholder's loss of an election and the succession to office of the winning party or candidate.*

The Politicians and the Army

Federalists took another ominous step when Adams asked Congress to create a military prepared for war. Adams wanted a stronger navy; Hamilton and others (who were becoming known as **High Federalists**) preferred a standing army. At the urging of Washington and against his own judgment, Adams appointed Hamilton inspector general, making him the de facto commander of the U.S. Army.

Congress authorized a 20,000-man army, and Hamilton proceeded to raise it. Congress also provided for a much larger army to be called up in the event of a declaration of war. When he appointed officers, Hamilton commissioned only his political friends. High Federalists wanted a standing army to enforce the Alien and Sedition Acts and to put down an impending rebellion in the South. Beyond that, there was little need for such a force. The Republicans, President Adams himself, and many other Federalists became convinced that Hamilton and his High Federalists were determined to destroy their political opponents, enter into an alliance with Great Britain, and impose Hamilton's statist designs by force.

To blunt the influence of the Hamiltonians, Adams began looking for ways to declare peace. He opened negotiations with France and stalled the creation of Hamilton's army while the talks took place. At first, Federalists in the Senate refused to send an envoy to France. They relented when Adams threatened to resign and leave the presidency to Vice President Jefferson. In the agreement that followed, the French canceled the obligations that the United States had assumed under the treaties of 1778, but they refused to pay reparations for attacks on American shipping since 1793—the very point over which many Federalists had wanted war. Peace with France cut the ground from under the more militaristic and repressive Federalists and intensified discord among the Federalists in general. It also damaged Adams's chances for reelection.

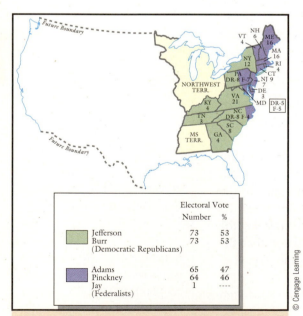

	Electoral Vote	
	Number	%
Jefferson	73	53
Burr	73	53
(Democratic Republicans)		
Adams	65	47
Pinckney	64	46
Jay	1	----
(Federalists)		

© Cengage Learning

Map 7.1 Presidential Election, 1800. *The electoral votes in 1800 split along starkly sectional lines. The South voted for Jefferson, New England voted for Adams, and the election was decided by close contests in Pennsylvania and New York.*

The Election of 1800

Thomas Jefferson and his Democratic Republicans approached the election of 1800 better organized and more determined than they had been four years earlier. Events in the months preceding the election also worked in their favor. The Federalists showed no sign of abandoning the Alien and Sedition Acts and the new military even when peace seemed certain, giving credence to the Republicans' allegation that the Federalists were using the crisis to their own political ends. The Federalists countered by warning that the election of Jefferson and his radical allies would release the worst horrors of the French Revolution in America.

After a heated campaign, Jefferson and his running mate, **Aaron Burr**, tied with 73 electoral votes each. Adams had 65 votes, and his running mate Charles Cotesworth Pinckney had 64 (see Map 7.1). Under the Constitution, a **lame-duck** Federalist Congress would decide whether Jefferson or Burr was to be president of the United States. After six days and 35 ballots, on which most Federalists voted for Burr, a compromise was reached whereby the Federalists turned in blank ballots and thus avoided voting for the hated (but victorious) Jefferson.

THE JEFFERSONIANS IN POWER

On the first Tuesday of March 1801, Thomas Jefferson left his rooms at Conrad and McMunn's boardinghouse in Washington and walked up Pennsylvania Avenue. Jefferson received military salutes along the way, but he forbade the pomp and ceremony that had ushered Washington into office. Accompanied by a few friends and a company from the Maryland militia, he joined Vice President Burr, other members of the government, and a few foreign diplomats in the unfinished Capitol's new Senate chamber.

FOCUS QUESTION

What were the principal reforms of the national government during Thomas Jefferson's administration? What were the implications of those reforms for the nature of republican government?

The Republican Program

Jefferson began his inaugural address with a plea for unity, insisting that "every difference of opinion is not a difference of principle. We have called by different names brethren of the same principle. We are all Republicans, we are all Federalists." He did not mean that he and his opponents should forget their ideological differences. He meant only to invite moderate Federalists into a broad Republican coalition. Jefferson went on to outline the kind of government a republic should have. He declared that Americans were a free people with no need for a European-style national state. A people blessed with isolation, bountiful resources, and liberty needed only "a wise and frugal Government, which shall restrain men from injuring one another, shall leave them otherwise free to regulate their own pursuits of industry and improvement, and shall not take from the mouth of labor the bread it has earned."

Jefferson's "wise and frugal" government would respect the powers of the states and preserve the liberties ensured by the Bill of Rights. It would be small, and it would pay its debts without incurring new ones, ending the need for taxation. It would rely for defense on "a disciplined militia" that would fight invaders while regulars were being trained, eliminating Hamilton's standing army. It would protect republican liberties from enemies at home and from the nations of Europe.

The simplicity of Jefferson's inauguration set the social tone of his administration. He reduced the number and grandeur of formal balls, levees, and dinners. Instead, he entertained senators and congressmen at small dinners that were served at a round table without formal seating. Jefferson presided over the meals without wearing a wig and dressed in old homespun and a pair of worn bedroom slippers. The casualness did not extend to what was served, however. The food was prepared by expert chefs and accompanied by fine wines, and it was followed by brilliant conversation. The president's dinners set examples of the unpretentious excellence through which Jefferson hoped to govern the republic that he claimed to have saved from monarchists.

Cleansing the Government

Jefferson cut the size and expense of government. He reduced the diplomatic corps and replaced officeholders who were incompetent, corrupt, or anti-republican. Legislation passed in March 1802 reduced the army to two regiments of infantry and one of artillery—a total of 3,350 officers and men. The goal, Jefferson explained, was to rely mainly on the militia for national defense but to maintain a small, well-trained professional army as well. At Jefferson's urging, Congress also abolished

PORTRAIT OF JEFFERSON, BY REMBRANDT PEALE, 1805.
A self-consciously plain President Jefferson posed for this portrait in January 1805, near the end of his first term. He wears an unadorned fur-collared coat, is surrounded by no emblems of office, and gazes calmly and directly at the viewer.

© Bettmann/ CORBIS

midnight judges *Federal judicial officials appointed under the Judiciary Act of 1801, in the last days of John Adams's presidency.*

impeachment *Act of charging a public official with misconduct in office.*

the direct tax of 1798 and repealed the parts of the Alien and Sedition Acts that had not already expired. Jefferson personally pardoned the 10 victims of those acts who were still in jail.

With a few strokes, Jefferson dismantled the oppressive apparatus of the Federalist state. And by reducing government expenditures, he reduced the government's debt. During Jefferson's administration the national debt fell from $80 million to $57 million, and the government built up a treasury surplus.

The Jeffersonians and the Courts

Jefferson next turned his attention to the federal courts. The First Congress had created circuit courts presided over by the justices of the Supreme Court, and only Federalists served on the Supreme Court under Washington and Adams. Jefferson's mistrust of the federal courts intensified when the lame-duck Federalist Congress passed a Judiciary Act early in 1801. The act reduced the number of associate justices of the Supreme Court from six to five, reducing Jefferson's chances of appointing a new member. It also took Supreme Court justices off circuit and created a new system of circuit courts. This change allowed Adams to appoint 16 new judges, along with marshals, federal attorneys, clerks, and justices of the peace. He worked until nine o'clock on his last night in office signing commissions for these "**midnight judges**." All of them were staunch Federalists.

Jefferson did replace the new federal marshals and attorneys with Republicans and dismissed some of the federal justices of the peace. But judges were appointed for life and could be removed only through **impeachment**. The Jeffersonians hit on a simple solution: They got rid of the new judges by abolishing their jobs. Early in 1802, Congress repealed the Judiciary Act and did away with the midnight appointees.

With the federal courts scaled back to their original size, Republicans in Congress went after High Federalists who were still acting as judges. They impeached John Pickering, a federal attorney with the circuit court of New Hampshire, and removed him from office. They failed, however, in their bid to remove Supreme Court Justice Salmon Chase.

William Marbury was one of the justices of the peace whom Jefferson had dismissed in his first few days in office. He sued Jefferson's secretary of state, James Madison, for his commission. Although Marbury never got his job, Chief Justice **John Marshall**, in his *Marbury v. Madison* decision, handed down a number of important rulings that laid the basis for the practice of **judicial review**—the Supreme Court's power to rule on the constitutionality of an act of Congress.

Louisiana

Europe remained at peace during Jefferson's first term and stayed out of American affairs. The one development that posed an international threat to the United States turned into a grand triumph: the **Louisiana Purchase** of 1803.

THE LOUISIANA PURCHASE. *This panorama of New Orleans celebrates the Louisiana Purchase of 1803. The patriotic caption promises prosperity for the city and (by inference) for the American settlements upriver. Here the power of the central government (in the form of money and the purchase of land) is shown to serve the spread of liberty.*

A View of New Orleans Taken from the Plantation of Marigny, Novermber, 1803 by Boqueto de Woiserie, Chicago Historical Society

By the beginning of the 19th century, a half-million Americans lived west of the Appalachians. Republicans saw westward expansion as the best hope for the survival of the republic. Social inequality would almost inevitably take root in the East, but in the vast lands west of the mountains, the republic could renew itself for many generations to come. To serve that purpose, however, the West needed ready access to markets through the river system that emptied into the Gulf of Mexico at New Orleans.

In 1800, Spain secretly ceded the Louisiana Territory (roughly, all the land west of the Mississippi drained by the Missouri and Arkansas rivers) to France. Napoleon Bonaparte had plans for a new French empire in America with the sugar island of Hispaniola (present-day Haiti and Dominican Republic) at its center. Late in 1802, the Spanish, who had retained control of New Orleans, closed the port to American commerce, creating rumors that they would soon transfer the city to France. President Jefferson sent a delegation to Paris early in 1803 with authorization to buy New Orleans for the United States.

By the time the delegates reached Paris, the slaves of Saint-Domingue (the French colony on Hispaniola), led by former slave Toussaint L'Ouverture, had revolted and defeated French attempts to regain control of the island. At the same time, another war between Britain and France seemed imminent. Napoleon decided to bail out of America and concentrate his resources in Europe. He astonished Jefferson's delegation by announcing that France would sell not only New Orleans but the whole Louisiana Territory for the bargain price of $15 million.

Jefferson, who had criticized Federalists when they violated the letter of the Constitution, faced a dilemma: The president lacked the constitutional power to buy territory, but the chance to buy Louisiana was too good to refuse. It would ensure Americans access to the rivers of the interior; it would eliminate a serious foreign threat on America's western border; and it would give American farmers enough land to sustain the agrarian republic for a long time to come. Swallowing his constitutional scruples, Jefferson told the American

John Marshall *Chief justice of the United States Supreme Court from 1801 to 1835.*

Marbury v. Madison *1803 case involving the disputed appointment of a federal justice of the peace in which Chief Justice John Marshall expanded the Supreme Court's authority to review legislation.*

judicial review *Supreme Court's power to rule on the constitutionality of congressional acts.*

Louisiana Purchase *Land purchased from France in 1803 that doubled the size of the United States.*

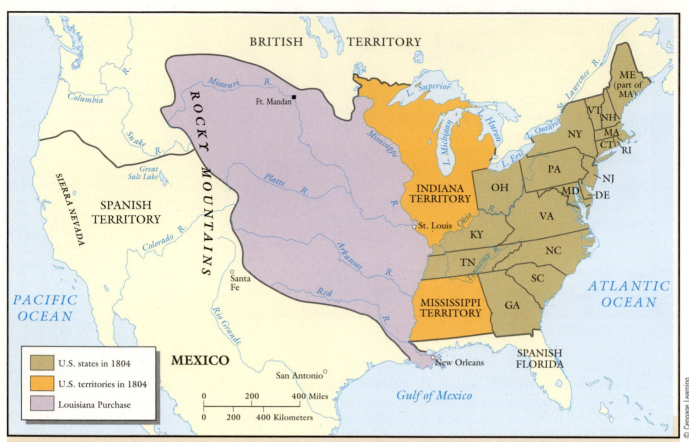

Map 7.2 **Louisiana Purchase.** *Jefferson's Louisiana Purchase nearly doubled the geographic size of the United States. It ended European competition for control of the North American interior and granted the United States the mouth of the Mississippi River, thus strengthening white settlements between the Appalachians and the Mississippi and increasing American control over those settlements.*

delegates to buy Louisiana. Republican senators quickly ratified the Louisiana treaty over Federalist objections, an act that met with overwhelming public approval (see Map 7.2).

Lewis and Clark

The Americans knew almost nothing about the land they had bought. Only a few French trappers and traders had traveled the plains between the Mississippi and the Rocky Mountains, and no white person had seen the territory drained by the Columbia River. In 1804, Jefferson sent an expedition under Meriwether Lewis and William Clark to explore the purchase. The two kept meticulous journals of one of the epic adventures in American history.

In May 1804, **Lewis and Clark** and 41 companions boarded a keelboat and two large canoes at St. Louis. They labored 1,600 miles up the Missouri River, passing through rolling plains dotted by the farm villages of the Pawnee, Oto, Missouri, Crow, Omaha, Hidatsa, and Mandan peoples. The villages of the lower Missouri had been cut off from the western buffalo herds and reduced to dependence by mounted Sioux warriors, who had begun to establish their hegemony over the northern plains.

Lewis and Clark traveled through Sioux territory and wintered at the fortified Mandan villages at the big bend of the Missouri River in Dakota

Lewis and Clark *Explorers commissioned in 1804 by President Jefferson to survey the Louisiana Purchase.*

country. In the spring they hired Toussaint Charbonneau, a French fur trader, to guide them to the Pacific. Charbonneau was useless, but his wife, a teenaged Shoshone girl named Sacajawea, was an indispensable guide, interpreter, and diplomat. With her help, Lewis and Clark navigated the upper Missouri, crossed the Rockies to the Snake River, and followed that stream to the Columbia River. They reached the Pacific in November 1805. They wintered there, then retraced their steps back to St. Louis, arriving in September 1806. They brought back volumes of drawings and notes, along with assurances that the Louisiana Purchase had been worth many, many times its price.

As Jefferson stood for reelection in 1804, he could look back on an astonishingly successful first term. He had dismantled the government's power to coerce its citizens, and he had begun to wipe out the national debt. The Louisiana Purchase had doubled the size of the republic at little cost, and, by eliminating France from North America, it had strengthened the argument for reducing the military and the debts and taxes that went with it.

The combination of international peace, territorial expansion, and inexpensive, unobtrusive government left the Federalists without an issue in the 1804 election. They went through the motions of nominating Charles Coteworth Pinckney of South Carolina as their presidential candidate and then watched as Jefferson captured the electoral votes of every state but Delaware and Connecticut.

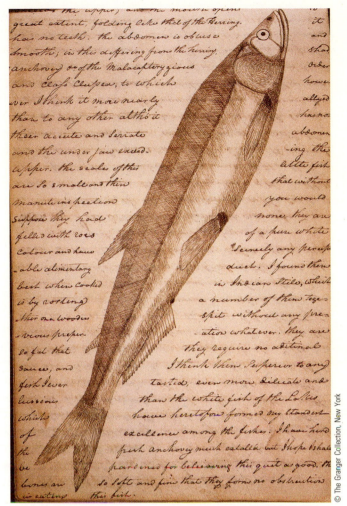

A PAGE FROM THE JOURNALS OF LEWIS AND CLARK. *Lewis and Clark traveled among peoples, flora, and wildlife that no American white person had ever seen. Their journals reveal both meticulous observation and a sense of wonder.*

THE REPUBLIC AND THE NAPOLEONIC WARS, 1804–1815

In spring 1803, Napoleon declared war on Great Britain. This 11-year war dominated the national politics of the United States. Most Americans wanted to remain neutral. Few Republicans supported Bonaparte, and none but the most rabid Federalists wanted to intervene on the side of Great Britain. Neither France nor Britain, however, would permit American neutrality.

The Dilemmas of Neutrality

At the beginning, both Britain and France encouraged the Americans to resume their role as neutral carriers and suppliers of food. Between 1803 and 1807, U.S. exports rose from $66.5 million to $102.2 million. Reexports—goods produced in the Caribbean, picked up by American vessels, and then reloaded in American ports onto American ships bound for Europe—rose even faster, from $13.5 million to $58.4 million.

FOCUS QUESTION

What was the situation of the United States within the international politics created by the Napoleonic Wars, and how did that situation degenerate into a second war with Great Britain?

In 1805, France and Great Britain began to interfere with that trade. Britain decided to use its naval supremacy to blockade Europe and starve the French into submission. The Essex Decision of 1805 empowered the Royal Navy to seize American ships engaged in the reexport trade with France. Then Britain blockaded long stretches of the European coast. Napoleon responded with the Berlin Decree, outlawing all trade with the British Isles. The British answered with an Order in Council that demanded that neutral ships trading with Europe stop first for inspection and licensing in a British port. Napoleon countered with the Milan Decree, which stated that any vessel that obeyed the British decrees or allowed itself to be searched by the Royal Navy was subject to seizure by France. The barrage of European decrees and counter-decrees meant that virtually all American commerce with Europe was outlawed by one or the other of the warring powers.

Trouble on the High Seas

The Royal Navy maintained a loose blockade of the North American coast, seizing hundreds of American ships, along with their cargoes and crews, as they left port. Under British law, the Royal Navy could impress any British subject into service during wartime. Many British subjects, including deserters from the Royal Navy, were hiding in the American merchant marine, avoiding the danger, low pay, and draconian discipline of the British navy. British ships commandeered those men. They also took Englishmen who had taken out U.S. citizenship (an act the British did not recognize) and, inevitably, native-born Americans. An estimated 6,000 American citizens were impressed into the Royal Navy between 1803 and 1812.

The kidnapping of American sailors nearly started a war. In June 1807, the American naval frigate *Chesapeake* signed on four English deserters from the British navy, along with some Americans who had joined the British navy and then deserted. Some of the deserters spotted their old officers from *H.M.S. Leopard* in Norfolk, Virginia, and taunted them on the streets. The *Leopard* left port and resumed its patrol of the American coast. On June 21, it caught the *Chesapeake* and demanded the return of the British deserters. When the American captain refused, the British fired, killing 3 Americans and wounding 18. The British then boarded the *Chesapeake*, seized the four deserters, and later hanged one of them.

The *Chesapeake* affair set off huge anti-British demonstrations in the seaport towns and angry cries for war throughout the country. President Jefferson responded by barring British ships from American ports and American territorial waters and by ordering state governors to prepare to call up as many as 100,000 militiamen.

Embargo

Jefferson had one more card to play: He could use trade as a means of "peaceable coercion" to ensure respect for American neutrality rights and keep the country out of war. Convinced that America's **yeoman** republic could survive without European luxuries more easily than Europe could survive without American food, Jefferson asked Congress to suspend all U.S. trade with foreign countries.

Congress passed the **Embargo** Act on December 22, 1807. Within a few months, it was clear that it would not work. The British found other markets and other sources of food. They encouraged the smuggling of American goods into Canada. American exports plummeted from $108 million in 1807 to $22 million in 1808. The economy slowed in every section of the country, but it ground to a halt in the cities of the Northeast. Federalists accused Jefferson of plotting an end to

yeoman *A farmer who owned his own farm.*

embargo *Government order prohibiting the movement of merchant ships or goods in or out of its ports.*

commerce and a reversion to rural barbarism, and they often took the lead in trying to subvert the embargo through smuggling and other means.

In 1808, James Madison, Jefferson's old ally and chosen successor, was elected president with 122 electoral votes to 47 for his Federalist opponent, Charles Cotesworth Pinckney. Although Republicans retained the presidency and control of both houses of Congress, Federalists made gains in Congress and won control of several state legislatures. Federalist opposition to the embargo, and to the supposed southern, agrarian stranglehold on national power that stood behind it, was gaining ground.

The Road to War

Early in 1809, Congress passed the Non-Intercourse Act as a replacement for the failing embargo. The new act retained the ban on trade with Britain and France but reopened trade with other nations. It also gave President Madison the power to reopen trade with either Britain or France once it had agreed to respect American rights. Neither complied, and the Non-Intercourse Act proved nearly as ineffective as the embargo.

In 1810, Congress passed Macon's Bill No. 2, which reopened trade with France and Britain but authorized the president to make a deal: If either belligerent ended its restrictions on U.S. trade, the United States would stop trading with the other nation. In September 1810, France promised to repeal the Berlin and Milan Decrees. Though the proposal was a clear attempt to lead the United States into conflict with Great Britain—and, in the end, France repealed only those sections that applied to the neutral rights of the United States—Madison felt he had no choice. He accepted the French promise and proclaimed in November 1810 that the British had three months to follow suit. The British refused to revoke their Orders in Council and told the Americans to withdraw their restrictions on British trade until the French had repealed theirs. The United States would either have to obey British orders or go to war.

The War Hawk Congress, 1811–1812

Republicans controlled both houses of Congress, but they were a divided majority. The Federalist minority was united against Madison. They were often joined by northeastern Republicans who followed the Federalist line on international trade, and by Republicans who wanted a more powerful military. Also opposed to Madison were the self-styled Old Republicans of the South, led by John Randolph.

In this confused situation a group of talented young congressmen came to power. Nearly all of them were Republicans from the South or the West. Called the **War Hawks**, these ardent nationalists wanted to declare war on England to protect U.S. rights. Through their organizational, oratorical, and intellectual power, they won control of Congress. Henry Clay of Kentucky, only 34 years old and serving his first term in Congress, was elected Speaker of the House. Clay controlled debate, packed key committees, worked tirelessly behind the scenes, and imposed order on his fellow congressmen.

In the winter and spring of 1811–1812, the War Hawks led Congress into a war. In November they voted military preparations, and in April they enacted a 90-day embargo—not to coerce the British but to return American ships safely into port before war began. On June 1, Madison sent a war message to Congress, and Congress declared war on June 18. The vote was far from unanimous. All 30 Federalists voted against the declaration. So did one in five Republicans, nearly all of them from the Northeast.

War Hawks *Members of the Twelfth Congress, most of them young nationalists from southern and western areas, who promoted war with Britain.*

American Strategy in 1812

Federalists and many northeastern Republicans expected a naval war; after all, the British had committed their atrocities on the ocean. Yet when Madison asked Congress to prepare for war, the War Hawks led a majority that strengthened the U.S. Army and left the navy weak. Reasoning that no U.S. naval force could challenge British control of the seas, they prepared instead for a land invasion of British Canada.

The decision to invade Canada led the Federalists, along with many of Randolph's Old Republicans, to accuse Madison and the congressional majority of planning a war of territorial aggression. Some members of Congress did want to annex Canada to the United States, but most saw the invasion as a matter of strategy. Lightly garrisoned and with a population of only half a million, Canada seemed the easiest and most logical place in which to damage the British. American policymakers reasoned that they could take Canada and hold it hostage while demanding that the British back down on other issues (see Map 7.3).

The Rise of Tecumseh

Native peoples east of the Mississippi River recognized alliances with Britain as a final chance to hold back American settlers. Relegated to smaller territory but still dependent on the European fur trade, Northwestern Indians now fell into competition with settlers and other Indians for the diminishing supply of game. The Creeks, Choctaws, and other tribes of the Old Southwest faced the same problem: Even when they chased settlers out of their territory, the settlers managed to kill or scare off the deer and other wildlife, ruining the old hunting grounds.

Faced with shrinking territories, the disappearance of wildlife, and diminished opportunities to be traditional hunters and warriors, many Indian societies sank into despair. Epidemics of European diseases (smallpox, influenza, measles) attacked peoples who were increasingly sedentary and vulnerable. Murder and clan revenge plagued the tribes, and depression and suicide became more common. The use of alcohol, which had been a scourge on Indian societies for two centuries, increased.

Out of this cultural wreckage emerged visionary leaders who spoke of a regenerated native society and the expulsion of all whites from the old tribal lands. The prophet who came closest to military success was **Tenskwatawa,** a fat, one-eyed, alcoholic Shawnee. When he went into a deep trance in 1805, the people thought he was dead. During preparations for his funeral, he awoke and told them he had visited heaven and hell and had received a prophetic vision. Indians must stop drinking and fighting among themselves. They must also return to their traditional food, clothing, tools, and hairstyles, and must extinguish all of their fires and start new ones without using European tools. All who opposed the new order must be put down by force. When all of that had been done, God (a monotheistic, punishing God borrowed from the Christians) would restore the world that Indians had known before the whites came over the mountains.

Tenskwatawa's message soon found its way to the native peoples of the Northwest. When converts flooded into the prophet's home village, he moved to Prophetstown (Tippecanoe) in what is now Indiana. There, with the help of his brother **Tecumseh,** he created an army estimated by the whites at anywhere between 650 and 3,000. Tecumseh, who took control of the movement, announced that he was the sole chief of all the Indians north of the Ohio River. The Indians of the Old Northwest united in an unprecedented stand against white encroachment.

Tenskwatawa *Brother of Tecumseh, whose religious vision of 1805 called for the unification of Indians west of the Appalachians and foretold the defeat and disappearance of the whites.*

Tecumseh *Shawnee leader who assumed political and military leadership of the pan-Indian religious movement began by his brother Tenskwatawa.*

Map 7.3 *War of 1812. Early in the war, Americans chose to fight the British in Canada, with costly and inconclusive results. Later, the British determined to blockade the whole coast of the United States and, late in the war, to raid important coastal towns. The results were equally inconclusive: Both sides could inflict serious damage, but neither could conquer the other. The one clear military outcome—one that the Americans were determined to accomplish—was the destruction of Indian resistance east of the Mississippi.*

Tecumseh's confederacy posed a threat to the United States. A second war with England was looming, and Tecumseh was receiving supplies and encouragement from the British in Canada. He was also planning to bring southern tribes into his confederacy. The prospect of unified resistance by the western tribes in league with the British jeopardized every settler west of the Appalachians. In 1811, William

Henry Harrison led an army toward Prophetstown. With Tecumseh away, Tenskwatawa ordered an attack on Harrison's army and was beaten at the Battle of Tippecanoe. But Tecumseh's confederacy remained a formidable adversary.

The War with Canada, 1812–1813

The United States attacked Canada in 1812, with disastrous results. The plan was to invade Upper Canada (Ontario) from the Northwest, cutting off pro-British Indian tribes from their British support. When General William Hull led an army of militiamen and volunteers into Canada from Detroit, he found the area crawling with British troops and their Indian allies. He retreated to the garrison at Detroit. British General Isaac Brock, who knew that Hull was afraid of Indians, sent a note into the fort telling him that "the numerous body of Indians who have attached themselves to my troops, will be beyond my controul the moment the contest commences." Without consulting his officers, Hull surrendered his army of 2,000 to the smaller British force. Hull was later court-martialed for cowardice, but the damage was done: The British and Indians occupied many of the remaining American garrisons in the Northwest and transformed the U.S. invasion of Upper Canada into a British occupation of much of the Northwest.

The invasion of Canada from the east went no better. In October a U.S. force of 6,000 faced 2,000 British and Indians across the Niagara River separating Ontario from western New York. The U.S. regular army crossed the river, surprised the British, and established a toehold at Queenston Heights. While the British prepared a counterattack, New York militiamen refused to cross the river to reinforce the regulars. The British regrouped and slaughtered the outnumbered, exhausted U.S. troops.

As winter set in, it was clear that Canada would not fall easily. The invasion, which U.S. commanders had thought would knife through an apathetic Canadian population, instead transformed the ragtag assortment of American loyalist émigrés, discharged British soldiers, and American-born settlers into a self-consciously British Canadian people.

Tecumseh's Last Stand

Tecumseh's confederacy, bruised but not broken in the Battle of Tippecanoe, allied itself with the British in 1812. A wing of the Creeks—who called themselves Red Sticks—joined him. The augmented confederacy provided stiff resistance to the United States throughout the war. The Red Sticks chased settlers from much of Tennessee. They then attacked a group of settlers who had taken refuge in a stockade surrounding the house of an Alabama trader named George Mims. In what whites called the Massacre at Fort Mims, the Red Sticks (reputedly with the collusion of black slaves within the fort) killed at least 247 men, women, and children. In the Northwest, Tecumseh's warriors, fighting alongside the British, spread terror throughout the white settlements.

A wiser U.S. Army returned to Canada in 1813. It raided and burned the Canadian capital at York (Toronto) in April and then fought inconclusively through the summer. In September 1813, Commodore Oliver Hazard Perry cornered and destroyed the British fleet at Put-in-Bay. Control of Lake Erie enabled the United States to cut off supplies to the British in the Northwest, and a U.S. Army under William Henry Harrison retook the area and continued on into Canada. On October 5, Harrison caught up with a force of British and Indians at the Thames River and beat them badly. In the course of that battle Richard M. Johnson, a War Hawk congressman acting as commander of the Kentucky militia, killed Tecumseh.

The following spring, General Andrew Jackson's Tennessee militia, aided by Choctaw, Creek, and Chero-kee allies, attacked and slaughtered the Red Sticks at Horseshoe Bend in Alabama. The military power of the Indian peoples east of the Mississippi River was broken.

The British Offensive, 1814

The British defeated Napoleon in April 1814, ending the war in Europe. They then turned their attention to the American war. During summer 1814, they began to raid the shores of Chesapeake Bay and marched on Washington, D.C. They chased the army and politicians out of town and burned down the Capitol building and the president's mansion. In September, the British attacked Baltimore but could not blast their way past the garrison that commanded the harbor from Fort McHenry. The battle inspired Francis Scott Key to write "The Star-Spangled Banner." When a British offensive on Lake Champlain stalled during the autumn, the war reached a stalemate: Britain had prevented the invasion of Canada and had blockaded the American coast, but neither side could take and hold the other's territory.

The British shifted their attention to the Gulf Coast, landing a large amphibious force near New Orleans. There they met an American army made up of U.S. regulars, Kentucky and Tennessee militiamen, clerks, workingmen, and free blacks from the city, and about a thousand French pirates—all under the command of Andrew Jackson. Throughout late December and early January, unaware that a peace treaty had been signed on December 24, the armies exchanged artillery barrages. On January 8, the British launched a frontal assault. A formation of 6,000 British soldiers marched across open ground toward 4,000 Americans concealed behind breastworks. After half an hour, 2,000 British soldiers lay dead or wounded. American casualties numbered only 70. Fought nearly two weeks after the peace treaty, the Battle of New Orleans had no effect on the outcome of the war or on the peace terms, but it salved the injured pride of Americans and made a national hero and a political power of Andrew Jackson.

DEATH OF TECUMSEH. *The Battle of the Thames relieved the Northwest of the British and Indian threat. It was remembered most strongly, however, as the day on which Richard M. Johnson killed Tecumseh.*

The Hartford Convention

While most Americans celebrated Jackson's victory, Federalist New England com-plained. New Englanders disliked Republican trade policies, and their congressmen had voted overwhelmingly against going to war. Some Federalists had openly urged resistance to the war. The British had encouraged that resistance by not extending their naval blockade to the New England coast, and throughout the first two years of the war New England merchants and farmers had traded freely with the enemy. In 1814, after the Royal Navy had extended its blockade northward and had begun to raid the towns of coastal Maine, some Federalists talked about seceding and making a separate peace with Britain.

THE BURNING OF WASHINGTON. *The United States suffered one of its greatest military embarrassments in 1814, when the British raided Washington, D.C., brushed off the opposition, and burned the president's house and the Capitol building.*

In an attempt to undercut the secessionists, moderate Federalists called a convention at Hartford in December 1814. The Hartford Convention proposed several amendments to the Constitution. The delegates wanted the "three-fifths" clause, which overrepresented the South in Congress, and the Electoral College (see Chapter 6) stricken from the Constitution. They wanted to deny naturalized citizens—who were strongly Republican—the right to hold office. They wanted to make it more difficult for new states, all of which sided with the Republicans, to enter the Union. Finally, they wanted to require a two-thirds majority of both houses for a declaration of war—a requirement that would have prevented the War of 1812.

The leaders of the Hartford Convention took their proposals to Washington in mid-January. They found the capital celebrating the news of the peace treaty and Jackson's victory at New Orleans. When they aired their proposals, they were branded as traitors. Although Federalists continued for a few years to wield power in southern New England, the Hartford debacle ruined any chance of a nationwide Federalist resurgence after the war.

The Treaty of Ghent

Britain's defeat of Napoleon spurred British and American efforts to end a war that neither wanted. In August 1814, they opened peace talks in the Belgian city of Ghent. As the war reached stalemate, negotiators on both sides began to withdraw their demands. The Treaty of Ghent, signed on Christmas Eve 1814, simply ended the war. The border between Canada and the United States remained where it had been in

1812; Indians south of that border—defeated and without allies—were left to the mercy of the United States; and British maritime violations were not mentioned.

Conclusion

In 1816 Thomas Jefferson was in retirement at Monticello, satisfied that he had defended liberty against the Federalists' love of power. The High Federalists' attempt to militarize government and to jail their enemies had failed. Their direct taxes were repealed. Their debt and their national bank remained in place, but only under the watchful eyes of true republicans. And their attempt to ally the United States with the anti-republican designs of Great Britain had ended in what many called the Second War of American Independence.

Yet for all his successes, Jefferson in 1816 saw that he must sacrifice his dreams of agrarianism. Jefferson's imagined yeomen traded farm surpluses for European manufactured goods—a system that encouraged rural prosperity, prevented the growth of cities and factories, and thus sustained the landed independence on which republican citizenship rested. Westward expansion, he had believed, would ensure the yeoman republic for generations to come. By 1816 that dream was ended. Arguing as Hamilton had argued in 1790, Jefferson insisted that "we must now place the manufacturer by the side of the agriculturalist."

CHAPTER REVIEW

Review Questions

1. What was the Federalist plan for organizing the national government and its finances? What were the Jeffersonian Republicans' principal objections to those plans?

2. What were the principal foreign and internal threats to the federal government in the years 1793–1797? How did Federalist administrations respond to those threats?

3. What were the principal reforms of the national government during Thomas Jefferson's administration? What were the implications of those reforms for the nature of republican government?

4. What was the situation of the United States within the international politics created by the Napoleonic Wars? How did that situation degenerate into a second war with Great Britain?

Critical Thinking Questions

1. In the 1790s Federalists and Democratic Republicans argued about the nature of the new national government. On what specific issues was this argument conducted? Was there a larger argument underlying these specifics?

2. Thomas Jefferson had a vision of the American republic and the role of the national government within it. In what ways did his presidency succeed in realizing that vision? In what ways did it fail?

Identifications

Review your understanding of the following key terms, people, and events for this chapter.

tariff, p. 161
Bill of Rights, p. 161
circuit court, p. 161
Alexander Hamilton, p. 161
excise tax, p. 163
abrogating a treaty, p. 164
Whiskey Rebellion, p. 165

impressment, p. 166
XYZ Affair, p. 167
naturalization, p. 167
aliens, p. 167
High Federalists, p. 168
Aaron Burr, p. 168
lame-duck administration, p. 168

midnight judges, p. 170
impeachment, p. 170
John Marshall, p. 170
Marbury v. Madison, p. 170
judicial review, p. 170
Louisiana Purchase, p. 170
Lewis and Clark, p. 172

yeoman, p. 174
embargo, p. 174
War Hawks, p. 175
Tenskwatawa, p. 176
Tecumseh, p. 176

DISCOVERY

In what ways did the ascension of the Jeffersonians to power in 1800 shape the future of America?

In thinking about this question, begin by breaking it down into the components shown below. A discussion of the significance of each component should appear in your answer.

Geography and Politics

Consider the map of the election of 1800. In what way was the country divided in this vote? How do you think the people in the western territories were likely to vote once the territories became states? What does this map foreshadow about the future of the Federalist Party? By the 1830s, Democratic Republicans called their party by a somewhat different name. Do you know what it was?

Political Culture

Compare the images of Washington and Jefferson on pages 161 and 170. If you didn't know anything about either man, would you say that one of them lived before the other? Which one looks more like a "modern" political leader? Why do you think so?

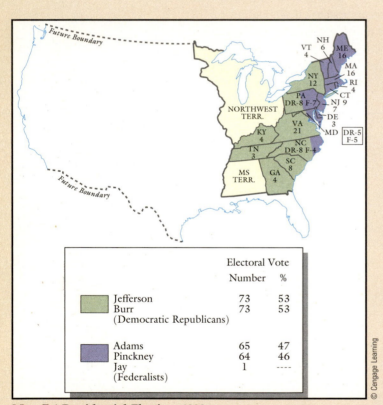

	Electoral Vote	
	Number	%
Jefferson	73	53
Burr	73	53
(Democratic Republicans)		
Adams	65	47
Pinckney	64	46
Jay	1	----
(Federalists)		

© Cengage Learning

Map 7.1 **Presidential Election, 1800**

CourseMate

Visit the CourseMate website at www.cengagebrain.com for additional study tools and review materials for this chapter.

NORTHERN TRANSFORMATIONS, 1790–1850

In 1790, American society approximated Jefferson's ideal: The United States was a nation of farmers who provided for themselves and sent surpluses overseas to be traded for manufactured goods. Americans sent timber, cured fish, wheat, tobacco, rice, and money to Europe (primarily Great Britain), and Europe (again, primarily Britain) sent manufactured goods—along with bills for shipping, insurance, banking, and tariff duties—back to America. In the 25 years following adoption of the Constitution, this old relationship fed significant economic growth in the United States, as European wars increased the demand for American produce and shipping.

Beginning in the 1790s and accelerating dramatically with the peace of 1815, the primary engine of northern economic development shifted from this North Atlantic trade to the internal development of the northern United States. Northeastern businessmen noted that rural markets were expanding, that imports were unreliable, and that a crowded countryside produced people eager to work for wages. They began to invest in factories. New factory towns, together with the old seaports and new inland towns that served a commercializing agriculture, provided the country's first significant domestic market for food. Governments of the northern states built roads and canals that linked farmers to distant markets, and farmers turned to cash-crop agriculture and bought necessary goods (and paid mortgages and crop loans) with the money they made. By 1830, a large and growing portion of New England, the mid-Atlantic, and the Northwest had transcended colonial economics to become an interdependent, self-sustaining market society.

1785	1790	1795	1800	1805	1810	1815	1820	1825	1830	1835

■ 1789
National government under the Constitution begins

■ 1790
Samuel Slater builds his first Arkwright spinning mill at Pawtucket, Rhode Island

■ 1793
Beginning of Anglo-French War
• Ohio enters the union as the 17th state

■ 1807
Robert Fulton launches first steamboat

■ 1812
Second war with Britain begins

■ 1813
Boston Associates erect their first textile mill at Waltham, Massachusetts

■ 1815
War of 1812 ends

■ 1818
National Road completed to Ohio River at Wheeling, Virginia

1825 ■
New York completes the Erie Canal between Buffalo and Albany

1828 ■
Baltimore and Ohio Railroad (America's first) completed

1835 ■
Main Line Canal connects Philadelphia and Pittsburgh

© Cengage Learning

This chapter describes the market revolution in the North. The succeeding chapter describes the very different patterns of change in the South in the same years.

POSTCOLONIAL SOCIETY, 1790–1815

FOCUS QUESTION

What was the nature of the northern agricultural economy and of agricultural society in the years 1790–1820?

In 1782 J. Hector St. John de Crèvecoeur, a French soldier who had settled in rural New York, explained American agrarianism through the words of a fictionalized farmer. First of all, he said, the American farmer owns his own land and bases his claim to dignity and citizenship on that fact: "This formerly rude soil has been converted by my father into a pleasant farm, and in return, it has established all our rights; on it is founded our rank, our freedom, our power as citizens, our importance as inhabitants of [a rural neighborhood]. . . ." Second, farm ownership endows the American farmer with the powers and responsibilities of fatherhood: "I am now doing for [my son] what my father did for me; may God enable him to live that he may perform the same operations for the same purposes when I am worn out and old!"

Farms

Few farmers in 1790 thought of farming as a business. Their first concern was to provide food and common comforts for their households. Their second was to create what rural folks called a **"competence":** the ability to live up to neighborhood

competence *Understood in the early republic as the ability to live up to neighborhood economic standards while protecting the long-term independence of the household.*

economic standards while protecting the long-term independence of their household—and thus the dignity and political rights of its head. Most farmers raised a variety of animals and plants, ate most of what they grew, traded much of the rest within their neighborhoods, and gambled surpluses on long-distance trade.

The world's hunger for American food, however, was growing. West Indian and European markets for American meat and grain expanded dramatically between 1793 and 1815, when war disrupted farming in Europe. Many northern farmers expanded production to take advantage of these markets. The prosperity and aspirations of hundreds of thousands of farmers rose, and their houses were sprinkled with tokens of comfort and gentility. The same markets also sustained traditions of household independence and neighborly cooperation. Farmers continued to provide for their families from their own farms and neighborhoods, and they risked little by increasing their surpluses and sending them overseas. They profited from world markets without becoming dependent on them.

Production for overseas markets did, however, alter rural households. Farm labor in post-revolutionary America was divided by sex. Men worked in the fields, and production for markets both intensified that labor and made it more exclusively male. In the grain fields, for instance, the long-handled scythe was replacing the sickle as the principal harvest tool. Women could use the sickle efficiently, but the long, heavy scythe was designed to be wielded by men. At the same time, farmers completed the substitution of plows for hoes as the principal cultivating tools—not only because plows worked better but because rural Americans had developed a prejudice against women working in the fields, and plows were male tools.

Household responsibilities, on the other hand, multiplied and fell more exclusively to women. Farmwomen's labor and ingenuity helped create a more varied and nutritious rural diet in these years. Although bread and salted meat were still the staples, by the 1790s improved winter feeding for cattle and better techniques for making and storing butter and cheese kept dairy products on the tables of the more prosperous farm families throughout the year. Chickens became more common, and farmwomen began to fence and manure their gardens, planting them with potatoes, turnips, cabbages, squash, beans, and other vegetables that could be stored.

Neighborhoods

Few farmers possessed the tools, the labor, and the food they would have needed to be truly self-sufficient. They regularly worked for one another, borrowed oxen and plows, and swapped one kind of food crop for another. Women traded ashes, herbs, butter and eggs, vegetables, seedlings, baby chicks, goose feathers, and the products of their spinning wheels and looms. Some cooperative undertakings—house and barn raisings and husking bees, for example—brought the whole neighborhood together, transforming a chore into a pleasant social event.

Few neighborhood transactions involved money. In 1790, no paper money had yet been issued by the states or the federal government. In New England, farmers kept

OLD MRS. HANSMAN KILLING A HOG. *This Pennsylvania farmwife seldom if ever worked in the fields, but her daily round of work was no dainty business. Along with other arduous and dirty labors, she killed and butchered hogs not only for her family but for some of her neighbors as well.*

"Butchering" from the journal of Lewis Miller (1796-1882), Volume 1 page 18. From the Collection of the York County Heritage Trust, York, PA.

careful accounts of neighborhood debts. In the South and West, farmers used a **"changing system"** in which they simply remembered what they owed. Yet farmers everywhere relied more on barter than on cash, conducting their economic lives within an elaborate network of neighborly and family obligations rather than by buying, selling, and calculating.

Country storekeepers and village merchants handled relationships between farmers and long-distance markets, and they were as much a part of their neighborhoods as of the wider world. In most areas, farmers brought produce to the storekeeper, who arranged its shipment to a seaport town. Some paid cash for produce, but most simply credited the farmer's account. Farmers also bought store goods on credit, and when bad crop years or bad luck made them unable to pay, storekeepers tended to wait for payment without charging interest. Storekeepers also played a role in local networks of debt, for it was common for farmers to bring their products to the store, and to have them credited to the accounts of neighbors to whom they were in debt, thus turning the storekeeper into a broker within the complicated web of neighborhood obligations.

Standards of Living

In 1790, most farmhouses in the older rural areas were small, one-story structures, and few farmers bothered to keep their surroundings clean or attractive. They repaired their fences only when they became too dilapidated to function. They rarely planted trees or shrubs, and housewives threw out garbage to feed the chickens and pigs that foraged near the house.

Inside, there were few rooms and many people. Beds stood in every room, and few family members slept alone. The hearth was the source of heat and light in most farmhouses. One great disparity between wealthy families and their less affluent neighbors was that the wealthy families could light their houses at night. Another disparity was in the outward appearance of homes. Wealthier families painted their houses white as a token of pristine republicanism, but their bright houses stood in stark contrast to the weathered, gray-brown clapboard siding of their neighbors.

Increased income from foreign markets did result in improvement. Farmers bought traditional necessities such as salt and pepper, gunpowder, tools, and coffee and tea, but these were now supplemented with luxuries such as crockery, flatware, finished cloth, mirrors, clocks and watches, wallpaper, and the occasional book. At mealtimes, only the poorest families continued to eat with their fingers or with spoons from a common bowl. By 1800, individual place settings with knives and forks and china plates, along with individual chairs instead of benches, had become common in rural America.

Inheritance

After 1790, overcrowding and the growth of markets caused the price of good farmland to rise sharply throughout the older settlements. Most young men could expect to inherit only a few acres of exhausted land or to move to wilderness land in the backcountry. Failing those options, they would quit farming altogether.

In revolutionary America, fathers had been judged by their ability to support and govern their households, to serve as good neighbors, and to pass

QUICK REVIEW

FARMING HOUSEHOLDS IN 1790

- Grew mixed array of plants and animals

- Used their produce to feed their families and trade with neighbors

- Organized their families along patriarchal lines

changing system *Elaborate system of neighborhood debts and bartering used primarily in the South and West, where little cash money was available.*

land on to their sons. After the war, fewer farm fathers were able to do that. Those in the old settlements had small farms and large families, which made it impossible for them to provide a competence for all their offspring. Most fathers tried to provide for all their heirs (generally by leaving land to their sons and personal property to their daughters). Few left all their land to one son, and many stated in their wills that the sons to whom they left the land must share barns and cider mills—even the house—on farms that could be subdivided no further. Such provisions fitted a social system that guaranteed the independence of the household head through complex relations with kin and neighbors, but they were also an indication that this system had reached the end of the line.

Outside New England, farm **tenancy** was on the increase. Farmers often bought farms in the neighborhood, rented them to tenants, then gave them to their sons when they reached adulthood. The sons of poorer farmers often rented a farm in the hope of saving enough money to buy it. Some fathers bought tracts of unimproved land in the backcountry—sometimes on speculation, more often to provide their sons with land they could farm. Others paid to have their sons educated, or arranged an apprenticeship to provide them with an avenue of escape from a crowded countryside. As a result, more and more young men left home. The populations of the old farming communities grew older and more female, while the populations of the rising frontier settlements and seaport cities became younger and more male.

The Seaport Cities

When the first federal census takers made their rounds in 1790, they found 94 percent of Americans living on farms and in rural villages. The rest lived in the 24 towns that had populations of more than 2,500. Only five communities, all seaport cities, had a population over 10,000: Boston (18,038), New York (33,131), Philadelphia (42,444), Baltimore (13,503), and Charleston (16,359).

When war broke out between Britain and France in 1793, the overseas demand for American foodstuffs and for shipping to carry products from the Caribbean islands to Europe further strengthened the seaport cities. The maritime economy during these years was disrupted by wars, bans on exports and imports, and trade embargoes, but by 1815, the seaports had been transformed. New York City had become the nation's largest city, with a population of 96,373 in 1810. Philadelphia's population had risen to 53,722, Boston's to 34,322, and Baltimore's to 46,555.

Seaport merchants amassed huge fortunes. To manage those fortunes, new institutions emerged. Docking and warehousing facilities expanded. Bookkeepers were replaced by accountants who were familiar with the new double-entry system of accounting, and insurance and banking companies were formed to handle the risks and rewards of wartime commerce.

The bustle of prosperity was evident on the waterfronts and principal streets of the seaport cities.

The main thoroughfares and a few of the side streets were paved with cobblestones and lined with fine shops and townhouses. But in other parts of the cities, the boom was creating unprecedented poverty. Narrow streets crowded with ragged children, browsing dogs and pigs, with garbage and waste filling the open sewers. Epidemics had become more frequent and deadly. New York City, for example, experienced six severe epidemics of yellow fever between 1791 and 1822.

tenancy *System under which farmers worked land that they did not own.*

PROCESSION OF VICTUALLERS, 1815.
The frequent and festive parades in the seaport cities included militia companies, political officials, clergymen, and artisans organized by trade. In this Philadelphia parade celebrating the end of the War of 1812, the victuallers, preceded by militia cavalrymen, carry a penned steer and a craft flag high atop a wagon, while butchers in top hats and clean aprons ride below. Behind them, shipbuilders drag a ship through the streets. Such parades were vivid displays of the system of interlocking labors that made up the city and of the value of artisans within that system.

The Historical Society of Pennsylvania, Procession of the Victuallers, by John Lewis Krimmel (Bc85 K89)

The slums were evidence that money created by commerce was being distributed in undemocratic ways. Per capita wealth in New York rose 60 percent between 1790 and 1825, but the wealthiest 4 percent of the population owned over half of that wealth. The wages of laborers rose, but the increase in seasonal and temporary employment, together with the recurring interruptions of foreign commerce, cut deeply into the security and prosperity of ordinary women and men.

Meanwhile, the status of artisans in the big cities was changing. In 1790, artisans constituted about half the male workforce of the seaport cities, and their respectability and usefulness, together with the role they had played in the Revolution, had earned them an honorable status. That status rested in large part on their independence. In 1790, most artisan workshops had been household operations with at most one or two apprentices and **journeymen**—wage earners who looked forward to owning their own shops one day. Most master craftsmen lived modestly (on the borderline of poverty in many cases) and aspired only to support their household in security and decency. They identified their way of life with republican virtue.

As in the countryside, however, the patriarchal base of that republicanism was eroding. With the growth of the maritime economy, the nature of construction work, shipbuilding, the clothing trades, and other specialized crafts changed. Artisans were being replaced by cheaper labor and being undercut by subcontracted "slop work" performed by semiskilled rural outworkers. Perhaps one in five master craftsmen entered the newly emerging business class. The others took work as laborers or journeymen. By 1815, most young craftsmen could not hope to own their own shops. In the seaport cities, the world of artisans like Paul Revere, Benjamin Franklin, and Thomas Paine was passing out of existence. Wage labor was taking its place.

The loss of independence undermined artisan husbands and fathers. Few wage earners could support a family without the earnings of a wife and children. Working-class women took in boarders and did laundry and found work as domestic servants or as peddlers of fruit, candy, vegetables, cakes, or hot corn. They sent their children out to scavenge in the streets. The descent into wage labor and the reliance on the earnings of women and children violated the republican, patriarchal assumptions of fathers.

journeyman *Wage-earning craftsman.*

FROM BACKCOUNTRY TO FRONTIER: THE NORTHWEST

The United States was a huge country in 1790, but most white Americans still lived on thin strips of settlement along the Atlantic coast and along the few navigable rivers that emptied into the Atlantic. Some were pushing their way into the wilds of Maine and northern Vermont, and in New York they had set up communities as far west as the Mohawk valley. Pittsburgh was a struggling new settlement, and two outposts had been established on the Ohio River: at Marietta and at what would become Cincinnati.

The Backcountry, 1790–1815

To easterners, the backcountry whites who were displacing the Indians seemed no different from the defeated aborigines. In fact, in accommodating themselves to a borderless forest used by both Indians and whites, many settlers had melded Indian and white ways. To clear the land, backcountry farmers simply **girdled** the trees and left them to die and fall. Then they plowed the land by navigating between the stumps. To easterners' minds, the worst offense was that women often worked the fields, particularly while their men, as did Indians, spent long periods away on hunting trips for food game and animal skins for trade.

Eastern visitors were appalled not only by the poverty, lice, and filth of frontier life but by the drunkenness and violence of the frontiersmen. Travel accounts tell of no-holds-barred fights in which men gouged the eyes and bit off the noses and ears of their opponents. Stories arose of half-legendary heroes like Davy Crockett of Tennessee, who wrestled bears and alligators, and Mike Fink, a Pennsylvania boatman who brawled and drank his way along the rivers of the interior until he was shot and killed in a drunken episode. Samuel Holden Parsons, a New Englander serving as a judge in the Northwest Territory, called the frontiersmen "our white savages."

Settlement

After 1789, settlers of the backcountry made two demands of the new national government: protection from the Indians and a guarantee of the right to navigate the Ohio and Mississippi rivers. The Indians were pushed back in the 1790s and finished off in the War of 1812, and in 1803 Jefferson's Louisiana Purchase (see Chapter 7) ended the European presence on the rivers. Over these years, the pace of settlement quickened. In 1790, only 10,000 settlers lived west of the Appalachians—about 1 American in 40. By 1820, two million Americans were westerners—1 in 5.

The new settlers bought land, built frame houses surrounded by cleared fields, planted marketable crops, and settled into the struggle to make farms out of the wilderness. Ohio entered the union in 1803, followed by Indiana (1816) and Illinois (1818). As time passed, the term *backcountry*, which easterners had used to refer to the wilderness, fell into disuse. By 1820 the term *frontier* had replaced it. The new settlements were no longer the backwater of American civilization. They were its cutting edge.

girdled trees *Trees with a line cut around them so sap would not rise in the spring.*

TRANSPORTATION REVOLUTION, 1815–1860

After 1815, dramatic improvements in transportation—more and better roads, steamboats, canals, and railroads—tied old communities together and penetrated previously isolated neighborhoods. These improvements made the transition to a market society physically possible.

FOCUS QUESTION

How did improvements in transportation actually channel commerce within and between sections?

Transportation in 1815

In 1815, the United States was a rural nation stretching from the old settlements on the Atlantic coast to the trans-Appalachian west, with transportation facilities that ranged from primitive to nonexistent. Americans despaired of communicating, to say nothing of doing business on a national scale. In 1816, a Senate committee reported that $9 would move a ton of goods across the 3,000-mile expanse of the North Atlantic. The same $9 would move the same ton of goods only 30 miles inland.

West of the Appalachians, transportation was almost entirely undeveloped. Until the 1820s, most northwesterners were southerners who settled near tributaries of the Ohio-Mississippi River system. They floated their produce downriver on jerry-built flatboats. At New Orleans it was transshipped to New York and other eastern ports. Most boatmen knocked down their flatboats, sold the lumber, and then walked home to Kentucky or Ohio.

Transporting goods *into* the western settlements was even more difficult. Keel boatmen navigated upstream using eddies and back currents, sailing when the wind was right, but usually poling their boat against the current. Skilled crews averaged only 15 miles a day. Looking for better routes, some merchants dragged finished goods across Pennsylvania and into the West at Pittsburgh, but transport costs made these goods prohibitively expensive. Consequently, the trans-Appalachian settlements remained marginal to the market economy.

TRAVEL BY STAGECOACH NEAR TRENTON, NEW JERSEY, 1815. *The coach is small and open to the weather, the passengers are crowded and uncomfortable (one of them has lost his hat), and the road is a dirt path with a steep incline—difficult when going uphill, dangerous when going down. The driver, like many of the people who worked with horses, is black. This was travel in one of the most developed parts of the country in 1815.*

Improvements

In 1816, Congress resumed construction of the National Road (first authorized in 1802) that linked the Potomac River with the Ohio River at Wheeling, Virginia. The road reached Wheeling in 1818. At about the same time, Pennsylvania extended the Lancaster Turnpike from Philadelphia to the Ohio River at Pittsburgh. The National Road enabled settlers and a few merchants' wagons to reach the West, but the cost of moving bulky farm produce over the road remained high. East-bound traffic on the National Road consisted largely of cattle and pigs, which carried themselves to market. Farmers continued to float their corn, cotton, wheat, salt pork, and whiskey south by riverboat and thence to eastern markets. It was the steamboat that first made commercial agriculture feasible in the Northwest. In 1807, **Robert Fulton** launched the *Clermont* on an upriver trip from New York City to Albany. Over the next few years Americans developed flat-bottomed steam-boats that could navigate rivers even at low water. The first steamboat reached Louisville from New Orleans in 1815. Two years later, with 17 steamboats already working western rivers, the *Washington* made the New Orleans-Louisville run in 25 days, a feat that convinced westerners that two-way river trade was possible. By 1820, 69 steamboats were operating on western rivers. The 60,000 tons of produce that farmers and planters had shipped out of the interior in 1810 grew to 500,000 tons in 1840. The steamboat had transformed the interior from an isolated frontier into a busy commercial region that traded farm and plantation products for manufactured goods.

In the East, state government created rivers where nature had made none. In 1817, Governor DeWitt Clinton talked the New York legislature into building a canal linking the Hudson River with Lake Erie, thus opening a continuous water route between the Northwest and New York City. The **Erie Canal** was a near-visionary feat of engineering, stretching 364 miles from Albany to Buffalo. Construction began in 1819, and the canal reached Buffalo in 1825. It was clear even before then that the canal would repay New York State's investment of $7.5 million many times over, and that it would transform the territory it served. By 1830, the corridor of the Erie Canal was one of the world's great grain-growing regions, dotted with market towns and new cities such as Syracuse, Rochester, and Buffalo.

The Erie Canal was an immense success, and legislators and entrepreneurs in other states joined a canal boom that lasted for 20 years. Northwestern states, Ohio in particular, built ambitious canal systems that linked isolated areas to the Great Lakes and thus to the Erie Canal. Northeastern states followed suit. A canal between Worcester and Providence linked the farms of central Massachusetts with Narragansett Bay. Another canal linked the coal mines of northeastern Pennsylvania with the Hudson River at Kingston, New York. In 1835, Pennsylvania completed a canal from Philadelphia to Pittsburgh. (See Map 8.1.)

The canal boom was followed quickly by a boom in railroads. The first of them connected burgeoning cities to rivers and canals. The Baltimore and Ohio Railroad, for example, linked Baltimore to the rivers of the West. Although the approximately 3,000 miles of railroads built between the late 1820s and 1840 helped the market positions of some cities, they did not constitute a national or even a regional rail network. A national system developed with the 5,000 miles of track laid in the 1840s and with the flurry of railroad building that gave the United States a rail network of 30,000 miles by 1860—a continuous, integrated system that created massive links between the East and the Northwest and that threatened to put canals out of business. In fact, the New York Central, which paralleled the Erie Canal, rendered that canal obsolete. (See Map 8.2.)

Robert Fulton *Builder of the* Clermont, *the first practical steam-driven boat.*

Erie Canal *Canal linking the Hudson River at Albany with the Great Lakes at Buffalo that helped to commercialize the farms of the Great Lakes watershed and to channel that commerce into New York City.*

Map 8.1 Rivers, Roads, and Canals, 1825–1860. *In the second quarter of the 19th century, transportation projects linked the North and Northwest into an integrated economic and social system. There were fewer improvements in the South: Farm produce traveled down navigable rivers from bottomland plantations to river and seaport towns, thence to New York for shipment overseas; southern legislatures and entrepreneurs saw little use for further improvements.*

Time and Money

The transportation revolution reduced the money it took to move heavy goods. Turnpikes cut the cost of wagon transport, but goods traveled most cheaply on water. In 1816, for example, freight rates on the Ohio–Mississippi system had been 1.3 cents per ton-mile for downriver travel and 5.8 cents for upriver travel. Steamboats cut both costs to a bit more than a third of a cent.

Improvements in speed were nearly as dramatic. The overland route from Cincinnati to New York in 1815 (by keelboat upriver to Pittsburgh, then by wagon

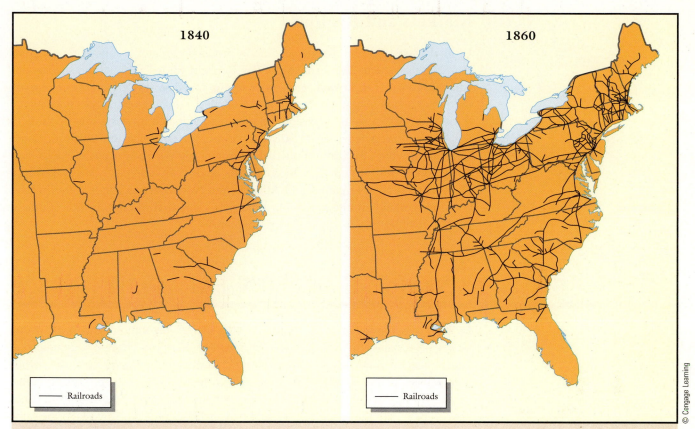

Map 8.2 **Railroads in the United States, 1840 and 1860.** *In these 20 years, both the North and South built railway systems. Northerners built rail lines that integrated the market economies of the Midwest and the East—connecting both sections and the towns within them. For the most part, Southern railroads linked the plantation belt with the ocean. Revealingly, only a few lines connected the North and South.*

the rest of the way) had taken a minimum of 52 days. By 1840, upriver steamboats carried goods to the terminus of the Main Line Canal at Pittsburgh, which delivered them to Philadelphia, which sent them on to New York City in a total transit time of 18 to 20 days. At about the same time, the Ohio canal system enabled Cincinnati to send goods north through Ohio, across Lake Erie, over the Erie Canal, and down the Hudson to New York City—an all-water route that reduced costs and made the trip in 18 days. By 1840, travel time between the big northeastern cities had been reduced to from one-fourth to one-eleventh of what it had been in 1790. Such improvements in speed and economy made a national market possible.

By 1840, improved transportation had made a market revolution. Foreign trade, which had driven American economic growth up to 1815, continued to expand. Exports (now consisting more of southern cotton than of northern food crops) continued to increase, and the flow of imported manufactured goods increased as well. Yet foreign trade now accounted for a smaller proportion of American market activity. Before 1815, Americans had exported about 15 percent of their total national product. By 1830, exports accounted for only 6 percent of a vastly increased national production. The great engine of economic growth in the North and West was not the old colonial relationship with Europe but self-sustaining domestic markets for farm produce and manufactured goods.

Markets and Regions

Until at least 1840, the market revolution produced greater results within regions than between them. The farmers of New England traded food for finished goods from Boston, Lynn, Lowell, and other towns in what was becoming an urban, industrial region. Although the Erie Canal created a huge potential for interregional trade, until 1839 most of its eastbound tonnage originated in western New York. In the West, farmers fed such rapidly growing cities as Rochester, Pittsburgh, and Cincinnati, which in turn supplied the farmers with tools, furniture, shoes, and other goods. Still, it was clear to politicians, and to anyone else who looked at a map, that the New England, mid-Atlantic, and Northwestern states were on their way to becoming an integrated market society—one that did not include southern plantations that grew for export (see Chapter 9).

NORTHEASTERN FARMS, 1815–1860

In the old communities of the Northeast, the market revolution sent many young people off to cities and factory towns and others to the West. Those who remained at home engaged in new forms of agriculture on a transformed rural landscape, while their cousins in the Northwest transformed a wilderness into cash-producing farms.

New Englanders who tried to grow grain on their rocky, worn-out soil could not compete with the farmers of western New York and the Northwest. At the same time, however, the factories and cities of the Northeast provided Yankee farmers with a market for meat and other perishables. Beef became the great New England cash crop. Dairy products were not far behind, and the proximity to city markets encouraged the spread of poultry and egg farms, fruit orchards, and truck gardens. The burgeoning shoe industry bought leather from the farmers, and woolen mills created a demand for wool.

The rise of livestock specialization reduced the amount of land under cultivation. Early in the century New Englanders still tilled their few acres in the old three-year rotation: corn the first year, rye the second, fallow the third. By the 1820s and 1830s, as farmers raised more livestock and less grain, the land that remained in cultivation was farmed more intensively. Farmers saved manure and ashes for fertilizer, plowed more deeply and systematically, and tended their crops more carefully. These improved techniques, along with cash from the sale of their livestock and the availability of food at stores, encouraged Yankee farmers to allocate less and less land to the growing of food crops.

The transition to livestock-raising transformed woodlands into open pastures. As farmers leveled the forests, they sold the wood to fuel-hungry cities. In the 1820s manufacturers began marketing cast-iron stoves that heated houses more cheaply and efficiently than open hearths, and canals brought cheap Pennsylvania anthracite to the Northeast. Farmers who needed pastureland could gain substantial onetime profits from the sale of cut wood. The result was massive deforestation.

With the shift to specialized market agriculture, New England farmers became customers for necessities that their forebears had produced themselves or had acquired through barter. They heated their houses with coal dug by Pennsylvania miners. They wore cotton cloth made by the factory women at Lowell. New Hampshire farm girls made straw hats for them, and the craftsmen of Lynn made their shoes. By 1830 or so, many farmers were even buying food. The Erie Canal and the western grain belt sent flour from Rochester into eastern neighborhoods where grain was no longer grown. Many farmers found it easier to produce specialized crops for market and to buy butter, cheese, eggs, and vegetables at country stores.

The turning point came in the 1820s. The storekeepers of Northampton, Massachusetts, for instance, had been increasing their stock in trade by about 7 percent per decade since the late 18th century. In the 1820s, they increased it 45 percent and now carried not only local farm products and sugar, salt, and coffee, but also bolts of New England cloth, sacks of western flour, a variety of necessities and little luxuries from the wholesale houses of New York City and Boston, and pattern samples from which to order silverware, dishes, wallpaper, and other household goods. Those goods were better than what could be made at home, and for the most part they were cheaper. But all of these things still cost money and committed farm families to increasing their cash incomes. Standards of living rose dramatically, but northeastern farmers depended on markets in ways that their fathers and grandfathers would have considered dangerous not only to family welfare but to the welfare of the republic itself.

THE NORTHWEST

One reason the market revolution in the Northeast went as smoothly as it did was that young people with little hope of inheriting land in the old settlements moved to towns and cities or to the new farmlands of the Northwest. Between 1815 and 1840 migrants from the older areas transformed the Northwest Territory into a working agricultural landscape.

Southern Settlers

In the Northwest until the 1820s, most settlers were yeomen from Kentucky and Tennessee, usually a generation removed from Virginia, the Carolinas, and western Maryland. They moved along the Ohio and up the Muskingum, Miami, Scioto, Wabash, and Illinois rivers to set up farms in the southern and central counties of Ohio, Indiana, and Illinois.

When southerners moved north of the Ohio River into territory that banned slavery, they often did so saying that slavery blocked opportunities for poor whites. But even those who rejected slavery seldom rejected southern folkways. Like their kinfolk in Kentucky and Tennessee, the farmers of southern and central Ohio, Indiana, and Illinois remained tied to the river trade and to a mode of agriculture that favored free-ranging livestock over cultivated fields. The typical farmer fenced in a few acres of corn and left the rest of his land in woods to be roamed by southern hogs known as "razorbacks" and "land sharks."

The southern-born pioneers of the Northwest, like their cousins across the Ohio River, depended more on their families and neighbors than on distant markets. Southerners insisted on repaying debts in kind and on lending tools rather than renting them, thus engaging outsiders in the elaborate network of "neighboring" through which transplanted southerners made their livings. As late as the 1840s, in the bustling town of Springfield, Illinois, barter was the preferred system of exchange.

Northern Farmers

Northeastern migrants entered the Northwest in the 1820s. Most of them were New Englanders who had spent a generation in western New York. The rest came directly from New England. Arriving in the Northwest along the market's busiest arteries, they practiced an intensive, market-oriented agriculture. They penned their cattle and hogs and fattened them up, making them bigger and worth more than those farther south. They planted their land in grain and developed one of the world's great wheat-producing regions. In 1820, the Northwest had exported only 12 percent of its agricultural produce. By 1840 that figure had risen to 27 percent, and it stood much higher among northern-born grain farmers.

The new settlers were notably receptive to improvements in farming techniques. They adopted cast-iron plows, which cut cleanly through oak roots four inches thick. By the 1830s, the efficient, expensive grain cradle had replaced the sickle as the principal harvest tool in northwestern wheat fields. Instead of threshing their grain by driving cattle and horses over it, farmers bought new horse-powered and treadmill threshers and used hand-cranked fanning mills to speed the process of cleaning the grain.

Some farmers rejected these agricultural improvements as expensive and unnatural. They thought that cast-iron plows poisoned the soil and that fanning mills made a "wind contrary to nater" and thus offended God. John Chapman, an eccentric Yankee who earned the nickname "Johnny Appleseed" by planting apple tree cuttings in southern Ohio and Indiana before the settlers arrived, planted only low-yield, common trees. He regarded grafting, which farmers farther north and east were using to improve the quality of their apples, as "against nature." Southerners scoffed at the Yankee fondness for mechanical improvements, the systematic breeding of animals and plants, careful bookkeeping, and farm techniques learned from books.

Conflict between intensive agriculture and older, less market-oriented ways reached comic proportions when the Illinois legislature imposed stiff penalties on farmers who allowed their small, poorly bred bulls to run loose and impregnate cows with questionable sperm, thereby depriving the owners of high-bred bulls of their breeding fees and rendering the systematic breeding of cattle impossible. When the poorer farmers refused to pen their bulls, the law was rescinded. A local historian explained that "there was a generous feeling in the hearts of the people in favor of an equality of privileges, even among bulls."

Farm families

FOCUS QUESTION

How did northern farm families experience the transition into commercial agriculture between 1815 and 1850?

Northern rural folk experienced this transformation not as individuals but as members of families, as commercialization changed relations between husbands and wives, parents and children, and their neighbors.

Households

The market revolution transformed 18th-century households into 19th-century homes. For one thing, Americans began to limit the size of their families. The decline was most pronounced in the North, particularly in commercialized areas. Rural birth rates remained at 18th-century levels in the southern uplands, in the poorest and most isolated communities of the North, and on the frontier. These communities practiced the old labor-intensive agriculture and relied on the labor of large families. For farmers who used newer techniques or switched to livestock, large families made less sense. Moreover, large broods hampered the ability of future-minded parents to provide for their children and conflicted with new notions of privacy and domesticity that were taking shape among an emerging rural middle class.

Before 1815, farmwives had labored in the house, the barnyard, and the garden while their husbands and sons worked in the fields. With the market revolution came a sharper distinction between male work that was part of the cash economy and female work that was not. Even such traditional women's tasks as dairying, vegetable gardening, and poultry raising became men's work once they became cash-producing specialties.

At the same time, new kinds of women's work emerged within households. Though there were fewer children to care for, the culture began to demand forms of child rearing that were more intensive, individualized, and mother-centered. Store-bought white flour, butter, and eggs and the new iron stoves eased the burdens of food preparation, but they also created demands for pies, cakes, and other fancy foods that earlier generations had only imagined. And while farmwomen no longer spun and wove their own cloth, the availability of manufactured cloth created the expectation that their families would dress more neatly and with greater variety than they had in the past, and women spent more time sewing, washing, and ironing. Similar expectations demanded greater personal and domestic cleanliness and taste, and farmwomen worked at planting flower beds; cleaning and maintaining prized furniture, mirrors, rugs, and ceramics; and scrubbing floors and children.

Housework was tied to new notions of privacy, decency, and domestic comfort. Before 1820, farmers cared little about how their houses looked, often tossing trash and garbage out the door for the pigs and chickens that foraged near the house. As farmers began to grow cash crops and adopt middle-class ways, they began to plant shade trees and kept their yards free of trash. They painted their homes, arranged their woodpiles into neat stacks, surrounded their houses with flowers and ornamental shrubs, and tried to hide their privies from view.

Inside, prosperous farmhouses took on an air of privacy and comfort. Separate kitchens and iron stoves replaced open hearths. The availability of finished cloth permitted the regular use of tablecloths, napkins, doilies, curtains, bedspreads, and quilts. Oil lamps replaced homemade candles, and the more comfortable families began to decorate their homes with wallpaper and upholstered furniture. Farm couples moved their beds away from the hearth and (along with the children's beds that had been scattered throughout the house) put them into spaces designated as bedrooms. They took the washstands and basins, which were coming into more common use, out of the kitchen and put them into the bedroom, thus making sleeping, bathing, and sex more private than they had been in the past. At the center of this new house stood the farmwife, apart from the bustling world of commerce, but decorating and caring for the amenities that commerce bought, and demanding that men respect the new domestic world that commerce had made possible.

A SOAP ADVERTISEMENT FROM THE 1850s. *The rigors of "Old Washing Day" lead the mother in this advertisement to abuse the children and house pets, while her husband leaves the house. With American Cream Soap, domestic bliss returns. The children and cats are happy, the husband returns, and the wife has time to sew.*

Neighborhoods

By the 1830s and 1840s the market revolution had transformed the rural landscape of the Northeast. The forests had been reduced, the swamps had been drained, and most of the streams and rivers were interrupted by mill dams. Bears, panthers, and wolves had disappeared, along with the beaver and many of the fish. Now there were extensive pastures and neatly cultivated croplands. Many towns, particularly in New England, had planted shade trees along the country roads, completing a rural landscape of straight lines and human cultivation, a landscape that made it easy to think of nature as a commodity to be altered and controlled.

Within that landscape, old practices and old forms of neighborliness fell into disuse. Neighbors continued to exchange goods and labor and to contract debts that might be left unpaid for years, but debts were more likely to be owed to profit-minded storekeepers and creditors, and even debts between neighbors were often paid in cash. Traditionally, storekeepers had allowed farmers to bring in produce and have it credited to a neighbor/creditor's account. In the 1830s, storekeepers began to demand cash payment or to charge lower prices to those who paid cash.

The farm newspapers that appeared in these years urged farmers to keep careful records of the amount of fertilizer used, labor costs, and per-acre yields, and discouraged them from relying on the old system of neighboring. Neighborly rituals like parties, husking bees, and barn raisings—with their drinking and socializing—were scorned as an inefficient and morally suspect waste of time.

By 1830, the efficient farmer concentrated on producing commodities that could be marketed outside the neighborhood and used his cash income to buy material comforts for his family, to pay debts, and to provide a cash inheritance for his children. Although much of the old world of household and neighborhood survived, farmers created a subsistence and maintained the independence of their households not through those spheres but through unprecedented levels of dependence on the outside world.

THE BEGINNINGS OF THE INDUSTRIAL REVOLUTION

FOCUS QUESTION

What was the relationship between urban-industrial growth and the commercialization of the northern countryside?

In the 50 years following 1820, American cities grew faster than ever before or since. The fastest growth was in new cities that served commercial agriculture and in factory towns that produced for a largely rural domestic market. Even in the seaports, growth derived more from commerce with the hinterland than from international trade. Paradoxically, the market revolution in the countryside had produced the beginnings of industry and the greatest period of urban growth in U.S. history.

Factory Towns: The Rhode Island System

Jeffersonians held that the United States must always remain rural. Americans could expand into the West, trade their farm surpluses for European finished goods, and thus avoid creating cities with their dependent social classes. Some Federalists argued that Americans, in order to retain their independence, must produce their own manufactured necessities. Proponents of domestic manufactures argued that people could enjoy the benefits of factory production without the troublesome blight of industrial cities. They believed that abundant waterpower would enable Americans to build their factories across the countryside. Such a decentralized factory system would provide employment for country women and children and thus subsidize the independence of struggling farmers.

The first factories were textile mills. The key to the mass production of cotton and woolen textiles was a water-powered machine that spun yarn and

HISTORY THROUGH FILM

A Midwife's Tale

Directed by Richard D. Rodgers (PBS)

The documentary *A Midwife's Tale*, based on the book by historian Laurel Thatcher Ulrich, is a close and imaginative analysis of the diary of Martha Ballard, a Maine farmwoman and midwife of the late 18th and early 19th centuries. Events Ulrich describes are reenacted; period modes of dress, housing, gardening, washing, coffin making, spinning and weaving, and other details are accurately reconstructed; the soundtrack consists of the sounds of footfalls, horses, hand looms, dishes, and an occasional cough, exclamation, or drinking song. The narrative is carried by an actress who reads passages from the diary, and Ulrich occasionally breaks in to explain her own experiences with the diary and its interpretation. The result is a documentary film that knows the difference between dramatizing history and making it up.

The Kennebec River, in the half-wild country in which Martha Ballard lived her busy and remarkably well-recorded life.

© Jerry and Marcy Monkman/ Aurora Photos

It also dramatizes the ways in which a skilled and sensitive historian goes about her work. Martha Ballard was a midwife in a town on the Kennebec River. She began keeping a daily diary at the age of 50 in 1785 and continued until 1812. Most of the film is about her daily life: delivering babies, nursing the sick, helping neighbors, keeping house, raising and supervising the labor of her daughters and niece, gardening, and tending cattle and turkeys. In both the book and the film, the busyness of an ordinary woman's days—and a sense of her possibilities and limits—in the early republic comes through in exhausting detail. The dailiness of her life is interrupted only occasionally: by a fire at her husband's sawmill, an epidemic of scarlet fever, a parade organized to honor the death of George Washington, the rape of a minister's wife by his enemies (including the local judge, who is set free), and a neighbor's inexplicable murder of his wife and six children.

There is also the process of getting old. At the beginning, Martha Ballard is the busy wife in a well-run household. As she ages and her children leave to set up households of their own, Ballard hires local girls who—perhaps because an increasingly democratic culture has made them less subservient than Ballard would like; perhaps because Ballard is growing old and impatient; perhaps both—tend to be surly. Her husband, a surveyor who works for merchants speculating in local land, is attacked twice in the woods by squatters, and spends a year and a half in debtor's jail—not for his own debts but because, as tax collector, he has failed to collect enough. While the husband is in jail and his aging wife struggles to keep the house going, their son moves his own family into the house. Martha is moved into a single room and is made to feel unwanted, a poignant and unsentimental case of the strained relations between generations that historians have discovered in the early republic.

A Midwife's Tale is a modest film that comes as close as a thorough and imaginative historian and a good filmmaker can to recreating the texture of lived experience in the northeastern countryside at the beginning of the 19th century. Students who enjoy the movie should go immediately to the book.

PAWTUCKET IN 1817. *Here is America's first textile milling town. It is set beside a waterfall that provides power for the mills. A bridge runs directly over the brink of the falls, and men and boys fish and play in the pool below them. It is a pastoral scene, the combination of nature and human artifice that early factory promoters held up as the ideal and attainable industrial landscape for the United States. But it is the factories and poor houses in the background, and not the river and its charms, that have a future.*

© The New York Public Library/Art Resource, NY

thread. The machine had been invented and patented by the Englishman Richard Arkwright in 1769, and the British government forbade the machinery or the people who worked with it to leave the country. Scores of textile workers defied the law and made their way to North America. One of them was Samuel Slater, who, working from memory, built the first Arkwright spinning mill in America at Pawtucket, Rhode Island, in 1790.

Slater's first mill was a small frame building tucked among the town's houses and craftsmen's shops. Although its capacity was limited to the spinning of cotton yarn, it provided work for children in the mill and for women who wove yarn into cloth in their homes. As his business grew and he advertised for widows with children, however, Slater was greeted by families headed by landless, impoverished men. Slater's use of children from these families prompted respectable farmers and craftsmen to pull their children out of Slater's growing complex of mills. More poor families arrived to take their places, and during the first years of the 19th century, Pawtucket became a disorderly mill town.

Soon Slater and other mill owners built factory villages in the countryside where they could exert better control over their operations and their workers. The practice became known as the Rhode Island or "family" system. At several locations in southern New England, mill owners built whole villages surrounded by company-owned farmland that they rented to the husbands and fathers of their mill workers. The workplace was closely supervised, and drinking and other troublesome practices were forbidden in the villages. Fathers and older sons worked either on rented farms or as laborers at the mills. By the late 1820s Slater and most other owners were getting rid of their outworkers and buying power looms, thus transforming the villages into disciplined, self-contained factory towns that turned raw cotton into finished cloth.

Factory Towns: The Waltham System

Francis Cabot Lowell *Wealthy Bostonian who, with the help of the Boston Associates, built and operated integrated textile mills in eastern Massachusetts.*

Touring English factory districts in 1811, wealthy Boston merchant **Francis Cabot Lowell** asked questions and made secret drawings of the machines. Returning home, Lowell joined with wealthy friends to form the Boston Manufacturing Company, soon known as the Boston Associates. In 1813, they built their first mill at Waltham, Massachusetts, and then expanded into Lowell, Lawrence, and other new towns near Boston during the 1820s. The company, operating under what became known as the Waltham system, built mills that differed from the early Rhode Island mills in two ways. First, they were heavily capitalized and as fully mechanized as possible; they turned raw cotton into finished cloth with little need for skilled workers. Second, the operatives who tended their machines were young, single women recruited from the farms of northern New England. The company provided supervised boardinghouses for them and enforced rules of conduct both on and off the job. The young women worked steadily, never drank, seldom stayed out late, and attended church faithfully. They dressed neatly—often stylishly—and read newspapers and attended lectures. They impressed visitors, particularly those who had seen factory workers in other places, as a dignified and self-respecting workforce.

The brick mills and prim boardinghouses set within landscaped towns and occupied by sober, well-behaved farm girls signified the desire of the Boston Associates to build a profitable textile industry without creating a permanent working class. The women would work for a few years in a carefully controlled environment, send their wages back to their family, and return home to live as country housewives. However, these young farmwomen did not send their wages home or, as was popularly believed, use them to pay for their brothers' college education. Some saved their money to use as dowries that their fathers could not afford. More, however, spent their wages on themselves, particularly on clothes and books.

The Waltham system produced a self-respecting sisterhood of independent, wage-earning women. Twice in the 1830s, the women of Lowell went on strike, proclaiming that they were not wage slaves but "the daughters of freemen." After finishing their stint in the mills, many Lowell women entered public life as reformers. Most of them married and became housewives, but not on the terms their mothers had known. One in three married Lowell men and became city dwellers. Those who returned home to rural neighborhoods remained unmarried longer than their sisters who had stayed on the farm, and then married men about their own age who worked at something other than farming.

The Boston Associates kept their promise to produce cotton cloth profitably without creating a permanent working class, but they did not succeed in shuttling young women from rural to urban paternalism and back again. Wage labor, the ultimate degradation for agrarian-republican men, opened a road of independence for thousands of young women.

Cities

The market revolution hit American cities with particular force. Here there was little concern for creating a classless industrial society: Vastly wealthy men of finance, a new middle class that bought and sold an ever-growing range of consumer goods, and the impoverished women and men who produced those goods lived together in communities that unabashedly recognized the reality of social class.

The richest men were seaport merchants who had survived and prospered during the world wars that ended in 1815. They carried on as importers and exporters, took control of banks and insurance companies, and made great fortunes in urban real estate. Below the old mercantile elite (or, in the case of the new cities of the interior, at the top of society) stood a growing middle class of wholesale and retail merchants, small manufacturers, and an army of lawyers, salesmen, auctioneers, clerks, bookkeepers, and accountants who processed the paperwork for the new market society. At the head of this new middle class were the wholesale merchants of the seaports who bought hardware, crockery, and other commodities from importers and then sold them in smaller lots to storekeepers from the interior. Slightly below them were the large processors of farm products.

QUICK REVIEW

THE WALTHAM SYSTEM

- Heavily capitalized by wealthy investors

- Integrated, mechanized cotton-to-cloth factories

- Workforce of young, single women

Another step down were specialized retail merchants who dealt in books, furniture, crockery, or other consumer goods. Alongside the merchants stood master craftsmen who had become manufacturers. With their workers busy in backrooms or in household workshops, they now called themselves shoe dealers and merchant tailors. At the bottom of this new commercial world were hordes of clerks, most of them young men who hoped to rise in the world. Both in numbers and in the nature of the work, this white-collar army formed a new class created by the market revolution.

In the 1820s and 1830s, the commercial classes transformed the look and feel of American cities. As retailing and manufacturing became separate activities (even in firms that did both), the merchants, salesmen, and clerks now worked in quiet offices on downtown business streets. Both in the seaports and the new towns of the interior, impressive brick and glass storefronts appeared on the main streets. Perhaps the most telling monuments of the self-conscious new business society were the handsome retail arcades that began going up in the 1820s, providing consumers with comfortable, gracious space in which to shop.

Metropolitan Industrialization

While businessmen were developing a new middle-class ethos, the people who made consumer goods were growing more numerous and subsequently were disappearing from view. With the exception of textiles and a few other commodities, few goods were made in mechanized factories before the 1850s. Most goods were made by hand. City merchants and master craftsmen met the growing demand by hiring more workers. The largest handicrafts—shoemaking, tailoring, and the building trades—were divided into skilled and semiskilled segments and farmed out to subcontractors who could turn a profit only by cutting labor costs. The result was the creation of an urban working class.

Take the case of tailoring. High rents and costly real estate, together with the absence of waterpower, prohibited locating large factories in cities, but the nature of the clothing trade and the availability of cheap labor gave rise to a system of subcontracting that transformed needlework into the first **"sweated"** trade in America. Merchants kept a few skilled male tailors to take care of the custom trade and to cut cloth into patterned pieces for ready-made clothing. The pieces were sent out to needleworkers who sewed them together in their homes. Male tailors continued to do the finishing work on men's suits, but most of the work was done by women who worked long hours for piece rates that ranged from 75 cents to $1.50 per week. Along with clothing, women in garrets and tenements manufactured the items with which the middle class decorated itself and its homes: embroidery, doilies, artificial flowers, fringe, tassels, fancy-bound books, and parasols. All provided work for ill-paid legions of female workers.

Other trades followed similar patterns. For example, northeastern shoes were made in uniform sizes and sent in barrels all over the country. Like tailoring, shoemaking was divided into skilled operations and time-consuming unskilled tasks. Men performed the skilled work of cutting and shaping the uppers. The drudgery of sewing the pieces together went to low-paid women. Skilled craftsmen could earn as much as $2 a day making custom boots and shoes. Men shaping uppers in boardinghouses earned a little more than half of that. Women binders could work a full week and earn as little as 50 cents. In this as in other trades, wage rates and gendered tasks reflected the old family division of labor, which was based on the assumption that female workers lived with an income-earning husband or father. In fact, increasing numbers of them were young women living alone or older women who had been widowed, divorced, or abandoned—often with small children.

sweated *Describes a type of work, mostly performed by women who worked in their homes producing items for subcontractors, usually in the clothing industry.*

Members of the new middle class entertained notions of gentility based on the distinction between manual and nonmanual work. Lowly clerks and wealthy merchants prided themselves on the fact that they worked with their heads and not their hands. They fancied that their entrepreneurial and managerial skills were making the market revolution happen, while manual workers simply performed tasks conceived by the middle class. The old distinction between proprietorship and dependence, which had placed master craftsmen and independent tradesmen, along with farm-owning yeomen, among the respectable "middling sort," disappeared. The men and women of an emerging working class struggled to create dignity and a sense of public worth in a society that hid them from view and defined them as "hands."

Conclusion

In the first half of the 19th century northern society became based in buying and selling. The Northeast sloughed off its old colonial status and moved from the periphery to the industrial and financial core of the world market economy. Other countries have made that transition by deemphasizing agriculture, drawing their populations into cities, and relying on the export of manufactured goods as their principal source of income. The American North, on the other hand, built factories and commercial farms at the same time and as parts of the same process. The market for American manufactures was in the American countryside. (Industrial exports from the United States were insignificant until the end of the 19th century.) The principal market for American food was in American towns and cities, and even on farms whose proprietors were too busy with staple crops to grow the old array of food. The result was a massive commercialization of the northwestern, mid-Atlantic, and New England states, and the beginnings of their integration into a unified northern capitalist democracy.

CHAPTER REVIEW

Review Questions

1. What was the nature of the northern agricultural economy and of agricultural society in the years 1790–1820?
2. How did improvements in transportation actually channel commerce within and between sections?
3. How did northern farm families experience the transition into commercial agriculture between 1815 and 1850?
4. What was the relationship between urban-industrial growth and the commercialization of the northern countryside?

Critical Thinking Questions

1. What were the sources of American economic growth in the years 1790 to 1820? What were the constraints upon growth, and how did those constraints help shape economic development in these years?
2. To what extent and in what ways was the transition to a market economy helped or hindered by the national and state governments?

Identifications

Review your understanding of the following key terms, people, and events for this chapter.

competence, p. 184
changing system, p. 186
tenancy, p. 187

journeyman, p. 188
girdled trees, p. 189

Robert Fulton, p. 191
Erie Canal, p. 191

Francis Cabot Lowell, p. 200
sweated, p. 202

DISCOVERY

What changes did the transportation and market revolutions bring to the United States? How did they also reinforce the existing social fabric and regional differences?

In thinking about this question, begin by breaking it down into the components shown below. A discussion of the significance of each component should appear in your answer.

Transportation and Regional Development

Based on your reading of this chapter, how did the Erie Canal and other canals transform New York and the rest of the United States? Look at the maps on pages 192 and 193. What areas experienced the greatest expansion of canals and railroads during the first half of the 19th century? How do you account for the differences in the development of transportation systems in America's regions? What were the economic and demographic consequences of these differences?

Transportation and Family Life

Study the advertisement. Where was American Cream Soap manufactured? Identify three or more ways American Soap Company says or suggests that its soap will improve the life of a "typical" middle-class family. Is this company aiming to sell its soap locally or nationally? Is there a relationship between the explosion of canals and railroads and the price and availability to this household of American Cream Soap? What differences do you see in the print advertising of the 1850s and today? What similarities do you see?

A SOAP ADVERTISEMENT FROM THE 1850s

 CourseMate

Visit the CourseMate website at www.cengagebrain.com for additional study tools and review materials for this chapter.

THE OLD SOUTH, 1790–1850

The southern states experienced a parallel market revolution, but it was transacted on southern terms. From the 1790s onward, international markets and technological innovation encouraged planters to grow cotton. Cotton became the great southern cash crop, and the plantation spread across an expanding Deep South. The planters sent mountains of cotton (along with tobacco from the Upper South, rice from the Georgia–Carolina coast, and sugar from Louisiana) to Great Britain. They made a lot of money, and they bought a lot of nice things.

Other southerners, however, were not as fortunate. Enslaved workers experienced longer hours and tighter discipline than in the past. They lost their families and friends to a soulless interstate slave trade, and they watched their masters' commitment to slavery harden into an unmovable political axiom. In addition, most white farmers moved to the edges of the commercial economy. They continued in the old-style mixed agriculture and traded relatively little beyond their neighborhoods. In the North, country people became the great consumer market that drove regional economic development. In the South, slaves and most whites bought little, and what they bought was made outside of the region. The South's reliance on cotton strengthened the region's neocolonial dependence on Great Britain and the northeastern United States. It also gave the South a labor system, a leadership class, and an economic and political culture that set the region apart from the burgeoning capitalist democracy of the North.

1792	1793	1796	1799	1800	1803	1808	1812	1817	1819	1822	1831

■ 1792
Kentucky enters the union as the 15th state

■ 1793
Eli Whitney invents the cotton gin

■ 1796
Tennessee enters the union as the 16th state

■ 1799
Successful slave revolution in Haiti

■ 1800
Gabriel's Rebellion in Virginia

■ 1808
International slave trade ends

■ 1817
Mississippi enters the union

1819 ■
Alabama enters the union

1822 ■
Denmark Vesey's slave conspiracy in South Carolina

1831 ■
Nat Turner's rebellion in Virginia

© Cengage Learning

OLD FARMS: THE SOUTHEAST

FOCUS QUESTION

What were the principal differences between the slave economies of the Chesapeake and the South Carolina–Georgia lowcountry?

In 1790, the planters of Virginia and South Carolina were among the richest men in the new republic. But international markets for their tobacco and rice were declining, and they faced uncertain futures.

The Chesapeake, 1790–1820

In the Chesapeake, the tobacco market had been falling since before the Revolution, and it continued to decline after 1790. Tobacco also depleted the soil, and by the late 18th century, tidewater farms and plantations were giving out. As lands west of the Appalachians opened to settlement, white tenants, laborers, and small farmers left the Chesapeake in droves. Many of them moved to Kentucky, Tennessee, or the western reaches of Virginia. Many others found new homes in nonslave states north of the Ohio River.

With tobacco profits falling, many Chesapeake planters switched to wheat, corn, and livestock. This transition left the Chesapeake with a huge investment in slaves who were less and less necessary, since grazing animals and raising wheat required less labor than tobacco. Planters with large numbers of slaves had to think up new uses for them. Some divided their land into small plots and rented both the plots and their slaves to white tenant farmers. Others hired out their slaves as artisans and urban laborers.

Race, Gender, and Chesapeake Labor

The increasing diversification of the Chesapeake economy assigned new chores to slave women and men. Wheat cultivation, for example, meant a switch from the hoes used for tobacco to the plow and grain cradle, both of which called for the upper-body strength of adult men. The grain economy also required carts, wagons, mills, and good roads and created a need for greater numbers of slave artisans, nearly all of whom were men. Many of these artisans were hired out to urban employers. In the new economy of the Chesapeake, male slaves did the plowing, mowing, sowing, ditching, and carting and performed most of the tasks requiring artisanal skills.

Slave women were left with the lesser tasks. Some were assigned to such chores as cloth manufacture, sewing, candle molding, and the preparation of salt meat, but most female slaves still did farmwork—hoeing, weeding, spreading manure, cleaning stables—that was monotonous, unskilled, and closely supervised. This new division of labor was clearly evident during the wheat harvest. On George Washington's farm, for example, male slaves, often working alongside temporary white laborers, moved in a broad line as they mowed the grain. Following them came a gang of children and women on their hands and knees binding wheat into shocks.

Flirting with Emancipation

Neither new crops nor new employments, however, erased the growing fact that Chesapeake proprietors needed less slave labor than they had in the past. Nothing, it seemed, could employ the great mass of enslaved people or repay the planters' huge investment in slaves. Some Chesapeake planters, particularly in Maryland and Delaware, began to manumit their slaves. Virginia's economic and cultural commitment to the plantation was stronger, but even in the Old Dominion there was a strong manumission movement. George Washington manumitted his slaves by will. Robert Carter, reputedly the largest slaveholder in Virginia, also freed his slaves, as did many others.

But emancipation moved slowly in Virginia for several reasons. First, few Virginia planters could afford to free their slaves without compensation. Second, white Virginians feared the social consequences of black freedom. Thomas Jefferson owned 175 slaves when he penned the phrase that "all men are created equal." He lived off their labor, sold them to pay his debts, gave them as gifts, sometimes sold them as a punishment, and kept one of them, a woman named Sally Hemings, as a mistress and fathered several children by her. Through it all he insisted that slavery was wrong, but he could not imagine emancipation without the colonization of freed slaves far from Virginia. A society of free blacks and whites, Jefferson believed, would end in disaster.

The Lowcountry and the Task System

The other center of plantation slavery in 1790 was lowcountry South Carolina and Georgia, where the principal crop was rice. Thousands of slaves in this region had either run away or been carried off by the British in the Revolution, and planters knew that the African slave trade was scheduled to end in 1808. Lowcountry planters, unlike their Chesapeake counterparts, could not imagine emancipating their slaves. They rushed to import as many Africans as they could in the time remaining. Between 1783 and 1808, between 100,000 and 190,000 captive people were brought directly from Africa to the United States, nearly all of them to Charleston and Savannah. It was the busiest period in the history of the slave trade in North America.

Collection of the Maryland Historical Society, Baltimore #III.21

QUICK REVIEW

THE TASK SYSTEM

- Slaves were assigned a task rather than specific hours of labor

- Slaves worked without supervision until the task was completed

- Remainder of the day belonged to the slave

private fields *Farms of up to five acres on which slaves working under the task system were permitted to produce items for their own use and sale in a nearby market.*

Slaves made up 80 percent of the population in the plantation counties of coastal South Carolina and Georgia. Farms and slave labor forces were big, and rice cultivation demanded intensive labor, often performed by workers forced to stand knee-deep in water. The work and the hot, sticky climate encouraged deadly summer diseases and kept white owners and overseers out of the fields. Planters instead organized slaves according to the so-called task system. Each morning the owner or manager assigned a specific task to each slave. When the task was done, the rest of the day belonged to the slave. Slaves who did not finish their task were punished, and when too many slaves finished early, the owners assigned heavier tasks.

The task system encouraged slaves to work hard without supervision, and slaves turned the system to their own uses. Often several slaves would work together until all their tasks were completed, and strong young slaves often helped older and weaker slaves. Once the day's work was done, the slaves shared their hard-earned leisure out of sight of the owner.

Slaves under the task system won the right to cultivate land as **"private fields"**—farms of up to five acres on which they grew produce and raised livestock for market. There was a lively trade in slave-produced goods, and by the late 1850s slaves in the lowcountry not only produced and exchanged property but also passed it on to their children. The owners tolerated such activity because slaves on the task system worked hard, required minimal supervision, produced much of their own food, and made money for their owners.

"AN OVERSEER DOING HIS DUTY." *In 1798 the architect and engineer Benjamin Latrobe sketched a white overseer smoking a cigar and supervising slave women as they hoed newly cleared farmland near Fredericksburg, Virginia. A critic of slavery, Latrobe sarcastically entitled the sketch "An Overseer Doing His Duty."*

NEW FARMS: THE RISE OF THE DEEP SOUTH

While the old centers of slavery and southern power stagnated or declined, planters discovered a new and promising cash crop. British textile factories had been buying raw **cotton** since the mid-18th century. But long-staple cotton was a delicate plant that thrived only on the Sea Islands off Georgia and South Carolina. The short-staple variety was hardier, but its sticky seeds had to be removed by hand before the cotton could be milled—an expenditure of slave labor that took the profit out of cotton.

In 1793, **Eli Whitney**, a Connecticut Yankee who had come south to work as a tutor, made a model of a cotton "gin" (a southern contraction of "engine") that combed the seeds from the fiber with metal pins fitted into rollers. A slave working with Whitney's machine could clean 50 pounds of short-staple cotton in a day. At a stroke, cotton became the great southern cash crop. Slavery and plantation agriculture had a new lease on life.

The Rise of the Cotton Belt

With the end of war in 1815, the plantation rolled west into a Cotton Belt that stretched beyond the Mississippi River. By 1834, the new states of Alabama, Mississippi, and Louisiana grew more than half of a vastly increased U.S. cotton crop. In 1810, the South produced 178,000 bales of ginned cotton, more than 59 times the 3,000 bales it had produced in 1790. With the opening of southwestern cotton lands, production jumped to 334,000 bales in 1820 and to 1,350,000 bales in 1840. In these years, cotton made up from one-half to two-thirds of the value of all U.S. exports. The South produced three-fourths of the world supply of cotton—a commodity that, more than any other, was the raw material of industrialization in Britain and Europe and, increasingly, in the northeastern United States (see Map 9.1).

cotton *Semitropical plant that produces white, fluffy fibers that can be made into textiles.*

Eli Whitney *The Connecticut-born tutor who invented the cotton gin.*

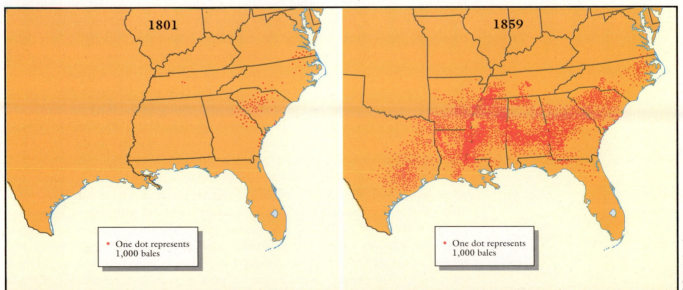

Map 9.1 Cotton Production, 1801 and 1859. *Short-staple cotton thrived wherever there was fertile soil, heat and humidity, low altitude, and a long growing season. As a result, a great belt of cotton and slavery took shape in the Lower South, from the midlands of South Carolina through East Texas.*

© Cengage Learning

The Interstate Slave Trade

With the international slave trade abolished in 1808, the source of slaves for the Southwest was the old seaboard states. During the 1790s, the Chesapeake sent 40,000 to 50,000 slaves south and west. The number rose to 120,000 in the 1810s. The slave families and slave communities of the Chesapeake lost 1 in 12 of their members in the 1790s, 1 in 10 between 1800 and 1810, and 1 in 5 between 1810 and 1820. In the 1820s, South Carolina and Kentucky joined the slave-exporting states. The trade in slaves reordered the human geography of the South. In 1790, planters in Virginia and Maryland had held 56 percent of all American slaves. By 1860, they owned only 15 percent. (See Map 9.2.)

Some enslaved migrants—estimates run as high as 30 percent—left their old neighborhoods in the company of masters (or masters' sons) and familiar fellow slaves. These slaves made new lives in the Southwest surrounded by some of the people they had known at home. But most were sold and resold in an interstate slave market that by 1820 had become an organized business with sophisticated financing, established prices, a well-traveled shipping route between Norfolk and New Orleans, and systems of slave pens and safe houses. With the exception of the plantation itself, the domestic slave trade was the biggest and most modern business in the South. The centrality of that trade advertised the nature of southern economic development: While northerners exchanged wheat, furniture, books, and shoes, Southerners exchanged slaves.

Cotton and Slave Labor

Southwestern plantations were among the most intensely commercialized farms in the world. Many of them grew nothing but cotton, while others grew supplementary cash crops and produced their own food. But nearly all of the plantation owners organized their labor in ways that maximized production and reinforced their own dominance.

Slaves from the Chesapeake and the rice coast experienced cotton cultivation as a difficult step down. Cotton required a lot of attention, but it did not demand much skill. Early in the spring the land was cleared and plowed, and gangs of slaves walked the furrows dropping seeds. During the growing season slaves constantly thinned the plants and cleared the fields of weeds, "chopping" the fields with hoes in the hot, humid Deep South summer. In a harvest season that could last long past Christmas, pickers swept through the fields selecting only the ripe bolls, then repeated the task over and over until the full crop was harvested. Slaves in the diversifying Chesapeake had made barrels and crates, boats, wagons, barns, and storage sheds; slaves on the rice coast farther south had built dikes and levees and had mastered the science of controlling large amounts of water. In the Cotton Belt they gave up those skills and went to work with axes, hoes, and their hands.

The work was relentless. Planters in the east had found it economical to allow slaves to work at varied tasks, at irregular times, or under the task system. They gave slaves only part of their food (often cornmeal and nothing else), then provided time and land with which slaves grew their own vegetables, chickens, and pigs. Planters on the cotton frontier did away with all that. Only a few retained the task system; most worked their slaves in gangs from dawn to dusk six days a week. Cotton land was too valuable to permit slave gardens. It made more sense to keep the slaves constantly at cotton cultivation and to supply them with all of their food. It was also a way of reducing the slaves' customary privileges within slavery, and of enforcing the master's role as the giver and taker of all things.

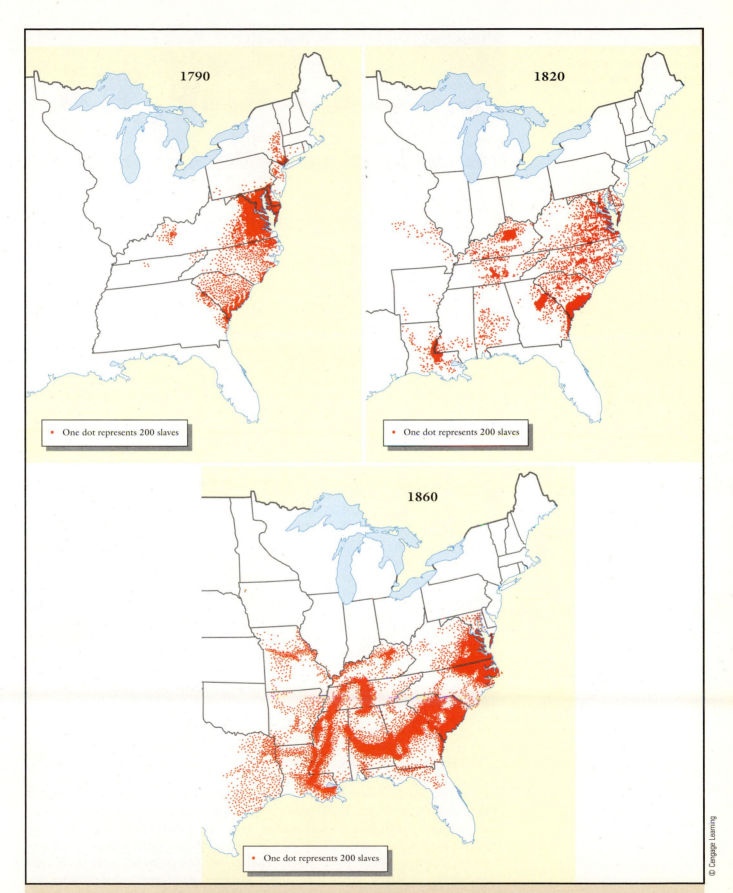

Map 9.2 **Distribution of Slave Population, 1790, 1820, and 1860.** *In 1790, slaves were concentrated in the Chesapeake and in the South Carolina and Georgia lowcountry. Over the next 70 years, Chesapeake planters put thousands of slaves into the interstate trade, which sold them into a Black Belt that stretched from the interior of the Carolinas to East Texas.*

"HAULING THE WHOLE WEEK'S PICKING." *William Henry Brown made this collage of a slave harvest crew near Vicksburg, Mississippi, in 1842. The rigors of the harvest put everyone, including small children, into the fields.*

The Historic New Orleans Collection, Accension #1975.931 & 2

The masters set harsher working conditions and longer hours than slaves had known in their old homes. Slaves could not hope to reinstitute the task system, the family gardens and little farms, the varied tasks, or the uneven hours of labor that they had known on the coast. Yet despite masters' lack of encouragement, gardens—some of them large and profitable—quickly appeared in the new slave quarters, and enslaved workers found that they could hold masters to standards of time and work. Masters who demanded longer than customary hours or labor on Sunday found the work going slower.

On the whole, the exploitation of slave labor after 1820 became both more rigorous and more humane. Planters imposed a new and more total control over their slaves, but they clothed it within a larger attempt to make slavery paternalistic and to portray themselves as gentlemen and not heartless slave drivers. Food and clothing seem to have improved, and individual cabins for slave families became standard. State laws often forbade the more brutal forms of discipline, and they uniformly demanded that slaves be given Sunday off.

Material standards seem to have risen. One rough indicator is physical height. On the eve of the Civil War, southern slaves averaged about an inch shorter than northern whites, but they were fully three inches taller than newly imported Africans, two inches taller than slaves on the Caribbean island of Trinidad, and an inch taller than British Marines. Slaves suffered greater infant mortality than whites, but those who survived infancy lived out "normal" life spans. Between 1790 and 1830 the slave population of the United States increased threefold. Unlike any other slave population in the Western Hemisphere, births outnumbered deaths among North American slaves.

But humane treatment came at a high price. At the same time that they granted slaves protection from the worst kinds of brutality, cotton-belt states enacted slave codes that defined slaves as persons without any of the rights enjoyed by the white men who owned the plantations, controlled the slaves, and wrote the laws.

Mastery as a Way of Life

Plantation masters were the acknowledged economic, social, cultural, and political elite of the South. Their authority rested on economic power and on their connections—often family relationships—with each other. But they dressed their power in gentility and an aura of mastery, a visible "right to rule" that few others, North or South, could match. That power and authority were tied to the ownership of slaves. When assessing a planter's standing, contemporaries seldom considered his acreage or his money. Instead, they counted slaves. In the most common calculation, the ownership of 20 slaves separated planters from farmers.

OLIVIER PLANTATION IN 1861. *The artist Marie Adrien Persac portrayed this southern Louisiana plantation as a site of white gentility, not of slavery and sugar production. The smoking chimneys of the processing plant at right tell us that work is going on. But the fields, the slave quarters, and the slaves themselves are hidden from view. We see only well-dressed whites strolling the grounds, transforming the plantation from a factory farm into a civilized and tranquil private park.*

The Olivier Plantation, 1861 (w/c on paper) by Persac, Adrien (1823-73) © Louisiana State Museum, USA/ The Bridgeman Art Library

It was a good enough measure, for the planter class made itself out of slaves. Slave labor bought the carpets, chandeliers, fine clothes, English chivalric novels, and racehorses with which planters displayed their social mastery. Just as important, slaves enabled planters and their ladies to distinguish themselves as gentlefolk who did not work. Southern farmers without slaves tended to sire very large families and to keep their children and wives in the fields. Southerners who owned slaves had fewer children, sent them to school, and moved their wives indoors. The skin of farmwomen was weathered, cracked, and darkened by the sun; plantation mistresses were less exhausted, and their skin was smoother and literally whiter.

The opposite of gentility was the South Carolina farmer who, according to a neighbor, "used to work [his daughters] in the fields like Negroes." According to northern visitors, this association of labor with slavery encouraged laziness among southern whites and robbed work of the dignity it enjoyed in other parts of the country. Most southern white farmers would have disagreed, but the association of black labor, white leisure, and white gentility was central to the plantation regime. The South would not have been the South without it.

Southern Families

Most southern whites regarded themselves less as individuals than as representatives of families. Southern boys often received the family names of heroes as their first names: Jefferson Davis, for example, or Thomas Jefferson (later, "Stonewall") Jackson. More often, however, they took the name of a related family—Peyton Randolph, Preston Brooks, Langdon Cheves. Children learned early that their first duty was to their family's reputation; in the white South, reputation and the defense of family honor were everything. A boy with a reputation for cowardice, for ineptness at riding or fighting, or for failure to

VISUAL LINK TO THE PAST

A Southern View of Slavery

Here is a southern representation of plantation society. The white family is genteel: a well-dressed, relaxed, and subdued father and mother, two well-dressed and well-behaved children, and a well-bred dog. The master/father assures us that he has inherited his slaves (he does not buy or sell them) and that he is devoting his fortune to their welfare and happiness. For their part, the slaves are contented. They live in whitewashed houses, they are nicely dressed, they play and dance, and healthy, contented old folks look on with pleasure.

Q How is slavery portrayed in this picture? What is missing? What are the postures and facial expressions of whites and blacks, and what do these say about the racial beliefs held by the artist and his audience?

Library of Congress, Prints and Photographs Division

control his emotions or hold his liquor was an embarrassment to his family. Among southern white men, wealth generally counted for less than did maintaining one's personal and family honor and thus winning membership in the democracy of honorable males.

The code of honor, although it forged ties of equality and respect among white men, made rigid distinctions between men and women and whites and blacks. Women and girls who misbehaved—with transgressions ranging from simple gossip to poor housekeeping to adultery—damaged not only their own reputation but also the honor of the fathers or husbands who could not control them. Such a charge could mean social death in a rural community made up of watchful neighbors.

When northerners attacked slavery because it denied the freedom of the individual, one southerner responded: "Do you say that the slave is held to involuntary service? So is the wife, [whose] relation to her husband, in the great majority of cases, is made for her and not by her." Few white southerners would have questioned the good sense of that response. Southern life was not about freedom, individual fulfillment, or social progress; it was about honoring the obligations to which one was born.

THE SOUTHERN YEOMANRY

Cotton rewarded **economies of scale:** planters with big farms and many slaves operated more efficiently and more profitably than farmers with fewer resources. The wealthier planter families bought up good cotton land with ready access to markets. They also bought up the majority of slaves. Only 30 percent to 35 percent of southern white families owned at least one slave in 1830, and that percentage dropped as time passed. Among the minority of southerners who were slave owners, half owned fewer than five, and less than 5 percent owned 20 or more.

FOCUS QUESTION

What factors encouraged southern yeoman farmers to enter regional, national, and international markets? What factors inhibited them?

Yeomen and Planters

Among southern whites, cotton produced not only an unequal distribution of wealth but a dual economy: plantations at the commercial center and a yeomanry on the fringes.

There were, of course, small farmers in the plantation counties. They tended to be commercial farmers, growing a few bales of cotton with family labor and perhaps a slave or two. Many of them were poor relatives of prosperous plantation owners. They voted the great planters into office, used their cotton gins, and tapped into their marketing networks. Some of them worked as overseers for their wealthy neighbors, sold them food, and served on local slave patrols. Economic disparities between planters and farmers in the plantation belt continued to widen, but the farmers remained tied to the cotton economy.

Most yeomen, however, lived away from the plantations in neighborhoods with few slaves and limited commercial activities. Most lived in the upcountry and the eastern slopes of the Appalachians from the Chesapeake through Georgia, the western slopes of the mountains in Kentucky and Tennessee, the pine-covered hill country of northern Mississippi and Alabama, and in swampy, hilly, heavily wooded lands throughout the southern states. All of these areas were unsuitable for plantation crops. Here the farmers built a yeoman society that shared many of the characteristics of the 18th-century countryside.

Many southern farmers stayed outside the market almost entirely. Farmers in large parts of the upcountry South preferred raising livestock to growing cotton or tobacco. They planted cornfields and let their pigs run loose in the woods and on unfenced private land. In late summer and fall, they rounded up the animals and sold them to drovers who herded them cross-country and sold them to flatland merchants and planters. This way of life sustained some of the most fiercely independent neighborhoods in the country.

A larger group of southern yeomen practiced mixed farming for household subsistence and neighborhood exchange, with the surplus sent to market. They put most of their land into subsistence crops and livestock, cultivating only a few acres of cotton. They grew more cotton as transportation made markets more accessible, but few southern yeomen allowed themselves to become wholly dependent on the market. With the income from a few bales of cotton, they could pay their debts and taxes and buy coffee, tea, sugar, tobacco, cloth, and shoes. But they entered and left the market at will, for their own purposes. The market served the interests of southern yeomen. It seldom dominated them.

economy of scale *Term used in both industry and agriculture to describe the economic advantages of concentrating capital, units of production, and output.*

Yeoman Neighborhoods

Since few farms were self-sufficient, yeomen farmers routinely traded labor and goods with each other. In the plantation counties, such cooperation tended to reinforce the power of planters, who put some of their resources at the disposal of their poorer neighbors. In the upcountry, cooperation reinforced neighborliness. Debts were generally paid in kind or in labor, and creditors often allowed their neighbors' debts to go unpaid for years.

Among southern neighborly restraints on entrepreneurialism, none was more distinctive than the region's attitude toward fences. In the North, well-maintained fences were a sign of ambitious, hardworking farmers. The poor fences of the South, on the other hand, were interpreted by northerners as a sign of laziness. Actually, the scarcity of fences in most southern neighborhoods was the result of local custom and state law. In country neighborhoods where families fished and hunted for food and where livestock roamed freely, the local economy required neighborhood use of privately owned land.

Southern farmers marketed their cotton and food surpluses at country stores, but they bought very little. A relatively prosperous backwoods farmer in South Carolina recalled that "I never spent more than ten dollars a year, which was for salt, nails and the like. Nothing to wear, eat or drink was purchased, as my farm provided all." Families such as these continued to live without carpets or curtains, to eat homegrown food from wooden or pewter plates, and to wear everyday cloth spun and woven by the women of the family, although many who could afford it wore clothing fashioned from machine-made cloth on Sunday. And yeomen seldom bought items or settled transactions in cash. While the northern countryside and the lowland plantation districts functioned in businesslike ways, the old barter economy—and the forms of family independence and neighborly cooperation on which it rested—persisted in the southern upcountry.

THE PRIVATE LIVES OF SLAVES

FOCUS QUESTION

Describe the cultural life that slaves made for themselves within the limits of slavery.

By 1790, slaves in the Chesapeake and along the South Carolina–Georgia rice coast had made a distinctively African American way of life within the boundaries of slavery. In the first half of the 19th century, hundreds of thousands of these people were torn from their communities and sold into the cotton states. It began a period of cultural destruction and reconstruction equaled only by the process of enslavement itself.

Slave Families

In law, in the census, and in the minds of planters, slaves were members of a plantation household over which the owner exercised absolute authority as owner, paternal protector, and lawgiver. Yet both slaveholders and slaves knew that slaves could not be treated like farm animals or little children. Wise masters learned that the success of a plantation depended less on terror and draconian discipline (though whippings—and worse—were common) than on the accommodations by which slaves traded labor and obedience for privileges and some measure of autonomy within the bounds of slavery. Hard-won privileges—holidays, garden plots,

VISUAL LINK TO THE PAST

A Slave Mother and the Slave Trade

In 1852, a slave mother from Virginia was caught up in the domestic slave trade. She wrote this to her husband:

Dear Husband I write you a letter to let you know of my distress my master has sold Albert to a trader on Monday court day and myself and other child is for sale also and I want you to let [me] hear from you very soon before next cort if you can I don't know when I don't want you to wait till Christmas I want you to tell Dr. Hamilton your master if either will buy me then can attend to it know and then I can go afterwards I don't want a trader to get me they asked me if I had got any person to buy me and I told them no they told me to the court house too they never put me up A man buy the name of brady bought albert and is gone I don't know whare they say he lives in Scottsville my things is in several places some is in stanton and if I would be sold I don't know what will become of them I don't expect to meet with the luck to get that way till I am quite heart sick nothing more I am and ever will be your kind wife Marie Perkins.

Q Slaves uniformly feared the unpredictability and destructiveness of the domestic slave trade. Within this simple letter, how many social and personal injuries can you count?

friendships, hunting and fishing rights—provided some of the ground on which slaves made their own lives.

The most precious privilege was the right to live in families. In the Chesapeake, most slaves lived in units consisting of a mother, a father, and their small children. At Thomas Jefferson's Monticello, most slave marriages were for life, and small children almost always lived with both parents. The most common exceptions were fathers who had married away from their own plantations and who visited **"broad" wives** and children during their off hours. Owners encouraged stable marriages because they made farms more peaceful and productive and because they flattered the owners' own religious and paternalistic sensibilities. For their part, slaves demanded families as part of the price of their labor.

Yet slave families had always been vulnerable. Many slaveholders coerced sex from female slaves. Some kept slaves as mistresses. They tended, however, to keep these liaisons within bounds. Slave sales threatened families, but most sales before 1800 or so took place within neighborhoods, damaging slave families without destroying them. The most serious threat was the death or bankruptcy of the slaveholder. Yet even these events usually kept slaves in the same extended neighborhood.

The Slave Trade and the Slave Family

That changed with the growth of the Cotton Belt and the interstate slave trade. Masters in the seaboard states claimed (often truthfully) that they tried to keep slave families together, and that they sold slaves to traders only out of dire necessity or only as a means of getting rid of troublesome individuals. The latter category could be used as a threat. Thomas Jefferson, reputedly the kindest of masters, punished a troublesome slave by selling him in 1803, declaring that he would be sent into "so distant an exile . . . as to cut him off completely from ever being heard of [again]."

"broad" wives *Wives of slave men who lived on other plantations and were visited by their husbands during off hours.*

Chesapeake planters and slaves knew, however, that the slave trade was more than a means of settling debts or punishing individuals. It had become an important source of income. Slaves in the exporting states continued to live in families that produced and nurtured their own children, but the children could expect to be sold into long-distance markets when they came of age. The systematic selling of teenaged and young adult slaves, who commanded the highest prices, became a standard way in which Chesapeake gentlemen maintained their status. Professional slave traders made no effort to hide their willingness to break slave families. Neither did the southwestern planters who bought slaves from the older states.

Separated from their kinfolk and communities, cotton-belt slaves began the old process of negotiation with their masters, and they reconstructed families. Cotton planters preferred young men for the labor of clearing the land, but they soon began importing nearly equal numbers of women and encouraging marriage. Families made for greater peace and quiet on the plantations, and they were a good long-term investment in the production of new slaves. Regardless of planter motivations, the slaves grasped the opportunity to form families. As early as the 1820s, 51 percent of rural Louisiana slaves lived in families composed of two parents and their children. That figure was smaller than it had been on the old farms, but in view of what the slaves had been through, it was surprisingly large.

Slaveholders who encouraged slave marriages knew that marriage implied a form of self-ownership in conflict with the slaves' status as property. Some conducted ceremonies in which couples "married" by jumping over a broomstick. Others had the preacher omit the phrases "let no man put asunder" and "till death do you part" from the ceremony. Slaves knew that such ceremonies had no legal force.

Slaves built their sense of family and kinship around such uncertainties. Because separation from parents was common, children spread their affection among adult relatives, treating grandparents, aunts, and uncles almost as though they were parents. In fact, slaves often referred to all their adult relatives as "parents." They also called nonrelatives "brother," "sister," "aunt," and "uncle," extending a sense of kinship to the slave community at large. Slaves chose as surnames for themselves the names of former owners, anglicized versions of African names, or names that

Five Generations of a Slave Family on a South Carolina Sea Island Plantation, 1862. *Complex family ties such as those of the family shown here were among the most hard-won and vulnerable cultural accomplishments of enslaved blacks.*

simply sounded good. They rarely chose the name of their current owner. Families tended to use the same given names over and over, naming boys after their father or grandfather, perhaps to preserve the memory of fathers who might be taken away. They seldom named girls after their mother, however. Unlike southern whites, slaves never married a first cousin. The origins and functions of some of these customs are unknown. We know only that slaves practiced them consistently, often without the knowledge of the slaveholders.

The Beginnings of African American Christianity in the Chesapeake

Until the mid-18th century, neither enslaved Africans nor their masters showed much interest in Christianizing slaves. That changed with the rise of evangelical Christianity in the South (see Chapter 10). In the slave communities of the Upper South, as well as the burgeoning free and semifree urban black populations in the towns, the evangelical revivals of the late 18th and early 19th centuries appealed to African Americans, who sensed that the bonds of slavery were loosening.

Between the Revolution and 1820, Chesapeake slaves embraced Christianity and began to turn it into a religion of their own. Slaves attended camp meetings, listened to **itinerant preachers**, and joined the Baptist and Methodist congregations of the southern revival. The revivalists, in turn, welcomed slaves and free blacks to their meetings and sometimes recruited them as preachers. Evangelical preaching, singing, and spiritual exercises were much more attractive than the cold, high-toned lectures of the Anglicans. So were the humility and suffering of the evangelical whites, many of whom were poor men and outsiders. Finally, the slaves gloried in the evangelicals' assault on the slaveholders' culture and in the antislavery sentiments of many white evangelicals. The result was a huge increase in the number of African American Christians.

These integrated congregations did not last. There were exceptions, but most congregations were in fact internally segregated, with blacks sitting in the back of the church, and with only whites serving in positions of authority. Blacks organized independent churches in Baltimore, Wilmington, Richmond, Norfolk, and the scattered villages that had risen to serve the Chesapeake's new mixed economy. By 1820, roughly 700 independent black churches operated in the United States. There had been none at all 30 years earlier. And on the plantations, slaves met informally—sometimes with the masters' permission, sometimes without it— to preach and pray.

Slave Theology

Slaves understood the message of Christianity in their own ways. The biblical notion that slavery could be punishment for sin and the white southern notion that God intended blacks to be slaves never took root among enslaved Christians. As one maid boldly told her mistress, "God never made us to be slaves for white people."

Another way in which slave religion differed from what was preached to them by whites was in the practice of conjuring, folk magic, root medicine, and other occult knowledge, most of it passed down from West Africa. Such practices provided help in areas in which Christianity was useless. They could reputedly cure illnesses, make people fall in love, ensure a good day's fishing, or bring harm to one's enemies. Sometimes African magic was in competition with plantation Christianity. Just as often, however, slaves combined the two. For instance, slaves

itinerant preachers *Ministers who lacked their own parishes and who traveled from place to place.*

sometimes determined the guilt or innocence of a person accused of stealing by hanging a Bible by a thread, then watching the way it turned. The form was West African; the Bible was not. The slave root doctor George White boasted that he could "cure most anything," but added that "you got to talk wid God an' ask him to help out."

While Christianity could not cure sick babies or identify thieves, it gave slaves something more important: a sense of themselves as a historical people with a role to play in God's cosmic drama. In slave Christianity, Moses the liberator (and not the slave-holders' Abraham) stood beside Jesus. The slaves' appropriation of the book of Exodus denied the smug assumption of the whites that they were God's chosen people who had escaped the bondage of despotic Europe to enter the promised land of America. To the slaves, America was Egypt, they were the chosen people, and the slaveholders were Pharaoh. The slaves' religious songs, which became known as **spirituals,** told of God's people, their travails, and their ultimate deliverance. In songs and sermons, the figures of Jesus and Moses were often blurred, and it was not always clear whether deliverance would take place in this world or the next. But deliverance always meant an end to slavery, often with a reversal of relations between slaves and masters.

Religion and Revolt

In comparison with slaves in Cuba, Jamaica, Brazil, and other New World planta-tion societies, North American slaves seldom went into organized, armed revolt. American plantations were relatively small and dispersed, and the southern white population was large, vigilant, and very well armed. Thousands of slaves demon-strated their hatred of the system by running away. Others fought slave owners or overseers, sabotaged equipment and animals, and stole from planters. But most knew that open revolt was suicide.

Christianity convinced slaves that history was headed toward an apocalypse that would result in divine justice and their own deliverance. But slave preachers almost never told their congregations to become actively engaged in God's divine plan, for they knew that violent resistance was hopeless. Slave Christians believed that God hated slavery and would end it, but that their role was to have faith in God, to take care of one another, to preserve their identity as a people, and to await deliverance. Only occasionally did slaves take retribution and deliverance into their own hands.

Gabriel's Rebellion

Masters who talked of liberty and natural rights sometimes worried that slaves might imagine that such language could apply to themselves. The Age of Demo-cratic Revolution took a huge step in that direction with the French Revolution in 1789. Among the first repercussions outside of France was a revolution on the Caribbean island of Saint-Domingue. That island's half-million slaves fought out a complicated political and military revolt that eventually led to the creation of the independent black republic of Haiti. Slave societies throughout the hemisphere heard tales of terror from refugee French planters and stories of hope from the slaves they brought with them.

Slaves from the 1790s onward whispered of natural rights and imagined themselves as part of the Democratic Revolution. This covert republic of the slaves sometimes came into the open. In Richmond in 1800, a slave blacksmith named Gabriel hatched a conspiracy to overthrow Virginia's slave regime. Gabriel had been hired out to Richmond employers for most of his adult life; he was shaped

spirituals *Term later devised to describe the religious songs of slaves.*

less by plantation slavery than by the democratic, loosely interracial underworld of urban artisans. Working with his brother and other hired-out slave artisans, **Gabriel's rebellion** was planned with military precision. They recruited soldiers among slave artisans, adding plantation slaves only at the last moment. Gabriel planned to march an army of 1,000 men on Richmond in three columns. The outside columns would set diversionary fires in the warehouse district and prevent the militia from entering the town. The center would seize Capitol Square, including the treasury, the arsenal, and Governor James Monroe.

Although his army would be made up of slaves, and although his victory would end slavery in Virginia, Gabriel hoped to make a republican revolution, not a slave revolt. His chosen enemies were the Richmond "merchants" who had controlled his labor. Later, a coconspirator divulged the plan: The rebels would hold Governor Monroe hostage and split the state treasury among themselves, and "if the white people agreed to their freedom they would then hoist a white flag, and [Gabriel] would dine and drink with the merchants of the city…" Gabriel expected what he called "the poor white people" and "the most redoubtable republicans" to join him. He would kill anyone who opposed him, but he would spare Quakers, Methodists, and Frenchmen, for they were "friendly to liberty." Unlike earlier slave insurgents, Gabriel did not plot violent retribution or a return to or reconstruction of West Africa. He was an American revolutionary, and he dreamed of a truly democratic republic for Virginia. His army would march into Richmond under the banner "Death or Liberty."

Gabriel recruited at least 150 soldiers who agreed to gather near Richmond on August 30, 1800. The leaders expected to be joined by 500 to 600 more rebels as they marched upon the town. But on the appointed day it rained heavily, washing out bridges and making roads impassible. Rebels could not reach the meeting point, and amid white terror and black betrayals, Gabriel and his henchmen were hunted down, tried, and sentenced to death. In all, the state hanged 27 supposed conspirators, while others were sold and transported out of Virginia. A white Virginian marveled that the rebels on the gallows displayed a "sense of their [natural] rights, [and] a contempt of danger."

Denmark Vesey

A second major slave conspiracy may not have been a conspiracy at all. In 1822, **Denmark Vesey**, a free black of Charleston, South Carolina (he had won a lottery and bought himself) stood trial for plotting rebellion. Vesey was a leading member of an African Methodist congregation that had seceded from the white Methodists and had been independent from 1817 to 1821. Vesey and some of the other members talked about their delivery out of Egypt. According to testimony coerced from slaves who wanted to avoid prosecution themselves, Vesey and his coconspirators planned the destruction of Charleston. A few dozen Charleston blacks would take the state armory, then arm rural slaves who would rise up to help them. They would kill the whites and commandeer ships in the harbor and make their getaway to Haiti.

We cannot know how much of that was true. But Charleston's white authorities pulled the story out of terrified blacks, believed it, and hanged Vesey and 35 other accused conspirators—22 of them in one day. For many years afterwards, frightened whites "knew" that most of the conspirators (estimates ranged from 600 to 9,000) remained at large and living among them.

Nat Turner

The revolt in Southampton County, Virginia, in August 1831 was real: Some 60 slaves shot and hacked to death 55 white men, women, and children. Their leader was **Nat Turner,** a Baptist lay preacher. Turner was, he told his captors, a Christian prophet and

Gabriel's rebellion *Carefully planned but unsuccessful rebellion of slaves in Richmond and the surrounding area in 1800.*

Denmark Vesey *Leader of a slave conspiracy in and around Charleston, South Carolina, in 1822.*

Nat Turner *Baptist lay preacher whose religious visions encouraged him to lead a slave revolt in southern Virginia in 1831 in which 55 whites were killed—more than in any other American slave revolt.*

NAT TURNER. *This contemporary woodcut depicts scenes from Nat Turner's rebellion. In this bloodiest of all North American slave revolts, 55 whites, most of them women and children, were shot and hacked to death.*

an instrument of God's wrath. As a child, he had prayed and fasted often, and the spirit—the same spirit who had spoken to the prophets of the Bible—had spoken to him. When he was a young man, he had run away to escape a cruel overseer, but God said he had not chosen him merely to have him run away, and Nat had returned. Turner knew that his master was God, not a slave owner.

Around 1830, Turner received visions of the final battle in Revelation, recast as a war between white and black spirits. Convinced by a solar eclipse in February 1831 that the time had come, Turner told other slaves about his visions, recruited his force, and launched a bloody and hopeless revolt that ended in mass murder, failure, and the execution of Turner and his followers.

The Gabriel, Vesey, and Turner revolts, along with scores of more limited conspiracies, deeply troubled southern whites. Slaveholders were committed to a paternalism that was increasingly tied to the South's attempt to make slavery both domestic and Christian. For their part, slaves recognized that they could receive decent treatment and pockets of autonomy in return for outward docility. Gabriel, Vesey, and Turner opened wide cracks in that mutual charade. A plantation mistress who survived Turner's revolt by hiding in a closet listened to the murders of her husband and children, then heard her house servants arguing over possession of her clothes. A Charleston grandee named Elias Horry, upon finding that his coachman was among the Vesey conspirators, asked him, "What were your intentions?" The formerly submissive slave replied that he had intended "to kill you, rip open your belly, and throw your guts in your face."

QUICK REVIEW

SLAVE RELIGION

- Incorporated Exodus as slave history
- Interpreted Revelation as deliverance, often by violence

A SOUTHERN MARKET REVOLUTION?

FOCUS QUESTION

What were the nature and limits of the market revolution in the South? Why?

The South experienced explosive economic growth between 1790 and 1860, but in different ways and with different results than in the North. The plantation was a profitable business, and it was big. In 1860 the cash value of the southern slave population was $3 billion. That was more than the value of investments in banking, railroads, and manufacturing combined.

Southern expansion, however, had its limits. Economic growth was concentrated on the largest farms, and prosperity and change did not reach far beyond those farms. Planters invested their profits in more slaves and more land. The result was a lack of diversification and an increasing concentration of resources in the hands of the planter class.

Most white farmers relied on the production of their households and neighbors, and they remained marginal to the market economy. They bought finished goods from the outside, but at a far lower rate than their northern counterparts. The slaves wore shoes and cheap cloth made in the Northeast and bought by their masters, and their trade in slave-made goods, while it was crucial to subsistence and a valued form of "independence" within slavery, resulted in only low-level (often furtive) entry into the market. The South continued to export its plantation staples and to pay outsiders for shipping, financial services, and finished goods. In contrast, the commercialization of northern farms created a rural demand for credit, banking facilities, farm tools, clothing, and other consumer goods and services—most of them provided by other northerners—and thus made a market revolution that included most northern families. In the South, economic growth produced more cotton and more slavery and comparatively little else.

Not that the South neglected technological innovation and agricultural improvement. Southerners developed the early cotton gin into big milling machines. They also developed a machine with a huge wooden screw powered by horses or mules to press ginned cotton into tight bales for shipping. Yet there were few such innovations, and they had to do with the processing and shipping of cotton. The truth is that cotton was a labor-intensive crop that discouraged innovation. Moreover, plantation slaves often sabotaged expensive tools and draft animals, scattered manure in haphazard ways, and passively resisted innovations that would have added to their drudgery. The cotton fields continued to be cultivated by people working with clumsy, mule-drawn plows that barely scratched the soil, by women wielding hoes, and by gangs who harvested the crop by hand.

Planters built their farms on alluvial land with access to the South's magnificent system of navigable rivers. They had little interest in expensive, state-supported internal improvements that their own neighborhoods did not need. Those whites in the upcountry who did want roads and canals seldom got their measures through planter-dominated legislatures.

Nor did the South build cities. The South used its canals and railroads mainly to move plantation staples to towns that transshipped them out of the region. Southern cities were located on the periphery of the region and served as transportation depots for plantation crops. Southern businessmen turned to New York City for credit, insurance, and coastal and export shipping. And it was from New York that they ordered finished goods for the southern market.

Conclusion

On the eve of the Civil War, James H. Hammond, a slaveholding senator from South Carolina, asked, "What would happen if no cotton was furnished for three years…. England would topple headlong and carry the whole civilized world with her save the south. No, you dare not make war on cotton. No power on earth dares to make war on cotton. Cotton is king."

Hammond and other planter-politicians argued that farmers at the fringes of the world market economy could coerce the commercial-industrial center. They were wrong. The commitment to cotton and slavery isolated the South politically. It had also deepened the South's dependence on the world's financial and industrial centers. The North transformed itself from a part of the old colonial periphery (the suppliers of food and raw materials) into a part of the core (the suppliers of manufactured goods and financing) of the world market economy. In contrast, the South, by exporting plantation staples in exchange for imported goods, worked itself deeper and deeper into dependence.

CHAPTER REVIEW

Review Questions

1. What were the principal differences between the slave economies of the Chesapeake and the South Carolina–Georgia lowcountry?

2. In what ways did the economy and society of the cotton belt differ from older plantation regions? How do you explain those differences?

3. What factors encouraged southern yeoman farmers to enter regional, national, and international markets? What factors inhibited them?

4. Describe the cultural life that slaves made for themselves within the limits of slavery.

5. What were the nature and limits of the market revolution in the South? Why?

Critical Thinking Questions

1. In what geographic areas and in what ways did slavery expand between 1790 and 1820? In what areas (and, again, in what ways) was the slave system called into question?

2. The central institutions of slave culture were the family and religion. Some have argued that these institutions helped slaves accommodate to slavery, whereas others have argued that they helped them resist it, and still others have argued that they did both. State your position on this question.

3. The principal differences between North and South as of 1850 stemmed from the fact that the North had experienced a thoroughgoing market revolution in the previous 50 years while the South had not. True or false?

Identifications

Review your understanding of the following key terms, people, and events for this chapter.

private fields, p. 208
cotton, p. 209
Eli Whitney, p. 209

economies of scale, p. 215
"broad" wives, p. 217

itinerant preachers, p. 219
spirituals, p. 220
Gabriel's rebellion, p. 221

Denmark Vesey, p. 221
Nat Turner, p. 221

DISCOVERY

How did regional differences manifest themselves in the United States? How might these differences have shaped its history?

In thinking about this question, begin by breaking it down into the components shown below. A discussion of the significance of each component should appear in your answer.

Culture and Society

Look at the maps on page 211 of the distribution of the slave population. Where was slavery most prevalent in 1790? In 1820? And in 1860? Are there any differences? Did any state or region lower its number of slaves during this time? Did any state or region significantly raise its number of slaves? What accounts for the differences?

What do you think the artist is trying to say about slavery in the illustration below? Does he have a particular view of white society in the South? Does gender play a role in this illustration at all?

Economics and Family Life

Look at the maps on page 209 showing cotton production. What factors combined to explain such growth in production between 1801 and 1859? Look at the illustration of hauling cotton on page 212. What are the roles of slave women and children in this harvest as depicted in this illustration? Do you think that the family labor patterns of white southerners were similar to those of slave families? Why or why not?

"An Overseer Doing His Duty"

Collection of the Maryland Historical Society, Baltimore #III.21

Visit the CourseMate website at www.cengagebrain.com for additional study tools and review materials for this chapter.

TOWARD AN AMERICAN CULTURE

Americans after 1815 experienced wave after wave of social and cultural change. Territorial expansion, the growth of the market, and the spread of slavery broke old social patterns. Americans reinvented family life. They created American forms of popular literature and art. They flocked to evangelical churches. They began to make a distinctively American culture, one based more or less uniformly on republicanism, capitalism, and Protestantism. But different kinds of Americans made different cultures out of the nation's revolutionary inheritance, market expansion, and revival religion. The result, visible from the 1830s onward, was an American national culture that was (and still is) less an accepted body of rules than an ongoing conversation.

1830	1835	1840	1845	1850	1855

■ **1830**
Charles Grandison Finney leads religious revival in Rochester • Joseph Smith founds the Church of Jesus Christ of Latter-day Saints

■ **1831**
First minstrel show is presented

■ **1843**
William Miller's Adventists expect the world to end

■ **1845**
George Lippard's lurid novel *Quaker City* becomes a best-seller

1849 ■
Astor Place theater riot in New York City leaves 20 dead

1852 ■
Harriet Beecher Stowe publishes *Uncle Tom's Cabin*

THE DEMOCRATIZATION OF CULTURE

The weakening of traditional authority created spaces that Americans filled in their own ways. Important pillars of old cultures, such as the Bible and revolutionary ideas of liberty and equality, remained. But the transportation network that carried goods out of rural neighborhoods brought new things in: furniture, clothing styles, forms of entertainment, information, aspirations. In part, Americans developed new ways of thinking and living as consumers of these cultural goods.

Among the items reaching Americans was information—newspapers, books, magazines, business communications, personal letters, and travelers who carried news. Information circulated among a public that was remarkably literate. In 1790, approximately 85 percent of adult men in New England and 60 percent of those in Pennsylvania and the Chesapeake could read and write. The literacy rate among women was lower—about 45 percent in New England—but on the rise. By 1820, all but the poorest whites could read and write. The United States, more than perhaps any other country, was a nation of readers.

FOCUS QUESTION

In what ways did literacy and print help to democratize American culture?

A Revolution in Print

The rise of a reading public was accompanied by a print revolution: Enterprising men (and a few women) made their livings by providing cheap Bibles and English novels, almanacs, newspapers, and other printed matter. Republican governments encouraged reading. The states provided common schools, and the national government helped the flow of print in unprecedented ways.

The governments of Great Britain and the European powers tried to control the circulation of information; they established few post offices, taxed newspapers, monitored what was said in the newspapers and even in the mail, and prosecuted people who put the wrong things in print. There were attempts to do such things in America, but the people defeated both the Stamp Act of 1765 and the Alien and Sedition Acts of 1798. The First Amendment guaranteed

BOOKS IN THE COUNTRYSIDE. *This crude woodcut of an American farm was produced in 1802. It is a typical scene: Cattle browse in an outlying pasture, the farmer tills his field, and his wife and children are occupied near the house. What is new is that the wife, the most prominent figure in the scene, sits by herself reading a book.*

freedom of the press, and the U.S. government (with the brief exception of the Alien and Sedition Acts) did not interfere. Just the opposite: Newspapers enjoyed discounted postal rates and circulated far beyond their points of publication. A law of 1792 allowed newspapers to mail copies to each other without cost. In this manner, the rise of an informed public was knowingly subsidized by the national government.

Newspapers were the most widely distributed publications. In 1790, there were 106 newspapers being published in the United States. In 1835, 1,258 were in publication, 90 of which were dailies. Though only 1 household in 10 subscribed to a newspaper, the democratic public knew what was in them. The papers were passed from hand to hand, read aloud in groups, and made available at taverns and public houses.

Improvements in distribution and printing technology encouraged other forms of popular literature as well. The emerging evangelical crusade printed and distributed **Sunday school** tracts and other religious materials. The American Bible Society devised a realistic plan to provide every household in America with a free Bible. Newspapers were men's reading, but the religious tracts tended to find their way into the hands of women. Women also were the principal readers of novels, a new form of reading matter that Thomas Jefferson and other authorities denounced as frivolous and aberrant.

Sunday schools *Schools that first appeared in the 1790s to teach working-class children to read and write but by the 1820s and 1830s became moral training grounds.*

The increase in literacy and in printed matter accelerated democratic individualism. Books and newspapers were scarce in the 18th century, and most Americans experienced the written word only as it was read aloud by fathers, ministers, or teachers. After 1790, private, silent reading of new kinds of texts became common. No longer were authority figures the sole interpreters of the world for families and neighborhoods. The new print culture encouraged Americans to read, think, and interpret information for themselves.

THE NORTHERN MIDDLE CLASS

FOCUS QUESTION

What were the central cultural maxims of the emerging northern middle class?

"The most valuable class in any community," declared the poet-journalist Walt Whitman in 1858, "is the middle class." At that time, the term **middle class** (and the social group that it described) was no more than 30 or 40 years old. Those who claimed the title were proprietors made by the market revolution: city and country merchants, master craftsmen turned manufacturers, and the mass of market-oriented farmers.

A New Middle Class

As the first center of factory production and a region of commercialized farms, New England played a disproportionate role in the making of middle-class culture. Yankee migrants dominated the commercial heartland of western New York and the northern regions of the Northwest. Even in the seaport cities, businessmen from New England were often at the center. This Yankee middle class invented cultural forms that became the core of an emerging business civilization. Liberty for them meant self-ownership and the freedom of action and ambition. Equality meant equality of opportunity. They upheld the autonomous and morally accountable individual against the traditional claims of neighborhoods and families. They cultivated an intensely private, mother-centered domestic life. Above all, they adhered to Protestant moral imperatives.

The Evangelical Base

In November 1830, the evangelist Charles Grandison Finney preached in Rochester, New York. Most in his audience were transplanted New Englanders, heirs of Yankee Calvinism. In their ministers' weekly sermons and in the prayers their children memorized, they reaffirmed the old Puritan beliefs in providence and original sin. The earthly social order (the fixed relations of power and submission between man and woman, rich and poor, parent and child, and so on) was necessary because humankind was innately sinful and prone to selfishness and disorder. Christians must obey the rules governing their station in life; attempts to rearrange the social order were both sinful and doomed to failure.

Yet while they embraced Puritan beliefs in church, the men and women in Finney's audience ignored them in their daily lives. Market expansion was clearly the result of human effort. Just as clearly, it added up to "improvement." As middle-class Christians improved the material and social worlds, their doctrines of natural depravity and their reliance on divine providence made less and less sense.

To such an audience, Charles Finney preached the organizing principle of northern middle-class evangelicalism: "God," he insisted, "has made man a moral free agent." Neither the social order nor the spiritual state of individuals was divinely ordained. People would make themselves and the world better by choosing right over wrong—though they would choose right only after submitting their rebellious wills to the will of God. This religion valued individual holiness over a permanent and sacred social order. It made the spiritual nature of individuals a matter of prayer, submission, and choice.

Yankee evangelists had been moving toward Finney's formulation since the turn of the 19th century. Like Finney, they borrowed revival techniques from the Methodists (weeklong meetings, meetings in which women prayed in public, an **"anxious bench"** for the most likely converts), but toned them down for their own more "respectable" audience. At the same time, middle-class evangelicals retained the Puritans' Old Testament sense of cosmic history. They enlisted personal holiness in a fight to the finish between the forces of good and evil in this world.

Domesticity

The Yankee middle class made crucial distinctions between the home and the world. Men in cities and towns now went off to work, leaving wives and children at home. The new middle-class evangelicalism encouraged this division of domestic labor. The public world of politics and economic exchange, said the preachers, was the sphere of men; women, on the other hand, exercised new kinds of moral influence within households.

The result was a feminization of domestic life. In the old yeoman-artisan republic, fathers were God's delegated authorities on earth, assigned the task of governing women, children, and other underlings. Middle-class evangelicals raised new spiritual possibilities for women and children. Mothers replaced fathers as the

middle class *Social group that developed in the early 19th century comprised of urban and country merchants, master craftsmen who had turned themselves into manufacturers, and market-oriented farmers—small-scale entrepreneurs who rose within market society in the early 19th century.*

anxious bench *Bench at or near the front of a religious revival meeting where the most likely converts were seated.*

A MIDDLE-CLASS NEW ENGLAND
FAMILY AT HOME, 1837. *The room is
carpeted and comfortably furnished.
Father reads his newspaper; books
rest on the table. Mother entertains
their only child, and a kitten joins the
family circle. This is the domestic
foundation of sentimental culture on
display.*

Abby Aldrich Rockefeller Folk Art Museum, The Colonial Williamsburg Foundation, Williamsburg, VA

QUICK REVIEW

DOMESTICITY

- Separation of home from economic and political life
- Mothers become the principal child-rearers
- Parental authority based in love, not power

Sarah Josepha Hale *Editor of
Godey's Lady's Book and an
important arbiter of domesticity and
taste for middle-class housewives.*

Uncle Tom's Cabin *Published by
Harriet Beecher Stowe in 1852, this
sentimental novel told the story of
the Christian slave Uncle Tom. It
became a best seller and the most
powerful antislavery tract of the
antebellum years.*

domestic fiction *Sentimental
literature that centered on household
and domestic themes that
emphasized the toil and travails of
women and children who overcame
adversity through religious faith and
strength of character.*

principal child-rearers, and they enlisted the doctrines of free agency and individual
moral responsibility in that task. Middle-class mothers sought to develop their
children's conscience and their capacity to love, to teach them to make good moral
choices, and to prepare them for conversion and a lifetime of Christian service.

Middle-class mothers could concentrate their efforts on household duties
because they had fewer children than their mothers or grandmothers had had,
meaning they could give each child closer attention. As a result, households were
quieter and less crowded; children learned from their mothers how to conduct
themselves. Mothers nurtured children who would be carriers of the new middle-
class culture, and male authorities recognized the importance of that job.

Middle-class women and girls became a huge market for new forms of
popular literature. There were cookbooks, etiquette books, manuals on housekeeping, sermons, and sentimental novels, many of them written and most of them read
by women. The works of popular religious writers such as Lydia Sigourney, Lydia
Maria Child, and Timothy Shay Arthur found their way into thousands of middle-
class homes. **Sarah Josepha Hale,** whose *Godey's Lady's Book* was the first mass-
circulation magazine for women, was an arbiter of taste not only in furniture,
clothing, and food but also in sentiments and ideas. By wide margins, novels by
women outsold Nathaniel Hawthorne's *The Scarlet Letter* and *The House of the Seven
Gables,* Ralph Waldo Emerson's essays, Henry David Thoreau's *Walden,* Herman
Melville's *Moby Dick,* and Walt Whitman's *Leaves of Grass.* Susan Warner's *The Wide,
Wide World* broke all sales records when it appeared in 1850. Harriet Beecher
Stowe's **Uncle Tom's Cabin** (1852) broke the records set by Warner.

Sentimental novels sacralized the middle-class home and the trials and triumphs of Christian women. The action takes place indoors, usually in the kitchen or
parlor, and the heroines are women who live under worldly patriarchy but triumph
through submission to God. The stories embody spiritual struggle and mother love.
The home is juxtaposed to the competition and callousness of the marketplace.
Unlike the female characters in British and European novels of the time, the women
in these American novels are intelligent, generous persons who grow in strength
and independence. In sentimental **domestic fiction,** women assume the role of
evangelical ministers, demonstrating Christian living. Female moral influence is at
war with the male world of power, greed, and moral compromise.

Despite the claims of some male critics, popular sentimental novels were not frivolous. They were subversive depictions of a higher spiritual reality that would move the feminine ethos of the Christian home to the center of civilization. That vision drove an organized public assault on irreligion, drunkenness, prostitution, slavery, and other practices and institutions that substituted passion and force for Christian love.

THE PLAIN PEOPLE OF THE NORTH

From the 1830s onward, northern reformers proposed their religious and domestic values as a national culture for the United States. But even in their own region they were outnumbered by those who rejected their leadership. The plain folk of the North were a varied lot: settlers in the lower Northwest who remained culturally southern; hill-country northerners; refugees from the countryside who had taken up urban wage labor; and increasing thousands of Irish and German immigrants. They did share a cultural conservatism that rejected sentimentalism and reformist religion out of hand.

FOCUS QUESTION

Within the North, what were the alternatives to middle-class culture?

The Decline of the Established Churches

The Founding Fathers had been indifferent to organized religion. Some, like George Washington, attended church out of a sense of obligation. Some, like Thomas Jefferson, subscribed to **deism**, the belief that God had created the universe but did not intervene in its affairs. Many simply did not think about religion. When asked why the Constitution mentioned neither God nor religion, Alexander Hamilton reportedly smiled and said, "We forgot."

In state after state, post-revolutionary constitutions withdrew government support from religion, and the First Amendment to the U.S. Constitution clearly prescribed the separation of church and the national state. Reduced to their own resources, the established churches went into decline. The Episcopal Church began to lose members. In 1780, nearly all of the 750 Congregational churches in the United States were in New England. In the next 40 years, although the nation's population rose from 4 to 10 million, the number of Congregational churches rose only to 1,100. Ordinary women and men were leaving the churches that had dominated the religious life of colonial America.

The Rise of the Democratic Sects

The collapse of established churches, the social dislocations of the post-revolutionary years, and the increasingly antiauthoritarian, democratic sensibilities of ordinary Americans provided fertile ground for the growth of new democratic sects. The Methodists and Baptists grew into the great popular denominations they have been ever since. Fiercely independent dropouts from older churches put together a loosely organized movement that would become the Disciples of Christ. At the same time, ragged, half-educated preachers spread the Universalist and Freewill Baptist messages in upcountry New England, while in western New York young Joseph Smith received the visions that would lead to Mormonism.

The fastest-growing sects shared a roughly similar style. First, they renounced the need for an educated, formally authorized clergy. **Crisis conversion** (understood

deism *Belief that God created the universe but did not intervene in its affairs.*

Crisis conversion *Understood in evangelical churches as a personal transformation that resulted from directly experiencing the Holy Spirit.*

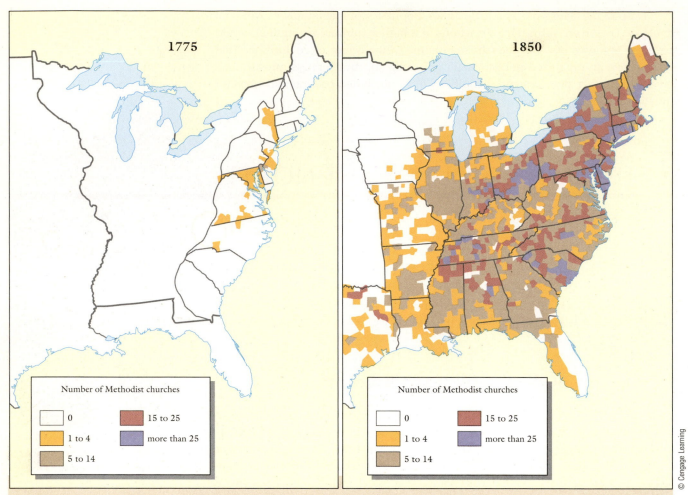

Map 10.1 Growth of American Methodism, 1775–1850. *This is a county-by-county map of the rise of American Methodism from the Revolution through the eve of the Civil War. In 1775 Methodism was almost nonexistent in British North America. By 1850 the Methodists were the largest Protestant denomination in the United States, and they were truly a national faith: There were Methodist churches in almost every county in the country.*

Restorationism *Belief that all theological and institutional changes since the end of biblical times were man-made mistakes and that religious organizations must restore themselves to the purity and simplicity of the apostolic church.*

circuit-riding preachers *Methodist ministers who traveled from church to church, usually in rural areas.*

as a spiritual transformation that resulted from direct experience of the Holy Ghost) was the necessary credential for preachers; a college degree was not. The new preachers substituted emotionalism and storytelling for Episcopal ritual and Congregational theological lectures. Stories attracted listeners, and they were harder for learned clergy to refute. The new churches also held up the Bible as the one source of religious knowledge, thus placing any literate Christian on a level with the best-educated minister. These tendencies often ended in **Restorationism**—the belief that theological and institutional changes since the end of biblical times were man-made mistakes and that religious organizations must restore themselves to the purity and simplicity of the church of the Apostles. In sum, these sects rejected learning and tradition and raised up the priesthood of all believers.

Baptists and Methodists were by far the most successful at preaching to populist audiences. (See Map 10.1.) By 1820, they outnumbered Episcopalians and Congregationalists by 3 to 1. Baptists based their appeal in localism and congregational democracy. Methodist success, on the other hand, entailed skillful national organization. Bishop Francis Asbury, the head of the church in its fastest-growing years, built a bureaucracy that seeded churches throughout the republic and sent **circuit-riding preachers** to places that had none.

Methodist preachers were common men who spoke plainly, listened carefully, and carried hymnals of tunes that anyone could sing. They shared traditional folk beliefs with their humble flocks. Some of the early circuit riders relied heavily on dreams; some could predict the future; many visited heaven and hell and returned with full descriptions. In the end, it was the hopefulness and simplicity of the Methodist message that attracted ordinary people. The Methodists rejected Calvinist determinism and taught that although salvation comes only through God, men and women can decide to open themselves to divine grace and play a decisive role in their own salvation.

The Providential Worldview

Northern plain folk favored churches as doctrinally varied as the people themselves. They included the most popular faiths (Baptists and Methodists came to constitute two-thirds of America's professing Protestants) and such smaller sects as Hicksite Quakers, Universalists, Adventists, Moravians, and Freewill Baptists. Yet for all their diversity, these churches had important points in common. Most shared an evangelical emphasis on individual experience over churchly authority. They favored democratic, local control of religious life and distrusted outside organization and religious professionalism. They rejected middle-class optimism and reformism, reaffirming humankind's duty to accept an imperfect world.

The most pervasive strain was a belief in providence—the conviction that human history was part of God's vast and unknowable plan, and that all events were willed or allowed by God. Middle-class evangelicals spoke of providence, too, but they seemed to assume that God's plan was manifest in the progress of market society and middle-class religion. Humbler evangelicals believed that the events of everyday life were parts of a vast blueprint that existed only in the mind of God—and not in the vain aspirations of women and men. They learned to accept misfortune with fortitude. They responded to epidemics, bad crop years, illness, and early death by praying for the strength to endure.

In a world governed by providence, the death of a child in particular was a test of faith that called for heroic acts of submission. Parents mourned the loss but stopped short of displaying grief that would suggest selfishness and lack of faith. Poor families washed and dressed the dead body themselves and then buried it in a churchyard or on a hilltop plot on the family farm. While the urban middle class preferred formal funerals and carefully tended cemeteries, humbler people regarded death as a lesson in the futility of worldly pursuits and in the need to submit to God's will.

CHILD'S GRAVESTONE. *Below the weeping willow on this baby girl's gravestone is an inscription affirming that death has set the child "free from trouble and pain" and has ushered her into a better life.*

Popular Millennialism

Middle-class evangelicals were **postmillennialists**: They believed that Christ's Second Coming would occur at the end of 1,000 years of social perfection brought about by the missionary conversion of the world. Ordinary Baptists, Methodists, and Disciples of Christ, on the other hand, assumed that the millennium would arrive with world-destroying violence, followed by 1,000 years of Christ's rule on earth. Most did not dwell on this terrifying premillennialism, assuming that God would end the world in his own time. But now and then, the ordinary evangelicals

postmillennialism *Belief (held mostly by middle-class evangelists) that Christ's Second Coming would occur when missionary conversion of the world brought about a thousand years of social perfection.*

of the North predicted the fiery day of judgment. People looked for signs of the approaching millennium in thunderstorms, shooting stars, eclipses, economic panics and depressions, and—especially—in hints that they believed God had placed in the Bible.

An avid student of those hints was William Miller, a Vermont Baptist who, after years of systematic study, concluded that God would destroy the world during the year following March 1843. Miller publicized his predictions throughout the 1830s, and near the end of the decade the Millerites (as his followers were called) gathered together thousands of believers, most of them conservative Baptists, Methodists, and Disciples in hill-country New England and in poor neighborhoods in New York, Ohio, and Michigan. As the end approached, the believers read the Bible, prayed, and attended meeting after meeting. Newspapers published stories alleging that the Millerites were insane and sexually licentious.

When the end of the year—March 23, 1844—came and went, most of the believers quietly returned to their churches. A committed remnant kept the faith and by the 1860s founded the Seventh-Day Adventist Church. The Millerite movement was a reminder that hundreds of thousands of northern Protestants continued to believe that the God of the Old Testament governed everything from bee stings to the course of human history, and that one day he would destroy the world in fire and blood.

Family and Society

Baptists, Methodists, Disciples of Christ, and the smaller popular sects evangelized primarily among people who had been bypassed or hurt by the market revolution. Often their rhetoric turned to criticism of market society, its institutions, and its centers of power. The Quaker schismatic Elias Hicks, a Long Island farmer who fought the worldliness and pride of wealthy urban Quakers, listed the following among the mistakes of the early 19th century: railroads, the Erie Canal, fancy food, the credit system, the city of Philadelphia, and the study of chemistry. William Miller expressed his hatred of banks, insurance companies, stockjobbing, chartered monopolies, personal greed, and the city of New York. In short, what the evangelical middle class identified as the march of progress, poorer and more conservative evangelicals condemned as a descent into worldliness that would provoke God's wrath.

Members of the popular sects often held to the patriarchal family form in which they had been raised. Hundreds of thousands of northern Protestants considered the erosion of domestic patriarchy a profound cultural loss and not, as it seemed to the middle class, an avenue to personal liberation. For some, religious conversion came at a point of crisis in the traditional family. William Miller, for example, had a strict Calvinist upbringing in a family in which his father, an uncle, and his grandfather were all Baptist ministers. As a young man he rejected his family, set about making money, and became a deist—actions that deeply wounded his parents. When his father died, Miller was stricken with guilt. He moved back to his hometown, took up his family duties, became a leader of the Baptist church, and (after reading a sermon entitled "Parental Duties") began the years of Bible study that resulted in his world-ending prophecies.

The Prophet Joseph Smith

The weakening of the patriarchal family and the attempt to shore it up were central to the life and work of one of the most unique and successful religious leaders of the

HISTORY THROUGH FILM

Gangs of New York (2002)

Directed by Martin Scorsese; starring Leonardo DiCaprio (Amsterdam Vallon), Daniel Day-Lewis (Bill "The Butcher" Cutting), and Cameron Diaz (Jenny Everdeane)

Martin Scorsese's movie about the Five Points of New York—the most dangerous neighborhood in mid-19th-century North America—is an operatic tragedy. An Irish boy (Leonardo DiCaprio) whose father, the leader of a gang called the Dead Rabbits, is killed by a nativist chieftain (Daniel Day-Lewis) in a gang fight, spends his childhood in an orphanage, and then returns to Five Points to take revenge. He becomes part of the criminal entourage of his father's killer, falls in love with a beautiful and talented female thief (Cameron Diaz) who had been raised (and used) by the same gang boss, and bides his time—tortured all the while by the prospect of killing a second father figure. In the end, the Irish boy resurrects his father's gang and challenges the nativists to a battle for control of the Five Points. The battle coincides with the Draft Riots of 1863, and the film ends (as it begins) in a horrendous bloodbath. The Irish thug kills the nativist thug, and the film ends with U2 singing "We Who Built America."

For those who can stomach close-up fights with clubs and hatchets, it is a good enough melodrama. Unhappily, Scorsese casts his story against real history and gets most of it wrong. The film takes pains to "reconstruct" Manhattan's Five Points, but our first view of the neighborhood is taken from a painting of a Brooklyn street. The oppressive noise and overcrowding that contemporary visitors described are mitigated by a large public space at the center of the Points—historically nonexistent, but a fine field for the gang fights that begin and end the movie. Historically, the gangs were headquartered at saloons and firehouses, but Scorsese's operatic sensibilities move the Dead Rabbits into catacombs beneath the Old Brewery—complete with torchlight, a crude armory, and an untidy pyramid of skulls. The nativists, on the other hand, prefer an Asian motif, holding their get-togethers in an ornate Chinese theater and social house that lends an air of orientalist extravaganza to a neighborhood that knew nothing of such things. The catalog of crimes against history could go on and on: The Dead Rabbits did not follow the cross into battle (Irish street gangs were not particularly religious); Irish priests did not look like Peter the Hermit; and Leonardo DiCaprio does not have a convincing Irish accent.

The "reformers" who minister to the Five Points receive equally silly treatment. The chiefs of the reformers are the aristocratic Schermerhorns. In fact, most Five Points missionaries were middle-class evangelicals who had little to do with the Schermerhorns or the other old families of New York. The movie reformers hold a dance for the neighborhood; in fact, the evangelicals hated dancing and parties. The reformers also attend a public hanging, cheering as four innocent men are put to death. But New York had outlawed public executions a generation earlier; felons were now hanged within prison walls before small invited audiences. Even if public hangings had persisted, reformers would not have attended them (they had stopped going to such spectacles soon after 1815), and had they been dragged out of their parlors to witness an execution, they would not have cheered. There is also an appearance by P. T. Barnum. Barnum had made his museum the premier middle-class entertainment spot in New York by eschewing low theater, cockfights, and other raucous and violent shows. Yet the movie had Barnum sponsoring a bare-knuckle prizefight—an act that would have cost him his reputation and his livelihood. The climactic riot includes another Barnum fabrication: Barnum's museum is set on fire; his menagerie escapes, and a terrified elephant romps through the burning streets. It almost certainly did not happen, but even the most fact-bound historian must bow to Scorsese's artistic license on that one.

Daniel Day-Lewis and his Five Points gang.

©Kobal/Picture Desk

period, the Mormon prophet **Joseph Smith** (see also Chapter 13). Smith's father was a landless Vermont Baptist who moved his wife and nine children to seven rented farms within 20 years. Around 1820, when young Joseph was approaching manhood, the family was struggling to make mortgage payments on a small farm outside Palmyra, New York. Despite the efforts of Joseph and his brothers, a merchant cheated the Smith family out of the farm. With that, both generations of the Smiths faced lifetimes as propertyless workers. To make matters worse, Joseph's mother and some of his siblings began to attend an evangelical Presbyterian church in Palmyra, apparently against the father's wishes.

Before the loss of the farm, Joseph had received two visions warning him away from existing churches and telling him to await further instructions. In 1827, the Angel Moroni appeared to him and led him to golden plates that translated into *The Book of Mormon.* It told of a light-skinned people, descendants of the Hebrews, who had sailed to North America long before Columbus. They had had an epic, violent history and had been visited by Jesus following his resurrection.

Joseph Smith later declared that his discovery of *The Book of Mormon* had "brought salvation to my father's house" by unifying the family. It eventually unified thousands of others under a patriarchal faith. The good priests and secular leaders of *The Book of Mormon* are farmers who labor alongside their neighbors; the villains are self-seeking merchants, lawyers, and bad priests. Smith carried that model of brotherly cooperation and patriarchal authority into the Church of Jesus Christ of Latter-day Saints, which he founded in 1830.

The new church was ruled not by professional clergy but by an elaborate lay hierarchy of adult males. On top sat the father of Joseph Smith, rescued from destitution and shame, who was appointed Patriarch of the Church. Below him were Joseph Smith and his brother Hyrum, who were called First and Second Elders. The hierarchy descended through a succession of male authorities that finally reached the fathers of households. An astute observer might have noticed the similarities between this hierarchical structure and the social order of the 18th-century North.

Joseph Smith *Poor New York farm boy whose visions led him to translate* The Book of Mormon *in the late 1820s. He became the founder and the prophet of The Church of Jesus Christ of Latter-day Saints (Mormons).*

A NEW POPULAR CULTURE

Not all northern plain folk spent their time in church. In cities and towns, they became both producers and consumers of a commercial popular culture.

Blood Sports and Boxing

Urban working-class neighborhoods were particularly fertile ground for popular amusements. Young working men formed a bachelor subculture that contrasted with the piety and self-restraint of the middle class. They organized volunteer fire companies and militia units that spent more time drinking and fighting rival groups than they did drilling or putting out fires. Gathering at firehouses, saloons, and street corners, they drank, joked, boasted, and nurtured notions of manliness based on physical prowess and coolness under pressure.

They also engaged in such **"blood sports"** as cockfighting, ratting, and dog fighting, even though many states had laws forbidding such activities. Such contests grew increasingly popular during the 1850s, often staged by saloon keepers. One of the best known was Kit Burns, who ran Sportsman Hall, a New York City

blood sports *Sporting activities emphasizing bloodiness that were favored by working-class men of the cities. The most popular in the early 19th century were cockfighting, rat baiting, dog fighting, and various types of violence between animals.*

saloon frequented by prizefighters, criminals, and hangers-on. Behind the saloon was a space—reached through a narrow doorway that could be defended against the police—with animal pits and a small amphitheater that seated 250, and regularly held 400 yelling spectators.

Although most spectators were working men, a few members of the old aristocracy also attended these events. Frederick Van Wick, scion of a wealthy old New York family, remembered an evening he had spent at Tommy Norris's livery stable, where he witnessed a fight between billy goats, a rat baiting, a cockfight, and a boxing match between bare-breasted women. "Certainly for a lad of 17, such as I," he recalled, "a night with Tommy Norris and his attraction was quite a night."

Prizefighting emerged from the same subterranean culture. Imported from Britain, boxing's popularity in the United States rose during the 1840s and 1850s. Many boxers had close ties with ethnic-based saloons, militia units, fire companies, and street gangs, and many labored at occupations with a peculiarly ethnic base. Some of the best American-born fighters were New York City butchers—a licensed, privileged trade from which cheap immigrant labor was excluded. Butchers usually finished work by 10 A.M. They could then spend the rest of the day idling at a firehouse or a bar and were often prominent figures in neighborhood gangs. A prizefight between an American-born butcher and an Irish day laborer would attract a spirited audience that understood its class and ethnic meaning.

An American Theater

In the 18th and early 19th centuries, all American theaters were in the large seaport cities. Those who attended were members of the urban elite, and nearly all the plays, managers, and actors were English. After 1815, new theaters and theater companies sprang up not only in New York and Philadelphia but also in dozens of other new towns, and traveling troupes carried theatrical performances to the smallest hamlets. Before 1830, the poorer theatergoers—nearly all of them men—occupied the cheap balcony seats; artisans and other workingmen filled benches in the ground floor area known as "the pit"; wealthier and more genteel patrons sat in the boxes. Those sitting in the pit and balcony ate and drank, talked, and shouted encouragement and threats to the actors.

As time passed, rowdyism turned into violence. Working-class theatergoers protested the elegant speech, gentlemanly bearing, and understated performances of the English actors, which happened to match the speech, manners, and bearing of the American urban elite. The first theater riot occurred in 1817 when the English actor Charles Incledon refused a New York audience's demand that he stop what he was doing and sing "Black-Eyed Susan." Such assaults grew more common during the 1820s. By the 1830s, separate theaters offered separate kinds of performances for rich and poor. But violence continued, culminating with an 1849 riot at the Astor Place Opera House in New York City. Twenty people lost their lives.

Playhouses that catered to working-class audiences continued to feature Shakespearean tragedies, but they now shared the stage with works written in the American vernacular. The stage "Yankee," rustic but shrewd, debuted at this time, and so did Mose the Bowery B'hoy, a New York volunteer fireman who performed feats of derring-do. Both frequently appeared in the company of well-dressed characters with English accents. The Yankee outsmarted them; Mose beat them up.

MUSICAL LINK TO THE PAST

"Oh Susanna"

Composer: Stephen C. Foster
Title: "Oh Susanna" (1847)

The most famous songs of Stephen C. Foster (such as "Camptown Races," "Old Folks at Home") represent the only example of a body of songwriting by an antebellum American to survive into the collective memory of the 21st century. One example of his songs' modern-day popularity occurred in 1998 when protesters, outside the White House wrote and sang new lyrics for "Oh Susanna" during President Clinton's videotaped grand jury testimony concerning his affair with Monica Lewinsky.

Foster also made inroads in the music business world. He was America's first full-time professional composer, making enough proceeds on his songs to support himself. However, Foster never became wealthy and for most of his life, barely made ends meet, mainly due to his habit of selling songs outright instead of obtaining royalties, and because the infrastructure of the modern popular music industry was not yet in place.

As author Ken Emerson suggested, "Oh Susanna" "pines for the past even as it hurtles into the future." The lyrics act as a bridge between rural and urban life, the latter being strongly on the rise in the United States. The song celebrates new technology, the steamboat and the telegraph, which helped make possible the interstate and international commerce fueling the growth of American cities. But "Oh Susanna" does not fail to recognize the danger of these new devices, particularly steamboats, which annually killed and injured hundreds of Americans during the 1840s.

"Oh Susanna" was also part of the minstrel culture of the period. Though Foster's minstrel songs were less offensive than most and attempted to portray blacks in a less derogatory and sometimes even in a positive manner, two racial epithets were featured in the original lyrics for "Oh Susanna." In 1855, African American author and activist Frederick Douglass pointed to Foster's later minstrel songs "Uncle Ned" and "My Old Kentucky Home" as songs that could "awaken the sympathies for the slave, in which anti-slavery principles take root and flourish."

In the history of American popular music, "Oh Susanna" became the first "shot heard round the world." Domestically, it swept the country, with 16 different publishers offering sheet music of the song (most of which paid no royalties to Foster). No previous American song had earned such wide international appeal; historian William Austin documented the song's popularity in Europe, India, and North Africa. Thanks to Foster, the modern American music industry had been born.

Q Why would a successful songwriter make more money from royalties than by selling his songs to a company outright? How do songwriters of today handle this situation?

Minstrelsy

The most popular form of theater was the blackface **minstrel show**. These shows were blatantly racist, and they were the preferred entertainment of working men in northern cities from 1840 to 1880. The first minstrel show was presented in 1831 when a white showman named Thomas Rice blacked his face and "jumped Jim Crow," imitating a black shuffle-dance he had seen on the Cincinnati docks.

Performances typically began with singing, dancing, and clapping. The audience then watched a conversation between three characters: Uncle Ned, a simple-minded plantation slave dressed in plain clothing; Zip Coon, a dandified, oversexed free black dressed in top hat and tails; and an interlocutor, the straight man—fashionably dressed, slightly pretentious, with an English accent. Their conversation included pointed political satire, skits ridiculing the wealthy and the educated, and sexual jokes that bordered on obscenity. The third and final section of a show featured songs, dances, and jokes.

minstrel show *Popular form of theater among working men of the northern cities in which white men in blackface portrayed African Americans in song and dance.*

AN EARLY PRINT OF "JIM CROW" RICE AT NEW YORK'S BOWERY THEATER. *The caption reads "American Theatre, Bowery, New York, Nov. 25th 1833. The 57th Night of Mr. T. D. Jim Crow Rice."*

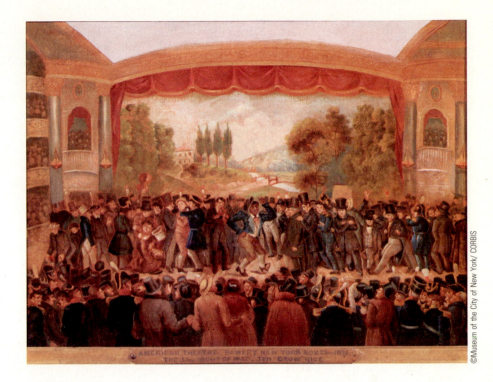

The minstrel shows introduced African American song and dance—in toned-down, Europeanized form—to audiences who would not have permitted black performers on the stage. They also reinforced racial stereotypes that were near the center of American popular culture. Finally, hiding behind masks, minstrel performers dealt broadly with aspects of social and political life that other performers avoided.

Novels and the Penny Press

Few of the commodities made widely available by the market revolution were more ubiquitous than newspapers and inexpensive books. Improvements in printing and papermaking enabled entrepreneurs to sell daily newspapers for a penny. Cheap "story papers" became available in the 1830s, "yellow-back" fiction in the 1840s, and dime novels from the 1850s onward. Although distributed throughout the North and the West, they found their first and largest audience among city workers.

Mass-audience newspapers were heavily spiced with sensationalism. The *Philadelphia Gazette* in late summer 1829, for instance, treated its eager readers to the following: "Female Child with Two Heads," "Bats," "Another Shark," "More Stabbing," "Fishes Travelling on Land," "Dreadful Steam Boat Disaster," "Raffling for Babies," and much more. These stories portrayed a haunted, often demonic nature that regularly produced monstrosities and ruined the works of humankind, as well as a human nature that, despite appearances, was often deceptive and depraved.

Working-class readers discovered a similarly untrustworthy world in cheap fiction. George Lippard's best seller *Quaker City* (1845) was a fictional exposé of the hypocrisy, lust, and cruelty of Philadelphia's outwardly genteel and Christian elite. Lippard and other adventure writers indulged in a pornography of violence that included cannibalism, blood drinking, and murder by every imaginable means. They also dealt with sex in unprecedentedly explicit ways. The yellow-back novels of the 1840s introduced readers not only to seduction and rape but to transvestitism, child pornography, necrophilia, miscegenation, group sex, homosexuality, and—perhaps most shocking of all—women with criminal minds and insatiable sexual appetites.

Popular fictions were melodramatic contests between good and evil. Heroes met a malign and chaotic world with courage and guile without hoping to change it. Indeed, melodramatic heroes frequently acknowledged evil in themselves while claiming moral superiority over the hypocrites and frauds who governed the world. A murderer in Ned Buntline's *G'hals of New York* (1850) remarks, "There isn't no *real* witue [virtue] and honesty nowhere, 'cept among the perfessional *dis*honest." By contrast, in middle-class sentimental novels, the universe was benign: Good could be nurtured, and evil could be defeated and transformed. For example, Harriet Beecher Stowe's slave driver Simon Legree is evil not because of a natural disposition toward evil, but because he has been deprived of a mother's love during childhood.

FAMILY, CHURCH, AND NEIGHBORHOOD: THE WHITE SOUTH

The southern states experienced cultural transformations of a more conservative nature—transformations grounded in localism, in the father-centered family, and in the influence of a traditionalist evangelical Christianity.

The Beginnings of the Bible Belt

In the first third of the 19th century, evangelical Protestantism transformed the South into what it has been ever since: the Bible Belt. Early southern evangelicals demanded a crisis conversion followed by a life of piety and a rejection of what they called "the world." To no small degree, "the world" was the economic, cultural, and political world controlled by the planters.

Southern Baptists, Methodists, and Presbyterians spread their message through the **camp meeting**. Though its origins stretched back into the 18th century, the first full-blown camp meeting took place at Cane Ridge, Kentucky, in 1801. Here the annual "Holy Feast," a three-day communion service of Scotch-Irish Presbyterians, was transformed into an outdoor, interdenominational revival at which hundreds experienced conversion. Estimates of the crowd at Cane Ridge ranged from 10,000 to 20,000 people. Converts fainted, jerked uncontrollably, and barked like dogs, visibly taken by the Holy Spirit. Such experiences affected women and men, whites and blacks, rich and poor, momentarily blurring social hierarchy in religious ecstasy.

Despite its critique of worldliness and its antiauthoritarian emphasis, southern Evangelicalism was at bottom conservative. The 19th-century Baptists, Methodists, and Presbyterians of the South, though they never stopped railing against greed and pride, lived comfortably with the region's system of fixed hierarchy and "God-given" social roles.

Slavery and Southern Evangelicals

Slavery became a major case in point. For a brief period after the Revolution, evangelicals opposed slavery (see Chapter 9). Methodists and Baptists preached to slaves as well as to whites. In 1780, a conference of Methodist preachers ordered

---

FOCUS QUESTION

In what specific ways did evangelical Protestantism act as a conservative force within southern culture?

QUICK REVIEW

EVANGELICAL RELIGION

- Bible as the one source of religious knowledge
- Crisis conversion needed
- Appeal to the middle and lower classes of society

camp meeting *Outdoor revival, often lasting for days; a principal means of spreading evangelical Christianity in the United States.*

circuit riders to free their slaves and advised all Methodists to do the same. In 1784, the Methodists declared that they would excommunicate members who failed to free their slaves within two years. Other evangelicals shared their views. As early as 1787, southern Presbyterians prayed for "final abolition," and two years later, Baptists condemned slavery as "a violent deprivation of the rights of nature and inconsistent with a republican government."

The period of greatest evangelical growth, however, came during the years in which the South committed irrevocably to plantation slavery. As increasing numbers of both slaves and slave owners came within the evangelical fold, the southern churches had to rethink their position on slavery. The Methodists never carried out their threat to excommunicate slaveholders. The Baptists and Presbyterians never translated their antislavery rhetoric into action. By 1820, evangelicals were coming to terms with slavery. Instead of demanding freedom for slaves, they suggested, as the Methodist James O'Kelly put it, that slave owners treat slaves as "dear brethren in Christ."

Gender, Power, and the Evangelicals

Southern white men distrusted the early evangelicals for more than their views on slavery. The preachers seemed even more grievously mistaken about white manhood and the integrity of white families. Southerners were localistic and culturally conservative. They distrusted outsiders and defended rural neighborhoods grounded in the sovereignty of fathers.

The early evangelicals threatened southern patriarchy. They preached individual salvation to women, children, and slaves—often hinting that the "family" of believers could replace blood ties. Churches sometimes intervened in family disputes or disciplined family members in ways that subverted patriarchal control. Perhaps worse, many preachers failed to act out the standards of southern manhood in their own lives. James McGready and other camp-meeting preachers often faced hecklers and rowdies. When attacked, they either ran off or quietly took their beatings. White men viewed such meekness (not to mention the celibacy of the Methodists) with suspicion and contempt. They felt the same about the hugging, kissing, crying, and bodily "exercises" acted out in evangelical meetings.

As they had with slavery, southern evangelicals came to terms with southern culture. Preachers learned to assert traditional forms of manhood. Their fathers and often themselves, they said, had fought the British and Indians heroically. They revealed that they had often been great drinkers, gamblers, fighters, and fornicators before submitting to God, and they also began fighting back when attacked. The preachers also made it clear that they would pose no threat to the authority of fathers. They discouraged the excesses of female and juvenile piety. At the same time, church disciplinary cases involving adultery, wife-beating, private drunkenness, and other offenses committed within families became more and more rare.

Pro-Slavery Christianity

In revolutionary and early national America, white southerners had been the most radical republicans. Jeffersonian planter-politicians led the fights for equal rights and the absolute separation of church and state, and southern evangelicals were the early republic's staunchest opponents of slavery. By 1830, however, the South felt increasingly embattled about slavery. The northern middle classes proclaimed a link between material and moral progress, identifying both with individual autonomy and universal rights. A radical northern minority was agitating for the immediate abolition of slavery.

QUICK REVIEW

PRO-SLAVERY RELIGIOUS ARGUMENTS

- Ancient Israelites held slaves

- Jesus did not denounce slavery

- All important relationships based in power and submission

Southerners met this challenge with an "intellectual blockade" against outside publications and ideas and with a moral and religious defense of slavery. The Bible provided plenty of ammunition. Southerners preached that the Chosen People of the Old Testament—Abraham in particular—had been patriarchs and slaveholders and that Jesus had lived in a society that sanctioned slavery and never criticized the institution. Some ministers claimed that blacks were the descendants of Ham and thus deserved enslavement. The most common religious argument was that slavery had given millions of heathen Africans the priceless opportunity to become Christians and to live in a Christian society.

Like their northern counterparts, southern clergymen applauded the material improvements of the age, but they insisted that moral improvement occurred only when people embraced the timeless truths of the Bible. Northern notions of progress through individual liberation, equal rights, and universal Christian love were wrong headed and dangerous. Southern pro-slavery intellectuals rejected Jefferson's "self-evident" equality of man; Edmund Ruffin, for instance, branded that passage of the Declaration of Independence as "indefensible" as well as "false and foolish."

The Mission to the Slaves

By the 1820s, slaveholders commonly attended camp meetings and revivals, and their churches taught them that slaves had immortal souls and that planters were responsible for their spiritual welfare. After Nat Turner's bloody slave revolt in 1831 (see Chapter 9), missions to the slaves took on new urgency: If the churches were to help create a family-centered, Christian society in the South, that society would have to include slaves.

To this end, Charles Colcock Jones, a Presbyterian minister from Georgia, wrote manuals on how to preach to slaves. He taught that no necessary connection linked social position and spiritual worth: There were good and bad slaveholders and good and bad slaves. He also taught that slaves must accept the master's authority as God's, and that obedience was their prime religious virtue. Jones warned white preachers never to become personally involved with their slave listeners—to pay no attention to their quarrels, their complaints about their master or about their fellow slaves, or about working conditions on the plantation. "We separate entirely their religious from their civil condition," he said, "and contend that one may be attended to without interfering with the other."

The evangelical mission to the slaves was not as completely self-serving as it may seem. For to accept one's worldly station, to be obedient and dutiful, and to seek salvation outside of this world were precisely what the planters demanded of themselves and their families. Safe and profitable plantations were to be achieved by Christianizing both slaveholders and slaves, a lesson that some slaveholders learned when they were expelled from their churches for mistreating their slaves.

RACE

Americans in the first half of the 19th century revised the racial order as well as the religious and domestic order of their society. White Americans had long assumed that Africans belonged at the bottom of society, but they assumed that others belonged there as well. In a colonial world in which many whites were indentured servants, tenants, apprentices, and workers who lived in their employers' homes, where increasing numbers of blacks were formally free and many others were hired out as semifree, few Americans made rigid distinctions concerning the "natural" independence of whites and the "natural" dependence of blacks. (All Americans, after all, were colonial subjects of the British king.) While the better-off whites were far from color blind, they wrote off poverty, disorder, drunkenness, and rioting as the work not of blacks but of an undifferentiated substratum of "Negroes, sailors, servants, and boys."

Modern racism—the notion that blacks were a separate and hopelessly inferior order of humankind—emerged from developments in the early 19th century: national independence and the crucial new distinction between Americans who were citizens and those who were not, the recommitment to slavery in the South, and the making of what would be called "free labor" in the North. Whites who faced lifetimes of wage labor and dependence struggled to make dignity out of that situation. At the same time, freed slaves entered the bottom of a newly defined "free-labor" society and tried to do the same. With plenty of help from the wealthy and powerful, whites succeeded in making white democracy out of the rubble of the old patriarchal republic. In the process, they defined nonwhites as constitutionally incapable of self-discipline, personal independence, and political participation.

Free Blacks

There had been sizable pockets of slavery in the northern states, but revolutionary idealism, coupled with the growing belief that slavery was inefficient, led one northern state after another to abolish it. By 1804, every northern state had taken some action, usually by passing gradual emancipation laws. By 1830, only a handful of aging blacks remained slaves in the North.

The rising population of northern free blacks gravitated to the cities, where they met a stream of free blacks and fugitive slaves from the Upper South. African Americans constituted a sizable minority in the rapidly expanding cities. Blacks in the seaport cities tended to take stable, low-paying jobs. A few became successful entrepreneurs, while others practiced skilled trades. Many worked as waiters or porters in hotels, as merchant seamen, as barbers, and as servants. Others worked as dockworkers and laborers. Still others became dealers in used clothing, draymen with their own carts and horses, or food vendors in streets and basement shops.

African Americans with money established businesses and institutions of their own. At one end were black-owned gambling houses, saloons, brothels, oyster cellars, and dance halls, which often served a mixed clientele. At the other end were institutions built by self-consciously "respectable" free blacks. Most prominent among these were churches. In Philadelphia, black preachers Richard Allen and Absalom Jones rebelled against segregated seating in St. George's Methodist Church and, in 1794, founded two separate black congregations; by 1800 about 40 percent of Philadelphia's blacks belonged to one of those two churches. The African Methodist Episcopal Church grew from Allen's church, and established itself as a national denomination in 1816. Schools and relief societies, usually associated with churches, grew quickly. Black Masonic lodges attracted hundreds of members. It was from this matrix of black businesses and institutions that black abolitionists—David Walker in Boston, Frederick Douglass in New Bedford and Rochester, the itinerant Sojourner Truth, and many others—would emerge to demand abolition of slavery and equal rights for black citizens.

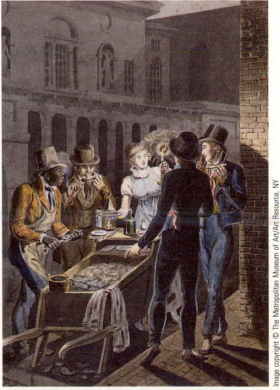

Image copyright © The Metropolitan Museum of Art/Art Resource, NY

A BLACK STREET VENDOR, SELLING OYSTERS IN PHILADELPHIA, CIRCA 1814. *In early 19th-century New York and Philadelphia, African Americans monopolized the public sale of oysters and clams.*

The Beginnings of Modern Racism

In post-revolutionary America, the most important social and political distinction was not between black and white or rich and poor. It was between the heads of independent households and the women, slaves, servants, apprentices, and others who were their dependents. Wage labor and tenancy reduced the number of independent northern whites. They fought that threat in a number of ways: Their skills and labor, they said, constituted a kind of property; their manhood conferred judgment and strength and thus independence. And along with the value of their labor and their manhood, white men discovered the decisive value of white skin.

Whites in the early 19th century began refusing to work alongside blacks. They chased blacks out of skilled jobs by pressuring employers to discriminate, and also by outright violence. As a result, African Americans disappeared from the skilled trades, while many unskilled and semiskilled blacks lost their jobs on the docks and in warehouses. As their old jobs vanished, blacks were systematically excluded from the new jobs that were opening up in factories.

There was trouble off the job as well. Black neighborhoods and institutions came under increasing attack. In the late 1820s and early 1830s, every northern city experienced antiblack rioting. In Philadelphia in 1834, for example, a riot broke out between working-class whites and blacks at a street carnival. Although blacks won the first round, the whites refused to accept defeat. Over the next few nights, they wrecked a black-owned tavern; broke into black households to terrorize families and steal their property; attacked whites who lived with, socialized with, or operated businesses catering to blacks; devastated the African Presbyterian Church; and destroyed a black church on Wharton Street by sawing through its timbers and pulling it down.

Above all, white populists pronounced blacks unfit to be citizens of the republic. The insistence that blacks were incapable of citizenship reinforced an equally natural white male political capacity. The most vicious racist assaults were often carried out beneath symbols of the revolutionary republic: Antiblack mobs in Baltimore, Cincinnati, and Toledo called themselves Minute Men and Sons of Liberty.

The more respectable and powerful whites had long been worried about the mixed-race underclass of the cities and towns. Now, as the disorder that they expected of the lower orders took the form of race riots, the authorities responded. But rather than protect the jobs, churches, schools, businesses, friends, and political rights of African Americans from criminal attack, they determined to stop the trouble by removing black people—from employment, from public festivities, and from their already-limited citizenship. Cities either excluded black children from public schools or set up segregated schools. Blacks were also excluded from white churches or sat in segregated pews. Even the Quakers seated blacks and whites separately.

CITIZENSHIP

As the nation transitioned from a republic to a democracy, patriarchal traditions were supplanted by new institutions of republican citizenship. The revolutionary constitutions of most states retained the colonial freehold (property) qualifications for voting. These granted the vote to from one-half to three-quarters of adult white men. Many of the disenfranchised were dependent sons who expected to inherit citizenship along with land. Some states dropped the freehold clause and gave the vote to all adult men who paid taxes, but with little effect on the voting population. Both the freehold and taxpaying qualifications tended to grant political rights to heads of households, reinforcing classical republican notions that granted full citizenship to independent fathers and not to their dependents.

Between 1790 and 1820, citizenship grounded in fatherhood and proprietorship gave way to a democratic insistence on equal rights for all white men. There were several reasons for that development. The proportion of adult white men who could not meet property qualifications multiplied at an alarming rate. In the new towns and cities, artisans and laborers and even many merchants and professionals did not own real estate. And in the west, new farms were often valued at below property qualifications. This became particularly troublesome after the War of 1812, when a large proportion of veterans could not vote.

In the early 19th century state after state extended the vote to all adult white men. In 1790, only Vermont granted the vote to all free men. Kentucky entered the Union in 1792 without property or taxpaying qualifications; Tennessee followed with a freehold qualification, but only for newcomers who had resided in their counties for less than six months. The federal government dropped the 50-acre freehold qualification in the territories in 1812. Of the eight territories that became states between 1796 and 1821, none kept a property qualification, only three maintained a taxpaying qualification, and five explicitly granted the vote to all white men. In the same years, one eastern state after another widened the franchise. By 1840, only Rhode Island retained a propertied electorate, primarily because Yankee farmers in that state wanted to retain power in a society made up more and more of urban, immigrant wage earners.

Suffrage reform gave political rights to propertyless men and took a long step away from the Founders' republic and toward mass democracy. At the same time, however, reformers explicitly restricted the vote to those who were white and male. New Jersey's revolutionary constitution had granted the vote to "persons" who met a freehold qualification. This loophole enfranchised property-holding widows, many of whom exercised their rights. A law of 1807 abolished property restrictions and gave the vote to all white men. The same law ended female voting. The question of woman suffrage would not be raised again until women raised it in 1848 (see Chapter 12). It would not be settled until well into the 20th century.

New restrictions also applied to African Americans. The revolutionary constitutions of Massachusetts, New Hampshire, and Vermont—northeastern states with small black minorities—granted the vote to free blacks. New York and North Carolina laws gave the vote to "all men" who met the qualifications, and propertied African Americans (a tiny but symbolically crucial minority) in many states routinely exercised the vote. Post-revolutionary laws that extended voting rights to all white men often specifically excluded or severely restricted votes for blacks. Free blacks lost the suffrage in New York, New Jersey, Pennsylvania, Connecticut, Maryland, Tennessee, and North Carolina. By 1840, fully 93 percent of blacks in the North lived in states that either banned or severely restricted their right to vote.

Thus the "universal" suffrage of which many Americans boasted was far from universal. Faced with the disintegration of Jefferson's republic of proprietors, the wielders of power had chosen to blur the emerging distinctions of social class while they hardened the boundaries of sex and race.

Conclusion

By the second quarter of the 19th century, Americans had made a patchwork of regional, class, and ethnic cultures. The new middle classes of the North and West compounded their Protestant and republican inheritance with a new entrepreneurial faith in progress. The result was a way of life grounded in the self-made and morally accountable individual and the sentimentalized (often feminized) domestic unit.

Yet most Americans did not live and think like the middle class. The poorer urban dwellers and farmers of the North remained loyal to the unsentimental, male-dominated families of their fathers and grandfathers, to new and old religious sects that preached human depravity and the mysterious workings of providence, and to the suspicion that perfidy and disorder lurked behind market economics and middle-class culture.

In the South, most white farmers persisted in a neighborhood-based, intensely evangelical, and socially conservative way of life. Southern planters, although they shared in the northern elite's belief in material progress and the magic of the market, were bound by family values, a system of slave labor, and a code of honor that was strikingly at variance with middle-class faith in an orderly universe and perfectible individuals. Slaves in these years continued to make cultural forms of their own. Despite their exclusion from the white world of liberty and equality, they tied their aspirations to the family, to an evangelical Protestant God, and to the individual and collective dignity that republics promise to their citizens.

CHAPTER REVIEW

Review Questions

1. In what ways did literacy and print help to democratize American culture?

2. What were the central cultural maxims of the emerging northern middle class?

3. Within the North, what were the alternatives to middle-class culture?

4. In what specific ways did evangelical Protestantism act as a conservative force within southern culture?

Critical Thinking Questions

1. Compare and contrast the domestic lives and family values of the northern middle class and the southern planter elite.

2. Compare and contrast the racial orders of the North and South in 1850. How do you explain the similarities and differences?

Identifications

Review your understanding of the following key terms, people, and events for this chapter.

Sunday schools, p. 228
middle class, p. 228
anxious bench, p. 229
Sarah Josepha Hale, p. 230

Uncle Tom's Cabin, p. 230
domestic fiction, p. 230
deism, p. 231
crisis conversion, p. 231

Restorationism, p. 232
circuit-riding preachers, p. 232
postmillennialism, p. 233

Joseph Smith, p. 236
blood sports, p. 236
minstrel show, p. 238
camp meeting, p. 240

DISCOVERY

What kind of culture emerged out of the market revolution that was discussed in Chapter 9? What was the impact on American families of the popular culture discussed in Chapter 10?

In thinking about this question, begin by breaking it down into the components shown below. A discussion of the significance of each component should appear in your answer.

The Impact of the Market on Family Life

Look at the illustration of domestic life on page 230. What does it suggest about how middle-class Americans saw their lives and their daily activities? What did the family want to reveal about their life at home? How does the illustration reflect the artist's definitions of *domesticity* and *sentimentality*? What would a photograph of your family suggest to future generations about the way you lived?

The Impact of the "New Popular Culture" on Family Life

Examine the image of an evening at the theater in the early 19th century. Does this activity seem to attract more men or women? How do you account for this gender difference? Is this gender difference important?

AN EARLY PRINT OF "JIM CROW" RICE AT NEW YORK'S BOWERY THEATER

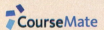

Visit the CourseMate website at www.cengagebrain.com for additional study tools and review materials for this chapter.

DEMOCRATS AND WHIGS

National political leaders from the 1820s onward faced two persistent problems. First, economic development and territorial expansion made new demands on government—demands that involved federal participation in state and local affairs. Second, a deepening rift between slave and free states rendered such involvement contested and dangerous.

The Whig Party proposed a solution that would solve both problems. The national government should subsidize roads and canals, foster industry with protective tariffs, and maintain a national bank to control credit and currency. The result would be a national market society. If the South, the West, and the Northeast profited by doing business with each other, the argument went, sectional jealousies would quiet down. Jacksonian Democrats, on the other hand, argued that the Whig plan violated the rights of states and benefited wealthy insiders. Most dangerous of all, they said, such an activist national government would anger the slaveholding South. To counter both threats, Jacksonians resurrected Jefferson's rhetoric of states' rights and inactive, inexpensive government—all of it inflected in the code of white male equality, domestic patriarchy, and racial slavery.

TIMELINE

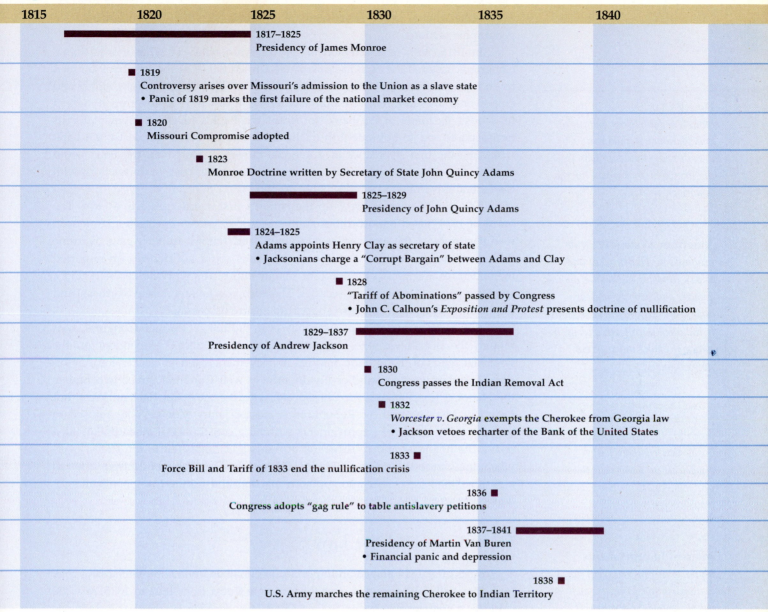

1815	1820	1825	1830	1835	1840

1817–1825
Presidency of James Monroe

1819
Controversy arises over Missouri's admission to the Union as a slave state
• Panic of 1819 marks the first failure of the national market economy

1820
Missouri Compromise adopted

1823
Monroe Doctrine written by Secretary of State John Quincy Adams

1825–1829
Presidency of John Quincy Adams

1824–1825
Adams appoints Henry Clay as secretary of state
• Jacksonians charge a "Corrupt Bargain" between Adams and Clay

1828
"Tariff of Abominations" passed by Congress
• John C. Calhoun's *Exposition and Protest* presents doctrine of nullification

1829–1837
Presidency of Andrew Jackson

1830
Congress passes the Indian Removal Act

1832
Worcester v. Georgia exempts the Cherokee from Georgia law
• Jackson vetoes recharter of the Bank of the United States

1833
Force Bill and Tariff of 1833 end the nullification crisis

1836
Congress adopts "gag rule" to table antislavery petitions

1837–1841
Presidency of Martin Van Buren
• Financial panic and depression

1838
U.S. Army marches the remaining Cherokee to Indian Territory

© Cengage Learning

THE AMERICAN SYSTEM

The 14th Congress, which met in the last days of 1815, was made up overwhelmingly of Jeffersonian Republicans. Nevertheless, the Congress reversed the positions taken by Jefferson's old party. The War of 1812 had demonstrated that the United States was unable to coordinate a fiscal and military effort. It had also convinced many Republicans that reliance on foreign trade rendered America dependent on Europe. The nation, they said, must abandon Jefferson's export-oriented agrarianism and encourage national independence through commerce and manufacturing.

FOCUS QUESTION

What were the components of the "American System"? What did the American System promise to accomplish?

National Republicans

Henry Clay headed the drive for what he called the **American System,** a program of **protective tariffs**, **internal improvements**, and a national bank. The American

Henry Clay *Speaker of the House, senator from Kentucky, and National Republican presidential candidate who was the principal spokesman for the American System.*

American System *Program proposed by Henry Clay and others to foster national economic growth and interdependence among the geographical sections. It included a protective tariff, a national bank, and internal improvements.*

protective tariff *Tariff that increases the price of imported goods that compete with American products and thus protects American manufacturers from foreign competition.*

internal improvements *Nineteenth-century term for transportation facilities such as roads, canals, and railroads.*

System, he argued, would foster national economic growth and harmony between geographic sections.

In 1816, with no discussion of the constitutionality of what it was doing, Congress chartered the Second Bank of the United States as the sole bank entitled to do business throughout the republic. It was headquartered in Philadelphia and empowered to establish branch offices wherever it saw fit. The government agreed to deposit its funds in the Bank, to accept the Bank's notes as payment for its transactions, and to buy one-fifth of the Bank's stock. Notes issued by the Bank would be the first semblance of a national currency. Moreover, the Bank could regulate the currency by demanding that state bank notes used in transactions with the federal government be redeemable in gold.

The same Congress drew up the nation's first overtly protective tariff. The Tariff of 1816 raised import duties an average of 25 percent, protecting American manufacturers at the expense of consumers and foreign trade. Again, wartime difficulties had paved the way: Since Americans could not depend on imported manufactures, Congress saw domestic manufactures as a patriotic necessity and a spur to commerce between the sections. The tariff was favored in the Northeast and the West, with enough southern support to ensure its passage.

Bills for transportation projects, however, did not get through Congress, even though the British wartime blockade had made Americans dependent on the wretched roads of the interior. Internal improvements were subject to local ambitions, and they were constitutionally doubtful as well. Congress agreed to complete the National Road linking the Chesapeake with the trans-Appalachian West, but President Madison and his Republican successor James Monroe both refused to support further internal improvements without a constitutional amendment. As a result, the financing and construction of roads and canals fell to the states, overwhelmingly the northern states. Henry Clay watched his vision of transportation as a nationalizing force turn into southern inaction and northern regionalization, a dangerous trend that continued throughout his long political life.

Commerce and the Law

The courts after 1815 played an important nationalizing and commercializing role. John Marshall, who presided over the Supreme Court from 1801 to 1835, saw the Court as a conservative hedge against Democratic legislatures. His early decisions

THE SECOND BANK OF THE UNITED STATES. *Located in downtown Philadelphia and modeled on the Parthenon in classical Athens, the new bank building was intended to be both republican and awesome. It was from here that gentlemen-directors attempted to impose their kind of order on the exploding monetary and credit systems of the 1820s and 1830s.*

protected the independence of the courts and their right to review legislation (see Chapter 7). From 1816 onward, his decisions encouraged business and strengthened the national government at the expense of the states.

Marshall's most important decisions protected the sanctity of contracts and corporate charters against state legislatures. For example, in *Dartmouth College v. Woodward* (1816), Marshall ruled that Dartmouth's corporate charter could not be altered by a state legislature. Though in this case the Supreme Court was protecting Dartmouth's chartered privileges, the decision also protected turnpike and canal companies, manufacturing corporations, and other ventures that held privileges under corporate charters granted by state governments. Once the charters had been granted, the states could neither regulate the corporations nor cancel their privileges. Corporate charters acquired the legal status of contracts, beyond the reach of democratic politics.

Two weeks after the *Dartmouth* decision, Marshall handed down the majority opinion in *McCulloch v. Maryland.* The Maryland legislature had attempted to tax the Baltimore branch of the Bank of the United States, and the Bank had challenged its right to do so. The Court decided in favor of the Bank. Marshall stated that the Constitution granted the federal government "implied powers" that included chartering the Bank, and he denied Maryland's right to tax the Bank or any other federal agency. "Americans," he said, "did not design to make their government dependent on the states." And yet many, particularly in Marshall's native South, remained certain that that was precisely what the Founders had intended.

Meanwhile, the state courts were working equally profound transformations of American law. In the early republic, state courts had often viewed property not only as a private possession but also as part of a neighborhood. When a miller built a dam that flooded upriver farms or impaired the fishery, the courts might make him take those interests into account, often in ways that reduced the business uses of his property. By 1830, New England courts routinely granted the owners of industrial mill sites unrestricted water rights, even when the exercise of those rights damaged their neighbors. As early as 1805, the New York Supreme Court in *Palmer v. Mulligan* had asserted that the right to develop property for business purposes was inherent in the ownership of property.

1819

Jacksonian democracy was rooted in two events that occurred in 1819. First, the debate on Missouri's admission as a slave state revealed the centrality and vulnerability of slavery within the Union. Second, a financial collapse led many Americans to doubt the market revolution's compatibility with the Jeffersonian republic. By 1820, politicians were determined to reconstruct the limited-government, states'-rights coalition that had elected Thomas Jefferson.

The Argument over Missouri

Early in 1819, slaveholding Missouri applied to become the first new state to be carved out of the Louisiana Purchase. New York congressman James Tallmadge, Jr., quickly proposed two amendments to the Missouri statehood bill. The first would bar additional slaves from being brought into Missouri. The second would emancipate Missouri slaves born after admission when they reached their 25th birthday.

FOCUS QUESTION

What enduring political issues were raised by the Missouri controversy and the Panic of 1819?

The congressional debates on the Missouri question were about sectional power, not the morality of slavery. Northerners resented the added representation in Congress and in the Electoral College that the "three-fifths" rule granted to the slave states (see Chapter 6). The rule had added significantly to southern power: In 1790, the South, with 40 percent of the white population, controlled 47 percent of the votes in Congress.

In 1819, the North held a majority in the House of Representatives. The South controlled a bare majority in the Senate. Voting on the Tallmadge amendments was starkly sectional: The House accepted them, but southern senators, with the help of the two Illinois senators and three northerners, defeated them. Deadlocked between a Senate in favor of admitting Missouri as a slave state and a House dead set against it, Congress broke off the angry debate and went home.

The Missouri Compromise

In the winter of 1819–1820, a new Congress passed the legislative package known as the **Missouri Compromise.** Massachusetts offered its northern counties as the new free state of Maine, neutralizing fears that the South would gain votes in the Senate with the admission of Missouri. Senator Jesse Thomas of Illinois then proposed the so-called Thomas Proviso: If the North would admit Missouri as a slave state, the South would agree to outlaw slavery in territories above 36°30′ N latitude—a line extending from the southern border of Missouri to Spanish territory. This opened Arkansas Territory to slavery and banned slavery in the remainder of the Louisiana Territory.

Congress admitted Maine with little debate, but the Thomas Proviso met northern opposition. A joint Senate–House committee separated the two bills. With half of the southern representatives and nearly all of the northerners supporting it, the Thomas Proviso passed. Congress next took up the admission of Missouri. With the votes of a solid South and 14 compromise-minded northerners, Missouri entered the Union as a slave state.

The Missouri crisis brought the South's commitment to slavery and the North's resentment of southern political power into collision. While northerners vowed to relinquish no more territory to slavery, southerners talked openly of disunion and civil war. Viewing the crisis from Monticello, the aging Thomas Jefferson was distraught: "A geographical line, coinciding with a marked principle, moral and political, once conceived and held up to the angry passions of men, will never be obliterated; every new irritation will mark it deeper and deeper. . . . This momentous question, like a fire-bell in the night, awakened and filled me with terror. I considered it at once the knell of the Union."

The Panic of 1819

Politicians debated the Missouri question against a backdrop of economic depression. The origins of the Panic of 1819 were international: European agriculture recovered from the Napoleonic wars, reducing the demand for American foodstuffs; revolution in Latin America cut off the supply of precious metals (the base of the international money supply); debt-ridden European governments hoarded the available specie; and American bankers and businessmen met the situation by expanding credit and issuing banknotes that were mere dreams of real money.

Congress had chartered the Second Bank of the United States partly to impose order on this situation, but the Bank itself became part of the problem. The western branch offices in Cincinnati and Lexington became embroiled in the speculative boom, and insiders at the Baltimore branch hatched schemes to enrich themselves.

Missouri Compromise
Compromise that maintained sectional balance in Congress by admitting Missouri as a slave state and Maine as a free state and by drawing a line west from the 36°30′ parallel separating future slave and free states.

In 1819, the Bank's president, Langdon Cheves of South Carolina, curtailed credit and demanded that state banknotes received by the Bank of the United States be redeemed in specie. By doing so, Cheves rescued the Bank from the paper economy created by state-chartered banks, but when the state banks were forced to redeem their notes in specie, they demanded payment from their own borrowers, and the national money and credit system collapsed.

A depression ensued. Businesses failed, and hundreds of thousands of workers lost their jobs. In Philadelphia, unemployment reached 75 percent. A tent city of the unemployed sprang up on the outskirts of Baltimore. The situation was no better in the countryside. Faced with a disaster that none could control and that few understood, many Americans directed their resentment onto the Bank of the United States.

REPUBLICAN REVIVAL

Without opposition, Jefferson's dominant Republican Party had lost its way. The nationalist Congress of 1816 had enacted much of the Federalist program under the name of Republicanism. The result, said the old Republicans, was an aggressive government that helped bring on the Panic of 1819. At the same time, the collapse of Republican unity in Congress had allowed the Missouri question to degenerate into a sectional free-for-all. By 1820, many Republicans were calling for a Jeffersonian revival that would limit government power and guarantee southern rights within the Union.

Martin Van Buren Leads the Way

Among those Republicans was Senator Martin Van Buren of New York. Van Buren had built his political career out of a commitment to Jeffersonian principles, personal charm, and party discipline. Although the Founders had denounced parties, Van Buren viewed them as necessary democratic tools. He insisted that competition and party divisions were inevitable and good, but that they must be made to serve the republic. Working with like-minded politicians, Van Buren reconstructed the coalition of northern and southern agrarians that had elected Thomas Jefferson. The result was the Democratic Party and, ultimately, a national two-party system that persisted until the eve of the Civil War.

The Election of 1824

Van Buren and his allies controlled the Republican **congressional caucus,** the body that traditionally chose the party's presidential candidates. They nominated William H. Crawford, a staunch Georgia Republican, in 1824. With Republican Party unity broken, the list of sectional candidates grew. John Quincy Adams, New England's **favorite son,** was the son of a Federalist president and secretary of state under Monroe. Henry Clay of Kentucky expected to carry the West. John C. Calhoun of South Carolina announced his candidacy, then dropped out and put himself forth as the sole candidate for vice president.

The wild card was **Andrew Jackson** of Tennessee, who in 1824 was known only as a military hero. He was also a frontier nabob with a reputation for violence. According to Jackson's detractors, impetuosity marked his public life as well.

What were the events and political motives that contributed to the Republican revival that formed around Andrew Jackson?

congressional caucus *In the early republic, the group of congressmen that traditionally chose the party's presidential candidates.*

favorite son *Candidate for president supported by delegates from his home state.*

Andrew Jackson *President of the United States (1829–1837) and founder of the Democratic Party who signed the Indian Removal Act, vetoed the Second Bank, and signed the Force Bill.*

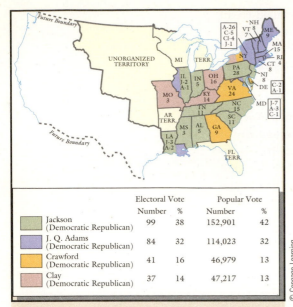

		Electoral Vote		Popular Vote	
		Number	%	Number	%
■	Jackson (Democratic Republican)	99	38	152,901	42
■	J. Q. Adams (Democratic Republican)	84	32	114,023	32
■	Crawford (Democratic Republican)	41	16	46,979	13
■	Clay (Democratic Republican)	37	14	47,217	13

© Cengage Learning

Map 11.1 Presidential Election, 1824. *Voting in the four-cornered contest of 1824 was starkly sectional. John Quincy Adams carried his native New England, while Crawford and Clay carried only a few states in their own sections. Only Andrew Jackson enjoyed national support: He carried states in every section but New England, and he ran a strong second in many of the states that were awarded to other candidates.*

As commander of U.S. military forces in the South in 1818, Jackson had, without orders, invaded Spanish Florida. He occupied Spanish forts, executed Seminoles whom he claimed were raiding into the United States, and hanged two British subjects. After being appointed governor of the newly acquired Florida, Jackson retired from public life in 1821. In 1824 eastern politicians knew Jackson only as a "military chieftain," "the Napoleon of the woods."

Easterners failed to take into account Jackson's popularity. In the 16 states that chose presidential electors by popular vote, Jackson polled 152,901 votes to Adams's 114,023 and Clay's 47,217. Crawford, who suffered a crippling stroke during the campaign, won 46,979 votes. Jackson's support was national. He carried 84 percent of the votes of his own Southwest; won in Pennsylvania, New Jersey, North Carolina, Indiana, and Illinois; and ran a close second in several other states.

"A Corrupt Bargain"

Jackson assumed that he had won: He had received 42 percent of the popular vote to his nearest rival's 32 percent, and he was clearly the nation's choice. But his 99 electoral votes were 32 shy of the plurality demanded by the Constitution. Acting under the Twelfth Amendment, the House of Representatives selected a president from among the top three candidates. As the candidate with the fewest electoral votes, Henry Clay was eliminated, but he remained Speaker of the House and had enough support to throw the election to either Jackson or Adams. Years later, Jackson claimed that Clay offered to support him in exchange for Clay's appointment as secretary of state—an office that traditionally led to the presidency. When Jackson turned him down, according to Jacksonian legend, Clay made Adams the same offer. Adams accepted what became known as the **"Corrupt Bargain."** Clay's supporters, joined by several old Federalists, switched to Adams, giving him a one-vote victory. President Adams appointed Henry Clay as his secretary of state. Reaction to the alleged Corrupt Bargain dominated the Adams administration and created a rhetoric of intrigue and betrayal that nourished a rising democratic movement.

"THE SYMPTOMS OF A LOCKED JAW." *In 1827, Henry Clay published a rebuttal of Jacksonian charges that he had participated in a Corrupt Bargain to deliver the presidency to John Quincy Adams. Here, a pro-Clay cartoonist displays Clay as a tailor in the act of sewing Andrew Jackson's mouth shut. Neither the rebuttal nor the cartoon worked: The long-term suspicions of the bargain with Adams ruined Clay's chances to become president.*

Library of Congress, Prints and Photographs Division

Jacksonian Melodrama

Andrew Jackson regarded the intrigues that robbed him of the presidency in 1825 as the culmination of a long train of corruption that the nation had suffered over the previous 10 years. Although in the campaign he had made only vague policy statements, he had firm ideas of what had gone wrong with the republic. He claimed that the Panic of 1819 had been brought on by self-serving miscreants in the Bank of the United States. The national debt was another source of corruption; it must be paid off and never allowed to recur. The federal government under James Monroe was filled with swindlers, and in the name of a vague nationalism they had taken power for themselves and schemed against the liberties of the people. Politicians had been bought off, said Jackson, and had stolen the presidency.

More completely than any of his rivals, Jackson captured the rhetoric of the revolutionary republic. And with his fixation on secrecy, corruption, and intrigues, he transformed both that rhetoric and his own biography into popular melodrama. With a political alchemy that his rivals never understood, Jackson submerged old notions of republican citizenship into a firm faith in majoritarian democracy: Individuals might become selfish and corrupt, he believed, but a democratic majority was, by its very nature, opposed to corruption and governmental excess. Thus the republic was safe only when governed by the will of the majority: "My fervent prayers are that our republican government may be perpetual, and the people alone by their virtue, and independent exercise of their free suffrage can make it perpetual."

Corrupt Bargain *Following the election of 1824, Andrew Jackson and his supporters alleged that, in a "corrupt bargain," Henry Clay sold his support during the House vote in the disputed election of 1824 to John Quincy Adams in exchange for appointment as secretary of state.*

ADAMS VERSUS JACKSON

While Jackson plotted revenge, John Quincy Adams assumed the duties of the presidency.

Nationalism in an International Arena

Adams had been an extraordinarily successful secretary of state under Monroe. In the Rush-Bagot Treaty of 1817 and the British-American Convention of 1818, Adams helped pacify the Great Lakes, restore American fishing rights off of Canada, and draw the U.S.–Canadian boundary west to the Rocky Mountains. He pacified the southern border as well. In 1819, the Adams-Onís Treaty procured Florida for the United States and defined the U.S.–Spanish border west of the Mississippi in ways that gave the Americans claims to the Pacific Coast in the Northwest.

Trickier problems had arisen when Spanish colonies in the Americas declared their independence. The European powers, victorious over Napoleon and determined to roll back the republican revolution, talked openly of helping the Spanish or of annexing South American territory for themselves. The Americans and the British opposed such a move. The British proposed a joint statement outlawing the interference of any outside power (including themselves) in Latin America, but Adams wanted the United States to make its own policy. In 1823 he wrote what became known as the **Monroe Doctrine.** It declared American opposition to any European attempt at New World colonization without (as the British had wanted) denying the right of the United States to annex new territory. Although the international community knew that the British navy, and not the Monroe Doctrine, kept Europe out of the Americas, Adams had announced the American intention to become the preeminent power in the Western Hemisphere.

FOCUS QUESTION

What were the principal events of the John Quincy Adams administration, and how did they contribute to his defeat in 1828?

Monroe Doctrine *Foreign policy doctrine proposed by Secretary of State John Quincy Adams in 1823. It denied the right of European powers to establish new colonies in the Americas while maintaining the United States' right to annex new territory.*

Nationalism at Home

As president, Adams tried to translate his fervent nationalism into domestic policy. In his first annual message to Congress, he warned against being "palsied by the will of our constituents" and outlined an ambitious program for national development under the auspices of the federal government: roads, canals, a national university, a national astronomical observatory ("lighthouses of the skies"), and other costly initiatives.

Congressmen could not believe their ears. Adams had received only one in three votes and had entered office accused of intrigues against the democratic will, and now he told Congress to pass an ambitious program and not to be "palsied" by the will of the electorate. Even congressmen who favored Adams's program were afraid to vote for it. Hostile politicians and journalists never tired of joking about Adams's "lighthouses to the skies." More lasting, however, was the connection they drew between federal public works projects and high taxes, intrusive government, the denial of democratic majorities, and expanded opportunities for corruption. Congress never acted on the president's proposals, and the Adams administration emerged as little more than a long prelude to the election of 1828.

The Birth of the Democratic Party

As early as 1825, it was clear that the election of 1828 would pit Adams against Andrew Jackson. With their candidate Crawford hopelessly incapacitated, Van Buren and other Republicans switched their allegiance to Jackson. They wanted Jackson elected not only as a popular hero but also as head of a new Democratic Party that would continue the states'-rights, limited-government positions of the old Jeffersonian Republicans.

Van Buren began preparations for 1828 with a visit to John C. Calhoun. Calhoun was moving along the road from postwar nationalism to states'-rights conservatism. He also wanted to stay on as vice president and thus keep his presidential hopes alive. After convincing Calhoun to support Jackson, Van Buren wrote a letter to Thomas Ritchie, editor of the *Richmond Enquirer* and leader of Virginia's Republicans. Van Buren proposed to revive the alliance of "the planters of the South and the plain Republicans of the North" that had elected Jefferson. A new Democratic Party, committed to states' rights and minimal government and dependent on the votes of both slaveholding and nonslaveholding states, would ensure democracy, the continuation of slavery, and the preservation of the Union.

The Election of 1828

The presidential campaign of 1828 was an exercise in slander rather than a debate on public issues. Jacksonians hammered away at the Corrupt Bargain of 1825, while the Adams forces attacked Jackson's character. A newspaper circulated the rumor that Jackson was a bastard and that his mother was a prostitute, but the worst slander centered on his marriage. In 1790, Jackson had married Rachel Donelson, who was estranged but not divorced from a man named Robards. Branding the marriage an "abduction," the Adams team screamed that Jackson lived with Donelson in a state of "open and notorious lewdness."

The Adams strategy backfired. While many voters agreed that Jackson's "passionate" nature disqualified him, many others criticized Adams for making Jackson's private life a public issue. Whatever the legality of their marriage, Andrew and Rachel Jackson had lived as models of marital fidelity for nearly 40 years. On the one hand, Jackson's supporters accused the Adams campaign of violating privacy and honor. On the other, they defended Jackson's marriage as a triumph of what was right and just over what was narrowly legal. The attempt to brand Jackson as a lawless man, in fact, enhanced his image as a melodramatic hero who battled unscrupulous, legalistic enemies by drawing on his natural nobility and force of will.

The campaign caught the public imagination. Voter turnout was double what it had been in 1824, totaling 56.3 percent. Jackson won with 56 percent of the popular vote and a margin of 178 to 83 in electoral votes. It was a clear triumph of democracy over genteel statesmanship, of limited government over expansive nationalism, and of the South and West over New England. Just as clearly, it was a victory of popular melodrama over old forms of cultural gentility. (See Map 11.2.)

A People's Inauguration

Newspapers estimated that 15,000 to 20,000 citizens witnessed Jackson's inauguration on March 4, 1829. They were "like the inundation of the northern barbarians into Rome," remarked Senator Daniel Webster. Jackson himself arrived at the Capitol in deep mourning. In December, his wife Rachel read the accusations that had been made against her and fainted on the spot. Although she had been in poor health, no one would ever convince Jackson that her death in January had not been caused by his political enemies.

Jackson's inaugural address was vague. He promised "proper respect" for states' rights and a "spirit of equity, caution, and compromise" on the question of the tariff. He promised to reform the civil service, and he vowed to retire the national debt. Beyond that, he said little, although he took every opportunity to flatter the popular majority. He had been elected "by the choice of a free people," and he pledged "the zealous dedication of my humble abilities to their service and their good." He finished by reminding Americans that a benign providence looked over them.

The crowd followed him to the White House, invading the mansion, muddying the carpets, tipping things over, breaking dishes, and standing in dirty boots on upholstered chairs. Jackson retreated to avoid being crushed, while his staff lured the crowd outside by moving the punch bowls and liquor to the lawn.

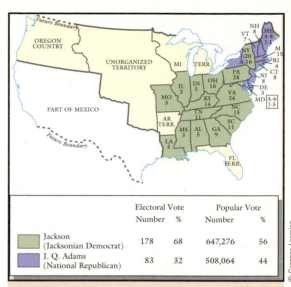

	Electoral Vote		Popular Vote	
	Number	%	Number	%
Jackson (Jacksonian Democrat)	178	68	647,276	56
J. Q. Adams (National Republican)	83	32	508,064	44

© Cengage Learning

Map 11.2 Presidential Election, 1828. *The 1828 presidential contest was a clear result of the organizing efforts that were building a national Democratic Party under the name of Andrew Jackson. Jackson picked up all of the states that had gone for Crawford or Clay in 1824, leaving only New England and small portions of the mid-Atlantic for John Quincy Adams.*

White House Collection

THE PRESIDENT'S LEVEE. *Robert Cruikshank drew Jackson's inaugural reception with men and women of all classes, children, dogs, and bucking horses celebrating the Old General's victory. Cruikshank subtitled his lithograph* All Creation Going to the White House.

The Spoils System

Martin Van Buren, who had mobilized much of the support for Jackson, was the new secretary of state—positioned to succeed Jackson as president—and Jackson's most valued adviser. Other appointments were less promising, for Jackson filled cabinet posts with old friends and political supporters who sometimes proved unfit for their jobs. Opponents complained that Jackson was replacing able public servants with political hacks. They soon had convincing evidence: Samuel Swarthout, whom Jackson had appointed collector of the Port of New York, stole $1.2 million and took off for Europe.

Actually, much of the furor over Jackson's **"spoils system"** was misdirected. He aimed, Jackson claimed, only to institute "rotation in office." Arguing that most government jobs could be performed by any honest, reasonably intelligent citizen, Jackson proposed ending the long tenures that, he said, turned the civil service into "support of the few at the expense of the many." Jackson removed about 1 in 10 executive appointees during his eight years in office, and his chosen replacements were as wealthy and well educated as their predecessors. They were, however, decidedly *political* appointees. Acting on his own need for personal loyalty and on the advice of Van Buren, Jackson filled vacancies with Democrats who had worked for his election.

spoils system *System by which the victorious political party rewarded its supporters with government jobs.*

JACKSONIAN DEMOCRACY AND THE SOUTH

FOCUS QUESTION

At the national level, how did Jacksonian Democrats and their rivals deal with widening differences between North and South?

Andrew Jackson was a national figure, but his base of his support was in the South, where he won 8 of every 10 votes in 1828. Southerners were wary of an activist government controlled by a northern majority. They looked to Jackson as a Tennessee planter and republican fundamentalist. But there was disagreement within the Jackson administration on how to protect southern interests. Vice President Calhoun believed that states had the right to veto federal legislation and even in extreme cases to secede from the Union. Secretary of State Van Buren insisted that the Union was inviolable and that the South's best safeguard was in a political party committed to states' rights within the Union.

Southerners and Indians

When Jackson entered office, a final crisis between frontier whites and the native people of the eastern woodlands was under way. By the 1820s, few Native Americans remained east of the Appalachians. But in the Old Southwest 60,000 Cherokees, Creeks, Choctaws, Chickasaws, and Seminoles remained on their ancestral lands, with tenure guaranteed by federal treaties that (at least implicitly) recognized them as sovereign peoples. Congress had appropriated funds for schools, tools, seeds, and training to help these Civilized Tribes make the transition to farming. Most government officials assumed that the tribes would eventually trade their old lands and use their farming skills on new land west of the Mississippi.

White farmers coveted the Indians' land, and states'-rights southerners denied the federal government's authority to make treaties or to recognize sovereign peoples within their states. Resistance centered in Georgia, where Governor George Troup brought native lands under the state's jurisdiction and then turned them over to poor whites by way of lotteries.

The Cherokees pressed the issue in 1827 by declaring themselves a republic with its own constitution, government, courts, and police. At the same time, a gold discovery on their land made it even more attractive to whites. The Georgia legislature promptly declared Cherokee law null and void, extended Georgia's authority into Cherokee country, and began surveying the lands for sale. Alabama and Mississippi quickly followed Georgia's lead by extending state authority over Indian lands and denying federal jurisdiction.

Indian Removal

President Jackson agreed that the federal government could not recognize native sovereignty within a state and declared that he could not protect the Civilized Tribes from state governments. Instead, he offered to remove them to federal land west of the Mississippi, where they would be under the authority of the federal government. Congress made that offer official in the **Indian Removal Act** of 1830.

The Cherokees had taken their claims of sovereignty to court in the late 1820s. In 1830, John Marshall's Supreme Court ruled in *Cherokee Nation v. Georgia* that the Indians were not sovereign peoples but "domestic dependent nations," dependents of the federal government and not of the state of Georgia, although somehow "nations" as well. In *Worcester v. Georgia* (1832), the court banned Georgia's extension of state law into Cherokee land. President Jackson ignored the decision, however, reportedly telling a congressman, "John Marshall has made his decision: *now let him enforce it!*" Jackson sat back as the southwestern states encroached on the Civilized Tribes. In 1838, his successor, Martin Van Buren, sent the U.S. Army to march the 18,000 remaining Cherokee to Oklahoma. Four thousand of them died along this "Trail of Tears," of exposure, disease, starvation, and white depredation.

Indian removal had profound political consequences. It strengthened Jackson's reputation as an enemy of the rule of law and a friend of local, "democratic" solutions. It also reaffirmed the link between racism and white democracy in the South and announced Jackson's commitment to state sovereignty and limited federal authority.

Southerners, the Tariff, and Nullification

In 1828, Jacksonians in Congress passed a tariff, hoping to win votes for Jackson in the upcoming presidential election. Assured of support in the South, they fished for

Indian Removal Act *(1830) Legislation that offered the native peoples of the lower South the option of removal to federal lands west of the Mississippi. Those who did not take the offer were removed by force in 1838.*

TRAIL OF TEARS. *In 1838 the U.S. Army marched 18,000 Cherokee men, women, and children, along with their animals and whatever they could carry, out of their home territory and into Oklahoma. At least 4,000—most of them old or very young—died on the march.*

The Trail of Tears (oil on canvas), Lindneux, Robert Ottokar (1871-1970) / Woolaroc Museum, Oklahoma, USA / Peter Newark Western Americana / The Bridgeman Art Library International

votes in the mid-Atlantic states and the Northwest by protecting raw wool, flax, molasses, hemp, and distilled spirits. The new tariff pleased northern and western farmers but worried the South. Protective tariffs diminished exports of southern cotton and other staples and raised the price of manufactured goods. Calling the new bill a "Tariff of Abominations," southern state legislatures denounced it as "unconstitutional, unwise, unjust, unequal, and oppressive."

South Carolina, guided by Vice President Calhoun, led the opposition. Calhoun concluded that southern states could protect themselves from national majorities only if they possessed the power to veto, or **nullify**, federal legislation within their boundaries. In his 1828 *Exposition and Protest*, Calhoun anticipated the secessionist arguments of 1861: The Union was a voluntary compact between sovereign states, states were the ultimate judges of the validity of federal law, and states could break the compact if they wished.

Nullification was extreme, and Calhoun and his friends tried to avoid using it. They knew that President Jackson was a states'-rights slaveholder and assumed that Vice President Calhoun would succeed to the presidency and would protect southern interests. They were wrong on both counts. Jackson favored states' rights but only within a perpetual Union. A tariff was ultimately a matter of foreign policy, clearly within the jurisdiction of the federal government. In Jackson's mind, to allow a state to veto a tariff would be to deny the legal existence of the United States.

Having rejected nullification, Jackson asked Congress to reduce the tariff rates in the hope that he could isolate the nullifiers from southerners who simply hated the tariff. The Tariff of 1832 lowered the rates but still affirmed the principle of protectionism. That, along with Boston abolitionist William Lloyd Garrison's declaration of war on slavery in 1831, followed by Nat Turner's bloody slave uprising in Virginia that same year (see Chapter 9), intensified southern white distrust of outside authority. South Carolina called a state convention that nullified the Tariffs of 1828 and 1832.

In Washington, President Jackson raged that nullification (not to mention the right of secession that followed logically from it) was illegal. Insisting that "Disunion . . . is *treason*," he asked Congress for a Force Bill empowering him to personally lead a federal army into South Carolina. At the same time, however, he supported the rapid reduction of tariffs. When Democratic attempts at reduction bogged down, Henry Clay, now back in the Senate, took on the tricky legislative task of rescuing his beloved protective tariff while quieting southern fears. The result was the Compromise Tariff of 1833, which, by lowering tariffs over the course of several years, gave southern planters the relief they demanded while maintaining moderate protectionism and allowing northern manufacturers time to adjust to the lower rates. Congress also passed the Force Bill. Jackson signed both into law.

With that, the nullification crisis came to a quiet end. No other southern state joined South Carolina in nullifying the tariff. Deprived of their issue and most of their support, the South Carolina nullifiers declared victory and disbanded their convention—but not before nullifying the Force Bill. Jackson overlooked that last defiant gesture because he had accomplished what he wanted: He had asserted a perpetual Union, and he had protected southern interests within it.

The "Petticoat Wars" and the Fall of Calhoun

The spoils system, Indian removal, nullification, and other questions of Jackson's first term were fought out against a backdrop of gossip and angry division within Jackson's government. The talk centered on Peggy O'Neal Timberlake, a Washington tavern-keeper's daughter who, in January 1829, had married John Henry Eaton, Jackson's old friend and soon to be his secretary of war. Eaton was middle-aged; his

nullification *Beginning in the late 1820s, John C. Calhoun and others argued that the Union was a voluntary compact between sovereign states, that states were the ultimate judges of the constitutionality of federal law, that states could nullify federal laws within their borders, and that they had the right to secede from the Union.*

HISTORY THROUGH FILM

Amistad (1997)

Directed by Steven Spielberg; starring Matthew McConaughey (Roger Baldwin), Morgan Freeman (Theodore Joadson), Anthony Hopkins (John Quincy Adams), Djimon Hounsou (Cinque)

In 1839 an American cruiser seized the Cuban slave ship *Amistad* off the shore of Long Island. The ship carried 41 Africans who had revolted, killed the captain and crew, and commandeered the ship—along with two Spanish slave dealers who had bargained for their lives by promising to sail the ship east to Africa, then steered for North America. The Africans were imprisoned at New Haven and tried for piracy and murder in federal court. The government of Spain demanded their return, and southern leaders pressured President Van Buren for a "friendly" decision. The legal case centered on whether the Africans were Cuban slaves or kidnapped Africans. (The international slave trade was by then illegal.) The New Haven court acquitted them, the federal government appealed the case, and the Supreme Court freed them again. The Africans were returned to Sierra Leone.

The Africans spend most of the movie in a dark jail or in court, and the film centers on them and their experiences with two groups of Americans: the abolitionists who are trying to free them and the political and legal officials who want to hang them, largely to keep their own political system intact. Spielberg's abolitionists are Lewis Tappan; a black activist (Morgan Freeman); an obscure young white lawyer (Matthew McConaughey); and, in the grand finale, congressman and former president John Quincy Adams (Anthony Hopkins). In the historical case, the defense was handled by veteran abolitionists or by persons who had been working with abolitionists for a long time. Spielberg shaped this group to tell his own story, beginning with reluctant and confused reformers and politicians who, along with the audience, gradually realize the moral imperatives of the case.

In one of the film's more powerful sequences the Africans' leader, Cinque (Djimon Hounsou), through a translator, tells his story to the lawyer: his village life in Sierra Leone (the one scene filmed in bright sunlight), his capture by Africans, his transportation to the slave fort of Lomboko, the horrors of the passage on the Portuguese slaver *Tecora*, the slave market in Havana, and the bloody revolt on the *Amistad*—all of it portrayed wrenchingly on the screen. The Africans' story continues in jail, as they study pictures in a Bible and try to figure out the American legal, political, and moral system. In court, they finally cut through the mumbo jumbo by standing and chanting "Give Us Free!"

In a fictive interview on the eve of the Supreme Court case, Cinque tells Adams he is optimistic, for he has called on the spirits of his ancestors to join him in court. This moment, he says, is the whole reason for their having existed at all. Adams, whose own father had helped lead the American Revolution, speaks for his and Cinque's ancestors before the Supreme Court. To the prosecution's argument that the Africans are pirates and murderers and to southern arguments that slavery is a natural state, Adams answers that America is founded on the "self-evident truth" that the one natural state is freedom. It is a fine courtroom speech: Adams has honored his ancestors, the justices (and the movie audience) see the moral rightness of his case, and the Africans are returned to Sierra Leone. (In a subscript, Spielberg tells us that Cinque returns to a village that had been destroyed in civil war, but the final ironic note is overwhelmed by the moral triumphalism of the rest of the movie.)

Amistad (1997) tells the story of 41 Africans who stage a revolt on the slave ship carrying them to Cuba and the trial that follows.

DreamWorks LLC/The Kobal Collection/Cooper, Andrew

bride was 29, pretty, flirtatious, and, according to Washington gossip, "frivolous, wayward, [and] passionate." Knowing that his marriage might cause trouble for the new administration, Eaton had asked for and received Jackson's blessings—and, by implication, his protection.

The marriage of John and Peggy Eaton came at a turning point in the history of both Washington society and elite sexual mores. Until the 1820s most officeholders had left their families at home, took lodgings at taverns and boardinghouses, and lived in a bachelor world. But the boardinghouse world eventually gave way to high society. Government officials were moving into Washington houses, and their wives presided over the round of dinner parties through which much of the government's business was done. Many of these political wives snubbed Peggy Eaton.

The shunning of Peggy Eaton split the Jackson administration in half. Jackson was committed to protect her. His grand romance with Rachel (as well as the gossip that surrounded it) was a striking parallel to the affair of the Eatons. That, coupled with Jackson's honor-bound agreement to the Eaton marriage, ensured that he would protect the Eatons to the bitter end. Noting that the rumormongers were not only politicians' wives but also prominent clergymen, Jackson blamed the "conspiracy" on "females with clergymen at their head."

In fact, Mrs. Eaton's tormentors included most of the cabinet members as well as Jackson's own White House "family." Widowed and without children, Jackson had invited his nephew and private secretary, Andrew Jackson Donelson, to live in the White House. Donelson's wife, serving as official hostess, shunned Peggy Eaton. Jackson assumed that schemers had subverted his own household. Before long, his suspicions centered on Vice President Calhoun, whose wife, Floride Bonneau Calhoun, was a leader of the assault on Eaton. Only Secretary of State Van Buren, a widower and an eminently decent man, included the Eatons in official functions. Sensing that Jackson was losing his patience with Calhoun, Van Buren's friends showed Jackson a letter revealing that while serving in Monroe's cabinet Calhoun had favored censuring Jackson for his unauthorized invasion of Florida in 1818. An open break with Calhoun became inevitable.

In 1831, Van Buren offered to resign his cabinet post and engineered the resignations of nearly all other members of the cabinet, allowing Jackson to remake his administration without firing anyone. Jackson replaced southern supporters of Calhoun with a mixed cabinet that included political allies of Van Buren. Jackson appointed Van Buren minister to Great Britain. He then replaced Calhoun with Van Buren as the vice presidential candidate in 1832 and let it be known that he wanted Van Buren to succeed him as president.

Petitions, the Gag Rule, and the Southern Mails

Democrats promised to protect slavery with a disciplined national coalition committed to states' rights within an inviolable Union. The rise of a northern antislavery movement (see Chapter 12) challenged that formulation. Middle-class evangelicals, who were emerging as the reformist core of the northern Whig Party, knew that Jacksonian Democrats wanted to keep moral issues out of politics. Jackson had rebuffed their petitions to stop movement of the mail on Sundays and to halt Indian removal. Evangelicals were also appalled by his defense of Peggy Eaton. Most of all, they disliked the Democrats' rigid party discipline, which in each case had kept questions of morality from shaping politics.

In the early 1830s a radical minority of evangelicals, seeking to abolish slavery, devised ways of making the national government confront the slavery question. In 1835, abolitionists launched a "postal campaign," flooding the mail with antislavery tracts. They bombarded Congress with petitions, most of them for the abolition of slavery and the slave trade in the District of Columbia (where Congress had undisputed jurisdiction), others against the interstate slave trade, slavery in the federal territories, and the admission of new slave states.

Some Jacksonians, including Jackson himself, wanted to stop the postal campaign with a federal censorship law. Calhoun and other southerners wanted state censorship. Knowing that state censorship of the mail was unconstitutional and that federal censorship would be a political disaster, Postmaster General Amos Kendall proposed an informal solution. Without changing the law, he simply looked the other way as local postmasters removed abolitionist materials from the mail. Almost all such materials were published in New York City and mailed from there. The New York postmaster, a loyal appointee, sifted them out of the mail and thus cut off the postal campaign at its source. The few tracts that made it to the South were destroyed by local postmasters.

The Democrats dealt similarly with antislavery petitions to Congress. Southern extremists demanded that Congress disavow its power to legislate on slavery in the District of Columbia, but Van Buren declared that Congress did have that power but should never use it. In dealing with the petitions, Congress simply voted at each session from 1836 to 1844 to **table** them without reading them, thus acknowledging that they had been received but sidestepping any debate. This procedure, which became known as the "gag rule," was passed by southerners with the help of most northern Democrats.

table a petition or bill *Act of removing a petition or bill from consideration without debate by placing it at the end of the legislative agenda.*

JACKSONIAN DEMOCRACY AND THE MARKET REVOLUTION

Jacksonian Democrats assumed power at the height of the market revolution, and they spent much of the 1830s and 1840s trying to reconcile the market and the republic. They welcomed commerce as long as it served the independence and rough equality of white men, but paper currency and the dependence on credit that came with the market revolution posed problems. The paper economy separated wealth from "real work" and encouraged an unrepublican spirit of luxury and greed. Worst of all, it required government-granted privileges that the Jacksonians branded "corruption." The Jackson presidency sought to curtail government involvement in the economy, to end special privilege, and thus to rescue the republic from the "Money Power."

The opposition to the Democrats favored an activist central government that would encourage orderly economic development through the American System. Jacksonian rhetoric about the Money Power and the Old Republic, they argued, was little more than the demagoguery of self-seeking politicians.

FOCUS QUESTION

How did Democrats and Whigs in the national government argue questions raised by economic development?

The Bank War

The argument between Jacksonians and their detractors came to focus on the Second Bank of the United States. Most businessmen valued the Bank, for it promised a stable paper currency and centralized control over the nation's monetary and credit system. But millions of Americans resented and distrusted the national bank, and President Jackson agreed with them. He insisted that both the Bank and paper money were unconstitutional. Above all, Jackson saw the Bank as a government-sponsored concentration of power that threatened the republic.

The charter of the Bank of the United States ran through 1836, but Senators Henry Clay and Daniel Webster encouraged Nicholas Biddle, the bank's brilliant, aristocratic president, to apply for recharter in 1832. They hoped to provoke the hot-tempered Jackson into a response that could be used against him in the election. Congress passed the recharter bill in early July 1832, and Jackson vetoed it.

Jackson's Bank Veto Message was a manifesto of Jacksonian democracy. He declared that the Bank was "unauthorized by the Constitution, subversive of the rights of the states, and dangerous to the liberties of the people." Its charter bestowed special privilege on the Bank and its stockholders. The Bank sucked resources out of the agrarian South and West and poured them into the pockets of northeastern gentlemen and their English friends. The granting of special privilege to such people (or to any others) threatened the system of equal rights that was essential in a republic. Jackson concluded with a call to conservative, God-centered Protestantism: "Let us firmly rely on that kind Providence which I am sure watches with peculiar care over the destinies of our Republic, and on the intelligence and wisdom of our countrymen."

The Bank Veto Message was a rambling attack that, in the opinion of the Bank's supporters, demonstrated Jackson's unfitness for office. Clay's supporters distributed Jackson's Bank Veto Message as *anti*-Jackson propaganda during the 1832 campaign. But most voters agreed with Jackson that the republic was in danger of subversion by parasites who grew rich by manipulating credit, prices, paper money, and government-bestowed privileges. Jackson portrayed himself as the protector of the old republic and a melodramatic hero contending with illegitimate, aristocratic powers. With the Bank and Jackson's veto as the principal issues, Jackson won by a landslide in 1832. (See Map 11.3.)

Jackson began his second term determined to kill the Bank before Congress could reverse his veto. He withdrew government deposits as they were needed and deposited new government revenues in state banks. By law, the decision to remove the deposits had to be made by the secretary of the treasury. After removing two secretaries who refused to comply with his order, Jackson appointed Roger B. Taney, a close adviser who had helped write the Bank Veto Message. Taney withdrew the deposits. In 1835, when the old Federalist John Marshall died, Jackson rewarded Taney by making him chief justice of the Supreme Court.

The Beginnings of the Whig Party

Conflict over deposit removal and related questions of presidential power united anti-Jacksonians into the Whig Party in 1834. The name of the party, as everyone who knew the language of the republic recognized, stood for legislative opposition to a power-mad executive. Whigs argued that Jackson had transformed himself from the limited executive described in the Constitution into King Andrew I. This process had begun with the spoils system and had become worse when Jackson began to veto congressional legislation. Jackson used the veto often—too often, said the Whigs, when the American System was at stake. In May 1830, for instance, Jackson vetoed an attempt by Congress to buy stock in a turnpike. Jackson questioned whether such federal subsidies were constitutional. More important, he announced that he was determined to reduce federal expenditures in order to retire

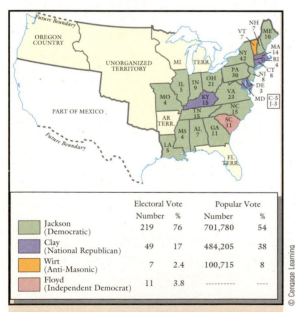

Map 11.3 Presidential Election, 1832. *The election of 1832 was a landslide victory for Andrew Jackson. The National Republican Henry Clay carried only his native Kentucky, Delaware, and southern New England. A defeated and resentful South Carolina ran its own candidate. Jackson, on the other hand, won in the regions in which he had been strong in 1828 and added support in New York and northern New England.*

	Electoral Vote		Popular Vote	
	Number	%	Number	%
Jackson (Democratic)	219	76	701,780	54
Clay (National Republican)	49	17	484,205	38
Wirt (Anti-Masonic)	7	2.4	100,715	8
Floyd (Independent Democrat)	11	3.8	----------	----

the national debt—hinting strongly that he would oppose all federal public works.

The bank veto conveyed the same message, and the withdrawal of the government deposits brought the question of "executive usurpation" to a head in 1834. Nicholas Biddle demanded that all loans be repaid to the Bank of the United States before it closed its doors. His demand undermined the credit system and produced a sharp financial panic. Congress received a well-orchestrated petition campaign to restore the deposits. Henry Clay led an effort in the Senate to censure the president, which it did in March 1834. Clay and Daniel Webster, a major supporter of the Bank, guided the old National Republican coalition into the new Whig Party. They were joined by southerners who resented Jackson's treatment of the South Carolina nullifiers.

A Balanced Budget

Jackson had removed the deposits in part because he anticipated a federal surplus revenue that, if handed over to the Bank of the United States, would have made it stronger than ever. The Tariffs of 1828 and 1832 produced substantial government revenue, and Jackson's frugal administration spent very little of it. The sale of public lands was adding to the surplus. In 1833, for the only time in its history, the United States paid off its national debt. Without Jackson's removal of the deposits, a growing federal treasury would have gone into the Bank and found its way into the hated paper economy.

Jackson and many members of his administration were deeply concerned about the inflationary boom that accompanied the market revolution. In 1836, Jackson issued a Specie Circular, which provided that speculators could buy large parcels of public land only with silver and gold coins, while settlers could continue to buy farm-sized plots with banknotes. Henceforth, speculators would have to bring wagonloads of coins from eastern banks to frontier land offices. With this provision, Jackson hoped to curtail speculation and to reverse the flow of specie out of the South and West. The Specie Circular was Jackson's final assault on the paper economy.

THE SECOND AMERICAN PARTY SYSTEM

KING ANDREW. *In this widely distributed opposition cartoon, "King Andrew," with a scepter in one hand and a vetoed bill in the other, tramples on internal improvements, the Bank of the United States, and the Constitution.*

In his farewell address in 1837, Jackson warned against a revival of the Bank of the United States and against all banks, paper money, and the spirit of speculation. The solution, as always, was a society of small producers, a vigilant democratic electorate, and a chaste republican government that granted no special privileges.

FOCUS QUESTION

What was peculiarly "national" about the Second Party System?

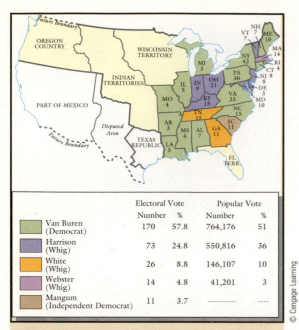

	Electoral Vote		Popular Vote	
	Number	%	Number	%
Van Buren (Democrat)	170	57.8	764,176	51
Harrison (Whig)	73	24.8	550,816	36
White (Whig)	26	8.8	146,107	10
Webster (Whig)	14	4.8	41,201	3
Mangum (Independent Democrat)	11	3.7	----------	----

© Cengage Learning

Map 11.4 **Presidential Election, 1836.** *In 1836, the Whigs tried to beat the Democrats' national organization with an array of sectional candidates, hoping to throw the election into the House of Representatives. The strategy failed. Martin Van Buren, with significant support in every section of the country, defeated the three Whig candidates combined.*

"Martin Van Ruin"

Sitting beside Jackson as he delivered his farewell address was his chosen successor, Martin Van Buren. In the election of 1836, the Whigs had acknowledged that Henry Clay, the leader of their party, could not win a national election. Instead, they ran three sectional candidates: Daniel Webster in the Northeast, the old Indian fighter William Henry Harrison in the West, and Hugh Lawson White of Tennessee, a turncoat Jacksonian, in the South. Whigs hoped to deprive Van Buren of a majority and throw the election into the Whig-controlled House of Representatives. But Van Buren had engineered a national Democratic Party that could avert the dangers of sectionalism, and he questioned the patriotism of the Whigs, asserting that "true republicans can never lend their aid and influence in creating geographical parties." That, along with his association with Jackson's popular presidency, won him the election. (See Map 11.4.)

Van Buren had barely taken office when the inflationary boom of the mid-1830s collapsed. Economic historians ascribe the Panic of 1837 and the ensuing depression largely to events outside the country. The Bank of England, concerned over the flow of British gold to American speculators, cut off credit to firms that did business in the United States. As a result, British demand for American cotton fell sharply, and the price of cotton dropped by half. With much of the speculative boom tied to cotton, the economy collapsed. In May 1837, New York banks, unable to accommodate people who demanded hard coin for their notes, suspended specie payments. Other banks followed suit, and soon banks all over the country went out of business. The financial and export sectors of the economy suffered most. In the seaport cities, one firm after another closed its doors, and about one-third of the workforce was unemployed.

Whigs blamed the depression on Jackson's hard-money policies. With economic distress the main issue, Whigs scored huge gains in the midterm elections of 1838, castigating the president as "Martin Van Ruin." Democrats blamed the crash on speculation and Whig paper money. Whigs demanded a new national bank, but Van Buren proposed the complete divorce of government from the banking system. Under this plan, the federal government would hold and dispense its money without depositing it in banks. He also required that customs and land purchases be paid in gold and silver coins or in notes from specie-paying banks, a provision that allowed government to regulate state banknotes without resorting to a central bank. Van Buren asked Congress to set up the Independent Treasury in 1837. The Independent Treasury Bill finally passed in 1840, completing the Jacksonian separation of bank and state.

The Election of 1840

Whigs were confident that they could defeat Van Buren in 1840. Trying to offend as few voters as possible, they passed over their best-known leaders, Clay and Webster, and nominated William Henry Harrison of Ohio as their presidential candidate. Harrison was the hero of the Battle of Tippecanoe (see Chapter 7) and a westerner whose Virginia origins made him palatable in the South. He was also a proven vote-getter who had carried seven states spread across different regions in 1836. Best of all, he was a military hero who had expressed few opinions on national issues and who had no political record to defend. As his running mate, the Whigs chose John Tyler, a states'-rights Virginian who had joined the Whigs out of hatred for Jackson. To promote this baldly pragmatic ticket, the Whigs came up with a catchy slogan: "Tippecanoe and Tyler Too."

Early in the campaign a Democratic journalist, commenting on Harrison's political inexperience and alleged unfitness for the presidency, wrote, "Give [Harrison] a barrel of hard cider, and settle a pension of two thousand a year on him, and my word for it, he will sit out the remainder of his days in his log cabin." Whigs, who had been trying to shake their elitist image, seized on the statement and launched what was known as the Log Cabin Campaign. The log cabin, the cider barrel, and Harrison's folksiness and heroism constituted the entire Whig campaign, while Van Buren was pictured as living in luxury at the public's expense.

Democrats howled that Whigs were peddling lies and refusing to discuss issues, but they knew they had been beaten at their own game. Harrison won only a narrow majority of the popular vote, but a landslide of 234 to 60 votes in the Electoral College. (See Map 11.5.)

The election of 1840 signaled the completion of the second party system—the most fully national alignment of parties in U.S. history. Andrew Jackson had won in 1828 with Jefferson's old southern and western agrarian constituency; in 1832 he won added support in the mid-Atlantic states and in northern New England. In 1836, Whigs broke the Democratic hold on the South by capitalizing on resentment of Jackson's defeat of Calhoun and nullification and mistrust of the New Yorker Van Buren. The election of 1840 completed the transition: Harrison and Van Buren received nearly equal levels of support in the slave and free states.

The election of 1840 also witnessed the high-water mark of voter turnout. Prospective voters met an avalanche of oratory, door-to-door canvassing, torchlight parades, and party propaganda. Democrats or Whigs could take no state for granted. They contested elections in nearly every neighborhood in the country, and the result was increased popular interest in politics. In 1824, about one in four adult white men had voted in the presidential election. Jackson's vengeful campaign of 1828 lifted the turnout to 56.3 percent, and it stayed at about that level in 1832 and 1836. The campaign of 1840 brought out 78 percent of the eligible voters, and the turnout remained at that high level for the rest of the 19th century.

In every part of the country, Whigs presented themselves as the party of active government and economic progress. They promised good roads, public schools, stable currency, and social harmony. In the North, the wealthiest men were Whigs (8 in 10 of the merchant elites in New York and Boston, for example). But the Whig Party received its core northern support among the market farmers, local merchants, and manufacturers created by the new market economy and the fires of middle-class revivals—supporters not only of Whig nationalism but also of internal improvements and a wide array of reforms in their own neighborhoods. In the South, Whigs ran well in plantation districts and in county-seat towns—the centers of southern wealth, commerce, and gentility. Many southern leaders came to dislike Jackson, and they took their personal followings into the Whig Party. Whigs also won votes in areas—eastern Tennessee and western North Carolina are examples—where farmers *wanted* to be brought into the flow of commerce. Put very simply, Whigs tended to be persons who were or wanted to be beneficiaries of the market revolution, and who embraced its attendant social and cultural transformations. They saw themselves as "improvers."

The Democrats, on the other hand, posed as defenders of the common (white) man and the old republic. They tended to be persons who had been hurt or

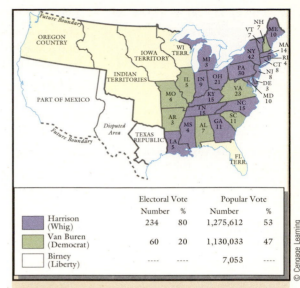

Map 11.5 Presidential Election, 1840. *In 1840, the Whigs united under William Henry Harrison, the one Whig candidate who had won national support four years earlier. Borrowing campaign tactics from the Democrats and inventing many of their own, Whigs campaigned hard in every state. The result was a Whig victory and a truly national two-party system.*

	Electoral Vote		Popular Vote	
	Number	%	Number	%
Harrison (Whig)	234	80	1,275,612	53
Van Buren (Democrat)	60	20	1,130,033	47
Birney (Liberty)	----	----	7,053	----

© Cengage Learning

bypassed by the market revolution, who belonged to conservative, otherworldly churches, and who distrusted Whigs who talked about progress, big government, and social homogeneity. In the South, Democrats were strong in districts with small farms, few slaves, and limited market activity. The northern Democrats were a coalition of small farmers, working people, and small businessmen, along with cultural minorities (Irish immigrants, for instance, were almost unanimously Democratic). North and South, Democrats were localists. They argued for the limited national government that since Jefferson's day had been a bulwark of the revolutionary republic, of white male democracy, and of chattel slavery.

Conclusion

Thus the party system answered the questions of slavery and economic development that had helped bring it into being. Nationally, Democrats stopped the American System. They dismantled the Bank of the United States, refused federal support for roads and canals, and revised the tariff in ways that mollified the export-oriented South. As a result, the stupendous growth of the American economy between 1830 and 1860 became a question of state and local—not national—government action. Neither the national commercial society envisioned by the Whigs nor the return to Jeffersonian agrarianism favored by many Democrats came into being. Instead, the United States experienced an almost inadvertent experiment in laissez-faire capitalism. On the political problems surrounding slavery, the two-party system did what Van Buren had hoped it would do: Because both Whigs and Democrats needed both northern and southern support, they avoided discussions of sectional questions. It worked that way until the party system disintegrated on the eve of the Civil War.

CHAPTER REVIEW

Review Questions

1. What were the components of the "American System"? What did the American System promise to accomplish?
2. What enduring political issues were raised by the Missouri controversy and the Panic of 1819?
3. What were the events and political motives that contributed to the Republican revival that formed around Andrew Jackson?
4. What were the principal events of the John Quincy Adams administration, and how did they contribute to his defeat in 1828?
5. At the national level, how did Jacksonian Democrats and their rivals deal with widening differences between North and South?
6. How did Democrats and Whigs in the national government argue questions raised by economic development?
7. What was peculiarly "national" about the Second Party System?

Critical Thinking Questions

1. Jacksonian Democrats represented themselves as a revival of Jeffersonian democracy. In what ways was that representation accurate? In what ways was it not?
2. Whigs claimed to be the party of economic progress. Yet, unlike modern *pro-growth* politicians, they demanded a powerful, interventionist national government. How did they argue that position?

Identifications

Review your understanding of the following key terms, people, and events for this chapter.

Henry Clay, p. 249
American System, p. 249
protective tariff, p. 249
internal improvements, p. 249

Missouri Compromise, p. 252
congressional caucus, p. 253
favorite son, p. 253

Andrew Jackson, p. 253
Corrupt Bargain, p. 254
Monroe Doctrine, p. 255
spoils system, p. 258

Indian Removal Act, p. 259
nullification, p. 260
table a petition or bill, p. 263

DISCOVERY

In what ways did Andrew Jackson change the presidency and politics?

In thinking about this question, begin by breaking it down into the components shown below. A discussion of the significance of each component should appear in your answer.

Politics and Geography

Compare the presidential election maps of 1824 and 1828. What conclusions can you draw between the victory of Andrew Jackson in 1828 and the image of Jackson's inaugural on page 257? Note how support for Jackson grew from one election to the next. Where was his support strongest?

Government and Law

Which groups in America disliked Jackson's policies? Look carefully at the cartoon of "King Andrew" on page 265. What is the significance of the "veto" he holds on the right? Why is he shown stepping on the Constitution of the United States? Is the representation of Jackson as royalty supposed to be in support of or in opposition to him? Based on what you have read in this chapter, is this a fair portrayal?

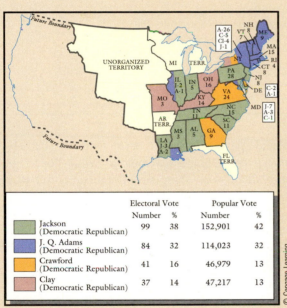

		Electoral Vote		Popular Vote	
		Number	%	Number	%
	Jackson (Democratic Republican)	99	38	152,901	42
	J. Q. Adams (Democratic Republican)	84	32	114,023	32
	Crawford (Democratic Republican)	41	16	46,979	13
	Clay (Democratic Republican)	37	14	47,217	13

© Cengage Learning

Map 11.1 Presidential Election, 1824

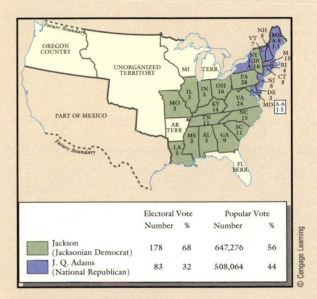

		Electoral Vote		Popular Vote	
		Number	%	Number	%
	Jackson (Jacksonian Democrat)	178	68	647,276	56
	J. Q. Adams (National Republican)	83	32	508,064	44

© Cengage Learning

Map 11.2 Presidential Election, 1828

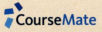 CourseMate

Visit the CourseMate website at www.cengagebrain.com for additional study tools and review materials for this chapter.

CHAPTER 12

ANTEBELLUM REFORM

T he politicians who built the Whig and Democratic parties tapped skillfully into the national patchwork of aspiration, fear, and resentment. Whigs envisioned smooth-running, government-sponsored transportation and financial systems. Such visions echoed the faith in cosmic order, material progress, and moral improvement that had become cultural axioms for the more prosperous and cosmopolitan Americans. Democrats, on the other hand, defended Jefferson's republic of limited government and white liberty and equality. They portrayed a haunted political universe in which trickery, deceit, and special privilege lurked behind the promises of the Whigs.

Whigs and Democrats constructed their coalitions largely at the neighborhood and state levels. Their arguments for and against state-supported internal improvements and state-chartered banks and corporations mirrored the national debate, and thus strengthened and nationalized party loyalties. Local cultural battles—arguments over alcohol, sexual morality, education, crime, and much more—also sharpened Democratic and Whig attitudes.

In the North, the churchgoing middle class provided the Whig Party with a political culture, a reform-oriented social agenda, and most of its electoral support. On a variety of issues, including prostitution, temperance, public education, and state-supported insane asylums and penitentiaries, Whigs used government to improve individual morality and discipline. Democrats argued that attempts to legislate morality were anti-republican and wrong. Not all reform movements, however, strengthened the party system. When some Whiggish northerners insisted upon women's rights and the immediate emancipation of all slaves, they attacked the foundations of the white republic and the party system, opening important questions that the political parties wanted to ignore.

TIMELINE

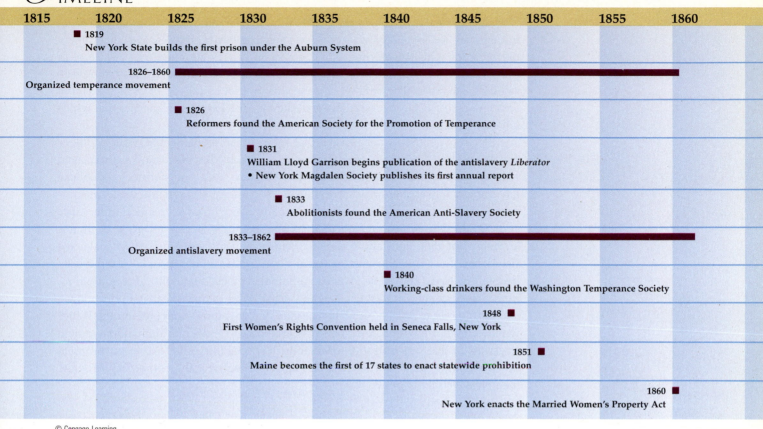

| 1815 | 1820 | 1825 | 1830 | 1835 | 1840 | 1845 | 1850 | 1855 | 1860 |

1819
New York State builds the first prison under the Auburn System

1826–1860
Organized temperance movement

1826
Reformers found the American Society for the Promotion of Temperance

1831
William Lloyd Garrison begins publication of the antislavery *Liberator*
• New York Magdalen Society publishes its first annual report

1833
Abolitionists found the American Anti-Slavery Society

1833–1862
Organized antislavery movement

1840
Working-class drinkers found the Washington Temperance Society

1848
First Women's Rights Convention held in Seneca Falls, New York

1851
Maine becomes the first of 17 states to enact statewide prohibition

1860
New York enacts the Married Women's Property Act

© Cengage Learning

THE POLITICS OF PROGRESS

Whigs assumed that both markets and government were agents of progress. Democrats preached that markets were good and governments were necessary, but that collaboration between the two produced corruption.

Markets and Governments

Whigs praised the new market economy as more than a means of producing national wealth. Markets created opportunities, and individuals who developed good work habits and moral discipline would prosper. The market would discourage laziness and ignorance and encourage social harmony, good manners, and disciplined ambition. At the same time, it would fill American homes with comfortable furniture and moral housewives. To poor farmers and city workers who believed that the market revolution undermined traditional forms of independence, Whigs promised social mobility within a new system of interdependence, but only to deserving individuals. Pointing to self-made Whigs such as Daniel Webster and Abraham Lincoln, Whigs promised national prosperity in a world that rewarded virtue.

As they did nationally, Whigs at the state and local levels wanted government to subsidize economic development and the moral improvement that would come along with it. Government should build roads, establish public schools, and create and oversee a stable, reliable currency. It should also foster virtue. "The government," remarked a New York City Whig in 1848, "is not merely a machine for making wars and punishing felons, but is bound to do all that is within its power to promote the welfare of the People."

FOCUS QUESTION

What were the Whig and Democratic conceptions of the duties and limits of government?

Democrats saw things differently. Few of them condemned market society, but they argued forcefully against activist government, high taxes, and government partnerships with private interests. Democrats saw government not as a tool of progress but as a potential evil—a concentration of power in the hands of imperfect, self-interested men. The only safe course was to limit its power. In 1837, the *United States Magazine and Democratic Review* declared: "The best government is that which governs least."

Most of all, Democrats insisted that Whig governments would create privilege and inequality. Corporate charters, banks, and subsidies to turnpike, canal, and railroad companies, they said, benefited insiders and transformed republican government into an engine of corruption and inequality. Jackson and the Democrats acknowledged that varying levels of talent and energy (not to mention inheritance and social connections) created inequalities, and they never talked of economic leveling. But they constantly accused Whigs of using government to make the rich richer. The Massachusetts Democrat George Bancroft concurred: "A republican people," he said, "should be in an equality in their social and political condition; . . . pure democracy inculcates equal rights—equal laws—equal means of education— and *equal means* of wealth also." By contrast, the government favored by the Whigs would enrich a favored few. Bancroft and other Democrats demanded limited government that was deaf to the demands of special interests. Neither government nor the market, they said, should be allowed to subvert the democracy of white men on which the republic rested.

Banks, Roads, Canals

Banking emerged as a central political issue in nearly every state, particularly after the widespread bank failures following the crash of 1837. Whigs defended banks as agents of economic progress, arguing that they provided credit for roads and canals, loans to businessmen and commercial farmers, and the banknotes that served as the chief medium of exchange. Democrats regarded banks as government-protected institutions that enabled a privileged few to make themselves rich at the public's expense.

In state legislatures, Whigs defended what had become a roughly standard system of private banks chartered by state governments—banks circulated banknotes and enjoyed **limited liability** to protect directors and stockholders from debts incurred by the bank. Many Democrats proposed abolishing all banks. Others proposed reforms. They demanded a high ratio of specie reserves to banknotes as a guard against inflationary paper money. They suggested eliminating banknotes in small denominations, thus ensuring that day-to-day business would be conducted in hard coin, protecting wage earners and small farmers from speculative ups and downs. Democrats also wanted to hold bank directors responsible for corporate debts and bankruptcies; some proposed banning corporate charters altogether.

By these and other means, Democrats in the states protected currency and credit from the government favoritism, dishonesty, and elitism that, they argued, enriched Whig insiders and impoverished honest Democrats. Whigs responded that corporate privileges and immunities and an abundant, elastic currency were keys to economic development, and they fought Democrats every step of the way.

Democrats in Congress and the White House blocked federally funded roads and canals (see Chapter 11). In response, the states launched the transportation revolution themselves, either by taking direct action or by chartering private corporations to do the work. State legislatures everywhere debated the wisdom of direct state action, of corporate privileges, of subsidies to canals and railroads, and

limited liability *Provisions that protected directors and stockholders of corporations from corporate debts by separating those debts from personal liabilities.*

of government debt. Whigs, predictably, favored direct action by state governments. Democrats often supported internal improvements, but they opposed "partial" legislation that would benefit part of a state at the expense of the rest. They also opposed projects that would lead to higher taxes and put state governments into debt. Beneath Whig plans for extensive improvements, Democrats argued, lay schemes to create special privilege, inequality, debt, and corruption—all at the expense of a hoodwinked people.

The argument about government and economic development in the states mirrored the national debate. Whigs wanted to use government and the market to make an economically and morally progressive—albeit hierarchical—republic. Democrats vowed to allow neither institution to subvert the equal rights and rough equality of condition that were, in their view, the preconditions of republican citizenship. Whig and Democratic arguments about banks and internal improvement were essentially the same in every state, and these state-level fights bolstered a national two-party system that did its best to ignore regional differences.

THE POLITICS OF SOCIAL REFORM

The establishment of public schools and institutions for criminals and the insane worked the same way. Whigs and Democrats agreed that such state-supported institutions had become necessary. But Whigs wanted them to improve the character and morals of their inmates, and were willing to spend money for that purpose. Democrats wanted to educate children and incarcerate criminals and the insane, but they wanted to do it cheaply.

FOCUS QUESTION

What were the Whig and Democratic positions on the issues of public schools, prisons, and asylums?

Public Schools

During the second quarter of the 19th century, local and state governments built systems of tax-supported public schools, known as **"common" schools**. Before that time, most children learned reading, writing, and arithmetic at home, in poorly staffed town schools, in private schools, or in charity schools run by churches or other benevolent organizations. Despite the lack of any system of education, most children learned to read and write, but literacy was more likely among boys than among girls, among whites than among blacks, and among northeasterners than among westerners or southerners.

By the 1830s Whigs and Democrats agreed that providing common schools was a proper function of government, and Democrats often agreed with Whigs that schools could equalize opportunity. More radical Democrats, however, wanted public schooling that would erase snobbery. A newspaper declared in 1828 that "the children of the rich and the poor shall receive a national education, calculated to make republicans and banish aristocrats."

The reformers who created the most advanced, expensive, and centralized state school systems were Whigs: Horace Mann of Massachusetts, Henry Barnard of Connecticut, Calvin Stowe (husband of Harriet Beecher) of Ohio, and others. These reformers talked more about character building than about the three Rs. They wanted schools that would downplay class divisions, but they were interested less in democratizing wealthy children than in civilizing the poor. William Seward, the Whig governor of New York, insisted that "education tends to produce equality, not by leveling all to the condition of the base, but by elevating all to the association of the wise and good."

common schools *Tax-supported public schools built by state and local governments.*

The schools taught a basic Whig axiom: that social questions could be reduced to questions of individual character. A textbook entitled *The Thinker, A Moral Reader* (1855) told children to "remember that all the ignorance, degradation, and misery in the world, is the result of indolence and vice." To teach that lesson, the schools had children read from the King James Bible and recite prayers acceptable to all of the Protestant sects. Such texts reaffirmed a common Protestant morality while avoiding divisive doctrinal matters.

Political arguments centered less on curriculum than on organization. Whigs wanted state-level centralization and proposed state superintendents and state boards of education, **normal schools** (state teachers' colleges), texts chosen at the state level, and uniform school terms. They also recruited young women as teachers. In addition to fostering Protestant morality in the schools, these women were a source of cheap labor. Salaries for female teachers in the northern states ranged from 40 to 60 percent lower than the salaries of their male coworkers.

Democrats preferred to give power to individual school districts, which would enable local school committees to tailor the curriculum, the length of the school year, and the choice of teachers and texts to local needs. Centralization, they argued, would create a metropolitan educational culture that served the purposes of the rich but ignored the preferences of farmers and working people. It was standard Democratic social policy: inexpensive government and local control.

Ethnicity, Religion, and the Schools

The argument between Whig centralism and Democratic parsimony dominated the debate over public education until the children of Irish and German Catholic immigrants entered schools by the thousands in the mid-1840s. Most immigrant families were poor and relied on their children's earned income. Consequently, the children's attendance at school was irregular at best. Moreover, most immigrants were Catholics. The Irish regarded Protestant prayers and the King James Bible as heresies. Some of the textbooks were worse. Olney's *Practical System of Modern Geography,* a standard textbook, declared that "the Irish in general are quick of apprehension, active, brave and hospitable; but passionate, ignorant, vain, and superstitious."

Many Catholic parents simply refused to send their children to school. Others demanded changes in textbooks, the elimination of the King James Bible, and tax-supported Catholic schools or at least tax relief for parents who sent their children to parish schools. Whigs, joined by many native-born Democrats, saw Catholic complaints as assaults on the Protestantism that they insisted was at the heart of American republicanism.

Some school districts, particularly in the rural areas to which many Scandinavian and German immigrants found their way, created foreign-language schools and provided bilingual instruction. In other places, state support for church-run schools persisted. But in northeastern cities, where immigrant Catholics often formed militant local majorities, demands for state support led to violence and to organized nativist (anti-immigrant) politics. In 1844, the Native American Party, with the endorsement of the Whigs, won the New York City elections. That same year in Philadelphia, riots that pitted Whig Protestants against Catholic immigrants, ostensibly over the issue of Bible reading in schools, killed 13 people.

QUICK REVIEW

WHAT WAS TAUGHT IN THE PUBLIC SCHOOLS

- Reading, writing, arithmetic

- Individual character development

- King James (English Protestant) Bible

normal schools *State colleges established for the training of teachers.*

Prisons

From the 1820s onward, state governments built institutions to house orphans, the dependent poor, the insane, and criminals. Americans in the 18th century (and many in the 19th century as well) had assumed that poverty, crime, insanity, and other social ills were among God's ways of punishing sin and testing the human capacity for both suffering and charity. Now reformers argued that deviance was the result of childhood deprivation. "Normal" people, they suggested, learned discipline and respect for work, property, laws, and other people from their parents. Deviants were the products of brutal, often drunken households devoid of parental love and discipline. The cure was to place them in a controlled setting, teach them work and discipline, and turn them into useful citizens.

In state legislatures, Whigs favored putting deviants into institutions for rehabilitation. Democrats regarded attempts at rehabilitation as wrongheaded and expensive. They wanted institutions that isolated the insane, warehoused the dependent poor, and punished criminals. Most state systems were a compromise between the two positions.

Pennsylvania built prisons at Pittsburgh (1826) and Philadelphia (1829) that put solitary prisoners into cells to contemplate their misdeeds and to plot a new life. This solitary confinement produced few reformations and numerous attempts at suicide. Far more common were institutions based on the model developed in New York at Auburn (1819) and Sing Sing (1825). In the **Auburn system,** prisoners slept in solitary cells and marched in military formation to meals and workshops. They were forbidden to speak to one another at any time. The rule of silence, it was believed, encouraged both discipline and contemplation. The Auburn system was designed both to reform criminals, the goal of the Whigs, and to meet the Democrats' goal of making a profit, for the prisons sold workshop products to the outside.

Auburn system *Prison system designed to reform criminals and reduce expenses through the sale of items produced in workshops. Prisoners slept in solitary cells, marched in military formation to meals and workshops, and were forbidden to speak to one another at any time.*

Prisoners at the State Prison at Auburn.

AUBURN PRISON. *Inmates at New York's Auburn Prison were forbidden to speak and were marched in lockstep between workshops, dining halls, and their cells.*

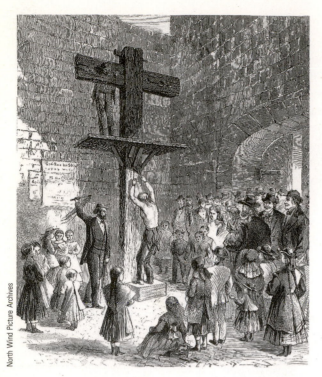

North Wind Picture Archives

Dorothea Dix *Boston reformer who traveled throughout the country campaigning for humane, state-supported asylums for the insane.*

THE WHIPPING POST AND PILLORY AT NEW CASTLE, DELAWARE. *Delaware was a slave state that continued to inflict public, corporal punishment on lawbreakers. Many of the witnesses to the whipping depicted here are small children, who are supposedly learning a lesson.*

Asylums

The leading advocate of humane treatment for the insane was **Dorothea Dix,** a Boston humanitarian. She traveled throughout the country pressuring state legislatures to build asylums committed to what reformers called "moral treatment." The asylums were to be clean and pleasant places, preferably outside the cities. Attendants were not to beat inmates or tie them up, although they could use cold showers as a form of discipline. Dix and other reformers wanted the asylums to be safe, nurturing environments in which the insane could be made well.

By 1860, the legislatures of 28 of the 33 states had established state-run insane asylums. Whig legislators, with minimal support from Democrats, approved appropriations for the more expensive facilities. Occasionally, Dorothea Dix won Democratic support as well. In North Carolina, she befriended the wife of a powerful Democratic legislator as the woman lay on her deathbed; the dying woman convinced her husband to support the building of an asylum. His impassioned speech won the approval of the lower house for a state asylum to be named Dix Hill. In the North Carolina senate, however, the proposal was supported by 91 percent of the Whigs and only 14 percent of the Democrats, a partisan division that was repeated in state after state.

THE POLITICS OF ALCOHOL

Central to party formation in the North was the fight between evangelical Whigs who demanded that government regulate public (and often private) morality and Democrats who feared both big government and the Whig cultural agenda. The most persistent issue in that argument was alcohol.

Ardent Spirits

Drinking had been a part of social life since the beginning of English settlement, but the withering of authority and the disruptions of the market revolution led to increased consumption, increased public drunkenness, and a perceived increase in the violence and social problems caused by alcohol. Per capita consumption of pure alcohol in all its forms increased from three to four gallons annually between 1790 and 1830, and most of the increase was in the form of cheap and potent whiskey. By 1830, per capita consumption of distilled spirits was more than five gallons per year—the highest it has ever been, and three times what it is in the United States today.

Beginning in the 1790s, physicians and a few clergymen attacked not only habitual drunkenness but also alcohol itself. For a short time after 1812, Federalist politicians and Congregational clergymen formed "moral societies" in New England that discouraged strong drink. Their imperious tone doomed them to failure.

INTERIOR OF AN AMERICAN INN, 1813. *In this democratic, neighborly scene in a country inn in the early republic, men of varying degrees of wealth, status, and inebriety are drinking and talking freely with each other. One man's wife and daughter have invaded this male domain, perhaps to question the time and money spent at the inn.*

John Lewis Krimmel, American, 1786-1821 Village Tavern, 1813-14, oil on canvas, 16 7/8 x 22 1/2 in. (42.8 x 56.9 cm) The Toledo Museum of Art, Toledo, Ohio; Purchased with funds from the Florence Scott Libbey Bequest in Memory of her Father, Maurice A. Scott

The temperance crusade began in earnest in 1826, when northeastern evangelicals founded the American Society for the Promotion of Temperance (soon renamed the American Temperance Society). The movement's manifesto was Lyman Beecher's *Six Sermons on the Nature, Occasions, Signs, Evils, and Remedy of Intemperance* (1826). Addressing the churchgoing middle class, Beecher declared alcohol an addictive drug that could turn even moderate drinkers into hopeless drunkards. Temperance, like other evangelical reforms, was presented as a contest between self-control and slavery to one's appetites. By encouraging total abstinence, reformers hoped to stop the creation of new drunkards while the old ones died out. As middle-class evangelicals eliminated alcohol from their own lives, they also ceased to offer it to their guests, buy or sell it, or provide it to their employees, and they encouraged their friends to do the same.

Beecher's crusade gathered strength in the middle-class revivals of the 1820s and 1830s. Charles Grandison Finney (see Chapter 10), in his revival at Rochester, made total abstinence a condition of conversion. Many other ministers and churches followed suit, and by the mid-1830s, the evangelical middle class had largely disengaged from alcohol and the people who drank it. Hundreds of evangelical businessmen refused to rent to merchants who sold liquor, sell grain to distillers, enter a store that sold alcohol, or hire employees who drank. Abstinence had become a badge of middle-class respectability.

By 1835, the American Temperance Society claimed 1.5 million members and estimated that 2 million Americans had renounced ardent spirits (whiskey, rum, and other distilled liquors). The society further estimated that 4,000 distilleries had gone out of business. Many politicians stopped buying drinks to win votes. In 1833, members of Congress formed the American Congressional Temperance Society. The U.S. Army put an end to the age-old liquor ration in 1832, and increasing numbers of militia officers stopped supplying their men with whiskey. The annual consumption of alcohol dropped by more than half in the 1830s.

The Origins of Prohibition

In the middle 1830s, Whigs made temperance a political issue. Realizing that voluntary abstinence would not end drunkenness, Whig evangelicals drafted coercive, prohibitionist legislation. First, they attacked the licenses granting grocery stores and taverns the right to sell liquor by the drink and to permit it to be consumed on the premises. The licenses were important sources of revenue for local governments. They also gave local authorities the power to cancel the licenses of troublesome establishments. Militant temperance advocates, usually in association with local Whigs, demanded that the authorities use that power to outlaw all public drinking places. In communities throughout the North, local parties organized around the licensing issue. The question first reached the state level in Massachusetts, when in 1838 a Whig legislature passed the "Fifteen-Gallon Law": Merchants could sell ardent spirits only in quantities of 15 gallons or more, thus outlawing every public drinking place in the state. In 1839, Massachusetts voters sent enough Democrats to the legislature to rescind the law.

Leading Democrats agreed with Whigs that Americans drank too much, but whereas Whigs insisted that regulating morality was a proper function of government, Democrats warned that government intrusion into areas of private choice would violate republican liberties. In many communities, alcohol became the defining difference between the two parties.

The Washingtonians

Democrats, despite their opposition to prohibition, often spoke out against drunkenness. Many craft unions denied membership to heavy drinkers, and hundreds of thousands of rural and urban Democrats quietly stopped drinking. Then, in 1840, former anti-prohibitionists launched a temperance movement of their own.

Six craftsmen were drinking at Chase's Tavern in Baltimore. As a joke, they sent one of their number to a nearby temperance lecture. He came back a teetotaler and converted the others. They then drew up a total abstinence pledge and promised to devote themselves to the reform of other drinkers. Within months a national movement, the Washington Temperance Society, had emerged. With a core membership of men who had opposed temperance in the 1830s, the Washingtonians differed from older temperance societies in several ways. First, they identified themselves as members of the laboring classes. Second, they were avowedly nonreligious. Third, the Washingtonians—at least those who called themselves True Washingtonians—rejected politics and legislation and concentrated on the conversion of drinkers through compassion and persuasion. Finally, they welcomed "hopeless" drunkards—and hailed them as heroes when they sobered up.

Temperance Schisms

Whig reformers welcomed the Washingtonians at first, but they soon had second thoughts. The nonreligious character of the movement disturbed those who saw temperance as an arm of evangelical reform. While the temperance regulars read pamphlets and listened to lectures by clergymen, lawyers, and doctors, the Washingtonians enjoyed raucous sing-alongs, comedy routines, barnyard imitations, dramatic skits, and even full-dress minstrel shows geared to temperance themes. Meetings featured experience speeches by reformed drunkards. Speaking extemporaneously, they omitted none of the horrors of an alcoholic life—attempts at suicide, friendships betrayed, fathers and mothers desolated, wives beaten and abandoned, children dead of starvation. Although Washingtonians had given up alcohol, their melodramatic tales, street parades, songbooks, and minstrel shows owed much to the popular culture Whig evangelicals opposed.

Nowhere did the Washingtonians differ more sharply from the temperance regulars than in their visions of the reformed life. Whig reformers expected men who quit drinking to withdraw from the male drinking world and retreat into the comfort of the newly feminized middle-class family. Washingtonians translated traditional male sociability into sober forms, and, more importantly, they called former drinkers back to the responsibilities of traditional fatherhood. Their experience stories began with the hurt drunkards had caused their wives and children and ended with their transformation into dependable providers and authoritative fathers. While the Whig temperance regulars tried to extend the ethos of individual ambition and the new middle-class domesticity into society at large, Washingtonians sought to rescue the self-respect and moral authority of working-class fathers.

The Washington Temperance Society collapsed toward the end of the 1840s, but its legacy survived. Among former drinkers in the North, it had introduced a new sense of domestic responsibility and a healthy fear of drunkenness. Along the way, the Washingtonians and related groups created a self-consciously respectable native Protestant working class in American cities.

Ethnicity and Alcohol

In the 1840s and 1850s, millions of Irish and German immigrants poured into neighborhoods stirred by working-class revivals and temperance agitation. The newcomers had their own time-honored relations to alcohol. The Germans introduced lager beer to the United States, thus providing a wholesome alternative for Americans who wished to give up spirits without joining the teetotalers. The Germans also built old-country beer halls, complete with sausage counters, oompah bands, group singing, and other family attractions. For their part, the Irish reaffirmed their love of whiskey— a love forged in colonial oppression and in a culture that accepted trouble with resignation, a love that legitimized levels of male drunkenness and violence that Americans, particularly the temperance forces, found appalling.

In the 1850s, native resentment of Catholic immigrants drove thousands of Baptist and Methodist "respectables" out of the Democratic coalition and into nativist Whig majorities that—beginning with Maine in 1851—established legal prohibition throughout New England, the middle states, and the Old Northwest. Many of these Democrats became part of the North's Republican majority on the eve of the Civil War.

The South and Social Reform

On economic issues, the legislatures of the southern and northern states divided along the same lines: Whigs wanted government participation in the economy; Democrats did not. On social questions, however, southern Whigs and Democrats both opposed moralizing legislation. The South was a rural, culturally conservative region of father-dominated households. Southern voters of both parties perceived attempts at "social improvement" as intrusive assaults on the autonomy of neighborhoods and families.

The southern states enacted school laws and drew up blueprints for state school systems, but the white South had little need for schools to enforce a common culture. Moreover, the South had less money and less faith in government. Consequently, southern schools tended to be locally controlled, to be infused with southern evangelical culture, and to have a limited curriculum and a short school year. In 1860, northern children attended school for an average of more than 50 days a year; white children in the South attended school for an average of 10 days annually.

By 1860, every slave state except Florida and the Carolinas operated prisons modeled on the Auburn system. Southern prisons stressed punishment and profits over rehabilitation. While northern evangelicals preached that criminals could be reformed, southerners demanded Old Testament vengeance, arguing that hanging, whipping, and branding were inexpensive, more effective than mere incarceration, and sanctioned by the Bible. Other southerners, defending the code of honor, charged that victims and their relatives would be denied vengeance if criminals were hidden away in prisons. Some southern prisons leased convict labor (and sometimes whole prisons) to private entrepreneurs.

The South did participate in temperance. By the 1820s, Baptists and Methodists had made deep inroads into southern society. Southern ministers preached against alcohol, while churchgoing women discouraged their husbands, sons, and suitors from drinking. But legal prohibition, which became dominant in the North, got nowhere in the South.

At bottom, southern resistance to social reform stemmed from a conservative, Bible-based acceptance of suffering and human imperfection and a commitment to the power and independence of white men who headed families. Any proposal that sounded like social tinkering or the invasion of paternal rights would fail. Many reforms—public schools, Sunday schools, prohibition, humane asylums—were seen as the work of well-funded and well-organized missionaries from the Northeast who wanted to fashion society in their own self-righteous image. The southern distrust of reform was powerfully reinforced after 1830, when northern reformers began to call for the abolition of slavery and the equality of the sexes—ideas that most white southerners found unthinkable.

THE POLITICS OF RACE

FOCUS QUESTION

How did Whigs and Democrats differ on questions of slavery and race?

Most whites in antebellum America believed in "natural" differences based on sex and race. God, they said, had given women and men and whites and blacks different mental, emotional, and physical capacities. Because humankind (female and nonwhite more than others) was innately sinful and prone to disorder, God ordained a fixed social hierarchy in which white men exercised power over others. Slaves and free blacks accepted their subordinate status only as a fact of life, not as something that was natural and just. Some women also questioned patriarchy. But before 1830, hierarchy based on sex and race was seldom questioned in public, particularly by persons who were in a position to change it.

In the antebellum years, as southerners and most northerners stiffened their defense of white supremacy, a radical minority of Whig evangelicals began to envision a world based on Christian love and individual worth and accomplishment, not "natural" differences. While conservative Christians insisted that relations based on dominance and submission were the lot of a sinful humankind, reformers argued that such relations interposed human power, too often in the form of brute force, between God and the individual spirit. They called for a world that substituted spiritual freedom and Christian love for every form of worldly domination. The result was a community of uncompromising radical reformers who attacked slavery as America's great national sin. In doing so, they assaulted the white republic and the core compromise of the American political system.

Democratic Racism

Neither Whigs nor Democrats encouraged the aspirations of slaves or free blacks, but it was the Democrats who incorporated racism into their political agenda. By the time of the Civil War, Democrats mobilized voters almost solely with threats of "amalgamation" and "Negro rule." Meanwhile, educated Democrats learned to think in racist terms. Among most scientists, biological determinism replaced historical and environmental explanations of racial differences. Many argued that whites and blacks were separate species—a "discovery" welcomed by Democrats. In 1850 the *Democratic Review* confided, "Few or none now seriously adhere to the theory of the unity of the races. The whole state of the science at this moment seems to indicate that there are several distinct races of men on the earth, with entirely different capacities, physical and mental."

As whites came to perceive racial differences as God-given and immutable, they changed the nature of those differences as well. In the 18th and early 19th centuries, whites had stereotyped blacks as ignorant and prone to drunkenness and thievery, but they had also maintained a parallel stereotype of blacks as loyal and self-sacrificing servants. From the 1820s onward, racists continued to regard blacks as incompetent, but they now saw all blacks as treacherous, shrewd, and secretive—individuals who only pretended to feel loyalty to white families and affection for the white children they took care of, while awaiting the chance to steal from them or poison them.

Colonization

Before 1830, few whites opposed slavery politically. The biggest organization that did address questions of slavery and race was the **American Colonization Society**, founded in 1816. This elite organization of white men never attacked slavery; the rising population of free blacks was their principal concern. They sought to colonize free blacks (but not slaves) in Liberia, on the west coast of Africa. Early members included Henry Clay, Andrew Jackson, and other political leaders of the West, the Middle States, and the Upper South. Blacks, they said, would continue to suffer from white prejudice and their own deficiencies as long as they stayed in the United States. They would exercise freedom and learn Christian and republican ways only if exported to Liberia.

Free blacks had agitated against slavery and legal racism for many years, demanding both abolition and equal rights. While a few sailed to Liberia, most insisted that colonization was not an offer of freedom but an attempt to round up black people and make them disappear. The black abolitionist James Forten spoke for many when he insisted that colonization "originated more immediately from prejudice than from philanthropy." Opposition to colonization created an immediatist, confrontational black antislavery movement—a movement that decisively shaped the later abolition crusade.

Abolitionists

Even though few white Americans openly contested slavery before 1830, the writing was on the wall. Emancipation in the North constituted an implicit condemnation of slavery in the South. So did events outside the United States. Toussaint L'Ouverture's successful slave revolution in Haiti threatened slavery everywhere (see Chapter 7). Mexico, Peru, Chile, Gran Colombia (present-day Colombia, Venezuela, Ecuador, and Panama), and other new republics carved out of the Spanish empire emancipated their slaves. The British outlawed the Atlantic slave trade in 1808, and the United States followed suit. The most powerful blow came in 1830, when the British Parliament emancipated the slaves of Jamaica, Bermuda, and other Caribbean islands ruled by Britain.

American Colonization Society *Established by elite gentlemen of the Middle States and the Upper South in 1816, this organization encouraged voluntary emancipation of slaves, to be followed by their emigration to the West African colony of Liberia.*

abolitionism *Movement begun in the North, circa 1830, to abolish slavery immediately and without compensation to owners.*

William Lloyd Garrison *Abolitionist and publisher of the first issue of the* Liberator.

American Anti-Slavery Society *Organization created by northern abolitionists in 1833 that called for immediate, uncompensated emancipation of the slaves.*

Historians usually date American **abolitionism** from 1831, when the veteran reformer **William Lloyd Garrison** published the first issue of the *Liberator* in Boston. Garrison condemned slavery not simply as a social problem or a bad idea but as America's great national sin. He demanded immediate emancipation and equal citizenship for African Americans. Garrison opposed discrimination as well as slavery, thus coupling southern slavery with the national question of race. From the beginning, he enjoyed the support and influence of northern free blacks. In its first year fully three-fourths of the *Liberator*'s subscribers and one-fifth of its writers were black, and when Garrison and his coworkers formed the New England Anti-Slavery Society in 1832, blacks made up one-fourth of the membership. They would form a larger organization, the **American Anti-Slavery Society**, the following year. Black orators such as Frederick Douglass and Sojourner Truth became stars of a well-organized abolitionist lecture circuit, and the heartfelt autobiographies of escaped slaves (many of them "as told to" white abolitionists) were mainstays of abolitionist literature, steering the movement away from the legalism of the colonizationists and toward personal, emotional appeals.

Moderates and latecomers to the abolitionist movement spoke of inherent racial characteristics but still tended to view blacks in benign (if condescending) ways. Harriet Beecher Stowe, for instance, portrayed blacks as simple, innocent, loving people who possessed a capacity for sentiment and emotionalism that most whites had lost. In 1852, Horace Mann told an audience of blacks in Ohio that "in intellect, the blacks are inferior to the whites, while in sentiment and affections, the whites are inferior to the blacks."

Radical abolitionists, however, remained committed not only to abolitionism but also to racial equality. Assuming that God had created blacks and whites as members of one human family, abolitionists opposed the "scientific" racism spouted by Democrats and many Whigs. Lydia Maria Child of New York City declared, "In the United States, colored persons have scarcely any chance to rise. But if colored persons are well treated, and have the same inducements to industry as others, they [will] work as well and behave as well."

THE RESURRECTION OF HENRY "BOX" BROWN. *One of the most resourceful of escaped slaves was Henry Brown of Richmond. Distraught at the sale of his wife and children, in 1849 he paid a white storekeeper to ship him as "dry goods" to James Miller McKim, a well-known abolitionist in Philadelphia. Brown was nailed into a small shipping crate and, after moving by two freight wagons, two trains, and a steamboat on which he was packed upside down, he arrived at McKim's house in free territory. He became a hero to abolitionists, who renamed him "Box" Brown. Afraid of recapture, he moved to England.*

VISUAL LINK TO THE PAST

An Abolitionist View of Slave Society

This provocative woodcut appeared in the *Anti-Slavery Almanac for 1840* (Boston, 1839). It pictures the lynching of slaves and their abolitionist allies by a southern mob. Surrounding the hanging tree are men (no women appear in the picture) engaged in other activities that northern reformers insisted grew from the brutality of slave society. Men duel with pistols and knives, engage in an eye-gouging wrestling match, gamble and drink, whip and torture slaves, and cheer for cockfights and horse races. The enemy here is not simply slavery but the debauchery, cruelty, and unbridled passions that abolitionists associated with it.

Q Compare this with "A Southern View of Slavery" on p. 214. Both pictures are extreme overstatements, but they overstate their cases in different ways. Why, do you think, did a southern apologist for slavery and a northern abolitionist choose these particular ways to portray the same society?

"OUR *PECULIAR* DOMESTIC INSTITUTIONS."

The radicalized abolitionists were a combination of old and new reformers. Some of them were cultivated Bostonians who opposed slavery as an affront to reason and humanity. Others were Quakers who added their antislavery experience and convictions to the cause. Abolitionists found their greatest support in southern New England, western New York, northern Ohio, and among the

©The Granger Collection, New York

WOMAN AND A SISTER. *For many years, the British antislavery forces had used the iconic image of a male slave, kneeling and holding up his chains, with the words "Am I not a man and a brother?" American abolitionists used that image as well, but added a similar image of a supplicant female slave, underlining the participation of women and the emerging centrality of women's issues in the American antislavery movement.*

Postal Campaign *Abolitionist tactic to force the nation to confront the slavery question by flooding the mails, both North and South, with antislavery literature. The hope was to raise controversy within an area that was the province of the federal government.*

new middle classes of the cities—ground that Yankee settlement, the market revolution, and Finneyite revivals had turned into the heartland of the northern Whig Party.

Agitation

Antislavery, unlike other reforms, was a radical attack on one of the nation's central institutions, and the movement attracted a minority even among middle-class evangelicals. Both Lyman Beecher and Charles Finney opposed the abolitionists in the 1830s, arguing that emancipation would come about sooner or later through the religious conversion of slave owners; antislavery agitation and the denunciation of slaveholders, they argued, would divide Christians, slow the revival movement, and thus actually delay emancipation. Other opponents, including some within the antislavery ranks, were outraged that blacks and whites and men and women met, organized, and socialized together, and that women and blacks delivered speeches to mixed audiences.

Radical abolitionists knew that they were a small, despised minority, and that government and most citizens wanted to ignore the question of slavery. The American Anti-Slavery Society staged a series of campaigns to force government and the public to face the South's "peculiar institution." In 1835, the society launched its **Postal Campaign,** flooding the nation's postal system with abolitionist tracts that southerners and most northerners regarded as incendiary. From 1836 onward, they petitioned Congress to abolish slavery and the slave trade in the District of Columbia and to deny the slaveholding Republic of Texas admission to the Union. Two-thirds of the signers of these petitions were women, prompting a Mississippi senator to declare that there would be less trouble "if the ladies and Sunday school children would let us alone."

From the beginnings of antislavery agitation, the public response was often violent. Riots aimed at blacks and their white friends exploded in nearly every northern city. Mobs destroyed black neighborhoods in New York and Philadelphia. A mob surrounded a convention of the Boston Female Antislavery Society in 1835, forced the women to leave, then went looking for Garrison. Garrison was roughed up, then escaped the mob by going into police custody, where he was charged with disturbing the peace. Southern whites had fewer free blacks or abolitionists to attack, but they found their own ways to respond. A committee in Mississippi invited Garrison and other antislavery leaders to come south and be hanged. And at the highest levels of government, President Jackson condoned mail censorship, and Congress authorized the gag rule on antislavery petitions (see Chapter 11).

In these ways, abolitionists demonstrated the complicity of the party system (and the Democrats in particular) in the institution of slavery, brought the slavery question to public attention, and tied it to questions of civil liberties in the North and political power nationally.

THE POLITICS OF GENDER AND SEX

Whigs valued a reformed masculinity that was lived out in the sentimentalized homes of the northern business classes or in the Christian gentility of the Whig plantation and farm. Jacksonian voters defended domestic patriarchy. Democrats often made heroes of men whose flamboyant, rakish lives directly challenged Whig domesticity. Whigs denounced Andrew Jackson for allegedly stealing his wife from her lawful husband; many Democrats admired him for the same reason. Richard M. Johnson of Kentucky, who was vice president under Martin Van Buren, openly kept a mulatto mistress and had two daughters by her; with his pistols always at hand, he accompanied her openly around Washington, D.C. "Prince" John Van Buren, the president's son and himself a prominent New York Democrat, met a "dark-eyed, well-formed Italian lady" who became his "fancy lady," remaining with him until he lost her in a high-stakes card game.

Whigs made Democratic contempt for sentimental domesticity a political issue. William Crane, a Michigan Whig, claimed that Democrats "despised no man for his sins" and went on to say that "brothel-haunters flocked to this party, because here in all political circles, and political movements, they were treated as nobility." Much of the Whig cultural agenda (and much of Democratic hatred of that agenda) was rooted in contests between Whig and Democratic masculine styles.

FOCUS QUESTION

How did Democrats and Whigs differ on questions of gender and sex? Knowing what you know about the political cultures of the two parties, how do you explain those differences?

Moral Reform

Sexual self-control became a badge of middle-class status. Men supposedly had the greatest difficulty taming their appetites. The old image of woman as seductress persisted in the more traditionalist churches and in the pulp fiction from which middle-class mothers tried to protect their sons. Whig evangelicals, on the other hand, discovered that women were naturally free of desire and that only men were subject to the animal passions. The middle-class ideal combined female purity and male self-control. For the most part, it was a private reform, contained within the home, but evangelical domesticity sometimes produced moral crusades to impose that ethos on the world at large. Many of these crusades were led by women from Whig families.

In 1828, a band of Sunday school teachers initiated an informal mission to prostitutes that grew into the New-York Magdalen Society. Taking a novel approach to an age-old question, the society argued that prostitution was created by brutal fathers and husbands who abandoned their young daughters or wives, by dandies who seduced them and turned them into prostitutes, and by lustful men who bought their services. Prostitution, in other words, was not the result of the innate sinfulness of prostitutes; it was the result of the brutality and lust of men. The solution was to remove young prostitutes from their environment, pray with them, and convert them to middle-class morality.

The Magdalen Society's *First Annual Report* (1831) inveighed against male lust and printed shocking life histories of prostitutes. Yet some men read it as pornography, and others used it as a guidebook to the seamier side of New York City. The wealthy male evangelicals who had bankrolled the Magdalen Society withdrew their support, and the organization fell apart. Thereupon many of the women reformers set up the Female Moral Reform Society, with a House of

REPORT

OF THE

WOMAN'S RIGHTS

CONVENTION,

Held at SENECA FALLS, N. Y., July 19th
and 20th, 1848.

Sarah Cowney

ROCHESTER:
PRINTED BY JOHN DICK
AT THE NORTH STAR OFFICE.

THE DECLARATION OF SENTIMENTS PUBLISHED BY THE FIRST
WOMEN'S RIGHTS CONVENTION IN 1848. *This account of the
proceedings and list of resolutions announced that there was an
organized women's rights movement in the United States. It also
announced that women's rights activists knew how to organize a
convention and how to publicize their activities in print. (Ties
between the women's and antislavery movements led the women to
have their report printed at the offices of the North Star, an
antislavery paper published by the black abolitionist Frederick
Douglass—the only male member of the convention—in
Rochester.)*

Sarah Grimke *Along with her
sister, Angelina, this elite South
Carolina woman moved north and
campaigned against slavery and
for temperance and women's
rights.*

Industry in which prostitutes were taught morality and household skills to prepare them for new lives as domestic servants in pious middle-class homes. This effort also failed, largely because few prostitutes were interested in domestic service or evangelical religion.

The Female Moral Reform Society was more successful with members of its own class. Its newspaper, the *Advocate of Moral Reform,* circulated throughout the evangelical North, eventually reaching 555 auxiliary societies with 20,000 readers. Now evangelical women fought prostitution by publishing the names of customers. They campaigned against pornography, obscenity, lewdness, and seduction and taught their sons to be pure, even when it meant dragging them out of brothels. They also publicized the names of adulterers, and they had seducers brought into court. In the process, women reformers fought the sexual double standard and claimed the power to define what was respectable and what was not.

Women's Rights

From the late 1820s onward, middle-class women in the North assumed roles that would have been unthinkable to their mothers and grandmothers. Evangelical domesticity made loving mothers (and not stern fathers) the principal rearers of children. Housewives saw themselves as missionaries to their families, responsible for the moral choices their children and husbands made. In that role, women became arbiters of fashion, diet, and sexual behavior. Many joined the temperance movement and moral reform societies, where they became public reformers while posing as mothers protecting their sons from rum sellers and seducers. They gained a sense of spiritual empowerment that led some to question their own subordinate status within a system of gendered social roles.

Nearly all early feminists were veterans of the antislavery crusade. Abolitionists called for absolute human equality and rejection of impersonal institutions and prescribed social roles. It became clear to some female abolitionists that the critique of slavery applied as well to inequality based on sex. Radical female abolitionists reached the conclusion that they were human beings first and women second. In 1837, **Sarah Grimke** announced, "The Lord Jesus defines the duties of his followers in his Sermon on the Mount . . . without any reference to sex or condition . . . never even referring to the distinction now so strenuously insisted upon between masculine and feminine virtues. . . . Men and women are CREATED EQUAL!" A women's rights convention put it just as bluntly in 1851: "We deny the right of any portion of the species to decide for another portion . . . what is and what is not their 'proper sphere'; that the proper sphere for all human beings is the largest and highest to which they are able to attain."

Such talk—and worse, the fact that women were delivering such speeches in public—aroused opposition even among abolitionists. While Garrison and the radicals supported full rights for women, others wished to win public favor and elect antislavery congressmen and state legislators. They argued that the woman question was at best a distraction. The result was a split in the antislavery crusade, largely over the question of women's rights.

Many women opposed gender inequality and had been talking about it for a long time. But it was the argument within the antislavery movement that spurred the first organized movement for women's rights. Beginning around 1840, women lobbied state legislatures against the common-law custom that women and children were under the protection and authority of their husbands and fathers, and thus had limited rights to property and over themselves. The reformers won significant changes in the laws governing women's rights to property, to the wages of their own labor, and to custody of children in cases of divorce. Fourteen states passed such legislation, culminating in New York's Married Women's Property Act in 1860.

Women's progress in achieving political rights, however, came more slowly. Elizabeth Cady Stanton and other feminist abolitionists organized the first Women's Rights Convention, held in 1848 at **Seneca Falls,** New York. The only male delegate was Frederick Douglass. Sojourner Truth, another prominent black opponent of slavery, also attended. Nearly all of the other delegates were white women abolitionists. Both as abolitionists and as feminists, they based their demands for equality not only on legal and moral arguments but also on the spirit of republican institutions. They issued a Declaration of Sentiments and Resolutions, based on the Declaration of Independence, which denounced "the repeated injuries and usurpations on the part of man toward woman."

Most of those "injuries and usurpations" were political. The central issue was the right to vote, for female participation in politics was a direct challenge to a male-ordained idea of women's place. A distraught New York legislator warned: "It is well known that the object of these unsexed women is to overthrow the most sacred of our institutions. . . . Are we to put the stamp of truth upon the libel here set forth, that men and women, in the matrimonial relation, are to be equal?" Later, Stanton recalled such reactions: "Political rights," she said, "involving in their last results equality everywhere, roused all the antagonism of a dominant power, against the self-assertion of a class hitherto subservient."

QUICK   REVIEW

DEMANDS OF THE WOMEN'S RIGHTS MOVEMENT

- Rejection of separate spheres
- Women's property rights
- Legal reforms on domestic issues
- Right to vote

Conclusion

By the 1830s, most citizens identified with either the Whig or Democratic Party, so much so that party affiliation was a big part of personal identity. In the states and neighborhoods, Whigs embraced commerce and activist government, arguing that both would foster prosperity, social harmony, and moral progress. Faith in progress and improvement led northern and western Whigs to entertain the hope that liberty and equality might apply to women and blacks. The Democratic response to this was grounded in a defense of white patriarchy and the old republic. They seldom doubted the value of commerce, but they worried that the market and its infrastructure of banking, credit, and paper money—all of it subsidized by government—forced inequality and dependence among the republic's white male citizenry. Democrats also looked with angry disbelief at attempts of Whigs to govern private and public behavior, and sometimes even to attack the "natural" and fundamental distinctions of sex and race.

In sum, Whigs reformulated the revolutionary legacy of liberty and equality, moving away from classical notions of citizenship and toward liberty of conscience and equality of opportunity within a market-driven democracy. They often attempted to civilize that new world by using government power to encourage commerce, social interdependence, and cultural homogeneity. When Democrats argued that Whig "interdependence" in fact meant dependence and inequality, Whigs countered with promises of success for individuals who were morally

Seneca Falls Convention (1848) *First national convention of women's rights activists.*

worthy of it. Democrats trusted none of that. Theirs was a Jeffersonian formulation grounded in a fierce defense of the liberty and equality of white men, and in a minimal, inexpensive, decentralized government that protected the liberties of those men without threatening their independence or their power over their households and within their neighborhoods.

CHAPTER REVIEW

Review Questions

1. What were the Whig and Democratic conceptions of the duties and limits of government?
2. What were the Whig and Democratic positions on the issues of public schools, prisons, and asylums?
3. How did Whigs and Democrats differ on questions of slavery and race?
4. How did Democrats and Whigs differ on questions of gender and sex? Knowing what you know about the political cultures of the two parties, how do you explain those differences?

Critical Thinking Questions

1. Choose a position either defending or attacking this statement: "Differences between Whigs and Democrats on economic policy, social reform, race, and gender boil down to differences in Whig and Democratic conceptions of white manhood."
2. What were the goals and assumptions that drove the movements for public schools, humane prisons and asylums, and temperance? Were those primarily Democratic or Whig assumptions?

Identifications

Review your understanding of the following key terms, people, and events for this chapter.

limited liability, p. 272
common schools, p. 273
normal schools, p. 274
Auburn system, p. 275

Dorothea Dix, p. 276
American Colonization Society, p. 281
abolitionism, p. 282

William Lloyd Garrison, p. 282
American Anti-Slavery Society, p. 282

Postal Campaign, p. 284
Sarah Grimke, p. 286
Seneca Falls Convention, p. 287

DISCOVERY

What broad social movements emerged during this period, and how did some try to stem these attempts at reform?

In thinking about this question, begin by breaking it down into the components shown below. A discussion of the significance of each component should appear in your answer.

Culture and Society

See the abolitionist depiction of slave society. Who is being lynched? What else are the southerners attending the lynchings doing? What does this suggest that the artist thinks about southern society and the effects of slavery on society? Is there any significance to the absence of women and children from this image?

AN ABOLITIONIST VIEW OF SLAVE SOCIETY

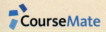

Visit the CourseMate website at www.cengagebrain.com for additional study tools and review materials for this chapter.

C H A P T E R

13

MANIFEST DESTINY: AN EMPIRE FOR LIBERTY—OR SLAVERY?

The United States became a transcontinental nation between 1845 and 1848, increasing in size by 50 percent. Through annexation, negotiation, and war, the United States gained more than one million square miles, with western migration and settlement playing an important role in making this territorial acquisition desirable.

Many Americans enthusiastically championed expansionism and celebrated this early version of U.S. empire. But expansionism aroused opposition as well. On both sides of the debate, the nation's politicians and its citizens worried over an increasingly fraught question: Was this new empire for liberty—or for slavery? The acquisition of vast new stretches of land reopened the issue of slavery's expansion and planted the bitter seeds of civil war.

1844	1846	1848	1850	1852	1854

■ **1844**
Expansionist James K. Polk elected president

1845 ■
U.S. annexes Texas

■ **1846**
U.S. declares war on Mexico

1847 ■
U.S. Army captures Mexico City

■ **1848**
Discovery of gold in California

1849 ■
Gold Rush to California

■ **1850**
Compromise of 1850

1851 ■
Fugitive slave rescues in North

■ **1852**
Uncle Tom's Cabin published

■ **1854**
William Walker invades Nicaragua

© Cengage Learning

GROWTH AS THE AMERICAN WAY

By 1850, older Americans had seen the area of the United States quadruple in their lifetime. Since the Louisiana Purchase of 1803, the American population had also quadrupled. Many Americans considered this growth evidence of God's benefi-cence to this virtuous republic. During the 1840s, a group of expansionists affiliated with the Democratic Party began to call themselves the **Young America movement.** They proclaimed that it was the **Manifest Destiny** of the United States "to over-spread and to possess the whole of the continent which Providence has given us for the development of the great experiment of liberty," as John L. O'Sullivan, editor of the *Democratic Review*, wrote in 1845.

For Native Americans, however, Manifest Destiny was a story of defeat and contraction. By 1850 the diseases and guns first introduced by whites had reduced the Indian population north of the Rio Grande to fewer than half a million, a fraction of the population of two or three centuries earlier. The relentless westward march of white settlements had pushed all but a few thousand Indians beyond the Mississippi. In the 1840s, the U.S. government decided to create a "permanent Indian frontier" at about the 95th meridian (roughly the western borders of Iowa, Missouri, and Arkansas). But white emigrants were already violating that frontier on the overland trails to the Pacific, and settlers were pressing against the borders of Indian territory. In little more than a decade, the idea of "one big reservation" in the West would give way to the policy of forcing Indians onto small reservations. The government "negotiated" with Indian chiefs for vast cessions of land in return for annuity payments that were often extracted by corrupt traders. Many Indians perished of disease, malnutrition, the alcohol first introduced by whites—and in futile efforts to break out of the reservations and regain their land.

FOCUS QUESTION

What impulses lay behind the Manifest Destiny of America's westward expansion?

Young America movement
A group of young members of the Democratic Party who were interested in territorial expansion in the 1840s.

Manifest Destiny *The belief that the United States was destined to grow from the Atlantic to the Pacific and from the Arctic to the tropics. Providence supposedly intended for Americans to have this area for a great experiment in liberty.*

VISUAL LINK TO THE PAST

Manifest Destiny

John Gast's 1872 painting, *American Progress*, with its Indians fleeing before a large figure of Columbia, has often been called a frontier allegory that celebrates "Manifest Destiny." But the painting doesn't just celebrate the conquering of western territory and peoples: Look closely to see how it also positions such technologies as the telegraph and the railroad.

Q What are some of the messages this painting conveys about how the process of westward expansion occurs?

Library of Congress, Prints and Photographs Division

Manifest Destiny and Slavery

Manifest Destiny also presaged a crisis in the history of black Americans. Territorial acquisitions had brought into the republic the slave states of Louisiana, Missouri, Arkansas, Florida, Texas, and parts of Alabama and Mississippi. Only Iowa, admitted in 1846, had joined the ranks of the free states.

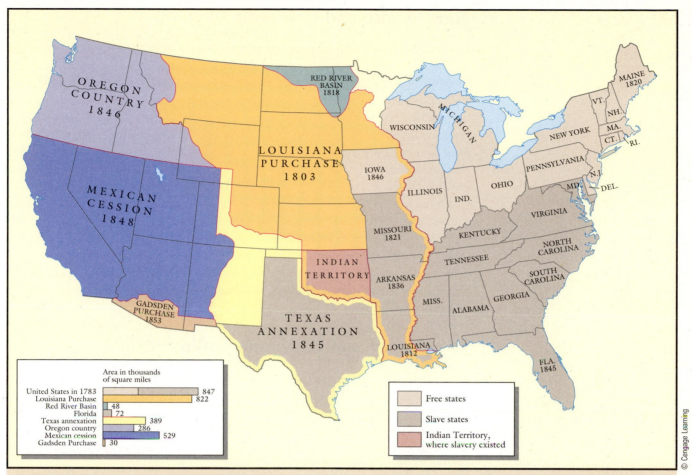

Map 13.1 **Free and Slave States and Territories, 1848.** *This map illustrates two developments of critical importance to the controversy over the expansion of slavery in the 1840s and 1850s: the larger number of slave than free states entering the Union from the territories acquired from France (Louisiana Purchase) and Spain (Florida) and the huge amount of new territory added by the acquisition of Texas and the Southwest from Mexico and the settlement of the Oregon boundary in the 1840s.*

Although the Compromise of 1820 had supposedly settled the division between slavery and freedom in the rest of the Louisiana Purchase, the expansion of slavery into new territories was an explosive issue. The issue first arose with the annexation of Texas, which helped provoke a war with Mexico that many antislavery northerners considered an ugly effort to expand slavery.

The Expansionist Impulse

Americans of European descent saw their future in the West. In the 1840s **Horace Greeley** urged, "Go West, young man." And to the West they went in unprecedented numbers, driven in part by the depression of 1837–1843 that prompted thousands to search for cheap land and better opportunity.

An earlier wave of migration had populated the region between the Appalachians and the Missouri River. Reports from explorers, fur traders, missionaries, and sailors filtered back from California and the Pacific Northwest, describing the bounteous resources and benign climate of those wondrous regions. Guidebooks rolled off the presses describing the prospects that awaited settlers who would turn "those wild forests, trackless plains, untrodden valleys" into "one grand scene of continuous improvements, universal enterprise, and unparalleled commerce."

Horace Greeley *Editor of the New York Tribune, one of the most influential newspapers in the country.*

New Mexico and California

By the time Mexico won its independence from Spain in 1821, some 80,000 Mexicans lived in portions of the region west of the 95th meridian. Three-fourths of them had settled in the Rio Grande valley of New Mexico and most of the rest in California. Colonial society had centered on the **missions** and the **presidios**. Intended to Christianize Indians, the missions also became an instrument to exploit their labor, while the presidios (military posts) protected the settlers from hostile Indians. Already in decline, the missions collapsed entirely after Mexican independence. The presidios, underfunded and understaffed, also declined, and the defense of Mexico's far northern provinces increasingly fell to the residents. But by the 1830s, many residents of New Mexico and California were more interested in bringing American traders in than in keeping American settlers out. A flourishing trade over the Santa Fe Trail from Independence, Missouri, brought American manufactured goods to Santa Fe, New Mexico (and points south), in exchange for Mexican horses, mules, beaver pelts, and silver. New England ships carried American goods all the way around the horn of South America to San Francisco and other California ports in exchange for tallow and hides produced by *californio* ranchers.

The Oregon and California Trails

At the depth of the economic depression in 1842 and 1843, Oregon fever swept the Mississippi valley. Thousands of farm families sold their land, packed their worldly goods in covered wagons along with supplies for five or six months on the trail, hitched up their oxen, and headed out from Independence or St. Joseph, Missouri, for the trek of almost 2,000 miles to the river valleys of Oregon or California. From 1840 to 1869, an estimated 50,000 emigrants made the trip.

Adult men outnumbered women on the western trails before the gold rush by more than 2 to 1. Many women were reluctant emigrants, and their diaries testified to their unhappiness: "What had possessed my husband, anyway, that he should have thought of bringing us away out through this God-forsaken country?" wrote one woman. She was sorry she had ever consented "to take this wild goose chase." For some families it did turn out to be a wild goose chase, but for many of those who stayed the course and settled in the far West, it was a success story in which women were critical in transforming settlements into communities.

On the way west, migrants passed through regions claimed by three nations—the United States, Mexico, and Britain—and they settled on land owned by Mexico (California) or claimed jointly by the United States and Britain (Oregon, which then stretched north to the border of Russian Alaska). But no matter who claimed it, the land was inhabited mostly by Indians. Few of the emigrants thought about settling down along the way, for this vast reach of arid plains, forbidding mountains, and burning wastelands was then known as the **Great American Desert.** Whites considered it suitable only for Indians and a disappearing breed of fur trappers. But one group did find its new home at the edge of the Great Salt Lake.

The Mormon Migration

Subjected to persecution that drove them from their original home in western New York to Ohio, Missouri, and eventually to Illinois, the **Mormons** established Nauvoo, Illinois, a thriving community of 15,000 souls, based on collective economic effort and theocratic discipline imposed by their founder and prophet, Joseph Smith. But the people of Illinois proved no more hospitable to the Mormons than the sect's previous neighbors. Smith's insistence that God spoke through him, his

---

missions *Outposts established by the Spanish along the northern frontier to aid in Christianizing the native peoples. They also were used to exploit their labor.*

presidios *Military posts constructed by the Spanish to protect the settlers from hostile Indians. They also were used to keep non-Spanish settlers from the area.*

Great American Desert *The treeless area in the plains most Americans considered unsuitable for settlement. It generally was passed over by settlers going to the Pacific coast areas.*

Mormons *Members of the Church of Jesus Christ of Latter-day Saints, founded by Joseph Smith in 1830; The Book of Mormon supplemented the Bible.*

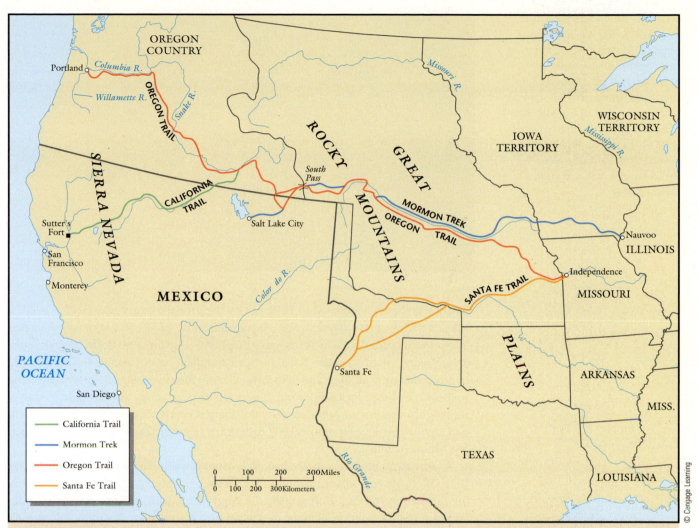

Map 13.2 Overland Trails, 1846. *The Santa Fe Trail was mainly a route for trade between the United States and the Mexican province (before 1848) of New Mexico. The other three trails carried hundreds of thousands of Americans to new homes in the West.*

autocratic suppression of dissent, and his assertion that the Mormons were the only true Christians and would inherit the earth provoked hostility. When a dissident faction of Mormons published Smith's latest revelation, which sanctioned **polygamy**, he ordered their printing press destroyed. The county sheriff arrested him, and in June 1844, a mob broke into the jail and killed him.

Smith's martyrdom prompted yet another exodus. His successor, Brigham Young, took the Mormons on the long trek westward. They arrived at the Great Salt Lake Basin on July 24, 1847. The Mormons made the desert bloom with grain and vegetables irrigated by water diverted from mountain streams. Young reigned as leader of the church, and from 1850 to 1857 as governor of the newly created Utah Territory. But relations with the government in Washington and with territorial officials were never smooth, especially after Young's proclamation in 1852 authorizing polygamy. When conflict between the Mormons and the U.S. Army broke out in 1857, Young surrendered his civil authority and made an uneasy peace with the government.

The Republic of Texas

As the Mormons were starting west, a crisis between Mexico and the United States was coming to a boil. The United States had renounced any claim to Texas in a

polygamy *The act of having more than one wife.*

MORMON EMIGRANTS ON THEIR WAY WEST. *This rare photograph depicts a Mormon wagon train snaking through a narrow mountain pass on its way to Salt Lake City. Beleaguered by neighbors in Illinois, the Mormons decided after Joseph Smith's murder in 1844 to emigrate to what was then Mexican territory— but would soon become part of the United States.*

Courtesy of the Church Archives, The Church of Jesus Christ of Latter-day Saints

treaty with Spain negotiated in 1819, but by the time the treaty was ratified in 1821, Mexico had won its independence. The new Republic of Mexico, seeking to develop its northern borderlands in Texas, gave Stephen F. Austin, a Missouri businessman, a large land grant to settle 300 American families there. Despite their pledge to become Roman Catholics and Mexican citizens, these immigrants and many who followed remained Protestants and Americans at heart. They also brought in slaves, in defiance of a recent Mexican law abolishing slavery. Despite Mexican efforts to ban any further immigration, 30,000 Americans lived in Texas by 1835, outnumbering Mexicans 6 to 1.

American settlers initially had little contact with Mexican *tejanos*. Then, in 1835, Mexico's new government became intent on consolidating its authority over the northern territories. In response, the Anglo-American settlers and the Mexican *tejanos* forged a political alliance to protest any further loss of autonomy in their province. When the Mexican government responded militarily, many Texans—both Anglo and American—fought back. In March 1836, the Anglo-Texans declared Texas the independent **Republic of Texas**.

It took the Texans less than seven months to win and consolidate their independence. Mexican General Antonio López de Santa Anna led the Mexican army that captured the **Alamo** (a former mission converted to a fort) in San Antonio on March 6, 1836, killing all 187 of its defenders, including the legendary Americans Davy Crockett and Jim Bowie. Rallying to the cry "Remember the Alamo!" Texans swarmed to the revolutionary army commanded by Sam Houston. When the Mexican army slaughtered another force of more than 300 men after they had surrendered at Goliad on March 19, the Texans were further inflamed. A month later, Houston's army, aided by volunteers from southern states, routed a larger Mexican force on the San Jacinto River and captured Santa Anna, who signed a treaty granting Texas its independence. The Mexican congress later repudiated the treaty but could not muster enough strength to reestablish its authority north of the Nueces River. The victorious Texans elected Sam Houston president of their new republic and petitioned for annexation to the United States.

The Annexation Controversy

President Andrew Jackson, wary of provoking war with Mexico or quarrels with antislavery northerners, rebuffed the annexationists. So did his successor, Martin Van Buren. The Texans turned their energies to building their republic. The British

---

tejanos *Spanish-speaking settlers of Texas. The term comes from the Spanish word* Tejas *for Texas.*

Republic of Texas *Independent nation founded in 1836 when a revolution by residents in the Mexican province of Texas won their independence.*

Alamo *Battle between Texas revolutionaries and the Mexican army at the San Antonio mission called the Alamo on March 6, 1836, in which all 187 Texans were killed.*

government encouraged them in the hope that they would stand as a buffer against further U.S. expansion. Texas leaders responded to some of the British overtures, probably in the hope of provoking American annexationists to take action. They did.

Vice President John Tyler had unexpectedly become president after the death of President William Henry Harrison from pneumonia in 1841, only weeks after his inauguration as the first Whig president. Tyler soon broke with the Whig Party that had elected him. A states'-rights Virginian who sought to create a new coalition to reelect him in 1844, Tyler seized on the annexation of Texas as "the only matter that will take sufficient hold of the feelings of the South to rally it on a southern candidate."

Tyler's secretary of state, John C. Calhoun, negotiated a treaty of annexation with the eager Texans, but then he made a mistake: He released to the press his letter informing the British minister to the United States that, together with other reasons, Americans wanted to annex Texas in order to protect slavery. This seemed to confirm abolitionist charges that annexation was a pro-slavery plot. Northern senators of both parties defeated the treaty in June 1844.

By then, Texas had become the main issue in the forthcoming presidential election. Whig candidate Henry Clay had come out against annexation, as had the leading contender for the Democratic nomination, former president Martin Van Buren. Van Buren's stand angered southern Democrats, who were determined to have Texas. Through eight ballots at the Democratic national convention, they blocked Van Buren's nomination; on the ninth, the southerners broke the stalemate by nominating one of their own, James K. Polk of Tennessee. Polk's nomination undercut President Tyler's hope of being reelected on the Texas issue, so he bowed out of the race.

Polk ran on a platform that called for not only the annexation of Texas but also the acquisition of all of Oregon up to 54°40' (the Alaskan border). That demand was aimed at voters in the western free states, who believed that bringing free territory in the Northwest into the Union would balance the expansion of slavery into Texas.

Texas fever swept the South during the campaign. So powerful was the issue that Clay began to waver, stating that he would support annexation if it could be done without starting a war with Mexico. This concession won him a few southern votes but angered northern antislavery Whigs. Many of them voted for antislavery Liberty Party candidate James G. Birney, who probably took enough Whig votes from Clay in New York to give Polk victory there and in the Electoral College.

QUICK REVIEW

MANIFEST DESTINY

- Impulses for western expansion in the 1840s

- Migration of midwestern farmers to Oregon and California and of Mormons to Utah

- Texas achieves independence, petitions for annexation to the United States, provokes controversy of the expansion of slavery

Acquisition of Texas and Oregon

Although the election was extremely close, Democrats regarded it as a mandate. Congress passed a **joint resolution** of annexation in March 1845, and Texas became the 15th slave state. Backed now by the United States, Texans claimed a southern and western border beyond the Nueces River all the way to the Rio Grande, which nearly tripled the area that Mexico had formerly defined as Texas. Mexico responded by breaking off diplomatic relations with the United States.

Meanwhile, Polk addressed his promise to annex Oregon. The United States and Great Britain had jointly "occupied" Oregon since 1818. Chanting the slogan "Fifty-four forty or fight!" many Americans demanded all of Oregon, as pledged in the Democratic platform. But Americans had settled only in the region south of the Columbia River, at roughly the 46th parallel. In June 1846, Polk accepted a compromise treaty that split the Oregon country between the United States and Britain at the 49th parallel.

joint resolution *An act passed by both houses of Congress with a simple majority rather than the two-thirds majority in the Senate.*

THE MEXICAN WAR

FOCUS QUESTION

What were the causes and consequences of the Mexican War?

Having avoided a war with Britain, Polk provoked one with Mexico. In 1845, he sent a special envoy to Mexico City with an offer to buy California and New Mexico for $30 million. To help Mexico make the right response, he ordered federal troops to the disputed border area between Mexico and Texas, dispatched a naval squadron to patrol the Gulf Coast of Mexico, and instructed the American consul at Monterey (the Mexican capital of California) to stir up annexation sentiment among settlers there. These strong-arm tactics provoked a political revolt in Mexico City that brought a militant anti-American regime to power.

Polk responded in January 1846 by ordering 4,000 soldiers under General Zachary Taylor to advance all the way to the Rio Grande. Recognizing that he could achieve his goals only through armed conflict, Polk waited for news from Texas that would justify a declaration of war. Finally, on May 9, 1846, word arrived that two weeks earlier Mexican troops had crossed the Rio Grande and had attacked an American patrol, killing 11 soldiers. Polk had what he wanted, and he sent a war message to Congress on May 11. Most Whigs opposed war with Mexico, but in the end, not wanting to be branded unpatriotic, all but a handful of them voted for what they called "Mr. Polk's War."

The United States went to war with a tiny regular army of fewer than 8,000 men, supplemented by 60,000 volunteers in state regiments. Mexican soldiers outnumbered American in most of the battles, but the Americans had higher morale, better leadership, better weapons (especially artillery), and the backing of a more determined, stable government and a far richer economy. The U.S. forces won every battle—and the war—in a fashion that humiliated Mexico and left a legacy of national hostility and border violence.

Military Campaigns of 1846

The Mexican War's first phase was carried out by Zachary Taylor, whose 4,000 regulars routed numerically superior Mexican forces on the Rio Grande in early May, even before Congress had declared war. Reinforced by several thousand volunteers, "Old Rough and Ready" Taylor pursued the retreating Mexicans to Monterrey and took the city in September 1846. Mexican resistance in the area had crumbled, and Taylor's force settled down as an army of occupation.

In the second phase of American strategy, General Stephen Watts Kearny led an army west from Fort Leavenworth toward Santa Fe in June 1846. Kearny's army occupied Santa Fe on August 18 without firing a shot. After receiving reinforcements, Kearny sent part of his army into the Mexican province of Chihuahua. In the most extraordinary campaign of the war, these troops marched 1,500 miles, foraging supplies along the way; fought and beat two much larger enemy forces; and finally linked up with Zachary Taylor's army near Monterrey.

Kearny led the other contingent across deserts and mountains to California. Events there had anticipated his arrival. In June 1846, a group of American settlers backed by Captain John C. Frémont captured Sonoma and raised the flag of an independent California, displaying the silhouette of a grizzly bear. This "bear-flag revolt" paved the way for the conquest of California by the *americanos*. The U.S. Pacific fleet seized California's ports and the capital at Monterey; sailors and soldiers together subdued Mexican resistance. Kearny's force arrived in December 1846, barely in time to help with the mopping up.

Military Campaigns of 1847

The Mexican government still refused to admit that the war was lost. Early in 1847, Santa Anna raised new levies and marched north to attack Taylor's army near Monterrey. Taylor was not as ready to withstand a counteroffensive as he had been a few weeks earlier. After capturing Monterrey, he had let the defeated Mexican army go and had granted an eight-week armistice in the hope that it would allow time for peace negotiations. Angry at Taylor's presumption in making such a decision and suspicious of the general's political ambitions, Polk canceled the armistice and named General-in-Chief

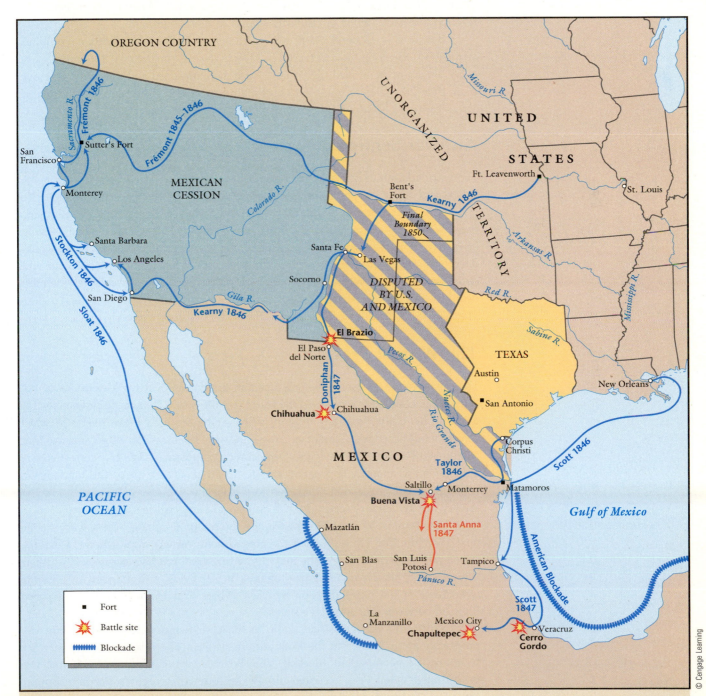

***Map 13.3* Principal Campaigns of the Mexican War, 1846–1847.** *This map provides a graphic illustration of the vast territory over which the Mexican War was fought; the distance from Veracruz to San Francisco is 2,500 miles.*

Winfield Scott to command the third phase of the war. A large, punctilious man, he had been nicknamed "Old Fuss and Feathers" for a military professionalism that contrasted with the homespun manner of "Rough and Ready" Zach Taylor. Scott decided to invade Mexico from a beachhead at Veracruz and in January 1847 ordered the transfer of more than half of Taylor's troops to his own expeditionary force.

Left with fewer than 5,000 men, most of them untried volunteers, an embittered Taylor nevertheless marched out to meet Santa Anna's army of 18,000. In a two-day battle on February 22 and 23 at Buena Vista, Taylor's force inflicted twice as many casualties as they suffered in a fierce struggle highlighted by the brilliant counterattack of a Mississippi regiment commanded by Jefferson Davis. The bloodied Mexican army retreated toward the capital. When news of the victory reached the East, Taylor's popularity soared to new heights.

But it was General Scott who actually won the war. With a combined army–navy force, he took Veracruz in March 1847. Over the next five months, his army, which never totaled more than 14,000 men, marched and fought its way over more than 200 miles of mountains and plains to Mexico City. Scott's outnumbered forces captured Mexico City on September 14.

Antiwar Sentiment

The war had enthusiastic support in the South and West and among Democrats, but Whigs and many people in the Northeast, especially in New England, considered it "wicked and disgraceful." While Democrats believed in expanding American institutions over *space*—in particular, the space occupied by Mexicans and Indians—Whigs believed in improving American institutions over *time*. "A nation cannot simultaneously devote its energies to the absorption of others' territories and the improvement of its own," said Horace Greeley. And antislavery people raised their eyebrows when they heard rhetoric about "extending the blessings of American liberty" to benighted regions. They suspected that the real reason was the desire to extend slavery.

The Wilmot Proviso

The slavery issue overshadowed all others in the debate over the Mexican War. President Polk could not understand the reason for the fuss. "There is no probability," he wrote in his diary, "that any territory will ever be acquired from Mexico in which slavery would ever exist." But other Americans were less sure. The issue came to a head in August 1846, when Pennsylvania Democratic Congressman David Wilmot offered an amendment to an army appropriations bill: ". . . that, as an express and fundamental condition of the acquisition of any territory from the Republic of Mexico . . . neither slavery nor involuntary servitude shall ever exist in any part of said territory."

This famous Wilmot Proviso framed the national debate over slavery for the next 15 years. The House passed the amendment. Nearly all northern Democrats joined all northern Whigs in the majority, while southern Democrats and southern Whigs voted almost unanimously against it. This outcome marked an ominous wrenching of the party division between Whigs and Democrats into a *sectional* division between free and slave states.

Northern Democrats had come to the conclusion that the South had disproportionate influence in the Polk administration. The resentment began when southern Democrats had blocked Van Buren's nomination in 1844 and was exacerbated when Polk accepted the 49° latitude for Oregon's northern boundary. The reduced rates of the Walker tariff in 1846 (sponsored by Robert J. Walker of Mississippi, Polk's secretary of the treasury) dismayed Democrats from Pennsylvania's industrial districts. Polk further angered Democrats from

QUICK REVIEW

THE MEXICAN WAR

- American military victories in 1846 and 1847 lead to capture of Mexico City

- Wilmot Proviso seeks to ban slavery in territory acquired from Mexico

- Treaty of Guadalupe Hidalgo reduces size of Mexico by one-half and increases size of United States by one-fourth

WAR NEWS FROM MEXICO. *Richard Caton Woodville's 1848 painting captures the excitement felt by some Americans as they read newspaper accounts of the Mexican War (1846–1848). But notice that the African American man and child, dressed in rags, are not part of the celebratory group gathered on the porch of the allegorical "American Hotel," although they appear interested in the war news. The painting reminds us that an underlying question of the Mexican War was whether slavery would be extended into new territory; it also reminds us that African Americans were not equal members of the American nation. At the far right we can see that an old woman peers out the window to see what is going on; she, too, is not part of the main group at the heart of the painting—just as women were not yet voting citizens of the American republic. The strong narrative thrust of Woodville's painting marks it as one of many "genre paintings" that in the 1830s, 1840s, and 1850s depicted ordinary Americans and often told allegorical stories of daily life and politics.*

Courtesy Crystal Bridges Museum of American Art, Bentonville, Arkansas

the **Old Northwest** by vetoing a rivers and harbors bill that would have provided federal aid for transportation improvements. The Wilmot Proviso was in part the product of these pent-up frustrations.

The slavery issue loomed as diplomat Nicholas Trist negotiated the terms of Mexican surrender. In the Treaty of Guadalupe Hidalgo, signed February 2, 1848, the United States agreed to pay Mexico $15 million for California, New Mexico, and a Texas border on the Rio Grande. The Senate approved the treaty on March 10 by a vote of 38 to 14. Half the opposition came from Democrats who wanted more Mexican territory and half from Whigs who wanted none. The treaty sheared off half of Mexico and increased the size of the United States by one-fourth.

Old Northwest *The region west of Pennsylvania, north of the Ohio River, and east of the Mississippi River.*

THE ELECTION OF 1848

The treaty did nothing to settle the question of slavery in the new territory, however. Mexico had abolished the institution two decades earlier; would the United States reintroduce it? Many Americans looked to the election of 1848 to decide the matter.

Four positions on the issue emerged, each identified with a candidate for the presidential nomination. (Polk did not seek renomination.) The Wilmot Proviso represented the position of those determined to bar slavery from all territories. The Liberty Party endorsed the proviso and nominated Senator John P. Hale of

FOCUS QUESTION

How did the question of slavery affect the election of 1848?

New Hampshire for president. Another candidate, southerner John C. Calhoun, formulated the "Southern-rights" position. Directly challenging the Wilmot Proviso, Calhoun introduced resolutions in the Senate in February 1847 affirming the right of slave owners to take their human property into any territory, pointing out that the Constitution protected the right of property.

Although most southerners agreed with Calhoun, the Democratic Party sought a middle ground. Secretary of State James Buchanan endorsed extending the old Missouri Compromise line of 36°30' to the Pacific. Another compromise position, which became known as **"popular sovereignty,"** proposed to let the settlers of each territory decide for themselves whether to permit slavery. This concept, identified with the fourth candidate, Senator Lewis Cass of Michigan, contained a crucial ambiguity: It did not specify *at what stage* the settlers of a territory could decide on slavery. Most northern Democrats assumed that a territorial legislature would make that decision as soon as it was organized. Most southerners assumed that it would not be made until the settlers had drawn up a state constitution, which normally happened only after several years as a territory. So long as neither assumption was tested, each faction could support popular sovereignty.

The Democratic convention nominated Cass for president, but, in an attempt to maintain party unity, its platform made no mention of popular sovereignty. The Whigs, on the other hand, tried to avoid controversy by adopting no platform at all. But the slavery issue would not die. In the eyes of many antislavery delegates who styled themselves **Conscience Whigs**, the party made itself ridiculous by nominating Zachary Taylor, a hero from a war that most of them had opposed, for president. The fact that Taylor was also a large slaveholder who owned several plantations was too much for the Conscience Whigs. They bolted from the party and formed a coalition with the Liberty Party and antislavery Democrats.

The Free Soil Party

The **Free-Soilers** met in convention in August 1848 and nominated former president Martin Van Buren. Speakers proclaimed slavery "a great moral, social, and political evil" and adopted a platform calling for "no more Slave States and no more Slave Territories."

The campaign was marked by futile efforts to bury the slavery issue. Free Soil pressure compelled both northern Democrats and Whigs to take a stand against slavery in the territories. Whigs pointed to their earlier support of the Wilmot Proviso, while Democrats said popular sovereignty would keep the territories free. In the South, though, the two parties presented other faces. Democrats pointed with pride to their expansionist record that had brought to the nation hundreds of thousands of square miles of territory—into which slavery might expand. But Taylor proved to be the strongest candidate in the South because he was a southerner and a slaveholder. Taylor carried 8 of the 15 slave states. Although he did less well in the North, he carried New York and enough other states to win the election. The Free-Soilers won no electoral votes but polled 14 percent of the popular vote in the North. They also elected nine congressmen and two senators.

The Gold Rush and California Statehood

In 1848, workers building a sawmill on the American River near Sacramento discovered flecks of gold in the riverbed. The news reached the East in August, and Polk confirmed the "extraordinary" discoveries of gold in his final message to Congress that December. By the spring of 1849, 100,000 gold seekers were poised to take off by foot on the

popular sovereignty *The concept that settlers of each territory would decide for themselves whether to allow slavery.*

Conscience Whigs *A group of antislavery members of the Whig Party.*

Free-Soilers *A term used to describe people who opposed the expansion of slavery into the territories. It came from the name of a small political party in the election of 1848.*

Courtesy of the California History Room, California State Library, Sacramento, California.

THE CALIFORNIA GOLD RUSH. *Prospectors for gold in the foothills of California's Sierra Nevada came from all over the world, including China. This photograph shows American-born and Chinese miners near Auburn, California, a year or two after the initial gold rush of 1849. It illustrates the original technology of separating gravel from gold by panning or by washing the gravel away in a sluice box, leaving the heavier gold flakes behind.*

overland trail or by ship—either around Cape Horn or to the isthmus of Central America, where, after a land crossing, they could board another ship to take them up the Pacific coast to the new boomtown of San Francisco. Men and women (outnumbered 10 to 1 by men) rushed to California from around the world. African Americans and Miwok Indians also worked as miners, but in 1850 land-hungry Anglo-Americans instituted discriminatory laws that not only privileged whites but forced the expulsion of Mexicans—many of whom were American citizens under the Treaty of Guadalupe Hidalgo. While few miners struck it rich, settlers kept arriving.

This population increase meant that the political organization of California could not be postponed. The mining camps needed law and order; the settlers needed courts, land and water laws, and mail service. In New Mexico, the 60,000 former Mexican citizens, now Americans, also needed a governmental structure for their new allegiance.

Still, the slavery question paralyzed Congress. In December 1848, lame-duck president Polk recommended extending the Missouri Compromise 36°30′ line to the Pacific. The Whig-controlled House defied him, reaffirmed the Wilmot Proviso, drafted a bill to organize California as a free territory, and debated abolishing the slave trade and even slavery itself in the District of Columbia. The Democratic Senate quashed all the bills. A southern caucus asked Calhoun to draft an address setting forth its position. He eagerly complied, producing in January 1849 a document that breathed fire against "unconstitutional" northern efforts to keep slavery out of the territories. But only two-fifths of the southern congressmen and senators signed it. Southern Whigs wanted nothing to do with it. They looked forward to good times in the Taylor administration and opposed rocking the boat.

They were in for a rude shock. Taylor viewed matters as a nationalist, not as a southerner. He proposed to admit California and New Mexico (the latter comprising present-day New Mexico, Arizona, Nevada, Utah, and part of Colorado) immediately as *states*, skipping the territorial stage.

From the South came cries of outrage. Immediate admission would bring in two more free states because slavery had not existed under Mexican law, and most of the forty-niners were Free Soil in sentiment. With the administration's support, Californians held a convention in October 1849, drew up a constitution excluding slavery, and applied to Congress for admission as a state. Taylor's end run would tip the existing balance of 15 slave and 15 free states in favor of the North, probably forever. Southerners vowed never to "consent to be thus degraded and enslaved" by such a "monstrous trick and injustice."

THE COMPROMISE OF 1850

FOCUS QUESTION

What issues were at stake in the congressional debates that led to the Compromise of 1850? How successfully did the compromise resolve these issues?

California and New Mexico became the focal points of a cluster of slavery issues. An earlier Supreme Court decision had found that the federal government bore the responsibility for enforcing the return of **fugitive slaves** who had escaped into free states. Southerners therefore demanded a strong national fugitive slave law (in utter disregard of their oft-stated commitment to states' rights). Antislavery northerners, on the other hand, were calling for an end to the slave trade in the national capital. And in the Southwest, a shooting war threatened to break out between Texas and New Mexico. Having won the Rio Grande as their southern border with Mexico, Texans insisted that the river must also mark their western border with New Mexico. This dispute also involved slavery because the terms of Texas's annexation authorized the state to split into as many as five states, and the territory it carved out of New Mexico would create the potential for still another slave state.

The Senate Debates

As he had in 1820 and 1833, Henry Clay sought to turn the crisis into an opportunity. A nationalist from the border state of Kentucky, he hoped to unite North and South in a compromise. On January 29, 1850, he presented eight proposals to the Senate. Clay grouped the first six of his proposals into three pairs, each pair offering one concession to the North and one to the South. The first pair would admit California as a free state but would organize the rest of the Mexican cession without restrictions against slavery. The second would settle the Texas boundary dispute in favor of New Mexico but would compensate Texas for the bonds it had sold when it was an independent republic. The third pair of proposals would abolish the slave trade in the District of Columbia but would guarantee the continued existence of slavery there unless both Maryland and Virginia consented to abolition. Of Clay's final two proposals, one affirmed that Congress had no jurisdiction over the interstate slave trade; the other called for a strong national fugitive slave law.

The final shape of the **Compromise of 1850** closely resembled Clay's package. But it required a long, grueling process of bargaining, including numerous set speeches in the Senate. Senators John C. Calhoun, Daniel Webster, and William H. Seward each spoke for one of the three principal viewpoints.

On March 4, Calhoun, suffering from consumption, sat shrouded in flannel as a colleague read his speech. Unless northerners returned fugitive slaves in good faith, he warned, unless they consented to the expansion of slavery into the territories and accepted a constitutional amendment "which will restore to the South, in substance, the power she possessed of protecting herself before the equilibrium between the two sections was destroyed," southern states could not "remain in the Union consistently with their honor and safety." Calhoun wanted to give slave states a veto power over any national legislation concerning slavery.

Webster's speech three days later was both a reply to Calhoun and an appeal for compromise. "I wish to speak to-day, not as a Massachusetts man, nor as a Northern man, but as an American," he announced. "I speak to-day for the preservation of the Union." Although Webster had voted for the Wilmot Proviso, he now urged Yankees

fugitive slaves *Runaway slaves who escaped to a free state.*

Compromise of 1850 *Series of laws enacted in 1850 intended to settle all outstanding slavery issues.*

not to insist upon it. Nature would exclude slavery from New Mexico. However, many of Webster's former antislavery admirers repudiated his leadership—especially since he also endorsed a fugitive slave law.

On March 11, Seward expressed the antislavery position. In reply to Calhoun's arguments for the constitutional protection of slavery in the territories, he invoked "a higher law than the Constitution," the law of God in whose sight all persons were equal. Instead of legislating the expansion of slavery or the return of fugitive slaves, the country should be considering how to bring slavery peacefully to an end.

Passage of the Compromise

While these speeches were being delivered, committee members worked behind the scenes to fashion compromise legislation. Clay lumped most of his proposals together in a single bill, hoping that supporters of any given part of the compromise would vote for the whole in order to win the part they liked. Instead, most senators and representatives voted against the package in order to defeat the parts they disliked. President Taylor continued to insist on the immediate admission of California (and New Mexico, when it was ready) with no quid pro quo for the South. Exhausted and discouraged, Clay fled Washington's summer heat, leaving a young senator from Illinois, **Stephen A. Douglas**, to lead the forces of compromise.

Douglas reversed Clay's tactics. Starting with a core of supporters made up of Democrats from the Old Northwest and Whigs from the upper South, he built a majority for each part of the compromise by submitting it separately and adding its supporters to his core: northerners for a free California, southerners for a fugitive slave law, and so on. This effort benefited from Taylor's sudden death on July 9. The new president, Millard Fillmore, a conservative Whig from New York, supported the compromise. One after another, in August and September, the separate measures became law. President Fillmore christened the Compromise of 1850 "a final settlement" of all sectional problems. Calhounites in the South and antislavery activists in the North branded the compromise a betrayal of principle.

The Fugitive Slave Law

The fugitive slave law generated the most controversy. The Constitution required that a slave who escaped into a free state must be returned to his or her owner, but it failed to specify how that should be done. Under a 1793 law, slave owners could take their recaptured property before any state or federal court to prove ownership. This procedure worked so long as officials in free states were willing to cooperate. But as the antislavery movement gained momentum in the 1830s, some officials proved uncooperative. And professional slave-catchers sometimes went too far, kidnapping free blacks and selling them. Several northern states passed antikidnapping laws that gave alleged fugitives the right of trial by jury and prescribed criminal penalties for kidnapping. The U.S. Supreme Court declared Pennsylvania's antikidnapping law unconstitutional, but it also ruled that enforcement of the Constitution's fugitive slave clause was a federal responsibility, thereby absolving the states of any need to cooperate in enforcing it. Nine northern states thereupon passed **personal liberty laws** prohibiting the use of state facilities in the recapture of fugitives.

Fugitive slaves dramatized the poignancy and cruelties of bondage more vividly than anything else. A man or a woman risking all for freedom was not an abstract issue but a real human being whose plight invited sympathy and help. Consequently, many northerners who did not necessarily oppose slavery felt outrage at the idea of fugitives being seized and returned. The **"underground railroad"**

Stephen A. Douglas *Senator from Illinois who emerged as a leading Democrat in 1850 and led efforts to enact the Compromise of 1850.*

personal liberty laws *Laws enacted by nine northern states to prohibit the use of state facilities such as jails or law officers in the recapture of fugitive slaves.*

underground railroad *A small group who helped slaves escape bondage in the South. It took on legendary status, and its role was much exaggerated.*

KIDNAPPING AGAIN! *This is a typical poster printed by abolitionist opponents of the fugitive slave law. It was intended to rally the citizens of Boston against the recapture and reenslavement of Anthony Burns, a fugitive slave from Virginia seized in Boston in May 1854.*

that helped spirit slaves out of bondage took on legendary status. Stories of secret chambers where fugitives were hidden, dramatic trips in the dark between stations on the underground, and clever or heroic measures to foil pursuing bloodhounds exaggerated the legend.

Probably fewer than 1,000 of a total three million slaves actually escaped to freedom each year. But to southerners the return of those fugitives, like the question of the legality of slavery in California or New Mexico, was a matter of honor and rights. Southerners regarded obedience to the fugitive slave law as a test of the North's good faith in carrying out the compromise.

The provisions of that law were extraordinary. It created federal commissioners who could issue warrants for arrests of fugitives and before whom a slaveholder would bring a captured fugitive to prove ownership. All the slaveholder needed for proof was an affidavit from a court or the testimony of white witnesses. Fugitives had no right to testify on their own behalf. The commissioner received a fee of $10 if he found the owner's claim valid, but only $5 if he let the fugitive go—a difference supposedly justified by the greater paperwork required to return the fugitive. The federal treasury would pay all costs of enforcement. The commissioner could call on federal marshals to apprehend fugitives, and the marshals could deputize citizens to help. A citizen who refused could be fined, and anyone who harbored fugitives or obstructed their capture could face imprisonment.

The Slave-Catchers

Abolitionists denounced the law and vowed to resist it. Opportunities soon came, as slave owners sent agents north to recapture fugitives, some of whom had escaped years earlier. In February 1851, for example, slave-catchers arrested a black man living with his family in Indiana and returned him to an owner who said he had run away 19 years before. In the first 15 months of the law's operation, 84 fugitives were returned to slavery and only 5 were released. (For the entire decade of the 1850s, the ratio was 332 to 11.)

Many blacks, with the support of white allies, resorted to flight and resistance. Thousands of northern blacks fled to Canada. In February 1851, slave-catchers arrested a fugitive who had taken the name Shadrach when he escaped from Virginia a year earlier. They rushed him to the federal courthouse, where deputy marshals held him, pending a hearing. But a group of black men broke into the courtroom, overpowered the deputies, and spirited Shadrach to Canada. This was too much for the Fillmore administration. In April 1851, another fugitive, Thomas Sims, was arrested in Boston, and the president sent 250 soldiers to help 300 armed deputies return Sims to slavery.

Continued rescues and escapes kept matters at fever pitch for the rest of the decade. In the fall of 1851, a Maryland slave owner and his son accompanied federal marshals to Christiana, Pennsylvania, a Quaker village, where two of the man's slaves had taken refuge. The hunters ran into a fusillade of gunfire from a house where a dozen black men were protecting the fugitives. When the shooting stopped, the slave owner was dead and his son was seriously wounded. Three of the blacks fled to Canada. This time Fillmore sent in the marines. They helped marshals arrest 30 black men and a half-dozen whites, who were indicted for treason. But the U.S. attorney dropped charges after a jury acquitted the first defendant, a Quaker.

Two of the most famous fugitive slave cases of the 1850s ended in tragedy. In the spring of 1854, federal marshals in Boston arrested a Virginia fugitive, Anthony Burns. Angry abolitionists poured into Boston to save him, but the new president, Franklin Pierce, would not back down. After every legal move to free Burns had failed, Pierce sent federal troops. While thousands of angry Yankees lined the streets, 200 marines and soldiers marched Burns back into bondage.

Two years later, Margaret Garner escaped from Kentucky to Ohio with her husband and four children. When a posse of marshals and deputies caught up with them, Margaret seized a kitchen knife and tried to kill her children and herself rather than return to slavery. She managed to cut her three-year-old daughter's throat before she was overpowered. After complicated legal maneuvers, the federal commissioner remanded the fugitives to their Kentucky owner—who promptly sold them down the river to Arkansas. In a steamboat accident along the way, one of Margaret Garner's sons drowned in the Mississippi.

Such events had a profound impact on public emotions. Most white northerners were not abolitionists, and few of them regarded black people as equals, but millions of them moved closer to an antislavery position in response to the shock of seeing armed slave-catchers on their streets. Several northern states passed

© Bettmann/CORBIS

HARRIET TUBMAN. *Born into slavery in Maryland around 1822, Harriet Tubman escaped to freedom in 1849, settling at first in Philadelphia. Despite the many dangers she faced, Tubman returned South over and over in the years before the Civil War, helping her own relatives as well as dozens of other slaves to escape north. Wanted posters throughout the upper South described this "Moses," as Tubman was called, but she eluded capture. During the Civil War, the intrepid Tubman worked for the Union army as a nurse and cook, as well as scout and spy in Confederate territory. Tubman was also active in the woman suffrage movement late in the century. Working by necessity in secret before the Civil War, today Tubman is remembered, along with Frederick Douglass, as one of the most prominent abolitionists of the 19th century.*

new personal liberty laws in defiance of the South. Although those laws did not make it impossible to recover fugitives, they made it so difficult, expensive, and time-consuming that many slave owners gave up trying.

Uncle Tom's Cabin

A novel inspired by the plight of fugitive slaves further intensified public sentiment. Harriet Beecher Stowe was a member of a prominent New England family of clergymen and writers, and was herself a short story writer. In the 1840s, while living in Cincinnati with her husband, a minister, she became acquainted with fugitive slaves who had escaped across the Ohio River. Outraged by the Fugitive Slave Act of 1850, in 1851 she began to write a new piece of fiction—managing to write a chapter a week after she had put her children to bed.

Uncle Tom's Cabin was first published in installments in an antislavery newspaper. When it was published as a book in the spring of 1852, it became a runaway best seller and was eventually translated into 20 languages. The novel's central theme was the tragedy of the breakup of families by slavery—dramatized in scenes that would become an important part of American popular culture, such as the slave Eliza's escape across the Ohio River to save her son from a slave trader. Throughout the novel Stowe spoke directly to white women readers, asking them to imagine being torn from their own children. Yet it was not just women who responded to her calls to end slavery: Men, too, wrote of being deeply affected by the tragic story she told.

Although banned in some parts of the South, *Uncle Tom's Cabin* found a wide but hostile readership there. Proslavery authors rushed into print with more than a dozen novels challenging Stowe's themes, but all of them together made nothing like the impact of *Uncle Tom's Cabin*. The book helped shape a whole generation's view of slavery.

FILIBUSTERING

If the prospects for slavery in New Mexico appeared unpromising, southerners could contemplate a closer region where slavery already existed—Cuba. Enjoying an economic boom based on slave-grown sugar, this Spanish colony only 90 miles from American shores had nearly 400,000 slaves in 1850. President Polk offered Spain $100 million for Cuba in 1848. The Spanish foreign minister stated that he would rather see the island sunk in the sea than sold.

Cuba

filibustering *A term used to describe several groups that invaded or attempted to invade various Latin American areas to attempt to add them to the slaveholding regions of the United States. The word originated from* filibustero, *meaning a freebooter or pirate.*

If money did not work, revolution might. Cuban planters intrigued with American expansionists in the hope of fomenting an uprising on the island. Their leader was Narciso López, a Venezuelan-born Cuban soldier of fortune. In 1849 López recruited several hundred American adventurers for the first **"filibustering"** expedition against Cuba (from the Spanish *filibustero*, a freebooter or pirate). When President Taylor ordered the navy to prevent López's ships from leaving New York, López shifted his operations to New Orleans, where he raised a new force. Port officials in New Orleans looked the other way when the expedition sailed in May 1850, but Spanish troops drove the filibusters into the sea after they had established a beachhead in Cuba.

Undaunted, López escaped and returned to a hero's welcome in the South, where he raised men and money for a third try in 1851. This time, William Crittenden of Kentucky commanded the 420 Americans in the expedition. Spanish soldiers defeated the filibusters, killing 200 and capturing the rest. López was garroted in the public square of Havana. Then 50 American prisoners, including Crittenden, were lined up and executed by firing squad.

These events dampened southerners' enthusiasm for Cuba, but only for a time. Democrat Franklin Pierce of New Hampshire won the presidency by a landslide in 1852. Although a Yankee, Pierce had a reputation as a "doughface"—a northern man with southern principles. To the delight of southerners, Pierce made annexing Cuba one of the top priorities of his new administration. He tried again to buy Cuba, instructing the American minister in Madrid, Pierre Soulé, to offer Spain $130 million. Soulé, a flamboyant Louisianan, managed to alienate most Spaniards by his clumsy intriguing. His crowning act came in October 1854 at a meeting with the American ministers to Britain and France in Ostend, Belgium. He persuaded them to sign what came to be known as the Ostend Manifesto. "Cuba is as necessary to the North American republic as any of its present . . . family of states," declared this document. If Spain persisted in refusing to sell, then "by every law, human and divine, we shall be justified in wresting it from Spain."

This "manifesto of the brigands," as antislavery Americans called it, caused an international uproar. The administration repudiated the manifesto and recalled Soulé. Nevertheless, acquisition of Cuba remained an objective of the Democratic Party. Meanwhile, American filibustering shifted its focus 750 miles south of Havana to Nicaragua.

The Gray-Eyed Man of Destiny

A native of Tennessee and a brilliant, restless man, William Walker had earned a medical degree from the University of Pennsylvania and had studied and practiced law in New Orleans before joining the 1849 rush to California. Weighing less than 120 pounds, Walker seemed an unlikely fighter or leader of men, but he fought three duels, and his luminous eyes won him the sobriquet "gray-eyed man of destiny."

Walker found his true calling in filibustering. At the time, numerous raids were taking place back and forth across the border with Mexico. In 1853, Walker led a ragged "army" of footloose forty-niners into Baja California and Sonora and declared the region an independent republic. Exhaustion and desertion depleted his troops, however, and the Mexicans drove the survivors back to California.

Walker decided to try again, with another goal. Many southerners eyed Nicaragua's potential for growing cotton, sugar, coffee, and other crops. The unstable Nicaraguan government offered a tempting target. Joining forces with rebel leaders there, Walker led a troop of filibusters into Nicaragua in 1855 and proclaimed himself commander in chief of the rebel forces. At the head of 2,000 American volunteers, he gained control of the country and named himself president in 1856. The Pierce administration extended diplomatic recognition to Walker's regime.

The other Central American republics soon formed an alliance to invade Nicaragua and overthrow Walker. To win support from the southern states, Walker reinstituted slavery in Nicaragua. Boatloads of new recruits arrived from New Orleans, but in the spring of 1857, they succumbed to disease and to the Central American armies.

Walker escaped to New Orleans, where he was welcomed as a hero. Southern congressmen encouraged him to try again. On this expedition, however, his ship struck a reef and sank. Undaunted, he wrote a book to raise funds for yet another invasion of Nicaragua, urging "the hearts of Southern youth to answer the call of honor. . . . The true field for the expansion of slavery is in tropical America." A few more southern youths answered the call, but they were stopped in Honduras. There, on September 12, 1860, the gray-eyed man met his destiny before a firing squad.

Conclusion

Within the three-year period from 1845 to 1848 the annexation of Texas, the settlement of the Oregon boundary dispute with Britain, and the acquisition by force of New Mexico and California from Mexico added 1,150,000 square miles to the United States. This expansion was America's Manifest Destiny, according to Senator Stephen A. Douglas of Illinois. "Increase, and multiply, and expand, is the law of this nation's existence," he proclaimed. "You cannot limit this great republic by mere boundary lines."

But other Americans feared that the country could not absorb such rapid growth without strains that might break it apart. At the outbreak of the war with Mexico, Ralph Waldo Emerson predicted that "the United States will conquer Mexico, but it will be as the man swallows the arsenic, which brings him down in turn." Emerson proved correct. The poison was the reopening of the question of slavery's expansion, which had supposedly been settled by the Missouri Compromise in 1820. The admission of Texas as a huge new slave state and the possibility that more slave states might be carved out of the territory acquired from Mexico provoked northern congressmen to pass the Wilmot Proviso. Southerners bristled at this attempt to prevent the further expansion of slavery. Threats of secession and civil war poisoned the atmosphere in 1849 and 1850.

The Compromise of 1850 appeared to settle the issue once again, but events would soon prove that this compromise had merely postponed the crisis. The fugitive slave issue and filibustering expeditions to acquire more slave territory kept sectional controversies smoldering. In 1854, the Kansas–Nebraska Act would cause them to burst into a hotter flame than ever.

CHAPTER REVIEW

Review Questions

1. What impulses lay behind the Manifest Destiny of America's westward expansion?
2. What were the causes and consequences of the Mexican War?
3. How did the question of slavery affect the election of 1848?
4. What issues were at stake in the congressional debates that led to the Compromise of 1850? How successfully did the compromise resolve these issues?

Critical Thinking Questions

1. Between 1803 and 1845 the territorial size of the United States expanded by only 5 percent (with the acquisition of Florida in 1819). Yet in the three years from 1845 to 1848 the size of the United States mushroomed by another 50 percent. How do you explain this remarkable phenomenon?
2. Why was the issue of slavery in the territories so important and controversial in the 1840s and 1850s when slavery already existed in half of the states?

Identifications

Review your understanding of the following key terms, people, and events for this chapter.

Young America movement, p. 291
Manifest Destiny, p. 291
Horace Greeley, p. 293
missions, p. 294
presidios, p. 294
Great American Desert, p. 294

Mormons, p. 294
polygamy, p. 295
Republic of Texas, p. 296
tejanos, p. 296
Alamo, p. 296
joint resolution, p. 297
Old Northwest, p. 301

popular sovereignty, p. 302
Conscience Whigs, p. 302
Free-Soilers, p. 302
fugitive slaves, p. 304
Compromise of 1850, p. 304

Stephen A. Douglas, p. 305
personal liberty laws, p. 305
underground railroad, p. 305
filibustering, p. 308

DISCOVERY

In what ways did Manifest Destiny provide opportunity but also sow the seeds of the Civil War?

In thinking about this question, begin by breaking it down into the components shown below. A discussion of the significance of each component should appear in your answer.

Geography and Culture

Look at the map of overland trails on page 296. Which parts of this journey do you believe would be most difficult? What kinds of problems and dangers might travelers along these trails encounter?

Geography and Politics

Look at the map of free and slave states and territories. In the area acquired in the Louisiana Purchase, were there more slave states or free states? How about in the Texas Annexation and the Mexican Cession? What impact did these three large acquisitions have on the controversy over the expansion of slavery in the 1840s and 1850s?

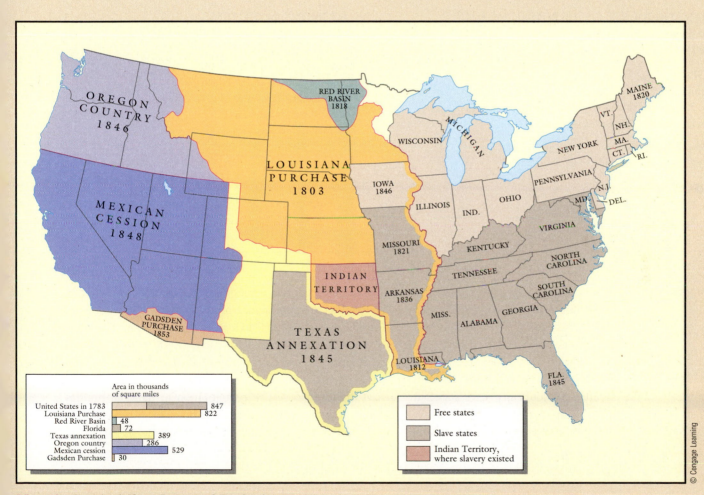

Map 13.1 Free and Slave States and Territories, 1848

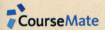

Visit the CourseMate website at www.cengagebrain.com for additional study tools and review materials for this chapter.

THE GATHERING TEMPEST, 1853–1860

KANSAS AND THE RISE OF THE REPUBLICAN PARTY	THE ECONOMY IN THE 1850S
The Kansas–Nebraska Act	"The American System of Manufactures"
The Death of the Whig Party	The Southern Economy
	The Sovereignty of King Cotton
IMMIGRATION AND NATIVISM	Labor Conditions in the North
Immigrants in Politics	The Panic of 1857
The Rise of the Know-Nothings	Sectionalism and the Panic
The Decline of Nativism	The Free-Labor Ideology
	The Impending Crisis
BLEEDING KANSAS	Southern Nonslaveholders
The Caning of Sumner	
	THE LINCOLN–DOUGLAS DEBATES
THE ELECTION OF 1856	The Freeport Doctrine
The Dred Scott Case	John Brown at Harpers Ferry
The Lecompton Constitution	

The wounds caused by the battle over slavery in the territories had barely healed when they were reopened. This time the strife concerned slavery in the Louisiana Purchase territory—an issue presumably settled 34 years earlier when the Missouri Compromise of 1820 admitted Missouri as a slave state but banned slavery from the rest of the Purchase north of 36°30'. To obtain southern support for the organization of Kansas and

Nebraska as territories, Senator Stephen Douglas consented to the repeal of this provision. Northern outrage at this repudiation of a "sacred contract" killed the Whig Party and gave birth to the antislavery Republican Party. In 1857, the Supreme Court further inflamed passions with the **Dred Scott** decision, which denied the power of Congress to restrict slavery from the territories. The reorientation of national politics along sectional lines was accompanied by a bloody civil war in Kansas and a raid on a federal arsenal in Virginia.

1852	1853	1854	1855	1856	1857	1858	1859

■ **1852**
Plenary Council of Catholic Church seeks tax support for parochial schools

■ **1853**
American Party emerges

■ **1854**
Congress passes Kansas–Nebraska Act • Republican Party organizes

■ **1855**
"Border Ruffian" legislature in Kansas legalizes slavery

■ **1856**
Civil war in Kansas • Preston Brooks
canes Charles Sumner on Senate floor

■ **1857**
Supreme Court issues Dred Scott decision

1858 ■
Kansas voters reject Lecompton constitution
• Lincoln–Douglas debates

1859 ■
John Brown's raid at Harpers Ferry

© Cengage Learning

KANSAS AND THE RISE OF THE REPUBLICAN PARTY

By 1853, settlers had pushed up the Missouri River to its confluences with the Kansas and Platte rivers. But settlement west of Missouri and land surveys for a transcontinental railroad required the organization of this region as a territory. Accordingly, in 1853 the House passed a bill creating the Nebraska Territory, embracing the area north of Indian Territory (present-day Oklahoma) up to the Canadian border. But the House bill ran into trouble in the Senate. Under the Missouri Compromise, slavery would be excluded from the new territory. Having lost California, the pro-slavery forces were determined to salvage something from Nebraska. Missourians were particularly adamant, because a free Nebraska would leave them almost surrounded on three sides by free soil.

The sponsor of the Senate bill was Stephen A. Douglas, chairman of the Senate Committee on Territories. In Douglas's opinion, allowing settlers to decide the slavery question for themselves in New Mexico and Utah had been the centerpiece of the Compromise of 1850. The initial draft of his Nebraska bill merely repeated the language used for those territories, specifying that when any portion of the Nebraska Territory came in as a state, it could do so "with or without slavery, as its constitution may provide."

This was not good enough for southern congressmen, who insisted on an explicit repeal of the Missouri Compromise. Sighing that this "will raise a hell of a storm," Douglas nevertheless agreed. He further agreed to divide the area into two territories: Kansas west of Missouri and Nebraska west of Iowa and Minnesota. To northerners this looked like a scheme to mark Kansas out for slavery.

FOCUS QUESTION

Why did the Whig Party die, and why did the Republican Party, rather than the American Party, emerge as the new majority party in the North?

Dred Scott *Missouri slave who sued for freedom on grounds of prolonged residence in a free state and free territory; in 1857, the Supreme Court found against his case, declaring the Missouri Compromise unconstitutional.*

The Kansas–Nebraska Act

The **Kansas–Nebraska Act** did indeed raise a hell of a storm. Douglas had failed to recognize the depth of northern opposition to the "slave power" and to the expansion of slavery. Millions of Americans regarded the expansion of slavery as a national question too important to be left to territorial voters. One of them was an old acquaintance of Douglas, **Abraham Lincoln**. An antislavery Whig who had served four terms in the Illinois legislature and one term in Congress, Lincoln was propelled back into politics by the shock of the Kansas–Nebraska bill. He acknowledged the right to hold slave property in states where it already existed, but he believed slavery was "an unqualified evil to the negro, the white man, and to the state." Stopping the further expansion of slavery was the first step on the long road to its "ultimate extinction."

Lincoln excoriated Douglas's "care not" attitude toward slavery. He branded the assertion that slavery would never be imported into Kansas because of the region's unsuitable climate as a "lullaby argument." The climate of eastern Kansas was similar to that of the Missouri River valley in Missouri, where slaves were busily raising hemp and tobacco. Missouri slaveholders were already poised to take their slaves into the Kansas River valley.

Lincoln's call to "Let us re-adopt the Declaration of Independence, and with it, the practices, and policy, which harmonize with it" gave voice to the feelings rising up against the Kansas–Nebraska bill. Abolitionists, Free-Soilers, northern Whigs, and even many northern Democrats formed anti-Nebraska coalitions, but they could not stop passage of the bill. It cleared the Senate easily, supported by a solid South and 15 of the 20 northern Democrats. In the House, it passed by a vote of 113 to 100.

The Death of the Whig Party

These proceedings destroyed the Whigs as a national party. In 1852, the Whig Party nominated General Winfield Scott for president. Though a Virginian, Scott took a national rather than a southern view. He was the candidate of the northern Whigs in the national convention, which nominated him on the 53rd ballot after a bitter contest. A mass exodus of southern Whigs into the Democratic Party enabled Franklin Pierce to carry all but two slave states in the election. The unanimous vote of northern Whigs in Congress against the Kansas–Nebraska bill was the final straw. The Whig Party never recovered its influence in the South.

It seemed to be on its last legs in the North as well. Antislavery Whig leaders like Seward and Lincoln hoped to channel anti-Nebraska sentiment through the Whig Party, but Free-Soilers and antislavery Democrats spurned the Whig label. Political coalitions arose under various names: Anti-Nebraska, Fusion, People's, Independent. The name that caught on was Republican.

The 1854 elections were disastrous for northern Democrats. One-fourth of Democratic voters deserted the party. The Democrats lost control of the House when 66 of 91 incumbent free-state Democratic congressmen went down to defeat. Combined with the increase in the number of Democratic congressmen from the South, this rout brought the party under southern domination.

The new Republican Party hoped to pick up the pieces of old parties in the North, but in urban areas hostility to immigrants created a tidal wave of **nativism** that threatened to swamp the anti-Nebraska movement. The anti-immigrant **Know-Nothings** won landslide victories in Massachusetts and Delaware, polled an estimated 40 percent of the vote in Pennsylvania, and did well elsewhere in the Northeast and border states.

Kansas–Nebraska Act *Law enacted in 1854 to organize the new territories of Kansas and Nebraska that effectively repealed the provision of the 1820 Missouri Compromise by leaving the question of slavery to the territories' settlers.*

Abraham Lincoln *Illinois Whig who became the Republican Party's first successful presidential candidate in 1860 and led the Union during the Civil War.*

nativism *Hostility of native-born Americans toward immigrants.*

Know-Nothings *Adherents of nativist organizations and of the American Party who wanted to restrict the political rights of immigrants.*

IMMIGRATION AND NATIVISM

In the 1840s, a combination of factors quadrupled the volume of immigration and changed its ethnic and occupational makeup. Whereas most earlier immigrants had come from Britain, the pressure of expanding population on limited land in Germany and successive failures of the potato crop in Ireland impelled millions of German and Irish peasants to emigrate. During the decade after 1845, three million immigrants entered the United States—15 percent of the total American population in 1845, the highest proportional volume of immigration in American history.

Many of these immigrants, especially the Irish, joined the unskilled and semi-skilled labor force in the rapidly growing eastern cities. They spoke foreign languages and observed alien customs. Most of them were Roman Catholics, and ethnic riots erupted between Protestant and Catholic workers. Established Americans perceived more recent arrivals as responsible for an increase in crime and poverty. In several eastern cities nativist political parties sprang up in the early 1840s with the intent of curbing immigrants' political rights.

FOCUS QUESTION

What were the origins of nativism? How did this movement relate to the slavery issue?

parochial schools *Schools associated with a church, usually Roman Catholic. The funding of these schools became a major political issue in the 1850s.*

Immigrants in Politics

Yet the political power of immigrants also grew. Most of the immigrants became Democrats, because that party welcomed or at least tolerated them and many Whigs did not. Foreign-born voters leaned toward the pro-slavery wing of the Democratic Party, even though seven-eighths of them settled in free states. Mostly working class and poor, they supported the Democratic Party as the best means of keeping blacks in slavery and out of the North. These attitudes sparked hostility toward immigrants among many antislavery people.

Attitudes toward immigrants had political repercussions. Two of the hottest issues in state and local politics during the early 1850s were temperance and schools. Temperance crusaders had grown confident and aggressive enough to go into politics. The drunkenness and rowdiness they associated with Irish immigrants became one of their particular targets. Twelve states had enacted prohibition laws by 1855. Though several of the laws were soon weakened by the courts or repealed by legislatures, they exacerbated ethnic tensions.

So did battles over public schools versus parochial schools. Catholics resented the Protestant domination of public education and the reading of the King James Bible in schools. The Church began to build **parochial schools** for the faithful, and in 1852, the first Plenary Council of American bishops decided to seek tax support for these schools or tax relief for Catholic parents who sent their children to them. This effort set off heated election contests in numerous northern cities and states. Anti-Catholic "free school" tickets won most of these elections by promising to defend public schools against the "bold effort" of this "despotic faith" to "uproot the tree of Liberty."

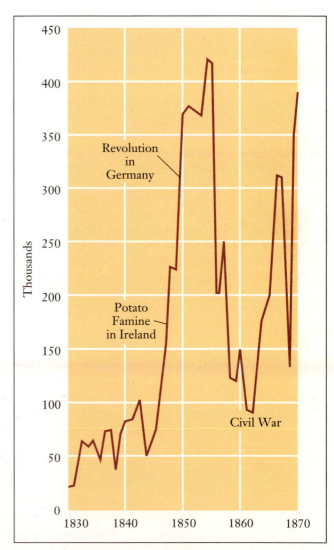

IMMIGRATION TO THE UNITED STATES
Source: Potter, Div & Stresses Reunion Paper, 1st, © 1973. Printed and electronically reproduced by permission of Pearson Education, Inc., Upper Saddle River, New Jersey.

MUSICAL LINK TO THE PAST

The Waltz: An Immoral Dance?

Composers: G. Jullien
Title: "Prima Donna Waltz" (circa late 1850s)

As tame and old-fashioned as the waltz may sound to modern ears, for many 19th-century observers, its arrival represented an alarming and morally dangerous development in American life. It did away with the niceties and social introductions of country dances, minuets, gavottes, and other dances championed previously in the American past. Those dances kept young people at a socially acceptable distance, constantly switching partners, never allowing a couple to concentrate on each other for an extended time. But couples who engaged in waltzing gripped each other in close embrace, intently gazed in each other's eyes at shockingly close range, and refused to share their partners or acknowledge other dancers on the floor. Worse yet, as reported by music historian Thornton Hagert, "The hypnotic effect of the unrelenting and mechanical turning, turning of the early waltz was thought to summon up uncontrollable passions that would surely lead to ridicule or even dishonor, disease and pregnancy." Despite numerous warnings of pernicious influence, waltz tempos steadily increased as the 19th century ambled forward, which presumably made dancers even dizzier and further clouded their personal judgment and morality. In addition, waltz steps were simplified as time went on, allowing more young people to participate in the waltz fad with little training.

The torrent of controversy surrounding the waltz presaged similar outcries against future American dance crazes such as the ragtime-influenced turkey trot of the 1910s, the jazz-inflected Charleston of the 1920s, the acrobatic Lindy Hop of the Big Band era, and the anarchic mosh-pit chaos of the 1970s punk rock scene. American youth have often seized music as an outlet and excuse to exhibit and play out emotions and feelings normally excluded from public view, to the chagrin of some of their elders. Musical expression by the American youth of the mid-20th century often featured distorted and screeching electric guitars, but such contraptions and the music they accompanied were probably no more threatening to American parents of the 1950s than the graceful bugle-led strains of the "Prima Donna Waltz" were for American parents of the 1850s.

Q Why do you think popular dances became simpler and less formal as the 19th century unfolded?

Q What do you think such cultural changes said about the character of the maturing United States?

 Listen to an audio recording of this music on the *Musical Links to the Past* CD.

The Rise of the Know-Nothings

It was in this context that the Know-Nothings (their formal name was the American Party) burst onto the political scene. The party resulted from the merger in 1852 of two secret fraternal societies that limited their membership to native-born Protestants: the Order of the Star-Spangled Banner and the Order of United Americans. Recruiting mainly young men in skilled blue-collar and lower white-collar occupations, the merged Order had a membership of one million or more by 1854. The Order supported temperance and opposed tax support for parochial schools. Members wanted public office restricted to native-born men and sought to lengthen the naturalization period before immigrants could become citizens. Members were pledged to secrecy; if asked about the Order, they were to reply "I know nothing."

Although the American Party drew voters from both major parties, it cut more heavily into the Whig constituency. Northern Whigs who had not already gone over to the Republicans flocked to the Know-Nothings. When the dust of the 1854 elections settled, it was clear that those who opposed the Democrats—either the Republicans or the Know-Nothings—would control the next House of Representatives.

The Decline of Nativism

In 1855, Republican leaders skillfully diverted the northern Know-Nothings from their crusade against Catholicism to a crusade against the slave power. Two developments helped them. The first was turmoil in Kansas, which convinced many northerners that the slave power was a greater threat than the pope. The second was an increase in nativist sentiment in the South. Violence erupted in several southern cities with large immigrant populations. The American Party won elections in Maryland, Kentucky, and Tennessee and polled at least 45 percent of the votes in five other southern states.

These developments had implications at the national level. Southern Know-Nothings were pro-slavery, while their Yankee counterparts were antislavery. The American Party, like the Whigs before them, foundered on the slavery issue. At the party's first national council in June 1855, most of the northern delegates walked out when southerners and northern conservatives joined forces to pass a resolution endorsing the Kansas–Nebraska Act. A similar scene occurred at an American Party convention in 1856. By that time, most northern members of the party had, in effect, become Republicans.

Nativism faded. The volume of immigration dropped by more than half in 1855 and stayed low for the next several years. Ethnic tensions eased, and cultural issues like temperance and schools receded. The real conflict turned out to be between North and South over the extension of slavery. That conflict led to civil war—and the war seemed already to have begun in the territory of Kansas.

BLEEDING KANSAS

When it became clear that southerners had enough votes to pass the Kansas–Nebraska Act, the stage was set for conflict. At first, Missouri settlers in Kansas posted the stronger numbers. But as the year 1854 progressed, settlers from the North came pouring in. Alarmed by this influx, bands of Missourians, labeled **"border ruffians"** by the Republican press, rode into Kansas prepared to vote as many times as necessary to install a pro-slavery government. In fall 1854, they cast at least 1,700 illegal ballots and sent a pro-slavery territorial delegate to Congress.

When the time came for the election of a territorial legislature the following spring, Senator David Atchison of Missouri led a contingent of border ruffians to Kansas. Nearly five thousand came and voted illegally to elect a pro-slavery legislature. When the territorial governor pleaded with President Pierce to nullify the election, Pierce removed him. Meanwhile, the new legislature legalized slavery and adopted a slave code that even authorized the death penalty for helping a slave to escape.

The so-called Free-State Party had no intention of obeying this "bogus legislature." By fall 1855, its members constituted a majority of legitimate settlers in Kansas. They called a convention, adopted a free-state constitution, and elected their own legislature and governor. By January 1856, two territorial governments in Kansas stood with their hands at each other's throats.

Kansas became the leading issue in national politics. The Democratic Senate and President Pierce recognized the pro-slavery legislature meeting in the town of Lecompton, while the Republican House recognized the antislavery legislature in Lawrence. Southerners saw the struggle as crucial to their future. "The admission of

FOCUS QUESTION

How was violence in Kansas related to the issue of slavery?

border ruffians *Term used to describe pro-slavery Missourians who streamed into Kansas in 1854 determined to vote as many times as necessary to install a pro-slavery government there.*

FREE-STATE MEN READY TO DEFEND LAWRENCE, KANSAS, IN 1856. *After pro-slavery forces sacked the free-state capital of Lawrence in 1856, northern settlers decided they needed more firepower to defend themselves. Somehow they got hold of a six-pound howitzer. This cannon did not fire a shot in anger during the Kansas troubles, but its existence may have deterred the "border ruffians."*

Kansas State Historical Society, Topeka, Kansas

Kansas into the Union as a slave state is now a point of honor," wrote Congressman Preston Brooks of South Carolina. On the other side, Charles Sumner of Massachusetts gave a well-publicized speech in the Senate on May 19 and 20 entitled "The Crime against Kansas." "Murderous robbers from Missouri," he charged, "from the drunken spew and vomit of an uneasy civilization" had committed the "rape of a virgin territory, compelling it to the hateful embrace of slavery." Among the southern senators Sumner singled out for special condemnation and ridicule was Andrew Butler of South Carolina, a cousin of Congressman Brooks. He accused Butler of having "chosen a mistress to whom he has made his vows . . . the harlot, Slavery."

The Caning of Sumner

Sumner's speech incensed Brooks, who decided to avenge his cousin. Two days after the speech, Brooks walked into the Senate chamber and beat Sumner bloody and unconscious with a heavy cane. News of the incident elated the South and enraged the North. Brooks resigned from Congress after censure by the House and was unanimously reelected. From all over the South came gifts of new canes, some inscribed with such mottoes as "Hit Him Again." But, in the North, the Republicans gained thousands of voters as a result of the affair. It seemed to prove their contentions about "the barbarism of slavery."

Republicans were soon able to add "Bleeding Kansas" to "Bleeding Sumner" in their repertoire of winning issues. As Sumner delivered his speech, an "army" of pro-slavery Missourians, complete with artillery, marched on the free-state capital of Lawrence. On May 21, they shelled and sacked the town, burning several buildings. A rival force of free-state men arrived too late to intercept them. One of the free-state "captains" was **John Brown**, an abolitionist zealot who considered himself anointed by the Lord to avenge the sins of slaveholders. When he learned of the sack of Lawrence, he declared that "Something must be done to show these barbarians that we, too, have rights." Leading four of his sons and three other men to a pro-slavery settlement at Pottawatomie Creek on the night of May 24–25, 1856, Brown dragged five men from their cabins and split open their heads with broadswords.

John Brown *Prominent abolitionist who fought for the antislavery cause in Kansas (1856) and led a raid to seize the Harpers Ferry arsenal in 1859.*

Brown's act set off a veritable civil war in Kansas. Not until President Pierce sent a tough new territorial governor and 1,300 federal troops to Kansas in September 1856 did the violence subside—just in time to save the Democrats from possible defeat in the presidential election.

THE ELECTION OF 1856

By 1856, the Republicans had become the largest party in the North. They were also the first truly sectional party in American history, for they had little prospect of carrying a single county in the slave states. At their first national convention, the Republicans wrote a platform that focused mainly on slavery but also incorporated the old Whig program of federal aid to internal improvements, including a railroad to California. For its presidential nominee, the party turned to John C. Frémont. This "Pathfinder of the West" had a dashing image as an explorer and for his role in the acquisition of California. With little political experience, he had few political enemies.

The Democrats chose as their candidate James Buchanan, a veteran of 30 years in various public offices. The Democratic platform endorsed popular sovereignty and condemned the Republicans as a "sectional party" that incited "treason and armed resistance in the Territories."

This would be a three-party election, for the American Party was still in the field. It nominated ex-Whig Millard Fillmore. The three-party campaign developed into a pair of two-party contests: Democrats versus Americans in the South; Democrats versus Republicans in the North. Fillmore, despite receiving 44 percent of the popular vote in the South, carried only Maryland. Considering Buchanan colorless but safe, the rest of the South gave him three-fourths of the electoral votes he needed for victory.

In the North, the turnout of eligible voters was a remarkable 83 percent. For many Republicans the campaign was a moral cause. Republican "Wide Awake" clubs marched in torchlight parades chanting "Free Soil, Free Speech, Free Men, Frémont!" Although the Republicans swept New England and the upper parts of New York State and the Old Northwest, the contest in the lower North was close. Buchanan needed only to carry Pennsylvania and either Indiana or Illinois to win the presidency, and the campaign focused on those states.

But the immigrant and working-class voters of the eastern cities and the rural voters of the lower Midwest were antiblack and anti-abolitionist in sentiment. They were ripe for Democratic propaganda that accused Republicans of favoring racial equality. "Black Republicans," declared an Ohio Democratic newspaper, intended to "turn loose . . . millions of negroes, to elbow you in the workshops, and compete with you in fields of honest labor."

Republicans in these areas denied that they favored racial equality. They insisted that the main reason for keeping slavery out of the territories was to enable white farmers and workers to make a living there without competition from black labor. Their denials were in vain: Support for the Republican Party by prominent black leaders, including Frederick Douglass, convinced hundreds of thousands of voters that the Black Republicans were racial egalitarians.

Democrats also charged that a Republican victory would destroy the Union. Buchanan set the tone in his instructions to party leaders: "The Black Republicans must be . . . boldly assailed as disunionists, and the charge must be re-iterated again and again." Southerners helped the cause by threatening to secede if Frémont won.

Black Republicans *Label coined by the Democratic Party to attack the Republican Party as believers in racial equality. The Democrats used this fear to convince many whites to remain loyal to them.*

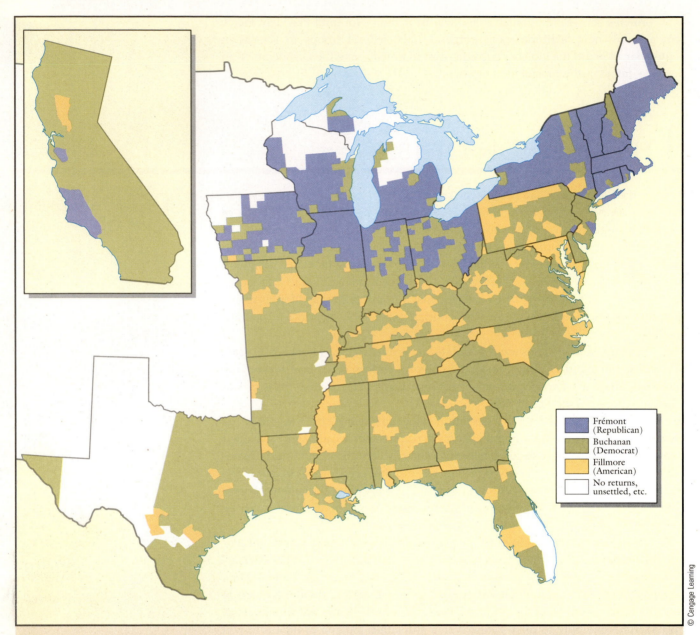

Map 14.1 Counties Carried by Candidates in the 1856 Presidential Election. *This map illustrates the sharp geographical division of the vote in 1856. The pattern of Republican counties coincided almost exactly with New England and the portions of other states settled by New England migrants during the two preceding generations.*

Fears of disruption caused many conservative ex-Whigs in the North to support Buchanan, who carried Pennsylvania, New Jersey, Indiana, Illinois, and California and won the presidency.

The Dred Scott Case

The South took the offensive at the outset of the Buchanan administration. Its instrument was the Supreme Court, which had a majority of five justices from slave states, led by Chief Justice Roger B. Taney of Maryland. Those justices saw the Dred Scott case as an opportunity to settle once and for all the question of slavery in the territories.

TABLE 14.1

POPULAR AND ELECTORAL VOTES IN THE 1856 PRESIDENTIAL ELECTION						
	Free States		Slave States		Total	
Candidate	Popular	Electoral	Popular	Electoral	Popular	Electoral
Buchanan (Democrat)	1,227,000	62	607,000	112	1,833,000	174
Frémont (Republican)	1,338,000	114	0	0	1,338,000	114
Fillmore (American)	396,000	0	476,000	8	872,000	8

© Cengage Learning

Dred Scott was a slave whose owner, an army surgeon, had kept him at military posts in Illinois and in Wisconsin Territory for several years before taking him back to Missouri. After the owner's death, Scott sued for his freedom on the grounds of his prolonged stay in Wisconsin Territory, where slavery had been outlawed by the Missouri Compromise. The case worked its way up from Missouri courts through a federal circuit court to the U.S. Supreme Court.

Chief Justice Taney issued the Court's ruling stating that Congress lacked the power to keep slavery out of a territory because slaves were property and the Constitution protects the right of property. For good measure, Taney also wrote that the circuit court should not have accepted the Scott case in the first place because black men were not citizens of the United States and therefore had no standing in its courts. The two non-Democratic northern justices were vigorous dissenters. They stated that blacks were legal citizens in several northern states and were therefore citizens of the United States. They cited Congress's constitutional power to make "all needful rules and regulations" for the territories. While modern scholars agree with the dissenters, in 1857 Taney had a majority, and his ruling became law.

referendum *Procedure that allows the electorate to decide an issue through a direct vote.*

The Lecompton Constitution

Instead of settling the slavery controversy, the Dred Scott decision intensified it. Several Republican state legislatures resolved that the ruling was "not binding in law and conscience." Meanwhile, pro-slavery forces, having won legalization of slavery in the territories, moved to ensure that it would remain legal when Kansas became a state. That required deft maneuvering, because legitimate antislavery settlers outnumbered pro-slavery settlers by more than two to one. In 1857, the pro-slavery legislature called for a constitutional convention at Lecompton to prepare Kansas for statehood. Because the election for delegates was rigged, Free Soil voters refused to participate. One-fifth of the registered voters thereupon elected convention delegates, who met at Lecompton and wrote a state constitution that made slavery legal.

Then a nagging problem arose. Buchanan had promised that the Lecompton constitution would be presented to the voters in a fair **referendum**. The problem was how to pass the pro-slavery constitution given the antislavery majority of voters. The convention came up with an ingenious solution. Instead of a referendum on the whole constitution, it would allow voters to choose between a constitution "with slavery" and one "with no slavery." Free-state voters branded the referendum a farce and boycotted it. One-quarter of the eligible voters went to the polls in December 1857 and approved the constitution "with slavery." Meanwhile, in a fair election policed by federal troops, the antislavery party won control of the new territorial legislature and promptly submitted both constitutions to a referendum that was boycotted by pro-slavery voters. This time, 70 percent of the eligible voters went to the polls and overwhelmingly rejected both constitutions.

QUICK REVIEW

REALIGNMENT OF POLITICAL PARTIES IN THE 1850S

- Kansas–Nebraska Act repealed prohibition of slavery in territories north of 36°30'
- Destruction of Whig Party and sectional split in Democratic Party
- Development of "Know-Nothings" (American Party), centered on anti-immigrant sentiment
- Emergence of Republican Party by 1856, as the American Party faded
- Split of Democratic Party by pro-slavery Dred Scott decision, Lecompton constitution, and a Buchanan administration dominated by southern Democrats

Although Buchanan had promised a fair referendum, southerners, who dominated both the Democratic Party and the administration, threatened secession if Kansas was not admitted to statehood under the Lecompton constitution "with slavery." Buchanan caved in. He sent the Lecompton constitution to Congress with a message recommending statehood.

What would Stephen Douglas do? If he endorsed the Lecompton constitution, he would undoubtedly be defeated in his bid for reelection to the Senate in 1858. And he regarded the Lecompton constitution as a travesty of popular sovereignty. He broke with the administration on the issue. He could not vote to "force this constitution down the throats of the people of Kansas," he told the Senate, "in opposition to their wishes and in violation of our pledges."

The fight in Congress was long and bitter. The South and the administration had the votes they needed in the Senate and won handily there, but the Democratic majority in the House was so small that the defection of even a few northern Democrats would defeat the Lecompton constitution. At one point a wild fistfight erupted between Republicans and southern Democrats. When the vote was finally taken, two dozen northern Democrats defected, providing enough votes to defeat Lecompton. Both sides then accepted a compromise proposal to resubmit the constitution to Kansas voters, who decisively rejected it. This meant that while Kansas would not come in as a slave state, neither would it come in as a free state for some time yet. Nevertheless, the Lecompton debate had split the Democratic Party, leaving a legacy of undying enmity between southerners and Douglas. The election of a Republican president in 1860 was now all but assured.

THE ECONOMY IN THE 1850S

FOCUS QUESTION

How did economic developments in the 1840s and 1850s widen the breach between North and South?

Beginning in the mid-1840s the American economy enjoyed a dozen years of growth and prosperity, particularly for the railroads. Most railroad construction took place in the Old Northwest, linking the region to the Northeast and continuing the reorientation of transportation networks from a north-south river pattern to an east-west canal and rail pattern. This reinforced the effect of slavery in creating a self-conscious "North" and "South." And although the Old Northwest remained predominantly agricultural, rapid expansion of railroads there laid the basis for its industrialization. During the 1850s the growth rate of industrial output in the free states west of Pennsylvania was twice as great as the rate in the Northeast and three times as great as the rate in the South.

Economic expansion considerably outstripped even the prodigious rate of population increase. While the number of Americans grew by 44 percent during these 12 years (1844–1856), the value of both exports and imports increased by 200 percent; mined coal tonnage by 270 percent; banking capital, industrial capital, and industrial output by approximately 100 percent; farmland value by 100 percent; and cotton, wheat, and corn harvests by about 70 percent. These advances meant a significant increase of **per capita** production and income, although the distance between rich and poor was widening—a phenomenon that has characterized all capitalist economies during stages of rapid industrial growth.

By the later 1850s, the United States had become the second-leading industrial producer in the world, behind only Britain. But the country was still in the early stages of industrial development. Agricultural processing and raw materials still played the dominant role. By 1860, the four leading industries, measured by value added in manufacturing, were cotton textiles, lumber products, boots and shoes, and flour milling.

per capita *Term used to measure the wealth of a nation by dividing total income by population.*

"The American System of Manufactures"

The United States had pioneered one crucial feature of modern industry: the mass production of **interchangeable parts**. High wages and a shortage of the skilled craftsmen who had traditionally fashioned guns, furniture, locks, watches, and other products had compelled American entrepreneurs to seek alternative methods. "Yankee ingenuity," already world-famous, came up with an answer: special-purpose machine tools that would cut and shape an endless number of parts that could be fitted together with other similarly produced parts to make whole guns, locks, clocks, and sewing machines in mass quantities. These products were less elegant and less durable than products made by skilled craftsmen, but they were also less expensive and thus more widely available to the "middling classes."

Such American-made products were the hit of the first World's Fair, the Crystal Palace Exhibition at London in 1851. British manufacturers were so impressed by Yankee techniques, which they dubbed "the American system of manufactures," that they sent two commissions to the United States to study them. The commissions cited the American educational system as an important reason for the country's technological proficiency. The British workman, trained by long apprenticeship "in the trade" rather than in school, lacked "the ductility of mind and the readiness of apprehension for a new thing" and was therefore "unwilling to change the methods he has been used to."

Whether this British commission was right in its belief that American schooling encouraged the "adaptative versatility" of Yankee workers, it was certainly true that public education and literacy were more widespread in the United States than in Europe. Almost 95 percent of adults in the free states were literate in 1860, compared with 65 percent in England and 55 percent in France. Nearly all children received a few years of schooling, and most completed at least six or seven years.

This improvement in education coincided with the feminization of the teaching profession, which opened up new career opportunities for young women. By the 1850s nearly three-quarters of the public school teachers in New England were women (who worked for lower salaries than male teachers), a trend that was spreading to the mid-Atlantic states and the Old Northwest as well.

interchangeable parts
Industrial technique using machine tools to cut and shape a large number of similar parts that can be fitted together with other parts to make an entire item such as a gun.

© Francis G. Mayer/CORBIS

THE COUNTRY SCHOOL. *This famous painting by Winslow Homer portrays the typical one-room rural schoolhouse in which millions of American children learned the three Rs in the 19th century. By the 1850s, elementary school teaching was a profession increasingly dominated by women, an important change from earlier generations.*

The Southern Economy

In contrast to the North, where only 6 percent of the population could not read and write, nearly 20 percent of the free population and 90 percent of the slaves in the South were illiterate. This was one of several differences between North and South that antislavery advocates pointed to as evidence of the backward, repressive, and pernicious nature of a slave society.

Still, the South shared in the economy's rapid growth. Cotton prices and production both doubled between 1845 and 1855. Similar increases in price and output emerged in tobacco and sugar. The price of slaves also doubled. Southern crops provided three-fifths of all U.S. exports, with cotton alone supplying more than half.

But a growing number of southerners deplored the fact that the **"colonial" economy** of the South was so dependent on the export of agricultural products and the import of manufactured goods. The ships that carried southern cotton were owned by northern or British firms; financial and commercial services were provided mostly by Yankees or Englishmen. Southerners must "throw off this humiliating dependence," declared James D. B. De Bow, the young champion of economic diversification in the South. In 1846, De Bow had founded a periodical, *De Bow's Review*, and he took the lead in organizing annual commercial conventions that met in various southern cities during the 1850s. In its early years, this movement encouraged southerners to invest in shipping lines, railroads, textile mills, and other enterprises.

Economic diversification in the South did make headway during the 1850s. The slave states quadrupled their railroad mileage, increased the amount of capital invested in manufacturing by 77 percent, and boosted their output of cotton textiles by 44 percent. But northern industry was growing even faster. In 1860, the North had five times more industrial output per capita than the South and three times the railroad capital and mileage per capita and per thousand square miles. Southerners had a larger percentage of their capital invested in land and slaves in 1860 than they had 10 years earlier. By contrast, the northern economy developed a strong manufacturing and commercial sector whose combined labor force almost equaled that of agriculture by 1860.

The Sovereignty of King Cotton

A good many southerners preferred to keep it that way. In the later 1850s, the drive for economic diversification in the South lost steam as cotton output *and* prices continued to rise, suffusing the South in a glow of prosperity. In a speech that became famous, James Hammond of South Carolina told his fellow senators in 1858 that "the slaveholding South is now the controlling power of the world. . . . No power on earth dares to make war on cotton. Cotton *is* king." Even the commercial conventions in the South seem to have embraced this gospel: By the later 1850s, one of their main goals was to reopen the African slave trade.

Southern whites continued to justify slavery as a positive good. Nowhere in the South, said defenders of slavery, did one see such "scenes of beggary, squalid poverty, and wretchedness" as one could find in any northern city. Black slaves, they insisted, enjoyed a higher standard of living than white "wage slaves" in northern factories. Black slaves never suffered from unemployment or wage cuts, they received free medical care, and they were taken care of in old age.

This argument reached its fullest development in the writings of George Fitzhugh, a Virginia farmer-lawyer whose newspaper articles were gathered into two books published in 1854 and 1857, *Sociology for the South* and *Cannibals All!* Free-labor capitalism, said Fitzhugh, was a competition in which the strong

colonial economy *Economy based on the export of agricultural products and the import of manufactured goods; sometimes used to describe the dependence of the South on the North.*

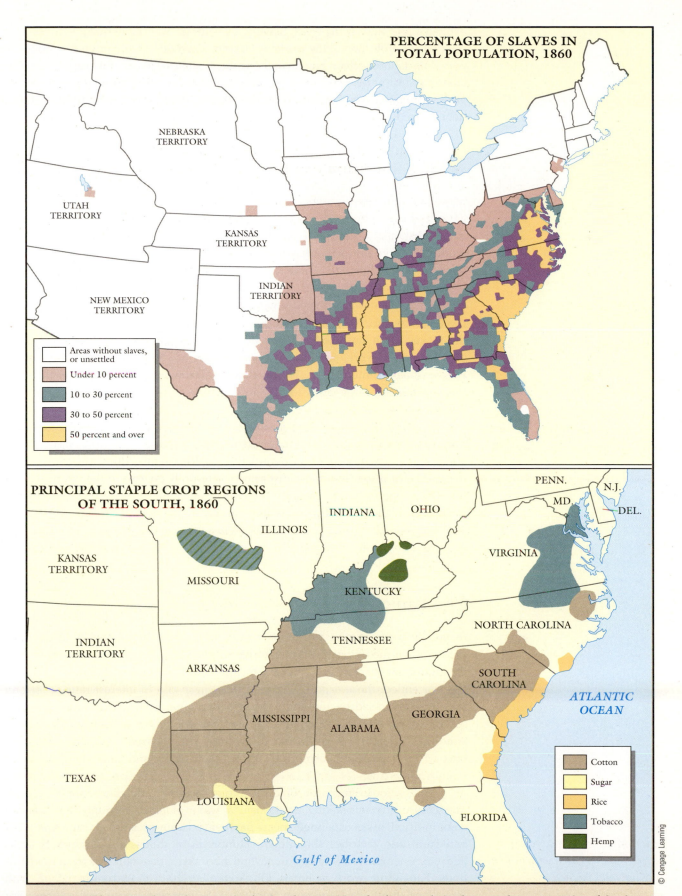

PERCENTAGE OF SLAVES IN
TOTAL POPULATION, 1860

Areas without slaves,
or unsettled

Under 10 percent

10 to 30 percent

30 to 50 percent

50 percent and over

PRINCIPAL STAPLE CROP REGIONS
OF THE SOUTH, 1860

Cotton

Sugar

Rice

Tobacco

Hemp

© Cengage Learning

Map 14.2 Slavery and Staple Crops in the South, 1860. *Note the close correlation between the concentration of the slave population and the leading cash crops of the South. Nothing better illustrates the economic importance of slavery.*

exploited and starved the weak. Slavery, by contrast, was a paternal institution that guaranteed protection of the workers. "Capital exercises a more perfect compulsion over free laborers than human masters over slaves," wrote Fitzhugh, "for free laborers must at all times work or starve, and slaves are supported whether they work or not. . . . What a glorious thing is slavery, when want, misfortune, old age, debility, and sickness overtake [the slave]."

Labor Conditions in the North

Some northern labor leaders did complain that the "slavery" of the wage system gave "bosses" control over the hours, conditions, and compensation of labor. To be sure, substantial numbers of recent immigrants, day laborers, and young single women in large northern cities lived in or on the edge of poverty. Many female seamstresses, shoe binders, milliners, and the like, who worked 60 or 70 hours per week in the outwork system, earned less than a living wage. The widespread adoption of the newly invented sewing machine in the 1850s only lowered per-unit piecework wages. Many urban working-class families could not have survived on the wages of an unskilled or semiskilled man. Women had to take in laundry, boarders, or outwork, and one or more children had to work. Much employment was seasonal or intermittent. The poverty, overcrowding, and disease in the tenement districts of large cities seemed to lend substance to pro-slavery claims that slaves were better off.

But they were not. There is no evidence that a northern workingman ever offered to change places with a southern slave. Average per capita income was about 40 percent higher in the North than in the South. Although that average masked large disparities, those disparities were probably less in the North than in the South. Opportunities for workers were greater in the North than anywhere else in the world. That was why four million immigrants came to the United States from 1845 to 1860 and why seven-eighths of them settled in free states. It was also why twice as many white residents of slave states migrated to free states than vice versa.

The Panic of 1857

In fall 1857, the relative prosperity of the North was interrupted by a financial panic. When the Crimean War in Europe (1854–1856) cut off Russian grain from the European market, U.S. exports mushroomed to meet the deficiency. After the war ended, those exports slumped. The sharp rise in interest rates in Britain and France, caused by the war, spread to U.S. financial markets and dried up sources of credit. The economic boom of the preceding years had caused the American economy to overheat: Land prices had soared, railroads had built beyond the capacity of earnings to service their debts, and banks had made too many risky loans.

This speculative house of cards came crashing down in September 1857. The failure of one banking house sent a wave of panic through the financial community. Banks suspended specie payments, businesses failed, railroads went bankrupt, and factories shut down. Hundreds of thousands of workers were laid off. Unemployed workers in several northern cities marched in demonstrations demanding work or bread. On November 10, a crowd gathered on Wall Street and threatened to break into the U.S. customs house and subtreasury vaults, where $20 million was stored. Soldiers and marines had to be called out to disperse the mob.

Library of Congress, Prints and Photographs Division

© The Granger Collection, New York

SOUTHERN PORTRAITS OF SLAVERY AND FREE LABOR. *Romanticized images of happy, well-fed slaves enjoying their work picking cotton were common in pro-slavery literature. Such images were often contrasted with the supposed harshness of life in northern tenement districts, as in this illustration of a communal pump that has run dry on a hot summer day in an immigrant neighborhood on New York's lower east side.*

But the country got through the winter with little violence, and the depression did not last long. By early 1858, banks had resumed specie payments, the stock market rebounded, factories reopened, railroad construction resumed, and by spring 1859, recovery was complete. The modest labor-union activities of the 1850s revived after the depression, as workers in some industries went on strike to bring wages back to pre-panic levels. In February 1860, the shoemakers of Lynn, Massachusetts, began the largest strike in U.S. history up to that time, eventually involving 20,000 workers in the New England shoe industry. Still, less than 1 percent of the labor force was unionized in 1860.

Sectionalism and the Panic

The Panic of 1857 intensified sectional animosities. The South largely escaped the depression. Its export-driven economy seemed insulated from domestic downturns. After a brief dip, cotton and tobacco prices returned to high levels and production continued to increase: The cotton crop set new records in 1858 and 1859. Southern boasts took on added bravado. "When thousands of the strongest commercial houses in the world were coming down," asked Senator James Hammond in March 1858, "what brought you up? . . . We have poured in upon you one million six hundred thousand bales of cotton. . . . We have sold it for $65,000,000, and saved you."

Northerners were not grateful. In fact, many blamed southern congressmen for blocking measures, especially higher tariffs, that would have eased the effects of the depression and helped not only manufacturers but also unemployed workers. In each session of Congress from 1858 through 1860, however, a combination of southerners and about half of the northern Democrats blocked Republican efforts to raise tariffs.

Three other measures acquired additional significance after the Panic of 1857. Republicans supported each of them as a means to promote economic health and to aid farmers and workers, but southerners rejected them as aimed at helping *northern* farmers and workers. One was the Homestead Act to grant 160 acres of public land to each farmer who settled and worked the land. Southern senators defeated this bill after the House had passed it in 1859. The following year both houses passed the Homestead Act, but Buchanan vetoed it and southern senators blocked an effort to override his veto. A similar fate befell bills for land grants to a transcontinental railroad and for building agricultural and mechanical colleges to educate farmers and workers.

The Free-Labor Ideology

By the later 1850s, the Republican antislavery argument had become a finely honed philosophy that historians have labeled a **"free-labor ideology."** It held that all work in a free society was honorable, but that slavery degraded the calling of manual labor by equating it with bondage. Slaves worked inefficiently, by compulsion; free men were stimulated to work hard and efficiently by the desire to get ahead. Social mobility was central to the free-labor ideology. Free workers who practiced the virtues of industry, thrift, self-discipline, and sobriety could move up the ladder of success. "I am not ashamed to confess," Abraham Lincoln told a working-class audience in 1860, "that twenty-five years ago I was a hired laborer, mauling rails, at work on a flat-boat—just what might happen to any poor man's son!" But in the free states, said Lincoln, a man knows that "he can better his condition. . . . The free labor system opens the way for all—gives hope to all, and energy, and progress, and improvement of condition to all."

Lincoln drew too rosy a picture, for large numbers of wage laborers in the North had little hope of advancing. But he expressed a belief that was widely shared. Americans could point to numerous examples of men who had achieved dramatic upward mobility. Faith in this "American dream" was most strongly held by Protestant farmers, skilled workers, and white-collar workers who had some real hope of getting ahead. These men tended to support the Republican Party and its goal of excluding slavery from the territories.

For slavery was the antithesis of upward mobility. Slaves could not hope to move up the ladder of success, nor could free men who lived in a society where they had to compete with slave labor. In the United States, social mobility often depended on geographic mobility. The main reason so many families moved into new territories was to get a new start, to get ahead. But, declared a Republican editor, if slavery goes into the territories, "the free labor of all the states will not. If the free labor of the states goes there, the slave labor of the southern states will not, and in a few years the country will teem with an active and energetic population."

Southerners contended that free labor was prone to unrest and strikes. Of course it was, said Lincoln in a speech to a New England audience during the shoemakers' strike of 1860. "I am glad to see that a system prevails in New England under which laborers *can* strike when they want to (*cheers*). . . . I *like* the system which lets a man quit when he wants to, and wish it might prevail everywhere (*tremendous applause*)." Strikes were one of the ways in which free workers could try

free-labor ideology *Belief that all work in a free society is honorable and that manual labor is degraded when it is equated with slavery or bondage.*

to improve their prospects. "I want every man," said Lincoln, "to have the chance—and I believe a black man is entitled to it—in which he can better his condition." That was why Republicans were determined to contain the expansion of slavery, for if the South got its way in the territories "free labor that can strike will give way to slave labor that cannot!"

The Impending Crisis

From the South came a maverick voice that echoed the Republicans. Living in up-country North Carolina, a region of small farms and few slaves, Hinton Rowan Helper had brooded for years over slavery's influence on southern development. In 1857, in a book entitled *The Impending Crisis of the South*, he pictured a South mired in economic backwardness, widespread illiteracy, poverty for the masses, and wealth for the elite. He contrasted this dismal situation with the prosperous northern economy and its near-universal literacy, neat farms, and progressive institutions. "Slavery lies at the root of all the shame, poverty, ignorance, tyranny, and imbecility of the South," he wrote. Slavery monopolized the best land, degraded labor, denied schools to the poor, and impoverished all but "the lords of the lash." Nonslaveholding whites, Helper argued, must organize and use their votes to overthrow "this entire system of oligarchical despotism."

The Impending Crisis was virtually banned in the South, and few southern whites read it, but it made a huge impact in the North. The Republican Party subsidized an abridged edition and distributed thousands of copies as campaign documents. During the late 1850s, a war of books (Helper's *Impending Crisis* versus Fitzhugh's *Cannibals All!*) exacerbated sectional tensions. Fitzhugh's book circulated freely in the North, whereas the sale or possession of Helper's book was a criminal offense in many parts of the South. Northern spokesmen did not hesitate to point out the moral: A free society could tolerate free speech and a free press, but a slave society could not.

Southern Nonslaveholders

How accurate was Helper's portrayal of southern poor whites degraded by slavery and ready to revolt against it? Planters felt uneasy about that question. After all, slaveholding families constituted less than one-third of the white population in slave states, and the proportion was declining as the price of slaves continued to rise. Open hostility to the planters' domination of society and politics was evident in the mountainous and upcountry regions of the South. These would become areas of Unionist sentiment during the Civil War and of Republican strength after it.

But Helper exaggerated the disaffection of most nonslaveholders in the South. Three bonds held them to the system: kinship, economic interest, and race. In the Piedmont and the lowcountry regions of the South, nearly half of the whites lived in slaveholding families. Many of the rest were cousins or nephews or in-laws of slaveholders in the South's extensive and tightly knit kinship network. Moreover, many young, ambitious nonslaveholders hoped to buy slaves eventually. Some of them *rented* slaves. And because slaves could be made to do menial, unskilled labor, white workers monopolized the more skilled, higher-paying jobs.

Even if they did not own slaves, white people owned the most important asset of all—white skin. White supremacy was an article of faith in the South (and in most of the North, for that matter). Race was a more important social distinction than class: "With us," said John C. Calhoun in 1848, "the two great divisions of society are not the rich and the poor, but white and black; and all the former, the poor as well as the rich, belong to the upper class, and are respected and treated as equals." The southern legal system, politics, and social ideology were based on the concept of domination by the "master race" of whites. Subordination was the Negro's fate, and slavery was the best means of subordination. Emancipation would loose a flood of free blacks on society and would undermine the foundations of white supremacy. Thus many of the "poor whites" in the South and immigrant workers or poorer farmers in the North supported slavery.

THE LINCOLN–DOUGLAS DEBATES

Lincoln–Douglas debates
Series of seven debates between Abraham Lincoln and Stephen Douglas in their contest for election to the U.S. Senate in 1858.

Courtesy of the Illinois State Historical Library

THE LINCOLN–DOUGLAS DEBATES. *The Lincoln–Douglas contest for the Senate in 1858 produced the most famous—and fateful— political debates in American history. At stake was nothing less than the future of the nation. Thousands of people crowded into seven towns to listen to these three-hour debates that took place outdoors from August to October in weather ranging from stifling heat to cold rain. Audiences were most friendly to Lincoln in antislavery northern Illinois, as portrayed in this illustration of the debate in Galesburg, home of Knox College and a hotbed of abolitionism.*

For Abraham Lincoln, slavery and freedom were incompatible. This became the central theme of a pivotal series of seven **Lincoln–Douglas debates** in 1858.

The debates were arranged after Lincoln was nominated to oppose Douglas's reelection to the Senate. State legislatures elected U.S. senators at that time, so the campaign was technically for the election of the Illinois legislature. But the real issue was the senatorship, and Douglas's prominence gave the contest national significance. Lincoln launched his bid with one of his most notable speeches. "A house divided against itself cannot stand," he said. "I believe this government cannot endure, permanently half slave and half free. . . . It will become all one thing, or all the other." What, asked Lincoln, would prevent the Supreme Court from legalizing slavery in free states? (A case based on this question was then before the New York courts.) Advocates of slavery were trying to "push it forward, till it shall become lawful in all the States." But Republicans intended to keep slavery out of the territories, thus stopping its growth and placing it "where the public mind shall rest in the belief that it is in the course of ultimate extinction."

In response, Douglas asked: Why could the country not continue to exist half slave and half free as it had for 70 years? Lincoln's talk about the "ultimate extinction" of slavery would provoke the South to secession. Douglas professed himself no friend of slavery, but if people in the southern states or in the territories wanted it, they had the right to have it. Lincoln's policy would not only free the slaves but would grant them equality. "Are you in favor of conferring upon the negro the rights and privileges of citizenship?" Douglas asked his supporters in the crowd. "Do you desire to strike out of our State Constitution that clause which keeps slaves and free negroes out of the State . . . in order that when Missouri abolishes slavery she can send one hundred thousand emancipated slaves into Illinois, to become citizens and voters on an equality with yourselves?"

Douglas's demagoguery put Lincoln on the defensive. He responded with cautious denials that he favored "social and political equality" of the races. The "ultimate extinc- tion" of slavery might take a century. It would require the voluntary cooperation of the South and perhaps be contin- gent on the emigration of some freed slaves from the country. But come what may, freedom must prevail. Americans must reaffirm the principles of the Founding Fathers. In Lincoln's words, a black person was "entitled to all the natural rights enumerated in the Declaration of Independence." Douglas, according to Lincoln, "looks to no end of the institution of slavery." By endorsing the Dred Scott decision, he instead looked to its "perpetuity and nationalization." Douglas was thus "eradicating the light of reason and liberty in this American people." That was the real issue, Lincoln insisted.

The Freeport Doctrine

The popular vote for Republican and Democratic state legislators in Illinois was virtually even in 1858, but because apportionment favored the Democrats, they won a majority of seats and reelected Douglas. But Lincoln was the ultimate victor, for his performance in the debates lifted him from political obscurity, while Douglas further alienated southern Democrats. In the Freeport debate, Lincoln had asked Douglas how he reconciled his support for the Dred Scott decision with his policy of popular sovereignty, which supposedly gave residents of a territory the power to vote slavery down. Douglas replied that even though the Court had legalized slavery in the territories, the enforcement of that right would depend on the people who lived there. This was a popular answer in the North, but it gave added impetus to southern demands for congressional passage of a federal slave code in territories like Kansas, where the Free Soil majority had by 1859 made slavery virtually null. In the next two sessions of Congress after the 1858 elections, southern Democrats, led by **Jefferson Davis**, tried to pass a federal slave code for all territories. Douglas and northern Democrats joined with Republicans to defeat it. Consequently, southern hostility toward Douglas mounted as the presidential election of 1860 approached.

John Brown at Harpers Ferry

Southern tempers were already high because of what had happened at **Harpers Ferry**, Virginia, in October 1859. After his exploits in Kansas, John Brown had disappeared from public view. But he had not been idle. He had worked up a plan to capture the federal arsenal at Harpers Ferry, arm slaves with the muskets he seized there, and move southward along the Appalachian Mountains, attracting more slaves to his army along the way until the "whole accursed system of bondage" collapsed.

Brown recruited five black men and seventeen whites, including three of his sons, for this reckless scheme. He also had the secret support of a half-dozen Massachusetts and New York abolitionists, who had helped him raise funds. On the night of October 16, 1859, Brown led his men across the Potomac and occupied the sleeping town of Harpers Ferry without resistance. Few slaves flocked to his banner, but the next day state militia units poured into town and drove Brown's band into the fire-engine house. At dawn on October 18, a company of U.S. marines commanded by Colonel Robert E. Lee and Lieutenant J. E. B. Stuart stormed the engine house and captured the surviving members of Brown's party. Four townsmen, one marine, and ten of Brown's men (including two of his sons) were killed; not a single slave was liberated.

John Brown's raid lasted 36 hours; its repercussions resounded for years. Brown and six of his followers were promptly tried by the state of Virginia, convicted, and hanged. This scarcely ended matters. Although no slaves had risen in revolt, the raid revived the fears of slave insurrection that were never far beneath the surface of southern consciousness. Exaggerated reports of Brown's network of

Jefferson Davis *Mississippi planter and prominent leader of the southern Democrats in the 1850s, who later served as president of the Confederacy.*

Harpers Ferry *Site of John Brown's 1859 raid on a U.S. armory and arsenal for the manufacture and storage of military rifles.*

THE LAST MOMENTS OF JOHN BROWN. *This famous 1882–1884 painting of John Brown by Thomas Hovenden reminds us that the memory of Brown's 1859 attack on Harpers Ferry resonated deeply in American culture. Here, a sentimental portrait of Brown portrays him about to kiss a baby, while the soldiers who will escort him to his death are positioned as an honor guard. Depicting Brown as a gentle hero and martyr to the antislavery cause, this genre painting avoids grappling with the ferocity and violence of Brown's actions, whether in Kansas or at Harpers Ferry.*

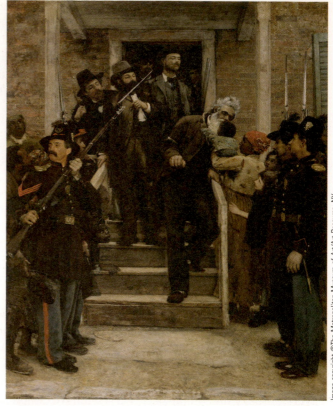

abolitionist supporters confirmed southern suspicions that a conspiracy was afoot. Republican leaders denied any connection with Brown and disavowed his actions, but few southerners believed them.

Many northerners, impressed by Brown's dignified bearing and eloquence during his trial, considered him a martyr to freedom. On the day of Brown's execution, bells tolled in hundreds of northern towns, guns fired salutes, and ministers preached sermons of commemoration. "The death of no man in America has ever produced so profound a sensation," commented one northerner. Ralph Waldo Emerson declared that Brown had made "the gallows as glorious as the cross."

Northern sympathy for Brown enraged southerners and weakened the already frayed threads of the Union. "I have always been a fervid Union man," wrote a North Carolinian, but "the endorsement of the Harpers Ferry outrage . . . has shaken my fidelity." A terror now descended on the South. Every Yankee seemed to be another John Brown; every slave who acted suspiciously seemed to be an insurrectionist. Hundreds of northerners were run out of the South in 1860, some wearing a coat of tar and feathers. Several "incendiaries," both white and black, were lynched. "Defend yourselves!" Senator Robert Toombs cried out to the southern people. "The enemy is at your door . . . meet him at the doorsill, and drive him from the temple of liberty, or pull down its pillars and involve him in a common ruin."

Conclusion

Few decades in American history witnessed a greater disjunction between economic well-being and political upheaval than the 1850s. Despite the recession following the Panic of 1857, the total output of the American economy grew by 62 percent during the decade. Yet a profound malaise gripped the country. Riots between immigrants and nativists in the mid-1850s left more than 50 people dead. Fighting in Kansas between pro-slavery and antislavery forces killed at least 200. A South

Carolina congressman bludgeoned a Massachusetts senator to unconsciousness with a heavy cane. Representatives and senators came to congressional sessions armed with weapons as well as with violent words.

The nation proved capable of absorbing a large influx of immigrants. It might also have been able to absorb the huge territorial expansion of the late 1840s had it not been for the reopening of the slavery issue by the Kansas–Nebraska Act of 1854. This legislation, followed by the Dred Scott decision in 1857, seemed to authorize the unlimited expansion of slavery. But within two years of its founding in 1854, the Republican Party emerged as the largest party in the North on a platform of preventing all future expansion of slavery. By 1860, the United States had reached a fateful crossroads. As Lincoln had said, it could not endure permanently half slave and half free. The presidential election of 1860 would decide which road America would take into the future.

CHAPTER REVIEW

Review Questions

1. Why did the Whig Party die, and why did the Republican Party, rather than the American Party, emerge as the new majority party in the North?
2. What were the origins of nativism, and how did this movement relate to the slavery issue?
3. How was violence in Kansas related to the issue of slavery?
4. How did economic developments in the 1840s and 1850s widen the breach between North and South?

Critical Thinking Questions

1. Why did the northern and southern economic systems develop in such different directions? Why did the effort by some southerners to escape from their "colonial" economic relationship fail?
2. One of the main points of contention in the Lincoln–Douglas debates was the question of whether the country could continue to endure half slave and half free. Why did Lincoln challenge Douglas's position that, because the nation had so endured for 70 years, there was no reason why it could not continue to do so?

Identifications

Review your understanding of the following key terms, people, and events for this chapter.

Dred Scott, p. 313
Kansas–Nebraska Act, p. 314
Abraham Lincoln, p. 314
nativism, p. 314

Know-Nothings, p. 314
parochial schools, p. 315
border ruffians, p. 317
John Brown, p. 318
Black Republicans, p. 319

referendum, p. 321
per capita, p. 322
interchangeable parts, p. 323
colonial economy, p. 324

free-labor ideology, p. 328
Lincoln–Douglas debates, p. 330
Jefferson Davis, p. 331
Harpers Ferry, p. 331

DISCOVERY

How did the United States find itself on the brink of the Civil War prior to the 1860 presidential election?

In thinking about this question, begin by breaking it down into the components shown below. A discussion of the significance of each component should appear in your answer.

Geography and Politics

Look at the map of counties in the 1856 presidential election. What regional patterns do you see in the counties that voted for each of the two major-party candidates (Frémont and Buchanan)? What does the distribution of votes for those two candidates suggest about the emerging sectional split in the country?

Demographics and Economy

Look at the maps of slavery and staple crops on page 327. What southern states had the highest percentages of slaves? The lowest? Compare the areas of highest percentages of slaves with the principal staple crop regions of the South. Which staple crops were most dependent on slave labor?

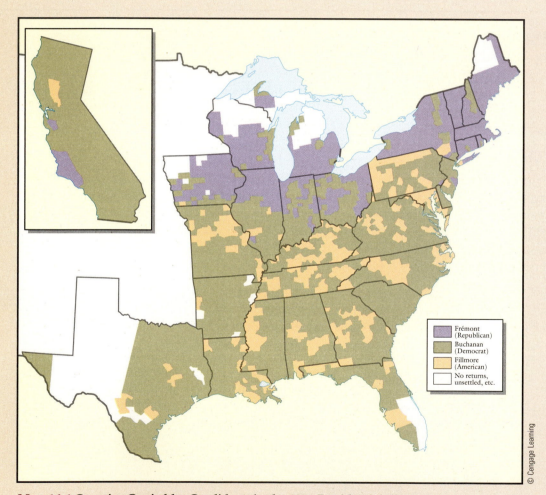

Frémont (Republican)
Buchanan (Democrat)
Fillmore (American)
No returns, unsettled, etc.

© Cengage Learning

Map 14.1 Counties Carried by Candidates in the 1856 Presidential Election

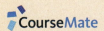

CourseMate

Visit the CourseMate website at www.cengagebrain.com for additional study tools and review materials for this chapter.

SECESSION AND CIVIL WAR, 1860–1862

I n April 1860, the Democratic Party, at its national convention in Charleston, South Carolina, split into northern and southern camps. This fissure virtually ensured the election of a Republican president. Such a prospect aroused deep fears among southern whites that a Republican administration might use its power to bring liberty and perhaps even equality to the slaves. When Abraham Lincoln won the election, the lower South states seceded from the Union. When Lincoln refused to remove U.S. troops from Fort Sumter, South Carolina, the new Confederate States army opened fire on the fort. Lincoln called out the militia to suppress the insurrection. Four more slave states seceded, and the country drifted into a civil war.

1860	1861	1862

■ **1860**
Lincoln elected president • South Carolina secedes

■ **1861**
Fort Sumter falls • Four more states secede to join Confederacy (April–May)
• Battle of Bull Run (Manassas)

1862 ■
Union capture of Forts Henry and Donelson (February 6 and 16)
• Naval battle of the *Monitor vs. Virginia (Merrimac)* • Battle of Shiloh
• Seven Days' Battles • Second Battle of Bull Run (Manassas)

© Cengage Learning

THE ELECTION OF 1860

A hotbed of southern-rights radicalism, Charleston turned out to be the worst possible place for the Democrats to hold their national convention. A Democratic Party rule requiring a two-thirds majority of delegates for a presidential nomination in effect gave southerners veto power. Although Stephen A. Douglas had the backing of a simple majority of the delegates, southern Democrats were determined to deny him the nomination.

The first test came in the debate on the platform. Southern delegates insisted on a federal slave code for the territories. Douglas could not run on a platform that contained such a plank, and if the party adopted it, Democrats were sure to lose every state in the North. By a slim majority, the convention rejected the plank and reaffirmed the 1856 platform endorsing popular sovereignty. Fifty southern delegates thereupon walked out of the convention. Even after they left, Douglas could not muster a two-thirds majority, nor could any other candidate. After 57 futile ballots, the convention adjourned to meet in Baltimore six weeks later to try again.

But the party was too badly shattered to be put back together—a fact that pleased pro-slavery radicals who hoped the election of a Republican would mobilize a southern majority for **secession**. In Baltimore, an even larger number of delegates from southern states walked out. They formed the Southern Rights Democratic Party and nominated John C. Breckinridge of Kentucky (the incumbent vice president) for president. When regular Democrats nominated Douglas, the stage was set for a four-party election. A coalition of former Whigs formed the Constitutional Union Party, which nominated John Bell of Tennessee. Bell had no chance of winning; the party's purpose was to exercise a conservative influence on a campaign that threatened to polarize the country.

The Republicans Nominate Lincoln

From the moment the Democratic Party broke apart, it became clear that 1860 could be the year the Republican Party elected its first president. The Republicans could expect no electoral votes from the 15 slave states. But in 1856 they had won all but five northern states, and with only two or three of those five they could win the presidency. The crucial states were Pennsylvania, Illinois, and Indiana. Douglas might carry them and throw the presidential election into the House, where anything could happen. Thus the Republicans had to carry at least two of the swing states to win.

The Republicans' leading prospect was William H. Seward of New York, who had served as governor and senator. However, Seward's antinativist policies had alienated some former members of the American Party, and he had a reputation for radicalism that might drive away voters in the swing states.

secession *The act of a state withdrawing from the Union. South Carolina was the first state to attempt to do this in 1860.*

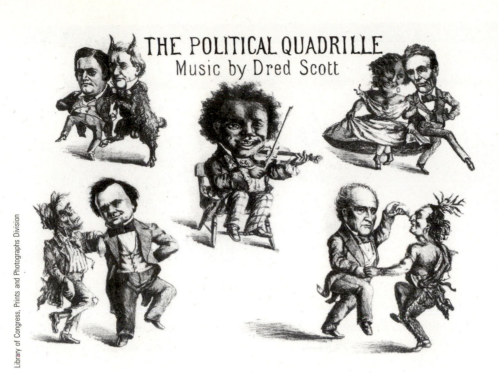

THE POLITICAL QUADRILLE
Music by Dred Scott

THE POLITICAL QUADRILLE. *This cartoon depicts the four presidential candidates in 1860. Clockwise from the upper left are John C. Breckinridge, Southern Rights Democrat; Abraham Lincoln, Republican; John Bell, Constitutional Union; and Stephen A. Douglas, Democrat. All are dancing to the tune played by Dred Scott, symbolizing the importance of the slavery issue in this campaign. Each candidate's partner represents a political liability: for example, Breckinridge's partner is the disunionist William L. Yancey, wearing a devil's horns, while Lincoln's partner is a black woman who supposedly gives color to Democratic accusations that Republicans believed in miscegenation.*

The next candidate to the fore was Abraham Lincoln. Although he too had opposed nativism, he had done so less prominently than Seward. His reputation was that of a more moderate man. He was from one of the swing states, and his rise from a poor farm boy and rail-splitter to successful lawyer and political leader perfectly reflected the free-labor theme of social mobility extolled by the Republican Party. By picking up second-choice votes from states that switched from their favorite sons, Lincoln won the nomination on the third ballot.

The Republican platform appealed to many groups in the North. Its main plank pledged exclusion of slavery from the territories. Other planks called for a higher tariff (especially popular in Pennsylvania), a homestead act (popular in the Northwest), and federal aid for transportation. This blend of idealism and materialism proved especially attractive to young people; a large majority of first-time voters in the North voted Republican in 1860.

Southern Fears

Militant enthusiasm in the North was matched by fear and rage in the South. Had not Lincoln branded slavery a moral, social, and political evil? Had he not said that the Declaration of Independence applied to blacks as well as whites? Had he not expressed a hope that excluding slavery from the territories would put it on the road to ultimate extinction? To southerners, the Republican pledge not to interfere with slavery in the states was meaningless.

A Republican victory in the presidential election would put an end to the South's control of its own political destiny. Even southern moderates warned that the South could not remain in the Union if Lincoln won. And what about the three-quarters of southern whites who did not belong to slaveholding families? Lincoln's election, warned an Alabama secessionist, would show that "the North [means] to free the negroes and force amalgamation between them and the children of the poor men of the South."

TABLE 15.1

VOTING IN THE 1860 ELECTION

	All States		Free States (18)		Slave States (15)	
	Popular	Electoral	Popular	Electoral	Popular	Electoral
Lincoln	1,864,735	180	1,838,347	180	26,388	0
Opposition to Lincoln	2,821,157	123	1,572,637	3	1,248,520	120
"Fusion" Tickets*	595,846	—	580,426	—	15,420	—
Douglas	979,425	12	815,857	3	163,568	9
Breckinridge	669,472	72	99,381	0	570,091	72
Bell	576,414	39	76,973	0	499,441	39

*In several states, the two Democratic parties and the Constitutional Union Party arranged a single anti-Lincoln ballot. These "fusion" tickets carried several counties but failed to win any state.

© Cengage Learning

Breckinridge carried 11 slave states. Bell won the upper-South states of Virginia, Kentucky, and Tennessee. Missouri went to Douglas—the only state he carried, although he came in second in the popular vote. While Lincoln received less than 40 percent of the popular vote, he won every free state and swept the presidency by a substantial margin in the Electoral College (see Table 15.1).

THE LOWER SOUTH SECEDES

FOCUS QUESTION

Why did political leaders in the lower South think that Lincoln's election made secession imperative?

Lincoln's victory provided the shock that southern **fire-eaters** had craved. According to the theory of secession, although each state, when it joined the Union, had authorized the national government to act as its agent in the exercise of certain functions of sovereignty, the states had never given away their fundamental sovereignty. Any state, by the act of its own convention, could withdraw from its "compact" with the other states and reassert its individual sovereignty. Although many conservatives and former Whigs, including Alexander H. Stephens of Georgia, shrank from the drastic step of secession, one after another the conventions voted to take their states out of the Union: South Carolina on December 20, 1860; Mississippi on January 9, 1861; Florida on the 10th; Alabama on the 11th; Georgia on the 19th; Louisiana on the 26th; and Texas on February 1. Delegates from the seven seceding states met in Montgomery, Alabama, in February to create a new nation to be called the Confederate States of America.

Northerners Affirm the Union

Most people in the North considered secession unconstitutional and treasonable. In his final annual message to Congress, on December 3, 1860, President Buchanan warned that secession would create a disastrous precedent that would make the United States government "a rope of sand." "The doctrine of secession is anarchy," declared a Cincinnati newspaper. "If any minority have the right to break up the Government at pleasure, because they have not had their way, there is an end of all government." Lincoln denied that the states had ever possessed independent sovereignty before becoming part of the United States. Rather, they had been colonies or territories that never would have become part of the United States had they not accepted unconditional sovereignty of the national government. "No State, upon its own mere motion, can lawfully get out of the Union. … They can only do so against law, and by revolution."

fire-eaters *Southerners who were eager, enthusiastic supporters of southern rights and later of secession.*

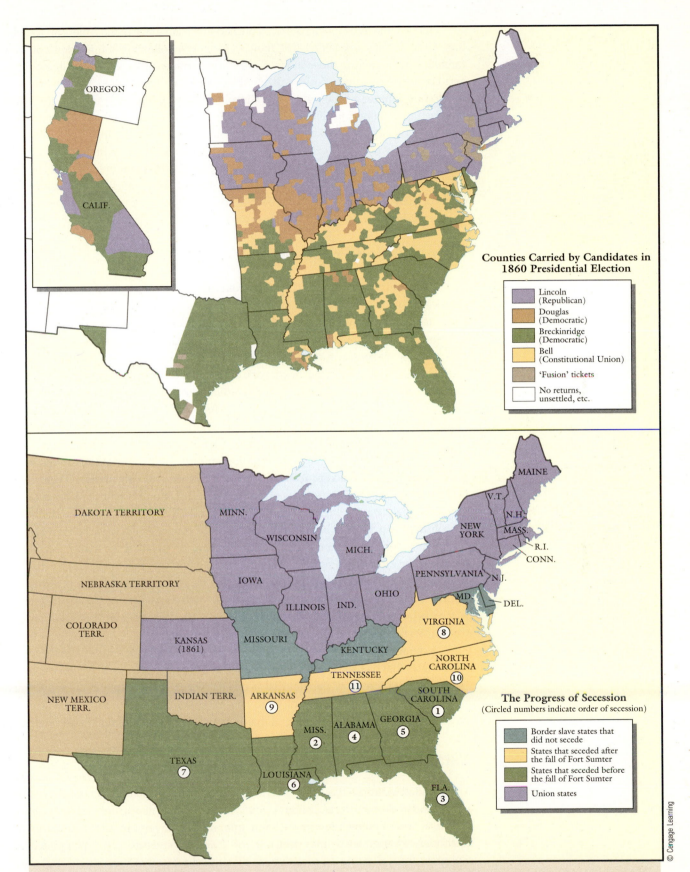

Counties Carried by Candidates in 1860 Presidential Election

- Lincoln (Republican)
- Douglas (Democratic)
- Breckinridge (Democratic)
- Bell (Constitutional Union)
- 'Fusion' tickets
- No returns, unsettled, etc.

OREGON

CALIF.

The Progress of Secession
(Circled numbers indicate order of secession)

- Border slave states that did not secede
- States that seceded after the fall of Fort Sumter
- States that seceded before the fall of Fort Sumter
- Union states

DAKOTA TERRITORY

MINN.

WISCONSIN

MICH.

MAINE

V.T.

N.H

NEW YORK

MASS.

R.I.

CONN.

NEBRASKA TERRITORY

IOWA

ILLINOIS   IND.   OHIO

PENNSYLVANIA   N.J.

MD.   DEL.

COLORADO TERR.

KANSAS (1861)

MISSOURI

KENTUCKY

VIRGINIA ⑧

NORTH CAROLINA ⑩

NEW MEXICO TERR.

INDIAN TERR.

ARKANSAS ⑨

TENNESSEE ⑪

SOUTH CAROLINA ①

TEXAS ⑦

MISS. ②   ALABAMA ④   GEORGIA ⑤

LOUISIANA ⑥

FLA. ③

***Map 15.1** Election of 1860 and Southern Secession. Note the similarity of the geographical voting patterns in the upper map to the map on p. 320. Another striking pattern shows the correlation between the vote for Breckinridge (upper map) and the first seven states to secede (lower map).*

Indeed, the secession debate was couched in the language of the American Revolution. Secessionists maintained that they were merely following the example of their forefathers in declaring independence from a government that threatened their rights and liberties. Northerners could scarcely deny the right of revolution, but "the right of revolution, is never a legal right," said Lincoln. "At most, it is but a moral right, when exercised for a morally justifiable cause. When exercised without such a cause revolution is no right, but simply a wicked exercise of physical power." The South, in Lincoln's view, had no morally justifiable cause. For southerners to cast themselves in the mold of 1776 was "a libel upon the whole character and conduct" of the Founding Fathers, said the antislavery poet and journalist William Cullen Bryant. They rebelled "to establish the rights of man . . . and principles of universal liberty," while southerners were rebelling to protect "a domestic despotism. . . . Their motto is not liberty, but slavery."

Compromise Proposals

Most people in the North agreed with Lincoln that secession was a "wicked exercise of physical power." The question was what to do about it. In December 1860, John J. Crittenden of Kentucky sponsored a compromise package in the Senate. The Crittenden Compromise consisted of a series of proposed constitutional amendments: to guarantee slavery in the states against federal interference; to prohibit Congress from abolishing slavery in the District of Columbia or on any federal property; to deny Congress the power to interfere with the interstate slave trade; to compensate slaveholders who were prevented from recovering fugitive slaves; and, most important, to protect slavery south of latitude 36°30' in all territories "now held *or hereafter acquired.*"

In the view of most Republicans, the latter clause might turn the United States into "a great slavebreeding and slavetrading empire." But some conservatives in the party were willing to accept it in the interest of peace and conciliation. Their votes, together with those of Democrats and upper-South Unionists whose states had not seceded, might have gotten the compromise through Congress. But President-elect Lincoln sent word to key Republican senators and congressmen to stand firm against compromise on the territorial issue. "Entertain no proposition for a compromise in regard to the *extension* of slavery," wrote Lincoln. "We have just carried an election on principles fairly stated to the people. Now we are told in advance, the government shall be broken up, unless we surrender to those we have beaten. . . . If we surrender, it is the end of us." Lincoln's advice was decisive: The Republicans voted against the Crittenden proposal and any other attempt to compromise.

Nothing that happened in Washington would have made any difference to the seven states that had seceded. No compromise could bring them back. No power could "stem the wild torrent of passion that is carrying everything before it," wrote former U.S. senator Judah P. Benjamin of Louisiana. Secession "is a revolution" that "can no more be checked by human effort . . . than a prairie fire by a gardener's watering pot."

Establishment of the Confederacy

The seceded states held a convention in Montgomery, Alabama, where they drew up a constitution and established a government for the new Confederate States of America. The Confederate constitution guaranteed slavery in the states and the territories, strengthened the principle of state sovereignty, and prohibited its Congress from enacting a protective (as distinguished from a revenue-raising) tariff. It limited the president to a single six-year term. Until elections could be held in November 1861, delegates constituted themselves a provisional Congress and elected Jefferson Davis and Alexander Stephens as provisional president and vice president.

LINK TO THE PAST

Cornerstone of the Confederacy

Alexander H. Stephens of Georgia had opposed the secession of his state in January 1861. But when Georgia seceded anyway, he "went with his state," as did so many other southerners who had initially counseled against secession. Stephens was subsequently elected vice president of the Confederate States of America. On March 21, 1861, he gave an address in Savannah, Georgia, which became known as the Cornerstone Speech, in which he proclaimed slavery to be the cornerstone of the new Confederacy.

The new Constitution [of the Confederate States] has put at rest forever all the agitating questions relating to our peculiar institution—African slavery as it exists among us—the proper status of the negro in our form of civilization. This was the immediate cause of the late rupture and present revolution.

[Thomas] Jefferson, in his forecast, had anticipated this, as the "rock upon which the old Union would split." He was right. . . . But whether he fully comprehended the great truth upon which that rock stood and stands, may be doubted. The prevailing ideas entertained by him and most of the leading statesmen at the time of the formation of the old Constitution were, that the enslavement of the African was in violation of the laws of nature; that it was wrong in principle, socially, morally, and politically. It was an evil they knew not well how to deal with; but the general opinion of the men of that day was, that, somehow or other, in the order of Providence, the institution would be evanescent and pass away. . . . Those ideas, however, were fundamentally wrong. . . .

Our new Government is founded upon exactly the opposite ideas; its foundations are laid, its cornerstone rests, upon the great truth that the negro is not equal to the white man; that slavery, subordination to the superior race, is his natural and moral condition. This, our new Government, is the first, in the history of the world, based upon this great physical, philosophical, and moral truth.

Q After the Civil War, Stephens wrote a two-volume history titled *The War Between the States,* in which he maintained that slavery was not the cornerstone of the Confederacy or the reason for secession. How might one explain the inconsistency between the Stephens of 1861 and the Stephens of 1868?

Davis and Stephens were two of the ablest men in the South. Davis had commanded a regiment in the Mexican War and had been secretary of war in the Pierce administration. But perhaps the main reason they were elected was to present an image of moderation and respectability to the eight upper-South states that remained in the Union. The Confederacy needed those states—at least some of them—if it was to be a viable nation, especially if war came. Without the upper South, the Confederate states would have less than one-fifth of the population (and barely one-tenth of the free population) and only one-twentieth of the industrial capacity of the Union states.

Confederate leaders appealed to the upper South to join them because of the "common origin, pursuits, tastes, manners and customs" that "bind together in one brotherhood the . . . slaveholding states." Residents of the upper South were concerned about preserving slavery, but they also boasted a strong heritage of Unionism. Virginia had contributed more men to the pantheon of Founding Fathers than any other state. Tennessee took pride in being the state of Andrew Jackson, who had struck down nullification years earlier. Kentucky was the home of Henry Clay, the "Great Pacificator" who had put together compromises to save the Union on three occasions. These states would not leave the Union without greater cause.

Fort Sumter *Fort in Charleston's harbor occupied by United States troops after the secession of South Carolina.*

The Fort Sumter Issue

As each state seceded, it seized the forts, arsenals, and other federal property within its borders. Still in federal hands, however, were two remote forts in the Florida Keys, another on an island off Pensacola, and Fort Moultrie in the Charleston harbor. In December 1860, the self-proclaimed republic of South Carolina demanded that the U.S. Army evacuate Moultrie. On the day after Christmas 1860, Major Robert Anderson, commander at Moultrie, moved his men to **Fort Sumter** on an artificial island in the channel leading into Charleston Bay. Sympathetic to the South but loyal to the United States, Anderson hoped that moving the garrison would ease tensions by reducing the possibility of an attack. Instead, it lit a fuse that eventually set off the war.

South Carolina sent a delegation to President Buchanan to negotiate the withdrawal of the federal troops. Buchanan surprised them by saying no. He even tried to reinforce the garrison. On January 9, an unarmed merchant ship carrying 200 soldiers for Sumter tried to enter the bay but was driven away by South Carolina artillery. Matters then settled into an uneasy truce, and the Confederates waited to see what the incoming Lincoln administration would do.

Lincoln knew that his inaugural address would be the most important in American history. His goal was to keep the upper South in the Union while cooling passions in the lower South. In his address, he demonstrated firmness in purpose to preserve the Union and forbearance in the means of doing so. He repeated his pledge not "to interfere with the institution of slavery where it exists." He assured the Confederate states that "the government will not assail *you*." But he also said that he would "hold, occupy, and possess the property, and places belonging to the government," without defining exactly what he meant or how he would do it.

Lincoln hoped to buy time to demonstrate his peaceful intentions and to enable southern Unionists (whose numbers Republicans overestimated) to regain the upper hand. But the day after his inauguration he was informed that provisions for the soldiers at Fort Sumter would soon be exhausted. The garrison must either be resupplied or evacuated. Any attempt to send in supplies by force would undoubtedly provoke a response from Confederate guns at Charleston. And such an action would

BOMBARDMENT OF FORT SUMTER, APRIL 12, 1861. *This colored illustration shows Confederate artillery in Fort Moultrie near Charleston, South Carolina, firing on Fort Sumter in the middle distance. Other Confederate guns are also firing on Fort Sumter from Fort Johnson, shown in the upper right portion of the picture. Confederate shells set the interior of Fort Sumter on fire, as portrayed here, forcing its surrender to forestall additional fires that might reach the powder magazine.*

© Bettmann/CORBIS

TABLE 15.2

SLAVERY AND SECESSION The higher the proportion of slaves and slaveholders in the population of a southern state, the greater the intensity of secessionist sentiment.		
Order of Secession	Percentage of Population Who Were Slaves	Percentage of White Population in Slaveholding Families
Seven states that seceded December 1860–February 1861 (South Carolina, Mississippi, Florida, Alabama, Georgia, Louisiana, Texas)	47	38
Four states that seceded after the firing on Fort Sumter (Virginia, Arkansas, Tennessee, North Carolina)	32	24
Four border slave states remaining in Union (Maryland, Delaware, Kentucky, Missouri)	14	15

© Cengage Learning

undoubtedly divide the North and unite the South, driving at least four more states into the Confederacy. Most members of Lincoln's cabinet, along with the army's general-in-chief, Winfield Scott, advised Lincoln to withdraw the troops from Sumter and abandon his pledge to "hold, occupy, and possess" national property.

Lincoln hit upon a different solution. He decided to send in unarmed ships with supplies but to hold troops and warships outside the harbor with authorization to go into action only if the Confederates used force to stop the supply ships. And he would give South Carolina officials advance notice of his intention. This stroke of genius shifted the decision for war or peace to Jefferson Davis. If Confederate troops fired on the supply ships, the South would stand convicted of starting a war by attacking "a mission of humanity." If Davis allowed the supplies to go in peacefully, the U.S. flag would continue to fly over Fort Sumter. The Confederacy would lose face at home and abroad, and southern Unionists would take courage.

Davis did not hesitate. He ordered General Pierre G. T. Beauregard to compel Sumter's surrender before the supply ships got there. At 4:30 a.m. on April 12, 1861, Confederate guns set off the Civil War by firing on Fort Sumter. After a 33-hour bombardment, the burning fort lowered the U.S. flag in surrender.

CHOOSING SIDES

News of the attack triggered an outburst of anger and war fever in the North. Because the tiny U.S. Army was inadequate to quell the "insurrection," Lincoln called on the states for 75,000 militia. The free states filled their quotas immediately. More than twice as many men volunteered as Lincoln had requested. Before the war was over, more than two million men would serve in the Union army and navy.

The eight slave states that were still in the Union rejected Lincoln's call for troops. Four of them—Virginia, Arkansas, Tennessee, and North Carolina—soon seceded and joined the Confederacy. As a former Unionist in North Carolina remarked, "The South must go with the South. . . . Blood is thicker than Water." Few found the choice harder to make than **Robert E. Lee** of Virginia. One of the most promising officers in the U.S. Army, Lee believed that southern states had no legal right to secede. Still, he felt compelled to resign after the Virginia convention passed an ordinance of secession on April 17. "I cannot raise my hand against my birthplace, my home, my children," Lee told a northern friend. While most southern whites embraced war against the Yankees with more enthusiasm, no one could know that before the war ended at least 260,000 Confederate soldiers would lose their lives.

Robert E. Lee *U.S. Army officer until his resignation to join the Confederacy as general-in-chief.*

The Border States

Except for Delaware, which remained firmly in the Union, the slave states that bordered free states were divided by the outbreak of war. Leaders in these states talked vaguely of neutrality, but they were to be denied that luxury.

The first blood was shed in Maryland on April 19 when a mob attacked a Massachusetts regiment traveling through Baltimore. The soldiers fired back, leaving 12 Baltimoreans and 4 soldiers dead. Confederate partisans burned bridges and tore down telegraph wires, cutting Washington off from the North for nearly a week until additional troops from Massachusetts and New York reopened communications and seized key points in Maryland. The troops also arrested many Confederate sympathizers. To prevent Washington from becoming surrounded by enemy territory, federal forces turned Maryland into an occupied state.

In Missouri, a showdown between Unionist and pro-Confederate militia turned into a riot in St. Louis on May 10 and 11, in which 36 people died. The Union commander, Nathaniel Lyon, then led a campaign that drove the Confederate militia into Arkansas. Reinforced by Arkansas regiments, these rebel Missourians invaded their home state and on August 10 defeated Lyon in the bloody battle of Wilson's Creek in the southwest corner of Missouri. The victorious Confederates marched northward, capturing a Union garrison at Lexington 40 miles east of Kansas City on September 20. Union forces then regrouped and drove the ragged Missouri Confederates back into Arkansas.

From then until the war's end, military power enabled **Unionists** to maintain political control of Missouri, even as continued guerrilla attacks by Confederate **"bushwhackers"** and counterinsurgency tactics by Unionist "jayhawkers" ravaged large areas of the state.

In elections held during the summer and fall of 1861, Unionists gained control of the Kentucky and Maryland legislatures. Kentucky Confederates, like those of Missouri, formed a state government in exile. When the Confederate Congress admitted both Kentucky and Missouri to full representation, the Confederate flag acquired its 13 stars. Nevertheless, two-thirds of the white population in the four border slave states favored the Union, though some of that support was undoubtedly induced by the presence of Union troops.

The war produced a fifth Union border state: West Virginia. A region of mountains, small farms, and few slaves, western Virginia's economy was linked more closely to Ohio and Pennsylvania than to the South. Most of the delegates from western Virginia had voted against secession. They returned home determined to secede themselves—from Virginia. The new state of West Virginia entered the Union in 1863.

Unionists *Southerners who remained loyal to the Union during the Civil War.*

bushwhackers *Confederate guerrilla raiders especially active in Missouri. Jayhawkers were the Union version of the same type of people. Both groups did a tremendous amount of damage with raids, arson, ambush, and murder.*

Indian Territory and the Southwest

To the south and west of Missouri, civil war raged for control of the Indian Territory (present-day Oklahoma). The Native Americans, who had been resettled there in the generation before the war, chose sides and carried on bloody guerrilla warfare with each other. The more prosperous Indians of the five Civilized Tribes (Cherokees, Creeks, Seminoles, Chickasaws, and Choctaws), many of them of mixed blood and some of them slaveholders, tended to side with the Confederacy. However, aided by white and black Union regiments operating out of Kansas and Missouri, the pro-Union Indians gradually gained control of most of the Indian Territory.

Map 15.2 **Principal Military Campaigns of the Civil War.** *This map vividly illustrates the contrast between the vast distances over which the armies fought in the western theater of the war and the concentrated campaigns of the Army of the Potomac and the Army of Northern Virginia in the East.*

In the meantime, Confederates had made their boldest bid to fulfill antebellum southern ambitions to win the Southwest. A small army composed mostly of Texans pushed up the Rio Grande valley into New Mexico in 1861. In February 1862, they launched a strike to capture Santa Fe. They hoped to push even farther westward and northward to the California and Colorado gold mines, which were helping to finance the Union war effort.

The Confederates won early victories in New Mexico, but Colorado miners had organized themselves into Union regiments. They fought the Texans in the battle of Glorieta Pass on March 26–28. The battle was a tactical draw, but the Coloradans destroyed the Confederate wagon train, forcing the southerners to retreat to Texas. Of the 3,700 who had started out to win the West for the Confederacy, only 2,000 made it back. The West and Southwest remained safe for the Union.

THE BALANCE SHEET OF WAR

FOCUS QUESTION

What were northern advantages in the Civil War? What were southern advantages?

The total population in the Union states in 1861 was 22.5 million, compared with 9 million people in the Confederate states, 3.7 million of them slaves. The Union eventually enlisted black soldiers and black sailors, but the Confederacy did not do so until the war was virtually over. Altogether, about 2.1 million men fought for the Union and 850,000 for the Confederacy. That was close to half of the North's male population of military age and three-quarters of the comparable Confederate white population. The Confederacy was able to enlist a larger proportion of its white population because its labor force consisted mainly of slaves. In economic resources, the Union states possessed nine-tenths of the country's industrial capacity, four-fifths of its bank capital, three-fourths of its railroad mileage, and three-fourths of its taxable wealth.

In a long war that mobilized the total resources of both sides, the North's advantages might prove decisive. But in 1861, both sides expected a short and victorious conflict. The South had some reason to believe that its martial qualities were superior. A higher proportion of southerners than northerners had attended West Point and other military schools, had fought in the Mexican War, or had served as officers in the regular army. As a rural people, southerners were proficient in hunting, riding, and other outdoor skills useful in military operations. The South had also begun to prepare for war earlier than the North. As each state seceded, it mobilized militia and volunteer military companies. Not until summer 1861 would the North's greater manpower begin to make itself felt in the form of a larger army.

Strategy and Morale

The North's superior resources did not guarantee success. Its military task was much more difficult than that of the South. The Confederacy had come into being in firm control of 750,000 square miles. To win the war, Union forces would have to invade, conquer, and occupy much of that vast territory and destroy its armies. To "win" the war, the Confederacy did not need to invade or conquer the Union or even to destroy its armies; it needed only to hold out long enough to convince northerners that the cost of victory was too high.

The important factor of morale also seemed to favor the Confederacy. To be sure, Union soldiers fought for powerful symbols: nation, flag, Constitution. But Confederates, too, fought for nation, flag, constitution, and liberty—of whites. In addition, they fought to defend their land, homes, and families. An army fighting in defense of its homeland generally has the edge in morale. "We shall have the enormous advantage of fighting on our own territory and for our very existence," wrote a Confederate leader.

Mobilizing for War

More than four-fifths of the soldiers on both sides were volunteers—citizen soldiers, not professionals. They carried peacetime notions of democracy and discipline with them into the army. The men elected their company officers and sometimes their field officers (colonel, lieutenant colonel, and major) as well. Political influence often counted for more than military training in the election and appointment of officers. In most regiments, the men in each company generally came from the same town or locality. Some Union regiments were composed of men of a particular ethnic group. These civilians in uniform were awkward and unmilitary at first, and some regiments suffered battlefield disasters because of inadequate training, discipline, and leadership. Even high-ranking generals, appointed on each side by the president,

HISTORY THROUGH FILM

The Red Badge of Courage (1951)

Directed by John Huston; starring Audie Murphy (The Youth) and Bill Mauldin (The Loud Soldier)

Stephen Crane's short novel *The Red Badge of Courage* became an instant classic when it was published in 1895. Civil War veterans praised its realistic descriptions of the confusion, terror, chaos, courage, despair, and adrenaline-driven rage of men in battle. A story of young Henry Fleming (The Youth) and his buddy Wilson (The Loud Soldier) in their first battle (Chancellorsville), the novel traces Henry's transition from boyhood to manhood, from raw recruit to veteran, over two days of violent combat. Intended by Crane as a portrait of soldiers facing the ultimate moment of truth in combat, the novel strives for universality rather than specificity as a Civil War story. Thus the battle is not actually named (although circumstances make clear that it is Chancellorsville, despite the film misleadingly dating it in 1862). The 304th New York regiment is fictional, and even the fact that it is a Civil War battle is scarcely mentioned. Crane did achieve a sort of universality; the novel is a story of men at war—not simply a story of the Civil War.

The film remains more faithful to the book than most movies based on novels. Most of the dialogue is taken directly from Crane. Henry Fleming's self-doubts, fears, and eventual heroism after he first runs away are brilliantly portrayed on the screen by action and dialogue against a background of a narrator's words. Fleming is played by Audie Murphy, America's most decorated soldier in the Second World War, and Wilson by Bill Mauldin, whose Willie and Joe cartoons provided the most enduring images of the American infantryman in that war. Their moving performances make the characters come alive.

Much of the credit for this success belongs to director John Huston, who brought out the best in his inexperienced actors. One of Hollywood's most prominent directors, Huston had lobbied Louis Mayer of MGM to produce the film. Believing that "Nobody wants to see a Civil War movie," Mayer finally gave in but provided Huston with a skimpy budget. When Huston flew to Africa immediately after the filming was completed to begin directing *The African Queen*, studio executives cut several of Huston's scenes and reduced the movie's length to 69 minutes. The studio also did little to promote the film, and because audiences failed to identify with its grim realism and mostly unknown cast, *The Red Badge of Courage* was a box-office failure. Like the novel, however, it has become a classic that is still, more than a half-century after it was filmed, one of the best cinematic portrayals of the psychology of men in combat.

Courtesy of The Everett Collection

Audie Murphy (Henry Fleming) and Bill Mauldin (The Loud Soldier), in The Red Badge of Courage.

were incompetent early on. In time, however, raw recruits became battle-hardened veterans commanded by experienced officers.

Weapons and Tactics

In Civil War battles, the infantry rifle was the most lethal weapon. Muskets and rifles caused 80 to 90 percent of the combat casualties. From 1862 on, most of these weapons were **"rifled"**—that is, they had spiral grooves cut in the barrel to impart a spin to the cone-shaped lead bullet, whose base expanded upon firing to "take" the rifling of the barrel. This made it possible to load and fire a muzzle-loading rifle two or three times per minute.

The rifle had greater accuracy and at least four times the effective range (400 yards or more) of the old smoothbore musket, but Civil War infantry tactics adjusted only gradually to its lethal accuracy. **Close-order assaults** against defenders equipped with rifles resulted in enormous casualties. The defensive power of the rifle became even greater when troops began digging into trenches. Massed frontal assaults became almost suicidal. Soldiers and their officers learned the hard way to adopt skirmishing tactics, taking advantage of cover and working around the enemy flank.

Logistics

The Civil War is often called the world's first "modern" war because of the role played by technology. Railroads and steamboats transported supplies and soldiers with unprecedented speed and efficiency; the telegraph provided rapid communication between army headquarters and field commanders.

Yet these modern forms of transport and communications were extremely vulnerable. Cavalry raiders and guerrillas could cut telegraph wires, burn railroad bridges, and tear up the tracks. Once the campaigning armies had moved away from their railhead or wharfside supply base, they returned to dependence on animal-powered transport. Union armies required one horse or mule for every two or three men. Thus a large invading Union army of 100,000 men would need about 40,000 draft animals. Confederate armies, operating mostly in friendly territory closer to their bases, needed fewer. The poorly drained dirt roads typical of much of the South turned roads into a morass of mud in wet weather.

These logistical problems initially did much to offset the industrial supremacy of the Union, but by 1862, the North's economy had fully geared up for war. Over the long haul, the South's industrial base proved inadequate. Particularly troublesome for the Confederacy was its inability to replace rails and rolling stock. Although the South produced plenty of food, the railroads deteriorated to the point that food could not reach soldiers or civilians. As the war went into its third and fourth years, the northern economy grew stronger and the southern economy grew weaker.

Financing the War

One of the greatest defects of the Confederate economy was finance. The Confederate Congress, wary of dampening patriotic ardor, was slow to raise taxes. And because most capital in the South was tied up in land and slaves, little was available for buying war bonds. Therefore, the Confederate Congress authorized a limited issue of treasury notes, to be redeemable in **specie** (gold or silver) within two years after the end of the war. The first modest issue was followed by many more because the notes declined sharply in value. By early 1863 it took eight dollars to buy what one dollar had bought two years earlier; just before the war's end, the Confederate dollar was worth one U.S. cent.

rifling *Process of cutting spiral grooves in a gun's barrel to impart a spin to the bullet. Perfected in the 1850s, it produced greater accuracy and longer range.*

close-order assault *Military tactic of attacking with little space between men. With the modern weapons used during the Civil War, such fighting produced a high casualty rate.*

specie *Metal money or coins, usually made of gold or silver.*

In 1863 the Confederate Congress tried to stem runaway inflation by passing a comprehensive law that taxed income, consumer purchases, and business transactions and included a "tax in kind" on agricultural products, allowing tax officials to seize 10 percent of a farmer's crops. In response, many farmers hid their crops and livestock or refused to plant, thereby worsening the Confederacy's food shortages. The Confederate government raised less than 5 percent of its revenue by taxes and less than 40 percent by loans, leaving 60 percent to be created by the printing press—a recipe for disaster.

In contrast, the Union government raised 66 percent of its revenue by selling war bonds, 21 percent by taxes, and only 13 percent by printing **treasury notes**. The Legal Tender Act authorizing these notes, the famous "greenbacks," was passed in February 1862. Instead of promising to redeem them in specie at some future date, as the South had done, Congress made them **"legal tender"**—that is, it required everyone to accept them as real money at face value. The North's economy suffered inflation during the war—about 80 percent over four years—but it was mild compared with the 9,000 percent inflation in the Confederacy.

The Union Congress also passed the National Banking Act of 1863. Before the war, the principal form of money had been notes issued by state-chartered banks. After Andrew Jackson's destruction of the Second Bank of the United States (Chapter 11), the number and variety of **banknotes** had skyrocketed until 7,000 different kinds of state banknotes were circulating in 1860. The National Banking Act of 1863 was an attempt to resurrect the centralized banking system and create a more stable banknote currency, as well as to finance the war. Under the act, chartered national banks could issue banknotes up to 90 percent of the value of the U.S. bonds they held. This provision created a market for the bonds and, in combination with the greenbacks, replaced state banknotes with a more uniform national currency.

National banknotes did have two defects, however, that would not be remedied until the creation of the Federal Reserve System in 1913. First, because the number of notes that could be issued was tied to each bank's holdings of U.S. bonds, the volume of currency available was dependent on the amount of federal debt rather than on the economic needs of the country. Second, the banknotes themselves tended to be concentrated in the Northeast, where most of the large national banks were located, leaving the South and West short.

treasury notes *Paper money used by the Union to help finance the Civil War. One type of treasury note was known as a greenback because of its color.*

legal tender *Any type of money that the government requires everyone to accept at face value.*

banknotes *Paper money, issued by banks, that circulated as currency.*

NAVIES, THE BLOCKADE, AND FOREIGN RELATIONS

To sustain its war effort, the Confederacy needed to import large quantities of material from abroad. To shut off these imports, on April 19, 1861, Lincoln proclaimed a **blockade** of Confederate ports. The task was formidable; the Confederate coastline stretched for 3,500 miles, with two dozen major ports and another 150 bays and coves where cargo could be landed. Although the U.S. Navy eventually placed several hundred warships on blockade duty, in 1861 the blockade was so thin that 9 of every 10 vessels slipped through it on their way to or from Confederate ports.

King Cotton Diplomacy

But the Confederacy inadvertently contributed to the blockade's success when it adopted King Cotton diplomacy. Textiles were at the heart of British industry, and three-fourths of Britain's supply of raw cotton came from the South. If that supply was cut off, southerners reasoned, British factories would shut down, unemployed

blockade *The closing of a country's harbors by enemy ships to prevent trade and commerce, especially to prevent traffic in military supplies.*

workers would starve, and Britain would face the prospect of revolution. Rather than risk such a consequence, Britain would recognize the Confederacy's independence and then use the powerful British navy to break the blockade.

Southerners were so firmly convinced of cotton's importance to the British economy that they kept the 1861 cotton crop at home rather than try to export it through the blockade. The strategy backfired. Bumper crops in 1859 and 1860 had piled up a surplus of raw cotton in British warehouses and delayed the anticipated "cotton famine" until 1862. The Confederacy missed its chance to ship out its cotton and store it abroad, where it could be used to purchase war matériel.

Moreover, the Confederacy's King Cotton diplomacy contradicted its own foreign policy objective: to persuade the British and French governments to deny the legality of the blockade. Under international law, neutral nations must respect a blockade if it is "physically effective." Confederate diplomats claimed that the Union effort was a mere "paper blockade," yet the dearth of cotton reaching European ports—as a result of the South's own embargo—suggested to British and French diplomats that the blockade was at least partly effective. And by 1862 it was. Although most **"blockade runners"** got through, the blockade had reduced the Confederacy's seaborne commerce enough to convince the British government to recognize it as legitimate. The blockade was also squeezing the South's economy. Although it lifted its cotton embargo in 1862, the Confederacy had increasing difficulty exporting enough cotton through the blockade to pay for the imports it needed.

Confederate foreign policy also failed to win diplomatic recognition by other nations. That recognition would have conferred international legitimacy on the Confederacy and might even have led to treaties of alliance or of foreign aid. The French emperor Napoleon III expressed sympathy for the Confederacy, as did influential groups in the British Parliament. But Britain did not want to recognize the Confederacy while it was engaged in a war it might lose, especially if recognition might jeopardize relations with the United States. By 1862, it had become clear that Britain would withhold recognition until the Confederacy had virtually won its independence, but such recognition would have come too late to help the Confederacy win.

The Confederate Navy

Lacking the capacity to build a naval force at home, the Confederacy hoped to use British shipyards for the purpose. Through a loophole in the British neutrality law, two fast commerce raiders built in Liverpool made their way into Confederate hands in 1862. Named the *Florida* and the *Alabama,* they roamed the seas for two years, capturing or sinking Union merchant ships and whalers. Altogether, Confederate privateers and commerce raiders destroyed or captured 257 Union merchant vessels and drove at least 700 others to foreign registry. But this Confederate achievement, although spectacular, made only a tiny dent in the Union war effort.

The *Monitor* and the *Virginia*

Though plagued by shortages on every hand, the Confederate navy department demonstrated great skill at innovation. Southern engineers developed "torpedoes" (mines) that sank or damaged 43 Union warships in southern bays and rivers. The South also constructed the world's first combat submarine. Another important innovation was the building of ironclad "rams" to sink the blockade ships. The most famous of these was the C.S.S. *Virginia,* commonly called the *Merrimac* because it was rebuilt from the steam frigate U.S.S. *Merrimack.* Ready for its trial-by-combat on March 8, 1862, the *Virginia* steamed out to attack the blockade squadron at Hampton Roads. It sank one warship with its iron ram and another with its 10 guns. Union shot and shells bounced off its armor plate.

blockade runner *A ship designed to run through a blockade.*

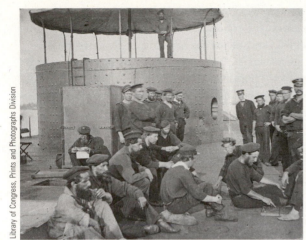

THE MONITOR AND VIRGINIA. *The crew of the Union ironclad* Monitor *stands in front of its revolving two-gun turret. In action, the sun canopy above the turret would be taken down and all sailors would be at their stations inside the turret or the hull, as shown in the painting of the famed battle, on March 9, 1862, between the* Monitor *and the Confederate* Virginia (Merrimac). *The* Virginia *was blown up by its crew two months later when the Confederates retreated toward Richmond because its draft was too deep to go up the James River.*

Panic seized Washington, but in the nick of time the Union's own ironclad, the U.S.S. *Monitor*, sailed into Hampton Roads and saved the rest of the fleet. Much smaller than the *Virginia*, with two 11-inch guns in a **revolving turret** (an innovation) set on a deck almost flush with the water, the *Monitor* looked like a "tin can on a shingle." It presented a small target and was capable of concentrating considerable firepower in a given direction with its revolving turret. The next day, the *Monitor* fought the *Virginia* in history's first battle between ironclads. It was a draw, but the *Virginia* limped home to Norfolk, never again to menace the Union fleet. Although the Confederacy built other ironclad rams, none achieved the initial success of the *Virginia*. By the war's end, the Union navy had built or started 58 ships of the *Monitor* class, launching a new age in naval history.

revolving turret *A low structure, often round, on a ship that moved horizontally and contained mounted guns.*

CAMPAIGNS AND BATTLES, 1861–1862

Wars can be won only by hard fighting. Some leaders on both sides overlooked this truth. One of them was Winfield Scott, general-in-chief of the U.S. Army. Scott, a Virginian who had remained loyal to the Union, evolved a military strategy based on his conviction that a great many southerners were willing to be won back to the Union. The main elements of his strategy were a naval blockade and a combined army–navy expedition to take control of the Mississippi, thus sealing off the Confederacy on all sides. The Northern press labeled Scott's strategy as the Anaconda Plan, after the South American snake that squeezes its prey to death.

FOCUS QUESTION

How did the Union's and Confederacy's respective military advantages manifest themselves in the campaigns and battles in 1861–1862?

The Battle of Bull Run

Most northerners believed that the South could be overcome only by victory in battle. Virginia emerged as the most likely battleground, especially after the Confederate government relocated its capital to Richmond in May 1861. In July, a Union army of 35,000 men moved toward the new capital. They got no farther than Bull Run, a sluggish stream 25 miles southwest of Washington, where a Confederate army commanded by Beauregard had been deployed to defend a key rail junction at Manassas.

Another small Confederate army in the Shenandoah Valley under General Joseph E. Johnston had traveled to Manassas by rail to reinforce Beauregard. On July 21, the attacking Union troops forded Bull Run and drove the rebels back. By early afternoon, the Union seemed to be on the verge of victory, but a Virginia brigade commanded by **Thomas J. ("Stonewall") Jackson** stood "like a stone wall," earning Jackson the nickname he carried ever after. By midafternoon, Confederate reinforcements had counterattacked and driven the exhausted and disorganized Yankees back across Bull Run.

The Battle of Manassas (or Bull Run, as Northerners called it) made a profound impression on both sides. Of the 18,000 soldiers actually engaged on each side, Union casualties (killed, wounded, and captured) were about 2,800 and Confederate casualties 2,000. The victory exhilarated Confederates and confirmed their belief in their martial superiority. It also gave them a morale advantage in the Virginia theater that persisted for two years. And yet, Manassas also bred overconfidence. Some in the South thought the war was won. Northerners, by contrast, were jolted out of their expectations of a short war. Congress authorized the enlistment of up to one million three-year volunteers. Hundreds of thousands flocked to recruiting offices in the next few months. Lincoln called General **George B. McClellan** to Washington to organize the new troops into the Army of the Potomac.

An energetic, talented officer only 34 years old, McClellan soon won the nickname "The Young Napoleon." He organized and trained the Army of the Potomac into a large, well-disciplined, and well-equipped fighting force. He was just what the North needed after its dispiriting defeat at Bull Run. When Scott stepped down as general-in-chief on November 1, McClellan took his place.

But as winter approached and McClellan did nothing to advance against the smaller Confederate army, whose outposts stood only a few miles from Washington, his failings as a commander began to show. McClellan was afraid to take risks; he never learned the military lesson that no victory can be won without risking defeat. He consistently overestimated the strength of enemy forces facing him and used these faulty estimates as a reason for inaction until he could increase his own force. When Republicans in Congress and in the press began to criticize him (he was a Democrat), he accused his critics of political motives. Having built a fine fighting machine, he was afraid to start it up for fear it might break. Lincoln removed him from command in November 1862.

Naval Operations

Because of McClellan, no further action occurred in the Virginia theater until spring 1862. Meanwhile, the Union navy won a series of victories over Confederate forts along the Atlantic and Gulf coasts. These successes provided new bases from which to expand and tighten the blockade, as well as takeoff points for operations. In February and March 1862, Union forces occupied several crucial ports on the North Carolina sounds and captured Fort Pulaski at the mouth of the Savannah River.

In April, the Union navy captured New Orleans, the Confederacy's largest city and principal fort. Most Confederate troops in the area had been called up the Mississippi to confront a Union invasion of Tennessee, leaving only some militia, an assortment of converted steamboats, and two strong forts flanking the river 70 miles below New Orleans. In a daring action on April 24, 1862, Union naval commander David G. Farragut led his fleet upriver past the forts and compelled the surrender of the city.

Fort Henry and Fort Donelson

Even more important than these naval operations were the Union victories won by the combined efforts of the army and fleets of river gunboats on the Tennessee and Cumberland rivers, which flow through Tennessee and Kentucky and empty into the Ohio River just before it joins the Mississippi. The unlikely hero of these Union victories was Ulysses

Thomas J. ("Stonewall") Jackson *A native of Virginia, he emerged as one of the Confederacy's best generals in 1861–1862.*

George B. McClellan *One of the most promising young officers in the U.S. Army, McClellan became principal commander of Union armies in 1861–1862.*

S. Grant, who had resigned from the military in 1854. Grant rejoined when war broke out, and his quiet efficiency and determined will won him promotion from Illinois colonel to brigadier general. When Confederate units entered Kentucky in September, Grant moved quickly to occupy the mouths of the Cumberland and Tennessee rivers.

With the help of a new class of ironclad gunboats designed for river warfare, Grant struck in February 1862. His objectives were Forts Henry and Donelson on the Tennessee and Cumberland rivers just south of the Kentucky–Tennessee border. The gunboats knocked out Fort Henry on February 6. Fort Donelson proved a tougher challenge. After its guns repulsed a gunboat attack, the 17,000-man Confederate army attacked Grant's besieging army, which had been reinforced to 27,000 men. With the calm decisiveness that became his trademark, Grant directed a counterattack that penned the defenders back up in their fort. Cut off from support by either land or river, the Confederate commander asked for surrender terms. Grant's reply made him instantly famous when it was published in the North: "No terms except an immediate and unconditional surrender can be accepted."

The victories had far-reaching strategic consequences. Union gunboats now ranged all the way up the Tennessee River to northern Alabama, enabling a Union division to occupy the region, and up the Cumberland to Nashville. Confederate military units pulled out of Kentucky and most of Tennessee and reassembled at Corinth in northern Mississippi. But by the end of March 1862, the Confederate commander in the western

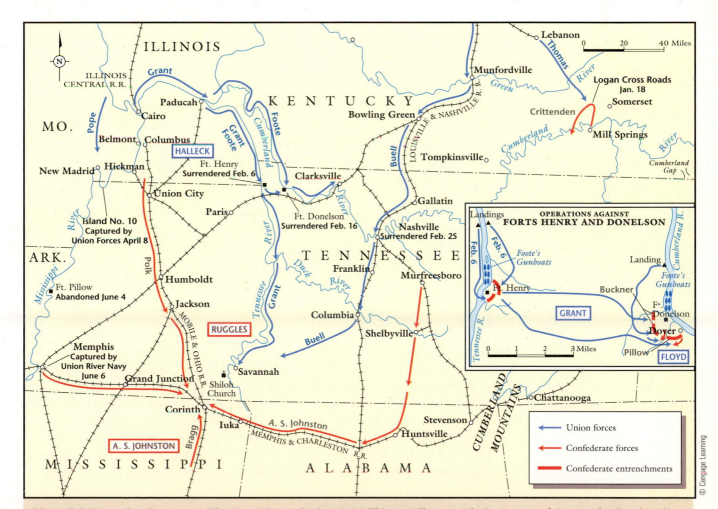

Map 15.3 Kentucky–Tennessee Theater, Winter–Spring 1862. *This map illustrates the importance of rivers and railroads as lines of military operations and supply. Grant and Naval Admiral Andrew Hull Foote advanced up the Tennessee and Cumberland rivers (southward), while General Don Carlos Buell moved along the Louisville and Nashville Railroad. Confederate divisions under the overall command of General Albert Sidney Johnston used railroads to concentrate at the key junction of Corinth.*

THE HORNET'S NEST AT SHILOH. *In the bloody fighting on April 6 at the Battle of Shiloh, portions of three Union divisions held out along a sunken farm road for several hours. Virtually surrounded by Confederate attackers, the 2,200 Union survivors surrendered in midafternoon. This was a costly Confederate success because General Albert Sidney Johnston was mortally wounded while directing the attack. The volume of fire from Union defenders was so great that the Confederates called the enemy position the "hornet's nest" because of the whizzing bullets coming from it. The stubborn Union fighting at the hornet's nest bought Grant time to establish a defensive line, from which he launched a successful counterattack the next day.*

theater, Albert Sidney Johnston (not to be confused with Joseph E. Johnston in Virginia), had built up an army of 40,000 men at Corinth. His plan was to attack Grant's force of 35,000, which had established a base 20 miles away at Pittsburg Landing on the Tennessee River just north of the Mississippi–Tennessee border.

The Battle of Shiloh

On April 6, the Confederates attacked at dawn near a church called Shiloh. They caught Grant by surprise and drove his army toward the river. After a day's fighting, with total casualties of 15,000, Grant's men brought the Confederate onslaught to a halt at dusk. One of the Confederate casualties was Johnston, the highest-ranking general on either side to be killed in the war. Beauregard took command after Johnston's death.

Some of Grant's subordinates advised retreat, but Grant would have none of it. Reinforced by fresh troops from a Union army commanded by General Don Carlos Buell, the Union counterattacked the next morning and, after 9,000 more casualties to the two sides, drove the Confederates back to Corinth. Although Grant had snatched victory from the jaws of defeat, his reputation suffered a decline for a time because of the heavy casualties and the suspicion that he had been caught napping.

Union triumphs continued. The combined armies of Grant and Buell, under the command of Henry W. Halleck, drove the Confederates out of Corinth at the end of May. Meanwhile, the Union gunboat fleet fought its way down the Mississippi, virtually wiping out the Confederate fleet in a spectacular battle at Memphis on June 6. At Vicksburg, the Union gunboats from the north connected with part of Farragut's fleet that had come up from New Orleans, taking Baton Rouge and Natchez along the way. The heavily fortified Confederate bastion at Vicksburg, however, proved too strong for the firepower of the Union naval fleet to subdue. Nevertheless, the dramatic succession of Union triumphs convinced the North that the war was nearly won.

The Virginia Theater

But affairs in Virginia were about to take a sharp turn in favor of the Confederacy. In the western theater, the broad rivers had facilitated the Union's invasion of the South, but in Virginia a half-dozen small rivers flowing west to east provided the Confederates with natural lines of defense. McClellan, still in command of the Army of the Potomac, persuaded a reluctant Lincoln to approve a plan to transport his army down Chesapeake Bay to the tip of the Virginia peninsula. That would shorten the route to Richmond and give the Union army a seaborne supply line.

This was a good plan in theory, but McClellan's failings again began to surface. A small Confederate blocking force at Yorktown held McClellan for the entire month of April, as he cautiously dragged up siege guns to blast through defenses that his large army could have punched through in days on foot. McClellan then slowly followed the retreating Confederate force up the peninsula to a new defensive line only a few miles east of Richmond.

Shortly thereafter, Stonewall Jackson's month-long campaign in the Shenandoah (May 8– June 9) demonstrated what could be accomplished through deception, daring, and mobility. With only 17,000 men, Jackson moved by rapid marches, covering 350 miles in one month and winning four battles against three separate Union armies, whose combined numbers surpassed Jackson's by more than 2 to 1.

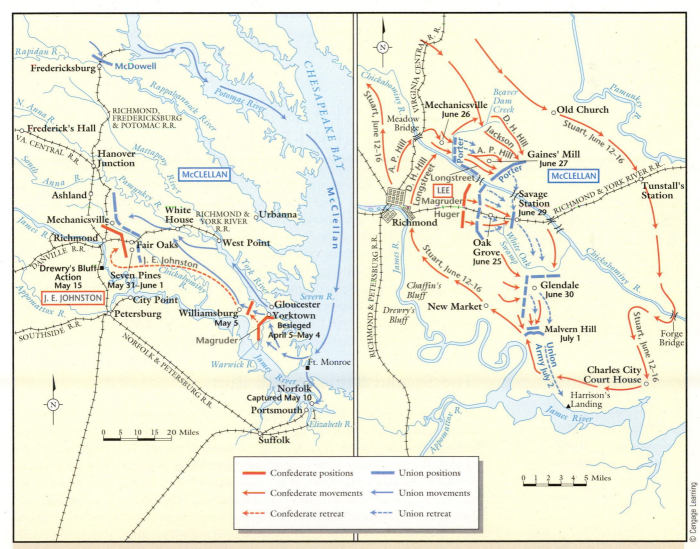

Map 15.4 **Peninsula Campaign, April–May 1862, and Seven Days' Battles, June 25–July 1, 1862.** *General McClellan used Union naval control of the York and James rivers to protect his flanks in his advance up the peninsula formed by these rivers (left map). When Robert E. Lee's Army of Northern Virginia counterattacked in the Seven Days' Battles (right map), McClellan was forced back to the James River at Harrison's Landing.*

Meanwhile McClellan's army continued toward Richmond. Although it substantially outnumbered the Confederate force defending Richmond, commanded by Joseph E. Johnston, McClellan overestimated Johnston's strength at double what it actually was. Even so, by the last week of May McClellan's army was within six miles of Richmond. A botched Confederate counterattack produced no result except 6,000 Confederate and 5,000 Union casualties. One of those casualties was Joseph Johnston, who had been wounded in the shoulder. Jefferson Davis named Robert E. Lee to replace him.

The Seven Days' Battles

That appointment marked a major turning point in the campaign. Lee's qualities as a commander manifested themselves when he took over what he renamed the Army of Northern Virginia. While McClellan continued to dawdle, Lee sent his cavalry commander, Jeb Stuart, to lead a reconnaissance around the Union army to discover its weak points; brought Jackson's army in from the Shenandoah valley; and launched a June 26 attack on McClellan's right flank in what became known as the Seven Days' Battles. Constantly attacking, Lee's army of 90,000 drove McClellan's 100,000 away from Richmond to a new fortified base on the James River. The offensive cost the Confederates 20,000 casualties (compared with 16,000 for the Union), but it reversed the momentum of the war.

CONFEDERATE COUNTEROFFENSIVES

The tide turned in the western theater as well. Union conquests in the spring had brought 50,000 square miles of Confederate territory under Union control. To occupy and administer this vast area, however, drew many thousands of soldiers from combat forces, which were left depleted and vulnerable deep in enemy territory. During the summer and fall of 1862 the cavalry commands of Tennessean Nathan Bedford Forrest and Kentuckian John Hunt Morgan staged repeated raids in which they burned bridges, blew up tunnels, tore up tracks, and captured supply depots and the Union garrisons trying to defend them. These raids paved the way for infantry counteroffensives. Even after southern forces were turned back at Corinth and Perryville in October, the Confederates in the western theater were in better shape than they had been four months earlier.

The Second Battle of Bull Run

Most attention, though, focused on Virginia. Lincoln reorganized the Union corps near Washington into the Army of Virginia under General John Pope. In August, Lincoln ordered the withdrawal of the Army of the Potomac from the peninsula to reinforce Pope for a drive southward from Washington. To attack Pope before McClellan could reinforce him, Lee shifted most of his army to northern Virginia, sent Jackson's foot cavalry on a deep raid to destroy the supply base at Manassas Junction, and then brought his army back together to defeat Pope's army near Bull Run on August 29 and 30. The demoralized Union forces retreated to Washington, where Lincoln reluctantly gave McClellan command of the two armies and told him to reorganize them into one.

Lee kept up the pressure by invading Maryland. On September 4, his weary troops splashed across the Potomac 40 miles upriver from Washington. This move presented momentous possibilities. Another victory by Lee might influence the U.S. congressional elections in November and help Democrats gain control of Congress,

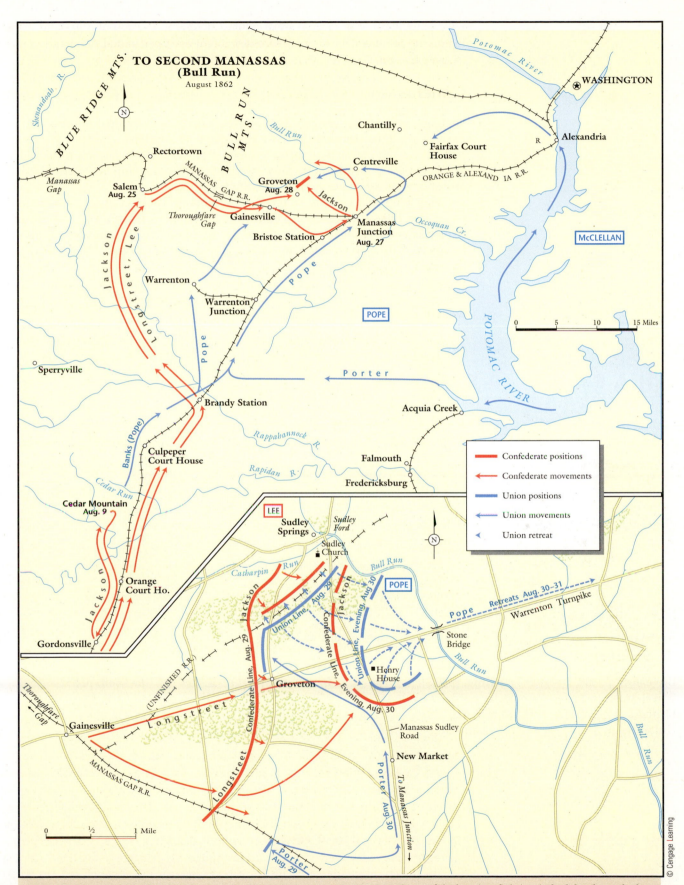

Map 15.5 Second Battle of Manassas (Bull Run), August 29–30, 1862. *Some of the heaviest fighting in both battles took place around the house owned by Judith Henry, which was destroyed. The elderly widow was killed in her house in the first battle.*

which might paralyze Lincoln's war effort. Successful invasion of Maryland, coming on top of other Confederate successes, might even persuade Britain and France to recognize the Confederacy.

Conclusion

Southern political leaders had maintained control of the national government for most of the time before 1860. That changed with Lincoln's election as the first president of an antislavery party, a national power shift of historic proportions. The Republicans, southerners feared, would launch a "revolution" to cripple slavery, and, worst of all, force racial equality on the South.

Thus the South launched a preemptive counterrevolution of secession to forestall a revolution of liberty and equality they feared would be their fate if they remained in the Union. Seldom has a preemptive counterrevolution so quickly brought on the very revolution it tried to prevent. If the Confederacy had lost the war in the spring of 1862, as appeared likely, the South might have returned to the Union with slavery intact. But the success of Confederate counteroffensives in the summer of 1862 convinced Lincoln that the North could not win the war without striking against slavery.

CHAPTER REVIEW

Review Questions

1. Why did political leaders in the lower South think that Lincoln's election made secession imperative?

2. What were northern advantages in the Civil War? What were southern advantages?

3. How did the Union's and Confederacy's respective military advantages manifest themselves in the campaigns and battles in 1861–1862?

Critical Thinking Questions

1. Given the North's advantages in population and economic resources, how could the Confederacy have hoped to prevail in the war?

2. How did the factors of geography, terrain, and logistics shape the strategy and operations of each side in the war?

Identifications

Review your understanding of the following key terms, people, and events for this chapter.

secession, p. 336
fire-eaters, p. 338
Fort Sumter, p. 342
Robert E. Lee, p. 343
Unionists, p. 344

bushwhackers, p. 344
rifling, p. 348
close-order assault, p. 348
specie, p. 348
treasury notes, p. 349

legal tender, p. 349
banknotes, p. 349
blockade, p. 349
blockade runner, p. 350
revolving turret, p. 351

Thomas J. ("Stonewall") Jackson, p. 352
George B. McClellan, p. 352

DISCOVERY

How significant was the role of slavery in bringing about secession and the outbreak of the Civil War? Why did the fighting occur where it did?

In thinking about this question, begin by breaking it down into the components shown below. A discussion of the significance of each component should appear in your answer.

Politics and Geography

Look at the map on the progress of secession on page 339. Note which states seceded before the fall of Fort Sumter and those that seceded after. Do these two groups form coherent subregions within the South? If so, what were their characteristics? For help in answering this question consult also Table 15.2 on page 345. What is the correlation between votes for Breckinridge (upper map) and the first seven states to secede?

Warfare

Look at the map of principal military campaigns. Where did most of the fighting occur? What is important or significant about the location(s) of the fighting? Why do you think the battles in the western theater were so dispersed and the ones in the East so concentrated? What different challenges do you suppose the troops in the East and West faced as a result of these varying circumstances?

Map 15.2 Principal Military Campaigns of the Civil War

Visit the CourseMate website at www.cengagebrain.com for additional study tools and review materials for this chapter.

A NEW BIRTH OF FREEDOM, 1862–1865

One great issue awaiting resolution as the armies moved into Maryland in September 1862 was emancipation of the slaves. The war had moved beyond the effort to restore the old Union. It now required the North to mobilize every resource that might bring victory or to destroy any enemy resource that might inflict defeat. Abolishing slavery would strike at a vital Confederate resource: slave labor. Slaves had already been escaping to Union lines by the tens of thousands.

Lincoln had decided to issue an emancipation proclamation and was waiting for a Union victory to give it credibility and potency.

This momentous decision would polarize northern public opinion and political parties. So long as the North fought simply to restore the Union, northern unity was impressive, but the events of 1862 raised the question of what kind of Union was to be restored. Would it be a Union without slavery, as abolitionists and radical Republicans hoped? Or would it be "the Union as it was," as Democrats desired?

1861	1862	1863	1864	1865

1861–1865
Abraham Lincoln presidency

■ **1862**
Battle of Antietam • Preliminary Emancipation Proclamation • Battle of Fredericksburg

■ **1863**
Final Emancipation Proclamation • Battle of Chancellorsville • Battle of Gettysburg • Fall of Vicksburg

1864 ■
Battles of the Wilderness, Spotsylvania, Cold Harbor • Siege of Petersburg • Fall of Atlanta • Reelection of Lincoln

1865 ■
Surrender of Lee at Appomattox • Ratification of 13th Amendment abolishing slavery

© Cengage Learning

SLAVERY AND THE WAR

In the North, the issue of emancipation was deeply divisive. Taking action against slavery in the South in 1861 could break up the fragile coalition Lincoln had stitched together to fight the war: Republicans, Democrats, and border-state Unionists. Spokesmen for the latter two groups served notice that, although they supported a war for the Union, they would not support a war against slavery. In July 1861, with Lincoln's endorsement, Congress passed a resolution affirming that the North sought not to overthrow slavery but only "to defend and maintain the supremacy of the Constitution and to preserve the Union."

Many northerners saw things differently. They insisted that a rebellion sustained *by* slavery in defense *of* slavery could be suppressed only by striking *against* slavery. As the black leader Frederick Douglass stated, "War for the destruction of liberty must be met with war for the destruction of slavery." When northerners discovered that they were not going to win an easy victory, many began to take a harder look at slavery. Slaves constituted the principal labor force in the South. They raised most of the food and fiber, built most of the military fortifications, and worked on the railroads and in mines and munitions factories. Why not convert this Confederate asset to a Union advantage by confiscating slaves as enemy property and using them to help the northern war effort?

FOCUS QUESTION

What factors led Lincoln to his decision to issue the Emancipation Proclamation?

The "Contrabands"

The slaves entered this debate in a dramatic fashion. As Union armies penetrated the South, a growing number of slaves voted for freedom with their feet. By twos and threes, by families, eventually by scores, they escaped from their masters and came over to the Union lines. By obliging Union officers either to return them to slavery or accept them, these escaped slaves began to make the conflict a war for freedom.

Although some commanders returned escaped slaves to their masters or prevented them from entering Union camps, most did not. When three slaves escaped to General Benjamin Butler's lines in May 1861, Butler refused to return them on the grounds that they were **"contraband of war."** For the rest of the war, slaves who came within Union lines were known as contrabands. On August 6, 1861, Congress passed an act authorizing the seizure of all property, including

contraband of war *Term used to describe slaves who came within the Union lines.*

A RIDE FOR LIBERTY. *This splendid painting of a slave family escaping to Union lines during the Civil War dramatizes the experiences of thousands of slaves who thereby became "contrabands" and gained their freedom. Most of them came on foot, but this enterprising family stole a horse as well as themselves from their master.*

A Ride for Liberty, or The Fugitive Slaves, c.1862 (oil on board), Johnson, Eastman (1824-1906) / © Brooklyn Museum of Art, New York, USA /The Bridgeman Art Library International

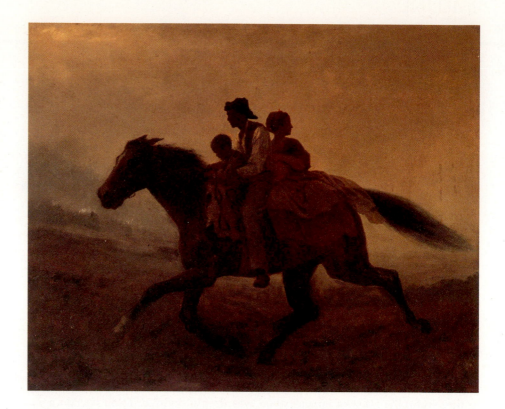

slaves, being used for Confederate military purposes. The following March, Congress forbade the return of slaves who entered Union lines.

The Border States

The problem of slavery in the loyal border states preoccupied Lincoln. On August 30, 1861, Union Major General John C. Frémont issued an order freeing the slaves of all Confederate sympathizers in Missouri. This caused such a backlash among border-state Unionists that Lincoln revoked the order.

In spring 1862, Lincoln tried persuasion instead of force. At his urging, Congress passed a resolution offering federal compensation to states that voluntarily abolished slavery. Lincoln told border-state leaders that the Confederate hope that their states might join the rebellion was keeping the war alive. Accept the proposal for **compensated emancipation**, he pleaded, and that hope would die. But border-state congressmen complained of being coerced, bickered about the amount of compensation, and wrung their hands over the prospects of economic ruin and race war. At a final meeting on July 12, Lincoln warned them that "If the war continue long . . . the institution in your states will be extinguished by mere friction and abrasion." Nevertheless, by a vote of 20 to 9 they again rejected the proposal for compensated emancipation.

The Decision for Emancipation

That very evening, Lincoln made the fateful decision to issue an emancipation proclamation. Several factors, in addition to the recalcitrance of the border states, impelled him. One was a growing demand from his own party for bolder action. Another was rising sentiment in the army to "take off the kid gloves" when dealing with "traitors." Finally, Lincoln's decision reflected his sentiments about the "unqualified evil" and "monstrous injustice" of slavery.

The military situation, however, rather than his moral convictions, determined the timing and scope of Lincoln's emancipation policy. Northern hopes that the war would

compensated emancipation
Idea that the federal government would offer compensation or money to states that voluntarily abolished slavery.

soon end had plummeted during the summer of 1862. Three courses of action seemed possible. One, favored by the so-called Peace Democrats, urged an armistice and peace negotiations to patch together some kind of Union, but that would have been tantamount to conceding Confederate victory. Republicans reviled the Peace Democrats as traitorous **Copperheads,** after the poisonous snake. A second alternative was to keep on fighting—in the hope that with a few more Union victories, the rebels would lay down their arms and the Union could be restored. Such a policy would leave slavery intact. The third alternative was to mobilize all the resources of the North and to destroy all the resources of the South, including slavery—a war not to restore the old Union but to build a new one.

On July 22, a week after his meeting with the border-state representatives convinced him there could be no compromise, Lincoln notified the cabinet of his intention to issue an emancipation proclamation. It was "a military necessity, absolutely essential to the preservation of the Union," he said. "We must free the slaves or be ourselves subdued." But Lincoln accepted the advice of Secretary of State Seward to delay the proclamation "until you can give it to the country supported by military success." Lincoln slipped his proclamation into a desk drawer and waited for a military victory.

New Calls for Troops

Meanwhile, Lincoln called for 300,000 new three-year volunteers for the army. In July, Congress passed a militia act giving the president greater powers to mobilize the state militias into federal service and to draft men into the militia if the states failed to do so. Although not a national draft law, this was a step in that direction. In August, Lincoln called up an additional 300,000 militia for nine months of service. The Peace Democrats railed against these measures and provoked antidraft riots in some localities. The government responded by arresting rioters and antiwar activists under the president's suspension of the writ of habeas corpus.[1]

Democrats denounced these "arbitrary arrests" as unconstitutional violations of civil liberties and added this issue to others on which they hoped to gain control of the House of Representatives in the fall elections. As morale declined following the defeat at Second Bull Run, prospects for a Democratic triumph seemed bright. One more military victory by Lee's Army of Northern Virginia might crack the North's will to continue the fight. Lee's legions began crossing the Potomac into Maryland on September 4, 1862.

The Battle of Antietam

Lee split his army into five parts. Three of them, under the command of Stonewall Jackson, occupied the heights surrounding the Union garrison at Harpers Ferry. The other two remained on watch in the South Mountain passes west of Frederick. But in a field near Frederick, two Union soldiers found a copy of Lee's orders for these deployments, apparently dropped by a careless officer. With this new information, Union commander George B. McClellan planned to pounce on the separated segments of Lee's army before they could reunite.

Copperheads *Term used by some Republicans to describe Peace Democrats to imply that they were traitors to the Union.*

© Bettmann/ CORBIS

CONFEDERATE DEAD ON THE BATTLEFIELD. *The new technology of photography came into its own during the Civil War, providing us with the first realistic portrayal of the human cost of war. This photograph of Confederate dead at Antietam, taken two days after the battle, conveyed "the terrible reality and suffering of war," in the words of a* New York Times *reporter who saw the pictures at an exhibit in the city. But, he added, "one phase . . . escaped photographic skill . . . the background of widows and orphans. . . . Broken hearts cannot be photographed."*

[1] A writ of habeas corpus is an order issued by a judge to law enforcement officers requiring them to bring an arrested person before the court to be charged with a crime so that the accused can have a fair trial. The U.S. Constitution permits the suspension of this writ "in cases of rebellion or invasion," so that the government can arrest enemy agents, saboteurs, or any individual who might hinder the defense of the country, and hold such individuals without trial.

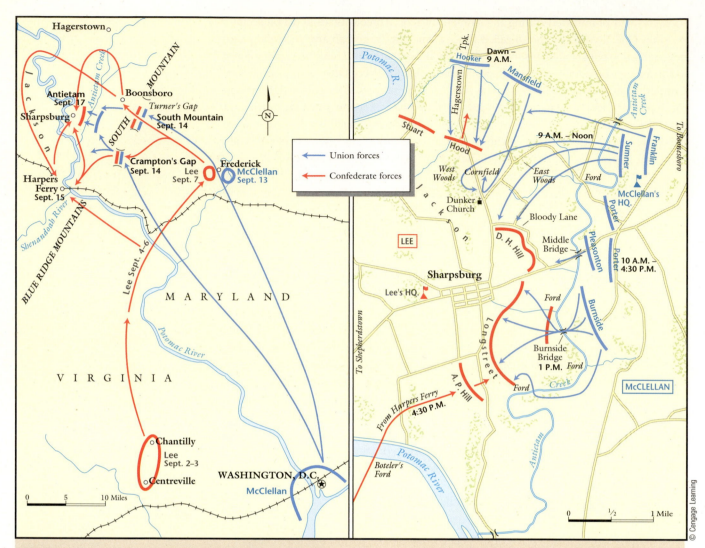

Map 16.1 Lee's Invasion of Maryland, 1862 [and] Battle of Antietam, September 17, 1862. *Both the advantages and disadvantages of Lee's defensive position in this battle are illustrated by the right-hand map. The Confederate flanks were protected by water barriers (the Potomac River on the left and Antietam Creek on the right), but the Confederates fought with their back to the Potomac and only Boteler's Ford as the single line of retreat across the river. If Burnside's attack on the Confederate right had succeeded before A. P. Hill's division arrived, Lee's forces could have been trapped north of the river.*

QUICK REVIEW

NORTHERN WAR BECAME A WAR FOR UNION AND EMANCIPATION

- Slaves classified as "contraband of war"

- Border states urged to undertake voluntary emancipation

- Emancipation Proclamation issued after Union victory at Antietam

Union troops overwhelmed the Confederate defenders of the South Mountain passes on September 14, but they advanced too slowly to save the garrison at Harpers Ferry, which surrendered 12,000 men to Jackson on September 15. Lee then managed to reunite most of his army near the village of Sharpsburg by September 17, when McClellan finally crossed Antietam Creek to attack. The battle of Antietam (called Sharpsburg by the Confederates) proved to be the single bloodiest day in American history, with more than 23,000 casualties (killed, wounded, and captured) in the two armies.

Although his men achieved potential breakthroughs near Sharpsburg, McClellan feared counterattacks. He held back 20,000 of his troops and failed to follow through. Thus the battle ended in a draw. The battered Confederates still clung to their precarious line, with the Potomac at their back. And even though he received reinforcements the next day and Lee received none, McClellan did not renew the attack. Nevertheless, the Confederates retreated to Virginia and gave up their campaign in Maryland.

"We Cannot Escape History": Abraham Lincoln

In the closing passage of his annual message to Congress in December 1862, Lincoln soared to an eloquence that matched the later Gettysburg Address and Second Inaugural Address. In this passage, Lincoln was supporting a plan for gradual and compensated abolition of slavery everywhere by constitutional amendment. He did not expect Congress to pass such an amendment or the Confederate states to accept it even if Congress did pass it. The real reference point for this passage was the forthcoming Emancipation Proclamation, which Lincoln issued a month later.

The dogmas of the quiet past, are inadequate to the stormy present. The occasion is piled high with difficulty, and we must rise with the occasion. As our case is new, so we must think anew, and act anew. We must disenthrall our selves, and then, we shall save our country.

Fellow-citizens, we cannot escape history. We of this Congress and this administration, will be remembered in spite of ourselves. No personal significance, or insignificance, can spare one or another of us. The fiery trial through which we pass, will light us down, in honor or dishonor, to the latest generation. . . . We—even we here—hold the power, and bear the responsibility. In giving freedom to the slave, we assure freedom to the free—honorable alike in what we give, and what we preserve. We shall nobly save, or meanly lose, the last best, hope of earth.

Q Why did Lincoln say that in giving freedom to the slave we assure freedom to the free? What did he mean by "the last best, hope of earth"?

The Emancipation Proclamation

This equivocal Union victory carried important consequences. Britain and France decided to withhold diplomatic recognition of the Confederacy. Northern Democrats failed to gain control of the House in the fall elections. And most significant of all, on September 22, Lincoln seized the occasion to issue his preliminary emancipation proclamation. It did not come as a total surprise. A month earlier, after Horace Greeley's editorial in the *New York Tribune* calling for action against slavery, Lincoln had responded with a public letter. "My paramount object in this struggle," wrote Lincoln, "*is* to save the Union. . . . If I could save the Union without freeing *any* slave I would do it, and if I could save it by freeing *all* the slaves I would do it; and if I could save it by freeing some and leaving others alone I would also do that." Lincoln had crafted these phrases carefully to maximize support for his proclamation. He portrayed emancipation not as an end in itself but as a *means* toward the end of saving the Union.

Lincoln's proclamation did not go into effect immediately. Rather, it stipulated that if any state, or part of a state, was still in rebellion on January 1, 1863, the president would proclaim the slaves therein "forever free." By New Year's Day no southern state had returned to the Union, and Lincoln signed the final proclamation.

The Emancipation Proclamation did not free all the slaves. It exempted the border states plus areas already under Union occupation because they were deemed not to be in rebellion. Lincoln was asserting his constitutional authority as commander in chief to confiscate enemy property. Even with this limitation, the proclamation essentially made the northern soldiers an army of liberation, however reluctant many of them were to risk their lives for that purpose.

A WINTER OF DISCONTENT

FOCUS QUESTION

What were the sources of internal dissent and dissension in the Confederacy? In the Union?

Although Lee's retreat from Maryland suggested that the Confederate tide might be ebbing, the tide soon turned. Displeased by McClellan's "slows" after Antietam, Lincoln replaced him on November 7, 1862, with General Ambrose E. Burnside. Burnside proposed to cross the Rappahannock River at Fredericksburg for a move on Richmond before bad weather forced both sides into winter quarters. Although Lee put his men into a strong defensive position on the heights behind Fredericksburg, Burnside attacked on December 13. He was repulsed with heavy casualties that shook the morale of both the army and the public.

News from the western theater did little to dispel the gloom. The Confederates had fortified Vicksburg on bluffs commanding the Mississippi River. This bastion preserved transportation links between the states to the east and west. To sever those links, in November 1862 Grant launched a two-pronged drive against Vicksburg. With 40,000 men, he marched southward from Memphis by land, while William T. Sherman came down the river with 32,000 men and a gunboat fleet. But Confederate cavalry raids destroyed the railroads and supply depots in Grant's rear, forcing him to retreat to Memphis. Meanwhile, Sherman attacked the Confederates at Chickasaw Bluffs in December, with no more success than Burnside had enjoyed at Fredericksburg.

Union forces under William S. Rosecrans did score a victory by driving the Confederates to retreat at the Battle of Stone River in Tennessee, but elsewhere matters went from bad to worse. Renewing the campaign against Vicksburg, Grant bogged down in the swamps and rivers that protected that Confederate bastion on three sides. Only on the east, away from the river, was there high ground suitable for an assault on Vicksburg's defenses. Grant's problem was to get his army, supplies, and transportation across the Mississippi to that high ground. For three months, he floundered in the Mississippi–Yazoo bottomlands, while disease and exposure depleted his troops.

The Rise of the Copperheads

During the winter of 1863, the Copperhead faction of the Democratic Party found an audience for its message that the war was a failure and should be abandoned. Ohio Congressman Clement L. Vallandigham, running for governor, asked northerners what this "wicked" war had accomplished: "Let the dead at Fredericksburg and Vicksburg answer." The Confederacy could never be conquered; the only trophies of the war were "debt, defeat, sepulchres." The solution was to "stop the fighting. Make an armistice. Withdraw your army from the seceded states." Above all, give up the unconstitutional effort to abolish slavery.

Vallandigham and other Copperhead spokesmen had a powerful effect on northern morale. Alarmed by a wave of desertions, the army commander in Ohio had Vallandigham arrested in May 1863. A military court convicted him of treason for aiding and abetting the enemy. The court's action raised serious questions of civil liberties. Was the conviction a violation of Vallandigham's First Amendment right of free speech? Could a military court try a civilian under **martial law** in a state where civil courts were functioning?

Lincoln was embarrassed by the swift arrest and trial of Vallandigham, which he learned about from the newspapers. To keep Vallandigham from becoming a martyr, Lincoln commuted his sentence from imprisonment to banishment—to the Confederacy. Union cavalry escorted Vallandigham under a flag of truce to Confederate lines in Tennessee. He soon escaped to Canada. There, from exile, Vallandigham conducted his campaign for governor of Ohio—an election he lost in October 1863.

martial law *Government by military force rather than by citizens.*

Economic Problems in the South

Southerners were buoyed by their military success but were suffering from economic problems caused by the Union blockade, the weaknesses and imbalances of the Confederate economy, the escape of slaves to Union lines, and enemy occupation of some of the South's prime agricultural areas. Despite the conversion of hundreds of thousands of acres from cotton to food production, the deterioration of southern railroads and the priority given to army shipments made food scarce in some areas. Prices rose much faster than wages. Even the middle class suffered. A war department clerk wrote that the rats in his kitchen were so hungry that they nibbled bread crumbs from his daughter's hand "as tame as kittens. Perhaps we shall have to eat them!"

Poor people were worse off, especially the wives and children of nonslaveholders who were away in the army. Some women took matters into their own hands. Decrying "speculators" who allegedly hoarded goods to drive up prices, they marched to stores, denounced "extortion," and took what they wanted without paying. On April 2, 1863, a mob of more than 1,000 women and boys looted several shops in Richmond before the militia forced them to disperse. The Confederate government subsequently released some emergency food stocks to civilians, and state and county governments aided the families of soldiers. Better crops in 1863 alleviated the worst shortages, but serious problems persisted.

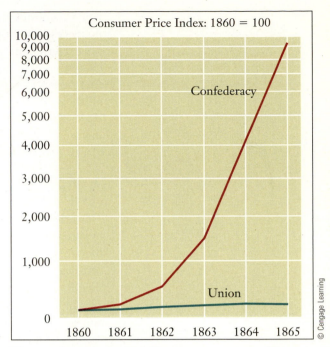

WARTIME INFLATION IN THE CONFEDERACY AND THE UNION

The Wartime Draft and Class Tensions

In both South and North, the draft intensified social unrest and turned it in the direction of class conflict. In April 1862, the Confederacy enacted a draft that made all white men aged 18 to 35 liable to conscription. A drafted man could hire a substitute, but the price of substitutes soon rose beyond the means of the average southern farmer or worker, giving rise to the bitter cry that it was "a rich man's war and a poor man's fight."

The cry grew louder in October 1862 when the Confederate Congress raised the draft age to 45 and added a clause exempting one white man from the draft on every plantation with 20 or more slaves. The purpose of this "overseer exemption" was to keep up production and prevent slave uprisings, but nonslaveholding farm families regarded the so-called **Twenty Negro Law** as blatant discrimination. The law provoked widespread draft dodging and desertions.

Similar discontent greeted the enactment of a conscription law in the North. In summer 1863 some 30,000 Union soldiers would be leaving military service, along with 80,000 of the nine-month militia called into service the preceding autumn. To meet the shortfall, Congress decreed in March that all male citizens aged 20 to 45 must enroll for the draft. The law was intended more to encourage volunteers to come forward than to draft men directly. The War Department set a quota for every congressional district and allowed 50 days for the quota to be met with volunteers before resorting to a draft lottery. Some districts avoided having to draft anyone by offering large bounties to volunteers. The bounty system produced glaring abuses, including **bounty jumpers** who enlisted and then deserted as soon as they got their money—often to enlist again under another name somewhere else.

The drafting process itself was also open to abuse. Like the Confederate law, the Union law permitted hiring substitutes. The Union law also allowed a drafted man to

Twenty Negro Law *Confederate conscription law that exempted from the draft one white man on every plantation owning 20 or more slaves.*

bounty jumpers *Men who enlisted in the Union army to collect the bounties offered by some districts to fill military quotas; these men would enlist and then desert as soon as they got their money.*

pay a **"commutation fee"** of $300 that exempted him from the current draft call (but not necessarily from the next one). That provision raised the cry of "rich man's war, poor man's fight" in the North as well. The Democratic Party nurtured this sense of class resentment, and racism intensified it. Democratic newspapers told white workers that the draft would force them to fight a war to free the slaves, who would then come north to take their jobs. Widespread violence occurred when the northern draft got under way in summer 1863. The worst riot occurred in July in New York City, where mobs consisting mostly of Irish Americans demolished draft offices, lynched several blacks, and destroyed huge areas of the city in four days of looting and burning.

A Poor Man's Fight?

The grievance that it was a rich man's war and a poor man's fight was more apparent than real. Taxes to sustain the war bore proportionately more heavily on the wealthy. In the South, the property of the rich suffered greater damage and confiscation than did the property of nonslaveholders. The war liberated four million slaves, the poorest class in America. Among those who volunteered in 1861 and 1862, the planter class was overrepresented in the Confederate army and the middle class in the Union forces.

Nor did conscription itself fall much more heavily on the poor than on the rich. Those who escaped the draft by decamping to the woods, the territories, or Canada were mostly poor. The Confederacy abolished substitution in December 1863. In the North, city councils, political machines, and businesses contributed funds to pay the commutation fees of drafted men who were too poor to pay out of their own pockets. In the end, it was neither a rich man's war nor a poor man's fight. It was an American war.

commutation fee *A $300 fee that could be paid by a man drafted into the Union army to exempt him from the current draft call.*

Blueprint for Modern America

The 37th Congress (1861–1863)—which enacted conscription, passed measures for confiscation and emancipation, and created the greenbacks and the national banking system (see Chapter 15)—also enacted three laws that provided what one historian has called "a blueprint for modern America." The Homestead Act granted a farmer 160 acres of land virtually free after he had lived on the land for five years and had made improvements on it. The Morrill Land-Grant College Act gave each state thousands of acres to fund the establishment of colleges to teach "agricultural and mechanical arts." The Pacific Railroad Act granted land and loans to railroad companies to spur the building of a transcontinental railroad from Omaha to Sacramento. Despite waste, corruption, and exploitation of the original Indian owners of this land, these laws helped farmers settle some of the most fertile land in the world, studded the land with state colleges, and spanned it with steel rails in a manner that altered the landscape of the western half of the country.

Women and the War

The war advanced many other social changes, particularly with respect to women. In factories and on farms, women replaced men who had gone off to war. More women entered the teaching profession, a trend that had begun in the Northeast and now spread to other parts of the country. The war also brought significant numbers of women into the civil service, as the huge expansion of government bureaucracies after 1861 and the departure of male clerks to the army provided openings.

QUICK REVIEW

THE HOME FRONTS

- Peace Democrats ("Copperheads") opposed war

- Crippling inflation in the South

- Conscription and antidraft riots created tensions in North

- Women provided crucial contributions to the war effort

Library of Congress, Prints and Photographs Division

Courtesy of the Illinois State Historical Library

FEMALE SPIES AND SOLDIERS. *In addition to working in war industries and serving as army nurses, some women pursued traditionally male wartime careers as spies and soldiers. One of the most famous Confederate spies was Rose O'Neal Greenhow, a Washington widow and socialite who fed information to officials in Richmond. Federal officers arrested her in August 1861 and deported her to Richmond in the spring of 1862. She was photographed with her daughter in the Old Capitol prison in Washington, D.C., while awaiting trial. In October 1864 she drowned off Wilmington, North Carolina, after a blockade runner carrying her in a lifeboat back from a European mission was run aground by a Union warship. The second photograph shows a Union soldier who enlisted in the 95th Illinois Infantry under the name of Albert Cashier and fought through the war. Not until a farm accident in 1911 revealed Albert Cashier to be a woman, whose real name was Jennie Hodgers, was her secret disclosed. Most of the other estimated 400 women who evaded the superficial physical exams and passed as men to enlist in the Union and Confederate armies were more quickly discovered and discharged—six of them after they had babies while in the army. A few, however, served long enough to be killed in action.*

Women's most visible impact was in the field of medicine. The outbreak of war prompted the organization of soldiers' aid societies, hospital societies, and other voluntary associations in which women played a leading role. Women helped the armies' medical branches provide more efficient, humane care for sick and wounded soldiers. Dr. Elizabeth Blackwell, the first American woman to earn an M.D. (1849), organized a meeting of 3,000 women in New York City on April 29, 1861. They organized the Women's Central Association for Relief, which became the nucleus for the most powerful voluntary association of the war, the U.S. Sanitary Commission. The Sanitary Commission was an essential adjunct of the Union army's medical bureau. Most of its local volunteers were women, as were most of the nurses it provided to army hospitals.

Nursing was not a new profession for women, but it had lacked respect as a wartime profession. The fame won by Britain's Florence Nightingale during the Crimean War six years earlier had begun to change that perception. Thousands of middle- and even upper-class women volunteers flocked to army hospitals. The nurses had to overcome the deeply ingrained suspicions of army surgeons and the opposition of husbands and fathers who believed that the shocking, physical atmosphere of an army hospital was no place for a respectable woman. But many thousands of women went to work, winning grudging and then enthusiastic admiration.

The war also bolstered the fledgling women's rights movement. It was no coincidence that Elizabeth Cady Stanton and Susan B. Anthony founded the National Woman Suffrage Association in 1869, only four years after the war. Although half a century passed before women won the vote, the movement could not have achieved the momentum that made it a force in American life without the work of women in the Civil War.

THE CONFEDERATE TIDE CRESTS AND RECEDES

The Army of Northern Virginia and the Army of the Potomac spent the winter of 1862–1863 on opposite banks of the Rappahannock River. With the coming of spring, Union commander Joe Hooker resumed the offensive. On April 30, Hooker crossed with his men several miles upriver and came in on Lee's rear. Lee quickly faced most of his troops about and confronted the enemy in dense woods near the crossroads mansion of Chancellorsville. Nonplussed, Hooker lost the initiative.

The Battle of Chancellorsville

Even though Union forces outnumbered the Confederates by almost 2 to 1, Lee boldly went over to the offensive. On May 2, Stonewall Jackson led 28,000 men on a stealthy march through the woods to attack the Union right flank late in the afternoon. The surprise was complete, and Jackson's assault crumpled the Union flank. Lee resumed the attack the next day. In three more days of fighting that brought 12,800 Confederate and 16,800 Union casualties (the largest number for a single battle so far), Lee drove the Union troops back across the Rappahannock. It was a brilliant victory for the Confederates. In the North, the gloom grew deeper.

The Gettysburg Campaign

Lee decided to parlay his tactical victory at Chancellorsville into a strategic offensive by again invading the North. A victory on Union soil would convince northerners and foreigners alike that the Confederacy was invincible. At first, all went well. The Confederates brushed aside or captured Union forces in the northern Shenandoah Valley and in Pennsylvania. Jeb Stuart's cavalry threw a scare into Washington by

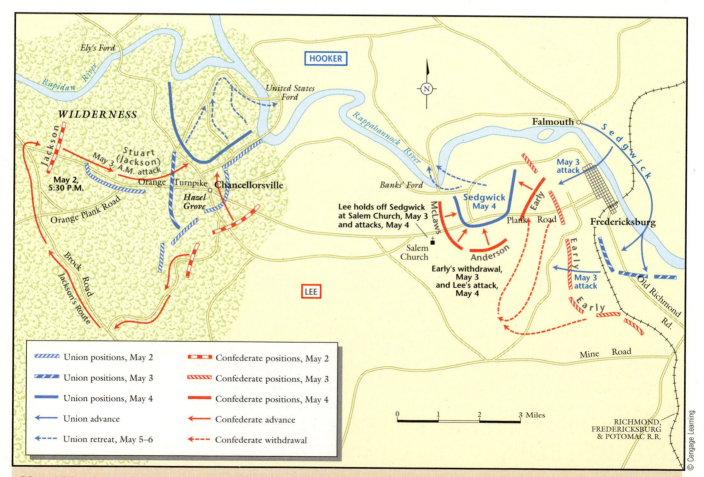

Map 16.2 **Battle of Chancellorsville, May 2–6, 1863.** *This map demonstrates the advantage of holding "interior lines," which enabled General Lee to shift troops back and forth to and from the Chancellorsville and Fredericksburg fronts over the course of three days while the two parts of the Union army remained separated.*

raiding behind Union lines into Maryland and Pennsylvania. That very success led to trouble. With Stuart's cavalry separated from the rest of the army, Lee lost vital intelligence. By June 28, several detachments of Lee's forces were scattered about Pennsylvania, far from their base and vulnerable.

At this point, Lee learned that the Army of the Potomac was moving toward him, now under the command of George Gordon Meade. Lee immediately ordered his own army to reassemble in the vicinity of Gettysburg. There, on the morning of July 1, the vanguard of the two armies met in a clash that grew into the greatest battle in American history.

As the fighting spread west and north of town, reinforcements were summoned to both sides. The Confederates got more men into the battle and broke the Union lines late that afternoon, driving the survivors to a defensive position on Cemetery Hill south of town. Judging this position too strong to take with his own troops, General Richard Ewell chose not to press the attack as the sun went down on what he presumed would be another Confederate victory.

But the next morning, the reinforced Union army was holding a superb defensive position. Lee's principal subordinate, First Corps commander James Longstreet, advised against attack, but Lee believed his army invincible. Pointing to the Union lines, he said: "The enemy is there, and I am going to attack him there." Longstreet reluctantly led the attack on the Union left. By the end of the day, Confederate forces had made small gains at great cost, but the main Union line had held firm.

Lee was not yet ready to yield the offensive. Having attacked both Union flanks, he thought the center might be weak. On July 3, he ordered a frontal attack on Cemetery Ridge, led by a fresh division under George Pickett. After a two-hour artillery barrage, Pickett's troops moved forward. "Pickett's Charge" was shot to pieces; scarcely half of the men returned unwounded to their own lines. It was the final act in a three-day drama that left some 50,000 men killed, wounded, or captured: 23,000 Federals and 25,000 to 28,000 Confederates.

Lincoln was unhappy with Meade for not cutting off the Confederate retreat. Nevertheless, Gettysburg was a great northern victory, and it came at the same time as other important Union successes in Mississippi, Louisiana, and Tennessee.

The Vicksburg Campaign

In mid-April, Grant had begun a move that would put Vicksburg in a vise. The Union ironclad fleet ran downriver past the big guns at Vicksburg with little damage. Grant's troops marched down the Mississippi's west bank and ferried across the river south of Vicksburg. There they kept the Confederate defenders off balance by striking east toward Jackson instead of marching north to Vicksburg. Grant sought to scatter the Confederate forces and to destroy the rail network so that his rear would be secure when he turned toward Vicksburg. It worked: Grant's troops trapped 32,000 Confederate troops and 3,000 civilians in Vicksburg.

Grant then settled down for a siege. Running out of supplies, the Vicksburg garrison surrendered on July 4. The Confederate garrison at Port Hudson, 200 river miles south of Vicksburg, surrendered on July 9. Northern forces now controlled the entire length of the Mississippi River. The Confederacy had been torn in two.

Chickamauga and Chattanooga

Northerners had scarcely finished celebrating the twin victories of Gettysburg and Vicksburg when they learned of an important—and almost bloodless—triumph.

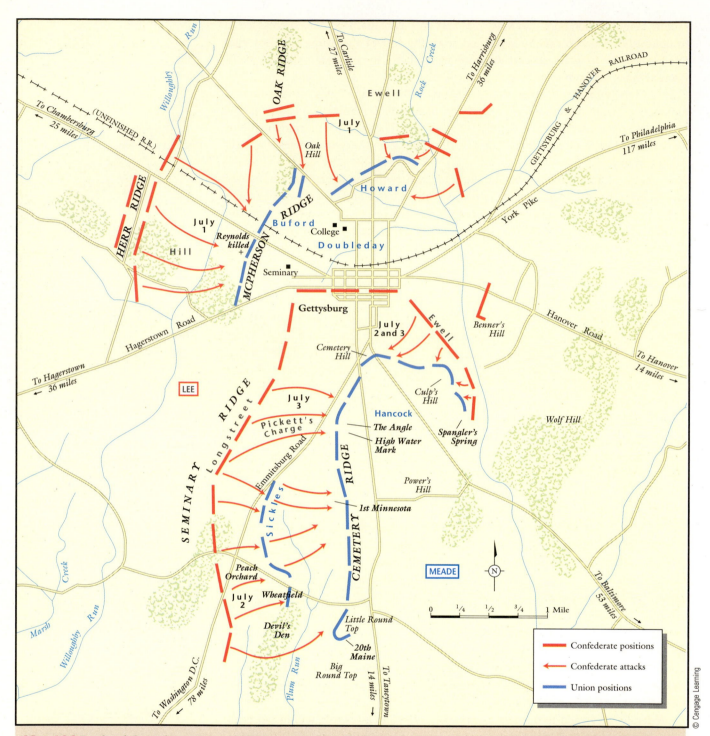

Map 16.3 **Battle of Gettysburg, July 1–3, 1863.** *On July 2 and 3, the Union army had the advantage of interior lines at Gettysburg, which enabled General Meade to shift reinforcements from his right on Culp's Hill to his left near Little Round Top over a much shorter distance than Confederate reinforcements from one flank to the other would have to travel.*

Union commander Rosecrans led his troops across east-central Tennessee and, by the first week of July, had pushed the Confederates back all the way to Chattanooga. After a pause for resupply, Rosecrans's army advanced again in August, this time in tandem with a smaller Union army commanded by Burnside. Again the outnumbered Confederates fell back, evacuating Knoxville and then Chattanooga. This action severed the South's only direct east-west rail link, and Union forces now stood poised for a campaign into Georgia. For the Confederacy it

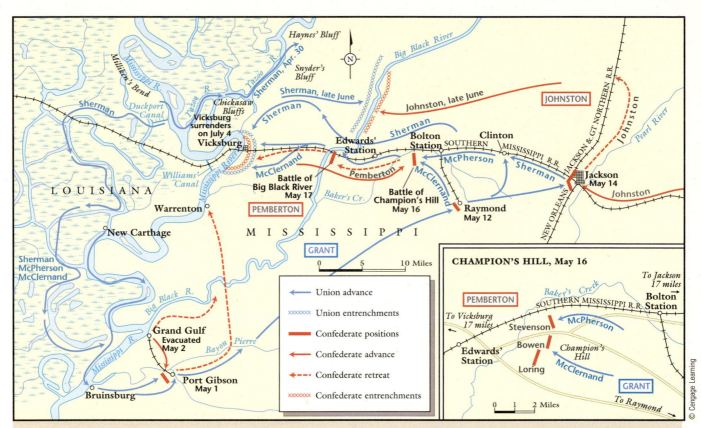

Map 16.4 Vicksburg Campaign, April–July 1863. *This map illustrates Grant's brilliant orchestration of the campaign that involved Sherman's feint at Haynes' Bluff (top of map) on April 30 while the rest of the Union forces crossed at Bruinsburg (bottom of map) and then cleared Confederate resistance out of the way eastward to Jackson before turning west to invade Vicksburg.*

was a stunning reversal of the situation only four months earlier, when the Union cause had appeared hopeless.

Confederate General Braxton Bragg reached into his bag of tricks and sent fake deserters into Union lines with tales of a Confederate retreat toward Atlanta. He then laid a trap for Rosecrans's troops as they advanced south of Chattanooga. On September 19, the Confederates turned and counterattacked Rosecrans's army in the valley of Chickamauga Creek. Over the next two days, in ferocious fighting that produced 35,000 casualties, the Confederates finally scored a victory. Only a firm stand by corps commander George H. Thomas prevented a Union rout. Lincoln subsequently appointed Thomas commander of the Army of the Cumberland to replace Rosecrans.

Lincoln also sent two army corps from Virginia under Hooker and two from Vicksburg under Sherman to reinforce Thomas, whose troops in Chattanooga were under virtual siege by Bragg's forces. More important, Lincoln put Grant in overall command of the beefed-up Union forces there. When Grant arrived in late October, he welded the various northern units into a new army and opened a new supply line into Chattanooga. On November 24, Hooker's troops drove Confederate besiegers off massive Lookout Mountain. The next day, an assault on Bragg's main line east of Chattanooga drove the Confederates south into Georgia.

These battles climaxed a string of Union victories in the second half of 1863. Jefferson Davis replaced Bragg with Joseph E. Johnston. Lincoln summoned Grant to Washington and appointed him general-in-chief of all Union armies. The stage was set for a fight to the finish.

QUICK REVIEW

THE PENDULUM OF WAR

- Confederate victory at Chancellorsville

- Union victories at Gettysburg and Vicksburg

- Confederate success at Chickamauga

- Union success at Chattanooga

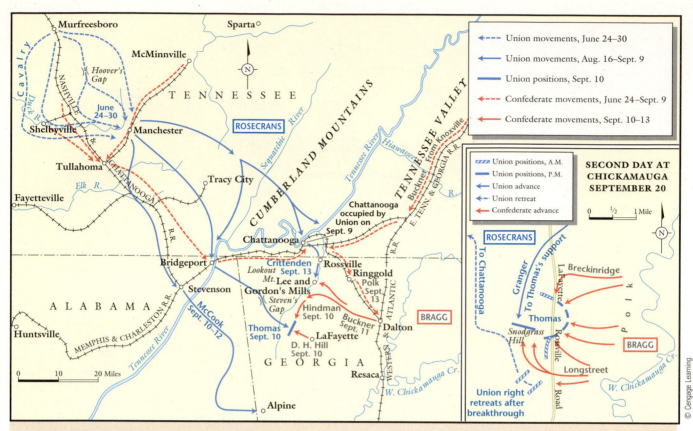

Map 16.5 Road to Chickamauga, June–September 1863. *From Murfreesboro to Chattanooga, Rosecrans's campaign of maneuver on multiple fronts, as shown on this map, forced Bragg's Army of Tennessee all the way south into Georgia in a campaign with minimal casualties before Bragg counterattacked at Chickamauga.*

BLACK MEN IN BLUE

FOCUS QUESTION

What contributions did women and African Americans make to the war efforts in both the North and South?

Northerners had not greeted the Emancipation Proclamation with great enthusiasm. Democrats and border-state Unionists continued to denounce it, and many Union soldiers resented the idea that they would now be risking their lives for black freedom. The Democratic Party had hoped to capitalize on this opposition, and on Union military failures, to win off-year elections. Northern military victories knocked one prop out from under the Democratic platform, and the performance of black soldiers fighting for the Union knocked out another.

Proposals to recruit black soldiers, Democrats said, were part of a Republican plot to establish "the equality of the black and white races." In a way, that charge was correct. Black men fighting for the Union would indeed advance the black race a long way toward equal rights. "Once let the black man get upon his person the brass letters, U.S.," said Frederick Douglass, "and a musket on his shoulder and bullets in his pocket, and there is no power on earth which can deny that he has earned the right to citizenship."

But it was pragmatism more than principle that pushed the North toward black recruitment. Putting black laborers in uniform was a compelling idea, especially as white enlistments lagged and the North had to enact conscription in 1863. Some Union commanders in occupied portions of Louisiana, South Carolina, and Missouri began to organize black regiments in 1862. The Emancipation Proclamation legitimized this policy with its proposal to enroll able-bodied male contrabands in new black regiments, although these units would serve as labor battalions, supply troops, and garrison forces rather than as combat troops. They would be paid less than white soldiers, and their officers would be white.

Black Soldiers in Combat

Continuing pressure from abolitionists, as well as military necessity, partly eroded this discrimination. Congress enacted equal pay in 1864. Above all, the regiments lobbied for the right to fight as combat soldiers. In May and June 1863, black regiments in Louisiana fought well at Port Hudson and Milliken's Bend, near Vicksburg. "The bravery of the blacks in the battle of Milliken's Bend completely revolutionized the sentiment of the army with regard to the employment of negro troops," wrote the assistant secretary of war.

Even more significant was the action of the 54th Massachusetts Infantry, the first black regiment raised in the North. Its officers, headed by Colonel Robert Gould Shaw, came from prominent New England antislavery families. On July 18, 1863, the 54th led an assault on Fort Wagner, part of the network of Confederate defenses protecting Charleston. Although the attack failed, the 54th fought courageously, suffering 50-percent casualties, including Colonel Shaw, who was killed. The battle occurred just after white mobs of draft rioters in New York had lynched blacks. Abolitionist and Republican commentators drew the moral: Black men who fought for the Union deserved more respect than white men who rioted against it.

Emancipation Confirmed

The Republicans swept the state elections that fall, a powerful endorsement of the administration's emancipation policy. But emancipation would not be assured of survival until it had been christened by the Constitution. On April 8, 1864, the Senate passed the Thirteenth Amendment to abolish slavery, but Democrats in the House blocked the required two-thirds majority there. Not until after Lincoln's reelection in 1864 would the House pass the amendment, which became part of the Constitution on December 6, 1865. In the end, though, the fate of slavery depended on the outcome of the war, and some of the heaviest fighting lay ahead.

PART OF COMPANY E, 4TH U.S. COLORED INFANTRY. *Organized in July 1863, most of the men were former slaves from North Carolina. The 4th fought in several actions on the Petersburg and Richmond fronts in 1864, helping to capture part of the Petersburg defenses on June 15. Of the 166 black regiments in the Union army, the 4th suffered the fourth-largest number of combat deaths.*

THE YEAR OF DECISION

During the winter of 1863–1864, desertions from Confederate armies increased, and inflation galloped out of control in the South. The Davis administration, like the Lincoln administration a year earlier, had to face congressional elections during a time of public discontent. Some antiadministration candidates ran on a quasi-peace platform (analogous to that of the Copperheads in the North) that called for an armistice and peace negotiations. The movement left unresolved the terms of such negotiations—reunion or independence—but any peace overture from a position of weakness was tantamount to conceding defeat. Still, antiadministration candidates made significant gains in the 1863 Confederate elections.

Out of the Wilderness

Shortages, inflation, political discontent, military defeat, high casualties, and the loss of thousands of slaves bent but did not break the southern spirit. Confederate armies no longer had the strength to invade the North or win the war with a knockout blow, but they could still fight a war of attrition. If they could hold out long enough and inflict enough casualties on the Union armies, they might weaken the northern will to continue fighting.

Northerners were vulnerable to this strategy. Military success in 1863 had created a mood of confidence, and people expected a quick, decisive victory in 1864. When Grant decided to remain in Virginia with the Army of the Potomac and to leave Sherman in command of the Union forces in northern Georgia, northerners expected these two heavyweights to floor the Confederacy with a one-two punch. Lincoln was alarmed by this euphoria, fearing that disappointment might trigger despair.

Lincoln was proved right. Grant ordered simultaneous offensives on all fronts, to prevent the Confederates from shifting reinforcements from one theater to another. These offensives began the first week of May. The heaviest fighting occurred in Virginia. When the Army of the Potomac crossed the Rapidan River, Lee attacked it in the flank in the thick scrub forest of the Wilderness, where Union superiority in numbers and artillery would count for little. The battle surged back and forth, with the Confederates inflicting 18,000 casualties and suffering 12,000 themselves. Having apparently halted Grant's offensive, they claimed a victory.

Spotsylvania and Cold Harbor

But Grant did not retreat. Instead, he moved toward Spotsylvania Courthouse, a key crossroads 10 miles closer to Richmond. Skillfully, Lee pulled back to cover the road junction. Repeated Union assaults left another 18,000 northerners and 12,000 southerners killed, wounded, or captured.

Having achieved no better than stalemate around Spotsylvania, Grant moved south around Lee's right flank in an effort to force the outnumbered Confederates into an open fight. Lee anticipated Grant's moves and confronted him from behind formidable defenses near the crossroads inn of Cold Harbor, only 10 miles northeast of Richmond. Believing the Confederates must be exhausted and demoralized by their repeated retreats, Grant attacked Cold Harbor on June 3—a costly mistake. Lee's troops were ragged and hungry but far from demoralized. Their withering fire inflicted 7,000 casualties in less than an hour.

Stalemate in Virginia

Now Grant moved all the way across the James River to strike at Petersburg, an industrial city and rail center 20 miles south of Richmond. If Petersburg fell, the Confederates could not hold Richmond. Once more Lee's troops raced southward and

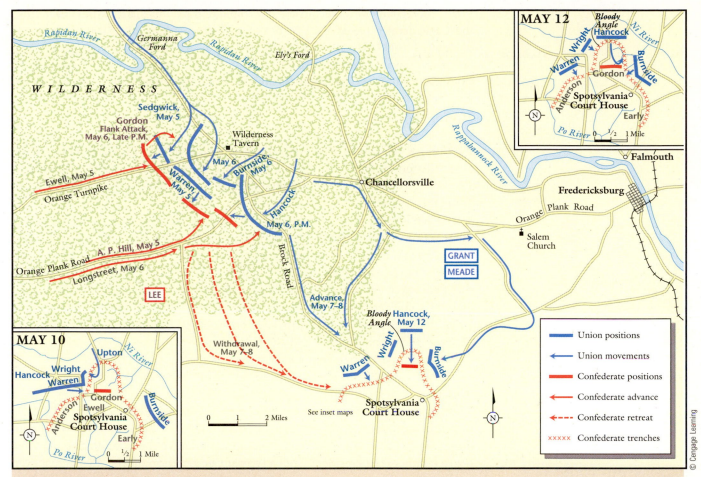

Map 16.6 Battle of The Wilderness and Spotsylvania, May 5–12, 1864. *Four major battles with a total of more than 100,000 casualties to both sides were fought within a few miles of Fredericksburg between December 1862 and May 1864. Compare this map with the Chancellorsville map on p. 370. The first battle of Fredericksburg on December 13, 1862 (described on p. 366) was fought in the same vicinity as the Fredericksburg fighting on May 3, 1863, shown on the Chancellorsville map.*

blocked Grant's troops. Four days of Union assaults produced another 11,000 northern casualties but no breakthrough. Such high Union losses in just six weeks cost the Army of the Potomac its offensive power. Grant reluctantly settled down for a siege along the Petersburg–Richmond front that would last more than nine grueling months.

Meanwhile, Benjamin Butler bungled an attack up the James River against Richmond and was stopped by a scraped-together army under Beauregard. A Union thrust up the Shenandoah valley was blocked at Lynchburg in June by Jubal Early. Early then led a raid all the way to the outskirts of Washington on July 11 and 12 before being driven back to Virginia. Union cavalry under Philip Sheridan inflicted considerable damage on Confederate resources in Virginia but again failed to strike a crippling blow.

The Atlanta Campaign

In Georgia, Sherman forced Johnston south toward Atlanta by constantly flanking him to the Union right, generally without bloody battles. By the end of June, Sherman had advanced 80 miles at the cost of 17,000 casualties to Johnston's 14,000—only one-third of the combined losses of Grant and Lee.

Jefferson Davis grew alarmed by Johnston's apparent willingness to yield territory without a fight. Sherman again flanked the Confederate defenses at Kennesaw Mountain in early July, then drove Johnston back to Peachtree Creek, less than five miles from Atlanta. Fearing that Johnston would abandon the city, Davis replaced him with John Bell Hood.

Hood counterattacked against the Yankees three times, in late July. Each time, the Confederates reeled back in defeat, suffering a total of 15,000 casualties to Sherman's 6,000. Hood finally retreated, but his army did manage to keep Sherman's cavalry and infantry from taking the two railroads leading into Atlanta from the south. Like Grant at Petersburg, Sherman seemed to settle down for a siege.

Peace Overtures

By August, the Confederate strategy of attrition seemed to be working. Union casualties on all fronts during the preceding three months totaled a staggering 110,000. "STOP THE WAR!" shouted Democratic headlines. "All are tired of this damnable tragedy."

Even Republicans joined the chorus of despair. "Our bleeding, bankrupt, almost dying country longs for peace," wrote Horace Greeley of the *New York Tribune*. Greeley became involved in abortive "peace negotiations" spawned by Confederate agents in Canada. Lincoln was skeptical, but given the mood of the North in midsummer 1864, he could not reject any opportunity to stop the bloodshed. He deputized Greeley to meet with the Confederate agents in Niagara Falls on the Canadian side of the border. At almost the same time (mid-July), two other northerners met under a flag of truce with Davis in Richmond. Lincoln had carefully instructed them—and Greeley—that his conditions for peace were "restoration of the Union and abandonment of slavery."

Davis would no more accept those terms than Lincoln would accept his. Although neither of the peace contacts came to anything, the Confederates gained a propaganda victory by claiming that Lincoln's terms had been the only obstacle to peace. Northern Democrats, too, focused on the slavery issue as the sole stumbling block. "Tens of thousands of white men must yet bite the dust to allay the negro mania of the President," ran a typical Democratic editorial. By August even staunch Republicans were convinced that Lincoln's reelection was impossible. Lincoln thought so too. "I am going to be beaten," he told a friend, "and unless some great change takes place, *badly* beaten."

Lincoln faced enormous pressure to drop emancipation as a condition of peace, but he refused to yield. He would rather lose the election than go back on the promise he had made in the Emancipation Proclamation. Some 130,000 black soldiers and sailors were fighting for the Union. They would not do so if they thought the North intended to forsake them.

At the end of August the Democrats nominated McClellan for president. The platform on which he ran declared that "after four years of failure to restore the Union by the experiment of war . . . [we] demand that immediate efforts be made for a cessation of hostilities." Democratic victory on that platform, said the *Charleston Mercury*, "must lead to peace and our independence" if "for the next two months *we hold our own and prevent military success by our foes.*"

The Prisoner-Exchange Controversy

The Democratic platform also condemned the Lincoln administration's "shameful disregard" of prisoners of war in Confederate prison camps. In 1862, the Union and Confederate armed forces had signed a cartel for the exchange of prisoners captured in battle. The arrangement had worked reasonably well for a year, making large prison camps unnecessary. When the Union army began to organize regiments of former slaves, however, the Confederate government announced that if they were captured, they and their white officers would be put to death. Although Lincoln threatened retaliation on Confederate prisoners of war if it did so, Confederate troops sometimes murdered black soldiers and their officers as they tried to surrender.

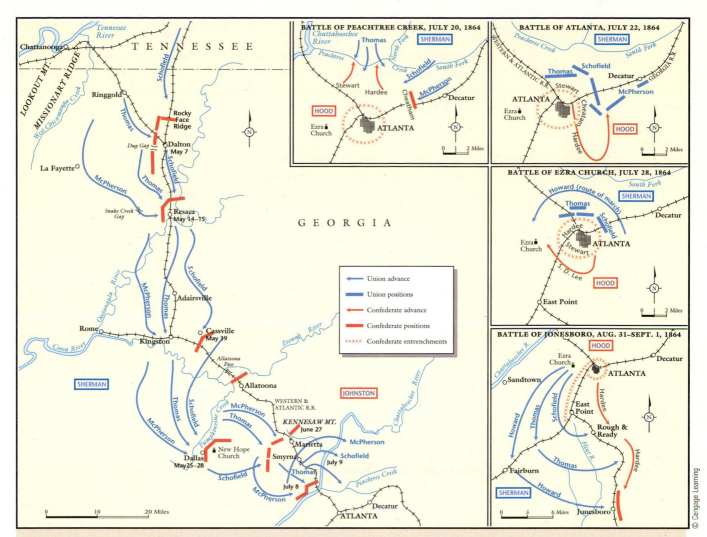

Map 16.7 **Campaign For Atlanta, May–September 1864.** *The main map illustrates Sherman's campaign of maneuver that forced Johnston back to Atlanta with relatively few battles. The first three inset maps show the Confederate counterattacks launched by Hood, and the fourth shows how the Union army got astride the last two railroads entering Atlanta from the south and forced Hood to evacuate the city.*

In most cases, Confederate officers returned captured black soldiers to slavery or put them to hard labor on southern fortifications. Outraged, the Lincoln administration in 1863 suspended the exchange of prisoners until the Confederacy agreed to treat white and black prisoners alike. The Confederacy refused.

There matters stood as the heavy fighting of 1864 poured thousands of captured soldiers into hastily contrived prison compounds that quickly became death camps. Prisoners were subjected to overcrowding, poor sanitation, contaminated water, scanty rations, inadequate medical facilities, and exposure to deep-South summer heat and northern winter cold. The suffering of northern prisoners was especially acute, because the deterioration of the southern economy made it hard to feed and clothe soldiers and citizens, let alone Yankee prisoners. Nearly 16 percent of all Union soldiers held in southern prison camps died.

The Lincoln administration came under pressure to renew exchanges, but the Confederates would not budge on the question of exchanging black soldiers. After a series of battles on the Richmond-Petersburg front in September 1864, Lee proposed an informal exchange of prisoners. Grant agreed, on condition that black soldiers captured in the fighting be included "the same as white soldiers." Lee refused, and Grant canceled the exchange. Lincoln backed this policy, even though local Republican leaders warned that many in the North "will work and vote against the President."

The Issue of Black Soldiers in the Confederate Army

During the winter of 1864–1865, the Confederate government quietly abandoned its refusal to exchange black prisoners, and exchanges resumed. One reason for this reversal was a Confederate decision to recruit slaves to fight for the South. Two years earlier, Davis had denounced the North's arming of freed slaves. But by February 1865, southern armies were desperate for manpower, and slaves constituted the only remaining reserve. Davis pressed the Confederate Congress to enact a bill for recruitment of black soldiers. The assumption that any slaves who fought for the South would have to be granted freedom generated bitter opposition. "What did we go to war for, if not to protect our property?" asked a Virginia senator. By three votes in the House and one in the Senate, the Confederate Congress finally passed the bill on March 13, 1865. Before any southern black regiments could be organized, however, the war ended.

LINCOLN'S REELECTION AND THE END OF THE CONFEDERACY

FOCUS QUESTION

Why did Lincoln expect in August 1864 to be defeated for reelection? What changed to enable him to win reelection by a substantial margin?

Battlefield events, rather than political controversies, had the strongest impact on U.S. voters in 1864. In effect, the election became a referendum on whether to continue fighting for unconditional victory. And suddenly the military situation changed dramatically.

The Capture of Atlanta

After a month of stalemate on the Atlanta front, Sherman's army moved to attack the last rail link into Atlanta from the south. At the battle of Jonesboro on August 31 and September 1, Sherman's men captured the railroad. (See Map 16.7 on p. 379.) Hood abandoned Atlanta to save his army. On September 3, Sherman sent a jaunty telegram to Washington: "Atlanta is ours, and fairly won." This news had an enormous impact on the election. The fall of Atlanta, the *Richmond Examiner* glumly declared, "came in the very nick of time" to "save the party of Lincoln from irretrievable ruin."

The Shenandoah Valley

In Virginia, Grant put Philip Sheridan in charge of a reinforced Army of the Shenandoah, telling him to "go after Early and follow him to the death." On September 19, Sheridan's men attacked Early's force near Winchester and after a daylong battle sent the Confederates flying to the south. With Sheridan in pursuit, Early's line collapsed, and his routed army fled 60 more miles southward.

But Jubal Early was not yet willing to give up. Reinforced by a division from Lee, on October 19 he launched a dawn attack that caught the Yankees by surprise and drove them back in disorder. At the time of the attack, Sheridan was at Winchester, returning to his army from Washington. He jumped onto his horse and sped to the battlefield. By sundown, Sheridan's charisma and tactical leadership had turned the battle from a Union defeat into another Confederate rout.

Sherman's and Sheridan's victories ensured Lincoln's reelection on November 8 by a majority of 212 to 21 in the Electoral College. Soldiers played a notable role in the balloting. Every northern state except three whose legislatures were controlled by Democrats had passed laws allowing absentee voting by soldiers. Seventy-eight percent of the military vote went to Lincoln, compared with 54 percent of the civilian vote. The men who were doing the fighting had sent a clear message that they meant to finish the job.

From Atlanta to the Sea

Many southerners got the message, but not Davis. The Confederacy remained "as erect and defiant as ever," he told his Congress in November 1864. It was this last-ditch resistance that Sherman set out to break in his famous march from Atlanta to the sea.

Sherman had concluded that defeating the Confederate armies was not enough to win the war; the railroads, factories, and farms that supported those armies must also be destroyed. The will of the civilians who sustained the war must be crushed. "We cannot change the hearts of those people of the South," he said, "but we can make war so terrible and make them so sick of war that generations would pass away before they would again appeal to it."

Sherman urged Grant to let him march through the heart of Georgia, living off the land and destroying all resources not needed by his army. Grant and Lincoln were reluctant to authorize such a risky move, especially with Hood's army of 40,000 men still intact in northern Alabama. Sherman assured them that he would send George Thomas to take command of a force of 60,000 men in Tennessee, who would be more than a match for Hood. With another 60,000, Sherman could "move through Georgia, smashing things to the sea. . . . I can make the march, and make Georgia howl!"

Lincoln and Grant finally consented. On November 16, Sherman's avengers marched out of Atlanta after burning a third of the city, including some nonmilitary property. Southward they marched 280 miles to Savannah, wrecking everything in their path that could by any stretch of the imagination be considered of military value.

The Battles of Franklin and Nashville

They encountered little resistance. Instead of chasing Sherman, Hood invaded Tennessee with the hope of recovering that state for the Confederacy. This campaign virtually destroyed his army. On November 30, the Confederates slaughtered part of the Union force at Franklin, 20 miles south of Nashville. Instead of retreating, Hood moved on to Nashville, where Thomas launched an attack that almost wiped out the Army of Tennessee. Its remnants retreated to Mississippi, where Hood resigned in January 1865.

Fort Fisher and Sherman's March through the Carolinas

Worse was yet to come for the Confederates. Lee's army in Virginia drew its dwindling supplies overland from the Carolinas and through the port of Wilmington, North Carolina, the only city still accessible to blockade runners. The big guns at Fort Fisher kept blockade ships at bay and protected the runners. In January 1865, though, the largest armada of the war—58 ships with 627 guns—pounded Fort Fisher for two days, disabling most of its big guns. Army troops captured the fort on January 15. That ended the blockade running, and Sherman soon put an end to supplies from the Carolinas as well.

At the end of January, Sherman's soldiers headed north from Savannah, eager to take revenge on South Carolina, which to their mind had started the war. Here, they made even less distinction between civilian and military property than they had in Georgia and left even less of Columbia standing than they had of Atlanta. Sherman's army pushed into North Carolina and brushed aside the force that Joseph E. Johnston had assembled to stop them.

The Road to Appomattox

The Army of Northern Virginia was now the only entity that kept the Confederacy alive, but it was on the verge of disintegration. Scores of its soldiers were deserting every day. On April 1, Sheridan's cavalry and an infantry corps smashed the right

SHERMAN'S SOLDIERS TEARING UP THE RAILROAD IN ATLANTA.
One of the objectives of Sherman's march from Atlanta to the sea was to demolish the railroads so they could not transport supplies to Confederate armies. The soldiers did a thorough job. They tore up the rails and ties, made a bonfire of the ties, heated the rails in the fire, and then wrapped them around trees, creating "Sherman neckties."

flank of Lee's line at Five Forks and cut off the last railroad into Petersburg. The next day, Grant attacked and forced Lee to abandon both Petersburg and Richmond. As the Confederate government fled its capital, its army set fire to all the military stores it could not carry. The fires spread and destroyed more of Richmond than the northern troops had destroyed of Atlanta or Columbia.

Lee's starving men limped westward, hoping to turn south and join the remnants of Johnston's army in North Carolina. Sheridan's cavalry raced ahead and cut them off at Appomattox, 90 miles from Petersburg, on April 8. It was the end. "There is nothing left for me to do," said Lee, "but to go and see General Grant."

The terms of surrender were generous. Thirty thousand captured Confederates were allowed to go home on condition that they promise never again to take up arms against the United States. (See Table 16.1.) After completing the surrender formalities on April 9, Grant introduced Lee to his staff, which included Colonel Ely Parker, a Seneca Indian. As Lee shook hands with Parker, he stared for a moment at Parker's dark features and said: "I am glad to see one real American here." Parker replied solemnly: "We are all Americans."

The Assassination of Lincoln

Wild celebrations broke out in the North at the news of the fall of Richmond, followed soon by news of Appomattox. Almost overnight, the celebrations turned to mourning. On the evening of April 14, Abraham Lincoln sought to relax by attending a comedy at Ford's Theatre. In the middle of the play, John Wilkes Booth broke into Lincoln's box. An aspiring actor, Booth was a native of Maryland and a frustrated, unstable egotist who hated Lincoln for what he had done to Booth's beloved South. He shot the president fatally in the head.

Lincoln's death in the early morning of April 15 produced an outpouring of grief throughout the North and among newly freed slaves in the South. The martyred president did not live to see the culmination of his great achievement in leading the nation to the victory that preserved its existence and abolished slavery. Within 10 weeks after Lincoln's death, his assassin was trapped and killed in a burning barn in Virginia (April 26), the remaining Confederate armies surrendered one after another (April 26, May 4, May 26, June 23), and Union cavalry captured the fleeing Jefferson Davis in Georgia (May 10). The trauma of the Civil War was over, but the problems of peace and reconstruction had just begun.

Conclusion

Northern victory in the Civil War resolved two fundamental questions left unresolved by the Revolution of 1776 and the Constitution of 1789: whether this fragile republican experiment in federalism called the United States would survive as one nation, and whether that nation, founded on a charter of liberty, would continue to exist as the largest slaveholding country in the world. Before 1861, the question of whether a state could secede from the Union had remained open. Eleven states did secede, but their defeat in a war that cost 625,000 lives ended the issue. Since 1865, no state has seriously threatened secession. And in 1865, the adoption of the Thirteenth Amendment to the Constitution confirmed the supreme power of the national government to abolish slavery and ensure the liberty of all Americans.

QUICK REVIEW

BATTLEFRONTS AND HOME FRONTS 1864–1865

- Stalemate in Virginia despite heavy fighting

- Failure of peace overtures in 1864

- Capture of Atlanta by Sherman and victories in the Shenandoah valley broke stalemate

- Reelection of Lincoln meant war to final victory at Appomattox

TABLE 16.1

CASUALTIES IN CIVIL WAR ARMIES AND NAVIES Confederate records are incomplete; the Confederate data listed here are therefore estimates. The actual Confederate totals were probably higher.							
	Killed and Mortally Wounded in Combat	Died of Disease	Died in Prison	Miscellaneous Deaths*	Total Deaths	Wounded, not Mortally	Total Casualties
Union	111,904	197,388	30,192	24,881	364,345	277,401	641,766
Confederate (estimated)	94,000	140,000	26,000	No Estimates	260,000	195,000	455,000
Both armies (estimated)	205,904	337,388	56,192	24,881	624,345	472,401	1,096,766

* Accidents, drownings, sunstroke, etc.

© Cengage Learning

The Civil War also accomplished a regional transfer of power from South to North. From 1800 to 1860, the slave states had used their leverage in the Jeffersonian Republican and Jacksonian Democratic parties to control national politics. In the 50 years after 1861, no native of a southern state was elected president, only one served as Speaker of the House and none as president pro tem of the Senate, and only 5 of the 26 Supreme Court justices appointed were from the South. In 1860 the South's share of the national wealth was 30 percent; in 1870 it was 12 percent.

The institutions and ideology of a plantation society and a caste system that had dominated half of the country before 1861 went down with a great crash in 1865—to be replaced by the institutions and ideology of free-labor capitalism. Once feared as the gravest threat to liberty, the power of the national government sustained by a large army had achieved the greatest triumph of liberty in American history. With victory and peace in 1865, the reunited nation turned its attention to the issue of equality.

CHAPTER REVIEW

Review Questions

1. What factors led Lincoln to his decision to issue the Emancipation Proclamation?

2. What were the sources of internal dissent and dissension in the Confederacy? In the Union?

3. What contributions did women and African Americans make to the war efforts in both the North and South?

4. Why did Lincoln expect in August 1864 to be defeated for reelection? What changed to enable him to win reelection by a substantial margin?

Critical Thinking Questions

1. How did a war that began, on the part of the North, with the goal of restoring a Union in which slavery existed in half of the country, become transformed into a war to give the nation a new birth of freedom?

2. In the winter of 1862–1863 northern morale was at rock bottom, and the prospects for Confederate success appeared bright. Yet two years later the Confederacy lay in ruins and its dream of independent nationhood was doomed. How and why did this happen?

Identifications

Review your understanding of the following key terms, people, and events for this chapter.

contraband of war, p. 361
compensated emancipation, p. 362

Copperheads, p. 363
martial law, p. 366
Twenty Negro Law, p. 367

bounty jumpers, p. 367
commutation fee, p. 368

DISCOVERY

What kinds of broad social changes did the Civil War bring?

In thinking about this question, begin by breaking it down into the components shown below. A discussion of the significance of each component should appear in your answer.

Warfare

Look at the photograph of the African American soldiers. Why was it more dangerous to be an African American soldier than a white soldier for the Union? What were the potential consequences? What effect(s) did the employment of black soldiers have on the movement toward equal rights?

Culture and Society

Consider the photos on page 369. What roles did women play in the war? What reasons might a woman have for secretly serving in a combat role? Both militaries seem to have discharged any woman discovered serving in the ranks. Why would the military not want women in the army?

Library of Congress, Prints and Photographs Division

PART OF COMPANY E, 4TH U.S. COLORED INFANTRY

Visit the CourseMate website at www.cengagebrain.com for additional study tools and review materials for this chapter.

RECONSTRUCTION, 1863–1877

From the beginning of the Civil War, the North fought to "reconstruct" the Union. Lincoln at first attempted to restore the Union as it had existed before 1861, but once the abolition of slavery became a northern war aim, the Union could never be reconstructed on its old foundations. Instead, it must experience a "new birth of freedom," as Lincoln had said at the dedication of the military cemetery at Gettysburg.

But precisely what did "a new birth of freedom" mean? At the very least it meant the end of slavery. But what would liberty look like for the four million freed slaves? Would they become citizens equal to their former masters in the eyes of the law? And on what terms should the Confederate states return to the Union? What would be the powers of the states and of the national government in a reconstructed Union?

TIMELINE

| 1863 | 1865 | 1867 | 1869 | 1871 | 1873 | 1875 | 1877 |

■ **1863**
Lincoln issues Proclamation of Amnesty and Reconstruction

■ **1865**
Andrew Johnson becomes president, announces his reconstruction plan

1865–1869
Andrew Johnson presidency

■ **1866**
Congress passes civil rights bill and expands Freedmen's Bureau over Johnson's veto and approves Fourteenth Amendment

■ **1867**
Congress passes Reconstruction acts over Johnson's vetoes

■ **1868**
Andrew Johnson impeached but not convicted

1869–1877
Ulysses S. Grant presidency

■ **1870**
Fifteenth Amendment ratified

1871 ■
Congress passes Ku Klux Klan Act

■ **1872**
Liberal Republicans defect from party
• Grant wins reelection

1873 ■
Economic depression begins with the Panic

■ **1874**
Democrats win House of Representatives

■ **1876**
Disputed presidential election causes constitutional crisis

1877 ■
Compromise of 1877 installs Rutherford B. Hayes as president

WARTIME RECONSTRUCTION

Lincoln initially feared that whites in the South would never extend equal rights to the freed slaves. In 1862, he encouraged freedpeople to emigrate to all-black countries like Haiti. Black leaders, abolitionists, and many Republicans objected to that policy. Black people were Americans. Why should they not have the rights of American citizens instead of being urged to leave the country?

Lincoln eventually embraced the logic and justice of that view. But in beginning the process of reconstruction, he first reached out to southern *whites*, whose allegiance to the Confederacy was lukewarm. On December 8, 1863, Lincoln issued his Proclamation of **Amnesty** and Reconstruction, which offered presidential pardon to southern whites who took an oath of allegiance to the United States and accepted the abolition of slavery. The plan allowed southern states to form new governments if the number of adult white males who took the oath equaled 10 percent of the number of voters in 1860.

Because the war was still raging, this policy could be carried out only where Union troops controlled substantial portions of a Confederate state: Louisiana, Arkansas, and Tennessee in early 1864. Lincoln hoped that the process might

amnesty *General pardon granted to a large group of people.*

snowball as Union military victories convinced more and more Confederates that their cause was hopeless. But those military victories were long delayed, and reconstruction in most parts of the South did not begin until 1865.

Radical Republicans and Reconstruction

Growing opposition within Lincoln's own party slowed the process as well. Many Republicans believed that white men who had fought *against* the Union should not be rewarded with restoration of their political rights while black men who had fought *for* the Union were denied those rights. If the freedpeople were landless, Radical Republicans said, provide them with land by confiscating the plantations of leading Confederates. Radical Republicans also distrusted oaths of allegiance sworn by ex-Confederates. Rather than simply restoring the old ruling class to power, they asked, why not give freed slaves the vote, to provide a genuinely loyal nucleus of supporters in the South?

These radical positions did not command a majority of Congress in 1864. Yet the experience of Louisiana, the first state to reorganize under Lincoln's more moderate policy, convinced even nonradical Republicans to block Lincoln's program. Enough white men in the occupied portion of the state took the oath of allegiance to satisfy Lincoln's conditions. They adopted a new state constitution and formed a government that abolished slavery and provided a school system for blacks. But the new government did not grant blacks the right to vote. It also authorized planters to enforce restrictive labor policies on black plantation workers. Louisiana's actions alienated a majority of congressional Republicans, who refused to admit representatives and senators from the "reconstructed" state.

At the same time, though, Congress failed to enact a reconstruction policy of its own. This was not for lack of trying. Both houses passed the Wade-Davis reconstruction bill (named for Senator Benjamin Wade of Ohio and Representative Henry Winter Davis of Maryland) in July 1864. That bill did not enfranchise blacks, but it did impose such stringent loyalty requirements on southern whites that few of them could take the required oath. Lincoln therefore vetoed it.

Lincoln's action infuriated many Republicans, and the bitter squabble threatened for a time to destroy Lincoln's chances of being reelected. Union military success in the fall of 1864, however, reunited the Republicans behind Lincoln. The collapse of Confederate military resistance the following spring set the stage for compromise on a policy for the postwar South. But Lincoln's assassination changed everything.

ANDREW JOHNSON AND RECONSTRUCTION

In 1864, Republicans had adopted the name Union Party to attract the votes of War Democrats and border-state Unionists who could not bring themselves to vote Republican. For the same reason, they also nominated Andrew Johnson of Tennessee as Lincoln's running mate.

Of "poor white" heritage, Johnson had clawed his way up in the rough-and-tumble politics of east Tennessee. This region of small farms and few slaves held little love for the planters who controlled the state. Johnson denounced the planters as "stuck-up aristocrats" who had no empathy with the southern yeomen for whom Johnson became a self-appointed spokesman. Johnson was the only senator from a seceding state who refused to support the Confederacy.

FOCUS QUESTION

What were the positions of Presidents Abraham Lincoln and Andrew Johnson and of moderate and radical Republicans in Congress on the issues of restoring the South to the Union and protecting the rights of freed slaves?

Booth's bullet therefore elevated to the presidency a man who still thought of himself as primarily a Democrat and a southerner. But the trouble this might cause in a party that was mostly Republican and northern was not immediately apparent. In fact, Johnson's enmity toward the "stuck-up aristocrats" whom he blamed for leading the South into secession prompted him to utter dire threats. "Traitors must be impoverished," he said. "They must not only be punished, but their social power must be destroyed."

Radical Republicans liked the sound of this. Johnson seemed to promise the type of reconstruction they favored—one that would deny political power to ex-Confederates and enfranchise blacks. They envisioned a coalition between these new black voters and the small minority of southern whites who had never supported the Confederacy. These men could be expected to vote Republican. Republican governments in southern states would pass laws to provide civil rights and economic opportunity for freed slaves.

Johnson's Policy

From a combination of pragmatic, partisan, and idealistic motives, therefore, Radical Republicans prepared to implement a progressive reconstruction policy. But Johnson unexpectedly refused to cooperate. Instead of calling Congress into session, he moved ahead on his own and issued two proclamations on May 29, 1865. The first provided a blanket amnesty for all but the highest-ranking Confederate officials and military officers and those ex-Confederates with taxable property worth $20,000 or more. The second named a provisional governor for North Carolina and directed him to call an election of delegates to frame a new state constitution. Only white men who had received amnesty and taken an oath of allegiance could vote. Similar proclamations soon followed for other former Confederate states. Johnson's policy was clear: He would exclude both blacks and upper-class whites from the reconstruction process.

Many Republicans supported Johnson's policy at first, but the radicals feared that restricting the vote to whites would open the door to the restoration of the old power structure in the South. They began to sense that Johnson (who had owned slaves) was as dedicated to white supremacy as any Confederate. "White men alone must govern the South," he told a Democratic senator. Although moderate Republicans believed that black men should participate to some degree in the reconstruction process, in 1865 they were not yet prepared to break with the president. They regarded his policy as an "experiment" that would be modified as time went on.

Southern Defiance

As it happened, none of the state conventions enfranchised a single black. Some of them even balked at ratifying the Thirteenth Amendment. Reports from the South told of neo-Confederate violence against blacks and their white sympathizers. Johnson seemed to encourage such activities by allowing the organization of white militia units.

Then there was the matter of presidential pardons. After talking fiercely about punishing traitors, and after excluding several classes of them from his amnesty proclamation, Johnson began to issue special pardons to many ex-Confederates, restoring property and political rights. Under the new state constitutions southern voters were electing hundreds of ex-Confederates to state offices. Even more alarming to northerners, who thought they had won the war, was the election to Congress of no fewer than nine ex-Confederate congressmen, seven ex-Confederate state officials, four generals, four colonels, and even the former Confederate vice president, Alexander H. Stephens.

Somehow the aristocrats and traitors Johnson had denounced in April had taken over the reconstruction process. They did so by flattering the presidential ego.

Thousands of prominent ex-Confederates or their tearful female relatives applied for pardons, confessing the error of their ways and appealing for presidential mercy. Johnson reveled in his power over these once-haughty aristocrats. More important, perhaps, was the praise and support Johnson received from leading northern Democrats. That party's leaders enticed Johnson with visions of reelection as a Democrat in 1868 if he could manage to reconstruct the South in a manner that would preserve a Democratic majority there.

The Black Codes

In fall 1865, these newly reconstructed state legislatures sought to define the rights of four million former slaves. The option of treating them exactly like white citizens was scarcely considered. Instead, the states excluded black people from juries and the ballot box, did not permit them to testify against whites in court, banned interracial marriage, and punished blacks more severely than whites for certain crimes. Some states defined any unemployed black person as a vagrant and hired him out to a planter, forbade blacks to lease land, and apprenticed black youths out to whites.

Northern Republicans saw these **"Black Codes"** as a brazen attempt to reinstate a quasi-slavery. "We tell the white men of Mississippi," declared the *Chicago Tribune*, "that the men of the North will convert the State of Mississippi into a frog pond before they will allow such laws to disgrace one foot of the soil in which the bones of our soldiers sleep and over which the flag of freedom waves." The Union army's occupation forces suspended the implementation of Black Codes that discriminated on racial grounds.

Land and Labor in the Postwar South

The Black Codes, though discriminatory, were designed to address a genuine problem. The end of the war had left black–white relations in the South in a state of limbo. The South's economy was in a shambles. Most tangible assets except the land itself had been destroyed. Law and order broke down in many areas. The war had ended early enough in the spring to allow the planting of at least some food crops. But who would plant and cultivate them? One-quarter of the South's white farmers had been killed in the war; the slaves were slaves no more. "I never did a day's work in my life," lamented a South Carolina planter, "and I don't know how to begin."

Despite all of this trouble, life went on. Slaveless planters and their wives and soldiers' widows and their children plowed and planted. Confederate veterans drifted home and went to work. Former slave owners asked their former slaves to work the land for wages or shares of the crop, and many did so. Others refused, because for them to leave the old place was an essential part of freedom.

Thus the roads were alive with freedpeople on the move in summer 1865. Many signed on to work at farms just a few miles from their old homes. Others moved into town. Some looked for relatives who had been sold away during slavery or from whom they had been separated during the war. Some wandered aimlessly. Whites organized vigilante groups to discipline blacks and force them to work.

The Freedmen's Bureau

Into this vacuum stepped the U.S. army and the **Freedmen's Bureau.** Tens of thousands of troops remained in the South until civil government could be restored. The

Black Codes *Laws passed by southern states that restricted the rights and liberties of former slaves.*

Freedmen's Bureau *Federal agency created in 1865 to supervise newly freed people. It oversaw relations between whites and blacks in the South, issued food rations, and supervised labor contracts.*

SHARECROPPERS WORKING IN THE FIELDS. *This photograph shows two families of sharecroppers picking cotton. Freed slaves resisted landowners' efforts to work them in gangs as they had in slavery, so the owners rented land to black families in return for a share of the crop. These croppers do not appear to be overjoyed with the new system.* Photographs and Prints Division, Schomburg Center for Research in Black Culture, The New York Public Library, Astor, Lenox and Tilden Foundations.

Freedmen's Bureau (its official title was Bureau of Refugees, Freedmen, and Abandoned Lands), created by Congress in March 1865, became the principal agency for overseeing relations between former slaves and owners. Staffed by army officers, the bureau established posts throughout the South to supervise free-labor wage contracts between landowners and freedpeople. The Freedmen's Bureau also issued food rations to 150,000 people daily during 1865, one-third of them to whites. Southern whites viewed the Freedmen's Bureau with hostility, but, without it, the postwar chaos in the South would have been much greater. Bureau agents encouraged black people to sign free-labor contracts and return to work.

In negotiating labor contracts, the bureau tried to establish minimum wages. Lack of money in the South, however, caused many contracts to call for **share wages**—that is, paying workers with shares of the crop. At first, landowners worked their laborers in large groups called gangs. But many black workers resented this system as reminiscent of slavery. Thus, a new system evolved, called **sharecropping**, whereby a black family worked a specific piece of land in return for a share of the crop produced on it.

Land for the Landless

Freedpeople, of course, would have preferred to farm their own land. "What's de use of being free if you don't own land enough to be buried in?" asked one black sharecropper (dialect in original source). Some black farmers did manage to save up enough money to buy small plots. Demobilized black soldiers purchased land with their bounty payments, sometimes pooling their money to buy an entire plantation on which several black families settled. Northern philanthropists helped some freedmen buy land. But most ex-slaves found the purchase of land impossible. Few of them had money, and even if they did, whites often refused to sell.

Several northern radicals proposed legislation to confiscate ex-Confederate land and redistribute it to freedpeople, but those proposals went nowhere. The most promising effort to put thousands of slaves on land of their own also failed. In January 1865, after his march through Georgia, General William T. Sherman had issued a military order setting aside thousands of acres of abandoned plantation land in the Georgia and South Carolina lowcountry for settlement by freed slaves. The army even turned over some of its surplus mules to black farmers. The expectation of **"40 acres and a mule"** excited freedpeople in 1865, but President Johnson's Amnesty Proclamation and his issuance of pardons restored most of this property to ex-Confederates. The same thing happened to white-owned land elsewhere in the South.

Education

Abolitionists were more successful in helping freedpeople get an education. During the war, freedmen's aid societies and missionary societies founded by abolitionists had sent teachers to Union-occupied areas of the South to set up

share wages *Payment of workers' wages with a share of the crop rather than with cash.*

sharecropping *Working land in return for a share of the crops produced instead of paying cash rent.*

40 acres and a mule *Largely unfulfilled hope of many former slaves that they would receive free land from the confiscated property of ex-Confederates.*

NEW YORK, SATURDAY, MAY 26, 1866.

Library of Congress, Prints and Photographs Division

THE BURNING OF A FREEDMEN'S SCHOOL. *Because freedpeople's education symbolized black progress, whites who resented and resisted this progress sometimes attacked and burned freedmen's schools, as in this dramatic illustration of a white mob burning a school during antiblack riots in Memphis in May 1866.*

schools for freed slaves. After the war, this effort was expanded with the aid of the Freedmen's Bureau. Two thousand northern teachers, three-quarters of them women, fanned out into every part of the South to train black teachers. After 1870, missionary societies concentrated on making higher education available to African Americans. They founded many of the black colleges in the South. The education crusade reduced the southern black illiteracy rate to 70 percent by 1880 and to 48 percent by 1900.

THE ADVENT OF CONGRESSIONAL RECONSTRUCTION

Political reconstruction shaped the civil and political rights of freedpeople. By the time Congress met in December 1865, the Republican majority was determined to take control of the process by which former Confederate states would be restored to full representation. Congress refused to admit the representatives and senators elected by the former Confederate states under Johnson's reconstruction policy and set up a special committee to formulate new terms. The committee held hearings at which southern Unionists, freedpeople, and U.S. army officers testified to abuse and terrorism in the South. Their testimony convinced Republicans of the need for stronger federal intervention to define and protect the civil rights of freedpeople. Many radicals wanted to grant the vote to black men, but because racism was still strong in the North, the special committee instead decided to draft a constitutional amendment that would encourage southern states to enfranchise blacks but would not require them to do so.

Schism between President and Congress

Meanwhile, Congress passed two laws to protect the economic and civil rights of freedpeople. The first extended the life of the Freedmen's Bureau and expanded its powers. The second defined freedpeople as citizens with equal legal rights and gave federal courts appellate jurisdiction to enforce those rights. Johnson vetoed both measures. He then gave a speech to Democratic supporters in which he denounced Republican leaders as traitors who did not want to restore the Union except on terms that would degrade white southerners. Democratic newspapers applauded the president for vetoing bills that would "compound our race with niggers, gypsies, and baboons."

The Fourteenth Amendment

With better than a two-thirds majority in both houses, congressional Republicans passed the Freedmen's Bureau and Civil Rights bills over the president's vetoes. Then, on April 30, the special committee submitted to Congress its proposed Fourteenth Amendment to the Constitution. After lengthy debate, the amendment received the required two-thirds majority in Congress on June 13 and went to the states for ratification. Section 1 defined all native-born or naturalized persons, including blacks, as American citizens and prohibited the states from abridging the "privileges and immunities" of citizens, from depriving "any person of life, liberty, or property without due process of law," and from denying to any person "the equal protection of the laws." Section 2 gave states the option of either enfranchising black males or losing a proportionate number of congressional seats and electoral votes. Section 3 disqualified a significant number of ex-Confederates from holding federal or state office. Section 4 guaranteed the national debt and repudiated the Confederate debt. Section 5 empowered Congress to enforce the Fourteenth Amendment by "appropriate legislation." The Fourteenth Amendment had far-reaching consequences. Section 1 has become the most important provision in the Constitution for defining and enforcing civil rights.

The 1866 Elections

During the campaign for the 1866 congressional elections, Republicans made clear that any ex-Confederate state that ratified the Fourteenth Amendment would be declared "reconstructed" and that its representatives and senators would be seated in Congress. Tennessee ratified, but Johnson counseled other southern legislatures to reject the amendment, which they did. Johnson then created a National Union Party made up of a few conservative Republicans who disagreed with their party, some border-state Unionists who supported the president, and Democrats. But many northern Democrats still carried the taint of having opposed the war effort, and most northern voters did not trust them. Further, race riots in Memphis and New Orleans bolstered Republican arguments that national power was necessary to protect "the fruits of victory" in the South. Perhaps the biggest liability was Johnson himself. In a whistle-stop tour through the North, he traded insults with hecklers and embarrassed his supporters.

Republicans swept the election. Having rejected the reconstruction terms embodied in the Fourteenth Amendment, southern Democrats now faced far more stringent terms. "They would not cooperate in rebuilding what they destroyed," wrote an exasperated moderate Republican, so "we must remove the rubbish and rebuild from the bottom."

The Reconstruction Acts of 1867

The new Congress enacted over Johnson's vetoes the Reconstruction acts of 1867. The acts divided the 10 southern states into five military districts, directed army officers to register voters for the election of delegates to new constitutional conventions, and enfranchised males aged 21 and older (including blacks) to vote in those elections. When a state had adopted a new constitution that granted equal civil and political rights regardless of race and had ratified the Fourteenth Amendment, it would be declared reconstructed, and its newly elected congressmen would be seated.

These measures embodied a true revolution. Southerners were shorn of political power, with their former slaves not only freed but also politically empowered. Blacks and their white allies organized **Union Leagues** to mobilize the new black voters into the Republican Party. Democrats branded southern white Republicans as **"scalawags"** and northern settlers as **"carpetbaggers."** By September 1867, the 10 states had 735,000 black voters and only 635,000 white voters registered. At least one-third of the registered white voters were Republicans.

President Johnson did everything he could to block Reconstruction. He replaced several Republican generals with Democrats. He had his attorney general issue a ruling that interpreted the Reconstruction acts narrowly, thereby forcing a special session of Congress to pass a supplementary act in July 1867. He encouraged southern whites to obstruct the registration of voters and the election of convention delegates. Johnson aimed to slow the process until 1868 in the hope that northern voters would repudiate Reconstruction in the presidential election of that year, when Johnson planned to run as the Democratic candidate.

Union Leagues *Organizations that informed African American voters of, and mobilized them to support, the Republican Party.*

scalawags *Term used by southern Democrats to describe southern whites who worked with the Republicans.*

carpetbaggers *Northerners who settled in the South during Reconstruction.*

THE IMPEACHMENT OF ANDREW JOHNSON

Johnson struck even more boldly against Reconstruction after the 1867 elections, which saw Republicans suffer setbacks in several northern states. In February 1868, he removed from office Secretary of War Edwin M. Stanton, who had administered the War Department in support of the congressional Reconstruction policy. This appeared to violate the Tenure of Office Act, passed the year before over Johnson's veto, which required Senate consent for such removals. By a vote of 126 to 47 along party lines, the House **impeached** Johnson on February 24. The official reason for impeachment was that he had violated the Tenure of Office Act. The real reason was Johnson's stubborn defiance of Congress on Reconstruction.

The impeachment trial before the Senate proved to be long and complicated, which worked in Johnson's favor by allowing passions to cool. The Constitution specifies the grounds on which a president can be impeached and removed: "Treason, Bribery, or other high Crimes and Misdemeanors." The issue was whether Johnson was guilty of any of these acts. His able defense counsel exposed technical ambiguities in the Tenure of Office Act that raised doubts about whether Johnson had actually violated it. Behind the scenes, Johnson strengthened his case by promising to appoint the respected General John M. Schofield as secretary of war and to stop obstructing the Reconstruction acts. In the end, seven Republican senators plus all Democrats voted for acquittal on May 16, and the final tally fell one vote short of the necessary two-thirds majority.

impeach *To charge government officeholders with misconduct in office.*

© CORBIS

TWO MEMBERS OF THE KU KLUX KLAN. *Founded in Pulaski, Tennessee, in 1866 as a social organization similar to a college fraternity, the Klan evolved into a terrorist group whose purpose was intimidation of southern Republicans. The Klan, in which former Confederate soldiers played a prominent part, was responsible for the beating and murder of hundreds of blacks and whites alike from 1868 to 1871.*

---

universal male suffrage
System that allowed all adult males to vote without regard to property, religious, or race qualifications or limitations.

Ku Klux Klan *White terrorist organization in the South originally founded as a fraternal society in 1866.*

The Completion of Formal Reconstruction

The impeachment trial's end cleared the poisonous air in Washington, and Johnson quietly served out his term. Constitutional conventions met in the South during winter and spring 1867–1868. The constitutions they wrote were among the most progressive in the nation. They enacted **universal male suffrage.** Some disfranchised certain classes of ex-Confederates for several years, but by 1872, all such disqualifications had been removed. The constitutions mandated statewide public schools for both races for the first time in the South. Most states permitted segregated schools, but schools of any kind for blacks represented a great step forward. Most of the constitutions increased the state's responsibility for social welfare.

Violence in some parts of the South marred the voting on ratification. The **Ku Klux Klan,** a night-riding white terrorist organization, made its first appearance during the elections. Nevertheless, voters in seven states ratified their constitutions and elected new legislatures that ratified the Fourteenth Amendment in spring 1868. That amendment became part of the U.S. Constitution the following summer, and the newly elected representatives and senators from those seven states, nearly all Republicans, took their seats in the House and Senate.

The Fifteenth Amendment

The remaining three southern states completed the Reconstruction process in 1869 and 1870. Congress required them to ratify the Fifteenth as well as the Fourteenth Amendment. The Fifteenth Amendment prohibited states from denying the right to vote on grounds of race, color, or previous condition of servitude. Its purpose was not only to prevent any future revocation of black suffrage, but also to extend equal suffrage to the border states and to the North.

But the Fifteenth Amendment still left women disfranchised, and debates over whether or not to support the amendment split the women's rights movement. In 1866, male and female abolitionists formed the American Equal Rights Association (AERA) to work for both black and woman suffrage. Most members supported the Fifteenth Amendment, believing that woman suffrage would have to wait until public opinion could be educated up to the standard of gender equality. Arguing instead that the amendment would establish "the most odious form of aristocracy the world has ever seen: an aristocracy of sex," radical suffragists Elizabeth Cady Stanton and Susan B. Anthony left the AERA and founded the National Woman Suffrage Association. The remaining AERA members reorganized themselves as the American Woman Suffrage Association. For the next two decades, these rival organizations, working for the same cause, remained at odds.

The Election of 1868

Just as the presidential election of 1864 was a referendum on Lincoln's war policies, so the election of 1868 was a referendum on the Reconstruction policy of the Republicans. Although the Republican nominee, General **Ulysses S. Grant,** had no political experience, he commanded greater authority and prestige than anyone else in the country. Grant agreed to run for the presidency in order to preserve in peace the victory for Union and liberty he had won in war.

The Democrats turned away from Andrew Johnson and nominated Horatio Seymour, the wartime governor of New York. They denounced the Reconstruction acts as "unconstitutional, revolutionary, and void." Their militant platform also demanded "the abolition of the Freedmen's Bureau, and all political instrumentalities designed to secure negro supremacy." The vice presidential candidate, Frank Blair of Missouri, declared that the Democrats sought to "allow the white people to reorganize their own governments."

The only way to achieve this bold counterrevolutionary goal was to suppress Republican voters in the South. Federal troops had only limited success in preventing the violence of the Ku Klux Klan. In Louisiana, Georgia, Arkansas, and Tennessee, the Klan or Klan-like groups committed dozens of murders and intimidated thousands of black voters. The violence helped the Democratic cause in the South, but probably hurt it in the North, where many voters perceived the Klan as an organization of neo-Confederate paramilitary guerrillas.

Seymour did well in the South, carrying five former slave states and coming close in others despite the solid Republican vote of the newly enfranchised blacks. But Grant swept the electoral vote 214 to 80. Seymour actually won a slight majority of the white voters nationally; without black enfranchisement, Grant would have had a minority of the popular vote.

THE GRANT ADMINISTRATION

Upon taking office, Grant's inexperience and poor judgment betrayed him into several unwise appointments of officials who were later convicted of corruption. His back-to-back administrations were plagued by scandals. His secretary of war was impeached for selling appointments to army posts and Indian reservations, and his attorney general and secretary of the interior resigned under suspicion of malfeasance in 1875.

Grant was too trusting of subordinates, and he appointed military colleagues and family members to offices for which they were scarcely qualified. But in an era notorious for corruption at all levels of government, many of the scandals were not Grant's fault. The Tammany Hall "Ring" of "Boss" William Marcy Tweed in New York City may have stolen more money from taxpayers than all federal agencies combined. In Washington, one of the most widely publicized scandals, the **Credit Mobilier** affair, concerned Congress rather than the Grant administration. Several congressmen had accepted stock in the Credit Mobilier, a construction company for the Union Pacific Railroad, which received loans and land grants from the government in return for ensuring lax congressional supervision.

What accounted for this explosion of corruption? During the war, expansion of government contracts and the bureaucracy had created new opportunities for the unscrupulous. Following the intense sacrifices of the war years came a relaxation of tensions and standards. Rapid postwar economic growth, led by an extraordinary

Ulysses S. Grant *General-in-chief of Union armies who led those armies to victory in the Civil War*

Credit Mobilier *Construction company for the Union Pacific Railroad that gave shares of stock to some congressmen in return for favors.*

rush of railroad construction, encouraged greed and get-rich-quick schemes of the kind satirized by Mark Twain and Charles Dudley Warner in their 1873 novel *The Gilded Age,* which gave its name to the era.

Civil Service Reform and Foreign Policy Issues

Some of the apparent increase in corruption during the Gilded Age was more a matter of perception, as reformers focused on the dark corners of corruption hitherto unilluminated because of the nation's preoccupation with war and reconstruction. In reality, during the Grant administration, several government agencies made real progress in eliminating abuses that had flourished in earlier administrations.

The chief target of civil service reform was the **"spoils system."** With the slogan "To the victor belongs the spoils," the victorious party in an election rewarded party workers with government appointments. The spoils system politicized the bureaucracy and staffed it with unqualified personnel who spent more time working for their party than for the government. Civil service reformers wanted to separate the bureaucracy from politics by requiring competitive examinations for the appointment of civil servants. This movement gathered steam during the 1870s and finally achieved success in 1883 with the passage of the Pendleton Act, which established the modern structure of the civil service. When Grant took office, he seemed to share the sentiments of civil service reformers, but many congressmen, senators, and other politicians resisted reform because patronage greased political machines that kept them in office. They managed to subvert reform, sometimes using Grant as an unwitting ally and turning many reformers against the president.

A foreign policy fiasco added to Grant's woes. The irregular procedures by which his private secretary had negotiated a treaty to annex Santo Domingo (now the Dominican Republic) alienated leading Republican senators, who defeated ratification of the treaty. Politically inexperienced, Grant acted like a general who needed only to give orders rather than as a president who must cultivate supporters. The fallout from the Santo Domingo affair widened the fissure in the Republican Party between "spoilsmen" and "reformers."

But the Grant administration had some solid foreign policy achievements to its credit. Hamilton Fish, the able secretary of state, negotiated the Treaty of Washington in 1871 to settle the vexing "Alabama Claims." These were damage claims against Britain for the destruction of American shipping by the C.S.S. *Alabama* and other Confederate commerce raiders built in British shipyards. The treaty established an international tribunal to arbitrate the U.S. claims, resulting in the award of $15.5 million in damages to U.S. shipowners and a British expression of regret.

Reconstruction in the South

During Grant's two administrations, the "Southern Question" was the most intractable issue. With the ratification of the Fifteenth Amendment, many people breathed a sigh of relief at this apparent resolution of "the last great point that remained to be settled of the issues of the war." But Reconstruction was not over; it had hardly begun. State governments elected by black and white voters were in place in the South, but Democratic violence protesting Reconstruction and the instability of the Republican coalition that sustained it portended trouble.

spoils system *System by which the victorious political party rewarded its supporters with government jobs.*

Blacks in Office

In the North, the Republican Party represented the most prosperous, educated, and influential elements of the population, but in the South, most of its adherents were poor, illiterate, and landless. About 80 percent of southern Republican voters were black. Although most black leaders were educated and many had been free before the war, the mass of black voters were illiterate ex-slaves. Neither the leaders nor their constituents, however, were as ignorant as stereotypes have portrayed them. Of 14 black representatives and two black senators elected in the South between 1868 and 1876, all but three had attended secondary school and four had attended college. Several of the blacks elected to state offices were among the best-educated men of their day. For example, Jonathan Gibbs, secretary of state in Florida from 1868 to 1872 and state superintendent of education from 1872 to 1874, was a graduate of Dartmouth College and Princeton Theological Seminary.

It is true that some lower-level black officeholders, as well as their constituents, could not read or write, but the fault for that situation lay not with them but with the slave regime that had denied them an education. Illiteracy did not preclude an understanding of political issues for them any more than it did for Irish American voters in the North, some of whom also were illiterate. Participation in the Union League and the experience of voting were forms of education. Black churches and fraternal organizations proliferated during Reconstruction and tutored African Americans in their rights and responsibilities.

Linked to the myth of black incompetence was the legend of the "Africanization" of southern governments during Reconstruction. The theme of "Negro rule" was a staple of Democratic propaganda, but blacks in fact held only 15 to 20 percent of public offices, even at the height of Reconstruction in the early 1870s. There were no black governors and only one black state Supreme Court justice. Nowhere except in South Carolina did blacks hold office in numbers anywhere near their proportion of the population.

"Carpetbaggers"

Next to "Negro rule," carpetbagger corruption and scalawag rascality have been the prevailing myths of Reconstruction. Carpetbaggers did hold a disproportionate number of high political offices in southern state governments during Reconstruction. A few did resemble the proverbial adventurer who came south with nothing but a carpetbag in which to stow the loot plundered from a helpless people. But most were Union army officers who stayed on after the war as Freedmen's Bureau agents, teachers in black schools, or business investors. They hoped to rebuild Southern society in the image of the free-labor North. Many were college graduates. Most brought not empty carpetbags but considerable capital, which they invested in what they hoped would become a new South. But they underestimated the hostility of southern whites, most of whom regarded them as agents of an alien culture.

"Scalawags"

Most of the native-born whites who joined the southern Republican Party came from the upcountry Unionist areas of western North Carolina and Virginia and eastern Tennessee. Others were former Whigs. Republicans, said a North Carolina scalawag, were the "party of progress, of education, of development."

But Democrats saw that the southern Republican Party they abhorred was a fragile coalition of blacks and whites, Yankees and southerners, hill-country yeomen and lowcountry entrepreneurs, illiterates and college graduates. The party was weakest along the seams where these disparate elements joined, especially the racial seam. Democrats attacked that weakness with every weapon at their command, including violence.

The Ku Klux Klan

The generic name for the secret groups that terrorized the southern countryside was the Ku Klux Klan, but some went by other names (the Knights of the White Camelia in Louisiana, for example). Part of the Klan's purpose was social control of the black population. Sharecroppers who tried to extract better terms from landowners, or black people who were considered too "uppity," were likely to receive a midnight whipping—or worse—from white-sheeted Klansmen. Scores of black schools, perceived as a particular threat to white supremacy, went up in flames.

The Klan's main purpose was political: to destroy the Republican Party by terrorizing its voters and, if necessary, murdering its leaders. No one knows how many politically motivated killings took place—certainly hundreds, probably thousands. Nearly all the victims were Republicans; most of them were black. In one notorious incident, the Colfax Massacre in Louisiana (April 18, 1873), a clash between black militia and armed whites left three whites and nearly 100 blacks dead. In some places, notably Tennessee and Arkansas, Republican militias suppressed and disarmed the Klan, but in most areas the militias were outgunned and outmaneuvered by ex-Confederate veteran Klansmen. Some Republican governors were reluctant to use black militia against white guerrillas for fear of sparking a racial bloodbath, as happened at Colfax.

In 1870 and 1871, Congress responded to southern violence with three laws intended to enforce the Fourteenth and Fifteenth Amendments. Interference with voting rights became a federal offense, and any attempt to deprive another person of civil or political rights became a felony. The third law, passed on April 20, 1871, and popularly called the Ku Klux Klan Act, gave the president power to suspend the writ of **habeas corpus** and send in federal troops to suppress armed resistance to federal law.

Armed with these laws, the Grant administration moved against the Klan. Although Grant used his powers with restraint, suspending the writ of habeas corpus only in nine South Carolina counties, there and elsewhere federal marshals backed by troops arrested thousands of suspected Klansmen. Federal grand juries indicted more than 3,000, and several hundred defendants pleaded guilty in return for suspended sentences. About 600 Klansmen were convicted. Most of them received fines or light jail sentences, but 65 went to a federal penitentiary for terms of up to five years.

The Election of 1872

These measures broke the back of the Klan in time for the 1872 presidential election. A group of dissident Republicans had emerged to challenge Grant's reelection. They believed that conciliation of southern whites rather than continued military intervention was the only way to achieve peace in the South. Calling themselves Liberal Republicans, these dissidents nominated Horace Greeley, the famous editor of the *New York Tribune*. Under the slogan "Anything to beat Grant," the

---

QUICK REVIEW

ACHIEVEMENTS OF SOUTHERN RECONSTRUCTION

- Election of Republican state governments

- Suppression of Ku Klux Klan

- Creation of black schools, churches, communities

---

habeas corpus *Right of an individual to have the legality of his arrest and detention decided by a court.*

HISTORY THROUGH FILM

Birth of a Nation (1915)

Directed by D. W. Griffith; starring Lillian Gish (Elsie Stoneman), Henry B. Walthall (Ben Cameron), Ralph Lewis (Austin Stoneman), George Siegmann (Silas Lynch)

Few films have had such a pernicious impact on historical understanding and race relations as *Birth of a Nation.* This movie popularized a version of Reconstruction that portrayed predatory carpetbaggers and stupid, brutish blacks plundering a prostrate South and lusting after white women. It perpetuated vicious stereotypes of rapacious black males. It glorified the Ku Klux Klan of the Reconstruction era, inspiring the founding of the "second Klan" in 1915 that became a powerful force in the 1920s (see Chapter 24). The first half of the film offers a conventional Victorian romance of the Civil War. The children of the northerner Austin Stoneman (a malevolent Radical Republican who is a thinly disguised Thaddeus Stevens) become friends with the children of the Cameron family, from South Carolina. The Civil War tragically separates the families. The Stoneman and Cameron boys enlist in the Union and Confederate armies and—predictably—face each other on the battlefield. Two Camerons and one Stoneman are killed in the war, and Ben Cameron, badly wounded, is captured, to be nursed back to health by Elsie Stoneman.

After the war the younger Camerons and Stonemans renew their friendship. The Stonemans visit South Carolina,

and Ben Cameron and Elsie Stoneman, and Phil Stoneman and Flora Cameron, fall in love. If the story had stopped there, *Birth of a Nation* would have been just another Hollywood romance. But Austin Stoneman brings south with him Silas Lynch, an ambitious, leering mulatto demagogue who stirs up the animal passions of the ignorant black majority to demand "Equal Rights, Equal Politics, Equal Marriage." A "renegade Negro," Gus, stalks the youngest Cameron daughter, who saves herself from rape by jumping from a cliff to her death. Silas Lynch tries to force Elsie to marry him. "I will build a Black Empire," he tells the virginal Elsie (Lillian Gish, the Hollywood beauty queen of silent films), "and you as my queen shall rule by my side."

Finally provoked beyond endurance, white South Carolinians led by Ben Cameron organize the Ku Klux Klan to save "the Aryan race." Riding to the rescue of embattled whites in stirring scenes that anticipated the heroic actions of the cavalry against Indians in later Hollywood westerns, the Klan executes Gus, saves Elsie, disperses black soldiers and mobs, and carries the next election for white rule by intimidating black voters. The film ends with a double marriage that unites the Camerons and Stonemans in a symbolic rebirth of a nation, one rightfully based on the supremacy of "the Aryan race."

The son of a Confederate lieutenant colonel, David Wark (D. W.) Griffith was the foremost director of the silent movie era. *Birth of a Nation* was the first real full-length feature film, technically and artistically superior to anything before it. Apart from its place in the history of cinema, though, why should anyone today watch a movie that perpetuates such wrongheaded history and noxious racial stereotypes? Precisely *because* it reflects and amplifies an interpretation of Reconstruction that prevailed from the 1890s to the 1950s, and thereby shaped historical understanding as well as contemporary behavior—as in its inspiration for the Klan of the 1920s.

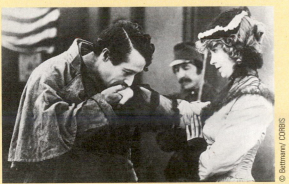

© Bettmann/ CORBIS

Colonel Ben Cameron (Henry B. Walthall) kissing the hand of Elsie Stoneman (Lillian Gish) in Birth of a Nation.

Democratic Party also endorsed Greeley's nomination. On a platform denouncing "bayonet rule" in the South, Greeley urged his fellow northerners to put the issues of the Civil War behind them.

Most voters in the North were still not prepared to trust Democrats or southern whites, however. Anti-Greeley cartoons by Thomas Nast showed Greeley shaking the hand of a Klansman dripping with the blood of a murdered black Republican. On Election Day Grant swamped Greeley. Republicans carried every northern state and 10 of the 16 southern and border states. But this apparent triumph of Republicanism and Reconstruction would soon unravel.

The Panic of 1873

The U.S. economy had grown at an unprecedented pace since recovering from a mild postwar recession. The first transcontinental railroad had been completed on May 10, 1869, at Promontory Summit, Utah Territory. But the building of a second transcontinental line, the Northern Pacific, precipitated a Wall Street panic in 1873 and plunged the economy into a five-year depression.

Jay Cooke's banking firm, fresh from its triumphant marketing of Union war bonds, took over the Northern Pacific in 1869. Cooke pyramided every conceivable kind of equity and loan financing to raise the money to begin laying rails west from Duluth, Minnesota. Other investment firms did the same as a fever of speculative financing gripped the country. In September 1873, the pyramid of paper collapsed. Cooke's firm was the first to go bankrupt. Like dominoes, hundreds of banks and businesses also collapsed. Unemployment rose to 14 percent, and hard times set in.

THE RETREAT FROM RECONSTRUCTION

FOCUS QUESTION

Why did a majority of the northern people and their political leaders turn against continued federal involvement in southern Reconstruction in the 1870s?

Democrats made large gains in the congressional elections of 1874, winning a majority in the House for the first time in 18 years. Public opinion also began to turn against Republican policies in the South. Intraparty battles among Republicans in southern states enabled Democrats to regain control of several state governments. Well-publicized corruption scandals also discredited Republican leaders. Although corruption was probably no worse in southern states than in many parts of the North, white Democrats scored propaganda points by claiming that corruption proved the incompetence of "Negro-carpetbag" regimes. Northerners grew increasingly weary of what seemed the endless turmoil of southern politics. Most of them had never had a very strong commitment to racial equality, and they were growing more and more willing to let white supremacy regain sway in the South.

By 1875 only four southern states remained under Republican control: South Carolina, Florida, Mississippi, and Louisiana. In those states, white Democrats had revived paramilitary organizations under various names: White Leagues (Louisiana); Rifle Clubs (Mississippi); and Red Shirts (South Carolina). Unlike the Klan, these groups operated openly. In Louisiana, they fought pitched battles with Republican militias in which scores were killed. When the Grant administration sent large numbers of federal troops to Louisiana, people in both the North and South cried out against military rule. The protests grew even louder when soldiers marched onto the floor of the Louisiana legislature in January 1875 and expelled several Democratic legislators after a contested election.

The Mississippi Election of 1875

The backlash against the Grant administration affected the Mississippi state election of 1875. Democrats there devised a strategy called the Mississippi Plan. The first step was to "persuade" the 10 to 15 percent of white voters still calling themselves Republicans to switch to the Democrats. Only a handful of carpetbaggers could resist the economic pressures, social ostracism, and threats.

The second step in the Mississippi Plan was to intimidate black voters, because even with all whites voting Democratic, the party could still be defeated by the 55 percent black majority. Economic coercion against black sharecroppers and workers kept some of them away from the polls, but violence was the most effective method. Democratic "rifle clubs" showed up at Republican rallies, provoked riots, and shot down dozens of blacks in the ensuing melees. Governor Adelbert Ames, a former Union general, called for federal troops to control the violence. Grant intended to comply, but Ohio Republicans warned him that if he sent troops to Mississippi, the Democrats would exploit the issue of bayonet rule to carry Ohio in that year's state elections. Grant yielded—in effect giving up for Ohio.

© Bettmann/ CORBIS

"The negroes of the South are free—free as air," says the parliamentary Watterson. This is what the *State*, a well-known Democratic organ of Tennessee, says, in huge capitals, on the subject: "Let it be known before the election that the farmers have agreed to spot every leading Radical negro in the county, and treat him as an enemy for all time to come. The rotten ring must and shall be broken at any and all costs. The Democrats have determined to withdraw all employment from their enemies. Let this fact be known."

"OF COURSE HE WANTS TO VOTE THE DEMOCRATIC TICKET!"
DEMOCRATIC "REFORMER." "You're as free as air, ain't you? Say you are, or I'll blow yer black head off!"

HOW THE MISSISSIPPI PLAN WORKED. *This cartoon shows how black counties could report large Democratic majorities in the Mississippi state election of 1875. The black voter holds a Democratic ticket while one of the men, described in the caption as a "Democratic reformer," holds a revolver to his head and says: "You're as free as air, ain't you? Say you are, or I'll blow your black head off!"*

LINK TO THE PAST

Frederick Douglass on the Supreme Court and Civil Rights

The Civil Rights Act of 1875 anticipated many of the provisions of the Civil Rights Act of 1964, which is the law of the land and has been upheld by the U.S. Supreme Court. But the law of 1875 was ahead of its time, or at least ahead of the Supreme Court of its time, which declared it unconstitutional on the grounds that the Fourteenth Amendment prohibited discrimination by states but not by individuals. The black civil rights leader Frederick Douglass denounced the Court's decision in language that anticipated the Supreme Court's reasoning in the last third of the 20th century.

This decision of the Supreme Court admits that the Fourteenth Amendment is a prohibition of the States. It admits that a State shall not abridge the privileges or immunities of citizens of the United States, but commits the seeming absurdity of allowing the people of a State to do what it prohibits the State itself from doing. . . . It is said that this decision will make no difference in the treatment of colored people; that the Civil Rights Bill

was a dead letter, and could not be enforced. There is some truth in all this, but it is not the whole truth.

That bill, like all advance legislation, was a banner on the outer wall of American liberty, a noble moral standard, uplifted for the education of the American people. . . .

This law, though dead, did speak. It expressed the sentiment of justice and fair play. . . . If it is a bill for social equality, so is the Declaration of Independence, which declares that all men have equal rights; so is the Sermon on the Mount, so is the Golden Rule . . . so is the Constitution of the United States.

FREDERICK DOUGLASS

From a speech in Washington, D.C., October 22, 1883

Q What is Douglass's response to the argument that the Civil Rights Act was a dead letter even before the Supreme Court declared it so?

The Mississippi Plan worked. In five of the state's counties with large black majorities, the Republicans polled 12, 7, 4, 2, and 0 votes, respectively. What had been a Republican majority of 30,000 in 1874 became a Democratic majority of 30,000 in 1875.

The Supreme Court and Reconstruction

Even if Grant had been willing to continue intervening in southern state elections, Congress and the courts would have constricted such efforts. The new Democratic majority in the House threatened to cut any appropriations intended for use in the South. In 1876, the Supreme Court handed down two decisions that declared parts of the 1870 and 1871 laws for enforcement of the Fourteenth and Fifteenth Amendments unconstitutional. In *U.S. v. Cruikshank* and *U.S. v. Reese,* the Court ruled that the Fourteenth and Fifteenth Amendments applied to actions by *states.* Therefore, the portions of these laws that empowered the federal government to prosecute *individuals* were unconstitutional. The Court did not say what could be done when states were controlled by white-supremacy Democrats who had no intention of enforcing equal rights.

Meanwhile, in the *Civil Rights Cases* (1883), the Court declared unconstitutional a civil rights law passed by Congress in 1875. That law banned racial discrimination in all forms of public transportation and public accommodations. If enforced, it would have effected a sweeping transformation of race relations—in the North as well as in the South. But even some of the congressmen who voted for the bill doubted its constitutionality, and the Justice Department had made little effort to enforce it. Several cases made their way to the Supreme Court, which in 1883 ruled the law unconstitutional—again on grounds that the Fourteenth Amendment applied only to states, not to individuals.

The Election of 1876

The mounting revelations of corruption at all levels of government ensured that reform would be the leading issue in the presidential election of 1876. Both major parties gave their presidential nominations to governors who had earned reform reputations in their states: Democrat Samuel J. Tilden of New York and Republican Rutherford B. Hayes of Ohio.

Democrats entered the campaign as favorites for the first time in two decades. It seemed likely that they could assemble an electoral majority from a "solid South" plus New York and two or three other northern states. To ensure a solid South, they looked to the lessons of the Mississippi Plan. In 1876, a new word came into use to describe Democratic techniques of intimidation: **bulldozing.** To bulldoze black voters meant to trample them down or keep them away from the polls. White vigilantes mobilized for an all-out bulldozing effort.

The most notorious incident, the Hamburg Massacre, occurred in the village of Hamburg, South Carolina, where a battle between a black militia unit and 200 Red Shirts resulted in the capture of several militiamen, five of whom were shot "while attempting to escape." This time Grant did send in federal troops. The federal government also put several thousand deputy marshals and election supervisors on duty in the South. Although they kept an uneasy peace at the polls, they could do little to prevent assaults, threats, and economic coercion in backcountry districts, which reduced the potential Republican tally in the former Confederate states by at least 250,000 votes.

Disputed Results

When the results were in, Tilden had carried four northern states, including New York with its 35 electoral votes, and all the former slave states except—apparently—Louisiana, South Carolina, and Florida, which produced disputed returns. Because Tilden needed only one of them to win the presidency, while Hayes needed all three, and because Tilden seemed to have carried Louisiana and Florida, it appeared initially that he had won the presidency. But fraud and irregularities reported from several bulldozed districts in the three states clouded the issue. For example, a Louisiana parish that had recorded 1,688 Republican votes in 1874 reported only 1 in 1876. The official returns ultimately sent to Washington gave all three states—and therefore the presidency—to Hayes, but the Democrats refused to recognize the results, and they controlled the House.

The country faced a serious constitutional crisis, and many people feared another civil war. The Constitution offered no clear guidance on how to deal with the matter. Congress created a special electoral commission consisting of five representatives, five senators, and five Supreme Court justices split evenly between the two parties, with one member, a Supreme Court justice, supposedly an independent—but in fact a Republican.

Tilden had won a national majority of 252,000 popular votes, and the raw returns gave him a majority in the three disputed states. But an estimated 250,000 southern Republicans had been bulldozed away from the polls. In a genuinely fair and free election, the Republicans might have carried Mississippi and North Carolina as well as the three disputed states.

The Compromise of 1877

In February 1877, three months after voters had gone to the polls, the electoral commission issued its ruling. By a partisan vote of 8 to 7—with the "independent" justice voting with the Republicans—it awarded all the disputed states to Hayes.

bulldozing *Using force to keep African Americans from voting.*

The Democrats cried foul and began a **filibuster** in the House to delay the final electoral count beyond the inauguration date of March 4. But, behind the scenes, a compromise began to take shape. Hayes promised his support as president for federal appropriations to rebuild war-destroyed levees on the lower Mississippi and federal aid for a southern transcontinental railroad. Hayes's lieutenants also hinted at the appointment of a southerner as postmaster general, who would have a considerable amount of patronage at his disposal. Most important, Hayes signaled his intention to end "bayonet rule." He believed that the goodwill and influence of southern moderates would offer better protection for black rights than federal troops could provide. In return for his commitment to withdraw the troops, Hayes asked for—and received—promises of fair treatment of freedpeople and respect for their constitutional rights.

The End of Reconstruction

Such promises were easier to make than to keep, as future years would reveal. In any case, the Democratic filibuster collapsed and Hayes was inaugurated on March 4. He soon fulfilled his part of the Compromise of 1877: Ex-Confederate Democrat David Key of Tennessee became postmaster general; in 1878, the South received more federal money for internal improvements than ever before; and federal troops left the capitals of Louisiana and South Carolina. The last two Republican state governments collapsed. Any remaining voices of protest could scarcely be heard above the sighs of relief that the crisis was over.

Conclusion

Before the Civil War, most Americans had viewed a powerful government as a threat to individual liberties. That is why the Bill of Rights imposed strict limits on the powers of the federal government. During the war and especially during Reconstruction, however, the national government had to exert an unprecedented amount of power to free the slaves and guarantee their equal rights as free citizens. That is why the Thirteenth, Fourteenth, and Fifteenth Amendments to the Constitution contained clauses stating that "Congress shall have power" to enforce these provisions for liberty and equal rights.

During the post–Civil War decade, Congress passed civil rights laws and enforcement legislation to accomplish this purpose. Federal marshals and troops patrolled the polls to protect black voters, arrested thousands of Klansmen, and even occupied state capitals to prevent Democratic paramilitary groups from overthrowing legitimately elected Republican state governments. But by 1875, many northerners had grown tired of or alarmed by this continued use of military power to intervene in the internal affairs of states. And the Supreme Court stripped the federal government of much of its authority to enforce certain provisions of the Fourteenth and Fifteenth Amendments.

The withdrawal of federal troops from the South in 1877 constituted both a symbolic and a substantive end of the era known as Reconstruction. Reconstruction had achieved the two great objectives inherited from the Civil War: to reincorporate the former Confederate states into the Union, and to accomplish a transition from slavery to freedom in the South. That transition was marred by the economic inequity of sharecropping and the social injustice of white supremacy. And a third goal of Reconstruction, enforcement of the equal civil and political rights promised in the Fourteenth and Fifteenth Amendments, was betrayed by the Compromise of 1877. In subsequent decades the freed slaves and their descendants suffered repression into segregated second-class citizenship.

filibuster *Congressional delaying tactic involving lengthy speeches that prevent legislation from being enacted.*

CHAPTER REVIEW

Review Questions

1. What were the positions of Presidents Abraham Lincoln and Andrew Johnson and of moderate and radical Republicans in Congress on the issues of restoring the South to the Union and protecting the rights of freed slaves?

2. Why was Andrew Johnson impeached? Why was he acquitted?

3. What were the achievements of Reconstruction? What were its failures?

4. Why did a majority of the northern people and their political leaders turn against continued federal involvement in southern Reconstruction in the 1870s?

Critical Thinking Questions

1. The two main goals of Reconstruction were to bring the former Confederate states back into the Union and to ensure the equal citizenship and rights of the former slaves. Why was the first goal more successfully achieved than the second?

2. Why have "carpetbaggers" and "scalawags" had such a bad historical image? Did they deserve it?

Identifications

Review your understanding of the following key terms, people, and events for this chapter.

amnesty, p. 386
Black Codes, p. 389
Freedmen's Bureau, p. 389
share wages, p. 390
sharecropping, p. 390

40 acres and a mule, p. 390
Union Leagues, p. 393
scalawags, p. 393
carpetbaggers, p. 393
impeach, p. 393

universal male suffrage, p. 394
Ku Klux Klan, p. 394
Ulysses S. Grant, p. 395
Credit Mobilier, p. 395

spoils system, p. 396
habeas corpus, p. 398
bulldozing, p. 403
filibuster, p. 404

DISCOVERY

Evaluate the success with which African Americans were integrated into American society during Reconstruction.

In thinking about this question, begin by breaking it down into the components shown below. A discussion of the significance of each component should appear in your answer.

Culture and Society

From your reading in this chapter and your examination of the illustrations shown here, what observations can you make about the role of violence and/or intimidation in suppressing Republican votes across the South in the 1870s? In the cartoon on the Mississippi Plan, how are the two gun-toting southern whites portrayed? Does this scene appear to represent a spontaneous, isolated incident or a systematic effort to influence votes? What is common between the two images?

© CORBIS

TWO MEMBERS OF THE KU KLUX KLAN

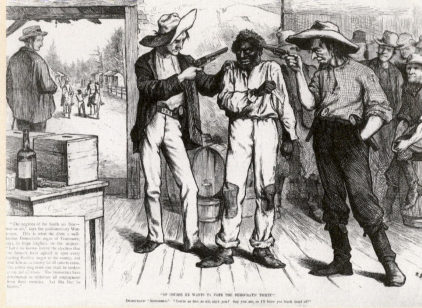

© Bettmann/ CORBIS

HOW THE MISSISSIPPI PLAN WORKED

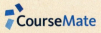

Visit the CourseMate website at www.cengagebrain.com for additional study tools and review materials for this chapter.

THE DECLARATION OF INDEPENDENCE

The Unanimous Declaration of the Thirteen United States of America

When in the Course of human events it becomes necessary for one people to dissolve the political bands which have connected them with another, and to assume among the Powers of the earth, the separate and equal station to which the Laws of Nature and of Nature's God entitle them, a decent respect to the opinions of mankind requires that they should declare the causes which impel them to the separation.

We hold these truths to be self-evident, that all men are created equal, that they are endowed by their Creator with certain unalienable Rights, that among these are Life, Liberty and the pursuit of Happiness. That to secure these rights, Governments are instituted among Men, deriving their just Powers from the consent of the governed. That whenever any Form of Government becomes destructive of these ends, it is the Right of the People to alter or to abolish it, and to institute new Government, laying its foundation on such principles and organizing its Powers in such form, as to them shall seem most likely to effect their Safety and Happiness. Prudence, indeed, will dictate that Governments long established should not be changed for light and transient causes; and accordingly all experience hath shewn, that mankind are more disposed to suffer, while evils are sufferable, than to right themselves by abolishing the forms to which they are accustomed. But when a long train of abuses and usurpations, pursuing invariably the same Object evinces a design to reduce them under absolute Despotism, it is their right, it is their duty, to throw off such Government, and to provide new Guards for their future security. Such has been the patient sufferance of these Colonies; and such is now the necessity which constrains them to alter their former Systems of Government. The history of the present King of Great Britain is a history of repeated injuries and usurpations, all having in direct object the establishment of an absolute Tyranny over these States. To prove this, let Facts be submitted to a candid world.

He has refused his Assent to Laws, the most wholesome and necessary for the public good.

He has forbidden his Governors to pass Laws of immediate and pressing importance, unless suspended in their operation till his Assent should be obtained; and when so suspended, he has utterly neglected to attend to them.

He has refused to pass other Laws for the accommodation of large districts of people, unless those people would relinquish the right of Representation in the Legislature, a right inestimable to them and formidable to tyrants only.

He has called together legislative bodies at places unusual, uncomfortable, and distant from the depository of their Public Records, for the sole Purpose of fatiguing them into compliance with his measures.

He has dissolved Representative Houses repeatedly, for opposing with manly firmness his invasions on the rights of the People.

He has refused for a long time, after such dissolutions, to cause others to be elected; whereby the Legislative Powers, incapable of Annihilation, have returned to the People at large for their exercise; the State remaining in the mean time exposed to all the dangers of invasion from without, and convulsions within.

He has endeavoured to prevent the Population of these States; for that purpose obstructing the Laws for Naturalization of Foreigners; refusing to pass others to encourage their migrations hither, and raising the conditions of new Appropriations of Lands.

He has obstructed the Administration of Justice, by refusing his Assent to Laws for establishing Judiciary Powers.

He has made Judges dependent on his Will alone, for the tenure of their offices, and the amount and payment of their salaries.

He has erected a multitude of New Offices, and sent hither swarms of Officers to harass our People, and eat out their substance.

He has kept among us, in times of peace, Standing Armies without the Consent of our legislatures.

He has affected to render the Military independent of and superior to the Civil Power.

He has combined with others to subject us to a jurisdiction foreign to our constitution, and unacknowledged by our laws; giving his Assent to their Acts of pretended Legislation: For Quartering large bodies of armed troops among us: For protecting them, by a mock Trial, from Punishment for any Murders which they should commit on the Inhabitants of these States: For cutting off our Trade with all parts of the world: For imposing Taxes on us without our Consent: For depriving us in many cases, of the benefits of Trial by Jury: For transporting us beyond Seas to be tried for pretended offences: For abolishing the free System of English Laws in a neighbouring Province, establishing therein an Arbitrary government, and enlarging its Boundaries so as to render it at once an example and fit instrument for introducing the same absolute rule into these Colonies: For taking away our Charters, abolishing our most valuable Laws, and altering fundamentally the Forms

Text is reprinted from the facsimile of the engrossed copy in the National Archives. The original spelling, capitalization, and punctuation have been retained. Paragraphing has been added.

of our Governments: For suspending our own Legislatures, and declaring themselves invested with Power to legislate for us in all cases whatsoever.

He has abdicated Government here, by declaring us out of his Protection, and waging War against us.

He has plundered our seas, ravaged our Coasts, burnt our towns, and destroyed the lives of our people.

He is at this time transporting large Armies of foreign Mercenaries to compleat the works of death, desolation and tyranny, already begun with circumstances of Cruelty and perfidy scarcely paralleled in the most barbarous ages, and totally unworthy the Head of a civilized nation.

He has constrained our fellow Citizens taken Captive on the high Seas to bear Arms against their Country, to become the executioners of their friends and Brethren, or to fall themselves by their Hands.

He has excited domestic insurrections amongst us, and has endeavoured to bring on the inhabitants of our frontiers, the merciless Indian Savages, whose known rule of warfare, is an undistinguished destruction of all ages, sexes and conditions.

In every stage of these Oppressions We have Petitioned for Redress in the most humble terms: Our repeated Petitions have been answered only by repeated injury. A Prince, whose character is thus marked by every act which may define a Tyrant, is unfit to be the ruler of a free People.

Nor have We been wanting in attentions to our British brethren. We have warned them from time to time of attempts by their legislature to extend an unwarrantable jurisdiction over us. We have reminded them of the circumstances of our emigration and settlement here. We have appealed to their native justice and magnanimity, and we have conjured them by the ties of our common kindred to disavow these usurpations, which, would inevitably interrupt our connections and correspondence. They too have been deaf to the voice of justice and of consanguinity. We must, therefore, acquiesce in the necessity, which denounces our Separation, and hold them, as we hold the rest of mankind, Enemies in War, in Peace Friends.

We, therefore, the Representatives of the United States of America, in General Congress, Assembled, appealing to the Supreme Judge of the world for the rectitude of our intentions, do, in the Name, and by Authority of the good People of these Colonies, solemnly publish and declare, That these United Colonies are, and of Right ought to be Free and Independent States; that they are Absolved from all Allegiance to the British Crown, and that all political connection between them and the State of Great Britain, is and ought to be totally dissolved; and that, as Free and Independent States, they have full Power to levy War, conclude Peace, contract Alliances, establish Commerce, and to do all other Acts and Things which Independent States may of right do. And for the support of this Declaration, with a firm reliance on the protection of divine Providence, we mutually pledge to each other our Lives, our Fortunes and our sacred Honor.

THE CONSTITUTION OF THE UNITED STATES OF AMERICA

We the People of the United States, in Order to form a more perfect Union, establish Justice, insure domestic Tranquility, provide for the common defence, promote the general Welfare, and secure the Blessings of Liberty to ourselves and our Posterity, do ordain and establish this Constitution for the United States of America.

Article I.

SECTION 1. All legislative Powers herein granted shall be vested in a Congress of the United States, which shall consist of a Senate and House of Representatives.

SECTION 2. The House of Representatives shall be composed of Members chosen every second Year by the People of the several States, and the Electors in each State shall have the Qualifications requisite for Electors of the most numerous Branch of the State Legislature.

No Person shall be a Representative who shall not have attained to the Age of twenty five Years, and been seven Years a Citizen of the United States, and who shall not, when elected, be an Inhabitant of that State in which he shall be chosen.

Representatives and direct Taxes[1] shall be apportioned among the several States which may be included within this Union, according to their respective Numbers, which shall be determined by adding to the whole Number of free Persons, including those bound to Service for a Term of Years, and excluding Indians not taxed, three fifths of all other Persons.[2]

The actual Enumeration shall be made within three Years after the first Meeting of the Congress of the United States, and within every subsequent Term of ten Years, in such Manner as they shall by Law direct. The Number of Representatives shall not exceed one for every thirty Thousand, but each State shall have at Least one Representative; and until such enumeration shall be made, the State of New Hampshire shall be entitled to chuse three; Massachusetts eight; Rhode Island and Providence Plantations one; Connecticut five; New York six; New Jersey four; Pennsylvania eight; Delaware one; Maryland six; Virginia ten; North Carolina five; South Carolina five; and Georgia three.

When vacancies happen in the Representation from any State, the Executive Authority thereof shall issue Writs of Election to fill such Vacancies.

The House of Representatives shall chuse their Speaker and other Officers; and shall have the sole Power of Impeachment.

SECTION 3. The Senate of the United States shall be composed of two Senators from each State, chosen by the Legislature thereof, for six Years; and each Senator shall have one Vote.[3]

Immediately after they shall be assembled in Consequence of the first Election, they shall be divided as equally as may be into three Classes. The Seats of the Senators of the first Class shall be vacated at the Expiration of the second Year, of the second Class at the Expiration of the fourth Year, and of the third Class at the Expiration of the sixth Year, so that one third may be chosen every second Year; and if Vacancies happen by Resignation, or otherwise, during the Recess of the Legislature of any State, the Executive thereof may make temporary Appointments until the next Meeting of the Legislature, which shall then fill such Vacancies.[4]

No Person shall be a Senator who shall not have attained to the Age of thirty Years, and been nine Years a Citizen of the United States, and who shall not, when elected, be an Inhabitant of that State for which he shall be chosen.

The Vice President of the United States shall be President of the Senate, but shall have no Vote, unless they be equally divided.

The Senate shall chuse their other Officers, and also a President pro tempore, in the Absence of the Vice President, or when he shall exercise the Office of President of the United States.

The Senate shall have the sole Power to try all Impeachments. When sitting for that Purpose, they shall be on Oath or Affirmation. When the President of the United States is tried, the Chief Justice shall preside: And no Person shall be convicted without the Concurrence of two thirds of the Members present.

Judgment in Cases of Impeachment shall not extend further than to removal from Office, and disqualification to hold and enjoy any Office of honor, Trust or Profit under the United States: but the Party convicted shall nevertheless be liable and subject to Indictment, Trial, Judgment and Punishment, according to Law.

SECTION 4. The Times, Places and Manner of holding Elections for Senators and Representatives, shall be prescribed in each State by the Legislature thereof, but the Congress may at any time by Law make or alter such Regulation, except as to the Places of chusing Senators.

The Congress shall assemble at least once in every Year, and such Meeting shall be on the first Monday in December, unless they shall by Law appoint a different Day.[5]

SECTION 5. Each House shall be the Judge of the Elections, Returns and Qualifications of its own Members, and a Majority of each shall constitute a Quorum to do Business; but a smaller Number may adjourn from day to day, and may be

---

Text is from the engrossed copy in the National Archives. Original spelling, capitalization, and punctuation have been retained.

[1]Modified by the Sixteenth Amendment.

[2]Replaced by the Fourteenth Amendment.

[3]Superseded by the Seventeenth Amendment.

[4]Modified by the Seventeenth Amendment.

[5]Superseded by the Twentieth Amendment.

authorized to compel the Attendance of absent Members, in such Manner, and under such Penalties as each House may provide.

Each House may determine the Rules of its Proceedings, punish its Members for disorderly Behaviour, and, with the Concurrence of two thirds, expel a Member.

Each House shall keep a Journal of its Proceedings, and from time to time publish the same, excepting such Parts as may in their Judgment require Secrecy; and the Yeas and Nays of the Members of either House on any question shall, at the Desire of one fifth of those Present, be entered on the Journal.

Neither House, during the Session of Congress, shall, without the Consent of the other, adjourn for more than three days, nor to any other Place than that in which the two Houses shall be sitting.

SECTION 6. The Senators and Representatives shall receive a Compensation for their Services, to be ascertained by Law, and paid out of the Treasury of the United States. They shall in all Cases, except Treason, Felony and Breach of the Peace, be privileged from Arrest during their Attendance at the Session of their respective Houses, and in going to and returning from the same; and for any Speech or Debate in either House, they shall not be questioned in any other Place.

No Senator or Representative shall, during the Time for which he was elected, be appointed to any civil Office under the Authority of the United States, which shall have been created, or the Emoluments whereof shall have been encreased during such time; and no Person holding any Office under the United States, shall be a Member of either House during his Continuance in Office.

SECTION 7. All Bills for raising Revenue shall originate in the House of Representatives; but the Senate may propose or concur with Amendments as on other Bills.

Every Bill which shall have passed the House of Representatives and the Senate shall, before it become a Law, be presented to the President of the United States; If he approve he shall sign it, but if not he shall return it, with his Objections to that House in which it shall have originated, who shall enter the Objections at large on their Journal, and proceed to reconsider it. If after such Reconsideration two thirds of that House shall agree to pass the Bill, it shall be sent, together with the Objections, to the other House, by which it shall likewise be reconsidered, and if approved by two thirds of that House, it shall become a Law. But in all such Cases the Votes of both Houses shall be determined by yeas and Nays, and the Names of the Persons voting for and against the Bill shall be entered on the Journal of each House respectively. If any Bill shall not be returned by the President within ten Days (Sundays excepted) after it shall have been presented to him, the Same shall be a Law, in like Manner as if he had signed it, unless the Congress by their Adjournment prevent its Return, in which Case it shall not be a Law.

Every Order, Resolution, or Vote to which the Concurrence of the Senate and House of Representatives may be necessary (except on a question of Adjournment) shall be presented to the President of the United States; and before the Same shall take Effect, shall be approved by him, or being disapproved by him shall be repassed by two thirds of the Senate and House of Representatives, according to the Rules and Limitations prescribed in the Case of a Bill.

SECTION 8. The Congress shall have power To lay and collect Taxes, Duties, Imposts and Excises, to pay the Debts and provide for the common Defence and general Welfare of the United States; but all Duties, Imposts and Excises shall be uniform throughout the United States; To borrow Money on the credit of the United States; To regulate Commerce with foreign Nations, and among the several States, and with the Indian Tribes; To establish an uniform Rule of Naturalization, and uniform Laws on the subject of Bankruptcies throughout the United States; To coin Money, regulate the Value thereof, and of foreign Coin, and fix the Standard of Weights and Measures; To provide for the Punishment of counterfeiting the Securities and current Coin of the United States; To establish Post Offices and post Roads; To promote the Progress of Science and useful Arts, by securing for limited Times to Authors and Inventors the exclusive Right to their respective Writings and Discoveries; To constitute Tribunals inferior to the supreme Court; To define and punish Piracies and Felonies committed on the high Seas, and Offences against the Law of Nations;

To declare War, grant Letters of Marque and Reprisal, and make Rules concerning Captures on Land and Water; To raise and support Armies, but no Appropriation of Money to that Use shall be for a longer Term than two Years; To provide and maintain a Navy; To make Rules for the Government and Regulation of the land and naval Forces; To provide for calling forth the Militia to execute the Laws of the Union, suppress Insurrections and repel Invasions; To provide for organizing, arming, and disciplining, the Militia, and for governing such Part of them as may be employed in the Service of the United States, reserving to the States respectively, the Appointment of the Officers, and the Authority of training the Militia according to the discipline prescribed by Congress; To exercise exclusive Legislation in all Cases whatsoever, over such District (not exceeding ten Miles square) as may, by Cession of particular States, and the Acceptance of Congress, become the Seat of the Government of the United States, and to exercise like Authority over all Places purchased by the Consent of the Legislature of the State in which the Same shall be, for the Erection of Forts, Magazines, Arsenals, dock-Yards, and other needful Buildings;—And To make all Laws which shall be necessary and proper for carrying into Execution the foregoing Powers, and all other Powers vested by this Constitution in the Government of the United States, or in any Department or Officer thereof.

SECTION 9. The Migration or Importation of such Persons as any of the States now existing shall think proper to admit, shall not be prohibited by the Congress prior to the Year one thousand eight hundred and eight, but a Tax or duty may be imposed on such Importation, not exceeding ten dollars for each Person.

The Privilege of the Writ of Habeas Corpus shall not be suspended, unless when in Cases of Rebellion or Invasion the public Safety may require it.

No Bill of Attainder or ex post facto Law shall be passed.

No Capitation, or other direct, Tax shall be laid, unless in Proportion to the Census or Enumeration herein before directed to be taken.

No Tax or Duty shall be laid on Articles exported from any State.

No Preference shall be given by any Regulation of Commerce or Revenue to the Ports of one State over those of another: nor shall Vessels bound to, or from, one State, be obliged to enter, clear, or pay Duties in another.

No Money shall be drawn from the Treasury, but in Consequence of Appropriations made by Law, and a regular Statement and Account of the Receipts and Expenditures of all public Money shall be published from time to time.

No Title of Nobility shall be granted by the United States: And no Person holding any Office of Profit or Trust under them, shall, without the Consent of the Congress, accept of any present, Emolument, Office, or Title, of any kind whatever, from any King, Prince, or foreign State.

SECTION 10. No State shall enter into any Treaty, Alliance, or Confederation; grant Letters of Marque and Reprisal; coin Money; emit Bills of Credit; make any Thing but gold and silver Coin a Tender in Payment of Debts; pass any Bill of Attainder, ex post facto Law, or Law impairing the Obligation of Contracts, or grant any Title of Nobility.

No State shall, without the Consent of the Congress, lay any Imposts or Duties on Imports or Exports, except what may be absolutely necessary for executing its inspection Laws: and the net Produce of all Duties and Imposts, laid by any State on Imports or Exports, shall be for the Use of the Treasury of the United States; and all such Laws shall be subject to the Revision and Controul of the Congress.

No State shall, without the Consent of Congress, lay any Duty of Tonnage, keep Troops, or Ships of War in time of Peace, enter into any Agreement or Compact with another State, or with a foreign Power, or engage in War, unless actually invaded, or in such imminent Danger as will not admit of delay.

Article II.

SECTION 1. The executive Power shall be vested in a President of the United States of America. He shall hold his Office during the Term of four Years, and, together with the Vice President, chosen for the same Term, be elected, as follows: Each State shall appoint, in such Manner as the Legislature thereof may direct, a Number of Electors, equal to the whole Number of Senators and Representatives to which the State may be entitled in the Congress: but no Senator or Representative, or Person holding an Office of Trust or Profit under the United States, shall be appointed an Elector.

The Electors shall meet in their respective States, and vote by Ballot for two Persons, of whom one at least shall not be an Inhabitant of the same State with themselves. And they shall make a List of all the Persons voted for, and of the Number of Votes for each; which List they shall sign and certify, and transmit sealed to the Seat of the Government of the United States, directed to the President of the Senate. The President of the Senate shall, in the Presence of the Senate and House of Representatives, open all the Certificates, and the Votes shall then be counted. The Person having the greatest Number of Votes shall be the President, if such Number be a Majority of the whole Number of Electors appointed;

and if there be more than one who have such Majority, and have an equal Number of Votes, then the House of Representatives shall immediately chuse by Ballot one of them for President; and if no Person have a Majority, then from the five highest on the List the said House shall in like Manner chuse the President. But in chusing the President, the Votes shall be taken by States, the Representation from each State having one Vote; A quorum for this Purpose shall consist of a Member or Members from two thirds of the States, and a Majority of all the States shall be necessary to a Choice. In every Case, after the Choice of the President, the Person having the greatest Number of Votes of the Electors shall be the Vice President. But if there should remain two or more who have equal Votes, the Senate shall chuse from them by Ballot the Vice President.[6]

The Congress may determine the Time of chusing the Electors, and the Day on which they shall give their Votes; which Day shall be the same throughout the United States.

No Person except a natural born Citizen, or a Citizen of the United States, at the time of the Adoption of this Constitution, shall be eligible to the Office of President, neither shall any Person be eligible to that Office who shall not have attained to the Age of thirty five Years, and been fourteen Years a Resident within the United States.

In Case of the Removal of the President from Office, or of his Death, Resignation, or Inability to discharge the Powers and Duties of the said Office, the Same shall devolve on the Vice President, and the Congress may by Law provide for the Case of Removal, Death, Resignation or Inability, both of the President and Vice President, declaring what Officer shall then act as President, and such Officer shall act accordingly, until the Disability be removed, or a President shall be elected.[7]

The President shall, at stated Times, receive for his Services, a Compensation, which shall neither be increased nor diminished during the Period for which he shall have been elected, and he shall not receive within that Period any other Emolument from the United States, or any of them.

Before he enter on the Execution of his Office, he shall take the following Oath or Affirmation:—"I do solemnly swear (or affirm) that I will faithfully execute the Office of President of the United States, and will to the best of my Ability, preserve, protect and defend the Constitution of the United States."

SECTION 2. The President shall be Commander in Chief of the Army and Navy of the United States, and of the Militia of the several States, when called into the actual Service of the United States; he may require the Opinion, in writing, of the principal Officer in each of the executive Departments, upon any Subject relating to the Duties of their respective Offices, and he shall have Power to grant Reprieves and Pardons for Offences against the United States, except in Cases of Impeachment.

He shall have Power, by and with the Advice and Consent of the Senate, to make Treaties, provided two thirds of the Senators present concur; and he shall nominate, and by and with the Advice and Consent of the Senate, shall appoint Ambassadors, other public Ministers and Consuls, Judges of

[6]Superseded by the Twelfth Amendment.
[7]Modified by the Twenty-fifth Amendment.

the supreme Court, and all other Officers of the United States, whose Appointments are not herein otherwise provided for, and which shall be established by Law; but the Congress may by Law vest the Appointment of such inferior Officers, as they think proper, in the President alone, in the Courts of Law, or in the Heads of Departments.

The President shall have Power to fill up all Vacancies that may happen during the Recess of the Senate, by granting Commissions which shall expire at the End of their next Session.

SECTION 3. He shall from time to time give the Congress Information of the State of the Union, and recommend to their Consideration such Measures as he shall judge necessary and expedient; he may, on extraordinary Occasions, convene both Houses, or either of them, and in Case of Disagreement between them, with Respect to the Time of Adjournment, he may adjourn them to such Time as he shall think proper; he shall receive Ambassadors and other public Ministers; he shall take Care that the Laws be faithfully executed, and shall Commission all the Officers of the United States.

SECTION 4. The President, Vice President and all civil Officers of the United States, shall be removed from Office on Impeachment for, and Conviction of, Treason, Bribery, or other high Crimes and Misdemeanors.

Article III.

SECTION 1. The judicial Power of the United States, shall be vested in one supreme Court, and in such inferior Courts as the Congress may from time to time ordain and establish.

The Judges, both of the supreme and inferior Courts, shall hold their Offices during good Behaviour, and shall, at stated Times, receive for their Services, a Compensation, which shall not be diminished during their Continuance in Office.

SECTION 2. The judicial Power shall extend to all Cases, in Law and Equity, arising under this Constitution, the Laws of the United States, and Treaties made, or which shall be made, under their Authority;—to all Cases affecting Ambassadors, other public Ministers and Consuls;—to all Cases of admiralty and maritime Jurisdiction;—to Controversies to which the United States shall be a Party;—to Controversies between two or more States;—between a State and Citizens of another State;[8]—between Citizens of different States,—between Citizens of the same State claiming Lands under Grants of different States, and between a State, or the Citizens thereof, and foreign States, Citizens or Subjects.

In all Cases affecting Ambassadors, other public Ministers and Consuls, and those in which a State shall be Party, the supreme Court shall have original Jurisdiction. In all the other Cases before mentioned, the supreme Court shall have appellate Jurisdiction, both as to Law and Fact, with such Exceptions, and under such Regulations as the Congress shall make.

The Trial of all Crimes, except in Cases of Impeachment, shall be by Jury; and such Trial shall be held in the State where the said Crimes shall have been committed; but when not committed within any State, the Trial shall be at such Place or Places as the Congress may by Law have directed.

SECTION 3. Treason against the United States, shall consist only in levying War against them, or in adhering to their Enemies, giving them Aid and Comfort. No Person shall be convicted of Treason unless on the Testimony of two Witnesses to the same overt Act, or on Confession in open Court.

The Congress shall have Power to declare the Punishment of Treason, but no Attainder of Treason shall work Corruption of Blood, or Forfeiture except during the Life of the Person attainted.

Article IV.

SECTION 1. Full Faith and Credit shall be given in each State to the public Acts, Records, and judicial Proceedings of every other State. And the Congress may by general Laws prescribe the Manner in which such Acts, Records and Proceedings shall be proved, and the Effect thereof.

SECTION 2. The Citizens of each State shall be entitled to all Privileges and Immunities of Citizens in the several States.

A Person charged in any State with Treason, Felony, or other Crime, who shall flee from Justice, and be found in another State, shall on Demand of the executive Authority of the State from which he fled, be delivered up, to be removed to the State having Jurisdiction of the Crime.

No Person held to Service or Labour in one State, under the Laws thereof, escaping into another, shall, in Consequence of any Law or Regulation therein, be discharged from such Service or Labour, but shall be delivered up on Claim of the Party to whom such Service or Labour may be due.

SECTION 3. New States may be admitted by the Congress into this Union; but no new State shall be formed or erected within the Jurisdiction of any other State, nor any State be formed by the Junction of two or more States, or Parts of States, without the Consent of the Legislatures of the States concerned as well as of the Congress.

The Congress shall have Power to dispose of and make all needful Rules and Regulations respecting the Territory or other Property belonging to the United States; and nothing in this Constitution shall be so construed as to Prejudice any Claims of the United States, or of any particular State.

SECTION 4. The United States shall guarantee to every State in this Union a Republican Form of Government, and shall protect each of them against Invasion; and on Application of the Legislature, or of the Executive (when the Legislature cannot be convened) against domestic Violence.

Article V.

The Congress, whenever two thirds of both Houses shall deem it necessary, shall propose Amendments to this Constitution, or, on the Application of the Legislatures of two thirds of the several States, shall call a Convention for proposing Amendments, which, in either Case, shall be valid to all Intents and Purposes, as Part of this Constitution, when

[8]Modified by the Eleventh Amendment.

ratified by the Legislatures of three fourths of the several States, or by Conventions in three fourths thereof, as the one or the other Mode of Ratification may be proposed by the Congress; Provided that no Amendment which may be made prior to the Year One thousand eight hundred and eight shall in any Manner affect the first and fourth Clauses in the Ninth Section of the first Article; and that no State, without its Consent, shall be deprived of its equal Suffrage in the Senate.

Article VI.

All Debts contracted and Engagements entered into, before the Adoption of this Constitution, shall be as valid against the United States under this Constitution, as under the Confederation.

This Constitution, and the Laws of the United States which shall be made in Pursuance thereof; and all Treaties made, or which shall be made, under the Authority of the United States, shall be the supreme Law of the Land; and the Judges in every State shall be bound thereby, any Thing in the Constitution or Laws of any State to the Contrary notwithstanding.

The Senators and Representatives before mentioned, and the Members of the several State Legislatures, and all executive and judicial Officers, both of the United States and of the several States, shall be bound by Oath or Affirmation, to support this Constitution; but no religious Test shall ever be required as a Qualification to any Office or public Trust under the United States.

Article VII.

The Ratification of the Conventions of nine States, shall be sufficient for the Establishment of this Constitution between the States so ratifying the Same.

Done in Convention by the Unanimous Consent of the States present the Seventeenth Day of September in the Year of our Lord one thousand seven hundred and Eighty seven and of the Independence of the United States of America the Twelfth. In witness whereof We have hereunto subscribed our Names,

Articles in Addition to, and Amendment of, the Constitution of the United States of America, Proposed by Congress, and Ratified by the Legislatures of the Several States, Pursuant to the Fifth Article of the Original Constitution.

Amendment I[9]

Congress shall make no law respecting an establishment of religion, or prohibiting the free exercise thereof; or abridging the freedom of speech, or of the press; or the right of the people peaceably to assemble, and to petition the Government for a redress of grievances.

Amendment II

A well regulated Militia, being necessary to the security of a free State, the right of the people to keep and bear Arms shall not be infringed.

Amendment III

No Soldier shall, in time of peace, be quartered in any house, without the consent of the Owner, nor in time of war, but in a manner to be prescribed by law.

Amendment IV

The right of the people to be secure in their persons, houses, papers, and effects, against unreasonable searches and seizures, shall not be violated, and no Warrants shall issue, but upon probable cause, supported by Oath or affirmation, and particularly describing the place to be searched, and the persons or things to be seized.

Amendment V

No person shall be held to answer for a capital or otherwise infamous crime, unless on a presentment or indictment of a Grand Jury, except in cases arising in the land or naval forces, or in the Militia, when in actual service in time of War or public danger; nor shall any person be subject for the same offence to be twice put in jeopardy of life or limb; nor shall be compelled in any criminal case to be a witness against himself, nor be deprived of life, liberty, or property, without due process of law; nor shall private property be taken for public use, without just compensation.

Amendment VI

In all criminal prosecutions, the accused shall enjoy the right to a speedy and public trial, by an impartial jury of the State and district wherein the crime shall have been committed, which district shall have been previously ascertained by law, and to be informed of the nature and cause of the accusation; to be confronted with the witnesses against him; to have compulsory process for obtaining witnesses in his favor, and to have the Assistance of Counsel for his defence.

Amendment VII

In suits at common law, where the value in controversy shall exceed twenty dollars, the right of trial by jury shall be preserved, and no fact tried by a jury, shall be otherwise reexamined in any Court of the United States, than according to the rules of the common law.

Amendment VIII

Excessive bail shall not be required, nor excessive fines imposed, nor cruel and unusual punishments inflicted.

Amendment IX

The enumeration in the Constitution, of certain rights, shall not be construed to deny or disparage others retained by the people.

---

[9]The first ten amendments were passed by Congress September 25, 1789. They were ratified by three-fourths of the states December 15, 1791.

Amendment X

The powers not delegated to the United States by the Constitution; nor prohibited by it to the States, are reserved to the States respectively, or to the people.

Amendment XI[10]

The Judicial power of the United States shall not be construed to extend to any suit in law or equity, commenced or prosecuted against one of the United States by Citizens of another State, or by Citizens or Subjects of any Foreign State.

Amendment XII[11]

The Electors shall meet in their respective States and vote by ballot for President and Vice-President, one of whom, at least, shall not be an inhabitant of the same State with themselves; they shall name in their ballots the person voted for as President, and in distinct ballots the person voted for as Vice-President, and they shall make distinct lists of all persons voted for as President, and of all persons voted for as Vice-President, and of the number of votes for each, which lists they shall sign and certify, and transmit sealed to the seat of the government of the United States, directed to the President of the Senate;—The President of the Senate shall, in the presence of the Senate and House of Representatives, open all the certificates and the votes shall then be counted;—The person having the greatest number of votes for President, shall be the President, if such number be a majority of the whole number of Electors appointed; and if no person have such majority, then from the persons having the highest numbers not exceeding three on the list of those voted for as President, the House of Representatives shall choose immediately, by ballot, the President.

But in choosing the President, the votes shall be taken by states, the representation from each state having one vote; a quorum for this purpose shall consist of a member or members from two-thirds of the states, and a majority of all the states shall be necessary to a choice. And if the House of Representatives shall not choose a President whenever the right of choice shall devolve upon them, before the fourth day of March next following, then the Vice-President shall act as President, as in the case of the death or other constitutional disability of the President.—The person having the greatest number of votes as Vice-President, shall be the Vice-President, if such number be a majority of the whole number of Electors appointed, and if no person have a majority, then from the two highest numbers on the list, the Senate shall choose the Vice-President; a quorum for the purpose shall consist of two-thirds of the whole number of Senators, and a majority of the whole number shall be necessary to a choice. But no person constitutionally ineligible to the office of President shall be eligible to that of Vice-President of the United States.

Amendment XIII[12]

SECTION 1. Neither slavery nor involuntary servitude, except as a punishment for crime whereof the party shall have been duly convicted, shall exist within the United States, or any place subject to their jurisdiction.

SECTION 2. Congress shall have power to enforce this article by appropriate legislation.

Amendment XIV[13]

SECTION 1. All persons born or naturalized in the United States, and subject to the jurisdiction thereof, are citizens of the United States and of the State wherein they reside. No State shall make or enforce any law which shall abridge the privileges or immunities of citizens of the United States; nor shall any State deprive any person of life, liberty, or property, without due process of law; nor deny to any person within its jurisdiction the equal protection of the laws.

SECTION 2. Representatives shall be apportioned among the several States according to their respective numbers, counting the whole number of persons in each State, excluding Indians not taxed. But when the right to vote at any election for the choice of electors for President and Vice-President of the United States, Representatives in Congress, the Executive and Judicial officers of a State, or the members of the Legislature thereof, is denied to any of the male inhabitants of such State, being twenty-one years of age, and citizens of the United States, or in any way abridged, except for participation in rebellion, or other crime, the basis of representation therein shall be reduced in the proportion which the number of such male citizens shall bear to the whole number of male citizens twenty-one years of age in such State.

SECTION 3. No person shall be a Senator or Representative in Congress, or elector of President and Vice-President, or hold any office, civil or military, under the United States, or under any State, who, having previously taken an oath, as a member of Congress, or as an officer of the United States, or as a member of any State legislature, or as an executive or judicial officer of any State, to support the Constitution of the United States, shall have engaged in insurrection or rebellion against the same, or given aid or comfort to the enemies thereof. But Congress may by a vote of two-thirds of each House, remove such disability.

SECTION 4. The validity of the public debt of the United States, authorized by law, including debts incurred for payment of pensions and bounties for services in suppressing insurrection or rebellion, shall not be questioned. But neither the United States nor any State shall assume or pay any debt or obligation incurred in aid of insurrection or rebellion against the United States, or any claim for the loss or emancipation of any slave; but all such debts, obligations, and claims shall be held illegal and void.

SECTION 5. The Congress shall have the power to enforce, by appropriate legislation, the provisions of this article.

Amendment XV[14]

SECTION 1. The right of citizens of the United States to vote shall not be denied or abridged by the United States or by any State on account of race, color, or previous conditions of servitude—

SECTION 2. The Congress shall have power to enforce this article by appropriate legislation.

Amendment XVI[15]

The Congress shall have power to lay and collect taxes on incomes, from whatever source derived, without apportionment among the several States, and without regard to any census or enumeration.

Amendment XVII[16]

The Senate of the United States shall be composed of two Senators from each State, elected by the people thereof, for six years; and each Senator shall have one vote. The electors in each State shall have the qualifications requisite for electors of the most numerous branch of the State legislatures.

When vacancies happen in the representation of any State in the Senate, the executive authority of such State shall issue writs of election to fill such vacancies: Provided, That the legislature of any State may empower the executive thereof to make temporary appointments until the people fill the vacancies by election as the legislature may direct.

This amendment shall not be so construed as to affect the election or term of any Senator chosen before it becomes valid as part of the Constitution.

Amendment XVIII[17]

SECTION 1. After one year from the ratification of this article the manufacture, sale, or transportation of intoxicating liquors within, the importation thereof into, or the exportation thereof from the United States and all territory subject to the jurisdiction thereof for beverage purposes is hereby prohibited.

SECTION 2. The Congress and the several States shall have concurrent power to enforce this article by appropriate legislation.

SECTION 3. This article shall be inoperative unless it shall have been ratified as an amendment to the Constitution by the legislatures of the several States, as provided in the Constitution, within seven years from the date of the submission hereof to the States by the Congress.

Amendment XIX[18]

The right of citizens of the United States to vote shall not be denied or abridged by the United States or by any State on account of sex.

Congress shall have power to enforce this article by appropriate legislation.

Amendment XX[19]

SECTION 1. The terms of the President and Vice-President shall end at noon on the 20th day of January, and the terms of Senators and Representatives at noon on the 3d day of January, of the years in which such terms would have ended if this article had not been ratified; and the terms of their successors shall then begin.

SECTION 2. The Congress shall assemble at least once in every year, and such meeting shall begin at noon on the 3d day of January, unless they shall by law appoint a different day.

SECTION 3. If, at the time fixed for the beginning of the term of the President, the President elect shall have died, the Vice-President elect shall become President. If a President shall not have been chosen before the time fixed for the beginning of his term, or if the President elect shall have failed to qualify, then the Vice-President elect shall act as President until a President shall have qualified; and the Congress may by law provide for the case wherein neither a President elect nor a Vice-President elect shall have qualified, declaring who shall then act as President, or the manner in which one who is to act shall be selected, and such person shall act accordingly until a President or Vice-President shall have qualified.

SECTION 4. The Congress may by law provide for the case of the death of any of the persons from whom the House of Representatives may choose a President whenever the right of choice shall have devolved upon them, and for the case of the death of any of the persons from whom the Senate may choose a Vice-President whenever the right of choice shall have devolved upon them.

SECTION 5. Sections 1 and 2 shall take effect on the 15th day of October following the ratification of this article.

SECTION 6. This article shall be inoperative unless it shall have been ratified as an amendment to the Constitution by the legislatures of three-fourths of the several States within seven years from the date of its submission.

[14]Passed February 26, 1869. Ratified February 2, 1870.
[15]Passed July 12, 1909. Ratified February 3, 1913.
[16]Passed May 13, 1912. Ratified April 8, 1913.
[17]Passed December 18, 1917. Ratified January 16, 1919.
[18]Passed June 4, 1919. Ratified August 18, 1920.
[19]Passed March 2, 1932. Ratified January 23, 1933.

Amendment XXI[20]

SECTION 1. The eighteenth article of amendment to the Constitution of the United States is hereby repealed.

SECTION 2. The transportation or importation into any State, Territory, or possession of the United States for delivery or use therein of intoxicating liquors, in violation of the laws thereof, is hereby prohibited.

SECTION 3. This article shall be inoperative unless it shall have been ratified as an amendment to the Constitution by conventions in the several States, as provided in the Constitution, within seven years from the date of the submission hereof to the States by the Congress.

Amendment XXII[21]

No person shall be elected to the office of the President more than twice, and no person who has held the office of President, or acted as President, for more than two years of a term to which some other person was elected President shall be elected to the office of the President more than once.

But this Article shall not apply to any person holding the office of President when this Article was proposed by the Congress, and shall not prevent any person who may be holding the office of President, or acting as President, during the term within which this Article becomes operative from holding the office of President or acting as President during the remainder of such term.

Amendment XXIII[22]

SECTION 1. The District constituting the seat of Government of the United States shall appoint in such manner as the Congress may direct: A number of electors of President and Vice President equal to the whole number of Senators and Representatives in Congress to which the District would be entitled if it were a State, but in no event more than the least populous State; they shall be in addition to those appointed by the States, but they shall be considered, for the purposes of the election of President and Vice President, to be electors appointed by the State; and they shall meet in the District and perform such duties as provided by the twelfth article of amendment.

SECTION 2. The Congress shall have power to enforce this article by appropriate legislation.

Amendment XXIV[23]

SECTION 1. The right of citizens of the United States to vote in any primary or other election for President or Vice President, or for Senator or Representative in Congress, shall not be denied or abridged by the United States or any State by reason of failure to pay any poll tax or other tax.

SECTION 2. The Congress shall have power to enforce this article by appropriate legislation.

Amendment XXV[24]

SECTION 1. In case of the removal of the President from office or of his death or resignation, the Vice President shall become President.

SECTION 2. Whenever there is a vacancy in the office of the Vice President, the President shall nominate a Vice President who shall take office upon confirmation by a majority vote of both Houses of Congress.

SECTION 3. Whenever the President transmits to the President pro tempore of the Senate and the Speaker of the House of Representatives his written declaration that he is unable to discharge the powers and duties of his office, and until he transmits them a written declaration to the contrary, such powers and duties shall be discharged by the Vice President as Acting President.

SECTION 4. Whenever the Vice President and a majority of either the principal officers of the executive department or of such other body as Congress may by law provide, transmit to the President pro tempore of the Senate and the Speaker of the House of Representatives their written declaration that the President is unable to discharge the powers and duties of his office, the Vice President shall immediately assume the powers and duties of the office of Acting President.

Thereafter, when the President transmits to the President pro tempore of the Senate and the Speaker of the House of Representatives his written declaration that no inability exists, he shall resume the powers and duties of his office unless the Vice President and a majority of either the principal officers of the executive department or of such other body as Congress may by law provide, transmit within four days to the President pro tempore of the Senate and the Speaker of the House of Representatives their written declaration that the President is unable to discharge the powers and duties of his office. Thereupon Congress shall decide the issue, assembling within forty-eight hours for that purpose if not in session. If the Congress, within twenty-one days after receipt of the latter written declaration, or, if Congress is not in session, within twenty-one days after Congress is required to assemble, determines by two-thirds vote of both Houses that the President is unable to discharge the powers and duties of his office, the Vice President shall continue to discharge the same as Acting President; otherwise, the President shall resume the powers and duties of his office.

[20]Passed February 20, 1933. Ratified December 5, 1933.
[21]Passed March 12, 1947. Ratified March 1, 1951.
[22]Passed June 16, 1960. Ratified April 3, 1961.
[23]Passed August 27, 1962. Ratified January 23, 1964.
[24]Passed July 6, 1965. Ratified February 11, 1967.

Amendment XXVI[25]

SECTION 1 The right of citizens of the United States, who are eighteen years of age or older, to vote shall not be denied or abridged by the United States or by any State on account of age.

SECTION 2. The Congress shall have power to enforce this article by appropriate legislation.

Amendment XXVII[26]

No law, varying the compensation for the service of the Senators and Representatives, shall take effect, until an election of Representatives shall have intervened.

[25]Passed March 23, 1971. Ratified July 5, 1971.
[26]Passed September 25, 1789. Ratified May 7, 1992.

GREENLAND
(Den.)

RUSSIA

ALASKA
(U.S.)

CANADA

UNITED
STATES

ATLANTIC

OCEAN

BAHAMAS

MEXICO

CUBA

DOMINICAN REP.

HAWAII
(U.S.)

JAMAICA HAITI

Puerto Rico (U.S.)
ST. KITTS
ANTIGUA

BELIZE

VIRGIN ISLANDS

DOMINICA

GUATEMALA HONDURAS

ST. LUCIA

BARBADOS

EL SALVADOR NICARAGUA

ST. VINCENT

GRENADA

GUINEA

PACIFIC

COSTA RICA

TRINIDAD & TOBAGO

PANAMA

VENEZUELA

GUYANA
SURINAME
FR. GUIANA

COLOMBIA

OCEAN

ECUADOR

PERU

BRAZIL

NAURU

KIRIBATI

SOLOMON
ISLANDS

TUVALU

TOKELAU

BOLIVIA

WEST.
SAMOA

AM.
SAMOA

PARAGUAY

VANUATU FIJI

TONGA NIUE
(N.Z.)

COOK
IS.
(N.Z.)

FRENCH
POLYNESIA

URUGUAY

NEW
CALEDONIA
(Fr.)

PITCAIRN
(U.K.)

CHILE

ARGENTINA

NEW
ZEALAND

FALKLAND IS.
(U.K.)